TEXAS POLITICS

W9-AJO-816

3 4026 00?0:

HARRIS COUNTY PUBLIC LIBRARY

320.497 Tex
Texas politics :
  individuals making a
  difference

$70.76
2nd ed.   ocm60668869

TEXAS POLITICS

Individuals Making a Difference

Second Edition

Nasser Momayezi
Texas A&M International University

W. B. Stouffer, Jr.
Texas State University

David M. Billeaux
Texas A&M University–Corpus Christi

José Angel Gutiérrez
University of Texas–Arlington

Eric Miller
Blinn College–Bryan Campus

Barry Price
Tarleton State University

Carol Waters
Texas A&M International University

HOUGHTON MIFFLIN COMPANY
Boston   New York

Vice President and Publisher: Charles Hartford
Sponsoring Editor: Katherine Meisenheimer
Development Editor: Terri Wise
Editorial Assistant: Kristen Craib
Project Editors: Reba Libby and Lindsay Frost
Senior Composition Buyer: Sarah Ambrose
Senior Art and Design Coordinator: Jill Haber Atkins
Senior Photo Editor: Jennifer Meyer Dare
Senior Manufacturing Coordinator: Marie Barnes
Executive Marketing Manager: Nicola Poser
Marketing Assistant: Kathleen Mellon

Cover image: Photograph © J.W. Burkey.

Credits appear on page C-1,
which constitutes an extension
of the copyright page.

"Texas in Context" boxed feature: Seal of the State of Texas. Reprinted by permission of the Office of the Secretary of the State of Texas.

Copyright © 2005 by Houghton Mifflin Company. All rights reserved.

No part of this work may be reproduced or transmitted in any form or by any means, electronic or mechanical, including photocopying and recording, or by any information storage or retrieval system without prior written permission of Houghton Mifflin Company, unless such copying is expressly permitted by federal copyright law. Address inquiries to College Permissions, Houghton Mifflin Company, 222 Berkeley Street, Boston, MA 02116-3764.

Printed in the U.S.A.

Library of Congress Catalog Number: 2004115699

ISBN: 0-618-43770-3

123456789-CRW-08 07 06 05 04

CONTENTS

CHAPTER 3   *Texas in the Federal System   53*

Join the Debate

Should a city be able to annex an adjacent area without the consent of the residents of that area?   102

CHAPTER 9   *The Executive Branch of Texas Government*   *251*

CHAPTER 11 *Criminal Justice Policy   320*

CHAPTER   **12** *Texas Health and Human Services*   *340*

Join the Debate

CHAPTER **13** *Education Policy*   *361*

CHAPTER **14** *The Budget*   *385*

TEXAS IN CONTEXT

JOIN THE DEBATE

Major Themes and Goals

This second edition, like the first, is dedicated to the idea that individuals, acting alone or in groups, can effect positive changes in their communities, their state, and their nation. As a society, we face a problem that has been familiar to political scientists since the time of Plato: if people interested in the common good don't participate in government, then the cynical and the greedy will dominate the affairs of the community in their own interests. We believe that our students make up the recruitment pool for future leadership. But too often they assume that the problems are so complex, the levers of power so difficult to reach, the system so corrupt, and the forces benefiting from the status quo so well entrenched that there is little they can do.

To demonstrate that individuals can make a difference, we begin every chapter with an example of one or more individuals who have made a difference. This vignette is linked to the content of the chapter and is usually mentioned in the chapter summary. By profiling both political leaders and ordinary Texans, we hope to promote interest and involvement in our political system. Thus, we explain how the political system works, how to play a role in it, and what the options are on some of the major issues that confront the system.

Each chapter also contains a feature called "Texas in Context," which reinforces the second major theme of this text—that Texas is a megastate and should be compared to the other large urbanized industrial states, such as California, Florida, and New York. We have much to teach to these states—performance review, for example—and much to learn from them. Several reforms enacted in Texas and based on the examples of other megastates are discussed throughout the book, and students are encouraged to consider working for (or against) them. These reform ideas include home rule for counties (Chapter 4), strengthening parties (Chapter 8), and reexamining the place system through which we elect council members in many cities (Chapter 4) and most of our judges at the district and state level (Chapter 10).

Changes to the Second Edition

Although the substantive framework of the text remains the same, we have made several improvements to the second edition. Naturally, we have included discussion and analysis of the many important political developments that have occurred since the first edition was published. Thus, in the new edition, we discuss the legislative redistricting controversy, the recent budget crisis and the increasing importance of the Comptroller of Public Accounts, and the 2004 election.

We have also made two pedagogical changes in every chapter. The first is the addition of a feature called "Join the Debate." In this feature, we present two sides of a current debate in Texas politics, which policymakers are grappling with and on which officials and citizens will have to make a decision in the next decade or so. For example, we examine the debates over whether the Texas governorship should be strengthened and whether the redistricting process should be reformed. We hope that this new feature will help students think critically about current policy issues and spur interesting classroom discussions.

Second, we have improved the end-of-chapter test preparation resources by splitting them into two parts. Each chapter now contains both Study Questions and Critical Thinking Questions. The Study Questions are intended to prepare students for multiple choice questions. In each chapter we provide examples of five short requests for information on which students are likely to be tested. We do not exhaust the possibilities but rather provide a start upon which students or instructors may build in order to cover the major points of the entire chapter. Following the Study Questions are Critical Thinking Questions, which prepare students for short essay exams. Although class size may prevent this kind of in-class exam, it may be possible to use Critical Thinking Questions for take home exams, short papers, or extra credit assignments.

Content and Organization

As in the first edition, our book begins by describing the political and constitutional structure of Texas government. Chapter 1 introduces the participatory and comparative themes of the book and describes the history, regions, and people of Texas. In this first chapter, we also point out that students are the recruitment pool for future leadership and provide some background on the dynamic relationship between Texas and the United States. Chapter 2 focuses on the constitutional development of Texas, while Chapter 3 places Texas within the U.S. federal system and presents a four-part definition of federalism. Chapter 4 describes local government in Texas and stresses the importance of the intergovernmental dimension.

Our focus then turns to describing political participation in Texas (Chapter 5) and the institutions for promoting it: interest groups (Chapter 6) and parties (Chapter 7). In Chapter 5, Powell's paradox is introduced as a way of understanding low voter turnout. Chapters 6 and 7 focus not only on interest groups and parties, but also on the dynamic relationship between them.

Next, we turn our attention to the major institutions of Texas government. Chapter 8 on the legislature includes the latest information from the seventy-eighth legislative session. Chapter 9 on the executive branch argues that the governorship of Texas is not as weak as most scholarly studies make it appear. Chapter 10 on the judicial branch includes an analysis and critique of our judicial system.

The text concludes with an examination of four key policy areas for the state of Texas. The first, criminal justice policy (Chapter 11), expands on the issues of Chapter 10. The important topics of human services and education also receive the attention of complete chapters (Chapters 12 and 13). The concluding chapter, Chapter 14, presents a concise treatment of taxation and budgeting and examines ways to reform our system.

Student and Instructor Support Materials

The supplements package for this edition has been revised to provide as much assistance as possible to instructors and students.

For instructors, new to this edition is the **HMClassPrep CD-ROM,** which aggregates electronic versions of the three key instructor ancillaries in one convenient resource. First, it contains the *Instructor's Resource Manual*, written by J. Aaron Knight of Houston Community College. The IRM includes chapter learning objectives and summaries, lecture topics, class activities and projects, and web resources. Second, the HMClassPrep CD contains *HMTesting* software, a complete computerized testing solution with test generation, classroom administration, and online testing features. Included in HMTesting are all of the questions from the *Test Bank* prepared by Evelyn Ballard of Houston Community College, including true-false, multiple choice, fill-in-the-blank, matching, and essay test questions for each chapter. Finally, the HMClassPrep CD-ROM includes chapter-specific *PowerPoint slides*, prepared by text author Eric Miller of Blinn College–Bryan Campus. The PowerPoint slides present lecture outlines for every chapter, along with key tables and figures from the text.

The IRM and PowerPoint slides are also available for download from the **Instructor Website** at politicalscience.college.hmco.com, along with web links and chapter outlines. Contact your Houghton Mifflin representative for the password.

For students, a **Study Guide** is now available with this text. Written by Evelyn Ballard of Houston Community College, the Study Guide contains chapter objectives, chapter summaries, key terms and definitions, Internet sources, and practice test questions in multiple choice, true-false, fill-in-the-blank, and essay formats.

Students will also benefit from the free study and review resources available on the **Student Website** at politicalscience.college.hmco.com, including ACE practice quizzes, prepared by Eric Miller of Blinn College–Bryan Campus; glossary flashcards; and chapter web links.

The *Texas Politics,* Second Edition, **WebCT and Blackboard courses** provide text-specific student study aids in customizable, Internet-based education platforms. Both platforms provide a full array of course management features for instructors who wish to incorporate educational technology in their traditional classrooms or for those who are teaching distance learning courses.

Acknowledgments

First, we'd like to thank our families for putting up with us during the writing and production of this second edition. We deeply appreciate your support and patience. They were essential to getting this project finished.

Second, we'd like to express our gratitude to the colleagues who took the time to review this edition and whose many suggestions helped this book realize its potential as an educational tool. Naturally, anything that detracts from it is our fault.

John C. Domino
Sam Houston State University

Timothy Hoye
Texas Woman's University

William Lester
Howard Payne University

J. D. Phaup
Texas A&M University, Kingsville

Roberto E. Villarreal
University of Texas, El Paso

Finally, we owe our thanks to the team at Houghton Mifflin who made this book possible. We are especially grateful to Katherine Meisenheimer, sponsoring editor, for her editorial suggestions and to Terri Wise, development editor, whose guidance through the writing stages was essential. Lindsay Frost and Reba Libby, who with humor and tact helped us work out the final glitches on our way through production, were excellent project editors. We owe a debt of gratitude to Marianne L'Abbate, who was not only a diligent copyeditor but a delightful correspondent, and to Bruce Carson, photo researcher *par excellence.* We are also grateful to Nicola Poser, executive marketing manager, Kristen Craib, editorial assistant, and Marie Barnes, senior manufacturing coordinator.

We welcome your questions, suggestions, and comments about this text. We can be reached at our respective institutions, or through the Houghton Mifflin website at politicalscience.college.hmco.com.

The Individual and the Megastate

When Robert Doerr (pronounced "door") learned that the Texas State University System Board of Regents had voted to table a name-change proposal for Southwest Texas State University (SWT), he was very disappointed. Doerr had supported the university president's idea to change the university name when it first surfaced the previous year. Now that President Jerry Supple was retiring, the Board of Regents felt that the new president, Denise Trauth, shouldn't have to deal with the name-change issue until she had a couple of years of experience. Some members of the board had ties to other schools in the state university system; some of these schools were not happy with the idea that SWT, the largest school in the system, would receive a name that implied flagship status. The name Texas State could be interpreted to mean that other schools in the Texas State University System were also-rans.[1]

It wasn't so much that Doerr, a graduating senior, was impatient, it was simply that he had done his homework and knew many reasons why the name change should take place. It seemed too obvious and so right. Now, he would probably graduate from a university with a name that was not only double directional but also inaccurate. Its home, San Marcos, Texas, is on the I-35 corridor in central Texas, far from the southwestern portion of Texas (think UTEP). South and West of San Marcos is San Antonio, the largest nearby metropolitan center. San Antonio considers itself the gateway to South—not Southwest—Texas.

Doerr was proud of his university, whatever its name, and it really didn't bother him too much that he would have to compete in the national job market with graduates from places like Iowa, Michigan State, or Georgia Tech. Within the state of Texas his university, Southwest Texas State, had a pretty good reputation, and thus the chances of his application being taken seriously were much better if he only looked for jobs in Texas—which he intended to do. He had good grades and was president of the Associated Student Government (ASG). The job market was a year away, however, and ASG faced several issues, including making sure it established good relations with Denise Trauth, the incoming president. Nevertheless, with Doerr sponsoring the bill, ASG voted (for the fourth time since the issue surfaced a few years earlier) to support the name change.[2]

As the opening of the 2003 legislative session drew near, Doerr arranged a visit with Texas State Senator Jeff Wentworth, who represented the district in which the university is located. Senator Wentworth and Doerr discussed a range of issues affecting students, including the proposal to allow universities to raise tuition and fees to offset cuts in state aid. Almost as an afterthought, Doerr mentioned that most members of Associated Student Government were sorry to learn that the name change had been tabled by the Board of Regents.

His curiosity piqued, the senator asked for more details. Then Wentworth shared with Doerr the fact that when he was president of the student body at Texas Agricultural and Mechanical University, he led the fight to get the name changed to Texas A&M. The idea of changing the name of the University in San Marcos to Texas State seemed like a great idea. If he introduced a bill in the Senate, would Doerr and the student government support it?

Doerr said yes and the project was on. Cosponsors were located in the House of Representatives; flyers were printed; and articles and op-ed pieces appeared in the student paper, *The University Star,* and in other papers in the area. As the session wore on, it became clear that many faculty members quietly supported the name change, as did the deans and vice presidents, but not everyone was in favor of it. Several alumni wrote to and called President Trauth, the Board of Regents, and their legislators expressing their opposition.[3] The Regents initially informed Senator Wentworth that they wouldn't support the bill and then later—but not unanimously— changed in favor of it.

The student body was not united in support of the name change, nor was the editorial board of *The University Star*. Informal polls taken of the student body and the alumni indicated a majority was opposed. Some called for a campuswide referendum. Nevertheless Doerr persevered in attempting to gather support in favor of the bill on campus and in the local community by testifying before legislative committees in the House and Senate. One heartening development was when one of the alumni, who liked the idea, pledged to underwrite the costs of the name change in terms of signs, stationery, and university literature.[4] This cost had been a point for the opposition, a point worth about $400,000.

Senator Wentworth persevered as well and the bill made its way through both houses and on to the governor's desk in June. Letters from both sides attempted to influence the sign or veto decision, and eventually the governor's office announced that he had signed the bill.[5] Southwest Texas State University became Texas State University at San Marcos on September 1, 2003. The university would refer to itself as Texas State. In deference to other schools with a long-time claim to the initials, TSU, Texas State pledged not to use TSU on any of its signs or literature. Those initials belong to either Texas Southern or Tarleton State, or both. At the ceremony celebrating the name change and in the official records of it, Robert Doerr is given a lot of credit for making the name change happen, as well he should.[6]

Individuals Make a Difference in Texas Politics

The story of Robert Doerr and the name change for his university is an appropriate place for us to begin our study of politics in Texas. It illustrates four noteworthy characteristics of politics—whether in Texas or Washington, D.C.

First, individuals can make a difference. Every day, somewhere in Texas, an ordinary individual is making a difference or preparing to become informed enough to be an extraordinary individual whose knowledge and expertise will be used to make Texas a better place. Preparing you for both is one of the goals of this book. On an issue that matters to you, you can make a difference. Had he been simply an ordinary student interested enough in the issue to bring it to the attention of his state senator, it is likely that Robert Doerr would have produced the same result. The fact that he was student body president was less important than the fact that he was willing to put his political resources to work for the name change.

Second, the name change shows that you can make a difference if you do a little homework. The Texas Legislature requires two semesters of U.S. and Texas politics courses before you graduate from a state-financed school. Knowing that fact is part of the homework we refer to. By the time you finish this course, you will have a better idea of how politics in Texas works, and we hope that you will be more motivated to get involved and make Texas an even better place in which to raise the next generation of Texans.

Third, the name-change process shows us that if you care about an issue, you are probably not alone. People around you may care as much as you do. But to make a difference, individuals have to let someone know what they want to accomplish. That way, an individual finds allies in the general population and in the institutions of government. Doerr could not have known that the name Texas State University had a special meaning to Senator Wentworth. It had been part of his life as an undergraduate, as a law student, and as a member of the Texas State University System Board of Regents before he became a state senator.

Texas State had been the name that a powerful Texas legislator chose for Texas Agricultural and Mechanical University when Wentworth was a student leader there. He and a few others had actively opposed that name and eventually carried the day in the Texas Legislature. When Wentworth was a law student at Texas Technological College, he had supported a name change to Texas State instead of Texas Tech.[7] On that debate, the other side won.

Had Doerr not brought the name-change issue to the senator's attention and indicated his enthusiastic support of it, it is likely that Senator Wentworth would have found lots of other issues on which to apply his legislative skills in the regular session of 2003. When you act, you are often the tip of a large iceberg that some political leaders are happy to see and some ignore at their peril.

Fourth, the majority doesn't always rule in a democracy. The name change took place despite determined opposition. As you will notice in Chapter 5 and elsewhere in the book, you'll note that dedicated minorities win lots of battles in our political system. Politics is more than taking public opinion polls. Naturally, the name change might not have happened in the face of unanimous opposition of the faculty senate, the alumni, the student body, and the Board of Regents. In the real world, however, it is rare to find a large collection of people who agree unanimously on any issue. Politics is more about mobilizing your support, than it is about convincing every single person that you are right.

Robert Doerr is one of several individuals you will meet in this book who, in large ways and small, have made a difference in Texas politics. The political system of Texas does respond to "we the people." However, it responds only if we act.

In his inaugural address in January 2001, the forty-third president of the United States, former governor of Texas George W. Bush, emphasized the importance of action in the political arena. He called it citizenship:

> What *you* do is as important as anything government does. I ask you to seek a common good beyond your comfort, to defend needed reforms against easy attacks, to serve your nation, beginning with your neighbor. I ask you to be citizens. *Citizens,* not spectators. *Citizens,* not subjects. *Responsible citizens,* building communities of service and a nation of character.[8]

If responsible citizenship were nothing more than making a few telephone calls to the state capitol in Austin, the Texas Legislature could simply issue everyone an Austin telephone book. But responsible citizenship is more than that. At a minimum, it involves taking an interest in what is good for our community, state, and nation and acting on that interest.

Because responsible citizenship is important to Texas, the Texas Legislature imposed that two-semester requirement. The legislators figured that because the state was subsidizing a college education, the state ought to see to it that its best and brightest were pointed in the direction of informed and responsible citizenship. After all, only about 20 percent of each generation of Texans earns a bachelor's degree.

About 24 percent of your generation will earn one.[9] Whether that percentage earns it in business or in botany, college graduates are likely to be the future leaders of Texas. Thus, a few courses in the history and politics of Texas might better equip them to lead wisely.

We do not know whether the Texas Legislature considered the fact that it might be a good idea to require future leaders to be exposed to courses that challenge the culture in which many of them were raised. The culture of Texas, reinforced by some radio talk shows and newspapers, promotes suspicion of, if not hostility toward, politics and government, so you as future leaders are destined to have your cages rattled at least a little. Our goal is not to convert you to a particular set of ideas; rather, it is to prepare you to be better able to lead and more inclined to do so in the context of a broader knowledge of how politics in Texas really works.

It is sobering to realize that when you graduate, you cease to be an average Texan. You will be part of that 24 percent with bachelor's degrees, and you will be expected to play a leadership role. For that reason, the taxpayers, philanthropists, and university administrators in Texas see to it that your effort to acquire a university education is heavily subsidized. In state-financed schools in Texas, your tuition and fees cover about 17 percent of what each university spends to provide your education. See Texas in Context 1.1. The rest comes from the state's taxpayers and your university's ability to raise money from alumni, philanthropists, government grants; its sale of books and T-shirts; and its collection of parking fines. Some states do not provide as much help as Texas does. Texas in Context 1.1 indicates the portion of the cost of education in ten of the most populous states that is paid for by tuition and fees. In addition, at many universities, the education subsidy also comes from low pay for secretaries, custodians, and cafeteria workers. You might want to say thank you the next time you deal with one of these people.

To call you the future leaders of Texas is not to suggest that each and every one of you is a future legislator or governor. You can make a difference in the politics of Texas without holding public office. Texas is a large, diverse state that needs enlightened leadership everywhere. You may be a leader in a shop or office of ten people, a town of 20,000, or a corporation with a market capitalization of $200 billion. Wherever you go and whatever you do, you will be in a position to make Texas a better place once you leave the university. Some manage to make a difference while they are still students in it. That is why we wrote this book: to help future leaders make sure that Texas changes for the better. Change is inevitable. Whether it is change for the better or change for the worse is up to you.

In addition to identifying the participatory theme of this text—helping to prepare you for leadership and showing evidence that you can make a difference—this chapter provides an overview of the context or the environment in which Texas politics and governance take place. This feature brings us to our second major theme of the book: the fact that Texas is not just one of fifty states in the United States of America—it is a megastate.

TEXAS in Context

1.1 Megastate Tuition and Fee Income as a Percentage of Expenditures

State	Tuition and Fees ($000)	Percentage of Expenditures from Tuition and Fees
California	2,415,485	12
Texas	**1,884,072**	**17**
Illinois	1,010,793	18
Florida	908,312	18
New York	1,724,619	22
Michigan	1,693,378	23
New Jersey	901,983	23
Massachusetts	518,152	24
Ohio	1,664,197	28
Pennsylvania	1,731,453	30

Source: U.S. Department of Education, National Center for Education Statistics, Integrated Post-secondary Education Data System (IPEDS), Finance Survey. This table was adapted by the authors from the table supplied by the Office of Institutional Research, Texas State University at San Marcos, February 2004.

Texas: The Largest Megastate

Megastate States that have large, highly urbanized populations and a large gross state product, which indicates a complex economy.

Gross state product The gross market value of the goods and services produced and delivered in a state.

It is important for us to use the comparative approach so we can learn from states with similar problems. We can also gauge how well we are doing in terms of meeting our obligation to create a decent and humane society in which individuals can reach their highest potential as human beings. In a sense, we have already introduced the comparative and megastate themes in our discussion of the degree to which states subsidize higher education. Every state we listed in Texas in Context 1.1 is a megastate.

In *Megatrends*,[10] John Naisbitt identified a **megastate** as one that is highly urbanized, experiencing rapid population growth, and destined to be among the first to experience the technological and urban changes that will take place in the twenty-first century. Naisbitt does not provide a list of ten megastates, although he identifies California, Texas, and Florida as among the states he is discussing. To provide a basis for comparing Texas to other states in a meaningful way, we have developed the Megastate Index. We identified the top ten megastates using three criteria: population, urbanization, and **gross state product**. The Megastate Index score for a state is an average of the three criteria ranks among the fifty states.

TEXAS in Context

1.2 Megastates Ranked by Megastate Index Score

	Population	Urbanization	Gross State Product	Index Score*
California	1	2	1	1
New York	3	5	2	2
Texas	**2**	**6**	**3**	**3**
Florida	4	4	5	4
Illinois	5	6	4	5
New Jersey	9	1	8	6
Pennsylvania	6	6	6	6
Ohio	7	11	7	8
Michigan	8	10	9	9
Massachusetts	13	3	12	10

Source: U.S. Census Bureau, *Statistical Abstract of the United States: 2000* (Washington, D.C.: U.S. Government Printing Office, 2000), pp. 24, 35, 454.

*This score was created by averaging the ranks of states among the fifty states on population, percentage of the population living in metropolitan areas, and gross state product.

In Texas in Context 1.2, we have listed the states by their ranks among the fifty states on the three criteria and their rank among the megastates on an index score computed by averaging the ranks.

In terms of wealth, population size, and urbanization, there is no doubt that Texas belongs among the megastates. Over 80 percent of our population lives in metropolitan areas.[11] Our economy, as measured by gross state product, is larger than that of all but two other states. Our population is second only to that of California. The 2000 U.S. Census figures reveal that our population has grown so rapidly that we gained two members in the U.S. House of Representatives in 2003, bringing our state delegation to thirty-two.

Megastates also have megaproblems, and megaproblems often cost megabucks. Rapid population growth and urbanization are but two of the factors that lead to the problems Texas faces as a megastate. But Texas is not a poor state, unable to pay for solutions to many of its problems. It is likely that we will have to change our approach to many policies in the decades to come, in areas from caring for the health of children to the way we raise revenues to pay for government.

From time to time throughout the rest of this book, we will indicate how Texas compares to the other megastates, and not to twenty or thirty states that don't have the resources that Texas does or the problems we face as a diverse industrial state. The fact that we pay our teachers more than Mississippi pays theirs is not only cold comfort to Texas teachers, whose salaries rank near the bottom among the megastates, it is irrelevant to the standard of living in Texas. Such comparisons are probably shortsighted in terms of how well equipped our schools are to prepare the next generation of leaders; for example, qualified teachers are leaving the classrooms of Texas in droves.[12]

The Context of Texas Politics: Diversity of Land, People, and Cultures

Texas politics takes place in a context, four features of which we have chosen to emphasize: location, regions particular to Texas, population, and political culture.

LOCATION: THREE DIMENSIONS

The politics and governments of Texas are heavily influenced by three dimensions of our location: Texas is situated within the United States of America, across the border from the United States of Mexico, and on the Gulf of Mexico.

Within the United States of America.   For most of Texas history, the vast majority of immigrants were Americans from other states. In 1845, Texas became the twenty-eighth state, and its citizens henceforth were American citizens. Forevermore, Texas would make a difference in the American political system. Many Texans have fought and died in America's wars. Texans have made significant contributions to America's economic, scientific, and cultural development. Texans have also played an important role in American politics. Dwight David Eisenhower (1953–1961) was the first president born in Texas, although he later moved to Kansas. Lyndon Baines Johnson (1963–1969) was the first president to have been born, raised, and buried in Texas. George Herbert Walker Bush (1989–1993) provides a link between Texas and one of the few other states to produce more than one or two presidents: He was born in Massachusetts (which has produced four presidents) and spent most of his adult life in Texas before being elected to the presidency. His son, President George Walker Bush (2001–), served one and one half terms as governor of Texas before moving to Washington.

Clearly, as a megastate and as a major actor in American politics, Texas has played a significant role in America's history. However, America has had an influence on Texas as well. For instance, the shape of Texas was determined in part by the U.S. government, which defended its southern boundary in war and negotiated its western boundary in peace.

On April 21, 1836, General Sam Houston's forces captured General Santa Anna alive at the Battle of San Jacinto. With the head of the Mexican government as a prisoner of war, Houston was able to negotiate the Treaty of Velasco. This treaty stipulated three requirements that are significant for the future of Texas and for the United States.

First, the treaty required the withdrawal of Mexican armed forces. These forces far outnumbered the Texans. Once the Mexican generals knew where the Texans were, the Mexican forces were quite capable of defeating Houston and his small, victorious band. However, the Texans had a military resource more important than troops and cannons: General Santa Anna. To save his life, the Mexican armies did as the treaty required and returned to the other side of the Rio Grande.[13]

The second significant feature of the Treaty of Velasco is that it recognized Texas independence. This gave Texas a legitimate claim for international recognition and support. It has also contributed to the mystique of Texas as the only state to have been an independent republic before becoming the Lone Star State.

The third significant feature of the treaty is that it included a territorial claim that seemed outrageous. Not only did the Texans claim the Tejas part of the Mexican State of Coahuilo y Tejas, but they also claimed half of the state of Tamaulipas and large chunks of the states of Nueva León, Chihuahua, and part of the unorganized territory of Santa Fe de Nuevo México. As soon as Santa Anna returned to Mexico, he repudiated the Treaty of Velasco.

Nevertheless, the Republic of Texas asserted that the treaty established its claim that the Texas border with Mexico was not the Nueces, which flows into the Gulf of Mexico at Corpus Christi, but the Rio Grande, over one hundred miles to the south. At that time, few Texas settlements existed in the area between the Nueces and the Rio Grande to support this claim. The southernmost of the original twenty-three organized counties under the Republic was San Patricio, on the north side of the Nueces.[14] Furthermore, the Republic of Texas was never able to back with force its claim to the territory beyond the Nueces or its claim to what is now the neighboring state of New Mexico. Two failed expeditions to assert the Texas claims, together with the temporary occupation of San Antonio by Mexican forces in 1842, demonstrated the military vulnerability of the Republic of Texas.[15]

After 1842, the idea of becoming part of the United States became even more attractive, and three years later, Texas joined the Union. At this point, Mexico broke off diplomatic relations with the United States and shortly after, war with Mexico began. After hostilities ended with the Treaty of Guadalupe Hidalgo in 1848, the boundaries of Texas were established.

It was not until Texas joined the Union that the land to the south of the Nueces was effectively occupied with the help of the U.S. Army. Thus, the current shape and territorial expanse of Texas is a product of its becoming one of the United States of America. The western boundary of Texas resulted from an 1850 compromise in which the U.S. government agreed to pay Texas $10 million in exchange for relinquishing its claim to New Mexico, which became the forty-seventh state in 1912.

Near the United States of Mexico. Can you name the states that border Texas? If you forgot to mention the Mexican states of Tamaulipas, Nueva León, Coahuila, and Chihuahua, you have left out an important part of Texas history, past and future. Although Texas has been politically independent of Mexico since 1836, the economies and the societies of both are permanently linked. In a study of the border region, John Sharp, a former comptroller of Texas, observes that:

> [I]n important, day-to-day ways, Texas and the four northern Mexican states that share its border—Chihuahua, Coahuilo, Nuevo León, and Tamaulipas—have a far greater stake in one another's economic prosperity than in the rest of their respective nations. . . . Economic promise isn't the only phenomenon that binds the region. Brewster County and Chihuahua have always been far less foreign to each other than either is to New York or Guadalajara.[16]

Unlike California, Texas has maintained good relations with Mexico for the last two decades of the twentieth century. Texas has not blamed economic downturns on Mexican immigrants and no longer promotes a statewide policy of excluding their children from Texas schools. We point this out to indicate that individual leadership matters. Former governors Ann Richards and George W. Bush both pursued welcoming policies toward Mexican immigrants (legal and illegal) and their children. Governor Pete Wilson of California, in contrast, built a political career on hostility toward immigrants and their children. In keeping with the new Texas tradition of good relations with Mexico, President George W. Bush chose Mexico as the first foreign nation he visited as president.

Besides common decency, other reasons form the basis for good relations with Mexico. Along both sides of the twelve-hundred-mile border is a commingling of cultures, workers, employers, and customers. Trade with Mexico is projected to surpass $200 billion by the end of the first decade of this century. Texas exports more to Mexico than does any other U.S. state. To point out the positive nature of good relations with Mexico is not to overlook the problems of truck traffic, drug trafficking, and illegal immigration. These problems need to be addressed; being a border state as well as a megastate is not without its challenges.

An interesting fact about illegal immigration to Texas is that it is less than half that of California and less per square mile than that of six other states. Almost as many immigrants enter the United States through the airports of Newark, New Jersey; New York City; and Boston, Massachusetts as those who cross the Texas border bridges at El Paso and Laredo. When these airport immigrants stay beyond their student and tourist visas, they become undocumented aliens with the same status as those who cross the Rio Grande. Although Texas (700,000) is second only to California (2 million) in terms of undocumented immigration, it is a distant second. Texas ranks seventh nationwide in illegal immigrants per square mile.[17]

Most of the population growth in Texas, however, stems from natural increase and the immigration of Americans from other states (955 a day). About half of the new immigrants to Texas in the past decade came from the other states. In 1993, 1994, and 1995, this immigration to Texas exceeded that of international immigration.[18]

On the Gulf of Mexico.   Our location on the Gulf of Mexico provides trade and tourism opportunities. Five Texas seaports are ranked in the top twenty ports in the nation in total tonnage, and the Port of Houston is America's top port in foreign tonnage.

Foreign trade brings foreign investment. Our top five export markets include three countries (the United Kingdom, Japan, and Canada) that are among the major foreign investors in the state's economic growth. In 1996, according to the comptroller of public accounts, foreign investment in Texas was $72.3 billion. Among the fifty states, Texas ranks second in investment value by foreign firms.[19]

Our beaches are a major asset. As a tourist attraction, they are second only to the Dallas metroplex. Tourism is one of the reasons that the economy of Texas is now diversified far beyond its historic bases of cattle, cotton, and oil. Naturally, our beaches and the sensitive environmental habitats they contain are also a major responsibility. (That assertion is a reminder about leadership.)

THE REGIONAL CONTEXT: PLANNING IN TEXAS

Texas has a land and water area of 267,277 square miles. It is as large as all of New England, New York, Pennsylvania, Ohio, and North Carolina combined.[20] The distance from Freer in the Panhandle to Brownsville on the south coast is over 800 miles as the crow flies and longer by road. The sheer size of Texas has consequences in terms of how politics is practiced and how public money is spent. Size means large distances to travel in serving the whole population of the state. It also means over 220,000 miles of roads, bridges, and highways to maintain.[21]

These distances between Texans lead to different perceptions of what the priorities for the government ought to be. When Ric Williamson, a talented former legislator from North Texas, was appointed by Governor Rick Perry in March 2001 to serve as one of the three state highway commissioners, Rio Grande Valley residents became concerned that the needs of the border regions would be ignored. In response, Commissioner Williamson has gone out of his way to reassure them. He pointed out in a newspaper interview that one of the top priorities assigned him by the governor was to "travel the border to talk to border legislators and city and county officials to hear their priorities on solving transportation problems in their areas" and then find a way to solve those problems.[22]

Distances also have political consequences beyond those of deciding which roads and bridges to improve first. Running for statewide office in Texas is a daunting task. The state contains 254 counties and more than twenty media markets in which radio and television ads must be purchased and personal appearances made. To pay for television spots and radio ads, candidates for major state offices must raise a lot of money. The relationship between money and politics is examined further in later chapters.

From coastal beaches and pine forests to rugged mountains and desert plains, Texas presents a range of geographical diversity appropriate for a state with such a large, diverse population. Texas can be divided into different regions based on different measures. The map in Figure 1.1 shows our seven regions of Texas. We have employed as our organizing unit the boundaries of the twenty-four state planning regions. Each of the 254 counties of Texas is located wholly within one of these regions.[23]

FIGURE 1.1   The Regions of Texas

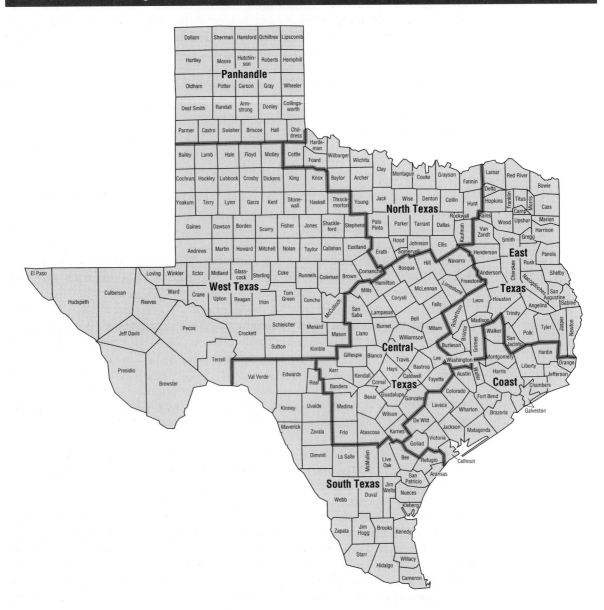

The regions themselves are based on natural geographic features, media coverage areas, labor markets, commuting patterns, economic market areas, and communities of interest among public officials.[24] Before we describe them, note that in almost all of them, you will find rich farmland, cattle ranches, and oil wells. Each region is, after all, part of Texas.

East Texas.   East Texas contains four planning areas: Ark-Tex, East Texas, Deep East Texas, and the Brazos Valley. Among its major cities are Texarkana, Tyler, Lufkin, and Longview.

East Texas is the land of the original settlements by Americans moving into Texas from the southern states. This region contains woodlands, some of the most beautiful in the state, and lakes, both humanmade and natural. Agriculture in East Texas has shifted from an emphasis on cotton to the production of a large rice crop on the coastal prairie, timber in Deep East Texas, and increasing amounts of beef and poultry.[25]

The development of a new poultry industry in East Texas has not been without environmental problems, which ultimately involve government at more than one level. East Texas chicken magnate Lonnie "Bo" Pilgrim has been accused of polluting many East Texas lakes and rivers. He has run afoul of residents in several communities and the Texas Commission on Environmental Equality (TCEQ). His company amassed over $900,000 in fines through more than sixty-eight violations (including seven federal water violations), twenty-five notices of violations, more than one hundred official complaints, and seven out-of-court settlements (agreed orders). The advocates of economic growth and of environmental protection often battle in Texas; sometimes interesting allies are drawn into the fray. In Pilgrim's case, his activities threaten to pollute Cypress Creek, which flows by the family home of Bill Ratliff, who served as the lieutenant governor and presiding officer of the Texas Senate during the Seventy-Seventh Texas Legislature.[26]

The Gulf Coast.   Although the Gulf Coast is located in the eastern part of the state, it merits a separate regional identity for two reasons: oil and urbanization. First, the oil industry has a wide economic penetration—not only because of its pumping from the ground but also because of the transformation of oil through the petrochemical industry into a wide range of goods shipped all over the world. Second, oil and shipping have led to increased urbanization in cities like Houston, Beaumont, Port Arthur, and Galveston. Urbanization alone would result in more diverse populations, but many of these cities are seaports with exposure to the traffic of the wider world. To the Gulf Coast has come diversity and urban institutions, such as the labor union movement, which is stronger in the petrochemical and transportation industries in Texas than in most other sectors.

The beginning of the separation of the Gulf Coast from East Texas moved dramatically forward in 1901, when the oil boom began near Beaumont. The history of Texas was changed forever with the explosion of the Spindletop gusher. Until the well was brought under control, it spewed over 70,000 gallons a day for nine days; thus also began the emergence of nonagricultural pollution in Texas. Within a few months, the oil business exploded in Texas as well. In 1901 alone, the state of Texas chartered 491 oil companies. Within a decade or so, oil had replaced cotton and cattle as the central feature of the Texas economy.[27]

West Texas.   West Texas is the land of the prairies, where cattle ranches and large irrigated fields of cotton, wheat, and sorghum provide much of the produce that makes Texas a leading agricultural state. In the high plains in the northern area around Lubbock, Abilene, and Big Spring, you can find irrigated cotton fields, grain crops, and feedlot cattle operations. In the middle belt, south of the Cap Rock escarpment, are the oil-producing counties of the Permian Basin. Midland and Odessa are the largest cities in that area. In San Angelo and southward are cattle ranches, occasional well pumps, and a fair number of goats essential to nearly half the world's production—and over 90 percent of the U.S. production—of mohair. In addition to productive agricultural land are miles of dry desert, and in the south are the rugged Davis Mountains, where Big Bend National Park is located. West Texas has five planning regions: South Plains, West Central Texas, Rio Grande, Permian Basin, and Concho Valley.

West Texas seems to have three centers of political orientation. First, Lubbock and Midland-Odessa are good-sized metropolitan areas influenced by immigration from midwestern and some eastern states. Politics in these areas is a little more cosmopolitan than in the second center of political orientation—the rural areas of West Texas, where the settlement, with a few exceptions, was an extension of the southern state settlement of East Texas. Southern Protestant fundamentalist churches dominate the small towns, and to some extent the small-town politics, of much of West Texas. The third area of influence is El Paso and the border counties, which are oriented as much toward Mexico as toward the United States. The tradition of Mexican radicalism and agrarian populism is what drives many voters and candidates concerned with the problems of the less fortunate and predisposes them to support policies that attempt to solve these problems.

Whatever their political orientation, however, West Texans share a sense of unity as West Texans. A little research on the Internet will yield a treasure trove of institutions and organizations with *West Texas* (WT) in their title scattered all over the regional map.

The Panhandle.   The Panhandle of Texas is the farthest north you can get and still be in Texas. Texline, near the New Mexico border, is closer to Bismarck, North Dakota, than it is to Brownsville. The largest Panhandle city, Amarillo, is closer to Kansas City than it is to Houston. The economy of the Panhandle is similar to that of West Texas: big irrigated farms and cattle ranches, oil and gas, and service industries. Using the Internet again as a research tool, we learn that West Texas institutions are spread evenly across West Texas, but Panhandle institutions are centralized in and around Amarillo. The Panhandle consists of one planning region: the Panhandle.

Although the Panhandle shares many characteristics of the northern part of West Texas, including the development of electricity-generating windmill farms, it merits separate treatment because of its cultural and economic link to the midwestern states. The railroad came to the Panhandle via Kansas City rather than New Orleans or Atlanta, and thus it brought midwestern farmers to settle there and introduce wheat as a cash crop. With the development of irrigation, the Panhandle has become a major producer of grain products and grain-fed cattle in large feedlots near Amarillo, a major shipping area by rail and truck. The twenty-six Panhandle counties produce about 25 percent of the nation's beef.

Panhandle farmers have been so successful at growing wheat and other grains through irrigation that they have put serious stress on the region's primary water supply, the Ogallala aquifer. Depletion, however, is not the only threat to the Ogallala. Seventeen miles north of Amarillo is the Pantex Nuclear Facility. It is at the center of numerous complex political issues, ranging from pollution of the aquifer with toxic chemicals and radioactive waste to abuse of employees seeking to maintain safety standards. On one side are supporters of Pantex, a major employer in the Amarillo area; on the other side are environmentalists, local farmers, and land owners who blame the facility for contaminated wells and for 400 cases of cancer in the nearby community of Panhandle, a town with a population of fewer than 3,000.[28]

North Texas.   North Texas contains three planning areas: Nortex, North Central, and Texoma. Its twenty-nine counties include one of the fastest-growing metropolitan areas in the country: the Dallas–Fort Worth metroplex. Dallas and Forth Worth were settled in part by midwesterners and have attracted more immigrants from those areas in the past twenty years. They have also been magnets for migrations from rural East and West Texas. This metroplex includes two other cities that rank in the top ten in Texas: Arlington, with a population of nearly 300,000, and Garland, the tenth largest Texas city, with a population of about 200,000.

The diverse economy of the metroplex area began with railroads. Today, it is linked by interstate highways to the rest of the nation and to the rest of the world by the Dallas–Forth Worth International Airport. Direct flights link the metroplex and Texas to Europe, Latin America, and Asia every day. In recent years, North Texas has become the relocation spot for the headquarters of several Fortune 500 corporations. The economy includes over 1,000 manufacturing plants, finance and insurance companies, and the high-tech industry, as well as defense, aerospace, and tourism. Outside the metroplex are oil and gas wells, as well as a healthy agricultural economy that includes beef and dairy farms and produces various crops, including wheat, peanuts, watermelon, and cantaloupe.[29]

North Texas has been the scene of some major progressive political organizing efforts. The Farmers' Alliance, a forerunner of the Populist party, met in Cleburne near Dallas in 1886 to issue a demand for the recognition of trade unions and cooperative stores. The cooperative stores were efforts by thousands of Texas farmers to find a way around the sharecropping system that kept many of them in poverty and in debt. Many large businesses refused to sell goods to the farmers' cooperative stores, preferring to deal though the so-called furnishing merchants, who sold goods on credit at high cost and high interest. For many years, the *Dallas Mercury* was one of the state's staunchest supporters of the efforts of farmers to organize themselves and promote social justice through the political system.[30]

Central Texas.   Central Texas contains four planning areas: the Heart of Texas, the Capital Area, the Alamo Area, and Central Texas. Its major urban centers are Austin and San Antonio, although Waco and Belton are not exactly rural crossroads. The whole Interstate 35 (I-35) corridor from San Antonio north beyond Austin to Waco is rapidly urbanizing and attracting immigrants from the Midwest as well as from California's electricity-starved Silicon Valley.

Austin, astride I-35, is clearly in Central Texas. No other region in Texas can reasonably claim the city. It could be argued that no other region wants to claim Austin because it seems to have an unusual concentration of liberal politicians in a state that tends to vote for conservative candidates. Thus, locating Austin in Central Texas is probably just fine with many Texans from other regions. San Antonio, on the other hand, could be considered part of South Texas. It is a gateway to Mexico from both I-35 south to Laredo and I-10 west to El Paso. However, part of San Antonio is in the hill country on the Edwards Plateau, a dominant feature of Central Texas. These rolling hills stretch for over a hundred miles westward from their emergence along I-35, which in this part of Texas is located on the Balcones fault line separating the Edwards Plateau from the Blackland prairie to the east.

San Antonio is the only major city in the United States that does not have a surface water supply. It depends on the Edwards underground aquifer for its water. This dependence has been a major political issue in this part of the state because the aquifer is often in danger of being depleted and even destroyed during droughts. With too much pumping, the freshwater pressure could drop, and saltwater could enter the aquifer, permanently polluting it. In 1993, a courageous individual used his authority to force Texas to take a giant step forward in saving not only the Edwards aquifer but also the Ogallala and other aquifers as well.

The court rulings of Lucius D. Bunton III, a federal judge, forced the region to face the issue of preserving a vulnerable water resource. His ruling in *Sierra Club v. Babbitt* in 1993 caused the Texas Legislature to create the Edwards Aquifer Authority, which had the mandate to limit and reduce pumping from the aquifer. According to the *Austin American-Statesman,* "Bunton . . . will go down in history as a jurist who fearlessly stood up to tradition, power and money and defied a century of Texas water law that gave property owners the right to pump limitless quantities of underground water."[31] Later, other authorities were also created, and in 1999 the Texas Legislature passed a sweeping water-protection law that reflects the efforts of individual Texans who brought the Sierra Club case before Judge Bunton and worked to keep water conservation on the public agenda.

Tourism, education, government, finance, high-tech industry, manufacturing, and agriculture are the bases of the Central Texas economy. The peach crop around Fredericksburg in Gillespie County is one of the biggest in the state and attracts thousands of tourists and Texans to the "pick 'em yourself" orchards that dot the landscape.

South Texas.   South Texas contains four planning areas: Middle Rio Grande, Lower Rio Grande, Coastal Bend, and South Texas. The region has a freshwater boundary on the west, Lake Amistad and the Rio Grande, and to the east is a saltwater boundary, the Gulf of Mexico.

The South Texas region reaches from the freshwater springs of the Edwards Plateau in the northwest to the salty beaches of the Texas Coast on the southeast. The economy of the region is based on goat and cattle raising, oil, and gas in the west and south; irrigated citrus and grain crops in the valley, where the famous ruby red grapefruit is grown; and fishing, shipping, and petrochemicals to the east. Both the coast and Lake Amistad attract tourism, and many South Texas communities gain population from midwestern snowbirds in the winter. Major cities include Corpus Christi; Aransas Pass on the coast; and Del Rio, Laredo, and Harlingen in the valley. Brownsville, a major seaport, is a few miles inland in the valley.

Many political issues in South Texas are linked to the fact that the region includes a large portion of the state's working poor. Some are recent immigrants from Mexico attempting to work their way north, and some are laborers living in the infamous *colonias*—collections of shacks and derelict mobile homes that lack sewer, water, and other basic services. South Texas is not the only Texas region in which poverty is a problem. This makes for potential alliances in the state legislature, to be discussed in Chapter 7. It also links the Texas Industrial Areas Foundation groups in different regions, which we will discuss in Chapter 6.

THE POPULATION OF TEXAS: A STUDY IN DIVERSITY

The Texas state motto is "Friendship," and with that motto, we acknowledge our debt to the Caddo and other peoples who were here when the Spaniards first arrived in 1528.[32] The Caddo word *Tejas* means "friends" or "allies." The Caddo people were members of the Hasinai Confederacy, which competed with others for land in eastern Texas and parts of Louisiana.[33] A brief examination of the Native American populations who competed and coexisted in Texas before the arrival of Europeans is a preview of the diversity and complex relations among the subgroups that make up the population of Texas today.

Native Americans.   The Native American populations were distributed across the state in different adaptations to the environments in which they lived. At least four cultural types have been identified: the plains peoples, such as the Lipan Apache and the Comanche; the coastal area tribes, such as the Karankawa; the agriculturists of the northeast, which included the Hasinai Confederacy; and the Jumano of West Texas, who combined agriculture and village life with buffalo hunting.[34]

Smallpox and other European diseases reduced the Native American population as much as did warfare, although some peoples were more vulnerable to warfare than others were. The villages and granaries of the Hasinai and Jumano were easier to find and destroy than were the food supplies of the more mobile buffalo hunters. It took a century longer to destroy the buffalo herds. The introduction of horses changed the nature of warfare on the plains to the advantage of the Comanche and Lipan Apache. Thus, change in the form of the arrival of Europeans did not affect all Native American peoples in Texas in exactly the same way, just as change today does not have the same impact on every region of the state.

Get involved in politics so these young Texans will grow up in a state even better than the one we've got.

Today, three tribal reservations are located in Texas: the Alabama-Coushatta in Polk County, the Tigua in El Paso County, and the Kikapoo south of Eagle Pass. Numerous cultural events celebrating the first native Texans occur annually in the state, including the Texas Red Nations Powwow in Dallas every November.[35]

A major issue in the relations between the Native Americans in Texas and the state government was the successful effort of former governor George Bush and former attorney general John Cornyn to shut down their gambling casinos. These casinos have the potential to bring millions of dollars into tribal communities, but they also have a darker side of gambling addiction. Some residents in their locales fear they will lower Texas Lottery ticket sales. Whether the casinos will ever open again remains to be seen. Bills aimed at giving them legal recognition failed to survive the 2003 session of the Texas Legislature.[36]

The 2000 U.S. Census recorded over 65,000 Native Americans in Texas.[37] Their numbers, however, understate their influence on the history and culture of the state as well as on the gene pool of its population. It is somewhat ironic that the Indians or Native Americans ceased to be the majority of the population 200 years after the first Europeans arrived, and the Anglo population, now a majority, will cease to be a majority long before the state of Texas is 200 years old. Although it will be difficult to overstate the influence of the Anglo population on Texas, Steve Murdock, the chief demographer at the Texas State Data Center at Texas A&M University, makes a point that future decisionmakers of Texas might find worth considering: "The future of Texas is tied to its minority population. How well they do is how well Texas will do."[38]

Anglos.   *Anglo,* short for *Anglo-Saxon,* is a term used in the southwestern states for persons classified as white and non-Hispanic on U.S. Census documents. Seldom noted is the fact that many people of Irish, Italian, or German heritage who are new to Texas are uncomfortable with being identified as "Anglo."

The Institute of Texas Cultures in San Antonio is a good place to see firsthand evidence of the diversity of the peoples who make up the population of Texas in general and, in particular the many European immigrants whose descendents are now considered Anglo. Although a majority of the original Anglo immigrants to Texas came from the southern states, large numbers also came from Germany and Czechoslovakia. In 1890, German Americans constituted the third largest ethnic category after Anglo Americans and African Americans.[39]

As Table 1.1 indicates, whites constitute a majority of the population, but not all whites are Anglos; some whites are self-identified as Hispanic. According to the Texas Data Center, however, Anglos could cease to be a majority after 2010

TABLE 1.1 Texas Population Categories: Race			
Texas		**Percentage of Total**	**Percentage of One Race**
Total population	21,215,494		
One race	20,758,706	97.85	
White	15,498,431	73.05	74.66
Black or African American	2,308,423	10.88	11.12
Native American	72,753	0.34	0.35
Asian	628,460	2.96	3.03
Pacific Islander*	13,112	0.06	0.06
Other	2,237,527	10.55	10.78
Two or more races	456,788	2.15	

*Includes Native Hawaiians

Source: American Community Survey Profile 2002, *Texas Table 1. U.S. Census Bureau, American Community Survey Office. Last revised: Tuesday September 02, 2003.*
census.gov/acs/www/Products/Profiles/Single/2002/ACS/Tabular/040/04000US481.htm
(accessed: 2/14/04). Calculations by author.

and could be outnumbered by the white and non-white Hispanic population in 2030.[40] The fact that every group will soon be a numerical minority is a good reason to attempt to understand the different population groups in Texas. Perhaps the first characteristic to point out is that not all Hispanics are Mexican Americans.

Mexican Americans.   With 86 percent of the Hispanic population, as Table 1.2 indicates, Mexican Americans are the largest component of this portion of the Texas population. The Hispanic population in Texas numbers some 7 million. Of the 15.5 million whites, only 10.8 million identify themselves as non-Hispanic or "white only." Thus, perhaps 4.6 million Hispanics are self-designated as whites. Of the 2.2 million Texans who identify as "some other race," many also identify themselves as Hispanic. Many people identify themselves as Hispanic and black, and Hispanic and Native American. Unfortunately, the census figures give us no information about those who would choose a La Raza (the new race—meztisos, or people of Castillan and Native American bio-cultural heritage) category if one were available. We assume such a category would include nearly 2.2 million people, that is, most of the "other" race category.

Among this diversity in the Hispanic population, which is symbolic of the diversity of the Texas population as a whole, Mexican Americans are the fastest-growing part of the population of Texas. The Mexican American portion of that population has the deepest historical claim to original citizenship in Texas.

The early Mexican Americans (Tejanos) were the first to establish ranches in South Texas and to challenge the domination of the Native Americans farther north. Later, many Tejanos fought beside the Anglo Texans in the War for Independence from Mexico. During the early years of Texas independence, many Anglos made life difficult for the Tejano population. Even heroes of the Battle of

TABLE 1.2 Texas Hispanic Population			
Texas Population Hispanic		**Percentage of Texas Population**	**Percentage of Hispanic Population**
Hispanic or Latino (of any race)	7,191,546	33.90	
Mexican	6,155,903	29.02	85.60
Puerto Rican	75,411	0.36	1.05
Cuban	21,751	0.10	0.30
Other Hispanic or Latino	938,481	4.42	13.05

Source: American Community Survey Profile 2002. *Texas Table 1. U.S. Census Bureau, American Community Survey Office. Last revised: Tuesday September 02, 2003.*
census.gov/acs/www/Products/Profiles/Single/2002/ACS/Tabular/040/04000US481.htm (accessed: 2/14/04). Calculations by authors.

San Jacinto, such as Juan Seguin, mayor of San Antonio, were forced to flee to Mexico.[41] Thus, the Tejano population decreased, and immigration from Mexico nearly stopped. In the twentieth century, as the economy developed and jobs became available on Texas farms and in Texas cities, Mexican immigration increased.

The African American population of Texas bore the brunt of nearly a century of segregation, but Mexican Americans suffered as well. Like the African American population, Mexican Americans had leaders and organizations that fought for equal rights. The GI Forum, for example, was founded in 1948 by Hector P. Garcia, a Corpus Christi physician who was a World War II combat veteran. (We hear more about him in Chapter 6.) Later, Willie Vasquez founded the Mexican American Legal Defense Education Fund, and José Angel Gutierrez worked in local politics to effect changes in Crystal City and he founded La Raza Unida party.

African Americans. The first persons of African ancestry to visit Texas arrived with the first persons of Spanish ancestry. Esteban the Moor, a slave of Andres Dorantes, arrived along with Cabeza de Vaca and Alonso del Castillo in 1528. They were the fortunate four out of a party of about 300 who survived a shipwreck near what is now Galveston. Captured by a coastal tribe, they were enslaved for six years before escaping. They wandered across Texas for eight months before reaching a Spanish settlement in Mexico in 1536.[42]

The first African Americans to arrive in any substantial numbers came to Texas before independence, as slavery spread across the southern United States. They were freedmen and fugitives from slavery. Some stayed in Texas, while others fled farther into Mexico, which had abolished slavery in 1829 but tolerated it in Tejas. After independence, slaveholders and their slaves came to Texas in increasing numbers. By the time of the American Civil War, the African American population was larger than the Tejano population.[43]

Despite over 600 lynchings and the constant threat of violence during the Jim Crow era (1872–1964), African Americans built churches, businesses, and a vibrant separate society in some of the larger cities, such as Houston and Galveston.[44] More than a dozen black newspapers, like the *Texas Freeman* and the *Houston Informer*, in cities from Galveston to Lubbock, called for an end to racial injustice, beginning with an end to lynching.[45] Courageous blacks challenged the segregation laws, and several key U.S. Supreme Court cases in Texas started America on the road to *Brown v. Board of Education* and the end of legal segregation. Today, African American leaders such as Rodney Ellis in the Texas Senate and Ron Kirk, former mayor of Dallas, promote progressive policies that seek to improve the lives of all Texans, whatever their racial identity.

The history of race relations in Texas also involves acts of courage and organizational skill among many Anglo Texans as well. For example, Jesse Daniel Ames created the Association of Southern Women for the Prevention of Lynching in the 1930s. In the same era, Ku Klux Klan leaders in Sonora entered a butcher shop to inform its owner that he should stop paying his African American butchers the same wage as he did his Anglo butchers. The owner, William George Ragsdale, chased them out with a meat cleaver.[46] Maurey Maverick, a congressman from San Antonio in the 1940s, was the first congressman from the South to vote in favor of an antilynching bill, and at a time when there were few black voters in his district.[47]

The Other Texans. Although the usual treatment of population categories in Texas puts those who are not identified as Anglo, African American, or Hispanic into an "other" category, this population is important for at least three reasons. First, it usually includes the entire Native American population, as discussed earlier. Second, after the 2000 U.S. Census, the category includes enough people from Asia and the Pacific Islands to make up a congressional district. A high percentage of those who immigrate here become naturalized citizens within a decade after arriving. Because most of these Texans do not live in the same part of the state, it is unlikely that a legislative district will be created in which they constitute a majority. Nevertheless, they play an important role in the economy as both producers and consumers. Many own businesses, and many work in high-tech industries.

A third reason for discussing the "other" Texans involves a change in the way the U.S. Census treats race and the increasing rate of marriage across racial lines. In 2000, for the first time, the U.S. Census enabled people to identify themselves as being in more than one category of race. The Census Bureau made this change because many Americans of mixed race—children and parents—testified before a congressional committee in favor of creating an additional census category: a multiracial category for people like them. Others were opposed to a new multiracial category because they didn't want to complicate the census further, and some were opposed because they feared their ethnic membership groups would be weakened by members shifting to a multiracial identification.

In a compromise measure (compromise is necessary for our diverse nation to make progress) Congress ordered the Census Bureau to make it possible for a U.S. citizen to identify him- or herself as being a member of more than one race. Although this solution satisfied neither side, it accomplished the goal of removing either-or thinking from this census category. As Table 1.2 indicates, based on the 2000 U.S. Census, the Census Bureau estimates that in 2002, there were over 21 million Texans. A little over 2 percent of these Texans identified themselves as members of two or more races. Although it may seem a small percentage, in real numbers that means 456,788 people, or the near-equivalent of another congressional district. At the state level, this population would be enough for two Texas House of Representatives districts.

To many Texans of mixed parentage, race is no longer an either-or choice. Being classified as one race or the other, for many Texans who are both, was uncomfortable and sometimes demeaning. In some families, children with skin lighter than their brothers or sisters are treated better in schools. This situation alone is a problem. Another occurs when children return to their neighborhoods and homes after being treated differently in the "Anglo" world.

The census change is a tribute to the efforts of individuals who made a difference byin testifying before congressional committees, attending meetings in their home states and hometowns, and participating in the political system to effect change. The census change is also an indication of changes occurring nationwide *and* in Texas.

In the years to come, increasing numbers of Texans will not be white, black, red, or yellow; they will be various shades of brown. These Texans will identify with more than one culture, and they will resist being put in a single racial box. This change will make for some interesting politics, yet another reason to study how the Texas political system works and how individuals can make it even better.

How people think of themselves is important; it influences the organizations they join and the policies they support. Equally important is how they think about politics. Our general orientation toward politics is taught to us during our pre-adult years through a process called **political socialization**. If you are fortunate enough to receive formal education, then you are better equipped to analyze what you have been brought up to think about politics. You can decide for yourself how you want to deal with those lessons. As part of this analytical process, we examine three American political cultures that influence Texas politics.

Political socialization The process through which we learn about politics and acquire our political culture.

POLITICAL CULTURE: INDIVIDUALISTIC, TRADITIONALISTIC, AND MORALISTIC

Political culture A pattern of attitudes toward and beliefs about politics, participation in politics, and the purpose of government.

Political culture consists of the attitudes, beliefs, and values that influence our political behavior. Of course, we are not simply robots programmed by our environment. However, there is strong evidence that environment does have an influence on our approach to politics.

Political scientist Daniel Elazar was one of the leading scholars whose ideas have shaped current research on political culture (and another example of the fact that one individual can make a difference). Elazar's work has been studied by scholars all over the world. Many have published research papers and books exploring the implications of Elazar's three American subcultures: moralistic, traditionalistic, and individualistic.[48] Virtually every state and local government textbook published since 1990, whether about a particular state or the politics of the fifty states, devotes several paragraphs, if not pages, to Elazar's three subcultures.

Texas became independent of Mexico mostly because its leaders were immigrants from America who shared the American vision of westward expansion to "civilize" a continent. The referendum held after independence to decide on the new Texas Constitution also asked voters to declare whether they wanted to become a state and join the United States of America. The response to both was an overwhelming "yes."[49] Thus, it makes sense to examine the three political cultures that emerged among the original thirteen American colonies and spread westward in the minds of those who migrated into new territories and eventually to Texas.[50] Other states have been influenced by only one or two of these cultures, but Texas has been influenced by all three. We will examine each culture in terms of its place of origin and its orientation toward politics, political participation, and government.

The Traditionalistic Culture.   The first American subculture to arrive in Texas was the traditionalistic, which emerged in the plantation economy of the slaveholding

South. In each county, a few wealthy plantation-owning families dominated politics and government. Government was one of several tools they used to protect the social hierarchy consisting of a landed aristocracy, a tiny middle class, poor whites, and slaves. Politics was the process of using any means possible, including government, to preserve the social order. Over the years "any means possible" to preserve the status quo ranged from nighttime terrorism to requiring full immediate repayment of loans at the local bank. The middle class tended to follow the lead of the aristocracy and sometimes would do its dirty work when it came to not loaning money for the next crop, or not hiring people "who didn't understand our ways," or boycotting a newspaper or business of a person "unsympathetic to our way of life." In some parts of the state, newspaper editors who published stories challenging the status quo were threatened with violence; at least one was shot and killed.[51]

Political participation was an obligation for the aristocracy, who used their talents to preserve their status, and a privilege earned by individual newcomers or members of the lower classes who had shown their respect for tradition and support for the social order. According to traditionalism, government as a tool for preserving the social order should be kept in the hands of those who understand "our way of life."

In South Texas, the traditionalistic political culture of the southern states blends with the hacienda culture because both involve a small class of large landowners and a larger class of workers, with a small middle class in between. *Patrones* who own large farms and ranches provide political leadership and economic support for their work forces, many of whom are extended family. Because of these ties, political leaders in many South Texas counties for much of the twentieth century could deliver the vote fairly predictably. Lyndon Baines Johnson won a Senate seat in South Texas in the 1948 election. In Jim Wells County, his margin of victory came from ballot box 13, to which 200 votes for Johnson had been added a few days *after* the election. The 200 voters who signed the polling sheet to get a ballot all had the same handwriting, and they voted in alphabetical order.[52] What is not usually mentioned is that Johnson lost an earlier election by being on the short end of similar practices.[53]

States and regions dominated by the traditionalistic culture are not likely to have high voter turnout rates or laws protecting workers and consumers. Political parties and labor unions, the two institutions that promote participation by the working class and the poor, are viewed with suspicion in traditionalistic states. A traditionalistic culture does not mean that change is impossible, but it is a challenge. As the Valley Interfaith example in Chapter 6 indicates, now there are a few institutions that challenge the status quo by mobilizing the working poor. Change can occur if individuals are willing to work for it.

The Individualistic Culture.   Although the name of this culture implies that individuals act alone, the name is somewhat misleading. According to Elazar, the individualistic culture provides a setting in which individuals can advance themselves in business or politics by forming alliances based on personal loyalty. This culture is associated with the cities, especially the port cities of the Middle

Atlantic states. To these highly diverse and dynamic cities came immigrants, often with families, from England and all over Europe seeking prosperity and a better life. With a diverse population, a clear definition of the common good was not as easy to define. However, everyone could understand the desire for a better life for oneself and for one's family and friends. Thus, politics was a process of more or less orderly competition, but competition nonetheless—and competition as part of a group or team, not as a "self-made man."

Politics in the individualistic culture is a game in which one competes to better oneself economically and socially. People went into business or into politics, or both. A paving contractor who contributed to the politicians who won the elections usually got the paving contracts. Thus, politics was a means of advancement for individuals who got there by working within organizations like businesses, political parties, or interest groups. "Political life within an individualistic political culture," says Elazar, "is based on a system of mutual obligations rooted in personal relationships."[54]

Political participation in the individualistic culture was neither an obligation nor a privilege but rather a right that one was free to exercise or not. Politics beyond voting was a game best left for those who understood the rules: the professional politicians. It was a game in which one might get a little sweaty or dirty, but the rewards were worth the effort. Amateurs and reformers were tolerated but largely ignored. Government was the prize won by those who successfully played the game of politics. Those who won control of all or part of government could reward friends and gain a share of the profits from the many projects on which growing cities spent money: road construction and repair, sewage systems, water-supply systems, public buildings, utilities, parks, and social services.

The major theme of this book is that the individual can make a difference, so it is important to clarify some of the confusion from linking Elazar's individualistic culture with laissez-faire capitalism and the notion of rugged individualism, both of which are somewhat hostile to using government as a tool for making society a better place. The individualistic political culture regards government as a prize; it is not hostile to it. Government is a means for advancing one's personal goals, just as the marketplace is. If one lives in a place where promoting a better society is a shared value, then the individualistic politician is happy to embrace that value to get elected. Thus, one of the goals of those interested in promoting a better Texas is the promotion of the idea that we have an obligation to make it a better place. If that value is widely shared, politicians—regardless of their cultural background—will pay attention to the values of those around them. After all, haven't we heard the phrase, "I share your values," a time or two in the most recent presidential campaign?

Although Texas is associated with the myth of rugged individualism, it has been our experience that many, if not most, Texans are cooperative, community-oriented folk. There are festivals and events celebrating community history in most Texas towns and cities. The appeal of the rugged individualism of the West is romantic and certainly has a scholarly literature asserting that its influence is felt in Texas, but to some scholars, individualism has been overemphasized.[55]

Quite often, whole communities migrated to Texas, and once there they engaged in the cooperative activities such as barn raising and community harvesting that improve everyone's chances of survival.[56] As any cowboy will tell you, it takes some cooperation from others to move cattle to market, even if the market is much easier to get to now than it was in the 1860s. According to Mody C. Boatright, a historian of the Texas West, "The reminiscences of the trail drivers of Texas stress mutual help, not individualism."[57] Even the wildcatters, those individuals who scratched up the money to drill wells (oil and dry) all over Texas, needed cooperative land owners, banks, roustabouts, and roughnecks to make their fortunes.[58] A visit to any Texas city, from Corpus Christi to El Paso, will provide you with ample opportunity to visit museums, chambers of commerce, and churches and find in the local telephone books long lists of community organizations that bring people together to solve common problems.

The Moralistic Culture.   This culture was probably the last to arrive in Texas and is still not as firmly established as the other two. It emerged in New England, where the population consisted largely of families working small farms clustered about a town. In this fairly homogeneous society, everyone was expected to participate in community decision making as well as in community service. The two went hand in hand. Almost everyone belonged to one of a handful of Protestant churches and thus entered public life with similar views of the relationship between church and state and the value of the individual human being.

Politics is not a dirty word in the moralistic culture. It is a process for solving community problems. Thus, a politician is one who dedicates his or her career to public service or public problem solving. Political participation is an obligation for all members of the community. Everyone has talents or ideas that can advance the public good. States with a moralistic culture were among the first to grant women the right to vote and were more likely than other states to support the proposed but unsuccessful equal rights amendment for women.[59]

Governments in states or communities with a moralistic culture are more likely than others to use government in innovative ways. Moralistic states are more likely to have consumer-protection laws, safe-workplace laws, government-sponsored recycling programs, and lower thresholds for defining drunk driving.[60]

The moralistic culture had a long way to travel through space and time to arrive in Texas. The first contingent of immigrants to Texas arrived during the nine-year period when Texas was an independent republic. They came to the Dallas and North Texas area from the Ohio Valley and the northeastern United States. The oil boom, the growth of military bases during World War II, and high-tech industry have brought successive waves of moralistic migration into Texas. Gradually, this culture has begun to have an influence, particularly in the Austin-Houston-Dallas triangle.

Perhaps the most obvious issue on which the moralistic culture has influenced Texas politics is its concern with corruption and the role of money in politics. The *Dallas Morning News* and other metropolitan dailies were instrumental in promoting ethics and campaign reform after the Sharpstown scandal in the 1970s and the indictment and conviction of Gus Mutscher, Speaker of the Texas House of Representatives, and three colleagues for conspiracy and bribe taking.[61] While the investigation of Speaker Tom Craddick by Travis County attorney Ronnie Earle seems a witch hunt to some Republicans, to others it is an extension of the moralistic concern about honesty in government. Articles making connections between Sharpstown and the 2003–2004 investigation appeared early in 2004.[62] Both the traditionalistic and individualistic cultures are a little more tolerant of the practice of helping one's relatives and friends by using either political power or funds from the public treasury, or both. Speaker Tom Craddick comes from West Texas, where the individualistic and traditionalistic subcultures predominate.

Several good-government organizations with headquarters in Austin, such as Common Cause, the League of Women Voters, and Public Citizen, have promoted ideas consistent with the moralistic political culture at the state level and in some communities. In January 2001, for example, the city council of Dallas passed a series of ethics-in-government ordinances, thanks in part to the efforts of local members of Texas Common Cause. The fact that the council passed them at all could be seen as consistent with a moralistic political culture and its concern with preventing corruption. The fact that such reforms were necessary indicates that the individualistic culture, with its more casual views of abuse of office, is also at home in Dallas.

Texas Culture. The three political cultures that Elazar identified influence the level of participation and attitudes toward government and politics. All three cultures embrace slightly different interpretations of the American creed. According to Elazar, the excesses of each culture seem to balance those of the others nationwide. However, in some states, such as Texas, one culture may overbalance the others. Most observers consider Texas to be more heavily influenced by the traditionalistic culture than any other. This situation is changing, however, because of migration patterns and political participation.

The Civic Culture: A New Analytical Model

Civic culture A culture that demonstrates four characteristics:

1. civic engagement;
2. political equality;
3. solidarity, trust, and tolerance
4. social structures of cooperation.

Political units with a civic culture are most likely to have democratic political systems and effective, responsive governments.

While Elazar developed his analysis of how different versions of our American culture moved westward, other scholars, including political scientist Robert Putnam, explored the concept of political culture in the broader comparative context of its relationship to democracy. Putnam compared the political cultures of the regions of Italy and the degree to which they supported democratic political systems. Putnam identified four traits that best prepared citizens for participation in a democracy and termed this collection of cultural characteristics the **civic culture**.[63]

FOUR TRAITS OF THE CIVIC CULTURE

Rice and Sumberg published one of the first studies of civic culture among the fifty American states. They used sometimes interesting and creative measures to develop the Civic Culture Index as a measure of the degree to which civic culture is found in each state:

- *Civic engagement*, which refers to high levels of participation in various political activities.

- *Political equality*, which promotes social and economic opportunity. Among the measures of political equality that Rice and Sumberg used are the percentage of schoolteachers who are men and the percentage of state legislators who are women.

- *Solidarity, trust, and tolerance*, which are linked to attempts to measure a sense of community and an openness of that community to new people and new ideas. A society in which people rarely sue one another would be one in which they trusted one another and tolerated differences of opinion. Thus, the lower the number of lawyers per capita, according to Rice and Sumberg, the more likely the society is to manifest solidarity, trust, and tolerance. Other measures are the crime rate and the default rate on student loans.

- *Social structures of cooperation*, which are measured by the number per capita of twenty-six types of nonprofit organizations, such as churches, civic volunteer organizations, and charities.[64]

CIVIC CULTURE IN THE FIFTY STATES

How do Texas and the other megastates rate according to the Civic Culture Index? Massachusetts ranks second. Texas and Florida, along with most other southern states, are in the bottom twenty. **The Civic Culture Index score** is highly correlated with measures of the quality of life in a state, the degree to which the state manifests a moralistic political culture, and the performance of state and local government. Thus, civic culture clearly has some relevance for future leaders of Texas because quality of life and effective government are important values.

Texas in Context 1.3 compares the megastates in terms of civic culture and government performance. To provide more context, we report the rank of the megastates among the fifty states rather than their index scores on the measure of civic culture. The government performance scores of New York and California place them first and second, respectively, among the fifty states. Texas ranks thirty-ninth, a higher government performance rank than its civic culture rank but nevertheless last among its peers: the megastates.

According to Rice and Sumberg, the higher a state's civic culture score, the more likely it is to have an effective, responsive government.[65] The rankings of the megastates indicate that, for all their wealth and urbanization, most of these states can improve considerably in terms of civic culture or government performance. An effective government seems to be a goal on which most Texans, liberal and conservative, can agree.

Whether you use all, part, or none of the civic culture traits as models for where you want Texas to be when you pass the torch of leadership to the next generation, we think you should be aware of the existence of the civic culture. It is a set of options and a standard that is being used to compare the degree to which nation-states in the international community embrace the values of democracy and effective government.

Civic Culture Index score A number that Rice and Sumberg compute by using data on the four elements of civic culture. Without accurate polling data, they use somewhat crude but sometimes interesting and creative measures, such as the percentage of schoolteachers who are men; the percentage of state legislators who are women; how well a state cares for the poor, especially children; the fairness of its tax system; and the existence of consumer-protection laws.

TEXAS in Context

1.3 The Megastates Ranked by Civic Culture Index*

	Civic Culture Index Rank	Government Performance Index Score
Massachusetts	2	1.13
New York	12	1.59
Illinois	21	0.63
Ohio	22	0.80
Pennsylvania	26	0.67
California	30	1.41
New Jersey	32	0.71
Michigan	33	0.87
Florida	42	0.04
Texas	**43**	**0.52**

*The Government Performance Index scores are provided for comparison.

Source: Tom W. Rice and Alexander F. Sumberg, "Civic Culture and Government Performance in the American States," *Publius* (Winter 1997): 104.

Summary and Preview

We began this chapter with a brief story—a vignette—that described how an individual, Robert Doerr, made a difference. Every chapter in this book features a similar vignette. In some, the individual affects his or her community; in others, he or she makes a difference in Texas politics. In large ways and small, individuals make a difference in politics at the local, state, and national levels. If more individuals try, more of them will make a difference. They will certainly be more likely to try if you exercise your leadership to set an example and to motivate.

We touched on the fact that you are destined for leadership in Texas and that the state is making an investment in you. We think you should know about some of the areas where leadership is needed to make Texas an even better place to live. That is why we introduce the megastate theme and return to it throughout this book. You should know how Texas compares to the other great states so that you will have a better idea of where our political resources are most needed. Clearly, Texas subsidizes its university population more than some other megastates do.

We conclude the text discussion in this chapter with another feature found in every chapter of this book. A box called Join the Debate discusses an issue in a format reminiscent of a television talk show where the participants sometimes raise their voices at one another.

The arguments (and questions) one finds in Join the Debate may not all be factual. Be advised that our Join the Debate feature does not always provide all the facts necessary to help you make an informed decision. Its purpose is to stimulate thinking, not to give you a canned answer. To understand an issue, you may have to obtain more information, which means doing some research.

JOIN THE DEBATE

THE ISSUE: Should tuition in Texas universities be increased?

AGREE

1. As Table 1.3 indicates, Texas ranks about average compared to both the fifty states and the megastates. Clearly we don't have a shortage of people with college degrees. Therefore we don't need to subsidize the people studying to obtain one.

2. Texas taxpayers are already overburdened. It's time for a little relief for the taxpayers rather than for college students.

3. The people best able to take advantage of the education system are the children of middle-class and upper-middle-class parents. Therefore, subsidizing a college education is probably going to benefit the haves rather than the have nots.

4. The top three states with relatively high percentages of college graduates do not subsidize students to the degree that the next three ranking states— Texas, California, and Illinois—do (see Texas in Context 1.1). Clearly, they are producing college graduates without subsidies. Thus, we don't need to subsidize higher education to produce college graduates.

DISAGREE

1. To ensure that our large, diverse population will be able to enjoy the American dream, we need leadership. Investing in leadership through education is the way to help everyone in Texas, not just the graduates themselves.

2. The idea of pitting one group of Texans against another is an old traditionalistic trick. It kept poor whites and poor blacks divided for nearly a century by playing the race card. We need a fair tax system in Texas that will provide the resources to pay the educational costs for more Texans, and to make it possible for working-class Texans to help pay for their own education, instead of subsidizing the light tax load of the wealthy.

3. The top two states in college degrees earned are smaller than Texas and have smaller populations than Texas does. Each one contains a major Ivy League institution. Many of the people with degrees who teach and who do graduate work at those institutions may have earned their degrees in other states.

4. The size of the tuition and fees bill for Texas students and their families is considerable. It is among the top two among the megastates. Could it be that Texas institutions of higher education with more students paying tuition are more efficient in using that money? If so, they enable the state to lower the percentage contributed through tuition and fees because of this efficiency.

TABLE 1.3	Education in Megastates: Percentage of Megastate Residents Age Twenty-Five and Over with College Degrees	
State	**Percentage of 25 and Over with College Degree**	**Rank Among Fifty States**
Massachusetts	35.5	1
New Jersey	31.6	6
New York	29.3	11
California	28.5	12
Illinois	28.1	13
Texas	**24.5**	**24**
Florida	24.1	26
Michigan	23.6	30
Pennsylvania	23.6	31
Ohio	21.9	40

Source: Ranking Tables 2002. "Percent of People with a Bachelor's Degree or More, Population 25 years and Over." U.S. Census Bureau American Community Survey Office
Last revised: Tuesday September 02, 2003
www.census.gov/acs/www/Products/Ranking/2002/R02T040.htm (accessed February 10, 2004).

In life beyond this book, be careful in discussions (arguments) to listen to the "facts" provided by others. The rules of formal debate—debating society debates—require the adherence to the facts. Inventing "facts," i.e., making stuff up, is not allowed. However, the rules of dormitory and barroom arguments do not rule out making up "facts." Rather than calling someone a liar on the spot, we suggest you listen. Later, do your homework and be better prepared to lead Texas. Decisions on important issues in Texas are not simply about winning arguments. It's not about egos; it's about making Texas a better place in which to raise the next generation.

In terms of providing some background on Texas, an important part of the American political system, we touched on some of our regional characteristics and provided a few examples of problems or areas where individuals can make or have made a difference. We also provided an overview of the diversity that characterizes the population of Texas.

We introduced two new sets of concepts that have comparative uses: the three American political cultures and the more universal civic culture. The three American political cultures tell us more about where we have been and where we are. The latter suggests some directions in which we may wish to go. In Texas, the traditionalistic culture is more influential than the individualistic and moralistic cultures. The latter two do exist in Texas, however, and their influence may be growing.

The civic culture is a measure of how well a political unit expresses values that promote democracy. It has real practical value because civic culture is closely associated with government that is both enlightened and effective. We assume that those two characteristics are worth working for in Texas and a direction in which we hope you will lead.

Some of the remaining features of each chapter in this book—the Key Terms, For Further Reading, and Internet Resources—are self-explanatory. However, the two sets of questions may seem one set too many. The Critical Thinking Questions are meant to challenge you; for the small classes using this book, they serve as potential sources of take-home essays.

The Study Questions should prepare you for the typical large-class multiple-choice and short-answer exams. We provide about five for each chapter on material in the beginning of the chapter. You need to write another five to ten on the rest of the chapter. If you type your answers to every question, you'll be better prepared than most of those who buy but don't really read this book. We hope both sets of questions demonstrate that we wrote this book with students in mind and that we are classroom teachers who cheerfully attempt to instruct real students every semester.

KEY TERMS

Megastate, p. 6
Gross state product, p. 6
Political socialization, p. 23

Political culture, p. 23
Civic culture, p. 27
Civic Culture Index score, p. 28

FOR FURTHER READING

The Council of State Governments, *The Book of the States: 2003* (Lexington, Ky.: The Council of State Governments, 2003).

Davidson, Chandler, *Race and Class in Texas Politics* (Princeton, N.J.: Princeton University Press, 1990).

Goodwyn, Lawrence, *Democratic Promise: The Populist Moment in America* (New York: Oxford University Press, 1976).

Harold, Stanley W., and Richard G. Niemi, *Vital Statistics on American Politics* (Washington, D.C.: Congressional Quarterly Press, 2003).

Horner, Louise L., *Almanac of the 50 States* (Palo Alto, Calif.: Information Publications, 2003).

Morgan, Kathleen O'Leary, and Scott Morgan, *State Rankings 2003* (Lawrence, Kans.: Morgan Quito, 2003).

Putnam, Robert, *Making Democracy Work* (Princeton, N.J.: Princeton University Press, 1993).

Shapiro, Thomas M. *The Hidden Cost of Being African American: How Wealth Perpetuates Inequality* (New York: Oxford University Press, 2004).

Stephens, Ray, and William M. Holmes, *Historical Atlas of Texas* (Norman: University of Oklahoma Press, 1989).

Vaca, Nicolas C., *The Presumed Alliance* (New York: HarperCollins, 2004).

STUDY QUESTIONS

1. What do Robert Doerr's activities regarding the name change at Texas State show us about politics?

2. According to George W. Bush, what does "responsible citizenship" mean, or what do responsible citizens do?

3. Define the term *megastate* and the items ranked in the megastate index.

4. Identify three dimensions that define Texas because of its location.

5. Identify the three requirements of the Treaty of Velasco.

CRITICAL THINKING QUESTIONS

1. In what ways has this chapter shown that individuals matter in Texas? Under what circumstances are they most likely to be effective?

2. Texas is a megastate. What does that mean in terms of the policies we may wish to pursue?

3. How has Texas been affected by joining the United States of America?

4. What are the major components of the Texas population, and what will that population look like in the middle of the twenty-first century?

5. Which of the three American political cultures do you think should expand in Texas? What are the staging points for this expansion?

6. Which region of Texas were you raised in? If you were not raised in Texas, then which region would you feel most comfortable living in?

INTERNET RESOURCES

www.Google.com   This search engine is useful and you are probably already aware of it. Professors at Texas State have used it to catch plagiarism on papers. It can also save you time if you have forgotten a URL or web address.

www.assignmenteditor.com   This site includes a good master list with lots of links. All journalism majors should know it already.

www.usnewspaperlinks.com/txnews.html   We found this site invaluable in researching the regions of Texas.

www.ccsi.com/~comcause   This site is sponsored by one of the original good-government organi-

zations still active in Texas, and it has useful links to other sites (click on "Other Sites of Interest"). The URL for Adam Rifkin's activism site is so long that it is better to find it through this site and then bookmark it. If you are interested in making a difference by doing volunteer work, check with Common Cause or with Adam Rifkin's site, which has numerous links.

www.cppp.org/ The Center for Public Policy Priorities tracks Texas policy dealing with children and the working poor.

CHAPTER 2

The Texas Constitution

The predominantly Hispanic Edgewood school district in West San Antonio had always been one of the poorest in the state of Texas. Many of the buildings in the district did not have air conditioning and were dilapidated. Many of the schools also lacked basic supplies and books. From his simple white frame house on Sylvia Avenue in the Edgewood district, Demetrio Rodriguez, a forty-eight-year-old sheet-metal worker at Kelly Air Force Base, could look across a dry, brown playing field and see a decaying Edgewood Elementary School where his two sons attended school. Not only had the top two floors of the school been condemned but almost half the teachers in the school were not certified.

In contrast, just ten minutes away, in northern San Antonio, was the affluent Alamo Heights Independent School District. For decades, Alamo Height's resources

His daughter didn't graduate from a school as well-equipped as Demetrio Rodriguez would have liked, but his daughter did graduate.

far surpassed those of its neighbor's. Teaching positions there rarely opened; when one did, candidates, heavy with credentials, vied for the job.

Under the Texas school finance system, rich school districts such as Alamo Heights could spend as much as nine times the money per pupil that a poorer district such as Edgewood could. To Rodriguez and his neighbors, it did not seem fair that a child who lived in a wealthy district would receive a better education than a child who did not.

Rodriguez and other concerned parents finally voiced their complaints privately to school administrators and state legislators. Rebuffed there, they went to court. On July 10, 1968, Rodriguez and seven other Edgewood parents filed a lawsuit on behalf of Texas schoolchildren who were poor or resided in school districts with low property-tax bases. Because Rodriguez challenged a state law on federal grounds, the case ultimately ended up in the U.S. Supreme Court. In this landmark case, *San Antonio Independent School District v. Rodriguez*, the Supreme Court ruled that the issue should be resolved by the state of Texas. The battle for educational equity continued.

Unsuccessful at the federal level, Rodriguez and others turned to the Texas state courts in 1984. This time, they prevailed. On October 2, 1989, the Texas Supreme

Court, in the historic *Edgewood v. Kirby* decision, unanimously declared the Texas school-finance system unconstitutional. The court would revisit the school-finance issue four times. After each of the first Edgewood cases, the legislature responded with a reformed finance system. Since Rodriguez started the fight for equal funding, the financial disparity among school districts in Texas has been reduced substantially. Nevertheless, a great deal remains to be done.

If Rodriguez and the other parents had not taken action, enormous disparities would still exist in school-district funding. Rodriguez and other parents acted as a group to improve the well-being of children in poor school districts. When the political system is not being effective, we cannot simply blame politicians or the constitution. We must act. If we do not, we should blame ourselves, not the politicians, for not taking an active role in our political system. People in a democratic system can rectify the flaws in the system through the legitimate participatory channels, as Rodriguez and others did.

The future of governance in Texas rests on the need for an involved, active, and informed citizenry. Otherwise, the quality of our lives in an open society could be threatened.

Historical Constitutional Development in Texas

Constitution A basic law that sets forth the institutional structure of government and the tasks these government institutions perform.

Separation of powers The principle of dividing governmental power among the executive, legislative, and judicial branches.

Limited government A government with limited authority. Usually the bill of rights and other provisions throughout the constitution place limits on governmental authority and power.

Bill of rights Amendments to the constitution that define basic liberties such as freedom of religion, speech, and the press, and offer protections against arbitrary searches by the police and being held without legal representation.

A written **constitution** is the foundation of democratic government. Constitutions, for nations and for states, have at least four common characteristics and common objectives. First, they prescribe the essential structure of government—a structure that invariably includes a chief executive, a legislature, and a court system. Second, they distribute responsibility among the executive, legislative, and judicial branches using the concept of **separation of powers.** In so doing, they establish limits of the power of government as a whole, that is, a **limited government.** Third, they set out a **bill of rights** restraining governmental interference with the liberties of individuals. Fourth, they provide ways to amend the constitution formally and sometimes ways to adapt laws and institutions to deal with change.

Texas has had considerable experience in constitution writing and development (whether a better constitution emerged each time is debatable). The first constitution was a joint constitution for Texas and Coahuila promulgated in 1827. The second constitution was drafted and adopted in 1836 for the Republic of Texas, and the third constitution was adopted when Texas became part of the United States in 1845. The fourth was written in 1861, when Texas joined the Confederacy at the start of the Civil War, and the fifth was written in 1866 to rejoin the Union. In 1869, Texas adopted what became known as the carpetbag constitution—its sixth. The seventh and last was adopted in 1876 following the Reconstruction government under the 1869 constitution.

Texas continues to operate under the 1876 constitution, although efforts have been made to replace it. To understand the current Texas constitution and politics of the state, it might help to understand the circumstances and conditions under which each constitution was drafted.

CONSTITUTION OF COAHUILA AND TEXAS (1827)

Texas was formerly part of Mexico and subject to the laws of Spain. In 1821, Mexico won independence from Spain. Following a period of internal strife, Mexico's political leaders wrote a constitution defining the powers of the federal government and several state governments.

Under an act of the Mexican Congress on May 7, 1824, Texas was joined temporarily with the Mexican state of Coahuila to form the single state of Coahuila y Tejas. In March 1827, a constitution was promulgated for the state. The Roman Catholic religion was declared a state religion, citizens were guaranteed individual rights and liberties, and restrictions were placed on the institution of slavery. Legislative power in Coahuila y Tejas was delegated to a legislative body with one chamber composed of twelve members, each elected for two years by popular vote. Tejas was allowed two representatives; the rest were to be chosen from the Mexican population of Coahuila.

In addition to limited representation, the religion and slavery clauses, and other features that the Texas colonists found objectionable, the administration of justice in Texas was neglected, and the rights of trial by jury were not guaranteed.[1] Laws were published in the Spanish language, which few of the Texas colonists knew. The interests of the two sections of the joint state were so diverse that they inevitably produced ill feeling between the peoples.[2]

After Santa Ana seized control of the Mexican government in 1834 and created a centralized government, the rapidly growing Anglo-Texan population became increasingly unhappy with his authoritarian rule. Political unrest and a keen desire for a separate state government finally led in 1836 to Texas's revolution and a declaration of independence from Mexico. These actions required a constitution for the Republic of Texas.

CONSTITUTION OF THE REPUBLIC (1836)

The Constitution of the Republic of Texas was written in 1836 by delegates assembled in a convention at Washington-on-the-Brazos. This new constitution resembled the U.S. Constitution written in Philadelphia in 1787, and the southern and border states from which most Anglo Texans at that time had come. This document, which was brief, concise, and flexible, provided a division of powers among the legislative, executive, and judicial branches of the government and a system of **checks and balances.** Regular elections guaranteed that the will of the people eligible to vote would prevail.

Checks and balances
A major principle of the U.S. government system whereby each branch of the government exercises a check on the actions of the other branches.

The 1836 constitution created a bicameral Congress composed of the Senate and the House of Representatives. House members, who had to be at least twenty-five years old, were chosen annually by districts. Each county was given at least one representative, and the House was never to exceed forty in number. Senators had to be at least thirty years old; they were elected from senatorial districts according to population and served three years.

The first president of Texas was to be elected by the people for a two-year term; subsequent presidents were to be elected for three years. No president could succeed himself. His powers and duties followed closely those of the president of the United States, but he was forbidden to lead the armies of the Republic except with the consent of the Texas Congress. No religion was shown a preference by the government. Negro slaves were to remain slaves; Congress was forbidden to emancipate slaves or legislate against their importation from the United States, but importation from any other country was declared piracy.

CONSTITUTION OF 1845

When Texans approved the Constitution of the Republic in 1836, they also gave a mandate for annexation to the United States. By so doing, say Texas historians Robert A. Calvert and Arnold De Leon, "[T]he majority revealed the deep-seated connection they felt to their country of origin."[3] The annexation was initially blocked by the issue of slavery. President Andrew Jackson feared a "northern reaction to the explosive issue: abolitionists saw talk of incorporating Texas as a conspiracy of southerners to expand slavery's domain."[4]

By the 1840s, however, annexation seemed more acceptable to the people in the United States. By then, the U.S. future was thought to be continental expansion, and Texas fell neatly into that idea.[5] When James K. Polk, the Democratic candidate for president, won election on an expansion platform, Congress began to rethink the fate of Texas.

The new constitution drafted in 1845 to allow Texas's annexation was approved by joint resolution of the U.S. Congress, and Texas was thus admitted into the Union on an equal footing with the original states. This constitution was also modeled after southern state constitutions and it was twice as long as the Constitution of 1836. U.S. Senator Daniel Webster called this constitution the best of all state constitutions of that day.[6]

The constitution created an elected legislature that met biennially and was composed of the House of Representatives and the Senate. The executive branch was similar to the federal strong-executive model in the U.S. Constitution. It provided for an elected governor and an elected lieutenant governor. The governor was afforded the opportunity to appoint many executive and judicial officers, including the attorney general, secretary of state, and supreme court and district court judges. However, the force of Jacksonian democracy, which advocated the election of executives, deprived the governor of Texas of his strong role by eliminating his appointive powers. In 1850, the voters of Texas amended the constitution to make almost all positions, executive and judicial, elective.[7]

CONSTITUTION OF 1861

When Texas seceded from the Union on the eve of the Civil War, the Constitution of 1861 went into effect. It was basically the same as the Constitution of 1845 except for changes required to conform with Texas's membership in the Confederate States of America. All officials were required to take an oath to support the constitution of Confederacy, clauses on slavery were changed to give greater emphasis and protection to that institution, and both the legislature and masters were forbidden to free any slaves.

CONSTITUTION OF 1866

On June 17, 1865, President Andrew Johnson appointed Andrew Jackson Hamilton, a former U.S. congressman from Texas and a Unionist, as provisional governor of Texas. The president instructed Hamilton to call a convention and to take the necessary steps to form a new civil government. Johnson's terms of reconstruction were lenient: The seceded states were to declare secession null and void; repudiate any Confederate war debt; and ratify the Thirteenth Amendment to the U.S. Constitution, which ended slavery.

Texas voters revived the Constitution of 1845 and amended it to include the stipulations required by the national government. This constitution declared the secession illegal, the debt repudiated, and slavery ended. But it denied blacks the right to vote, hold office, attend state-financed public schools, or serve on juries.[8]

Johnson's mild reconstruction policies had never been popular with northern congressmen.[9] After Radical Republicans captured the U.S. Congress in the November 1866 election, they began to impose on the South a series of policies known collectively as Reconstruction. The Congressional Reconstruction Act of 1867, which was passed over President Johnson's veto, required southern states—including Texas—to draft new constitutions granting African Americans suffrage, ratifying the Fourteenth Amendment, and including other provisions acceptable to the Congress. The Fourteenth Amendment made all persons born or naturalized in the United States citizens of the nation and provided federal protection for citizens' rights. The states are required to provide equal protection under the law and due process of law. The new constitution was invalidated by the U.S. Congress, and Texas went back to the drawing board to devise yet another constitution.

CONSTITUTION OF 1869

A constitutional convention was called in 1869 to draft a constitution acceptable to the Radical Republicans in the U.S. Congress. This document was duly accepted by the electorate and by the U.S. Congress, and Texas was readmitted into the Union in 1870. This constitution, formulated under pressure from Washington, did not represent the sentiment of white native Texans, however: It enfranchised African Americans and disenfranchised former Confederate soldiers and persons who held public office under the Confederate system. To pay for the protection of the western counties from Comanche raids and the establishment of law and order in the rest of the state, the tax burden under this constitution was heavy. In this political climate, Radical Republicans gained control of the Texas legislature and elected as governor Edmund J. Davis, a Radical Republican and former Union army general.

According to the Constitution of 1869, the legislature met annually, the governor served a four-year term, and judges were appointed by the governor rather than being elected to office. Salaries for government officials significantly increased. The governor was also given complete control over the registration of voters. Both the militia and the state police were under the control of the governor, whose power was reinforced by a provision enabling him to establish martial law in any troublesome district. Davis's administration in Texas was believed by some to be "one of oppression, corruption, graft and blackmail."[10] To others, it was typical of state governments of the time. Clearly, the thousands of returning unhappy Confederate veterans made protection of the African American population difficult, if not impossible. According to Fred Gantt, Irving Luther and G. Haggard, "[t]he Constitution of 1869 sought to centralize the government and brought about a large growth in government expenditures, an increase in taxation, and rapid accumulation of a comparatively heavy debt."[11]

Davis's party received a severe blow when a Democratic majority was elected to the legislature in the election of 1872. In the gubernatorial election the next year (called the most fraudulent election in Texas history), Davis was defeated by Richard Coke, a former Confederate officer and nominee of the Democrats.[12] The stage was set for drafting a new constitution that was satisfactory to the Anglo majority.

CONSTITUTION OF 1876

In the elections of 1872, 1873, and 1874, the Democrats successfully wrested control of the legislature, the governor, and the courts from the Republicans. Having regained control of the legislative and executive branches of government, they determined in 1874 to replace the unpopular Constitution of 1869.[13] In August 1875, voters approved a convention to meet in September and selected three delegates from each of the thirty senatorial districts to write the new document.

The constitutional convention was composed of ninety men: seventy-five Democrats and only fifteen Republicans, six of them black. Forty-one were farmers, twenty-nine were lawyers, and twenty were representatives of other walks of life.[14] Not one had been a member of the convention of 1868–1869.

Particularly influential in the convention proceedings were forty-one delegates who were members of the Society of the Patrons of Husbandry, soon called the **Grange.** The Grange was an organization of farmers, and its main goals were to restrict the size and scope of state government and to control the excesses of big business, particularly the banks that controlled credit and the railroads that moved their crops to markets in the eastern cities. The Grange, which was formed in Dallas in October 1873, emerged as the most organized and effective force espousing a restrictive constitution. In the convention, the Grange members acted as a block and therefore set the tone of the convention.[15]

The delegates to the Constitutional Convention of 1875 were determined to strip government of the power they believed the Republicans had misused. They set out to erase all vestiges of Reconstruction, including protection of African American Texans, and to initiate a concept of government even more limited than in the pre–Civil War constitutions. They restricted the governor's power and term

The Grange An organization of farmers. The Texas Grange was organized in 1873.

of office, severely curbed the taxing and spending powers of the legislature, and lowered the salaries of public officials. They also included in the constitution as many safeguards as possible to prevent any abuse of power. In doing so, they also limited the legitimate use of power. As a result, the 1876 Constitution has been amended frequently so that the state government could solve problems.

Ratification of the Constitution of 1876 was accomplished without effective opposition, but without impressive enthusiasm either. Nevertheless, by a vote of 53 to 11, the convention adopted the constitution on November 24, 1875, and arrangement was made to submit it to the largely Anglo male electorate for approval. In spite of vigorous criticism of the constitution, it was approved overwhelmingly. The vote for adoption, in a remarkably quiet election, was 136,606 to 56,652.[16]

As might be expected, rural sections of the state voted overwhelmingly for ratification because many of the constitution's provisions were in their interest. Farmers distrusted big business, particularly big banks, and preferred instead smaller, locally owned banks whose managers would be more understanding during hard times. Framers of the constitution prohibited branch banking, a business practice whereby a single, large bank conducts business from several locations. This provision ensured that large banks would be locally owned. Most of the large towns and cities, including Dallas, Galveston, Houston, and San Antonio, voted against adoption of this constitution.

Texas Constitution Today

The Constitution of 1876, now with 432 amendments, is still the fundamental law of Texas. It was a product of reaction, or overreaction, to the Radical Republican regime in Texas. Its framers thus set out to restrain a state government that they believed had grown too large and too expensive.

The limitations placed on the executive and legislative branches represent examples of overreaction. The legislature was to be made up of two houses: a Senate of thirty-one members and a House of Representatives not to exceed 150 members. The term of senators was reduced from six to four years. To reduce the cost of government, the new constitution provided for biennial sessions of legislature (instead of the annual sessions required by the 1869 document and by the current constitution of all the other megastates). The constitution itself specified also how much lawmakers were to be paid. As of 1975, when the most recent amendment about salaries was ratified, legislators are paid $7,200 per year plus per-diem and travel allowances. To prevent government from squandering money and increasing the state's debt, the delegates forbade the state to incur indebtedness in an amount greater than $200,000 and severely limited the taxing power of the legislature.[17]

The new constitution reduced the term of the governor from four years to two. (This stipulation has been changed for the governor and the rest of the executive branch by later constitutional amendments.) It also reduced the salary of the governor and limited his or her powers by setting forth the governor's duties in great detail. Aside from express limits on gubernatorial power, other means were used to make it difficult for any future government to abuse its powers, or to use power in a positive way. Article IV decentralized the executive authority by vesting executive power in seven executive officers, all of whom (except the secretary of state) were to be elected by the voters.

The governor's powers and duties were set forth in considerable detail. He might convene the legislature in special session, call out the militia and declare martial law to suppress insurrections, and fill various vacancies by appointments (subject, however, to approval of the Senate by a two-thirds vote). He was given power to veto laws and veto items in appropriations bills, but his veto might be overridden by a two-thirds vote of both houses. It was declared that the governor, as the chief executive of the state, should cause the laws to be "faithfully executed," but the powers granted to him were not equal to such great responsibilities. He was given no formal authority over local officers and other elected state executive officers. In summary, Article IV set the stage for a fragmented and therefore weak executive branch.

Having hemmed in the legislature and executive on almost every side, the delegates to the Constitutional Convention of 1876 then turned to limiting the power of the state courts. Under the 1869 constitution, the governor had the power to appoint all judges. Article V of the 1876 Constitution, however, provided that all judges be elected by popular vote, with terms of four years for district judges and six years for judges of higher courts. With the establishment of a dual system of appeals courts, the convention provided for a supreme court with power to review civil cases only and for a court of criminal appeals with appellate jurisdiction over all criminal cases and certain classes of civil cases. Texas is one of only two states (Oklahoma is the other) that does not have a single court at the top of the judicial pyramid.

Despite contemporary criticism of the Constitution of 1876, it reflected fairly well the views of the majority of the Anglo public. As historians A. J. and Ann Thomas contend, "The main effort of the Constitutional Convention of 1875, without question, was devoted to the restraining of individuals in governmental roles from wrongdoing."[18] This effort can be compared to child rearing: How can people (or children) learn if they are prevented from making any mistakes at all? What happens if they do make mistakes?

BASIC PRINCIPLES OF THE TEXAS CONSTITUTION

The ideas of political philosophers, especially John Locke and the French philosopher Montesquieu, have heavily influenced all constitution writing in the United States. One part of Locke's theory is the idea of limited government by way of the separation of powers. Article II of the Texas Constitution explicitly establishes the separation of power among the three branches; no one can hold a position in more than one branch at a time. To prevent the concentration of power, checks and balances have been added: the executive and judicial branches share some powers, and no branch has exclusive domain over any activity. To put it another way, the operation of government requires that the three branches cooperate and compromise occasionally.

Popular sovereignty
A political concept in which the voters in a political system are the ultimate and supreme source of all authority.

Also found in the Texas Constitution is the idea of **popular sovereignty**. It is sometimes stated directly as a principle, and it is sometimes implied by the fact that all public officials are either elected or receive their appointments from those who are elected, and can exercise only the powers given to them by elected officials or by the people themselves. Popular sovereignty is the theoretical underpinning for a written constitution, which is how the people limit the powers of their government. A bill of rights is a basic limitation on the power of the government and is another feature of the Texas Constitution.

Popular sovereignty can be applied differently, however, depending on which level of the political system exercises this sovereignty. The founding fathers clearly placed sovereignty at the state level and in the constitution they wrote. If you want to raise legislative salaries or give the citizens of a county the power to restructure their own county government, then you have to change the state constitution.

The Texas Bill of Rights is contained in the first article of the constitution and has twenty-nine sections. Many of the civil rights set forth in this document are identical to those found in the first eight amendments to the U.S. Constitution. The article declares, for example, that all free men have equal rights and that the writ of habeas corpus (the legal doctrine that a person who is arrested must have a timely hearing before a judge) cannot be suspended or unduly delayed.[19] It forbids unreasonable searches, and it guarantees liberty of speech and the press, the right of the accused to obtain bail and to be tried by a jury, and the right of citizens to keep and bear arms. Also included are various guarantees and declarations not found in the U.S. Bill of Rights, such as the provisions that forbid imprisonment for debt and religious tests for public office.

The Texas Constitution spells out in detail the organization and power of local governments, especially of counties. In legal theory, local governments depend on the state government for their formal powers, and under the Texas Constitution, the state legislature is authorized to enact legislation involving local governments (except county governments). The structure of county government cannot be changed except by constitutional amendment.

Criticisms of the Texas Constitution

Since its adoption in 1876, the Texas Constitution has been criticized for its excessive length, detail, and restrictiveness. It has also been blamed for the difficulty that state and local governments face in trying to cope with many contemporary problems.

TOO MUCH DETAIL

Scholars believe that a state constitution should be brief and explicit and include general principles rather than specific legislative provisions. In other words, the constitution should establish the basic power relationships among various components of government. It should not attempt to define in detail the purposes for which that power may be used. The more detailed aspects of law should be left to legislative statute.

The Texas Constitution does not conform to this model. Rather, it is a hodge-podge of legislative rules, statutory materials, and a limited amount of fundamental law. It is less a set of basic governmental principles than a compilation of detailed statutory language that renders it inflexible. For example, it contains detailed provisions on several issues: the teachers' retirement fund, rural fire-protection districts, limitations on state appropriation of anticipated revenue, the issuance and sale of bonds by the state to create the Texas Water Development Board, and a tax levy authorized for Confederate soldiers and salaries as well as for their widows. These various issues could have been included more effectively in state statutes or administrative provisions rather than in the state constitution had the legislature been less restricted. Unlike the U.S. Constitution, which lists specific tasks given to Congress and then grants Congress the powers "necessary and proper" to carry out those tasks, the Texas Constitution of 1876 contains no "necessary and proper" clause for the legislature—just a limited number of specific tasks.

LENGTH AND NUMBER OF AMENDMENTS

State constitutions typically are excessively long and detailed. In contrast to the U.S. Constitution, which has about 8,700 words, the average state constitution has 30,000. The Texas Constitution, with its seventeen articles and 432 amendments, is the longest constitution of the megastates (see Texas in Context 2.1). It contains over 90,000 words, and it is exceeded in length only by the constitution of Alabama, with a whopping 315,000 words. Only California, with 500 amendments, has changed its constitution more than Texas has.[20]

As a result of its great length and detail, the Texas Constitution is highly inflexible. More and more decisions must be referred directly to the electorate through the process of amendment. The large number of amendments has further increased its complexity and detail.

Unlike the Texas Constitution, the U.S. Constitution has been amended only twenty-seven times since its adoption in 1789, and it is a concise document that outlines broad, basic principles of authority and governance. It has been made adaptable through interpretation by judicial, executive, and legislative actions rather than formal amendment.

THE LONG BALLOT AND DECENTRALIZED ADMINISTRATIVE SYSTEM

The framers of the Constitution of Texas had little confidence in state government because of their widespread fear of and frustrating experience with Reconstruction rule. They didn't have much confidence in local government either. They believed that less government—state or local—meant that people were better off. The result of their efforts was a restrictive and poorly drafted document.

TEXAS in Context

2.1 Constitutions of the Megastates

State	Estimated Length (Number of Words)	Number of Amendments Submitted to Voters	Number of Amendments Adopted
Texas	**93,000**	**606**	**432***
California	54,645	846	507
Florida	52,421	127	96
New York	51,700	288	215
Ohio	36,900	265	160
Massachusetts	36,700	148	120
Michigan	27,649	61	23
Pennsylvania	27,503	34	28
New Jersey	22,956	67	54
Illinois	13,700	17	11

*Based on information provided by Legislative Reference Library of Texas Online at http://www.lrl.state.tx.us/legis/constAmends/lrlhome.com.

Source: The Book of the States 2003 (Lexington, Ky.: Council of State Governments, 2003), p. 10.

In the executive branch, the Texas Constitution dispersed authority to such a degree that firm executive leadership is difficult to achieve. For example, the constitution permits the direct election of a series of executive branch officials (including the attorney general, treasurer, land commissioner, and comptroller), allowing them to operate with little influence from the governor's office.

The objective of this direct election (or long ballot) was to establish popular control over the operation and functions of government. In practice, the long ballot has not often lived up to expectations.[21] The electorate is not generally familiar with the responsibilities of all the administrative offices or with the qualifications of the candidates seeking them. Voters' interest in such offices is seldom high. Such officeholders may become closely allied with special interests concerned with the work of their specific office. These interest groups finance the election campaigns of candidates who may be sympathetic to their point of view. Public officials may not become corrupted once in office, but the process lets interest groups pick their own regulators. Thus, it appears that the people exercise little or no control over the activities of such officeholders even though, in theory, they elect them. If you can organize your fellow Texans to take a closer look at the system, however, then perhaps you can make sure that elected officials serve the people, not the special interests. The biggest spenders don't always win.

Social Changes and Constitutional Adaptation

The Texas of 1876 is significantly different than the Texas of 2005. Changes in our society have required Texas government to adapt to technology, urban sprawl, and the migration of people, plants, diseases, and ideas. These changes have required us to change our constitution many times. Whether or not 432 amendments were absolutely necessary, we have them. Because so many amendments have been required, it has become quite normal for interest groups to slip a few unnecessary amendments into the process. In 2002, for example, we limited the power of the state to tax raw cocoa. Does this belong in our constitution?

Constitutions are adapted to modern conditions by amendment, by judicial decisions, or by laws and executive actions. All three methods merit some attention.

CONSTITUTIONAL AMENDMENT

Constitutional rules, like all rules, can and do change over time. Constitutional changes in many states come about in three specific ways: (1) legislative proposal, (2) constitutional convention, and (3) popular initiative.[22] Article XVII of the Texas Constitution provides only one method of amending. "The legislature," reads the constitution, "at any regular session or at any special session when the matter is included within the purposes for which the session is convened, may propose amendments revising the constitution." The proposed amendment or amendments must be approved by a two-thirds vote of all members elected to each chamber. At least 100 House representatives and twenty-one senators would have to vote in favor of an amendment. The governor has no power to veto or otherwise legally impede what the legislature determines.

Once approved by the Texas legislature, an amendment must be put before the voters in a special election or it is appended to the ballot in the general election. If the majority of those who vote in the election approve, then the governor issues a proclamation to that effect. A 1972 amendment to the constitution requires that proposed amendments have to be published twice, but not in full. All newspapers in the state qualifying for the publication of legal notices are required to publish a synopsis of the amendment. In addition, the entire text of each amendment must be posted at the courthouse of each county. Normally, the electorate does not show much interest in the proposed amendments. The turnout for elections on constitutional amendments is considerably low: Only a small fraction of registered voters cast ballots in these elections.[23]

Almost annually, Texas voters decide what changes will be made to the state constitution. From its adoption in 1876 through September 2004, the constitution has been amended 432 times from a total of 606 amendments that were submitted to the voters for their approval. Only Louisiana, California, and Alabama have adopted more amendments to their constitution. As shown in Table 2.1, more than half of these amendments were adopted in the previous three decades. During this period, voters considered 247 amendments, adopted 191 of them, and turned

TABLE 2.1	Constitutional Amendments Proposed and Adopted				
Year Proposed	Number Proposed	Number Adopted	Year Proposed	Number Proposed	Number Adopted
1879–1889	16	8	1951–1959	43	37
1891–1899	15	9	1961–1969	84	56
1901–1909	20	11	1971–1979	67	42
1911–1919	36	10	1981–1989	99	84
1921–1929	26	15	1990–1999	81	64
1931–1939	45	32	2001–2003	42	42
1941–1949	35	22			

Source: *Texas Legislative Council*, Analyses of Proposed Constitutional Amendments (September 2003).

down fifty-six. During this time, the Lone Star State was in the midst of a great transition from a rustic frontier to a complex, highly urbanized, and highly industrialized state. The 1970s particularly were boom years for the state compared with the nation as a whole. From 1970 to 1980, per-capita personal income in Texas increased 25.7 percent, compared to 13.3 percent for the nation as a whole.[24] At the same time, the population in the state rose from 11.2 million in 1970 to 14.2 million in 1980, an increase of 26.8 percent, which is well above the 11.4 percent increase in population nationally.[25]

With this growth came new problems that were unheard of a century ago. Texans had to adapt themselves to these new situations. They amended the constitution frequently to keep the state administration at least partially in touch with the increasingly complex social demands. The fact that so many amendments have been adopted and others continue to be submitted by the legislature is persuasive proof that the constitution should be revised in a comprehensive and orderly fashion. It is almost impossible now to make any basic changes in the Texas constitutional system through amendments. Indeed, many amendments are poorly drafted and have to be changed.

In the past six constitutional amendment elections, turnout has ranged from 6.9 percent to 12.6 percent. The high point came in 1993, when a special election for the U.S. senator was also on the ballot. In November 2003, only 12 percent of the 12 million registered voters in Texas approved twenty-two more amendments to the Constitution. This turnout was in fact higher than average in a constitutional amendment election because of the controversial Proposition 12, which was at the center of fierce public debate during the election. This proposition allows the legislature to place caps on noneconomic damages in medical malpractice suits. It became a big-money battle pitting doctors against plaintiffs' lawyers as both sides tried to rally voters to their cause. Supporters and opponents of the proposition raised at least $13 million for the fight. Despite well-funded, organized, and vocal opposition around the state, Proposition 12 won by less than 25,000 votes out of nearly 1.5 million ballots cast. To put it another way, 100 more votes in each of the 254 counties could have altered the outcome.

It is unfortunate that the Texas Constitution can be manipulated by wealthy special interests like the insurance industry. If voters withdraw from judgment and do not participate in the voting process, democracy will be captured by a small minority that will steer government mostly for its own benefit. Ultimately that outcome will also destroy democracy. As a citizen of this state, you have the obligation and ample opportunity to learn about every aspect of government. Information is the key for making appropriate judgments about the great experiments such as voting for constitutional amendments.

CONSTITUTIONAL REVISION OF 1974

Progressive leaders have long advocated that the Texas Constitution be either revised or replaced with a new document that provides for a more accountable and efficient state government. Spearheaded by the League of Women Voters, the Texas Bar Association, and other civic groups, the Texas legislature in 1972 approved an amendment to the Texas Constitution authorizing the creation of a constitutional revision commission to study the need for constitutional change and to report its recommendations to members of the legislature by November 1, 1973.

Under the authority of the 1972 amendment, a six-member committee (the governor, the lieutenant governor, the Speaker of the House, the attorney general, the chief justice of the Texas Supreme Court, and the presiding judge of the Court of Criminal Appeals) selected thirty-seven persons to serve on the Constitutional Revision Commission, which was chaired by a former Texas chief justice, Robert W. Calvert. After holding hearings at various locations around the state, the commission prepared a draft constitution, or working model. The proposed new constitution was much shorter and more generally phrased than the existing one. It included major changes such as greater administrative powers for the governor, annual legislative sessions, and the elimination of much of the unnecessary details in the existing constitution.[26]

With Speaker of the House Price Daniel, Jr., as the presiding officer, the 181 members of the legislature met as planned in January 1974 to consider the revision commission's recommendations. After much debate and compromise, the convention completed an eleven-article constitution in July. When the proposed constitution was voted on by the legislature, however, it fell three votes short. The legislature failed to approve its own work. Thus, the document was not presented to the voters.[27]

At least four factors contributed to the failure of the convention to submit a new constitution to the voters. First, the delegates were also legislators, and they were subject to pressure from interest groups because of the impact their votes might have on their political future. Second, the convention was hampered by the lack of positive leadership. Governor Dolph Briscoe, Jr., assumed a neutral stance on the proposed constitution. Speaker Daniel, who chaired the convention, had already taken himself out of the running for the Speaker's job in the next session of the legislature. As a lame duck, he was a less effective leader. Third, some emotional issues, especially the proposed insertion of the right-to-work provision prohibiting union membership as a required condition of employment, served to polarize the delegates. Texas has had a right-to-work statute on the books since 1947, and the prospects of inserting it into the new constitution was more than progressive delegates could stomach. Finally, the required two-thirds vote was blamed for the failure of the convention. A large majority voted at one time or another for each resolution, but a two-thirds vote proved impossible for the entire document.

The legislature in 1975 revived the constitutional revision issue. It essentially took the proposal that the convention had drafted and parceled it into eight proposed amendments, minus the right-to-work provision. In November 1975, approximately twenty-five percent of the eligible voters went to the polls and overwhelmingly rejected all eight proposed amendments by a margin of 3 to 1.[28] The brunt of the blame for this failure goes to the general lack of citizen interest in the work of the constitutional convention.[29]

RECENT ATTEMPTS AT REVISION

During the 1999 session of the legislature, Senator Bill Ratliff and Representative Rob Junell proposed a new state constitution that would streamline and modernize the existing constitution. It would trim outmoded restrictions and unnecessary detail best left to statute. It would cut the constitution from 376 sections and 82,800 words to 150 sections and 19,000 words, leaving a much clearer, more easily understood outline of the duties and powers of the state government. The new constitution would remove nineteenth-century limits on the governor's authority, thus allowing the chief executive to appoint a cabinet of department heads, as the U.S. president and many other state governors do.

Ratliff's and Junell's proposed constitution died in House and Senate committees. Although its opponents agreed that a new constitution is needed, they opposed the legislature's rewriting it in a single session. They advocated the creation of a constitutional convention to concentrate solely on constitutional revision.

Texas will not have a new constitution unless a large enough coalition agrees on what it should contain. How can you, as an individual, help to rewrite the constitution? If you think it is time to change the constitution and thus streamline the system, you can work with the League of Women Voters and the State Bar Association. (The Internet Resources at the end of this chapter provides website addresses for both organizations.) These two organizations believe that Texas should have a new state constitution. They charge that the existing document is so long and detailed, and so often amended, that many citizens do not understand it.

You may also write or send an e-mail to your state representative and senator to urge them to consider proposing a new constitution in the next legislative session. To find your representative's name and e-mail address, go to the website provided in the Internet Resources section at the end of the chapter and click on Who Represents Me?

JOIN THE DEBATE

THE ISSUE: Should the Constitution of 1876 be revised?

AGREE

1. It has been amended 432 times.
2. It can be amended by a small fraction of voters.
3. It is too long and complex. Constitutions should be brief and explicit.
4. It is inflexible.
5. The long ballot and decentralized administrative system did not provide real popular control over the operations of government.
6. It has created biennial legislative sessions. Large states like Texas need annual legislative sessions.

DISAGREE

1. If it ain't broke, don't fix it.
2. Safeguards were created to prevent the abuse of power.
3. Judges are not appointed; they are elected by popular vote instead.
4. Citizens were guaranteed individual rights and liberties.
5. The legislative session is limited.
6. The governor's power is reduced.

Review and discuss the constitution introduced by Representative Rob Junell and Senator Bill Ratliff with your teacher and fellow classmates. If you believe that the proposed constitution would make Texas government more efficient, contact your representatives (particularly Senator Ratliff, who served as lieutenant governor in 2001 and 2002) to urge them to introduce it again in the legislature. The address of the website for the proposed constitution is in the Internet Resources section.

Summary

Like most other states, Texas has had many different constitutions over the years. The constitution is important because it organizes the branches of government, distributes powers and privileges among agencies and officeholders, and imposes limits and restrictions on governmental activities.

Texas currently operates under a constitution that was written in the latter decades of the nineteenth century, when state and local governments were plagued by corruption. Attempts to thwart the chicanery led to the inclusion of many lengthy and restrictive constitutional provisions. Although the final document was exceedingly detailed and lengthy, it provided an adequate government at the time of its adoption. But changing social and economic conditions resulting from population and industrial growth have revealed the inadequacy of government to meet situations unimagined by the framers of the 1876 constitution. To keep abreast of the times, a great number of amendments have been added to the constitution. Some of them are for interest groups and not for the general public.

Numerous efforts have been made in recent decades to overhaul the Texas Constitution so that the state can have a more efficient modern government. Proponents of constitutional revision typically seek a shorter and less restrictive document, a shortened ballot, and elimination of numerous antiquated irrelevancies. All attempts, including the last one at sweeping reform, have failed. Consequently, the state has been forced to amend the document continually on a piecemeal basis. A successful revision effort may have to wait until the majority of the citizens of Texas realize that it is time for a change.

KEY TERMS

Constitution, p. 36
Separation of powers, p. 36
Limited government, p. 36
Bill of rights, p. 36

Checks and balances, p. 37
The Grange, p. 40
Popular sovereignty, p. 43

FOR FURTHER READING

Calvert, Robert A., and Arnold De Leon, *The History of Texas* (Arlington, Ill.: Harlan Davidson, 1990).

Gantt, Fred, Jr., *Governing Texas: Documents and Reading* (New York: Crowell, 1966).

May, C. Janice, "Trends in State Constitutional Amendment and Revision," in *The Book of the States* (Lexington, Ky.: The Council of State Governments, 2003).

Stanford, G., "Constitutional Revision in Texas: A New Chapter," *Public Affairs Comment 2* (February 1974).

Stewart, Frank M., and Joseph L. Clark, *The Constitution and Government of Texas* (Boston, Mass.: D.C. Heath, 1949).

Thomas, A. J., Jr., and Ann Van Wynen Thomas, "The Texas Constitution of 1876," *Texas Law Review* 1957.

STUDY QUESTIONS

1. Identify Demetrio Rodriguez and the action he took.

2. What is the function of a constitution?

3. What are the basic principles of the Texas Constitution?

4. What are the similarities and differences between the Texas and the U.S. constitutions?

5. What was the impact of the Grange on the Texas Constitution that remains in effect?

CRITICAL THINKING QUESTIONS

1. Texas has operated under seven constitutions. In your opinion, which one do you believe functioned most effectively and efficiently? Why?

2. Article IV of the 1876 Texas Constitution set the stage for a weak executive branch. What are some of the disadvantages of an executive branch with limited powers?

3. Under the 1869 constitution, the governor had the power to appoint all judges. What could be some of the advantages of appointing individuals in governmental roles?

4. The Texas Constitution has been criticized for its excessive length, detail, and restrictiveness. What are some positive aspects of having an inflexible government?

5. What could be done to get the public interested in the work of rewriting or replacing the constitution?

INTERNET RESOURCES

www.prairienet.org/~scruffy/f.htm   Go to this site to compare the Texas Constitution with the constitutions of other states.

www.findlaw.com   Most state constitutions can be accessed at this website.

www.lwv.org   The League of Women Voters is one of the organizations interested in altering and improving the Texas Constitution. Choose the Texas link.

www.texasbar.com   The Texas Bar Association is another organization interested in altering and improving the Texas Constitution.

www.senate.state.tx.us/75r/senate/members/dist1/dist1.htm   Contact Bill Ratliff, who was one of the sponsors of a new constitution for Texas proposed at the Seventy-Sixth Legislature when he was a senator.

CHAPTER 3

Texas in the Federal System

In 1787, James Madison submitted a proposed amendment to Congress concerning congressional pay raises, along with ten other amendments that eventually became the U.S. Bill of Rights. Madison argued that "there is a seeming impropriety in leaving any set of men without control to put their hand in the public coffers, to take out money to put in their pocket; there is seeming indecorum in such power." Six states approved the amendment immediately, far short of the eleven then needed for ratification.[1] This amendment then languished for almost 200 years, until 1992, when the requisite three-fourths of the states approved it. Now the Twenty-Seventh Amendment to the U.S. Constitution, it states: "No law varying the compensation for the services of the Senators or Representatives shall take effect, until an election of Representatives shall have intervened."

The story of the approval of this amendment began in 1982, when Gregory Watson was writing a paper for his government class at the University of Texas at Austin and came across the proposed amendment. At that time, only eight states had ratified it. Watson argued in his paper that the proposed amendment could still be ratified because no time limit had been placed on ratification, as has been the case with proposed amendments ever since. His instructor disagreed with him and assigned a C to the paper.

Strongly believing in his argument, Watson started a one-man crusade to have the amendment approved by the remaining states. His research turned up a U.S. Supreme Court ruling in 1939 that any amendment without a deadline is still pending business. One state at a time, Watson began sending letters to members of the legislatures in states that had not yet ratified the amendment. In April 1983, he achieved his first success, in Maine. Then in April 1984, it was Colorado. The snowball began to roll as Watson's efforts caught national attention. Texas ratified the amendment in 1989. On May 7, 1992, the Michigan state legislature became the crucial thirty-eighth state to ratify the amendment, 203 years after its proposal.

Watson's hard work and determination helped to make ratification of the Twenty-Seventh Amendment to the U.S. Constitution a reality. Although others tried to take credit for its passage, a Michigan state senator, John F. Kelly, was widely quoted as giving Watson the credit he deserved. Kelly asserted that "Watson's persistence paid off. The beauty of our system is that every individual counts, if they want to."[2]

Watson's story links an individual to both state and national governments. It reminds us both that the U.S. Constitution can be amended only if the state governments approve and that these governments exist to serve us, the citizens. These governments exercise *our* sovereignty, not their own. This point is important to remember in dealing with subjects like federalism and intergovernmental relations, which focus on governments and unintentionally tend to shut individuals out of the discussion. Nevertheless, we as individuals need to understand how these governments interact to make sure they interact in our interests.

The American Federal System

In many discussions of federalism, those who hold the *states rights position* express a concern about national government encroachment on what they view as the sovereignty of the states. The *individual rights position,* in contrast, asserts that the sovereignty of the people matters. From the perspective of individual rights, the power of both the states and the federal government has grown since 1787, not one at the expense of the other.

When a federal judge like Lucius Bunton III, who also happens to be a Texan, tells the government of San Antonio and private landowners that they cannot pump the Edwards aquifer dry, that judge is looking out for the interests of the hundreds of thousands of individual Texans who need the aquifer protected. The fact that he is a federal judge is less important than the fact that he is protecting individual rights to water for generations to come. A federal judge can take this action because of a law passed in the U.S. Congress (which some congressmen from Texas voted for and some voted against). That interaction between judicial and legislative actors who are also Texans is part of the dynamics of the federal system. This system attempts to exercise the sovereignty of the people in serving the interests of individuals by spreading power among a collection of over 87,000 governments, about 4,700 of which are located in Texas.[3]

Americans have always felt ambivalent about government, any level of government, and Texans even more so. © 2004 Austin American-Statesman. *Reprinted with permission of* Universal Press Syndicate. *All rights reserved.*

CONCEPT OF FEDERALISM

The Federal system, of which Texas is a part, was created in 1787 when our founders met in Philadelphia, Pennsylvania, to amend our first constitution—the Articles of Confederation. The government under the Articles was so weak and so ineffective at resolving the growing disputes among the thirteen member states that George Washington threw his support behind an effort to create a new constitution instead of simply amending the Articles. Disgusted by the quarrels among the several states, Washington wrote to a friend shortly before the convention: "I do not conceive we can exist long as a nation without having lodged somewhere a power which will pervade the whole Union in as energetic a manner as the authority of the state governments extends over the several states."[4]

Washington was the presiding officer at the constitutional convention. Once the Constitution was written, it was no small matter to get the people of the several states to ratify it. Like many accomplishments in politics, it took a lot of individual time and energy. To get the proposed constitution ratified in New York, three leaders at the convention—James Madison, Alexander Hamilton, and John Jay—wrote a series of articles published in the local papers or printed up as handbills. Collected together, these articles are called the *Federalist Papers* and have become the best known source for understanding our federal system. The writers of the U.S. Constitution devised a governmental framework that created a national government whose powers were sufficient to provide stability for the nation. At the same time, they placed few restrictions on the states as long as they did not interfere with each other or the national government's constitutional authority.

The system of **federalism** described in the U.S. Constitution has become more complex in the years since 1789, just as the world in which it operates has become more complex. However, the Constitution has been amended only twenty-seven times, the last time as a result of an assignment that linked a Texas college student with James Madison, the primary author of the Constitution.

The American version of federalism can be defined as a political system that is (1) a union of governments, (2) a union of people, (3) recognized by a constitution that grants the sovereignty of the people to the central government, and (4) guarantees the continued existence of the member governments:[5]

1. *A union of governments:* The importance of states in federalism becomes apparent when we consider that this system could not have come into existence if the state governments had not allowed elections to take place for choosing representatives to ratifying conventions, and then allowed the conventions themselves to take place in each state.
2. *A union of people:* The notion of dual citizenship—that one is a citizen of a state and of the United States of America—is a key feature of American federalism. In creating the U.S. Constitution (which starts with "We the people of the United States"), the framers limited the national government's ability to oppress its citizens and amended the Constitution to add a Bill of Rights, which provides additional protections.
3. *Recognized by a constitution that grants the sovereignty of the people to the central government:* Although the idea that state and local governments might oppress their citizens was certainly addressed by Madison in *Federalist Paper No. 10*, it took nearly 100 years for the Fourteenth Amendment of the U.S. Constitution to be passed. In the name of the people of the United States of America, it grants the federal government the authority to require every state to provide every U.S. citizen with equal protection under the law, thus establishing the basis for holding the states to the same standards as the U.S. government for treating citizens fairly. Dual citizenship means being simultaneously citizens of both the state and the nation.
4. *Guarantees the continued existence of the member governments:* The notion of guarantees to the states is critical for understanding the American federal system. It is just as important as the notion of dual citizenship. Not all countries that have adapted federalism to their needs have built in this guarantee. Although other guarantees protect the integrity of the states, the **litmus test of American federalism** is not tied to a specific formula. It simply requires a reasonable role for the states by asking one simple question: "Does the Constitution protect the states by giving them a role in amending it?" Without that protection, a system may be called federal, but it does not follow the American model of federalism. We require that three-fourths of the states ratify an amendment before it becomes part of the Constitution. As Gregory Watson knows well, that requirement means thirty-eight of fifty states.

Federalism The philosophy that describes the governmental system in which power is divided between a central government and regional governments.

Litmus test of American federalism Does the Constitution protect the states by giving them a role in amending it?

In 1789, we invented federalism and, in a sense, we are still inventing it. Each generation adds new features to a core of concepts that remains unchanged. As our form of federalism became better understood in practice, other political systems have attempted to adopt and modify it to their own situation; India, Mexico, Germany, Canada, Nigeria, and Australia all have slightly different forms of federalism—some in the American style, some not. In Canada, for example, it takes unanimous consent of the provinces to amend the Canadian constitution; it is rarely amended.

THE WHOLE AND ITS PARTS: THREE ARRANGEMENTS

Today, almost every American government textbook neatly differentiates unitary, federal, and confederate systems. This differentiation was not possible before the development of our federal Constitution because *federal* and *confederate* meant essentially the same thing. *Federalism* now refers to a form of government that divides authority between a strong central government and a set of regional (state) governments, in a system that provides a role for both governments to deal directly with citizens. A **unitary system,** in contrast, vests all authority in the central government. Citizenship is national, not both regional and national. In a **confederacy,** the central government is weak and cannot deal directly with citizens, and regional governments are powerful. In a confederacy, the powers of the central government are limited to those powers delegated to it by the member governments (see Table 3.1).

Unitary system A system of government in which all powers reside in the central government.

Confederacy A league of independent states in which the central government has only limited powers over the states.

In terms of developing the American version of federalism we have today, it took a civil war to establish the fact that once a political unit joined the United States of America by becoming a state, it could not leave (secede). In fact, the U.S. Supreme Court case that acknowledges that principle originated in Texas: *Texas v. White* (1868). Chief Justice Salmon Chase declared in his majority opinion, "The Constitution . . . looks to an indestructible Union, composed of indestructible states."[6]

In 1997, a group calling themselves the Republic of Texas attempted unsuccessfully to challenge the legality of the way Texas joined the Union in 1845. The leaders are now in prison not because they exercised their freedom of speech, but because they went far beyond it to commit several crimes, including kidnapping, assault with a deadly weapon, and mail fraud. We mention this example because it is important

TABLE 3.1 The Relationship Among the Central Governments, Major Subunits, and Citizens			
Government Type	**Citizenship**	**Alter Constitution**	**Examples**
Unitary	Central only	Central only and citizens	France, Great Britain
Federal	Central and major units	Central and major units	United States, Mexico
Confederate	Major units only	Major units only	United Nations, North Atlantic Treaty Organization

to note that a few people in the Texas political system still do not regard it as our legitimate system. The fact that individuals attempt to make a difference by tearing the system down is all the more reason to get involved and improve it so that it comes closer to meeting the needs of everyone.

DEVELOPMENT OF FEDERALISM

For much of the history of the United States, controversies over jurisdiction were almost entirely legalistic; they depended on court interpretations of the Constitution. Before the industrial revolution tied Americans more closely together, the idea of a distant government in the District of Columbia having much to do with ordinary Americans was an alien concept. America was an idea. People were proud to be Americans, but they regarded state and local governments as being the governments that really affected them.

Between 1865 and 1933, a relationship known as **dual federalism** assumed a clear legal separation between the powers of the national government and those belonging to the states. The theory of dual federalism emerged before the American economy developed to the point that every state is larger in gross state product and in population than many members of the international community. We are not thinking just of the megastates; Rhode Island is bigger than one or two members of the United Nations. Some of our Texas counties are larger than Rhode Island, and they could also be independent countries.

The Great Depression of the 1930s profoundly changed the nature of relationships among national, state and local governments. The depression followed the stock market crash of 1929 and led the way to the election of Franklin D. Roosevelt (FDR) as president. Rampant unemployment (historians estimate it was as high as 40 to 50 percent) and poverty increased the demands on the states, with their limited budgets and amateur legislatures. No government programs at any level had dealt before with such severe poverty and economic loss. Roosevelt's administration introduced the New Deal: economic and social programs together with necessary economic regulations.

President Roosevelt's remedy for the economic ills of the nation focused on serving individual Americans and included innovative involvement by the national government in areas traditionally dealt with by the governments of the states, counties, and cities. The relationships that developed following the 1930s established a new phase of federalism, sometimes called **cooperative federalism,** in which the states and national government cooperate in solving complex common problems. The New Deal programs of Franklin Roosevelt, for example, frequently required joint action by both the national government and the states. Federal grants were given to the states to help pay for housing assistance, Aid to Families with Dependent Children, unemployment compensation, and other programs.

Constitutionally, of course, the powers of the states and the national government remained separate, but the lines of distinction became blurred in cooperative federalism. If dual federalism was a **layer cake,** with the national government and the states in two distinct layers, cooperative federalism became more like a **marble cake**

Dual federalism A system of government in which states and the national government remain supreme within their own sphere.

Cooperative federalism A system of government in which powers and policy assignments are shared between states and the federal government.

Layer cake A phrase that is used to describe federalism in which the top layer is the national government and the bottom layer is comprised of all the state governments. This picture of federalism indicates a formal, legal separation of the activities of the national government and the state governments.

Marble cake A phrase used to describe the relationships among governments in which national, state, and local government activities are swirled together with no clear lines of separation. This picture of federalism incorporates the idea of all governmental levels sharing in making and carrying out decisions.

with mingled responsibilities and no clear delineation between spheres of influence.[7] This new relationship between the whole and its parts is called intergovernmental relations.

Intergovernmental Relations and the Constitution

Intergovernmental relations A term that describes the working relationships of governments in modern American federalism as they interact with each other at all levels.

Since the 1930s, interpretations of federalism have continued to change. The workings of the federal system are sometimes called **intergovernmental relations (IGR).** This term refers to the entire set of interactions among national, state, and local governments found in modern federalism. To understand intergovernmental relations today, it is necessary to consider not only constitutional and statutory influences, but also the formal and informal interactions among local, state, and national governments. As we shall see, politics and individuals also play an important part in a dynamic, evolving federalism.

The U.S. Constitution and fifty state constitutions establish the framework for our system of intergovernmental relations in which the various levels of government share functions and each level can influence the others. Viewing the relationship between the more inclusive unit of government and the units that make it up is called *vertical IGR.* In examining the relationships between states or between units of local government, we use the term *horizontal IGR.*

VERTICAL AND HORIZONTAL INTERGOVERNMENTAL RELATIONS

Vertical relations among governments refer to those between the national government and states, the national government and local governments, and states and local governments. Horizontal relations concern relationships between states and other states, and local governments and other local governments. These relationships between governments entail constitutional and legal as well as formal and informal interaction.

An important feature of our system is often overlooked in discussions of vertical federalism: While Article VI of the U.S. Constitution states that the laws and treaties of the U.S. government are the supreme law of the land, it qualifies this statement in an important way. The laws and treaties that are in keeping with the Constitution, not the national government itself, are the supreme law of the land. It sets forth the conditions under which that government exercising the sovereignty of the people can act, and it must act in accord with the Constitution. Otherwise, those acts can be declared unconstitutional by the U.S. Supreme Court, as long as someone from within the political system brings forward a legitimate case against the law or treaty.

In Texas and other states, the state government exercises similar sovereignty for the citizens of the state in making rules affecting local governments. The state government isn't supreme within the state; the people of the state are. State supreme courts also can and do declare state laws unconstitutional.

STATE RELATIONS WITH NATIONAL GOVERNMENT

In the United States, the formal allocation of power between state and national government is constitutionally described. The Constitution gives express powers primarily or exclusively to the national government. Other powers, known as *concurrent powers,* are shared with the states, which must exercise those powers within the limits set by the Constitution, including the authority to tax and borrow money, establish courts, make and enforce laws, charter banks and corporations, spend money for the general welfare, and take private property for public purposes after providing just compensation for it. Still other unspecified powers are reserved to the states and the people under the Ninth and Tenth amendments to the U.S. Constitution.

In the development of the intergovernmental system, three types of actions by the national government merit attention: federal court orders, legislative regulations and mandates, and preemptive legislation. It is important to remember that in almost all these actions, individuals in government are making decisions about individual citizens of states who are also Americans.

Federal Court Orders. The U.S. Supreme Court has played a major role in defining the relationships and marking the boundaries between national and state functions. To a significant extent, the growth in federal power is the cumulative result of Supreme Court interpretations of the Constitution. The Supreme Court, for ex-

Long lines of semitrailers approach the border between Texas and Mexico. The North American Free Trade Agreement (NAFTA) and truck traffic are still issues in Texas politics.

ample, expanded the power of the national government in the important case of *McCulloch v. Maryland* (1819). John Marshall, the chief justice of the Court, declared that the Constitution emanated from the sovereign people. The people had made their national government supreme over all rivals within the sphere of its powers. This case laid the foundation for an expansion of the national government in the years ahead.

As the umpire of our federal system, the Supreme Court has claimed the power of judicial review over state actions; increased the power of Congress to regulate interstate transactions, particularly those related to commerce; and enlarged the executive powers it deemed necessary to the fulfillment of the Constitution. In so doing, it has extended the protection of individuals from government abuse (both national and state), and it has also made it possible for the federal government to make state governments more efficient and broaden the range of services they provide.

The most notable development in the history of the judiciary was the ratification in 1868 of the Fourteenth Amendment, with its broad restrictions on the ability of those in charge of state government to abuse their power. The Fourteenth Amendment requires that every citizen be given due process of law when life, liberty, and property are at risk. The due process clause has been interpreted to extend most of the prohibitions of the Bill of Rights to actions of state and local governments.

The application of the Bill of Rights to states allows for increased federal judicial supervision of state courts, especially in cases dealing with the rights of people accused of crimes. The federal Constitution establishes a minimum level of protection for individual rights to which states must adhere. State constitutions and their bills of rights may give greater protection from state and local authorities than the federal Constitution does. The U.S. Supreme Court has agreed that persons found guilty of capital crimes may be executed if the process by which they were convicted is devoid of racial prejudice. Texas is one of thirty-eight states that execute persons convicted of capital crimes, one of thirty-two that execute by lethal injection.

The U.S. Supreme Court was instrumental in beginning what has been referred to as the second American Revolution: the civil rights revolution. In *Brown v. Board of Education of Topeka, Kansas* (347 U.S. 483, 1954), the Supreme Court (by a unanimous vote) ordered states to cease segregating children by race in their public schools. This case is a watershed in the development of modern federalism for at least three reasons.

First, it was a unanimous decision by the Court. In an unusual show of unity, all nine justices voted to abolish segregation. In recent years, numerous decisions have been by 5–4 majorities, a demonstration that every vote counts.

Second, *Brown* established the principle that the federal government was no longer going to ignore the rights of individual Americans just because they lived in a particular state. In 1954, this decision was courageous. It took the actions of many more courageous individuals to bring an end to legal segregation, but the Court in effect gave their actions a legitimacy they might not otherwise have enjoyed.

A third reason that the *Brown* case is so important for federalism is that it clearly demonstrates the evolving nature of our system. In 1896, the U.S. Supreme Court declared that segregation was constitutional. In 1954, the same institution declared it was unconstitutional.[8] When new people join our federal institutions, old decisions may be changed. As we observed in Chapter 1, change may be for the better or for the worse, which is why your participation is critical: to make sure our institutions do not change for the worse.

Another landmark decision came in 1973. In *Roe v. Wade,* the Supreme Court made it unconstitutional for states to prohibit abortion in the first three months of pregnancy.[9] This case points to an important characteristic of our political system: for large, complex political systems to survive, leaders who disagree must often compromise on issues important to them. The American federal system was based on compromise. The Connecticut Compromise, the three-fifths compromise, and the agreement to postpone regulating (abolishing) the slave trade were all essential for the Constitution to get out of Philadelphia for ratification by the states. These compromises, together with the promise of a future bill of rights, were necessary for the Constitution to be ratified. Benjamin Franklin, in supporting the adoption of the Constitution, a document about which he had some reservations, asked that each of his colleagues "doubt a little of his own infallibility" and vote to approve it.[10]

Roe v. Wade is another compromise on an important moral issue. At one extreme are those who want all abortions abolished; on the other extreme are those who want women to have the unlimited right to control their own reproductive systems. Each side tries to put forth its own views in several ways. Some who advocate the right to life have murdered doctors who perform abortions, picketed their homes, and humiliated their children, and they have sought to abolish birth control pills as well as abortions and outlaw counseling on family planning. Abortion on demand, including the right to abort fetuses because of gender or fetuses ready for birth, are among the positions held by those who advocate complete freedom of choice. Each side has moderates and extremists. Each side feels strongly and has moral grounds for its position. *Roe v. Wade* is a compromise because it neither completely prohibits abortion nor allows absolute freedom of choice. It allows individual states to legislate.

In a 1985 Texas case that required deciding whether the rights of an employee should be nullified if he worked for a state or local government, the Supreme Court decided in favor of the employee. In *Garcia v. San Antonio Metropolitan Transit Authority,* it held that Joe Garcia, an employee of the San Antonio transit authority, was entitled to overtime pay (time-and-a-half) under the National Fair Labor Standards Act. The Court rejected as unsound in principle and unworkable the practice of protecting traditional governmental functions, such as fire and police protection, sanitation, public health administration, and administration of parks and recreation, from congressional regulation. Rather than protecting the states by declaring certain subjects off limits, the Court said that the states were more than adequately protected by the dynamics of the Constitution, by "procedural safeguards inherent in the federal system."[11]

These safeguards include the fact that members of Congress are elected from the states. After hearing from mayors and state legislators, and a governor or two, that the time-and-a-half requirement would cost state and local governments millions of dollars and might lead to tax increases that would be blamed on Congress, Congress responded just as the Court probably figured it would. Congress allowed state and local governments, but not private companies, an exemption in the Fair Labor Standards Act. They could give compensatory time, at time-and-one-half, rather than actual cash; that is, someone who worked overtime would be paid in time off later. This case protected the rights of a U.S. citizen, Joe Garcia, while also protecting the ability of state and local governments to offer transportation services.

In the 1990s, with the addition of justices appointed by Presidents Reagan and Bush, both conservatives, the Supreme Court appears to have tempered the legislative license to protect individuals that it had given the federal government. In an important 1995 decision, *United States v. Lopez,* the Court appeared to put some new limits on Congress's authority to use the commerce clause in Article I of the Constitution as justification for federal legislation in areas deemed to be reserved to the states. In that decision, the Court invalidated the Gun-Free School Zones Act of 1990, a federal statute banning the possession of a firearm in or within 1,000 feet of a school. Writing for the majority, Chief Justice William Rehnquist asserted that the Gun-Free School Zones Act was "a criminal statute that by its terms had nothing to do with 'commerce' or any sort of enterprise, however broadly one might define those terms."[12]

Two years later, in 1997, the Supreme Court (in *Printz v. United States*) struck down provisions of the federal Brady Handgun Violence Prevention Act, which required local law enforcement officers to conduct background checks on gun purchasers. The Court declared that the "federal government may neither issue directives requiring the states to address particular problems, nor command the states' officers, or those of their political divisions, to administer or enforce federal regulatory programs."[13] Yet the Court acknowledged that the federal government can establish federal programs and use federal funds to entice state or local participation, as it does in a wide variety of existing federal programs.

In another Texas case, *City of Boerne, Texas v. Flores* (1997), the Court intended to delimit the scope of congressional power. This case involved a dispute between the city of Boerne and St. Peter Catholic Church. The church wanted to expand its historic building to accommodate a growing parish. The city objected that the expansion would violate the city's ordinance creating a historic district, which included a church. The church responded that the city's ordinance violated the national Religious Freedom Restoration Act of 1993, which prohibits a government from substantially burdening a person's exercise of religion unless the government can show that the restriction furthers a compelling governmental interest and is the least restrictive means of furthering that interest.

In striking down the Religious Restoration Act of 1993, the Supreme Court was concerned that Congress was using its legislative authority in furtherance of a right not explicitly protected by the Fourteenth Amendment. In *Boerne,* the Court faced a choice between a local church and a local government. It chose the local

JOIN THE DEBATE

THE ISSUE: Should gun control be left to the states rather than to national government?

AGREE

1. The Constitution leaves such matters to states as part of the reserved powers (Amendment 10).

2. The states can reflect the policy preferences of their residents more effectively. People may differ on gun control from state to state. Texas, for example, allows citizens to carry concealed weapons if they get a state permit to do so.

3. The national government cannot use state police powers to enforce gun control; it must be a state effort.

4. Requirements such as gun permits and mandatory training can be carried out more effectively by the states.

5. State and local police are the agencies that will have to respond to gun incidents, so states should have the right to make decisions about gun control.

DISAGREE

1. The U.S. Constitution, Amendment 2, guarantees the right to keep and bear arms. It also asserts that "[a] well regulated militia" is necessary to a free state. In a federal system both levels can regulate.

2. Different state laws on gun control will allow criminals to obtain weapons from states with loose controls and take them to states with stricter controls, thus negating the laws of states that prefer tight gun control legislation.

3. With homeland security concerns, weapons should be controlled consistently nationwide.

4. A national registry for guns, for example, will be more effective than uncoordinated state registries.

5. The national government is in a better position to enforce gun control laws because a concern is bringing weapons in from other nations (counterterrorism regulations).

government, while at the same time giving Congress notice about the limits of its authority.[14]

Legislative Regulations and Mandates.   Not all of the increase in national power came at the expense of states' rights. The national government mandates compliance with some of its objectives, but more often it relies on inducements to achieve its ends. These inducements or incentives generally take the form of financial assistance that is made available to governments willing to pursue national goals. These programs, called *grants-in-aid,* are voluntary, but in almost all cases, the amount of assistance is attractive enough to enlist state and local participation—under the supervision of national agencies and subject to national guidelines, of course. Congress can use these grants-in-aid to buy cooperation from state policymakers who might otherwise be reluctant to endorse national legislation. Federal aid to state and local governments often comes with strings attached.

Although officials of state and local government do not welcome mandates from the national government, they willingly accept grants-in-aid, even those with strings attached. Grants allow officials to do more for their constituents without raising state and local taxes, or at least without raising taxes in proportion to spending increases. Financial grants-in-aid are the chief incentives by which national policymakers induce state governments to enact programs and policies intended to serve national objectives.

First, Congress may employ cross-cutting regulations that are across-the-board requirements affecting all or most federal assistance programs. They involve provisions that prohibit the use of funds from any national source in programs that discriminate on the basis of race, ethnicity, gender, or religious practice, for example. Another familiar cross-cutting regulation requires the preparation of an environmental impact statement for any construction project involving national funds. State and local governments must provide evidence of compliance with these regulations, and they incur administrative costs for preparing the necessary scientific and technical reports.

Second, national officials may terminate or reduce funding or aid in a specified program if state and local officials do not comply with the requirements of another grant-in-aid program. This action is a *cross-over sanction.* National highway funds are often used in this way to force states to adopt policies preferred by Congress.[15] Under a 1984 law, states that refused to raise the minimum drinking age to twenty-one forfeited 5 percent of their national highway funding. The penalty increased by 10 percent for each subsequent year in which the states failed to act. All states eventually complied with this demand.

The federal government often requires states to carry out certain activities without providing the funds to do so, an action called an unfunded mandate. The 1990 Americans with Disabilities Act (ADA), for example, required state and local governments to modify their government facilities to make them accessible to individuals with disabilities. Carrying out these unfunded federal mandates required the expenditure of billions of dollars that were not provided by Congress. During the 1980s and early 1990s, state or local governments were required by federal law to implement stricter water-pollution regulations, establish programs to protect workers against certain dangerous chemicals, and submit reports on measures to protect more than 150 new endangered species, among other things.[16] As the cost of mandated expenditures goes up, the ability of state and local governments to set their own policy priorities goes down. Critics of mandates argue that the federal government should not impose programs on state and local governments without paying for them. The Republican leadership in the U.S. House of Representatives incorporated mandate reform in their 1994 Contract with America and required the Congressional Budget Office to disclose the costs of legislative mandates on state and local governments. In March 1995, a mandate reform bill that had bipartisan support in Congress was signed into law by President Clinton, once again demonstrating the dynamics of federalism.[17] Congress responds to state and local voices often—but not always.

Preemptive Legislation.   The third type of regulation, partial preemption, often rests on the commerce clause of the Constitution. By engaging in this type of regulation, the national government essentially sets national minimum standards by issuing appropriate regulations for, say, air or water quality if a state refuses to regulate. Should a state refuse to enforce standards issued by an agency of the national government, then the agency assumes jurisdiction for enforcement. States are entitled to adopt and implement more stringent standards, but weak or nonexistent standards are preemptively denied by Congress.[18]

Regulation, Federalism and the Business Community.   Government regulation is of particular concern to businesses whose profits may be affected. The interaction between profits and regulation has at least three dimensions in our intergovernmental system. First, the costs of complying with any regulations—environmental, historic preservation, work safety, or equal opportunity—has an effect on business and thus may affect profits. Second, it can be difficult for national and international firms to deal with regulations that vary from state to state or county to county. The uniformity of federal regulations is a definite preference if this is the only dimension examined. Third, some businesses are local while others are organized on a national or international level. Thus, the business community itself may be divided on what the best regulations might be and who ought to do the regulating.

Clearly, the issue of regulation goes beyond the apparent conflict between state's rights and federal encroachment. Politics sometimes enters the arena when some professions and businesses try to get rules passed at the state or national level that make it difficult for newcomers to compete with those already established. Firms that operate only in states where business interest groups are influential may prefer state regulations because they are able to get the kind of regulations they want from the state legislatures. Firms that operate nationwide may want the convenience of using the same set of plans to build a hamburger stand in Minnesota and in Texas. In a few cases, an industry whose leaders feel it is too heavily regulated in one or two states may decide to push for uniformly weaker regulations at the federal level.[19]

The Dynamics of Federalism Revisited.   Interactions between states and the national government often have an electoral component. For example, Texas is one of a few states that lay claim to oil lands ten and a half miles beyond its shores. For other states, the limit is three miles; beyond that, the oil lands on the continental shelf belong to the federal government. This special treatment for Texas did not come about through victory at sea, in the courtroom, or on the battlefield; it was the result of a presidential election victory. In the presidential election of 1952, Dwight David Eisenhower won thanks in part to the vote in Texas, and he granted state control of the tidelands to Texas, thus reversing the policies of the previous administration.[20]

STATE RELATIONS WITH LOCAL GOVERNMENTS

Local governments include counties, townships, cities, and special-purpose districts. Texas does not have townships, but counties, cities, and special-purpose districts are important forms of local government in the state. (All of these forms are discussed more fully in Chapter 4.) Counties are considered arms of state government, performing the dual roles of serving the needs of the state and acting as local governments with locally elected officials who are responsive to the concerns of local constituents. Special-purpose districts include school districts and various other governments that are established by the state to serve particular purposes. Examples of special-purpose districts in Texas include hospital districts and water-conservation districts.

Because Texas is an urbanized state, with approximately 85 percent of the population living in cities, the city is of particular economic, social, and political importance. Allowing city officials to handle many of their own problems frees legislators to deal with issues that affect the state as a whole. Also, as the state became less rural and agricultural and more urban, an increasing number of voters lived in municipalities. Certainly, these voters prefer local control and have a greater understanding of their own local needs.

State elected officials are receptive to the desires of voters in cities. For these reasons, the state has been willing to delegate powers of self-government to cities, but that power is not absolute. Cities must follow state law in regard to their powers; the state limits what cities may do, what taxes they may levy, and how they may exercise their powers of governance. In Texas, as in the rest of the nation, cities remain creatures of the state, subject to state law.

NATIONAL RELATIONS WITH LOCAL GOVERNMENTS

Because the U.S. Constitution makes no mention of local governments, interaction between them and the national government was minimal (though existing) before the 1930s. Now, the national government is involved with issues in local government such as crime and pollution control. Grants-in-aid and loans are available from the national government to local governments, though it is more common for the national government to provide grants to states, which then pass the money on to localities.

National funding for schools and other purposes is an important source of revenue for local governments. The national government also interacts with localities through technical assistance and advice and through emergency assistance in times of disaster. In the 1980s, President Reagan reduced direct national and local interaction in line with his New Federalism initiative, but President Clinton repeatedly expressed his administration's desire to form a national government partnership with localities to address their needs.

Officials at the local level may influence national government policies through organizations such as the National League of Cities, the U.S. Conference of Mayors, the International City/County Management Association, councils of government, and the National Association of Counties. These organizations are instrumental in horizontal intergovernmental relations among localities; each one also provides information for the national government and exerts influence on national policies that affect them.

Just as in the relationship between states and the national government, local governments tend to appreciate the monetary assistance provided in national and local grants but resent, at least to some extent, the controls that accompany the financial assistance. Many benefits are provided by national grants. They enable local government to provide facilities and services without raising local taxes, but they may infringe on local control by distorting the policy preferences of local residents.

HORIZONTAL INTERGOVERNMENTAL RELATIONSHIPS

Horizontal relationships are those among peers, as in state-state and local-local interaction. In these cases, shared citizenship is sometimes missing from the equation. On the other hand, officials of the same type of government have a basis for rapport. The notion of horizontal federalism gets a little complex within the rather diverse category of local governments. A county may contain several cities, school districts, and various kinds of special districts. Some of these units may be larger than others or may have a more affluent tax base than others.

Relationships Among State Governments.   Horizontal relationships among states are addressed in the U.S. Constitution; those among localities have developed over time. Article IV, section 2 of the U.S. Constitution says, "Citizens of any state are entitled to all privileges and immunities of citizens in the several states."

Interpretation of this section has been variable. States cannot discriminate against nonresidents by forbidding them access to jobs and to equal treatment in the courts and before the law. They cannot levy taxes that only nonresidents must pay. But the courts have allowed states to charge different rates of tuition for nonresidents in state universities, for instance, and to require a registered nurse licensed by one state to get a new license to practice in a different state.

Article IV, section 1 requires that states give "full faith and credit" to the decisions made in other states. A court judgment in one state requiring an individual to pay a sum of money to another individual will be enforceable even if the people concerned relocate to another state. This section is also the basis of the extradition of an accused criminal from one state to another. The governor of each state has the power to order extradition of an accused or convicted criminal. Extradition is not an automatic process, but governors are generally not eager to retain criminals within their borders. In 1934, the national government made it less attractive for a criminal (for instance, a Texas bank robber) to flee to another state by passing a law making it a federal crime to cross state lines to avoid prosecution or imprisonment.

Formal and informal communications among states also allow innovative programs in one state to be shared with others and allow the officials in one state to benefit from the experiences of another. Elected officials have several formal channels of communication through organizations such as the National Association of Governors, the Council of State Governments, and the National Conference of State Legislatures.[21] These organizations also provide a means of pressuring the national government. Position statements from the National Association of Governors, for example, have been influential in the development of Washington's changing attitude toward federalism.

Public servants in state agencies also share information about public programs and their experiences in solving problems. Professional organizations and informal networks allow state agencies to influence each other. For instance, state law enforcement officials from California, Arizona, Texas, and New Mexico may meet to confer about drug smuggling problems along the U.S.-Mexico border. A good idea offered by a Texas official may be taken up by a California state official and eventually be adopted as policy by the California legislature. In these days of e-mail and Internet communication, ideas may be shared among policy experts and agencies on a frequent, informal basis.

Article 1, section 10 of the U.S. Constitution says that no state shall enter into an agreement with other states without the permission of Congress. By inference, this section allows states to make such agreements as long as Congress approves. In Texas, communities on the border of another state may make interlocal agreements with adjacent communities in the neighboring state to share services and facilities.[22]

Similarly, states on an international border may enter into agreements with adjoining nations. Many programs, such as drug interdiction and health, are related to problems that transcend national boundaries. In Texas, the Seventy-Sixth Legislature (1999) addressed the problem of exchanging health information with Mexico, empowering the Texas Department of Health to find ways of communicating more effectively with their counterparts in Mexico about disease detection and surveillance.[23] The legislature recognized that viruses and germs do not have to go through customs to pass from one nation to another! This example shows how the interaction of national and state governments in our federal system supports communication among bureaucrats in a pragmatic effort to improve the lives of people in the United States and in Mexico.

Many issues that involve more than one state are subject to cooperative efforts between states, but conflicts can also arise. The most common sources of conflict between states stem from economic differences, spillover effects, differential effects of policies, and boundary disputes.

Economic disparities among states may produce conflicts when a poor state is next door to a wealthier state. People in a wealthier state may resent the residents of poorer states commuting to jobs in their state and using facilities provided by the wealthier state.

Spillover effects
Unintended effects of the policies or practices of a government that may produce negative or positive consequences on those outside the policy area.

A more pervasive problem may be created by **spillover effects,** a term that refers to a problem in one state that is caused by activities in another. A hypothetical example would be an industry in Louisiana that produces pollution affecting Texas residents. It is likely that the situation would create conflict between the two states because Texas would be receiving problems but no benefits from that industry.

Boundary disputes have occurred among states from time to time. The historic dispute over territory in what is now the state of New Mexico predates the Civil War. Many Texans believed the area east of the Rio Grande had been won in the 1836 revolution and thus was rightly a part of Texas. But the largely Hispanic residents of the New Mexico territory resisted Texas's claim to land east of the Rio Grande. The Texas Legislature created county governments that included small villages such as Taos and Albuquerque and the larger trading center of Santa Fe and attempted unsuccessfully to organize those counties. By 1847, the Texas governor was proposing to take the area by force.

Of course, the U.S. Congress got involved in the dispute and attempted to find a compromise satisfactory to both parties. It is likely that congressional efforts would also have been futile except that eastern bondholders were demanding payment on Texas's outstanding preannexation debt. A bill sponsored by Senator James A. Pearce of Maryland established the existing western border of Texas so that Texas yielded 98,300 square miles of land. The bill easily passed Congress and was approved by Texans in a special referendum. The Texas Legislature accepted the measure in a special session. In return, Congress appropriated $10 million plus a supplementary $2.5 million for the services of the Texas Rangers during the Mexican-American War. That appropriation allowed Texas to retire the debt of the Republic and to become solvent for the first time in its history.[24]

Most disputes between states are settled by negotiation and political exchanges, but some require legal action. To be heard by a national court, the disputes must be between two states rather than between a state and a few people in another state. Also, a problem occurs if one state refuses to comply with a court order because courts do not have enforcement ability. Often, Congress must take action by passing new laws to address a situation. And taking an issue to court may actually increase interstate conflicts and become a political tool for candidates running for office.

Relationships Among Local Governments. Horizontal relationships are also important among local governments. Local-local relationships may be cooperative or competitive. They may include legal contracts or interlocal agreements, as when two or more local governments work together to provide services or purchase equipment (thus saving costs by pooling resources). Interaction among local governments is often facilitated by councils of government.

Councils of government (COGs) Voluntary associations of local governments formed under state law to deal with the problems and planning needs that cross the boundaries of individual governments or that require regional attention.

Councils of government (COGs) are entities that serve the needs of other governments at the local level. They are voluntary associations of counties, cities, and special-purpose districts that assist these member governments with regional problems and interests. COGs are yet another example of the dynamic nature of our federal system. Alert public servants or bureaucrats in a federal agency learned of the success of a COG created in Wayne County, Michigan.[25] A clause was added to a grant program encouraging states or local governments to create them, and the federal government would help with the funding. Now, COGs exist in every state, and have central organizations to represent them. In Texas, the organization is called the Texas Association of Regional Councils.

COGs have no power to regulate or compel the member governments to act; their role is advisory only. They do, however, have a coordinating role in grant applications and have developed as a local agency with the expertise to help local governments navigate the complicated system of federal and state grant-in-aid programs. At a minimum, COGs save taxpayers money by not having two or more overlapping governments spend state or federal tax money on the same service. Beyond that, COGs can claim a lot of credit for helping to bring money home to Texas cities, counties, and school districts. Grant applications do not go far in the federal system unless the local COG has signed off on them. This situation creates a real inducement toward information-sharing and cooperation in applying for grants.

Although few Texans know the name of the COG in the planning region in which they live, every square mile of Texas, rural and urban, is served by a COG. For example, a COG serving South Texas, the South Texas Development Council (STDC), includes the cities of Laredo, La Grulla, Rio Grande City, and Roma. Four counties, eight school districts, and seven special districts are also part of the STDC. This COG promotes cooperation among these governments in a large, sparsely populated area to solve regional problems and encourage economic development. By contrast, the East Texas Council of Governments (ETCOG) comprises fourteen counties, seventy-two cities, forty school districts, and thirteen special districts in the twelve-county planning area. With a more concentrated population and with more member governments, ETCOG addresses different problems than does STDC. The activities of COGs are largely dependent on the needs of their members. Although they do have many differences, almost all Texas COGs are active in several programs, including multicounty rural transportation services (usually in vans and small buses), meals on wheels, maintenance of emergency 911 systems, as well as criminal justice program planning and regional law enforcement training.[26]

COGs provide a mechanism for intergovernmental relations among local governments. Two COGs in Texas include members in other states, which facilitates interaction on issues common to the states concerned. They are particularly valuable to the many small cities across the state, giving city officials an opportunity to engage in joint endeavors with others and thus making more efficient use of resources. COGs may also provide a conduit of information from national and state government agencies and may offer classes for agency officials on new state and national laws.

Informal Vertical and Horizontal Relationships.   Communication networks have grown up among agency officials at all levels of government. When the national government issues a mandate to a state or local government or when a state or local government receives a grant-in-aid from the national government to undertake a project, the persons responsible for carrying out the task are not usually elected officials; rather, they are bureaucrats who work for government agencies with particular expertise in the area of concern. These agents of government often have considerable power to affect the policy that elected officials have passed into law. Laws are often vague, leaving much decisionmaking about how to implement the policy to the experts in public agencies.

Most agencies at the national level have equivalent state, and often local, agencies with related goals and responsibilities. The people who work in the agencies at each level of government may have similar values, interests, and educational backgrounds. For example, the federal Department of Health and Human Services may have reason to interact frequently with agencies under the Texas Health and Human Services Commission and with local, city, or metropolitan health departments.

Two models have been created to describe this phenomenon: picket fence federalism and bamboo fence federalism. *Picket fence federalism* portrays the power of bureaucrats at different levels of government to affect what government does in particular policy areas. Figure 3.1A illustrates the connection of bureaucrats at national, state, and local levels of government as they share information, influence policy, and interact to deliver policy. This model illustrates the power that may be exercised by agency officials operating, to some extent, outside the influence of the elected officials at all levels. *Bamboo fence federalism* (see Figure 3.1B) includes the concepts of picket fence federalism and the influence of other actors at each governmental level (vertical relationships) who work in related policy areas (horizontal relationships). For example, the Texas Department of Family and Protective Services may interact frequently with the Texas Department of Health Services; local health departments may share information with each other. This model incorporates the idea of networks of policy specialists who interact to work out problems and set standards within areas where they have decisionmaking power and responsibility.

Both picket fence federalism and bamboo fence federalism also incorporate the concept of the influence of iron triangles on policy outcomes. *Iron triangles* consist of agency officials, interest group representatives, and legislative or congressional committees interested in the same policy area. The idea of iron triangles emphasizes the control of these actors over policy, often to the detriment of the general public good. Although such influences exist, it is also true that the general public, you and I, can exert influence on government policy through communicating our desires to elected representatives and agency officials and through interest group membership. These models perform the valuable function of making us aware of the existence of an informal, less visible influence on what government does, a view that is important to us as active citizens.

In Chapter 1, we introduced the concept of megastates and showed that Texas is the largest in area and the second largest in population. Texas in Context 3.1 helps us understand why the megastates are so important within the federal system. They contain over half the U.S. population and produce over half of the U.S. gross national product (GNP). That GNP, by the way, is so large in terms of the rest of the world that you would have to subtract the GNP of the top three megastates

FIGURE 3.1 Models of Federalism

A. Picket Fence Federalism

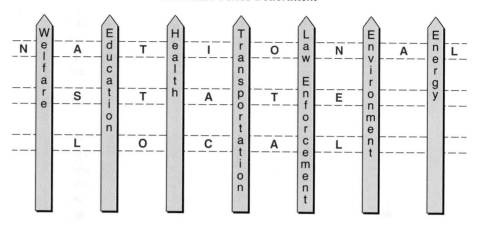

B. Bamboo Fence Federalism

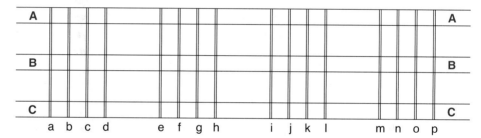

A: national government
B: state government
C: local government
a: primary and secondary education
b: higher education
c: special education
d: vocational education
e: public health
f: Medicaid
g: health research
h: training health practitioners

i: air transportation
j: road transportation
k: rail transportation
l: water transportation
m: unemployment compensation
n: aid to families with dependent children
o: supplementary security income
p: job training

before the GNP of the United States would drop to second in the world, behind the GNP of Japan.

In the context of politics and presidential elections, why do you suppose the megastates with more than half of the U.S. population have fewer than half of the presidential electors? It has something to do with one of the compromises that created and hold our federal system together. Every state, regardless of population gets two seats in the Senate and one in the House of Representatives. Hence, a perfect match between population and the number of electors does not exist.

As the American federal system has changed over time, so has Texas. Today, it is no longer a rural state providing cattle, cotton, and oil for other states to process and sell on the world market. It is now the second largest state in population and one of the richest and most influential states in the Union. Four Texans have been elected president of the United States. Texans have also played major roles in the U.S. Congress. Since the 1940s, Democrats Sam Rayburn and Jim Wright served as Speaker, and in the 105th Congress, Republicans Dick Army and Tom DeLay served as majority leader and majority whip.

Other famous Texans making their mark in our nation's capital include Maury Maverick, Sr., the progressive San Antonio congressman who was one of FDR's staunchest supporters; Wright Patman and Henry B. Gonzales, both of whom served brilliantly as a voice of the people by looking carefully at political initiatives of the banking industry; and Senator Ralph Yarborough, whose record in protecting the environment, consumers, and blue-collar workers has been unequaled. Barbara Jordan, the first African American elected to the Texas State Senate in the twentieth century, served in the U.S. House of Representatives as a strong voice of reason and with distinction on the House Judiciary Committee during the Watergate hearings. Henry Cisneros, another former mayor of San Antonio like Maverick and Gonzales, served in the Clinton administration as secretary of housing and urban development.

The National Performance Review, which was issued by Vice President Albert Gore in the fall of 1993, made several recommendations for reinventing federalism. This policy review process was developed in Texas by Comptroller John Sharp, who was asked to serve on the National Performance Review Commission. The era of the 1990s has been called the devolution revolution because both the national and state governments favored increasing the power of the states to control complex programs. The National Performance Review helped launch a determined effort to form partnerships with states and localities that would give the smaller units greater freedom in trying new programs. For certain policy areas that have historically been controlled by the national government, provision was made to allow states to qualify for waivers that allow state initiatives differing from national guidelines.

Many states, including Texas, took advantage of this opportunity. In the costly area of delivering government-supported health care, Texas got a waiver to modify the provision of Medicaid. Texas then gradually introduced managed care in various regions of the state and invited input from concerned citizens and health care providers in these regions with the idea of saving costs, extending health care to

TEXAS in Context

3.1 Texas in a System of States and Megastates

	Gross Domestic Product (Billions of Dollars)	Megastate Percentage of U.S. Gross Domestic Product	Population (Millions)	Megastate Precentage of U.S. Population	Presidential Electors	Megastate Percentage of Electors
United States	7,262.9		281.4		538	
California	927.5	13	33.9	12	53	10
Florida	338.1	5	16.0	6	25	5
Illinois	358.1	5	12.4	4	19	4
Massachusetts	197.8	3	6.3	2	10	2
Michigan	246.4	3	9.9	4	15	3
New Jersey	260.9	4	8.4	3	13	2
New York	579.7	8	19.0	7	29	5
Ohio	291.4	4	11.7	4	18	3
Pennsylvania	305.3	4	12.3	4	19	4
Texas	**544.0**	**7**	**20.9**	**7**	**32**	**6**
Megastate total	4,049.2	56	150.8	53	233	44

Sources: U.S. Census Bureau, *Statistical Abstract of the United States: 2000* (Washington, D.C.: U.S. Government Printing Office, 2000), p. 455; Texas State Data Center, TAMU.//census.tamu.edu/Data/Apport/table1.php (June 15, 2001).

those in need, and accommodating regional preferences in health care delivery. (As we will see in Chapter 12, however, Texas has some room for improvement in this area.)

NEW DIRECTIONS IN INTERGOVERNMENTAL RELATIONS

George W. Bush's New Federalism. Federalism was primarily a legal concept to the Constitution's framers, but as we have seen, political interpretations as well as court decisions have affected the relative power of the national government and state governments. Political interpretations of federalism often change in response to circumstances. As noted earlier, Ronald Reagan's New Federalism differed from the Federalism of William Clinton. Subsequent presidents influenced the relationship between the national government and states, moving further toward devolution of power through the administrations of George Herbert Walker Bush and William Clinton. The current president, George W. Bush, initially articulated a strong version of New Federalism with even more emphasis on reducing national government power.[27] As governor, Bush had been adamant about the need to keep the national government from interfering with state business. As president, he pledged to return more power to the states, but in practice he has supported policies that move significantly away from the concept of devolution.

For example, even though education is generally considered to be a matter within state control, Bush's campaign pledge to improve schools led him to support a bill, passed in Congress, mandating states to conduct annual education achievement tests.[28] In a similar vein, the Bush administration has supported strong national measures on crime control and abortion. The president's belief that these issues are of great national importance may explain why, despite a commitment to devolving power to the states, he has sought greater national government control.

Even more striking are the changes in national, state, and local relations following the September 11, 2001, terrorist attacks on the World Trade Center and the Pentagon. The terrorist attacks stunned the nation and resulted in several changes in the way both the president and the public view intergovernmental relations. After September 11, the president created, almost immediately, a new federal Department of Homeland Security charged with prevention of terrorist attacks. From the outset, it was apparent that securing safety of the populace from random terrorists would require greater cooperation among national, state, and local agencies.

Homeland Security and the States.   Perhaps the greatest challenge to our system of intergovernmental relations so far is the task of developing a cooperative defense system against the threat of terrorist attacks. Renowned political scientist Donald Kettl says, "It's the hardest thing in our history we've ever tried to do."[29] Kettl, along with other experts on federalism and intergovernmental relations, met in March 2003 to assess the progress made in developing a seamless web of connections among all governments to prevent terrorist attacks and to respond in the case of attacks. They concluded that states and local governments have worked hard on planning but have made little substantive progress toward increasing the overall level of protection. The system of multiple, autonomous governments that has served so well in providing laboratories for innovative policies and practices has proven difficult to coordinate toward a common goal. Levels of preparedness differ from community to community across the United States. While achieving cooperation among federal agencies is difficult under the new Department of Homeland Security, developing working partnerships among the myriad of states and local governments is even more daunting.

The intrinsic competition for resources among local governments and among states has created a culture that is not conducive to cooperative efforts. While classic intergovernmental relationships emphasize flexibility at state and local levels, a system of nationwide coordination requires top-down control and planning. Even if states and localities are willing to submit to direction from the top, complications come from the variations among states and localities. Agencies of the many, almost autonomous governments across the nation have developed, over time, operational practices and communication systems that are incompatible with those of other jurisdictions. Federal dollars are an important component of standardizing communication systems nationwide, but differences in economic well-being among various governments makes allocation of federal dollars complex. A key problem is providing money to fund new technology and training, but questions of policy remain.

Should the emphasis be on prevention or on response? Prevention seems to require a broad plan under national leadership. Response is the purview of states and local governments, at least at first. Because local officials are logically the first responders in the case of an attack, they favor increasing resources to enable quick reaction. The matter is further complicated at the state and local level by the question, Response to what? Terrorist attacks could range from the use of weapons of mass destruction to sabotage of water supplies and food sources, to attacks with biological and chemical weapons. Indeed, it is difficult to find a limit to the possibilities in the realm of terrorist actions. How can government be ready when the vehicle of attack is unpredictable? The broad array of possibilities requires changes at all levels of government to be able to identify the first responders and the necessary interagency efforts.

Fire departments and law enforcement agencies would naturally be involved in any response to an attack, but other agencies should also be included in a defensive plan. Health departments at all levels of government can provide the expertise needed in a biological or chemical attack but have not traditionally been included in planning strategies. Other agencies, particularly those that deal with water and wastewater, are obvious centers of expertise in the event of sabotage. Agencies that control infrastructure, such as international bridges and state roadways, could be crucial to the prevention of and the response to attacks on those facilities. In short, both protection and response must involve almost every public agency at all levels of government. Development of many new interagency channels of communication is necessary, which presents a sharp learning curve for the officials involved. According to political scientist, Paul Posner, reluctance among agencies about sharing information must be changed. Questions about access to information, privacy, and identification of those who are part of the intergovernmental security network are likely to be raised in the immediate future.[30]

Money to support state and local efforts must come, to a large extent, from the national government. In 2003, many states, including Texas, faced budget shortfalls, which presented major barriers to the initiation of new programs. States continue to wrestle with the problem of ensuring security against terrorist attacks. Like other states, Texas is grappling with these issues.

Texas and Homeland Security.   Texas has several characteristics that make it an attractive target to terrorists. It is a large state located on an international border, it is a key state in the agricultural economy of the nation, and increasing urbanization has created many vulnerable areas of concentrated population. It also has vast underpopulated areas that are difficult to monitor. It has nuclear facilities such as the Pantex weapons plant in the Panhandle and a nuclear power plant at Comanche Peak, as well as defense contractors Lockheed, Bell, and Raytheon with offices in the state. It has petrochemical plants, large supplies of oil and other raw materials, and high-tech manufacturing plants. Texas has major international airports and economic centers and multiple sites of international commerce, such as the Houston ship channel and several international bridges. An attack on Texas would have a major effect on the nation as a whole.

Even before September 11, policymakers in the state had taken measures to protect the population from disasters. The Texas Disaster Act of 1975 recognized the need to prevent, prepare for, respond to, and recover from various emergencies and disasters. The act created the Texas Division of Emergency Management (DEM) in the office of the governor but later placed it under the Department of Public Safety (DPS). Now the agency reports to the governor *and* to the DPS. This law defined *disaster* broadly but includes hostile military or paramilitary action, which is relevant today. The state is required to develop an emergency operations plan, and state officials are mandated to assist local governments in developing their own plans. Over time, Texas has created two bureaus to deal with disasters, one for mitigation and recovery and one for preparedness and response. Lawmakers also established a public information branch and regional field operations offices. If local jurisdictions cannot cope as first responders, they must notify the state-appointed regional liaison officer personally, by telephone or through any state trooper. Information is passed to the DEM coordinator, the director of DPS, and the governor. The governor can declare a disaster and implement a state emergency operations plan. In 1999, Texas developed a handbook to be used in case of attack by terrorists or an attack using weapons of mass destruction. The handbook provides training for some municipalities to help them respond to attacks. Exercises are scheduled regularly in various jurisdictions throughout the state to ensure readiness.

With the increased emphasis on security after September 11, Texas agencies have developed a plan to expand the organizational roles of state and local entities in the event of a terrorist attack. Following September 11, the governor created a task force to deal with terrorism. It is a multidisciplinary group, including a DEM coordinator, a Texas land commissioner, several senators, retired military officials, a county sheriff and chair of (TPS) Texas Public Safety committee, chair of the Texas Railroad Commission, and others. The twenty-four councils of government were charged with the task of establishing a mechanism for regional coordination and have produced a policy guide called "Strategies for Texas First Responder Preparedness." This guide also outlines what individual jurisdictions must do to be eligible for the state disaster program. The Texas plan relies to a great extent on utilizing existing warning systems to communicate safety information to the public.

Of major concern is addressing problems with communication. Texas has more than 1,000 fire departments, 254 sheriff's departments, and many other agencies. Radio frequencies are not always compatible, but the cost of making all systems compatible is high. Long ago, Texas tried to improve the situation by establishing three frequencies for statewide mutual aid, but the system didn't work very well. Many jurisdictions need money to improve communication equipment.

Some funding for new programs has come from the national government through the Terrorism Consequence Management Program Assistance Grants. These grants have improved the communication equipment available in a few jurisdictions, but much more is needed to ensure communication capability among all governments. Federal funding has helped Texas to add personnel to new positions related to terrorism, but some local jurisdictions chafe under the strict rules that accompany federal funding. Federal funding requirements tend to change frequently so that smaller jurisdictions in particular have difficulty interpreting the fluctuating maze of rules. Questions abound concerning personnel reimbursement in the event of response to areas outside the employing jurisdiction. Some jurisdictions are better able to bear the expense of response.

The federal Department of Justice (DOJ), the Centers for Disease Control (CDC), and the Federal Emergency Management Agency (FEMA) have worked with Texas state and local governments and have provided money and training plans. In 2002, the state began working with Mexico to develop plans to deal with terrorism. The Texas Department of Criminal Justice dedicated $1 million for training law enforcement about terrorism, but continued allocations of state money depends greatly on the fiscal health of Texas during the upcoming years.

Texas has moved toward the goal of improving security for residents within the state, but a lot of work must still be done. Individual citizens will have a key role in the prevention of terrorism and responding to attacks. One of the recommendations of the governor's task force is the establishment of call centers for reporting suspicious activity. Informed individuals, going about daily activities, are in the best position to be the eyes and ears of the state because terrorists can lurk in unexpected places. Individual citizens have a key role in advising officials as they form policies to deal with terrorism and in supporting governmental efforts to keep the state safe.

Summary

Texas is part of a complex system of vertical and horizontal intergovernmental relations that was made possible by the system of federalism established by the U.S. Constitution. These relationships have been and continue to be characterized by dynamic change as a result of Supreme Court interpretations of the Constitution, changes in statutory law, and changing political preferences of citizens. Since the 1980s, state governments have established their role as innovators in the federal system, displaying an improved capacity for action and changing public expectations about the function of state governments.

But fundamental changes in American intergovernmental relations have occurred in the past two decades, including devolution of responsibility for policy in key domestic areas. These changes may be undermined to an extent by the post-9/11 emphasis on intergovernmental cooperation under centralized guidance to promote homeland security. At least in the short term, innovation by state governments may take a back seat to federal initiatives. With the reelection of George W. Bush in November 2004, the trend towards centralization of homeland security policy may be expected to continue. The costs of increased security may limit policy choices by states and localities in many domestic policy areas. A growing national deficit and budgetary stresses at the state level may also affect the ability of state governments to fund programs related to pollution control, health and welfare, and education, to name but a few.

What does this discussion of intergovernmental relations have to do with you? You may be less interested in the development of federalism than in policies that affect you personally and your community. However, a better understanding of the relationships among the governments to which you pay taxes is important in becoming a more effective actor in the political system of Texas.

KEY TERMS

Federalism, p. 56
Litmus test of American federalism, p. 56
Unitary system, p. 57
Confederacy, p. 57
Dual federalism, p. 58
Cooperative federalism, p. 58

Layer cake, p. 58
Marble cake, p. 58
Intergovernmental relations, p. 59
Spillover effects, p. 70
Councils of government (COGs), p. 70

FOR FURTHER READING

Frantzich, Stephen, *Citizen Democracy: Political Activism in a Cynical Age* (Boulder, Colo.: Rowman & Littlefield, 1999).

Kettl, Donald F., "The States and Homeland Security, Building the Missing Link" (New York: The Century Foundation, 2003).

Nice, David C., and Patricia Fredericksen, *Federalism, The Politics of Intergovernmental Relations* (New York: St. Martin's Press, 1987).

Saffell, David, and Harry Basehart, *State and Local Government: Politics and Public Policies*, 7th ed. (New York: McGraw-Hill, 2001).

STUDY QUESTIONS

1. List three types of federalism and explain the differences among them.

2. What are the differences between dual federalism and cooperative federalism?

3. Define the term *intergovernmental relations* and provide an example.

4. List and explain the three concurrent powers.

5. Explain picket fence federalism and bamboo fence federalism.

CRITICAL THINKING QUESTIONS

1. Should the national government force state compliance with certain rules?

2. Should state governments exercise more authority over certain areas such as health, welfare, crime, and educational problems?

3. Can state governments create and implement statewide programs that address the diverse needs of different local communities?

4. Should the national government return more power to the states?

5. What are the effects of the complex relationships among governments on the ability of citizens to affect what government does?

INTERNET RESOURCES

www.statesnews.org The home page of this website for the Council of State Governments provides a network for identifying and sharing ideas with state leaders.

www.gsa.gov/fdac/queryfdac.htm This home page lists financial and nonfinancial assistance programs administered by departments and establishments of the federal government.

http://lcweb2.loc.gov/const/fed/fedpaper.txt This website provides a copy of the Federalist Papers. Compare and contrast the view of federalism found in the original writings with your perception of federalism today.

www.txregionalcouncil.org/regions.htm This website provides information about all regional councils of government in Texas.

Local Government in Texas

Hickory Creek, Texas, nestled quietly next to the bustling city of Dallas, is populated by a mere 2,200 residents who enjoy the tranquility of suburban life, convenient access to the city, and the availability of recreational facilities found in the nearby federally protected Westlake Park. Who would have expected these peaceful, typical Texas citizens to rise up against their own city government and engage in a difficult, energy-consuming political struggle? But in 1999, the residents of Hickory Creek proved that it is possible for ordinary citizens to fight town hall and win.

It all began when the Hickory Creek town council decided to consider a plan proposed by entrepreneur Peter Brody to build an indoor-outdoor soccer facility, to be called Blue Sky Soccer Arena, in Westlake Park. When residents overflowed town hall during the council meeting to discuss the arena, the surprised mayor postponed the meeting and rescheduled it to take place in the high school auditorium.

Flyers were distributed informing the community about the public forum on the proposed facility. Concerned residents flocked to the high school to hear the details; many did not like what they heard. Some people, including a few from outside Hickory Creek, spoke in favor of the plan, citing the inevitability of development and the economic advantages it would provide for the town. Soccer fans, in particular, were in favor of the arena. Others, mostly Hickory Creek residents, spoke against it; they were concerned with the impact of the soccer arena on traffic and on the environment of the park. After the city council approved the Blue Sky plan in a split 3–2 vote, the heretofore sleepy little town quickly became a beehive of activity as many residents prepared to protest the plan.

Webpage designer and animal lover Nita Van Cleave telephoned those who had spoken against the plan at the council meeting. They provided the core of activists who met at the Van Cleaves' home to begin mobilizing the community against Blue Sky. Cheryl Roemmele, a school counselor who had led a fight against opening a drive-through wildlife preserve in Westlake Park years before, offered constructive ideas about tactics. Diane Ciarloni, editor of a small paper about horses, supplied the names of others who would help; those people supplied even more names. Door-to-door canvassing drew in others. One of the protesters contacted the Sierra Club and other conservation groups for information about the impact of the proposed arena on the environment.

After learning that Westlake Park is located on a floodplain, Randy King, owner of a boat storage business, explored the details of the financing of the arena. Another resident went to the attorney general's office in Austin to get information on floodplain development. Marvoureen Mathews, a former mayor, learned from the city water department that the arena would require installation of a costly sewer system, which would have to be provided at city expense. Diane Ciarloni and several others called reporters and ran ads in the newspaper to get the attention of the public. Another resident had Stop Blue Sky T-shirts made and sold them to raise money for the protesters' expenses. Butch Mallam, the mayor pro tem of nearby Copper Canyon (who used Westlake Park for his model airplanes), assisted the efforts of the anti–Blue Sky group; the town of Copper Canyon passed a resolution supporting the protesters.

The protesters wrote to the Army Corps of Engineers and contacted national, state, and local officials. They distributed flyers created by a resident at her printing business and circulated petitions to residents. Gary Van Cleave, an air traffic controller at the Dallas–Forth Worth airport, and Nita Van Cleave created a webpage to keep residents and others informed of minute-by-minute changes.

A rally near Westlake Park attracted citizens ranging from elderly conservatives to bikers in support of the protesters, and more signatures were added to petitions. The rally also attracted the attention of the media. The protesters had gathered 350 of the 400 signatures needed on the petition to stop the project when the Army Corps of Engineers made additional efforts unnecessary. The Army Corps representative informed the council that, because of the issues raised by the protest group, an environmental impact study would have to be done, costing up to $500,000 and taking up to two years to complete. The council members then realized that the Blue Sky plan was effectively dead, at least for now.

Although Hickory Creek has in many ways settled back into a comfortable routine, its residents do not intend to be complacent about their city government. The protesters have formed a watchdog group to monitor the actions of government in their beloved town and to encourage participation. Gary Van Cleave served for a time on the Hickory Creek town council. Nita Van Cleave received the Hickory Creek Citizen of the Year award in 2001 in recognition of her efforts in defeating the Blue Sky Project and in recognition of the service provided by her webpage, Nita's Hickory Creek, which includes many items of interest as well as a discussion page that allows citizens to express their views about ongoing issues. Through the Blue Sky experience, the residents of this small town discovered the power of the ordinary citizen's voice in government.[1]

Why Have Local Government?

Our representatives in Washington, D.C., and even state officials in Austin may seem far away to the average Texan, but local government is just next door. The elected officials and the employees of local government are often neighbors with whom we play baseball and attend church. Local government officials have stakes in our communities in a way that higher-level officials do not because our communities are their communities.

Not only do we feel closer to local government than to state and national government, but it affects our daily lives more intimately. Local government has the primary responsibility for ensuring that clean water comes from our taps, controlling traffic so that we can reach our destinations safely, removing and disposing of wastes, and enforcing laws so that our neighborhoods are safe.

Maintaining streets and alleys, controlling business activity and location, and educating children are other major activities of local government that are of great importance to Texans. Local provision and maintenance of public parks, swimming pools, and similar recreational facilities benefit residents at low cost to the users. Public libraries and adult education programs offer opportunities to people of all ages and economic levels. Indeed, the quality of life in communities is largely controlled by local government.

Because residents can influence the activities and services offered by local government, individual communities may reflect the unique preferences of citizens in that area. Levels of service and the types of service provided can vary from locality to locality according to the needs and wishes of citizens and their willingness to pay the cost. For example, a community may strongly support youth recreational facilities and opt to provide generous funding for them. A community with fewer children may prefer emphasizing activities for senior citizens. In the case of Hickory Creek, residents wanted to preserve natural flora and fauna rather than attract commercial ventures. Citizens can make a difference in what local government does.

In addition to providing necessary services and facilitating participation, local government relieves state government of much decisionmaking responsibility about community issues. The power given to local government by the state allows control to those who are most affected by a decision. Local school boards in Texas, for example, are given decisionmaking power over education policy because the needs of children in Dallas may be quite different from the needs of children in Laredo or the rural areas of West Texas. The power of the local government to control local issues is not complete, but it has developed throughout history.

What Is Local Government?

Statutory law Statutory law is created by the legislature rather than established in the state constitution.

General-purpose governments Governments that provide various services and perform various functions. The most common general-purpose local governments are counties and cities.

Special-purpose governments Governments that provide only one or just a few related services.

The term *local government* encompasses counties, cities (municipal corporations), school districts, and other special districts. Some states have townships or boroughs, which are similar to counties. All of these governments exist below the state level for the purpose of serving the needs of citizens. States establish local governments through either their constitution or laws passed by their legislatures (that is, **statutory law**). Each form of government created in this way is given powers and responsibilities, which may be defined in the state constitution, statutory law, or a charter (which is a type of local constitution). These governments can be divided into general-purpose governments and special-purpose governments. **General-purpose governments,** most commonly cities and counties, provide various services and usually have legislative, executive, and judicial branches. In contrast, **special-purpose governments** are established to perform just a few related functions. In Texas, as in all other states, exchange of information among these types of governments is facilitated by COGs, which were discussed in Chapter 3. COGs serve a valuable function for governments, linking regional officials with common concerns. As the number of governments increases, this communication is increasingly important. See Texas in Context 4.1 for the numbers of local governments in the megastates. The term *subcounty governments* refers to cities, towns, and villages.

General-Purpose Governments in Texas

General-purpose governments, cities and counties, are familiar to most people because they provide important services to residents. However, not everyone has a clear understanding of the structure and function of these units.

COUNTIES

The most basic general-purpose government in the majority of states, as well as in Texas, is the county. Only two states, Connecticut and Rhode Island, do not have counties.[2] Counties were established to act as arms of the state and to provide minimal services in an era when agriculture was the primary economic base and a large number of people lived in rural, sparsely populated areas.

TEXAS in Context

4.1 Numbers of Local Governments in Megastates Compared to Population

Megastate	County Governments	Subcounty Governments	Nonschool Special Districts	Population
California	57	475	2,830	34,501,130
Florida	66	404	626	16,713,149
Illinois	102	2,722	3,145	12,600,620
Massachusetts	5	351	403	6,427,801
Michigan	83	1,775	366	10,050,446
New Jersey	21	568	276	8,484,431
New York	57	1,545	1,135	19,157,532
Ohio	88	2,250	631	11,421,267
Pennsylvania	66	2,564	1,885	12,335,091
Texas	**254**	**1,196**	**2,245**	**21,779,893**

Source: U.S. Census Bureau, Government Organization: 2002 Census of Governments (Washington, D.C.: U.S. Government Printing Office, 2003).

Texas has 254 counties that vary extensively in size and population. Historically, counties had few responsibilities and provided only basic services, such as building and maintaining roads in rural areas. County officials have been charged more and more often with increasingly complex tasks, making administration of the county a growing challenge in many parts of Texas today. In spite of the increased demands on county government, the structures that were created to govern in simpler times remain almost unchanged, and all counties have the same form of government.

County Officials.   Regardless of the varying size and diversity of counties, all (with a few exceptions) have the same set of officials.

County Judge.   The county judge is the chief administrator of the county and the judge of county court. He or she is chosen by citizens of the county in a partisan election for a four-year term. The duties of the judge vary according to the population of the county but generally include heavy administrative responsibilities. Candidates for this office are not required to have a law degree, even though the responsibilities of the position may be extremely demanding.

Commissioners Court.   The county judge presides over commissioners court, which is not a court in the usual sense but a legislative body composed of four commissioners elected from single-member districts, and the county judge. Each commissioner represents a specific geographical district or precinct in the county that, by ruling of the U.S. Supreme Court, must contain approximately the same number of people as do the other three districts. Equal division of the population within districts ensures that citizens have equal representative power, a guarantee established by the U.S. Supreme Court decision in *Avery v. Midland County*.[3] This ruling applied the one person–one vote rule to local government representation, including counties and cities. County commissioners are elected in partisan elections every four years. The terms of the four commissioners are staggered so that an election is held for two commissioners every two years.

Commissioners court is responsible for setting the tax rate and passing the budget, making personnel decisions, and generally performing many administrative tasks. As is true of any other amateur group, the expertise and management skills of the county judge and the commissioners are variable.

Constables.   Constables are law enforcement officers elected for a four-year term from single-member districts; their duties vary by county. They are required to have a high school education or equivalent and be bonded; that is, they must obtain a surety bond that guarantees a sum of money to cover the potential cost of damages caused by the actions of the constable. The amount of the bond is determined by the commissioners court and is usually between $500 and $1,500. In 1999, the Texas Legislature passed a bill requiring constables to be certified peace officers.[4] With the permission of commissioners court, a constable may appoint a deputy. In all counties, they execute warrants and citations, and in more populous counties, they may have greater law enforcement responsibilities.

County Sheriff.   The county sheriff is elected to a four-year term as the chief law enforcement officer in a county. The duties encompass enforcing the law in the county, operating the county jail, and executing court orders. Each sheriff must have a high school diploma or its equivalent and be bonded. A sheriff in Texas who is not a commissioned peace officer may be required by the State Commission on Law Enforcement Standards to attend up to forty hours of instruction in law enforcement. The state commission approves content and standards for the courses. The county served by the sheriff is financially responsible for the cost of the instruction. The requirement for instruction may be waived by the commission if the sheriff can demonstrate that attending classes would be a hardship. A sheriff may appoint deputies and guards for the county jail. In counties with a population of 210,000 or more, the sheriff may appoint—subject to the approval of commissioners court—a police force and a police chief.[5]

Justice of the Peace.   The justice of the peace adjudicates cases involving misdemeanors and some civil matters, and serves as the county coroner in counties with no medical examiner. The qualifications for office are minimal, but justices of the peace are required to have forty hours of education in criminal justice. They are elected to a four-year term.

County Attorney.   The county attorney prosecutes cases in county court and acts as a legal adviser to the commissioners and other county officials. This person is elected to a four-year term (the position may be appointive in larger counties). In larger counties, the district attorney (a state rather than a county official) assumes most of the responsibilities for prosecuting cases.

Generally, the county attorney is responsible for prosecuting criminal misdemeanor cases; appearing in civil suits affecting the county; and handling other matters such as child support, bond forfeitures, and commitment procedures. The district attorney, on the other hand, is usually responsible for prosecuting felony cases in district court. Distinguishing the duties of the county attorney and the district attorney is difficult because their responsibilities may coincide in some counties. In fact, in some instances, the district attorney may prosecute misdemeanors, and the county attorney may appear in district court.[6]

County Clerk.   The county clerk, elected for a four-year term, serves as the chief record keeper and election officer. This person serves as the clerk for county commissioners court; records deeds, mortgages, wills, and contracts; issues marriage licenses and maintains certain records of births and deaths; serves on the county election board; certifies candidates running for county office; and preserves the results of state, county, and special district elections. In counties with a population over 8,000, the district clerk also assumes the role of record keeper for district court.

County Financial Officers.   The county tax assessor-collector, treasurer, and auditor are financial officers for the county. The tax assessor-collector, elected for a four-year term, collects county taxes and fees and some state taxes and fees; registers voters; and assesses the value of property for the purposes of collecting **ad valorem taxes,** which are levied on property owners after the value of the property has been determined by the tax assessor-collector or the appraisal district. In counties located within a tax-appraisal district, this person may act as the chief appraiser for the district.

Ad valorem taxes Taxes levied on real property, that is, land and buildings, based on the assessed value of the property.

The treasurer, also elected for a four-year term, receives, deposits, and disburses funds. Some counties have abolished the office of treasurer and transferred the duties to a county auditor. The county auditor, an appointed rather than an elected official, reviews county financial records and countersigns treasurer's warrants issued by the treasurer's office. Treasurer's warrants (issued by the treasurer) are official statements of money to be received or paid by the county. In counties with over 225,000 people or with taxable property worth more than $15 million, the auditor assumes the county judge's role as chief budget officer.

Unelected Positions.   In addition to the elected officials who serve the county, several other nonelected positions are important in delivering services to county residents. They vary but may include, in addition to the county auditor, the county engineer, the county purchasing agent, and the elections administrator.

County Funding.   A tax on land and buildings located in the county provides the largest source of revenue for Texas counties. The state also provides counties with a portion of state motor vehicle and license fees and other motor vehicle taxes and fees. Counties may also levy a sales tax of ½% to 1% as long as the combined state-local tax does not exceed 8.25%.

Citizen Influence on County Government. Commissioners court holds regular meetings that are open to the public. You can contact your local county commissioner or your county judge to find out the time and place of meetings. Most Texas counties provide a webpage that includes the names of elected officials, the agenda of the next court meeting, and often the minutes of previous meetings. A visit to commissioners court will provide an opportunity to witness how decisions are made about services offered by the county as well as how funding and taxing decisions are made. You may even want to speak to the court about a county issue that concerns you. In that case, contact the county judge and ask to be included on the agenda of the next meeting. You can also contact your commissioner at any time to voice your opinions about county matters. Commissioners are your neighbors, so they are likely to welcome input regarding issues that affect your area. They are also elected officials who are in place to serve your interests. Part of that job is responding to the concerns of voters like you.

CITIES

Municipal corporation
Another name for an incorporated city.

As the nation urbanized, another general-purpose government, the **municipal corporation** (city), became the civic and economic center of activity for increasing numbers of people. As important as cities are today, it is surprising to some people that the U.S. Constitution does not mention cities at all. Under the federal system of government, national and state governments have powers derived from the U.S. Constitution; cities do not.

The legal status of cities in the United States was controversial as the nation became more urbanized during the nineteenth century. The controversy was settled and the status of cities was established by the famous Dillon's Rule.[7] In 1872, Judge John Dillon established the following limits on local governments: they have only those powers that are (1) expressly granted to them by the state and (2) clearly implied by the expressly granted powers.

Dillon's Rule is still accepted doctrine with regard to the relationship of cities and states. Judge Dillon made it clear that if doubt exists about whether a local government has a particular power, it does not have it. Thus, cities are completely dependent on the state for the powers they have. Why, then, do municipalities have so much control over their own activities today? We can explain this current trend by considering the difficulty that a state legislature would have if it had to make every decision for each city in the state. State legislators realized that local decisions can be made more effectively by local people who are familiar with the complexities of particular issues in a community. Allowing local officials to handle many of their own problems also frees the legislators to deal with issues that affect the state as a whole.

In addition, as the nation became less rural and agricultural and more urban, an increasing number of voters were living in municipalities. Certainly, these voters preferred local control and had a greater understanding of local needs. As elected officials, state legislators were receptive to the desires of voters in cities. For these reasons, states were willing to delegate powers of self-government to cities. That power is not absolute, however; cities must follow state law with regard to their powers. The specific structure and powers of a city are granted through municipal charters, which vary from state to state.

City Charters.   If a group of people living in close geographical proximity wish to become a municipal corporation (referred to as becoming incorporated), they must file an application with the county judge of the county in which the community is located or, if the community is located in two counties, with the county judge in either of the counties. The county judge then determines whether the community is eligible to incorporate. If it is, the judge orders an incorporation election. If the majority of votes cast by qualified voters in the community favor incorporation, the county judge records in the files of commissioners court that the community is incorporated. The new status of the community is effective the date of the entry in commissioners court records. The new city is granted a charter to establish and describe its status and powers. The Texas Constitution describes how a populated area can become incorporated and the powers that it will have as a municipal corporation. Statutory law also specifies the state's regulations that apply to these entities.

General law charter
A city charter that establishes the legal status of smaller cities, setting down the type of government the city has and establishing the powers of the city.

You can find two basic types of city charters in the state of Texas: a **general law charter** and a home rule charter. A small city, under 5,000 in population, has a general law charter, which describes the structures of the municipal corporation's government and specifies its powers. General law charters in Texas are classified as Type A, Type B, or Type C, categories related to the number of residents and the area occupied by the community. According to state law, the type of general law charter issued determines the kind of city government the municipality will have and the powers available to it. However, the Texas Legislature also allows certain general law cities, by a majority vote in a popular election, to adopt a manager-council form of government. The powers and duties of the city manager in a general law city are specifically outlined in the Local Government Code.

General law cities in Texas may enact ordinances or resolutions by following the procedure outlined in the Local Government Code, but they are closely regulated by state law; those regulations are linked to the size and area of the city. We know that the population and the size of cities tend to change over time, however, with some cities gaining inhabitants and expanding land area and others shrinking in size. A municipal corporation in Texas does not automatically change to a different type as it grows or shrinks. Each incorporated area must petition the state for a change of designation if its inhabitants want to do so. As a general law city grows larger, reaching 5,000 in population, the residents may decide to become a home rule city.

Home rule charter A city charter that may be adopted by larger cities. It allows the city greater self-governing power.

Home rule charters in Texas are granted to larger cities (5,000 or more in population) whose citizens have chosen to become a home rule city; that is, when at least two-thirds of the governing body of the municipality, on petition of at least 10 percent of the qualified voters of the city, order an election on the question: "Shall a commission be chosen to frame a new charter?"[8] If voters agree to frame a new charter, the charter is written by a commission selected by voters in a ballot, appointed by the governing body of the city, selected at a mass meeting of citizens, or appointed by the mayor. The charter, and subsequent amendments to it, must be approved by a majority vote of the qualified voters in the city. The home rule city charter is filed with the Texas secretary of state.

In drafting their charter, residents of a home rule city may use any of the several structures of city government. They do not have to use a standard form like the residents of counties and general law cities do. Home rule residents can give their government greater authority to determine its revenue sources. A home rule charter gives city residents greater flexibility in dealing with local problems. In addition to being able to draft the city's charter and thus establishing the structure of its government, the home rule citizens can alter the city charter as needs or preferences change without appealing to the state legislature for permission.

For example, many home rule cities in Texas use direct democracy to a greater extent than does the state. The powers of initiative, referendum, and recall allow citizens greater power over the actions of city government and city officials. **Initiative** is the power of citizens to draft a proposal through a process of collecting signatures on a petition favoring the proposal. It is a way in which citizens can write or change law themselves. **Referendum** is the power of citizens to bring a proposal to a vote. **Recall** is the right of citizens, through a petition process, to remove an elected official from office before his or her term is over.

City Government Structure. The structure of city governments varies widely throughout the United States, but we can classify them into three primary forms: mayor-council, council-manager, and commission.

Mayor-Council Government. Patterned after the British model, mayor-council is the oldest form of government in the United States. Today, with the exception of the large cities of Houston and El Paso, only smaller Texas cities use the classic mayor-council form. In all of these forms, a prescribed number of officials (council members or commissioners) are elected to represent the citizens and act as the legislative branch of city government. These representatives may be elected in an **at-large election,** meaning each represents and is elected by the whole city, or they may be elected from single-member districts (sometimes called **by-district elections**). Some cities have a mixed method of election, with some representatives elected by district and some elected at-large.

In addition, Texas city elections are **nonpartisan elections,** meaning that candidates do not run for office under a political party label. For single-member district elections, the city is divided into separate geographical areas (districts), each with approximately the same number of citizens. A council member or commissioner is elected from each district by the citizens of that district. The mayor in a mayor-council form of government, usually elected at-large, may be a strong mayor or a weak mayor. It is important to understand that these terms refer to the amount of power that is given to the mayor by the city charter, not to the character and ability of this official. A strong mayor has executive powers; a weak mayor often has no more power than a council member.

Initiative The power of citizens to draft a proposal through a process of collecting signatures on a petition favoring the proposal. It is a way in which citizens can write or change law themselves.

Referendum The power of citizens to bring a proposal to a vote.

Recall The right of citizens, through a petition process, to remove an elected official from office before his or her term is over.

At-large election One in which the entire political unit—for example, a city—votes for a candidate for office. The winner thus represents all citizens in the political unit.

By-district election One in which the political unit is divided into parts or districts. A candidate for office is selected by the citizens of each district and thus represents only that part of the political unit.

Nonpartisan elections Elections in which the candidates are not identified by a political party label. This type of election is the most common city election.

A strong mayor acts as the chief executive of the city, with veto power over votes of the council and sometimes the authority to appoint heads of city agencies and boards. In strong mayor cities, a system of checks and balances may allow the council to control the mayor through powers such as approval of the mayor's appointments and approval of the city's budget.

In a weak mayor system, the mayor's responsibilities are largely symbolic. He or she presides over council meetings and cuts ribbons for new facilities. Any executive power is limited and is often shared with other elected or appointed officials.

Council-Manager Government.   A more recent type of city government has become popular in Texas (and throughout the rest of the nation). The council-manager form of city government originated during the period when the spoils system was reformed. The first recorded use of a city manager was in Staunton, Virginia, in 1908.[9] The supposedly politically neutral expertise provided by the city manager proved valuable during that era because governing cities had become increasingly complex. As a result, many other cities throughout the United States adopted that plan. In fact, the city manager form is the most common type of city government in Texas.

In this form, the city council is the elected representative body for the municipality. The mayor, usually a weak one, may be elected by the people or chosen by the council itself from among its members. But executive responsibility for the day-to-day operation of the city is vested in a city manager, hired for his or her administrative skills. Although the manager is formally empowered only to carry out the wishes of the council, this person is in fact a powerful actor in city government because of his or her expertise.

Commission Form of City Government.   The commission form of local government, little used today, originated in Galveston, Texas, in 1901 as another product of progressive reforms.[10] In this form of government, the elected representatives (that is, the commissioners) essentially wear two hats. First, each is elected at-large and represents the citizens in much the same way as do council members in a mayor-council form of government. One of the commissioners may be designated as mayor, a title that is largely symbolic. Second, each is also the head of a city department; for example, one commissioner may be the commissioner of parks and another the commissioner of streets. The flaws of this form are apparent: no separation exists between executive and legislative functions. The commissioners as a group make decisions as the legislators for the city, and each individual commissioner is responsible for executing those decisions in her or his particular department or agency. Conflicts are difficult to resolve because each commissioner tends to support his or her particular department at the expense of others. And consider the difficulty of finding an individual who is both an effective representative and has the skills and knowledge necessary to administer a city department. In the commission form of government, leadership is weak or nonexistent, and the persons elected often lack the expertise needed to perform their duties.

Although the commission form seems to work well enough in small cities, many U.S. cities today, even Galveston, Texas, have abandoned it. Nevertheless, Texas

Local Government Code requires that Type C general law cities have a commission form of government. A few cities, such as Amarillo, label their type of government as the commission form but have modified it so that the commissioners act more as council members than as classic commissioners. Also, the city has a professional manager to oversee government agency activities.

Funding. Ad valorem property taxes are the most important sources of revenue for Texas cities. Cities are also permitted by Texas law to charge a sales tax on goods sold within the city. Sales taxes are collected by the Texas comptroller of public accounts, who then returns to the city its portion of the sales tax.

Almost every Texas city levies a sales tax, a source of revenue important to city finance, but other sources of revenue are also available. User fees are charged for the use of a city-owned facility; for example, the city may charge an admission fee to a city swimming pool or park. Rental charges are collected from individuals who rent city-owned property, such as a convention center or an athletic facility. Even parking meters are a way of charging rent for leaving one's vehicle on a city street. Permit fees are charged to those who engage in certain occupations or services. Examples are building permits, restaurant permits, alcohol sales permits, and even garage sale permits (in some cities). Hotel and motel occupancy taxes are important sources of revenue for cities whose economy depends on tourism. Gambling provides some revenue for Texas cities in the form of taxes on bingo games. Texas cities also get a small portion of the state lottery. Revenue for cities also comes from federal grants-in-aid and from the sale of bonds.

Citizen Input in City Government. All Texas cities are governed by the people of the city through elected officials. Residents of a city can attend meetings of the town council or city council to learn how decisions are made in their locality. The time and place of these meetings and the agenda of the next meeting must be posted in a public place. Generally, you can find out about the meetings by calling one of the elected officials or the city secretary. You can arrange, through the city secretary or the mayor's office, to be included on the agenda whenever you want to address an issue. And you can contact your elected officials at any time to express your opinions. Elected officials depend on input from voters as they consider options to address city issues.

Special-Purpose Governments in Texas

Special-purpose districts provide services that other levels of government do not wish to perform or are not empowered to perform. These governments have often been created to deal with issues that transcend municipal or county boundaries. For example, a special-purpose district may be created to address a problem presented by a floodplain that encompasses several counties and includes several cities. In such a case, one county or city cannot deal with the problem effectively, so a special unit of government is created. In other cases, a city or county government may lack the resources or the willingness to increase taxes for their residents to cope with a problem, so they favor leaving it to a state-created special-purpose district. Because new problems continually arise, special-purpose districts are the fastest-growing form of local government today.

The megastates all have numerous special districts created to serve their various needs. Illinois has the most special districts, not only among the megastates but among all fifty states; Pennsylvania, with approximately the same population as Illinois, has fewer special districts. Population does not seem to be directly related, however, to the number of special districts among states. (Refer again to Texas in Context 4.1 for a comparison of the number of local governments in the megastates.)

Special-purpose districts in Texas are not as visible to the average citizen as are counties and cities, but they are quite numerous and serve various needs that other governments do not fulfill. They may be contiguous with the geographical boundaries of a county or city, or they may encompass all or parts of a number of cities or even counties.

Of all special districts, school districts are the most numerous throughout the United States, and independent school districts are the most prevalent. The distinction between independent and dependent school districts is the degree of self-governance and autonomy given to the district. In many states, school districts are under the authority of a governmental unit, such as a municipality or county. Texas has long preferred independent units governed by a local school board. Independent school districts were established by the Texas Constitution as a reaction to the centralized school administration of the Reconstruction governor, E. J. Davis. These districts afford a great deal of local control of public schools, a condition most Texans favor.

As you can see in Texas in Context 4.2, Texas has only one dependent school district, the Windham School District (WSD), located in Huntsville. It was established by the Texas Legislature in 1969 to serve prisoners incarcerated in the Texas prison system. The school board for WSD, the Texas Board of Criminal Justice, is comprised of members appointed by the governor. This unique school district operates within prisons, providing training in agriculture and industry operations, food service, laundry, and laundry services, among others. WSD has a superintendent who oversees four regions, each of which has a regional administrator who in turn supervises the principals of schools within the region. The goal of WSD is to provide Texas offenders with skills that will enable them to be productive members of society after their release from prison. All other school districts in Texas are governed by local citizens.

Citizen Input in School Districts.   School districts other than WSD in Texas are operated through elected boards composed of local citizens who make decisions about school issues. School board meetings are open to the public. Attending one of their meetings is a way to learn about the concerns of local schools and affords an opportunity to address those issues. The qualifications for becoming a school

Texas in Context

4.2 Numbers of Public School Districts in Megastates

Megastate	Independent School Districts	Dependent School Districts	Total	Population
California	1,047	60	1,107	34,501,130
Texas	**1,089**	**1**	**1,090**	**21,779,893**
Illinois	934	—	934	12,600,620
Michigan	580	159	739	10,050,446
New York	683	32	715	19,157,532
Ohio	667	—	667	11,421,267
New Jersey	549	75	624	8,484,431
Pennsylvania	516	—	516	12,335,091
Massachusetts	82	248	330	6,427,801
Florida	95	—	95	16,713,149

Source: U.S. Census Bureau, Government Organization: 2002 Census of Governments (Washington, D.C.: U.S. Government Printing Office, 2003).

board member are not stringent; the Texas Association of School Boards even provides a website to assist anyone who is interested in serving.[11] While running for any office requires a commitment of time and energy, many individuals with no experience in politics have been successful in school board races. If you are concerned about the schools in your area, perhaps you should consider becoming a member of the school board.

Nonschool Special Districts. Other special districts were created over time and are still being created to address particular problems, such as water conservation and drainage. The most common function of special districts is control of natural resources. For this purpose, drainage and flood-control districts as well as irrigation, soil-conservation, and water-conservation districts have been created in many states. Special districts to deal with fire protection, housing, community development, and sewerage are also common among the states. Additional examples of special districts are airport authorities, hospital districts, metropolitan rapid transit authorities, and more recently crime control and prevention districts. At least 90 percent of all special districts throughout the United States are single-purpose districts. Less than 10 percent are charged with performing multiple but related functions, generally involving water supply and sewerage.

Municipal utility districts (MUDs) provide an example of multiple-function special districts in Texas. The Texas Legislature established MUDs in 1917 as conservation and reclamation authorities to control water and sewerage provision in developments and to protect the environment. These special districts have been somewhat controversial, with detractors saying that they allow developers to pass on the financial burden of improvements to home buyers. For some time, the Texas Legislature has allowed MUDs to build parks and recreation facilities as a component of their constitutionally imposed authority to conserve and protect water supplies, but they were not allowed to sell bonds prior to the Seventy-Eighth Legislature.

The question of whether conservation and reclamation districts could develop a purely recreational facility (when the project was not a facet of conservation efforts) arose in 1980 when a resident of Harris County challenged the right of the Harris County Water Control and Improvement District No. 110 to develop a facility that had a community center, a swimming pool, and tennis courts. In this case, the court found that the district did not have the right to build a facility because the recreational facilities did not further its constitutional purpose.[12] Subsequently, when the Upper Guadalupe River Authority planned to build a reservoir, the Texas attorney general found that it could provide swimming and boating areas along with the reservoir because the primary purpose of the reservoir was to provide water for the city of Kerrville, in keeping with the constitutional purpose of the authority. The power of conservation and reclamation districts was enhanced and expanded in 2003, when voters approved Proposition 4, a constitutional amendment authorizing the financing of recreational facilities through the sale of guaranteed bonds by MUDs in the Tarrant Regional Water District or in a district in any of ten counties: Bexar, Bastrop, Waller, Travis, Williamson, Harris, Galveston, Brazoria, Fort Bend, and Montgomery.

Those who supported the amendment argued that the present law was unclear and that specifically empowering districts to create parks and recreational facilities would increase the number of those facilities available for residents. Because financing them with bonds requires voter approval, the measure would give the residents greater decisionmaking power. Proponents also argued that the proposal would facilitate provision of recreational facilities in areas outside cities or in areas where neither the city nor the county provided adequate facilities.

Those opposed to the amendment objected to allowing districts in the designated areas to use tax dollars for recreational facilities but not allowing the practice in other parts of the state. They also argued that county and city governments are adequate to provide needed facilities, and that conservation and reclamation districts should concentrate on their constitutional objectives. Perhaps the strongest objection from opponents was that some conservation and reclamation districts were created as a result of actions by developers who use the recreational developments to enhance private sales of land; however, the proponents of the amendment prevailed.[13]

Special districts are created in one part of the state to deal with regional problems particular to that area. Often, debt limits or resource limits on existing governments have made it easier to create a new governmental unit to address an issue rather than burdening an existing local government with a problem that would result in additional demands on its revenue sources. Problems such as flood control or water conservation often extend over the boundaries of several local governments, making it unlikely that any one locality would be willing to shoulder the whole cost of the solution. Each special district has been created through a process outlined in state law, sometimes requiring approval by voters in an affected area.

The sources of revenue for special districts in Texas vary, although most get some funding from property tax, user fees, permits, fees, bonds, and grants. Intergovernmental transfers from the state or from the national government are important sources of funding for many special districts, particularly independent school districts and junior college districts.

Because special districts are created in regions, different parts of the state have their own individual mix of these unique governments. Look at a property-tax statement in your area. Chances are that it will itemize the special districts that are funded with ad valorem taxes. (You may discover the existence of governments in your own community with which you were unfamiliar.) When you understand what special districts exist in your area, you are empowered to sort out the responsible units among the growing and complex morass of governments that affect particular concerns you may have and thus you may control what they do more effectively. Remember that knowledge is power: the more you understand how government functions, the more effective you will be as a citizen. Each special district serves a unique purpose in the community. Many were created with the consent of voters like you. As we see in the example of MUDs in Texas, voters are sometimes asked to make decisions about the powers of special districts.

Issues in Texas Local Government

As future leaders of Texas, you will doubtlessly find that part of your political time will be devoted to issues that affect the communities where you live and work. Here are a few areas in which you may need to develop some background.

ELECTION LAWS

We have already noted that cities make decisions about their election laws. Because the rules of the game have some influence on the outcome, the kinds of laws that cities adopt have an effect on election results. We want to remind you that election laws are decisions made by previous generations and that you can change these decisions. Perhaps the most influential decision has been a way of organizing elections called the place system. Let's review the options available for organizing elections to put this concept in context. A political unit (city or state) can elect some officials by one of the following methods: generic at-large, at-large with the place system, at-large with cumulative voting, and single-member districts.

Generic at-Large. *Generic at-large* is a term we have coined to describe a system in which officials such as city council members are all elected from the whole political unit. In a small city, everyone can be reached by door-to-door campaigning.

BOX 4.1   Different Election Systems: Different Outcomes

Conditions

Seats—Three to be filled in this Election. Each voter has three votes.

Candidates—One Mexican American (Hernandez), and five Anglos.

Voters—Thirty-four Mexican Americans and sixty-six Anglos.

GENERIC AT-LARGE METHOD:

Mexican Americans use only one of their three votes; they single-shot to elect one candidate.

Vote Candidate	Mexican American			Anglo			Total
	First	Second	Third	First	Second	Third	
Hernandez	34			0	0	0	34
Jones	0	0	0	40	6	15	61
Smith	0	0	0	14	35	15	64
Poteet	0	0	0	5	15	10	30
Crown	0	0	0	6	6	10	22
Davis	0	0	0	1	4	16	21
Votes Used	34	0	0	66	66	66	

The larger the city, the more necessary it is to reach voters with mass media, which costs money and gives an advantage to candidates who can raise the necessary cash. In an at-large election with no modifications, however, the disadvantage of being from a poor neighborhood or of being a member of an ethnic minority group can be overcome. Candidates can organize their followers to use their vote only once in an election in which more than one candidate is to be elected. In other words, they do not use their second or third vote for candidates from the majority or candidates able to raise the majority of the money. This one-vote tactic is called single shotting.

If you look at the election outcomes in Box 4.1, you will see how single shotting works. Both tables assume an Anglo majority of sixty-six and a Mexican American minority of thirty-four, with three officials to be elected.

At-Large System with Places (Place System).

The generic, or unmodified, at-large system without places gives minorities a chance, even though it is an at-large election. A modification that significantly reduces their chances is the introduction of places. In the place system, minority candidates are forced to run head-to-head against members of the majority group. More often than not, they lose (see Box 4.1). In some communities, minorities have lost so often that they have sued to change the system. City governments that refuse to change often lose.

The at-large system with places can lead to the systematic exclusion of Mexican Americans and African Americans from public office. If they do not have a seat at the table, the needs and issues that affect these groups may be ignored, and consequently their belief in the political system may be weakened. In some communities, the generic at-large system was modified to prevent single-shotting and thus deny representation of these communities. Check to see if this situation has happened in your community. Another example of the rules being changed to keep minority issues off the table occurred in 1987, in Victoria, Texas, where a Mexican American female was elected to a local school board. The Anglo majority promptly changed the rules for getting issues on the agenda. Henceforth, it would take two votes, not just one, to place an item on the agenda.[14]

Thus, in a diverse society like Texas, certain categories of Texans can be denied representation by people like themselves. This lack of representation is against federal law if it occurs consistently over time. Federal law does not guarantee a proportion of seats to minorities equal to their percentage of the population; it simply requires that minorities get some representation if they have demonstrated that they have tried and failed to elect candidates.

Generic at-Large Election with Cumulative Voting.

The difference between the cumulative method and the generic at-large system is that in a cumulative system, an individual voter can use all of his or her votes for one candidate. In most electoral systems with multiple candidates, a voter has only one vote per seat, and he or she can use all of those votes or not. A few communities in Texas have adopted this method, but it is used more frequently in other states.

Many school boards are elected from single-member districts, but in those that have an at-large system, a 1995 change in voting procedure has benefited minority candidates.[15] Governor George W. Bush signed into law a provision for cumulative voting in at-large school board elections, which allows each voter to vote for as many candidates as there are vacancies on a board. In other words, if three at-large positions are open, each voter may cast three votes. The winners are the three candidates with the highest number of votes. This system has been especially favorable to minority candidates, who could not prevail in the former winner-take-all system.

Single-Member Districts.   In single-member district systems, the political unit is divided into districts, each of which elects an official. Counties are divided into single-member districts for electing county commissioners, for example. A minority candidate usually wins in a district in which his or her minority group is actually a majority. The problem with single-member districts is that they have to be redrawn every ten years after the census. This stipulation inserts an extra election into the election cycle and means extra work and a reshuffling of the staggered terms. (The possibility for fraud in the redrawing of district boundaries, called gerrymandering, will be discussed in Chapter 8.)

In sum, you may wish to consider several options if your community still has the place system. Clearly, at-large elections are not the problem for representation in a diverse community. The place system is the problem, a point we revisit in Chapter 10 when we discuss judicial elections. As Box 4.2 indicates, representation and democracy don't have to mean that 60 percent of the population makes 100 percent of the decisions.

EXTRATERRITORIAL JURISDICTION

Texas cities grew rapidly in the twentieth century as immigrants from the Northeast and Midwest sought a more favorable environment to raise their families and to work. Lower taxes and weaker unions attracted businesses to Texas. Of course, most businesses located in urban areas of the state. As cities grew, the more prosperous residents gravitated to residential areas outside the city limits, with less traffic and crime, more fresh air, and freedom from city taxes. Living outside the city limits did not always ensure complete freedom from city government, however.

Extraterritorial jurisdiction (ETJ) The geographical area outside the boundaries of a city over which the city has some control and some responsibility.

By state law, municipal corporations are responsible for an area outside the city within what is called the city's **extraterritorial jurisdiction (ETJ).** The Texas Legislature established ETJs to "promote and protect the general health, safety, and welfare of persons residing in and adjacent to the municipalities."[16] The size of the ETJ is determined by the number of residents in the city, ranging from a half-mile beyond the city limits for cities of fewer than 5,000 inhabitants to five miles beyond the city limits for municipalities with 100,000 or more inhabitants.

Until 2001, authority to control the ETJ was given to the adjacent city and to the county, with no stipulation about which unit was responsible for particular services. The Seventy-Seventh Legislature determined that the city and county cannot both regulate the ETJ. In 2003, HB1204, passed by the Texas Legislature and signed by the governor, requires cities with over 100,000 in population to have an agreement with the county concerning control of the ETJ by January 1, 2004. Smaller cities must have a similar agreement with their counties by January 1, 2006.

ANNEXATION

Annexation The practice of a city extending its borders to include areas that were formerly not within the city limits.

The city can enlarge its boundaries through a process called **annexation,** thus expanding its ETJ. Annexation is a legal process whereby a city extends its borders to encompass a new area, which then becomes part of the city. Annexing an area can be costly because state law requires that cities extend services such as water and

---

BOX 4.2   A Child's Approach to Decisionmaking

In "Tyranny of the Majority," a collection of essays, Lani Guinier shares a lesson learned from her four-year-old son, Nikolas. While reading *Sesame Street Magazine* together, they came to a picture in which readers were asked to decide what would happen next. Six children in the picture were deciding on a game to play. Four children had their hands raised to vote for tag, and two had their hands down because they wanted to play hide and seek.

Nikolas responded to the question, "What game will the children play?" with the answer, "They will play both. First they will play tag. Then they will play hide-and-seek." With the wisdom of a child, he had looked beyond the lesson in counting in a democracy that was being taught and cut to the larger issue for a just society.

"Why agree to play with people who won't give you a turn?" he asked.

To some children, it is natural and fair to take turns. Adult rulemakers and questioners too often miss this point in stressing all-or-nothing decisionmaking, in which 51 percent of the population make 100 percent of the decisions.

Source: Lani Guinier, *The Tyranny of the Majority: Fundamental Fairness in Representative Democracy* (New York: Free Press, 1995), p. 2.

---

sewer to annexed areas within four and a half years and that they extend essential services such as police, fire, and health services immediately. This cost is sometimes, but not always, offset by the increased revenue gained by city taxes on the newly annexed property. Because cities depend primarily on ad valorem property taxes, the addition of an area with expensive houses will generate more revenue than will an area that has undeveloped property.

Texas Local Government Code, Chapter 43 establishes the right of cities to annex surrounding territory and sets the conditions necessary for them to do so. Cities are generally limited to annexing unincorporated areas within their extraterritorial jurisdiction but, under some circumstances, large home rule cities may annex small incorporated areas with the consent of the voters in that area.[17] In some cases, a city may engage in defensive annexation to prevent an adjacent area from incorporating. In the 1980s, Lubbock, a city that prohibits package sales of alcoholic beverages, quickly annexed a distressed area on its western border to prevent the area from incorporating and legalizing alcohol sales.

Annexation laws in Texas have been liberal in the past, and it remains difficult for a small community to resist annexation by a larger neighbor. In some cases now, consent of the voters in the larger city and the smaller, contiguous area is necessary, but by state law, Texas cities can annex up to 10 percent of their ETJ in a one-year period without the consent of the residents of that area. They can now even annex incorporated communities with a population of 600 or less. In that case, the incorporation of the small city is abolished.

Residents of suburbs may prefer to remain independent of a large neighboring city, thus keeping their own tax base, local government, and schools. A smaller city

JOIN THE DEBATE

THE ISSUE: Should a city be able to annex an adjacent area without the consent of the residents of that area?

AGREE

1. The economic viability of the state depends on the ability of cities to expand as needed.

2. Many of the residents of the ETJ work in the city and enjoy its benefits, so they should contribute to the tax base of the city.

3. The majority of those concerned in any annexation live in the city, so they should be able to override the opinions of the minority living outside the city.

4. When a city encroaches on a neighboring settled area, events such as fires and loose dogs affect the city, so the city should be able to take over and control those problems.

5. Businesses in an ETJ have an advantage over those in the city with which they compete because they pay less in taxes. Annexation would level the playing field for those in the city.

6. Unsafe conditions such as inadequate waste disposal and questionable drinking water can be a problem in rural areas. Cities can regulate such issues more easily, so they should be able to take over if they can.

DISAGREE

1. Business interests should not be the state's priority. Rural farmland should be protected from being gobbled up by a nearby city.

2. Residents are outside the city because they chose to be and should not be forced to become city residents against their will.

3. Becoming part of a city will raise taxes for residents. They should have a say about the level of their taxes.

4. Residents of an ETJ may have allegiance to their area, not the city, and thus they will not be good citizens of the city.

5. Being annexed by the city may affect how property owners can use their land, especially if it is zoned for different uses than the owners want.

6. It may be a long time before the city provides services to an annexed area, but the residents will be paying taxes during that time. Is that fair?

that is adjacent to the big city has control over its area and can provide the benefits of small-town living with the convenience of easy access to the city's workplaces, shopping centers, and recreational facilities. The idea of being swallowed up by the large city may be horrifying to residents.

In a recent instance, many citizens of Guadalupe County opposed the annexation of several historic farms by the city of New Braunfels in 2003. Residents feared higher taxes, the encroachment of industrial property into their agrarian community, and the potential for rezoning agricultural land to allow commercial enterprises. In protest, one angry farmer said, "We grow everything for everybody, our farms are disappearing. Who are we going to buy our food from? Iraq?"[18] Despite their protests and a resolution by the Guadalupe County Commissioners Court, the annexation took place. New Braunfels leaders wanted their city to grow, as all city officials do. This incident illustrates the control that the state exercises over cities, and also that individuals who want to influence issues such as annexation must bring their concerns to officials at the state level if they want change.

Annexation has been controversial in many instances. SB 89, passed into law in 1999, required cities to develop an annexation plan that details the availability of city services to an area of proposed annexation and offers residents of that area an opportunity to comment. In 2003, failed HB 568 would have required the approval of the voters in any area before annexation could take place. Why is annexation important to Texas cities? As urban areas have grown more populous, some states have developed cooperative agreements among central cities, suburbs, and counties in a metropolitan area. Instead, Texas has assured the ability of cities to expand as needed through liberal annexation laws. As the Texas Legislature was considering HB 568 in 2003, the Texas Municipal League commissioned a study of the impact of reducing the rate of annexation. In this study, the Perryman Group argued that, because 92 percent of the state's economic activity takes place in urban areas, those areas are vital to the well-being of the state as a whole. Says Perryman, any restriction on annexation would reduce annual gross state product by $305.7 billion by 2030 and result in a loss of 1,234,760 permanent jobs by that same year, and it would reduce personal income and annual retail sales by a substantial amount.[19]

Resistant residents in Guadalupe County might disagree with giving priority to economic growth, and they might feel that their case should be an exception. It is apparent, though, that the issue of annexation may well pit the interests and preferences of a local area against the economic interests of the state as a whole. Annexation promises to be a subject for debate for many years.

SUBURBANIZATION

Suburb A residential community that has grown up outside the city limits of a larger city and may exist as one of many contiguous suburbs.

Over time, cities like San Antonio and Dallas have become surrounded by smaller cities called **suburbs.** Some of these suburbs are independent, incorporated cities; others may have been absorbed by the larger city; and still others may be unincorporated communities. Texans in these regions are accustomed to driving from one small suburb into another, often without realizing when they have crossed a city boundary. Suburbs that are incorporated cities gain a reputation among locals.

Sometimes the reputation is positive, for example, for excellent schools or other facilities; sometimes it is negative, for example, for ardent enforcement of traffic laws. These suburbs provide choices for residents and greater control over their local government than they might find in the larger city, but suburbanization can also cause problems.

As more prosperous residents move into suburbs, older cities are left with poorer citizens who are less able to pay taxes and often with aging infrastructure and streets in need of repair. Problems of crime, homelessness, poverty, traffic congestion, and air pollution increase when revenue declines. Suburban residents may continue to use the facilities of the city, drive on its streets, work in its businesses, and use its recreational and entertainment facilities but pay most of their local taxes to their suburbs.

Gentrification A term used to describe the renovation of an older area of a city to make it attractive to middle-class people.

To combat this problem, cities may adopt strategies to attract people to the inner city to live. **Gentrification** programs are designed to restore older historic neighborhoods and make them attractive to young, middle-class families. Renewal projects, particularly popular in the 1970s, spent money to revitalize downtown areas by tearing down dilapidated structures and replacing them with specialty shops, restaurants, theaters, and apartments intended to attract middle-class residents. A negative side effect of urban renewal projects has been displacement of poor people who lived in the dilapidated buildings that were torn down, which in turn resulted in an increase in homelessness. Older large cities have to work to solve complex problems with decreasing resources. Often the solution to one problem generates yet another. People who live in cities increasingly need to make their voices heard in local government.

ZONING

Cities have authority for establishing and enforcing several codes intended to provide for the health, safety, and welfare of persons living within their boundaries. Building codes, traffic ordinances, parking ordinances, and zoning ordinances are some of the most significant. Zoning laws, for example, illustrate the fact that an attempt to solve a problem may have potential negative side effects. Most Texas cities have laws that control the use of land within the boundaries of the city to protect the quality of life within the area. **Zoning laws** regulate where particular types of activities may be conducted. For instance, some areas of the city may be reserved for residential dwellings, some for commercial enterprises, some for light manufacturing, and some for heavy manufacturing. In the days before zoning laws were common, nothing stopped a person from building a rendering plant next to a restaurant or an adult entertainment club next to a school. Zoning laws protect property value by preventing conflict in land use. Residential areas are separated from commercial areas so that homeowners are not bothered by heavy traffic caused by adjacent businesses. Few would dispute that zoning laws often have a positive effect. And in most Texas cities, an individual who believes a zoning restriction causes a hardship can appeal for an exception to the planning and zoning board. For example, zoning laws usually restrict businesses from being

Zoning laws The control of land use and development in a particular area.

opened in a residential area because of the increased traffic they may draw into the neighborhood. An individual may argue before the zoning board that his or her proposed type of business (perhaps a mail-order operation) will not increase local traffic and thus should be granted an exception from the prohibition against locating in a residential area.

On the negative side, zoning laws have been used to exclude certain racial groups or others deemed undesirable by a community. Exclusionary zoning can take many forms. A residential area may be expensive to move into because lot sizes must be large or because all homes must have a particular construction. In some areas, multifamily dwellings such as apartments may be prohibited. If these laws discriminate intentionally against a racial group, they may be unconstitutional. Zoning laws that discriminate on the basis of poverty, however, are not subject to constitutional challenge. Some people may challenge exclusionary zoning laws as discriminatory, but others argue that they provide a means for a community to control its environment.

The power of citizens in controlling their community through zoning restrictions is illustrated by the defeat of a proposed zoning change in Hickory Creek, the small town mentioned in the vignette at the beginning of this chapter. In September 2003, the Hickory Creek town council responded to citizen protests against allowing a high-density subdivision to be constructed in the town.[20]

PROPERTY TAX

Taxes became a major focus of the 2003 legislative session, when property owners in many areas of the state called for reform of property-tax laws, particularly the so-called Robin Hood plan (through which wealthy school districts helped to support poorer districts). This plan harkens back to a 1970s lawsuit that charged the children of the state's poor school districts were discriminated against by a system in which schools were largely supported by local property taxes, resulting in a great disparity between resources available to children in poor and rich districts. After much wrangling, the present system, which requires sharing of local revenues from wealthier districts, was adopted. By 2003, however, the appraised values of property in many areas had skyrocketed, creating what many felt was an unfair burden on owners. In some areas, school property taxes had risen 70 percent in a decade.[21] Indeed, while the tax burden on Texans is less than the tax burden on residents of other states, the property-tax burden is higher.[22]

Legislators sought to remedy the problem without much success in the 2003 legislative session. Lieutenant Governor David Dewhurst introduced a plan to reduce local school property taxes by establishing a state property tax and increasing sales taxes by almost two cents, and then applying revenues from those sources to supporting public schools. The Dewhurst plan was roundly criticized on the grounds that it would not generate sufficient revenue for schools and would hurt the poorest Texans. By the end of the legislative session, the only property tax relief bill that was passed was HB 3504, a mild reform that made it easier for an elderly or disabled person to receive a tax deferral on a homestead.[23]

Why is Texas unable to fix the problem of finding fair taxation to support schools? Common Cause Texas alleged that lawmakers keep trying to tweak a flawed system rather than find a new solution to our dilemma. Part of the problem is the political aversion in Texas to other sources of revenue used by most states, particularly a state income tax. While many agree that both sales and property taxes are regressive (that is, they unfairly burden the poor), the more equitable income tax is political poison for any legislator with the temerity to propose it.

The debate over property taxes continued through the fourth special session of the Seventy-Eighth Legislature. The debate over property taxes continued through the fourth special session of the Seventy-Eighth Legislature. In September 2004, State District Judge John Dietz ruled that the Robin Hood system of school finance is unconstitutional.[24] The debate is sure to be an issue in 2005. It is imperative that we consider the alternatives and communicate our ideas to our elected officials. This issue will affect everyone in the state. (More discussion about tax reform appears in Chapter 14.)

ETHICS IN GOVERNMENT

One principle of democratic governance is accountability of elected officials to voters. Making sure that our officials keep the public trust is a responsibility of citizens in a democracy. Officials at the state and national level are subject to more scrutiny by the media and the general public than are those at the local level, but even at the local level, the power to do evil or good is an intrinsic part of elected office. How can we hold local officials accountable to us, the voters? Or should we assume that, because they are our neighbors, local officials do not need to be watched as closely as those in higher office?

In 2002, the Miami-Dade County Commission on Ethics and Public Trust surveyed local governments nationwide to ascertain what mechanisms were in place to promote ethics and accountability. Among other findings, only 25 percent of local governments reported having an ethics board or commission, and only 40 percent provided some form of ethics training for employees. Only 17 percent of elected officials were required to participate in ethics training. Of the major concerns expressed by respondents, 80 percent were concerned with conflict-of-interest issues, while 37 percent were worried about lack of public trust.[25]

A similar concern about the ethics of local government officials in Texas was shown by the passage of HB 1606 in 2003. This bill requires officials in each city with over 100,000 in population to file financial disclosure statements in a place available to the public. This bill was supported by Common Cause Texas; Public Citizen, Inc.; Campaigns for People; and the Texas Daily Newspaper Association. On the other hand, the Texas Municipal League (TML) lobbied strongly against it. TML believes that this requirement will unfairly target the most economically successful Texans, discouraging them from running for a frequently unpaid, volunteer office. What do you think? Should local officials be required to disclose their financial records? Should other requirements be in place to ensure accountability of elected officials at local level?

These folks listen as well as speak. Let them know what you think on issues that matter to you.

Texas Local Governments in the Twenty-First Century

Many challenges face the local governments of Texas in the twenty-first century. Some of them are new and some are old issues that state and local leaders have faced for a long time. Homeland security is an issue for governments at all levels. Local governments are in a position to be first responders in case of a terrorist attack. New security measures are in place in most Texas local governments as they take on the unprecedented role of partner with state and national government in protecting our citizens. Security measures in themselves may affect local governments; for example, tightening federal border control requirements reduces the number of shoppers and tourists coming into Texas from Mexico. At the same time, cities, counties, and other local governments may face budget cuts unless the overall economy of the state improves. Texas local governments are less dependent on the state than are localities in most other states. Even so, cuts in state programs have a strong impact on local governments who must make up for the reductions in state programs such as health care and welfare programs.

CITIES

Municipal corporations, or cities, are home to over 85 percent of Texas residents. They have become the primary economic centers of the state and the locus of most political activity. Texas in Context 4.3 illustrates the growth of the largest cities in the megastates from 1990 to 1999.

As the population of Texas cities increases, problems grow more complex and expensive. A priority of almost all cities is economic growth. The prosperity of the city directly affects the well-being of residents; the means by which that growth is fostered is a political decision for the residents and officials. Sometimes the goals of economic growth may conflict with other legitimate goals. This situation has made managing a city increasingly fraught with difficulties.

Governing Magazine recently presented the results of a project, undertaken in cooperation with the Maxwell School of Citizenship and Public Affairs at Syracuse University, to rate the management of selected cities in the United States on five dimensions: financial management, human resources management, information technology, capital management, and managing for results.[26] The Texas cities included were Austin, Dallas, Houston, and San Antonio. The average grades on all dimensions ranged from Austin's A– to Houston's B–. But as officials in any Texas city would admit, those high grades do not mean that problems don't exist in urban Texas.

An article in *Texas Town and City* predicts that cities in the twenty-first century will face changes that will require replacing the traditional municipal planning of the past with more modern and citizen-driven planning strategies.[27] City officials will have to respond to new interests created by changes in demographics. As Hispanics become the largest minority, more women enter the workforce, and the population of senior citizens increases, these groups will express policy preferences that may differ from those of the past. The article suggests that the increasing diversity of cities will boost the importance of citizen input and government response.

Encouraging participation by citizens is increasingly a priority of cities throughout Texas. San Angelo is an example of a city proactively seeking input. Mayor J. W. Lown instituted the Take Charge Initiative, which created several citizen committees to offer advice on numerous issues. Among them are committees on neighborhood development, arts and humanities, economic development, natural resources, and equality and opportunity. The latter received a $5,000 grant from La Raza to assist their efforts, and other committees are seeking grants to further their endeavors. The city of Arlington has posted an online citizen action request form that asks for suggestions, ideas, and problems from residents and visitors to the city.[28] In fact, e-government initiatives that provide information and access to the public through e-mail are becoming common throughout Texas and in most other states as well. Contacting local government is becoming easier with these technological advances.

Cities want to attract residents and businesses, foster construction, and welcome tourists and conventioneers. At the same time, they want to reduce traffic

TEXAS in Context

4.3 Population Changes of Selected Cities in Megastates

State	City	2000 Population	Percentage Change from 1990
California	Los Angeles	3,694,820	+5.67
Florida	Jacksonville	735,617	+13.65
Illinois	Chicago	2,896,016	+3.88
Massachusetts	Boston	589,141	+3.03
Michigan	Detroit	925,051	−10.01
New Jersey	Newark	273,546	−0.61
New York	New York City	8,008,278	+8.56
Ohio	Columbus	711,470	+11.04
Pennsylvania	Philadelphia	1,517,550	−4.29
Texas	**Houston**	**1,953,631**	**+16.54**

Source: U.S. Census Bureau, http://www.census.gov/population/estimates.metrocity/SC100KT1.txt.

congestion, control air pollution, and provide a safe environment for residents. Obviously, these goals require tradeoffs and compromise. Balancing the needs and desires of multiple interests invites participation by citizens who will be affected by each city's policies.

COUNTIES

Texas counties also face challenges in the new millennium. Their governing structures are largely the same in populous Harris and Dallas counties and in rural King County. Although the problems facing counties are increasingly complex and diverse, the counties themselves lack the flexibility they need to cope with changing demands. Unlike many other states, Texas lacks provision for home rule counties, an alternative that would allow greater autonomy for counties in highly populated areas. Even in areas of less population density, limits on county government have allowed some problems to fester, particularly on the Texas-Mexico border.

Colonias Residential developments found in South Texas, particularly along the Texas-Mexico border, that are lacking in acceptable water and sewer services and contain substandard structures.

BORDER AREAS

Border issues have received legislative attention recently because representatives have sought solutions to the multifaceted problems presented by the South Texas *colonias.* **Colonias** are communities that have arisen in rural areas inhabited by extremely poor, mostly Hispanic residents. Because counties, in general, lack the authority to enforce strict building and zoning regulations, many of the structures in the *colonias* are substandard shacks, hot in the summer and cold in the winter. Many *colonias* lack a clean water supply and sanitary sewage disposal facilities. In the 1999 legislative session, Senator Eddie Lucio (Brownsville) and Representative Henry Cuellar (Laredo) sponsored a bill (SB 1421), which was passed, allowing border counties to establish planning commissions and begin inspection of subdivisions to ensure compliance with development requirements.

The bill also includes other provisions to provide assistance to *colonias* residents in getting safe water and sewage facilities. Border counties and cities have experienced unprecedented growth in the past decade as a result of vastly increased trade after passage of the North American Free Trade Agreement (NAFTA). Growth brings with it an increased demand for services, road maintenance and construction, schools, and other facilities to accommodate a mushrooming population.

Legislation passed in the Seventy-Sixth Legislature, such as SB 501, addressed the need for state attention to border regions. SB 501, sponsored by Senator Eliot Shapleigh (El Paso), requires state agencies to include in their strategic plans an analysis of how the agency can increase its presence on the Texas-Mexico border and on the borders of Texas and other states.

A report issued in November 2003 by State Comptroller Carole Keeton Strayhorn recognized some improvement in the conditions of border residents but lamented that the poverty rate on the border is still 24.1 percent compared to a state average of 14.5 percent, with 35.5 percent of border children living in poverty. Unemployment on the border remains higher than in much of the state, and both the education level and per-capita income remain below the state average.[29] Continued efforts will be necessary to improve the conditions of these areas.

GRASSROOTS POWER

Individuals who want to influence government often find that they are most successful when they get together with other people who share their concerns. The right to assemble peacefully, guaranteed by the First Amendment to the U.S. Constitution and Article I of the Texas Constitution, ensures that we can join with others to work together for change in government. Interest group activity is well known at the national level, but local-level groups have received less attention.

Many neighborhood groups in Texas cities have successfully lobbied city government for tax abatement, changes in zoning, improved housing, and other goals that are specific to the group. City officials often welcome input from citizens and citizen participation. For example, the city of Austin has sponsored workshops to train potential community activists, giving them tips on how to start a neighborhood association. Many other Texas cities have also fostered the development of groups that offer interested citizens an opportunity to participate in community planning and development.

Some interest groups at the local level have been particularly successful in Texas. An example is Communities Organized for Public Service (COPS) in San Antonio, founded in 1974 by twenty community groups that joined together to work for the interests of the mostly Hispanic minority population of San Antonio. The group has been effective in winning support for local programs that benefit poor neighborhoods. A key actor in the formation of COPS, Ernie Cortes, also helped to create Valley Interfaith, mentioned in Chapter 1 of this text. His effort is another example of an individual making a difference in Texas. Through its work, COPS has brought new streets, drainage, sidewalks, libraries, parks, and streetlights to poor San Antonio neighborhoods and has effectively changed the political power structure of the city. People living in poor areas now have an active voice in government.

In addition to locally based grassroots organizations, local interests are linked to state and national concerns. Interest groups such as Common Cause provide a way for citizens to influence the state legislature or Congress about issues that have a local impact. The Sierra Club is an example of a nationwide organization with a local impact. This organization, devoted to the protection of the environment, works through local chapters to address the environmental concerns of communities.

The people represented by interest groups range from those who seek solutions for problems of the poor to those who are concerned with the problems facing more affluent Texans. COPS represents the interests of poor, minority citizens, whereas other groups, such as the Stop Blue Sky coalition mentioned at the beginning of this chapter, represent the interests of the middle class. At the local level, citizens from all walks of life can influence government.

Summary

Local government in Texas refers to counties, cities, and special districts. These governments are by far the closest to individuals and have the most direct effect on our daily lives. The direct effects and closeness of local government enhance the potential for residents to affect the decisions made by elected officials.

The Stop Blue Sky group illustrates how ordinary citizens can make a difference in their communities. Each of us can affect the quality of life in our communities through participation in local government. We can discover what our local government is doing by attending city council meetings and the meetings of commissioners courts.

Do you know the agenda of your local zoning board or school board? Becoming familiar with the individuals in our communities who make decisions that directly affect us is essential if we are to control what is done. In fact, getting involved in local decisionmaking is more convenient and easier than participation at higher levels of government. Those who are interested may find that running for office and serving on boards puts them in the driver's seat in their local community.

If you look back through this chapter, you will see the great power that citizens of a community have over the way local government works. Local government is set up to be responsive to citizens, from the need for voter assent in the creation of a city to deciding who the elected officials are and what they do in office. Citizen participation in elections, on boards and commissions, and in public meetings gives individuals a voice in each Texas community. Membership in neighborhood associations and other groups helps each person to shape the policies of local government.

The first step in active participation in your local government is learning how your local government works. The examples in this chapter and throughout the rest of this book show that individuals like you and me can make Texas a better place to live.

KEY TERMS

Statutory law, p. 85
General-purpose governments, p. 85
Special-purpose governments, p. 85
Ad valorem taxes, p. 88
Municipal corporation, p. 89
General law charter, p. 90
Home rule charter, p. 90
Initiative, p. 91
Referendum, p. 91
Recall, p. 91

At-large election, p. 91
By-district election, p. 91
Nonpartisan elections, p. 91
Extraterritorial jurisdiction (ETJ), p. 100
Annexation, p. 100
Suburb, p. 103
Gentrification, p. 104
Zoning laws, p. 104
Colonias, p. 109

FOR FURTHER READING

Beyle, Thad L. (ed.). 2004. *State and Local Government 2004-2005: Politics, Legislatures, Media, Courts, and Bureaucracies.* Washington: CQ Press.

Coplin, William D. and Carol Dwyer. 2001. *Does Your Government Measure Up? Basic Tools for Local Officials and* Citizens. Syracuse: Syracuse University Press.

Johnson, David R. and Richard Harris. 2000. Books on Demand.

Saxe, Allan A. 2001. *Politics of Arlington: An Era of Continuity and Growth.* Eakin Press.

Veselka, Robert E. and Kenneth Foote (ed). 2000. *The Courthouse Square in Texas.* Austin: University of Texas Press.

STUDY QUESTIONS

1. What is a general-purpose government? Name at least two.

2. What is a special-purpose government? Name at least two.

3. What is the governing body or bodies of a city in Texas?

4. How are the officials of a city government chosen?

5. What is the governing body of a Texas county?

CRITICAL THINKING QUESTIONS

1. What are the reasons for having local government? How would Texas be different if it did not have local government in place?

2. What issues are most appropriate for local government decisionmaking? (Name at least three.) What issues are most appropriate for

state level decisionmaking? What issues should be taken to the national level?

3. Should counties in Texas all have the same governing structure? Why or why not?

4. What changes in county government structure are needed to help counties solve increasingly complex problems?

5. Why are the conditions of cities increasingly important to Texas citizens? What are the advantages of living in a city? What are the disadvantages?

6. Are zoning laws good or bad for a city? Explain.

7. Should Texas annexation laws be reformed to make it more difficult for a city to annex parts of its surrounding area? Why or why not?

8. What problems are created by suburbanization? What are some possible solutions?

9. Why does Texas have so many special-purpose governments? Does the number of special-purpose governments make it easier or harder for Texans to hold public officials accountable?

10. Should local elected officials have to submit financial disclosure statements? Why or why not? Are financial disclosure statements sufficient to ensure ethical conduct?

11. How can local governments work to encourage greater input from citizens? What is your local government doing now?

12. What are the particular problems on the Texas-Mexico border? Why are these problems of concern to all Texans?

INTERNET RESOURCES

www.tsha.utexas.edu/handbook/online/ The Handbook of Texas Online is a multidisciplinary encyclopedia of Texas history, geography, and culture.

www.tsl.state.tx.us/ref/abouttx/index.html This website has many links to a wide variety of statistics and information about Texas.

www.riceinfo.rice.edu/armadillo/Texas/index.html The Rice University information page has general information about Texas and links to newspapers, magazines, and other media.

www.texasalmanac.com/ This online Texas almanac provides frequently updated information on Texas government, culture, history, education, and environment.

www.tded.state.tx.us/ The Texas Department of Economic Development website has financial and economic information about Texas.

www.capitol.state.tx.us/ Texas Legislature Online has links to the activities of the legislature, including bills, committees, and representatives.

www.governor.state.tx.us/ The Texas governor's page has information about his or her priorities for Texas, as well as other news.

www.county.org/ The Texas Association of Counties website has information about county government and activity in Texas.

www.txregionalcouncil.org/ The Texas Association of Regional Councils has links to all councils of government in Texas, as well as the latest information on membership and activity.

Political Participation

Despite the beautiful weather on a fine May morning in 1999, Lynda French was incredibly annoyed. She had just learned that IBM had cut her pension and that of her husband, Tom. Between them, they had been loyal employees for nearly forty years. Over those years, they had given up several opportunities to move to better-paying jobs. They had always been encouraged to stay with IBM on the grounds that IBM took care of its people with a generous retirement package. Now, IBM had announced that it was changing its pension plan from the traditional pension into a so-called cash balance method, which is more portable for new employees. It is also cheaper for IBM. In Tom's case, it reduced his pension by 37 percent. Workers who had been with the firm for twenty-five years or more suffered similar losses. Lynda was allowed to choose between the two plans, but her husband, because of his age and seniority, was not.[1]

State government can regulate conditions of labor, including the way individuals such as yourself or members of your family are treated by their employers. Economic power is a form of political power. IBM was using its economic power and its political influence when Lynda French decided to do something about it. We have something to learn from her.

Although French was no expert on pension plans, she could see that IBM's actions would result in a significant reduction in lifestyle after she and her husband retired. To determine what the situation would be, she looked for information on the Internet about pension plans, but she found little help there. Figuring that others were looking for help on the Internet, she created a website to share information. From her website grew an organization, IBM Employee Benefits Action Coalition (IEBAC), linking IBM employees in Austin and in other cities to one another and to employees at other companies who were being treated the same way.

Press releases and articles about Lynda French and IEBAC in newspapers and magazines across the country brought attention to IBM's broken promises. On March 27, 2000, the California Public Employees Retirement System (CALPERS), the largest pension plan in the United States, announced that it would vote its 9.2 million shares of IBM stock in favor of a stockholder resolution that would require the company to give all of its 145,000 U.S. workers the choice of remaining under its traditional pension system or switching to the cash balance plan.[2] Although the proposal did not pass, it drew enough votes to get the attention of IBM management.

The publicity drawn by the case made it easier to find attorneys with the experience to sue IBM on the basis of age discrimination. In response to the publicity and the lawsuits, IBM has modified its plan to provide pension options for several thousand (though not all) employees. The U.S. Senate has held hearings on pension plans (with special attention on the IBM plan), and other agencies of state and local government are carefully scrutinizing the IBM pension plan. Two federal court rulings in 2003 against IBM's pension plan changes have shifted the advantage to Lynda French and the employees.[3]

Little of this change would have occurred without the spark and the organizational drive of Lynda French. "Her site was key to the IBM revolution," says Karen Friedman of the Pension Rights Center, a nonprofit pension watchdog group.[4] Lynda French provides an example of an individual who has made a difference. She also provides an example of a course of action: get involved and bring other people along.

Concepts of Political Participation

Political participation
Any activity that seeks to influence public decisions.

Political participation can be defined as any activity that attempts to influence public decisions. Public decisions are not made only by governments. Influencing IBM's decisions on pensions certainly qualifies as political participation because

IBM affects a significant portion of the public. You are probably a long way from retirement, but members of your family may not be. The way retirees are treated is an important political issue in both the public and the private sector. Political participation by people like Lynda French helps keeps decisionmakers aware of the impact of their decisions on real people as well as on the bottom line.

Political activities do not have to be traditional types of activities. They include any activity intended to influence public decisions, either directly or indirectly. By "any activity," we include baking a cake or babysitting. If you bake a cake to raise funds for a political organization or to feed volunteers, or if you are babysitting (even if you are being paid) at least partially because you want to free the child's parents to vote or attend a meeting or campaign, then you are engaged in political participation.

You can participate as an individual or as a member of an organization. To be effective, you often need to bring a few friends with you. We urge you to test our "few friends" thesis. On the evening of the next primary election in Texas, take a few friends along to vote for you to be a delegate to the county convention. We are pretty sure that you will be elected.

Most individuals who participate eventually join a party or an interest group, and probably both. We have devoted one chapter to each of those institutions. In this chapter, we explore some important features of participation that involve you and those around you.

TWO CHARACTERISTICS OF POLITICAL PARTICIPATION

Hierarchical Arranged in order of increase or decrease according to a characteristic. Political participation can be arranged in a hierarchy according to increasing opportunity costs and decreasing percentages of the population involved.

Political participation is **hierarchical** because political activities can be arranged in a hierarchy according to increasing opportunity costs and decreasing percentages of the population involved. Another way to view political activities is as investments in the community and your own future. Thus, activities that require more time or energy or thinking (or all three) are investments rather than costs.

Some political activities involve little investment of time or energy; registering to vote is an example. Other activities, such as casting an informed vote in a local election, require more investment. You may have to read a newspaper article or two before you vote. When it comes to attending meetings or campaigning or engaging in volunteer activities, we are talking about even more serious investment. Because the investment of political resources increases as one moves up the hierarchy of activities, it is no surprise that we find fewer and fewer people involved in these activities. This tradeoff is a second way of looking at the hierarchy: More resources invested means fewer people investing.

Cumulative To increase by adding on instead of increasing by substituting new activities for old ones.

The second feature of political activities is that they are **cumulative** because those who participate in higher-cost activities add them to what they have already been doing. For example, they do not stop expressing an opinion or voting when they decide to run for office or campaign for a candidate or cause.

POLITICAL SOCIALIZATION

In Chapter 1, we discussed the three political cultures that influence Texas politics. We noted that many Texans are brought up to believe a certain way about politics

Political socialization
The process of learning about politics as we learn our language and culture.

and about participation in it. Political scientists call the process by which we learn our political culture and basic beliefs about politics **political socialization.**

The major agents of political socialization are families, neighborhoods, schools, churches, and the mass media. The lessons they teach may be overt; that is, the lessons are intended to be taught. When our parents teach us about stop signs and red, yellow, and green lights or when a newspaper informs us how to register to vote, we are learning lessons they intend to teach. Sometimes, however, the lessons are indirect or covert. A family member may not be aware that he or she is teaching about politics when he or she expresses contempt for a particular officeholder or political institution. The person may simply be voicing an opinion. Depending on how often a person expresses this contempt, as well as our age and impressionability, we may be learning to distrust all political leaders or to regard political participation as something to avoid.

During our early years, the many lessons we learn direct us toward one or more of the political cultures and guide us toward our definitions of what it means to be an American and a Texan. For most people, these early lessons are seldom contradicted by experience in adulthood. People seldom change their political orientations once they are established for at least two reasons.

The first is the number of distractions. In Sam Houston's time, political speeches were a major form of entertainment, but now we have an incredible number of entertainment choices competing with political events for our attention. A second reason people seldom change is that few obtain a higher education and learn to examine political beliefs critically and interact with people from different backgrounds and beliefs. Remember that as members of the recruitment pool for future leaders, you will constitute less than 25 percent of your age group.

In short, people tend to emerge from adolescence with orientations and attitudes about politics that are unlikely to change much because they have neither the training nor the time to examine them critically. We do not mean to imply that no one changes or learns anything new outside the college classroom; that too few do is simply part of the reason that political systems change so gradually.

DEMOGRAPHIC FACTORS ASSOCIATED WITH PARTICIPATION

Socioeconomic status (SES) The rank one has in a hierarchy that is determined by occupational prestige, income, education, and wealth.

Just as activities can be ranked in a hierarchy, so can people. In fact, many students confuse the two hierarchies. In terms of **socioeconomic status (SES),** those near the top of the hierarchy are more likely to participate than those at the bottom. Nevertheless, the relationship is not perfect. Some poor people with little formal education participate at a higher rate than many high-income people. They figure out for themselves the relationship between their lives and the larger political system.

Some of those who figure it out for themselves become activists and explain it to others. Cesar Chavez led farm workers in the Rio Grande valley into the political system, Irma Tenayuka led pecan shellers in San Antonio, Rosemary Galdiano of Fort Worth helped organize Allied Communities of Tarrant (ACT), and dozens of other people of modest education and income across Texas have made a difference. Given the odds against which they labor, they could use some help.

Some groups organize the transmittal of information about why it makes sense to participate and how to do so. They increase the likelihood that someone will participate (so can you). In persuading others to participate, they attempt to influence one or more of six conditions, which we discuss below.

INCREASING THE PARTICIPATION OF OTHERS

At least six conditions can influence how you increase the participation of others; all have to do with altering how people think or feel about politics (you cannot change their socioeconomic status):

1. *Individuals who see the link between benefits to themselves and participation are more likely to participate.* Benefits are often classified in three categories: material (jobs, tax savings, and other pocketbook issues), solidarity (which has to do with meeting interesting people and being part of a movement or group that is doing something worthwhile), and purposive (which is associated with doing something worthwhile, such as getting a bill passed, a law changed, a qualified person elected to office). Thus, someone who explains to people in a neighborhood how electing a candidate who will make sure potholes in their neighborhood streets get fixed will save them money on tires and car repairs is making linkages that the people might not make for themselves between material benefits and political participation. The haves are in a position to make this connection easily; the have-nots sometimes need more information. The benefits of participation are also clear to people who own or run businesses. They know how government decisions on taxes, labor policy, and the environment affect them. However, their employees might not make the connection that perhaps their interests in terms of taxes, labor policy, and pollution are often not the same as their employer's.

2. *Individuals who understand the difference among alternatives are more likely to participate.* Explanation of the differences in the choices available often happens for upper-income people at business meetings, during civic association luncheons, and in the locker room after a round of golf. Many other workers do not have similar meetings, and thus someone must perform this function for them.

3. *Individuals who are self-confident are more likely to participate.* A political science term for self-confidence in the political arena is a sense of *political efficacy*. People who are successful in business or sports or who accomplished the significant task of graduating from college are more likely to feel confident about participating at many levels in the political system. People who lack similar accomplishments can be induced to participate if they are confident in the person encouraging them to do so. You can make others feel better about themselves and thus increase their sense of efficacy. This approach is a long-run project, but it is worth starting, and it can also have career payoffs. People who have social skills do well in new settings, like an interview or a new job. Making people feel comfortable is a social skill.

4. *Individuals who believe the outcome will be negative unless they take action are more likely to participate.* In some cases, this approach means explaining how close the election is despite how well one's candidate is doing in a neighborhood, or explaining why attending a meeting is essential for the outcome to be positive.

5. *Individuals who believe they possess relevant skills or knowledge are more likely to participate.* In some cases, this approach means taking away an excuse rather than demonstrating that one has relevant skills or knowledge. For example, it takes no special knowledge to occupy a chair at a meeting.

6. *Individuals who believe that the investment of political resources is not too high will participate.* Although this item in the list seems like a restatement of the first condition, people may need to hear how little time or effort is required to accomplish a goal. ("It takes just five minutes to register. It takes you that long just to find matching socks in the morning.")

REASONS WHY PEOPLE DON'T PARTICIPATE

The reasons why people don't participate probably outnumber the reasons why they are likely to participate. Many of the reasons for nonparticipation also have to do with the way the rules for participation, particularly voting, are organized. You can do something about these reasons also. In *The Vanishing Voter*, Thomas Patterson, a professor at Harvard, notes five reasons why too many people do not vote. These reasons have to do with the way elections are organized.

1. *Early poll closing:* In Texas and twenty-five other states, polls close at 7:00 P.M. local time, and voting must be over by 7:30 P.M. or earlier. In twenty-four other states, seven of them megastates, the polls are open until 8:00 P.M. or later. It is no surprise that voter turnout is higher in the latter group of states.[5]

2. *Registration:* In *The Vanishing Voter* study, 21 percent of nonvoters interviewed indicated that a change of address was the reason they weren't registered. In Idaho, Maine, Minnesota, New Hampshire, Wisconsin, and Wyoming, one can register at the polls on Election Day; in North Dakota, registration isn't necessary. Citizens in these states turn out to vote at a rate that is 15 percent higher than in the states that require earlier registration.[6]

3. *Frequent elections:* Thirty-nine of the fifty states elect governors in off-years, that is, years other than presidential election years. This setup depresses the vote in both election years. In many European democracies, fewer municipal elections and special elections mean less drain on the attention and energy of the potential voting public. Primary elections, which are used only in the United States, add one more series of elections. Runoffs (required by state law in Texas to force a majority rather than a plurality decision) add yet another election.

4. *The Electoral College:* According to Patterson, the fact that candidates and the media pay more attention to the states where the presidential election will be close affects the election in three ways: It skews candidate effort, it draws

---

JOIN THE DEBATE

THE ISSUE: Should the Electoral College be abolished?

AGREE

1. The Electoral College and the Supreme Court gave Bush an election in 2000 that he had no business winning. It could happen again. Gore received 537,431 more popular votes nation-wide than Bush did. Furthermore, by "mistakenly" confusing them with felons with similar names, the state of Florida removed 50,000 Black voters from the rolls. If we used only the national vote totals, those 50,000 potential democratic votes in Florida would not have mattered. However, when they were taken out of an election "decided' by 537 votes, it resulted in a serious miscarriage of justice defying common sense and all rules of fair play.

2. Many responsible organizations that have studied and worked in American elections for years agree that the Electoral College should be replaced by popular vote. This list of organizations includes the League of Women Voters, which has supported this idea since 1970, and Harvard professor Thomas E. Patterson, who describes his position in some detail in *The Vanishing Voter*.

3. The Gore–Bush election is not the only time the popular decision has been thwarted. President Grover Cleveland lost to Benjamin Harrison in the 1888 election, even though he had a popular majority. The Hayes–Tilden election of 1848 is yet another example of election manipulation, this time in three states (including Florida). Several close calls have involved pluralities. A switch of only 2,000 votes in California could have given the 1916 presidential election to Charles Evans Hughes instead of Woodrow Wilson, who had more than a 500,000 popular vote advantage nationwide.

4. The Electoral College system promotes overemphasis—in the campaigns and in the media—on a few states and leaves voters in the rest of the country less informed and thus less likely to vote.

5. The Constitution does not bind electors to vote for the person they were chosen to support. We could have another constitutional crisis if this happens on a large scale in only one state. In 1948, 1960, and 1976, at least one elector did not vote for his party's candidate.

---

media attention to the battleground states, and it makes voter acquisition of information harder in states where the parties and candidates exert less effort.[7] As a result, with fewer voters participating in presidential elections, races further down the ballot for important positions such as state senator, state representative, and county commissioner also lack voter participation. The decision to use the all-or-nothing determination of a state's Electoral College votes is a state decision, but to Patterson, this decision is beside the

JOIN THE DEBATE

DISAGREE

1. The problem with the simple idea that democratic legitimacy involves numbers alone ignores several American traditions that protect the rights of minorities. The distribution of seats in both the Senate and the House illustrate this principle, as does the ability of a minority of senators to filibuster, or a one-third-plus-one minority of either house to prevent a proposed amendment, and also a one-quarter-plus-one minority of states to prevent ratification of a constitutional amendment.

2. The amendment process (which one can observe from the frequently, and sometimes frivolously, amended Texas Constitution) is one that should be entered into carefully. Right now a president from Texas is trying to amend the Constitution to prevent gay marriages. Yet another constitutional initiative on the Electoral College could lead to the cluttering of our Constitution with trivial amendments.

3. The Electoral College is part of our federal tradition. To abandon it is to weaken the source of legitimacy for our political system. Successful candidates must create a nationwide coalition to win. A popular vote decision would encourage candidates to focus only on the populous states and even limit their campaign efforts to regions. This approach would hurt our federal system.

4. More often than not, the Electoral College tends to magnify a president's electoral vote and his legitimacy rather than challenge it. Both of President Clinton's electoral victories were by pluralities rather than majorities. Yet his Electoral College majorities were impressive. Take away the magnifier effect of large Electoral College majorities and we will have a series of presidents with slim popular victories and questionable claims to govern.

5. Changing the rules so dramatically could have untold negative effects on the electoral game itself. A popular election approach would encourage numerous minor-party candidates to deny both leading candidates a victory and would lead to decisions in Congress or runoff elections, further depressing turnout and faith in the American system. The only way to avoid this situation is to have pure plurality election, no matter how small the plurality. Thus, we could have a candidate who gets 31 percent of the vote being declared the winner.

point. For him, the problem is with the Electoral College system itself. About the Bush–Gore election, he asks, "In what other democracy in the world would 537 votes in one state outweigh a nationwide margin of 537,179 votes?"[8] (See Join the Debate.)

5. *Election Day:* In most industrial democracies, Election Day is a national holiday and workers have all day to vote. In the United States, workers have to show up at the polls before or after work.

Although voting is an essential activity in a democracy, political participation involves a wide range of additional activities, many of which reinforce voting behavior or are closely related, from babysitting so parents can vote or attend a meeting to trying to change people's attitudes and providing them with new information about candidates, issues, or cause-and-effect relationships. These activities are usually associated with one or more participation strategies.

Participation Strategies

Although participation involves many kinds of activities, at least seven clusters of activities can be called strategies. Almost all seven can be performed by ordinary individuals as well as by groups. Although more than seven clusters of activities are available, you will undoubtedly be using one or more of the clusters listed here if you attempt to influence public decisions. Several of them directly or indirectly involve attempting to influence public opinion.

LOBBYING

Lobbying Personally contacting a public official to influence a decision.

Lobbying is personally contacting a public official to influence a decision. This contact can be face to face or by letter, fax, e-mail, or telephone. These contacts can take place in the public official's office, at his or her home, or at social occasions. To be effective, make your case briefly and ask for support. Staff people are also worth lobbying because they often make recommendations to public officials that influence decisions.

Perhaps the most important idea to remember about lobbying is the iceberg effect. When public officials meet ordinary citizens who are motivated enough to bring their views about issues to them, they know many other ordinary citizens are as concerned but do not themselves do any lobbying. Thus, when you contact a public official, you represent many more people than yourself.

GRASSROOTS LOBBYING

Grassroots lobbying Attempting to influence others to contact a public official personally.

Grassroots lobbying is attempting to influence others to contact a public official personally. You will always be more effective if you bring a few friends along, whether to a meeting or the voting booth.

When organizations buy advertising designed to foster goodwill toward the general public—for example, "General Motors is people," or "Plastic saves lives"—they are engaged in long-term grassroots lobbying. You can take this approach too, albeit on a smaller budget. Your volunteer activity builds you credibility in your

Picking up, hauling off, reading to little kids, painting a house. . . . Your time and talent are needed in your community. Volunteering is not only good for the soul, it's good for your social life and future career prospects as well.

community. It also brings you in contact with leaders and future leaders of your community. (It might also make you feel better about yourself.)

Short-term grassroots lobbying occurs when an organization attempts to mobilize people to act on issues; for example, they urge, "Write your representative in Congress," "Call your city council," or "Come to the rally on Tuesday." Grassroots lobbying multiplies influence. The more people you can get to contact public officials, the more likely that the officials will pay attention. This one-on-one contact is so effective that a technique has been created to fake it. **Astroturf lobbying** is a term used to describe the activities of public relations firms that attempt to generate personal contacts with public officials. These expensive campaigns usually involve a phone bank. People working the phone bank ask respondents to answer a few questions in a sort of a minisurvey. Those who provide unwelcome answers are screened out. People who agree with the astroturf campaigner are then asked if they will sign a letter that the public relations firm will send to them, which in turn will go directly to a public official. They can even provide letterhead for the respondent.

Top-dollar campaigns involve asking the "correct" respondents if they would like to talk to their representative in Congress or state legislator. Then they are patched through by telephone to that official's office. Staff members on the other end have no idea how the call was generated. So far, this tactic is used mainly at the national level to influence Congress and federal agencies. It will not be long, however, before

Astroturf lobbying The use of various techniques by public relations firms to simulate lobbying by individuals. It is regarded as artificial grassroots lobbying.

this tactic appears in the megastates, especially the top three, which includes, of course, Texas.[9] Your participation counts so much that people are willing to fake it.

ATTENDING A PUBLIC HEARING

Public hearing A meeting at which decisionmakers listen to the public to gather information.

A **public hearing** is a meeting at which decisionmakers listen to the public to gather information before making a decision. Public hearings take place at the national, state, and local levels. Members of both the legislative and executive branches conduct them. This stage is so important in the political process that the leadership in many organizations spend a high percentage of their time in such meetings. Decisionmakers are more likely to hear from leaders of organizations than they are the general public. The general public needs to know about this opportunity to influence decisions. To some extent, that task will be one of your jobs as a future leader: Mobilizing people to attend meetings is an important leadership function.

At the state and national levels, legislative committees meet to hear from the public on proposed legislation. At the local level, many school board and city council meetings perform two different functions on the same evening. First, the public hearing takes place, and decisionmakers hear from citizens concerned with proposals to pass laws, raise taxes, or change the zoning in a neighborhood; second, members of the decisionmaking body discuss the issue before voting. Note that it is a considerable step forward that councils, boards, and commissions conduct this decisionmaking in public and not behind closed doors or at the coffee shop before the regular meeting. During the discussion or deliberation phase of the meeting, however, members of the public are simply an audience and may not be able to make contributions. At the state level, legislative committees or executive agencies such as the Texas Commission on Environmental Quality may hold public hearings on one day and then meet on a separate day make a decision. But being an audience member is an important part of participation, which is the reason behind open-meeting laws: They make sure that decisionmakers act in the public interest because they have to do so in public.

Representatives from various lobbying organizations are present at most public hearings. It is an important place to learn what the other side has to say, as well as to make clear the position of one's group. In a 1998 study of interest groups in state politics, the activity mentioned most frequently by lobbyists and lobbying organizations was testifying at legislative hearings.[10]

APPOINTMENTEERING

Appointmenteering An attempt to influence appointments to public office.

Appointmenteering is an attempt to influence appointments to public office. You can volunteer to be the appointee, you can recruit someone else to serve, or you can try to influence whether someone gets appointed.

It is important to remember that not all public officials who influence our lives are elected. Many are appointed by city councils (the planning commissioners, the library board members, the employee grievance committee), the county

When voters show up, office-holders pay attention. Decisions can be changed by what happens at a public hearing.

commissioners courts (election judges, members of special districts created by the county), and the governor.

ELECTIONEERING

Electioneering A wide range of activities involved in getting someone elected to public office.

Retail politics Personal contact with citizens by telephone or door-to-door canvassing to mobilize them to vote or participate in some other way.

Wholesale politics The use of the mass media to reach voters.

Electioneering involves a wide range of activities, all involved in getting someone elected to public office. One of the key distinctions in understanding how electoral politics works is the distinction between retail and wholesale politics. **Retail politics** involves personal contact. A volunteer rings the doorbell of a potential voter or calls that person on the telephone to urge him or her to vote a particular way.

Wholesale politics is the use of the mass media. A well-financed organization buys an advertisement or gives money to a party to buy ads that enter thousands of homes the same night at the same time with exactly the same message. The importance of getting a message into homes during a campaign is a clear indication of why volunteers are so important. Volunteer hours are worth a lot of money to an underfunded campaign.

José Angel Gutiérrez, a founder of La Raza Unida, was always on the lookout for new electoral strategies. In high school, he noticed that the Anglo students, a numerical minority, managed to get one of their own elected to most high school offices. The Anglos voted as a bloc for just one Anglo candidate, while the Mexican Americans would spread their votes over many Mexican American candidates. Later, Gutiérrez put this technique to use for the benefit of Mexican American candidates in school and in local elections.[11] As we noted in Chapter 4, this tactic is called single shotting.

When working in a city council election campaign in the 1970s, Gutiérrez noticed that the Chicano women in charge of getting out the vote in the barrio conserved their scarce resources by getting as many residents as they could gather on one or two blocks each day to vote absentee. The next day, they would focus on another block or two in the community. With limited personnel to mobilize voters on Election Day, this pre–Election Day effort of 200 votes or so a day paid off handsomely for a community short on volunteer activists.[12] Thus, in large ways and small, an organized minority can affect the outcome of elections by conserving their votes on the ballot or by systematically using their volunteer time and energy in getting voters to the polls.

Both wholesale and retail politics deliver a message, but the retail contact is more likely to mobilize people to vote than is the wholesale contact alone. Personal contact with potential voters increases their turnout by approximately 15 percent.[13]

DEMONSTRATING

Demonstrating Group attempts to bring public attention to an issue and make public officials aware of the intensity of group feelings.

Demonstrating is usually a group attempt to accomplish two goals simultaneously: bring attention to a public issue and make one or more public officials aware of the intensity of feelings on an issue. Sometimes a poorly organized demonstration can do more harm than good to a cause. Here are a few conditions associated with a successful demonstration:

- *Define your public.* Are you trying to reach residents of a small town or the wider public? In Greenville, North Carolina, the college students who defied segregation laws in 1962 by sitting in at lunchroom counters had a wider audience in mind than that of the voters of Greenville.

- *Make sure your public agrees with the ideas or principles you are trying to promote.* Otherwise, it is like trying to teach a pig to sing: It will not work, and it will annoy the pig.

- *Have a simple, acceptable remedy available for the problem.* Two examples are a drafted piece of legislation or a petition. Otherwise, you appear well-meaning but vague and ineffective.

- *Be prepared to take the consequences for your action.* If people throw objects at you or call you names, do not fight back. If you have people in your group who will fight, then keep them home or choose another tactic.

- *Make sure the media are aware of your activity.* Otherwise, you are a tree falling in the forest with no one around to hear the sound. Saturday morning is usually a slow period for the news media, so it is a good time to schedule an event.

Almost 1,000 Texans rallied at the state capitol in support of legislation affecting children's health and education. Participants also opposed the weakening of rules affecting the development of colonias.

Politics and political participation involve luck as well as good planning and hard work.

Demonstrations have a long history in American politics, from the Boston Tea Party to the suffragettes, to the civil rights movement. The tactic is most often conducted by groups of people. However, sometimes an individual engages in demonstration and is occasionally taken seriously. Such an individual was Granny D—Doris Haddock, an eighty-nine-year-old retired secretary from New Hampshire who decided to bring attention to the need for campaign reform by walking across the United States. Starting from the Rose Bowl Parade in California on New Year's Day 1999, she headed east toward Washington, D.C. In early March, she entered Texas at El Paso; walking ten miles a day, six days a week, she exited Texas at Texarkana on July 17, 1999. Along the way, she got lots of press attention, was taken to Austin for a rally on the steps of the capitol, and spoke to audiences at numerous events, including rodeos, rallies in high school auditoriums, the Texas Reform party state convention, and lots of luncheons and community dinners. She arrived in Washington just after her ninetieth birthday and led a parade to another rally on the steps of the Capitol in Washington, D.C.

Not all demonstrations meet with immediate success. To the thousands of people in Texas who walked with Granny D or heard her speak, just making it through the heat of a Texas summer was a success. The passage of the McCain-Feingold campaign reform bill was due in part to the attention Granny helped bring to this cause.

LITIGATING

Litigating Using the legal system to influence public policy.

Using the legal system to influence public policy—that is, **litigating**—sounds rather abstract. However, when a landlord decides to let a piece of rental property deteriorate and it affects a neighborhood, his or her decision becomes a public one that you may wish to influence. An organization called Safe Streets Now has helped neighbors organize to deal with nuisance properties. Their approach involves four steps:

1. Organize by creating a neighborhood association. Agree to meet and discuss tactics.
2. Gather information; document the nuisance and the damage it is doing with photos and formal signed statements called affidavits.
3. Negotiate with the property owner.
4. Sue in small claims court if the owner fails to respond constructively. Each person whose property is being damaged by the nuisance should sue.

Suing in small claims court (the justice of the peace court in most parts of Texas) does not require a lawyer. The individual amounts may seem trivial to the owner of a nuisance, but they have a real attention-getting impact when they are added together. Ten or twenty families each suing a single person for $5,000 becomes significant if the court finds in their favor. If the offender does nothing to stop the nuisance, each day of doing nothing may count as a separate offense.

Individuals and groups use the courts in many other ways. Laws, executive decisions, and lower court decisions can be challenged in court. Individuals can get an order from a judge, known as a *writ of mandamus,* to require a public official to enforce a law or perform a duty that he or she is unwilling to do. This action puts the court on the side of the individual because ignoring a court order puts the official in contempt of court, and perhaps will make him or her subject to serious fines or even jail time as a result.

As officers of the court, attorneys expect to do a certain amount of free legal work, known as *pro bono work,* for the public good. Legal aid societies can help those who can prove that they do not have the resources for necessary legal assistance. In most parts of Texas, *legal aid* is listed in the telephone book.

Public Opinion

Public opinion is the expression of an attitude or belief about a public issue. Thus, unless one acts, one's feelings or attitudes do not become part of the political system. Expressing an opinion is a political activity.

Political leaders, especially those whose jobs depend on elections, care what the public is thinking, but they are mostly concerned with those thoughts that are expressed. People who care enough to express an idea are more likely to act on it. Political leaders watch four characteristics of public opinion closely: direction, salience, intensity, and stability.

DIRECTION

If public opinion unanimously points in one direction, it gives clear guidance to a political leader. If 65 percent of the people are in favor of an issue and the rest are undecided, that information is also useful. If the public is split fifty-fifty, however, then little guidance is given. Thus, direction is based on the distribution of opinions among the public. Sometimes public opinion gives no guidance.

SALIENCE

Salience The condition of being strikingly conspicuous; prominent.

Salience means standing out, being conspicuous. This dimension of public opinion helps us understand the fact that not everyone has an opinion on every issue. Some issue publics are very large, like the public for the abortion issue. Some issue publics are small and thus provide political leaders with little or no guidance. In some cases, they are influenced by a small issue public, such as their major campaign contributors. For this reason, it is often important to increase the size of an issue public so that more average working Texans are represented.

One of your jobs on issues that you care about is to make sure as many people as possible know about it. In other words, you want to make sure the issue is salient to the general public—that it has a large issue public. Once people learn the facts, they may agree with your position. Even if they do not, the issue is still a salient one: public officials have to pay attention to it.

INTENSITY

When people feel strongly about an issue, they are more likely to act on it. If only 30 percent of the electorate is for or against something and if they care intensely enough to make campaign contributions and phone calls or write letters to the editor, then public officials pay attention. This feature of public opinion runs counter to the general public's view of democracy. Governments should do what the majority wants, shouldn't they? The answer is no if the majority does not care strongly enough to back up its opinions with other political resources.

The notion of intensity is essential for understanding the role of public opinion and of participation in our democracy. It has considerable relevance in the context of change. Today's intense minority may use its political resources to persuade enough of the uncommitted to join them so that they become a new majority on their issue, which is why freedom of speech, freedom of assembly, and freedom of the press are so important to the dynamics of our political system.

STABILITY

If direction, the size of the issue public, or the distribution of intensity do not change over time, then public officials do not have to change their positions on issues. If any one of the first three characteristics changes, then this change may influence the behavior of public officials.

Powell's Paradox in Texas

According to political scientist Bingham Powell, Americans are more predisposed to participate than are citizens in most other industrial democracies.[14] They have a greater sense of political efficacy, they express a willingness to meet with the purpose of solving problems, and they belong to voluntary organizations at a higher rate than do people in other countries. In spite of their predisposition and other behavior, Americans vote at a lower rate than do citizens in most other industrial democracies, a fact called **Powell's paradox.** Although Powell's explanation for this phenomenon was written nearly two decades ago, it is still particularly relevant for Texas today. His observation that voting regulations depress turnout has been reconfirmed by many other researchers, including (as we have already observed) Thomas Patterson in *The Vanishing Voter.*

Powell's paradox Despite the fact that they are more predisposed to participate and that they participate in some activities more than people in other countries do, Americans vote at a lower rate than do citizens in other industrial democracies.

VOTING REGULATIONS

Both Powell and Patterson agree that if the registration barrier could be lifted, many more people would vote. Registration is an important reason why voter turnout in Texas is lower than in other megastates. In the 2000 presidential election, Texas ranked forty-eighth among the fifty states in voter turnout, just as it did in 1996.[15]

Some scholars have suggested that the state's history of resistance to making voting easy has established patterns that take a long time to change. Among the restrictions on the ballot that lasted until federal law or constitutional amendments removed them are male-only suffrage (1920), a poll tax of a day's wages or more (1966), the white primary (1944), denial of the vote to those enlisted in the

service (1965), annual registration (1971), and the requirement of property ownership to vote in local elections (1975). However, the last of these restrictions was removed thirty years ago, so the answer for low voter turnout today is probably
found elsewhere.[16]

INSTITUTIONS FOR MOBILIZING THE PUBLIC

Although voting regulations are a limiting factor, they could be partially overcome
with institutions for mobilizing those less likely to participate. Institutions for mobilizing the public are weaker in the United States than in other industrial democracies. Powell points to the fact that in the United States, both labor unions and
political parties are more limited by federal and state law than they are in other
democracies. This suggestion opens several lines of inquiry regarding voter turnout and participation in Texas. First, let's examine the concept of *the public* that
needs mobilizing.

All Texans are not equally in need of mobilization. In fact, those in the upper
echelons of corporations, banks, insurance companies, and government institutions do not need much mobilizing. Like wealthy people in the other major industrial democracies, they participate at a higher rate than workers do.[17] They see the
link between their participation and state and local policy regarding taxes, labor
relations, the environment, and other issues important to them. When it comes to
making campaign contributions, those in the upper-income brackets not only see
the logic of contributing, they also have the resources to contribute.[18] When CEOs
and other top executives make 500 times what the average blue-collar employee
makes, a rather large discrepancy exists in the political resources available to
each group.[19]

TABLE 5.1 Shares of Family Income in Texas	
Percentage of Population	**Average Income**
Lowest 20 percent	$ 9,300
Second 20 percent	19,700
Middle 20 percent	31,900
Fourth 20 percent	52,500
Top 20 percent	
The bottom 15 percent of the top 20 percent	95,300
The next 4 percent of the top 20 percent	202,000
Top 1 percent	$1,081,000

*Source: Robert S. McIntyre, Robert Denk, Norton Francis, Matthew Gardner, Will Gomaa, Fiona Hsu, and
Richard Sims.* Who Pays? A Distributional Analysis of the Tax System in All 50 States, *2d ed.(Washington, D.C.:
Institute on Taxation and Economic Policy 2003), p. 102.*

The less educated, the working poor, and middle-income families in which both adults work (and sometimes work at more than one job) are the groups for whom mobilizing is necessary to increase participation. These groups often do not see the connections between participation and policies that are in their interest regarding taxes, the environment, and labor relations. These groups are most in need of retail politics.

Retail politics has a personal touch; human beings explain person-to-person how political participation is linked to public decisions. In retail politics, people are available to organize events and bring others together to identify and solve problems. As we have already pointed out, for the upper classes, this political mobilization occurs at business luncheons, during country club and charitable dinners, and in the corporate boardroom itself. The working poor and the middle class need another set of institutions. Without organizations like strong parties, labor unions, or community service coalitions to promote their interests, the middle class and working poor receive most of their political information through wholesale politics—media campaigns funded largely by corporations and the business community. Although labor unions use the mass media, they are outspent about 11 to 1.[20] Their messages explaining that their issues are often middle-class issues are frequently drowned out by messages from the other side.

Institutions for Mobilizing the Moderate Middle

One of the real concerns expressed by many observers of the social and economic changes that took place in the 1990s was the rapid growth of the wealth of the top 1 percent of families in America and the potential for a decline in the middle class.[21] Most Texans and most Americans think of themselves as middle class. It is worth considering how many families belong in that class and what their interests are. Table 5.1 indicates the average income of each 20 percent (or quintile) of the Texas population, from the very poor to the very wealthy. Most Texas families— poor, middle class, and moderately well-off—earn five figure incomes ($10,000 to $99,999). Thus, on economic and workplace issues, they have a lot in common. When we reach the top 20 percent of income earners, we find a large range of incomes reaching the hundreds of millions, which is why the category for the top 20 percent is presented differently. Among the families in the top 1 percent, we find the range of very high incomes whose average is in the six figures but we also find families with seven- and eight-figure incomes.

Because the poverty line is about $18,850 for a family of four, and because the top 1 percent of income earners includes people with incomes of over $1 billion, it is clear that the bottom four categories of income earners have much in common. These groups are the people who vote in large numbers in European democracies because they are mobilized by labor unions and strong political parties. The labor unions tend to mobilize the blue-collar workers and the working poor, and the parties tend to mobilize the middle class. Once mobilized, the middle class (with its superior civic skills—speaking, writing, and organizing meetings) also tends to help parties with the task of mobilizing the working poor.

In America and in Texas, the middle class is more likely to identify with and support the issues of the upper classes, in part because the right has been able to confuse liberalism and socialism in the American mind. This trend is one product of a weak labor union movement, which in most states has not been able to make its issues known to the middle class through the mass media. The fact that 44 percent of nonunion workers surveyed nationwide would like to have the chance to join a union indicates that some communication about labor unions is getting through.[22]

Many union members earn incomes that place them squarely in the middle class. The American Medical Association voted in 1999 to support the efforts of physicians to create unions that would bargain with health maintenance organizations (HMOs) and insurance companies. Thus, it is worth considering the possibility that the middle class has more in common with labor union members than most middle-class workers think they do.[23]

In Texas, these institutions are largely missing from the political environment, and so the link is difficult for many to make. The chambers of commerce in many Texas communities recruit new businesses by stating that their community has no unions and pointing out that Texas is a right-to-work state. The weakness of labor unions in a state goes hand-in-hand, however, with weak parties. Both mobilize people untouched by business and upper-class institutions. The politics that result from this mobilization require both the conservative and the liberal parties to appeal to the vast majority of the population, which occupies the moderate ideological position in the middle. The problem is that mobilizing the moderate majority, which consists of the working and middle classes, will take some effort and will require some long-run changes in how we do politics in Texas. Let's examine the three types of institutions that mobilize people in the middle.

POLITICAL PARTIES IN TEXAS

Political parties in Texas are important components of the political system. Studying parties as we do in Chapter 7, will help us understand how to make them better at mobilizing voters in Texas and rendering Texas government more accountable. In Texas, the selection of candidates and the organization of government are not controlled or even heavily influenced by party leaders. Many reasons explain this situation, but what concerns us here is that in Texas, parties are weak and business-dominated interest groups are strong. Thus, the nomination of candidates is influenced by interest groups as much as or more than it is by parties.

In most industrial democracies, party leaders nominate candidates; in Texas and many other states, they are nominated in open elections (primaries) in which interest groups have a great deal of influence through campaign contributions. In other industrial democracies, the parties organize the government after elections. In the Texas Legislature, the parties have less control over committee assignments or over the election of the presiding officer of either body. Without the power to organize the legislature, party leaders have little influence over their members in the legislature. A few years ago a study of voting behavior in the Texas Legislature found that while party label is the best single predictor of a U.S. congressman's vote, there was no significant statistical relationship existing between the voting behavior of a Texas legislator and his or her party.[24] Recent events suggest that such a relationship may exist. Nevertheless, political parties in Texas need to be better equipped to engage in retail politics to make the link between participation and influence clearer to the ordinary Texans who make up the majority of the state's population. Stronger parties can increase their influence over public policy.

LABOR UNIONS IN TEXAS

Collective bargaining
The right of workers, after winning a majority in an organizing election, to bargain with management on working conditions such as safety, wages, and benefits.

The issue associated with the right to work has been decided in Texas and many other southern states by previous generations, just as the issue of segregation was decided from 1878 to the 1950s. "Right to work" was once a slogan in an ongoing debate about labor unions. The other side of the debate used the slogan "right to bargain collectively." This right of **collective bargaining** is protected by federal law—the National Labor Relations Act—and is further protected by state law in many states. The right to bargain collectively is seldom exercised in Texas, however. State law makes it difficult for workers to organize and thus bargain as a group and easy for management to defeat them when they try.

The right to bargain collectively is exercised only when a majority of the workers in a factory or shop have voted to organize and thus bargain as a group with management over the working conditions in the factory. Working conditions include safety equipment to prevent industrial accidents and deaths, workers' compensation for families when injuries or death occur, wages, hours of work, health insurance, retirement benefits, and the right to appeal decisions made by supervisors. By creating a bargaining agreement or contract, the workers have some influence over an important part of their daily lives: their jobs.

After workers have organized to bargain as a group with management, the transition to attempting to influence the larger political system is more easily made. Victory in the workplace can convince workers that their votes matter; in the real world, those active in unions organize volunteers and activities to promote participation, explain issues, and help make that link. Texas in Context 5.1 illustrates that workers do make this transition and that labor unions do have an impact on the politics of the states in which they are strong.

The relationship between voter turnout in a state and whether that state has a significant level of labor union membership is noticeable. It is stronger in congressional election years like 1998 than it is in presidential election years like 2000. Once workers have organized to bargain collectively, they have also been mobilized to take a more active role in the environment that affects their lives. Voting in state and local elections is easy compared to organizing a factory.

As the years go by and new people come to work at the factory, they may not wish to join the union. They want the right to work at the factory without paying the cost of maintaining the collective bargaining agreement. From the point of view of those who pay dues, the person who receives the benefits of an organized

TEXAS in Context

5.1 Union Membership in the Megastates and Voter Turnout

	Percentage of Workers Who Are Union Members	Voter Turnout in 1998	Voter Turnout in 2000
Texas	**5.8**	**24.6**	**43.2**
Florida	6.8	10.8	50.7
Massachusetts	14.3	37.9	56.9
California	16.0	33.7	44.1
Pennsylvania	16.9	32.4	53.7
Ohio	17.3	40.8	55.8
Illinois	18.6	37.1	52.8
Michigan	20.8	41.3	57.5
New Jersey	20.8	30.0	51.0
New York	25.5	31.8	49.4

Sources: Bureau of Labor Statistics, //stats.bls.gov/news.releas/union2t05.htm. For voter turnout, see www.uselectionatlas.or/USPRESIDENT/GENERAL/pe2000vto.html.

shop without contributing to the cost of maintaining the collective bargaining agreement is a parasite. Political scientists have a value-neutral term for an employee who wants to exercise the right to work without paying union dues: **free rider.**

Free rider Someone who enjoys collective benefits without making a contribution to obtaining or defending them.

As Mancur Olson points out in *The Logic of Collective Action,* free riders are problems for all organizations that work to obtain benefits enjoyed collectively by large numbers of people. **Collective benefits** are advantages that we enjoy without having worked to get them, such as the clean-air and clean-water regulations that environmental organizations have worked hard to obtain. Unless we contribute to those organizations, we are free riders.

Collective benefits Benefits we enjoy whether we helped obtain them or not.

SAUL ALINSKY ORGANIZATIONS

In addition to parties and labor unions (which tend to mobilize the middle class), a third type of organization in the United States mobilizes the working poor. They can be called community service organizations, and they exist somewhat under the radar of most studies of interest groups. Usually they are classified under the general rubric of neighborhood associations. Community service organizations are much less concerned with protecting middle-class homeowners from zoning changes and the construction of low-cost housing; in fact, most community service agencies would be in favor of low-cost housing.

Another way of classifying these organizations is to link them with Saul Alinsky, a community organizer who helped create the Back of the Yards association among the people who worked in the slaughterhouses of Chicago, and later the Woodlawn Association among the black neighborhoods near the University of Chicago. Alinsky created an organization to train organizers to respond to requests for assistance in other parts of the country. One of his most famous students is Ernesto (Ernie) Cortes, who helped found Communities Organized for Public Service (COPS) in San Antonio.

Eventually, Cortes founded the Texas Industrial Areas Foundation (Texas IAF), which has led to the creation of a network of over forty community-based organizations in urban centers. According to sociologist Mark Warren, a noted author on community studies, "It is the most successful community organizing network in the country."[25] Texas IAF professional organizers work with church leaders to build local organizations that address various local issues, including affordable housing, job training, school reform, and community policing.

Although the organization operates through a lengthy process of consultation and coalition building, from time to time it mobilizes people to vote or attend mass meetings to get the attention of political leaders on issues of concern. In 1986, for example, Allied Communities of Tarrant (ACT) negotiated with the city of Fort Worth for specifically identified projects worth $57 million to be completed in ACT neighborhoods as part of its support for a larger bond package being offered by the city. To help get approval for the package, ACT registered more than 7,000 new voters and worked to pass the bond issue in forty voting precincts in ACT neighborhoods. City officials credit ACT for the crucial votes that provided the margin of victory in passing the bond package.[26]

Alinsky organizations exist in Texas, but they are no substitute for parties or unions. They seldom get involved in elections beyond the city level, and it is difficult to expand their membership base much beyond the member churches. Nevertheless, they provide training in leadership, and some of their members move on to the wider political arena.

Future leaders of Texas should know about these organizations because they are an important part of the networks that link the poorer communities in Texas cities to one another and to the larger system. They may provide key resources should a systematic attempt ever be made to mobilize the working poor and middle class in Texas to participate at the same level that the upper class does.

Summary

Political participation can be defined as any activity that attempts to influence public decisions. Individuals in Texas can participate alone, or they can join parties and interest groups that influence the way government works. Participation requires action. Some actions require a greater investment of political resources than others. You will make a difference if you act, just as Lynda French, Ernesto Cortes, José Gutiérrez, and Saul Alinsky did. More often than not, you will make an even greater difference if you bring along a few friends. The effort invested in bringing them along is itself political participation.

In trying to initiate change in Texas, you will sooner or later attempt to influence public opinion. Political leaders watch public opinion closely because those who express an opinion are more likely to act than those who remain silent.

Powell's paradox may continue in Texas as long as each generation decides to be disgruntled taxpayers instead of active citizens. However, you can change this situation by becoming active in your political party and attempting to strengthen it. You may also help your church link with a politically oriented community service coalition and mobilize parishioners, friends, and neighbors into making Texas a better place.

While joining a labor union is probably unlikely for most college students destined for careers in the professions and the business community, attempting to understand these institutions and helping promote a more tolerant attitude toward them is a step away from the conditions of Powell's paradox. Many white-collar workers and even physicians are beginning to see the value of organizing to influence their terms of employment.

KEY TERMS

Political participation, p. 115
Hierarchical, p. 116
Cumulative, p. 116
Political socialization, p. 117
Socioeconomic status (SES), p. 117
Lobbying, p. 122
Grassroots lobbying, p. 122
Astroturf lobbying, p. 123
Public hearing, p. 124
Appointmenteering, p. 124

Electioneering, p. 125
Retail politics, p. 125
Wholesale politics, p. 125
Demonstrating, p. 126
Litigating, p. 128
Salience, p. 129
Powell's paradox, p. 130
Collective bargaining, p. 134
Free rider, p. 135
Collective benefits, p. 135

FOR FURTHER READING

Burns, Nancy, Kay Lehman Schlozman, Sidney Verba, *The Private Roots of Public Action: Gender, Equality, and Political Participation.* (Cambridge, Mass.: Harvard University Press, 2000).

Gutiérrez, José Angel, *The Making of a Chicano Militant: Lessons from Cristal* (Madison: University of Wisconsin Press, 1998).

Mort, Jo-Ann, ed., *Not Your Father's Union Movement: Inside the AFL-CIO* (New York: Verso, 1998).

Palast, Greg, *The Best Democracy Money Can Buy* (New York: Penguin Putnam, 2003).

Patterson, Thomas E., *The Vanishing Voter: Public Involvement in an Age of Uncertainty* (New York: Random House, 2002).

STUDY QUESTIONS

1. Identify Lynda French.

2. Identify the six conditions that you can influence to increase the political participation of others.

3. List Patterson's five reasons that people don't vote.

4. Describe seven participation strategies.

5. List and describe briefly the four characteristics of public opinion that political leaders watch most closely.

CRITICAL THINKING QUESTIONS

1. Explain the following observation: "Political participation is often hierarchical and cumulative."

2. Do you think we ought to abolish the Electoral College? Why?

3. Which of the strategies of participation are most appealing to you and why? Which strategy would require the most effort to get you involved?

4. Identify the characteristics of public opinion that political leaders watch most closely and are most clearly linked to a strategy of participation that you might engage in.

5. Discuss Powell's paradox in the context of changing it in Texas and what might be done to change its associated conditions further.

INTERNET RESOURCES

www.lwv.org/   Like Common Cause, the League of Women Voters is a mainstream, nonpartisan, activist organization engaged in promoting participation by ordinary people.

www.sos.state.tx.us/function/elec1/results   Turn to this election results website for information on voter registration and turnout in Texas.

www.trinity.edu/~mkearl/strat.html   This website explores the fact that the gap between rich and poor in the United States is greater now than at any other time in the past seventy-five years and greater than in any other industrialized nation. It has links to many scholarly studies, tables, and graphs.

www.tcf.org/   The Century Foundation, founded in 1919, undertakes timely and critical analyses of major economic, political, and social institutions and issues. It is nonprofit and nonpartisan. The website leads to studies on the media and society, inequality, and the economy.

www.inequality.org/Inequality   This website explores the notion of class and inequality and the political consequences of huge disparities in income, and provides useful links to other sites.

www.ufenet.org/   United for a Fair Economy publicizes issues of economic injustice and income disparity. The group attempts to bring public attention to the big difference between the salaries of corporate CEOs and those of working Americans.

www.responsiblewealth.org/   This website for Responsible Wealth is sponsored by wealthy Americans who believe in a fair tax system and policies that benefit ordinary Americans. It contains a thought-provoking list of research papers with titles like "Paying a Living Wage Is Good for Business" and "Top Paid CEOs Don't Deliver Top-Notch Results."

www.ksg.harvard.edu/inequality/Focus/focus.htm   This Harvard University website provides links to academic research on poverty and policies dealing with inequality.

CHAPTER 6

Participation and Interest Groups

Returning from World War II a decorated veteran with six battle stars and the Bronze Star, Dr. Hector P. Garcia had already made a difference when he set up a medical practice in Corpus Christi and became a medical examiner for the Veterans Administration. His military service would be only the beginning, however. Little did he know that his work for the Veterans Administration would set him on a path that would lead to the Medal of Freedom, the highest honor the president can bestow on a civilian.

For Garcia, making a difference in politics started with a problem he encountered getting prompt hospital care for his patients who were veterans. The closest veterans' hospital was in San Antonio, which created a hardship for his patients. They had to miss work while going and coming, many were too sick to travel, and others had no way to travel so far. The situation was particularly frustrating because medical care was available at the nearby Naval Hospital in Corpus Christi. But that hospital treated only military personnel, not veterans. Garcia approached other community hospitals for help, but he met with little success.

Finding this hardship for men who had served their country in World War II intolerable, Garcia organized a group of veterans with the goal of applying pressure for change by bringing this humanitarian cause to the attention of the public and federal officials. The group succeeded in getting the Naval Hospital and the Veterans Administration to agree to provide hospital care at the Naval Hospital for Corpus Christi veterans on a contractual basis. Encouraged by this success, the veterans, almost all of them Mexican Americans, decided to remain organized on a permanent basis and address other problems under Garcia's leadership.

Calling itself the American G.I. Forum of the United States, the group turned first to the matter of illiteracy and the general lack of education among Hispanic veterans. Most had only a few years of formal education and were unable to find jobs even in the fast-developing postwar economy. The American G.I. Forum, in conjunction with the Veterans Administration and the local school system, set up schools with the specific purpose of addressing adult illiteracy and joblessness with schooling and job training. The group also began to advocate for programs such as free school lunches, scholarships for the needy, and various other social programs long before they became part of national policy.

In 1949, one incident transformed the American G.I. Forum into a major national player in the struggle for civil rights. The G.I. Forum learned that a funeral home in Three Rivers had refused to allow the use of its chapel for Felix Longoria, a Mexican American infantryman killed in the Philippines in World War II and whose body was finally being returned to the United States for burial. The group mounted a public protest, and Garcia contacted several elected officials, including U.S. Senator Lyndon Johnson. Although Johnson could not change the situation in Three Rivers, he did intercede to arrange for Longoria to be buried in Arlington National Cemetery near Washington, D.C., with full military honors. The G.I. Forum provided the money to bring his family to Washington for the ceremony.

The Longoria case generated a lot of publicity, including a considerable amount of local criticism of Senator Johnson and the American G.I. Forum in this racially and ethnically charged period. It also brought discrimination against Mexican Americans to the attention of the nation and cast the American G.I. Forum in the role of combating it. It is worth remembering today that Mexican Americans were generally treated as second-class citizens, that they were subject to segregated school systems, discrimination in hiring for jobs in both the public and private sectors, and denial of public accommodations such as restaurants and hotels. Garcia himself once publicly recalled a sign outside a restaurant that read "No Dogs or Mexicans Allowed."

Garcia and the G.I. Forum contributed to changing these conditions. The organization used electioneering techniques to get greater Hispanic representation on elected bodies in state and local government. Registration efforts, voter education, and strategic mobilization helped the Hispanic community gain a political toehold. Litigation was also used to establish the rights of Mexican Americans as a class, a legal foundation on which a more general political and social attack on ethnic prejudice could be mounted.

In the process, Garcia's national reputation and recognition grew. President John F. Kennedy appointed him an ambassador to the United Nations, and President Lyndon Johnson appointed him to a five-man White House commission to study the problems of Hispanics. And for his contributions, President Ronald Reagan awarded him the Medal of Freedom in 1984. Today, the American G.I. Forum has reduced its activist role, but it remains an important legacy to Garcia, with chapters in twenty-four states and its national headquarters in Washington, D.C.[1]

Interest Groups, Participation, and Democracy

Interest group A formal organization through which individuals seek to promote or defend a shared interest by influencing public policy.

Public policy Decisions that determine what government does or does not do.

Interest groups are organizations through which individuals seek to promote or defend a shared interest by influencing **public policy.** They are one of the principal means through which individuals participate in politics and play a central role in our democratic political system. They stimulate debate, raise issues that the public or political leaders may not be aware of, and sometimes help prevent bad policy from being enacted or—in the case of Hector Garcia and the G.I. Forum—keep a bad policy from being continued.

Interest groups can also be harmful to democracy when their activity undermines the broader public interest. The Founding Fathers long ago cautioned against the rise of factions for just this reason, and modern analysts often lament the influence of pressure groups possessed of too much power and too little concern for the broader society beyond their narrow special or even single interest. Such powerful organized interests may damage the democratic value of political equality, making some interests far better represented in the policy process than others. In the hope that the battle between interests would best be carried out in the open rather than in secret, the Founding Fathers recognized the importance of the people's right to organize (assemble) and petition government. They added it to the U.S. Constitution through the Bill of Rights. Texas, like most other states, includes a similar provision in its Bill of Rights.

Modern defenders of political interest groups also argue that interest groups constitute the most effective and just means of representing society.[2] Some defenders even argue that politics can be understood only by looking at the interaction of groups.[3] They also suggest that the Founding Fathers could not have foreseen how a more complex society would produce some interest groups representing not the narrow economic interests of their members but their perceptions of what is in the public interest. Such groups expand and enrich the role of interest groups as representative institutions, reducing their threat to the public interest.

JOIN the DEBATE

THE ISSUE: Are interest groups beneficial?

AGREE

1. Interest groups provide an effective means for citizens to participate freely in government.

2. Everyone has an equal legal right to organize and participate, so interest groups stimulate a more active and involved citizenry and thus a more full democratic representation.

3. Interest groups articulate specific citizen concerns, thus enhancing government responsiveness.

4. Interest groups ensure representation of minority interests and help avoid abuse of minority rights by majorities in the political system.

5. Interest group activity helps educate the public on important issues.

6. Interest groups perform an important watchdog function, keeping an eye on government activity for citizens.

DISAGREE

1. Only a minority of people actually join groups and most of those people participate only by contributing money, so they contribute little to the quantity or quality of democratic participation for the average citizen.

2. Involvement in interest groups is concentrated among those with relevant resources in skills and money, so taken as a whole, interest group articulation of interests is not representative of the majority opinion.

3. Interest group organizations are not internally democratic: They have largely self-selected leadership that provides little democratic accountability for citizen members.

4. Representation through interest groups tends to benefit organized groups with narrow goals and divisible (selfish) interests rather than the general collective or majority public interest.

5. Unavoidable disparities in money resources among interest groups result in a bias in the responsiveness of government that weakens the democratic legitimacy of government.

6. Interest groups tend to isolate interests, making them more rigid in their demands and less willing to compromise for the common interest.

Three features of interest groups are included in most definitions: organization, shared interest, and intent to influence public policy. To these three, we add another dimension that is often overlooked: irresponsibility. We discuss each of these interest group features in the following subsections.

ORGANIZATION

In Chapter 5, we discussed issue publics in terms of public opinion. The larger the issue public, the more likely it is that leaders will pay attention to that issue. An issue public, however, is not necessarily organized; an interest group is. It has a name, usually an e-mail as well as a postal address, a telephone number, and designated leaders. You can write a letter to or call an interest group on the telephone; you cannot do either with an issue public, an interest, or an ethnic group.

When members of any of those collections of people become organized, then and only then do they become an interest group. All students are members of various issue publics, but not all students have joined interest groups. Even as a member of an issue public, you "make a difference," but your impact is enhanced if you participate more actively through an organization representing your interest. Organization may simply be passing around a legal pad at a city council meeting so members of a neighborhood stay in contact and hold a subsequent meeting of their own. Until that first step is taken, however, those neighbors are an interest or an issue public, not an interest group.

This simple characteristic of interest groups is surprisingly important because it means interest groups are almost always a subset (and sometimes a tiny subset) of those who share the interest represented. In other words, interest groups are not designed to represent the whole society accurately. Instead, they represent only those parts of society willing and able to organize. This distinction is important because the influence of organized interests may distort democratic representation in important ways.

Equal and fair representation is a fundamental political value in the United States, so it is important that we understand how interest groups might pose a threat to that value.[4] First, the individuals in the organized subset of a larger group may not accurately represent the interests of the whole. The organization's leadership is often not democratically elected or accountable to the whole in any way. They are often the more or less self-appointed voice of the larger group and may or may not faithfully represent its actual views and interests. Indeed, the more individuals in the group, the less likely it is that any single organization can accurately represent its interests.

Second, some interests are far better represented in the interest group system than others are. This characteristic distorts the representativeness of the system, making it more likely that policies enacted will benefit some interests and not others. We mention here just two of the many reasons for this phenomenon. The first reason for unequal representation is that small interest populations with narrow concerns are somewhat easier to organize than are larger populations with more diverse interests. Interest groups representing smaller populations have the advantage of both greater unity and clearer common interests, making potential members more willing to organize. People sharing such an interest can see that they have much to gain from group membership and how their personal contribution will make a difference to the group effort. In contrast, interest groups representing large populations tend to suffer from the **free rider** problem. When interest populations are large, each potential member is less able to see how his or her personal contribution to the group goal is making a difference.

Free rider Someone who enjoys collective benefits without making a contribution to obtaining or defending them.

Collective benefits Benefits we enjoy whether we helped obtain them or not.

As we saw in Chapter 5, the free rider problem is especially true for groups pursuing a **collective benefit,** which cannot be withheld from nonmembers. The temptation is strong for the individual to avoid the costs and effort of group membership when their contribution does not seem important. Besides, they will automatically share in any benefit gained by the group. Indeed, it is rational in a narrow, self-interested sense for each individual to remain a nonmember of a group in such circumstances and to free-ride on any benefits that the group achieves.

Of course, if everyone acted in this narrow, self-interested way, no groups with large potential memberships pursuing collective interests would ever form. Clearly such groups, like labor unions, environmental groups, and consumer groups do form and sometimes find ways to cope with this organizational disadvantage. But partly because of the free rider problem with large populations, small populations with narrow interests tend to be overrepresented and disproportionately effective in the political process.[5]

The second reason that some groups and their populations are better represented is that they are more able to organize. Organization is partly a function of resources, and some interests simply have more money and organizational talent at their disposal than others do. Corporate and professional interests often have plenty of organizational talent and money; small businesses, minorities, and the poor have little of either. This bias in the interest group system is systematic and a real problem for equal representation in a democracy where interest groups play such a central role. Organization is what group politics is all about, and interests that are well organized are much more likely to be effective than those that are not. As the renowned political theorist E. E. Schattschneider observed many years ago about the interest group system, "The flaw . . . is that the [interest group] chorus sings with a strong upper class accent."[6]

SHARED INTERESTS

A second element of our definition of political interest groups is that these organizations form around shared interests. This characteristic has a couple of important implications. First, notice that the idea of a political interest group implies no restriction regarding the type of interest that might be represented. No limit is set on the number and kind of interests that might be organized. Interest groups can be as varied and diverse as society itself.

The second implication of shared interests is that they need not be personal interests. People may have an interest in promoting causes that do not directly benefit themselves, or the causes may even involve costs to them. Organizations formed to defend and further the interests of children, the prevention of rare diseases, and the environment are often formed and maintained by people not directly or uniquely benefited by the activities of the group.

INFLUENCE ON PUBLIC POLICY

By definition, an interest group seeks to influence public policy. An organization may have been created to worship God, manufacture automobiles, cure the sick, or help keep members of an occupation up to date on technology. When that organization becomes involved in attempting to influence public policy on same-sex marriages, taxation, labor relations, or Medicare payments, that organization becomes an interest group.

IRRESPONSIBILITY

This characteristic is sometimes discussed in dealing with interest groups, and we include it in our definition. We cannot hold an interest group responsible for being successful in politics. When schoolchildren are shot and killed, we cannot hold the National Rifle Association accountable. When people die from secondhand smoke, we cannot hold the National Tobacco Institute accountable. A few years ago, an interest group was able to get the Texas Legislature to delay the date on which a vehicle inspection law would take effect. In the time before it took effect, a truck with faulty brakes ran into a school bus, killing several children. That interest group cannot be held accountable.

We can try to hold government accountable. We can vote public officials out of office or vote against the slate of a political party if we do not like the policies it has enacted or failed to enact. Thus, we can hold someone accountable. That someone is never an interest group, which is simply the nature of the way the political system works. You and I can create an interest group to ask government to achieve certain goals. If government does them and they do not work out, no one can punish us. This characteristic is both the good news and the bad news about interest groups.

Types of Interest Groups

One of the most widely recognized and best-documented changes in the second half of the twentieth century was the vast growth in the number and types of interest groups active in U.S. politics. The growth in activity was almost certainly a reflection of the rapid socioeconomic and technological changes of the period. Rapid socioeconomic changes brought new industries and occupations and led to the decline of others. New industries and occupations brought new groups to further new interests. Declining industries also became better organized to try to defend themselves from the effects of change.

General prosperity resulted in a better-educated citizenry with greater motivation and resources to organize politically. Growth in government provided further motivation for organization, with more programs and regulations distributing benefits and burdens to be sought and avoided. Finally, advances in technology made organization more possible. New communication technology and computers to handle information have brought sophisticated organizational tools within the reach of the vast majority of Americans. Younger Americans have led the way in making a difference through the use of the Internet. Young people have been instrumental in using the Internet to organize around issues ranging from animal rights to international trade on both the national and even the international level.

These changes affected Texas as much as or more than the rest of the nation. From a fairly narrow range of influential groups—especially oil, banking, insurance, and attorneys' interests—has emerged a full range of interest organizations in Texas. Although the traditional interests are still powerful in Texas, its interest group system, like its economy, has become much more diversified.

We can categorize the various types of groups in many ways, but for simplicity we will list only seven general categories: business groups, agricultural groups, professional associations, organized labor, sociocultural groups, public interest groups, and cause groups. Some of these categories could be gathered under a general label of groups concerned with economic well-being. For some of them, however, other factors are clearly involved. For example, some professional organizations lobby for public interest issues like better health care or safer streets. Labor unions endeavor to get the minimum wage raised when clearly labor union members will not directly benefit from it because they already make more than the minimum wage. Others appear to be citizen groups concerned with the public good; however, neighborhood groups, for example, in addition to wanting the neighborhood safe, are also concerned about property values in which they have a personal economic stake. Thus, we resist the temptation to generalize too widely and simply present our seven types of interest groups in the following subsections.

BUSINESS GROUPS

Often taking the form of trade associations (groups that represent a particular industry), business organizations constitute by far the most numerous and best-organized political interest groups in Texas.[7] Business interests have both a high stake in public policy and enjoy a natural advantage in resources, so it is natural that they would be numerous and well organized. At least three reasons explain why business has a stake in state government.

First, state government has regulatory authority over nearly every type of economic activity in Texas. Businesses want regulatory policy that will not interfere with profit-making or in some cases will secure market advantages that actually improve opportunities for profit. Second, state government spends billions of dollars for goods and services that private business provides. It is a profitable source of business for many producers and an essential customer for some, like highway contractors, that cannot exist without lucrative government contracts.

Finally, if government is spending billions of dollars annually, it is also collecting billions of dollars in taxes each year. Like the rest of us, businesses want to pay as little in taxes as possible. For all these reasons, business has a high stake in state government and so will you. You may, and many of your fellow students certainly will, go into business either independently or as part of management of a large corporation. Making a difference in that case may involve activity in business groups or specific trade associations. Even if you choose a profession outside business, your economic interests will be tied to business interests. Making a difference will involve helping to promote or oppose the interests of business groups.

Business groups are also particularly well situated to defend their interests because they enjoy a natural advantage in financial resources, which are so necessary to successful interest advocacy. Corporations are particularly at an advantage; unlike other types of interest groups, they do not have to charge membership dues or conduct fundraisers to finance their activities. Their political costs can be paid for from money generated by the goods and services they sell. These resources allow business groups to be well organized and acquire highly skilled experts to help promote their positions. As a result, business and trade groups are the most powerful groups in both national and Texas politics. These groups have probably been even more important in Texas politics in the past because they have had the advantage of operating in an environment with a weaker party system and far fewer competing interest organizations than at the national level.

Business and trade groups remain the most powerful interest in Texas, but they are not as dominant today as they once were. Part of the reason is that some of the most powerful business groups in Texas—those representing the oil and gas, real estate, and banking industries—no longer enjoy the financial dominance they once did. This trend is in large part due to the oil slump of the 1980s, which not only dried up some of their financial resources but also prompted diversification of the Texas economy. With greater diversification of the economy comes greater diversification of the interests of business and greater likelihood that these interests will clash and limit each other's influence.[8] Differing business organizations often have conflicting goals and thus compete, rather than cooperate, in interest advocacy. All business groups also face more competition from the increasing number of nonbusiness and noneconomic groups, which further reduces the dominance of business interests.

AGRICULTURAL GROUPS

Farm groups represent a special type of business interest that has always been important in Texas politics. Because Texas was once a predominantly rural and agricultural state, farm interests had the votes and major land owners had the resources to dominate state politics. As you know from the discussion in Chapter 2 of the origins in 1875 of the current Texas Constitution, a farmers' organization known as the Grange was the most important political force shaping the document. Overrepresentation of rural areas in the state legislature, excellent organization, and political savvy allowed farm groups to wield disproportionate power well into the twentieth century.

Traditional farm groups are still influential, but they have been weakened politically as the state has become more urban and industrialized.[9] Redistricting to give each district approximately the same population has also ended the overrepresentation of rural areas in the state legislature. Although the Grange once held limiting and controlling big business as a central political goal, much of agriculture in Texas today has itself become agribusiness. Run by large corporations, this form of agricultural interest has all the advantages and political resources of big business at its disposal. Thus, agricultural interests today can increasingly be thought of as a special form of business interest.

PROFESSIONAL ASSOCIATIONS

Professional associations—organizations of doctors, lawyers, realtors, and other professionals—have also been among Texas's more influential interest groups. The relatively high socioeconomic status of their members gives them the resources to make their voices heard. And many elected officials have been professionals, especially lawyers, before seeking public office. In addition to furthering the interests of their profession generally, professional groups are also often concerned with matters such as standards of admission to a profession or licensing of practitioners.

ORGANIZED LABOR

Organized labor in Texas is not as active or powerful as is business or, for that matter, as is organized labor in much of the rest of the country. Not only does labor lack the resources of business and professional groups, it is especially hampered in Texas by a relatively hostile political culture. Like other southern states, union membership is low in Texas and declining. The prevalence of antilabor laws certainly contributes to this trend, and the workforce itself is given little information to counter the anti-union bias of the political culture.

Labor organizations are not entirely powerless. Two labor organizations are generally regarded as significant participants in the political process: the Texas American Federation of Labor–Congress of Industrial Organizations and the Texas Oil, Chemical, and Atomic Workers Union. Not surprisingly, organized labor is strongest in the relatively urban and heavily industrialized areas of the state, such as the Houston and Dallas–Fort Worth areas, as well as the Golden Triangle area of Beaumont, Port Arthur, and Orange. Labor has also benefited from its political alliances to some extent. Unions have associated themselves with the Democratic party, which has historically been dominant in the state. They have certainly benefited politically by this association, despite the fact that they have been allied with the liberal, and weaker, wing of the party. Also, labor benefits from the fact that its interests sometimes coincide with those of business. Labor and business battle over many workplace issues such as labor relations laws and occupational safety regulations, but they also find common ground in favoring policies that promote jobs in the state and in opposing those, like environmental regulations, that might threaten the loss of jobs due to plant closings. So it would be incorrect to think that labor is always on the losing side politically.

The antilabor orientation of Texas's laws clearly reflects the fact that labor groups in Texas have been ineffective in promoting the issues that matter most to them. Benefits such as unemployment insurance and workers' compensation insurance are lower than comparable benefits in most other industrial states. Generally, the labor relations laws are restrictive rather than supportive of union activity. Texas is a right-to-work state. **Right to work** means that the state outlaws the closed shop, the union shop, and any arrangement that prevents an employee who benefits from the union's efforts from being required to help pay for it. The right to work, in essence, is the right to be a free rider. Paying for the cost of collective bargaining is vital for unions to avoid the crippling effects of the free rider problem (mentioned earlier) to which unions are vulnerable. In addition, law also prohibits the tools of labor organization such as check-off systems of union dues, secondary boycotts, and even mass picketing.

Right to work The legal prohibition of collective bargaining agreements that contain any provisions for compulsory union membership.

The future does not look bright for organized labor in Texas. The cultural animosity toward unions that has characterized the state shows no sign of weakening, leaving labor in a difficult catch-22 situation. Labor has little hope of developing organizationally with the restrictive labor laws currently in place and little chance of generating the political power necessary to change the laws without developing stronger organizations. The Democratic party's political fortunes in the state seem to be waning, a development that can only erode labor's already limited political prospects.

SOCIOCULTURAL GROUPS

Although not as well organized as the business groups that make up the large majority of interest groups, an increasing number and variety of other types of groups are active in Texas politics. Among them are groups attempting to better the lives of various social categories and cultural identity groups.

Racial and Ethnic Organizations. Latinos and African Americans are the largest and most politically active minority groups in Texas. Organizations representing Latinos are both more numerous and more local to Texas than are African American organizations. The League of United Latin American Citizens (LULAC) was founded in Corpus Christi in 1929. Its focus has been on achieving full citizenship rights for Latinos and equal educational opportunities.[10] The American G.I. Forum, discussed at the beginning of the chapter, has successfully pursued similar goals.

The Texas Democratic Party harbors both the Tejano Democrats and the Mexican American Democrats, organizations that seek to further the interests of Latinos through the Democratic party and its elected officials. In addition, the nationally based Mexican American Legal Defense Fund has sought political and legal equality for Latinos through the courts in Texas.

Important African American political organizations in Texas, most notably the National Association for the Advancement of Colored People, the Urban League, and the Congress of Racial Equality, are also nationally based. These organizations have fought discrimination and sought greater representation for African Americans in political office.

With federal court rulings and the Voting Rights Act of 1965, Latinos and African Americans are much more influential in Texas politics today than they once were. They have become a significant voting bloc and cannot be ignored in statewide elections or especially in citywide elections in the state's larger cities. However, they are not as powerful as many other groups or as influential as they might be. Many minority citizens are not registered to vote or fail to participate, the groups that represent them sometimes compete rather than cooperate, and none of these groups has ready access to adequate resources. As a result, they have been only modestly successful in achieving their goals, particularly in fighting poverty and achieving economic equality for the citizens they represent.

Religious Groups.   Churches and other religious organizations have long been the foundation for political activism, particularly in the South. Indeed, churches have been instrumental in the organization of African Americans for the pursuit of civil rights.[11] Other Protestant and Roman Catholic churches have helped organize political groups in poor and minority neighborhoods to work toward providing or securing social services and stimulating local political activism. The Christian Coalition has recently emerged as the most significant religious group in Texas politics. Working primarily within and through the Republican party, the Christian Coalition is comprised of citizens holding conservative social views who are concerned that society has lost its moral bearings. Abortion and homosexual rights, prayer in schools, and gun control are among their central issues.[12]

The Christian Coalition, which developed rapidly as an organization during the 1990s, has attempted to influence politics primarily by recruiting candidates for local school board elections and gaining influence within the Republican party. It has had considerable success in both endeavors, becoming an important force on local school boards and effectively capturing control of the Republican party machinery. As successful groups often do, however, it has stimulated the formation of more liberal Christian organizations in opposition. Liberal pastors have formed the Texas Faith Network to try to counter the Christian Coalition, and the Texas Freedom Network has attempted to mobilize liberal Christian Democrats to run for local school boards. Moral questions and Christian argument about them are thus likely to be prominent features of Texas politics in the foreseeable future.

PUBLIC INTEREST GROUPS

Groups that seek government policies to serve what they believe to be the broad interests of society as a whole are public interest groups. Unlike business groups, they are not primarily interested in direct economic gain. This characteristic does not mean that they focus on all of society's collective interests or that the public itself is involved in selecting which collective interests will be addressed by any group. All public interest groups focus on some broad interests and not others, and those interests chosen by any group reflect the goals and concerns of the group's leadership rather than that of the general public.

Often calling themselves *consumer groups* or *citizens' groups,* some public interest groups have a broad focus, pursuing policy goals in several areas at a time and in different areas at different times. Common Cause, for example, describes itself as the citizens' lobby and works for political reforms in campaign finance laws, ethics regulations for public officials, and various other causes. The extended network of consumer organizations associated with Ralph Nader—represented in Texas by the Texas Public Interest Research Group—watches for and responds to threats to consumers posed by products of all kinds.

Other public interest organizations are focused on a narrow range of issues or even a single policy area. Environmental groups like the Sierra Club and Greenpeace, for example, serve the public interest by focusing their efforts entirely on policies designed to protect and conserve the environment. Most environmental groups also tend to narrow their focus even further, seeking primarily to influence policy in a specific area, such as pollution reduction or wilderness preservation. Other examples include the American Civil Liberties Union (ACLU), which seeks to serve as guardian of the constitutional rights of all individuals, and the League of Women Voters, which seeks to encourage political participation through simplifying voter-registration procedures, publishing voter guides, and sponsoring candidate forums and debates.

CAUSE GROUPS

Cause groups seek to aid particular segments of society that are in need but are politically weak or to promote a particular element of public policy they regard as especially important. Groups that work to promote the interests of individuals with a particular debilitating or deadly disease have a clear and encompassing cause, for example. The Coalition for the Homeless also takes up the cause of a segment of society too weak politically to fend for itself, as does the Children's Defense Fund.

Other cause groups focus on an issue their members care deeply about. Perhaps the most famous example of such a group, and one that is important in Texas as well as nationally, is the National Rifle Association (NRA). The NRA is an organization of gun enthusiasts who believe in the absolute right to possess firearms, and thus it has worked hard to block efforts to regulate gun ownership at both the national and state levels. The current controversy over the legal status of abortion has produced cause-oriented groups on both sides of the issue. In Texas, the Texas Right to Life Committee opposes abortion, while the Texas Abortion Rights Action League defends the right to choose. Mothers Against Drunk Driving (MADD) is another nationally based cause group that has had some success in Texas promoting stronger drunk-driving laws. Even marijuana has its organized defenders in the National Organization for Repeal of Marijuana Laws (NORML).

The number of public interest organizations has expanded rapidly in recent years, and public interest organizations can be found lobbying today on almost every imaginable issue, leaving few issue publics, potential issues, interests, or causes completely unrepresented. Together, they offer plentiful opportunities for people to join like-minded individuals in making a difference on issues and concerns they care about. However, many of these organizations, like NORML, operate on a shoestring budget in Texas and have yet to go much beyond making the issue public aware of certain issues.

What Groups Do: Techniques for Influence

The general goal of interest groups is to influence governmental policy in ways favorable to the group and its members. To accomplish this goal, groups must influence the thinking and behavior of those who make policy decisions. Groups attempt to influence these decisionmakers using all the participation strategies discussed in Chapter 5. Organized interests engage in these strategies using somewhat different techniques from those used by individuals because of their distinct goals and resources. It is worth noting also that not all interest groups use the same methods. Some groups emphasize certain strategies more than others, and some use certain approaches exclusively while avoiding others entirely. The choice of approach depends most fundamentally on the money and membership resources available to the group and the nature of the goals that the group seeks. Group leadership will try to match their techniques to the particular resources and goals of the group to maximize its effectiveness. Clearly, organizations with big budgets and prominent members who are leaders in the business community use different techniques than do ordinary workers or people of modest means. Not too many people in thousand-dollar suits march and stand for hours in picket lines under the hot sun. Below, we revisit the major participation strategies with an eye to how interest groups employ them to pursue their goals.

LOBBYING

Lobbying Any attempt to influence public policy decisions through direct contact with decision-makers.

Lobbying is probably the activity that comes to mind first for most people when they think of interest groups and their activities. Once done on a catch-as-catch-can basis in the corridors and lobbies of capitol buildings (thus the origin of the term), **lobbying** has come to refer to a range of activities, all involving the attempt to influence policymakers through direct contact of some kind. Lobbying can involve formal or informal contacts and, as we have seen in Chapter 5, can be engaged in by anyone from the average citizen to highly paid professional lobbyists. It can take the form of everything from personal, one-to-one conversations to formal testimony before committees, to the more impersonal phone call, letter, or telegram. Professional lobbyists employ all these forms, while the rest of us are usually limited to the more formal and impersonal forms of contact.

A professional lobbyist is someone designated by an interest group to represent its interests to government policymakers. Sometimes these representatives work for lobbying firms or law firms that provide lobbying services. Such firms are frequently a source of employment for former government officials and officeholders, whose expertise and contacts developed while in office are valuable resources for lobbying after their terms have ended. Other professional lobbyists are employees of the organization or business, and lobbying is a large part or all of their job responsibilities. Professional lobbyists are expensive and thus are used primarily by financially strong groups. While professional lobbyists can be found representing all the categories of groups we have discussed above, they are most likely to be found plying their trade for business and professional groups.

The key to successful lobbying is direct personal communication with policy-makers. Professional lobbyists seek to establish and maintain access to legislators so that their case can be made directly and their interests can be articulated effectively. Such access can be cultivated through informal contacts of various kinds designed to get the lobbyist on a first-name basis with the legislators. Lobbyists will try to see as many legislators as possible, as often as possible. Just stopping by, buying lunch, or shaking a hand are key elements of the trade. Lobbyists also hold social events of various kinds for legislators with the intention of providing a circumstance in which to develop stronger personal relationships. Indeed, lobbying in Texas once occurred largely in the context of informal entertainment provided evenings and weekends for the legislators. While still an important way to create personal relationships that lead to access, a changing social climate and legal limitations have made more formal means of communicating information to legislators increasingly important.[13]

Formal lobbying contacts can take several forms. Most coveted by lobbyists is the private meeting with a legislator. To present the group's information and argument

A legislator is used to the guys in the expensive suits. When you show up, his curiosity is often piqued.

in a one-on-one meeting in which the lobbyist has the undivided attention of the decisionmaker provides the best opportunity to persuade. Legislators' time is a limited and scarce resource, and such access is an especially valuable asset. Lobbyists will also seek contacts with important members of a legislator's staff. Winning the endorsement of a trusted aid who has the confidence of the legislator may be as effective as, or in some cases more effective than, speaking to the legislator directly.

The relationship between lobbyists and policymakers is not a one-way street. To achieve their ends, lobbyists need access to policymakers to communicate their interests, but policymakers also need lobbyists for their information and expertise. For this reason, lobbyists are often invited to testify before legislative committees on policy areas relevant to their interests. Such testimony is an opportunity to communicate with exactly those legislators who are most important in shaping pending legislation that the group cares about. Lobbyists can use this opportunity to make it clear why a new regulation is harmful or beneficial, or how it might be changed and improved.

Individual legislators also often become dependent on trusted lobbyists as a source of valuable policy information. Groups with the money will often do or pay for extensive research, gathering information that it would be nearly impossible for the legislators to generate on their own. Interest organizations and their professional lobbyists are often the source of policy ideas and innovations that legislators can use to further their political careers. In fact, close, trusted, professional lobbyists may even help write legislation and advise legislators on political strategies for getting the legislation passed.

To reach this high level of access and influence, it is clear that a lobbyist must know how to approach public officials and know the subject matter important to their groups. Lobbyists will get to know legislators as individuals, learn their interests and needs, and learn how best to present arguments that have a positive impact. They will understand that they trade primarily in information, and that the quality and integrity of that information will be crucial in developing a long-term relationship with a legislator based on trust. If a legislator is to depend on a lobbyist, he or she must trust that the lobbyist's information and advice will never result in public embarrassment. Misleading a legislator for short-term gain can mean the loss of access in the long run. Threats and arm-twisting are also tactics that are rarely used because they are harmful to the creation and maintenance of the amicable relationships that are the basis of real success in lobbying. In some ways, professional lobbying is thus self-regulating because the business of interest representation depends on persuasion, and the ability to persuade is built on a foundation of integrity and trust.

ATTENDING A PUBLIC HEARING

The importance of public meetings was emphasized in Chapter 5. These opportunities for the general public to be heard are also important opportunities for organizational leadership to influence decisions. Although intended as a forum for individual citizens to communicate their views and concerns, representatives of organized interests are often the dominant participants at these functions. Presence and participation at school board meetings, city council meetings, and the public hearings of state executive and regulatory agencies can be an important part of making a difference in government. Lobbyists and interest group leaders recognize the importance of the access that these meetings and hearings provide, and they rarely miss the opportunity to make the group's case heard. Group leadership may also encourage membership to pack a meeting, even providing transportation to group members, to ensure that the organization and its interests are well (and vocally) represented in the audience.

GRASSROOTS LOBBYING

A more indirect form of lobbying, but one that is still orchestrated by group leadership and lobbyists, is grassroots lobbying, the mobilization of group membership to contact elected representatives by letter, phone, or e-mail, or even personally. Groups with large memberships or members who can be politically influential because they control economic resources, are opinion leaders, or are just likely to vote often find grassroots lobbying a useful tactic. Groups notify their members of a problem and encourage them to contact their legislators or other appropriate officeholders. They will make it as easy as possible to do so, providing the names, addresses, telephone numbers, and e-mail addresses of the individual member's legislators. They may even organize transportation for the members to Austin and have the lobbyist arrange for the members, or selected individuals, to see the appropriate officeholders.

Members of the legislature pay attention to opinion expressed through such contacts, especially if it comes in great volume from potential voters, or if it comes from individuals in their districts who are important campaign contributors or in any way politically important. Of course, legislators will often know that a wave of contacts from a particular group has been stimulated by the group leadership and has not occurred spontaneously. To make political sense of the messages they are receiving, they must assess the intensity of feeling behind the contact, especially if they are similarly worded letters, e-mails, fax messages, postcards, or telephone calls. Separating the true grassroots sentiment from the artificial astroturf (defined and discussed in Chapter 5) is a vital political skill for policymakers. It is hardly an exact science, however, and the precise impact of grassroots lobbying efforts is difficult to determine. Most legislators will err on the side of caution, however, and are likely to be swayed by either a large number of contacts from potential voters or a few contacts by politically influential constituents.

Another way to influence political decisions is to shape the climate of opinion in the general political community. The conventional means of mobilizing public opinion (or what is sometimes called "going public") is through some sort of public relations campaign. Normally, this means extensive use of mass media and advertising. Groups may promote causes by purchasing ads in magazines, on billboards, on the radio, and on television. One such campaign that has had some success was launched by Citizens Against Lawsuit Abuse, which advocates tort reform. The group was attempting to convince the public that they faced an epidemic of frivolous lawsuits and that greedy trial lawyers were encouraging outrageous jury awards in personal injury and product liability cases to line their own pockets.

The real purpose of the campaign was to help insulate the insurance and other business interests backing the group from damaging civil settlements. In this case, the group focuses on an issue because people might not be as sympathetic to the cause if it was clear the citizens involved were representing large corporate interests. In other cases, a group may engage in institutional advertising, in which they try to create a more favorable image for the group itself in the eyes of the public. The goal is to create a supportive climate in which to operate politically, where opposition will be less likely and slower to develop. Groups as diverse as labor unions, teachers, and the National Rifle Association (NRA) have engaged in this sort of effort in recent years. Like the NRA's We Are the NRA campaign, these efforts typically try to portray an organization and its members as unassuming regular people, neighbors, and responsible members of the community that we need not fear.

Persuasion on a mass basis is an expensive undertaking, however, always involving the investment of a lot of money on media. Groups without extensive financial resources will not be able to afford the costs or the risks of the conventional means of going public.

DEMONSTRATING

Groups that can't afford the public relations experts, media advisers, and paid advertising of going public can, however, pursue similar goals by means of protest activity. The basic goal of this unconventional tactic is to mobilize public opinion. The hope is that a demonstration or rally will draw the attention of the news media, which raise public awareness of a problem in a context that will result in public pressure on lawmakers on behalf of the group's cause. As discussed in Chapter 5, however, it is a risky strategy that can fail to mobilize public opinion in a way favorable to the group and can actually turn public opinion against the group and its goals. Therefore, such tactics must be planned carefully to ensure success.

Unconventional interest group tactics can range from legal activities to illegal civil disobedience, to the use of violence or terrorism. Peaceful marches, picketing, boycotts, and rallies are all unconventional but legal ways to try to sway public opinion and public policy. Sometimes the goal of a group is to change what it sees to be an unfair or oppressive law. In such cases, a group may turn to **civil disobedience,** which involves a public act committed to break an objectionable law (or a law linked to an objectionable practice or policy). Classic examples of civil disobedience from the civil rights movement include Rosa Parks refusing to yield her seat on the bus and sit-ins by African Americans in segregated restaurants. An example of breaking a law linked to an objectionable policy was protesting the Vietnam War by publicly burning one's draft card. Civil disobedience involves peacefully breaking a law and a willingness to accept the punishment for this act without resistance. The purpose is not to get away with breaking the law but to make

Civil disobedience The intentional, public, non-violent violation of a law to protest the unjustness of the law or a public policy related to or represented by the law.

Demonstrations are useful political tactics. They do require some organizational skills. That may be where you come in.

the authorities enforce an objectionable law and thus publicize its unfairness or illegitimacy. Civil disobedience, while an illegal form of protest, also supports the broader political system by accepting the government's right to enforce the law.

While legal protest and civil disobedience have sometimes been successful in achieving their ends, often they are not. When change is too slow or does not happen at all, a group or some members of a group may become frustrated and turn from peaceful protest to violence. Along with instances of legal protest and civil disobedience, Texas has seen its share of violent protest activity. Instances date back as far as the 1870s when violence by the Ku Klux Klan attracted attention. Populist farmers used violence against the railroads and banks in the last decades of the nineteenth century. All sorts of groups, from organizations of poor people to African Americans, Mexican Americans, welfare mothers, anti-abortion activists, and even religious conservatives and college students, have resorted to violence at various times. The common denominator is people organized around a cause or interest they feel strongly about, but who lack the resources to feel they can make the system respond to their concerns through peaceful means.

APPOINTMENTEERING

Interest groups are keenly aware that unelected bureaucrats are also important decisionmakers in the policy process. In making administrative decisions concerning implementation of policy, bureaucrats shape the meaning and impact of policy in ways that are significant to interest groups. In addition, because bureaucrats develop great expertise in particular policy areas, they are often the source of new policy ideas and initiatives that legislators pick up and enact into law. By influencing appointments to administrative agencies and lobbying administrators once in office, a technique known as **appointmenteering,** interest groups can affect policy of concern to them at both the initiation and implementation stages. Interest group lobbyists are also useful sources of information for agencies and can serve as sources of political support when an agency's programs or budget are under review by the legislature or the governor. It would be an unwise agency head who failed to cultivate political contacts and support from interest groups, as well as an unwise interest group that ignored the option of appointmenteering.

Appointmenteering An attempt to influence appointments to public office.

ELECTIONEERING

Influencing officeholders, both elected and appointed, is much easier, of course, if they are already sympathetic to a group's interests. An important way that an interest group can obtain a more sympathetic set of officeholders is through the process of electioneering—helping to nominate and elect persons to public office. Because elected officials are responsible for appointing many of the unelected administrative leaders of agencies, electioneering can also help secure more sympathetic bureaucrats. Most groups engage in some form of electioneering, depending on the nature of the group and its resources. The various electioneering activities can be divided into two basic forms: campaign assistance and campaign contributions.

Groups with substantial memberships but lacking great financial resources are most likely to focus their electioneering efforts on campaign assistance. Basic to such assistance are efforts to get out the voters favorable to a particular candidate. This approach can take the form of endorsements of a favored candidate in newsletters to the group members or in local newspapers to the wider public. Such endorsements can serve as a guide to members and others in the community sympathetic to the interests of the organization. The organization may also use its membership to provide basic elements of retail politics such as telephone and door-to-door canvassing to solicit votes, stage public rallies in favor of a candidate, and provide transportation for voters going to the polls on Election Day.

A group can also give a favored candidate special access to the group's members. Providing a candidate with group membership information and mailing lists, using group members for campaign-related research, and inviting candidates to speak at group events are all valuable assets to a candidate's campaign.

Political campaigns are an expensive undertaking, and they are becoming more expensive with each successive election. Money is an increasingly vital resource to politicians; as a result, many interest groups view campaign contributions as an increasingly vital means of influencing politicians. Not only can significant campaign contributions help elect a sympathetic officeholder, they can ensure more effective access to him or her for lobbyists. Legislators naturally tend to listen to the groups that have helped to finance their campaigns.

Teachers can use your help. Students need a role model, a friend, or simply a break in the routine. Just call a school or a school district to get the ball rolling.

Political action committee (PAC) An organization created by an interest group, corporation, labor union, or other organization to raise money for the purpose of spending on and contributing to political campaigns.

The mechanism for interest group contributions to political campaigns is the **political action committee (PAC).** Thus, while corporate interests and labor unions cannot, by law, contribute directly to individual candidates, these and other groups can form PACs that will perform the task of soliciting voluntary contributions from members and the general public and then distribute the money to candidates. National law sets a limit on the amount of money a PAC can contribute to a candidate for national office, but no such restrictions exist on PACs contributing to candidates for Texas government. The only requirement is that they report contributions greater than $100 so that the public can know which PACs are backing a particular candidate.

PAC contributions have followed fairly regular and predictable patterns. First, it is clear that the largest amounts of PAC money come from interests with a substantial stake in the regulatory and spending decisions of the Texas Legislature. Business associations are the biggest of the big-money contributors, and prominent among them are companies that bid on state highway contracts, as well as insurance and utility companies whose rates are set by the state. Realtors and developers whose profit opportunities often depend on state tax subsidies and transportation decisions have active PACs. PACs representing teachers' groups, whose members' salaries are directly affected by the state legislature, are also prominent players in the campaign contribution game.

A second pattern concerns the candidates to whom PACs give their contributions. Several factors may guide a PAC's choices. Campaign contributions are viewed as an investment in policy influence, and basically PACs want to get the most for their money. Thus, they want to contribute to legislators in a position of leadership and power. The powerful speaker of the Texas House, for example, will draw more contributions than the average member. So will those legislators who chair committees important to big-money interests.

PACs also want to invest in candidates they believe have the best chance to win. Campaign contributions buy no access and influence unless the candidate wins. Thus, incumbents attract far more money than challengers do because those in office are proven winners. As a result, PACs are more comfortable giving money to a strong and proven candidate, even one that is only moderately supportive of the group's interests, than they are giving money to a strongly supportive long-shot

Sargent © 2004 Austin American-Statesman. *Reprinted with permission of* Universal Press Syndicate.

Texas in Context

6.1 PAC Contributions in the Megastates (in Millions of Dollars)

Megastate	1998	2002	Percentage Increase Between 1998 and 2002	2002 Megastate Rank
Texas	**7.1**	**9.7**	**36.6**	**4**
California	10.2	13.8	35.3	2
Pennsylvania	4.7	6.1	29.8	7
New Jersey	4.2	5.4	28.6	8
Illinois	11.9	14.3	20.2	1
Michigan	5.3	6.3	18.9	5
Ohio	5.8	6.1	15.1	6
Massachusetts	2.0	2.3	15.0	10
New York	9.8	11.2	14.3	3
Florida	3.2	3.5	9.3	9

Source: Open Secrets, www.opensecrets.org (accessed February 28, 2004).

challenger. Spending money on a projected loser is close to throwing the money away. Of course, when a race is competitive, the PAC is free to back the candidate more sympathetic to its interests or even to contribute to both candidates to hedge the group's bets. Sometimes a PAC will back a weaker candidate in a specific race to try and unseat or at least embarrass an enemy incumbent. The hope is often not so much that the enemy incumbent will be defeated but that he or she will have to work hard for reelection and expend a lot of resources. The political enemy may then be more cautious about opposing the group's goals, or the political enemy's electoral scare may serve to give pause to other less secure politicians when they consider opposing the group's interests.

A final pattern is that the amount of money flowing through PACs into Texas state elections is continuing to increase rapidly. In the 2002 election, PACs of various kinds poured just over $56.1 million into state election contests, up by almost 9 percent over the $51.5 million in the 2000 cycle. Of the $56.1 million, business groups accounted for just over $45 million (80 percent), while labor spent $2.2 million (3.8 percent). The remaining $8.9 million (15.9 percent) was contributed by sociocultural, public interest, and cause groups. The latter category has been experiencing the greatest growth in PAC spending in recent years.[14]

Much of the total spending and recent growth in spending has come in the form of so-called soft-money contributions. The elimination of this form of unlimited contributions to party organizations by the McCain-Feingold Campaign Reform

Act will certainly have an impact on the volume and patterns of spending in the future. Texas in Context 6.1 presents another way to consider PAC activity in Texas. The feature examines hard-money contributions (those subject to limits in amount that can be made directly to candidates) and compares them to the amounts contributed in other megastates. We can see that Texas ranks high (fifth among all states) and has experienced a greater percentage growth in PAC contributions between 1998 and 2002 than any of the other megastates.

LITIGATION

It is said that almost every important political conflict eventually finds its way to a resolution in the courts. This statement may be an exaggeration, but interest groups often have an important stake in the outcome of judicial decisions, and the courts are an increasingly significant focus of interest group activity. The most basic way that groups attempt to influence public policy through the courts is by filing lawsuits, or litigation. For some groups, such as the National Association for the Advancement of Colored People (NAACP), the American Civil Liberties Union (ACLU), and the Mexican-American Legal Defense and Education Fund (MALDEF), litigation is the primary means of influencing public policy. Many other groups use litigation as part of their policy efforts or to defend themselves against hostile interests that are more actively using the courts.

As the examples above suggest, litigation has often been the tool of groups in society that have lacked resources vital to making other tactics effective. As discussed in Chapter 5, the Safe Streets Now organization has helped neighbors organize to deal with nuisance properties through small claims court. This example is a dramatic illustration of how a small group or even an individual with few resources can make a difference through the legal system.

To bring a case to court, a group must have standing to sue, which means that the group or an individual associated with the group must be able to show that the group (or the group's membership) have been or will be harmed by a current policy or by the government's failure to implement a policy properly and fully. For groups like racial and ethnic minorities, this stipulation presents little problem because the issues they care about clearly present real legal and constitutional questions for their members. For economic groups, however, the courts are less likely to be the site of policy initiatives and are more likely to be the site of the defense of privilege challenged by minority rights or environmental groups.

All groups can involve themselves in litigation by providing free legal services for those drawn into legal disputes that have potential consequences for the group's interests. Many of the groups with a legal defense fund offer this sort of legal service to selected clients. All groups can also file a "friend of the court" **amicus curiae brief,** supporting the arguments of litigants whose interests parallel their own.

Litigation tactics take time (sometimes years), legal expertise, and money: resources that groups may not have or may be unable to maintain for the long run. Nothing can guarantee that bringing a matter to court will result in a successful judgment. Playing this game successfully takes a favorable case suited to the

Amicus curiae brief A legal brief filed by an individual or group that has an interest in a court case but is not a party to that case in an effort to influence its outcome.

group's ends and judges who share the group's perspective. It helps to have judges who have a legal philosophy and political ideology sympathetic to the group and its goals. Even at the national level, groups are not above attempting to influence the selection of judges, pushing presidents to appoint and senators to confirm judges who share their perspectives on matters such as abortion and civil rights. In Texas, where the judiciary is elected, groups engage in the same kind of election-eering in judicial elections as they do for legislative elections. Judges need money for their election races too, and groups who have a high stake in litigation are ready to provide it.

Interest Group Power in Texas

The question of interest group power in Texas really involves two somewhat re-lated questions. First, how powerful are interest groups in Texas politics in general? (Are they central or peripheral political actors, more or less important than in other states, and why?) Second, which particular interest groups in Texas are more powerful than others, and why?

HOW POWERFUL ARE INTEREST GROUPS IN TEXAS POLITICS?

Interest groups in some states are much more influential political actors than in other states. This variation comes from factors external to the groups themselves, involving differences in the state-to-state political environment in which they op-erate. Texas is considered to be among the states in which interest groups exercise a strong influence on politics and public policy. As Texas in Context 6.2 indicates, on a scale of 1 to 5 for describing interest group strength in the state political sys-tem, Texas is a 4. One state, Florida (the other southern megastate), is a 5.[15] Several factors help to explain why organized interests have traditionally been and remain powerful in Texas: the nature of the political culture, the basic political structure, the degree of professionalism, the strength of the party system and the nature of partisan competition, and the degree of development of the economy.

Political Culture.   As discussed in Chapter 1, Texas has a predominantly tradition-alistic political culture, with increasing influence from both the individualistic and moralistic cultures (the former is far ahead of the latter). A traditionalistic culture supports leadership by an economic elite, which is represented by strong business interest groups; the individualistic political culture accepts the advancement of private interests through political activity. Thus, the political culture of Texas not only encourages interest group activity but also tends especially to legitimize that of the social elite as being in the interests of the entire population.

Political Structure.   Also partly a function of the state's political culture is the nature of the basic political structure. A consolidated political structure helps to limit the access points to government and thus the power of interest groups. A consolidated political structure is one characterized by a strong executive with appointment power over top-level administrators. As we have seen, for cultural and historical reasons, the Texas Constitution creates a remarkably fragmented political structure that is characterized by a weak governor surrounded by independent boards and commissions and other elected executive officials in a plural executive establishment. These independent boards, commissions, and other elected officials provide multiple sites for group influence. This structure was created to serve the needs of a much different time, but it has survived the cultural changes in the state as well as the development of a large urban population and a diversified economy. These changes have fostered the creation of numerous interest groups that find a great many opportunities for influence in Texas's traditionalistic political structure.

Professionalism.   Generally, the greater the level of professionalism in state government, the greater the government's strength and independence from interest groups. Professionalism in state government is indicated by characteristics such as well-paid elected officials, public employees who are adequately paid and who are selected and promoted on the basis of merit, and extensive staff support for both the governor and legislature. On all these dimensions, the Texas government rates as relatively unprofessional, and thus it is comparatively weak and more susceptible to interest group influence. An unprofessional government is weak relative to private interest groups because it depends heavily on interest groups for vital resources and services that a professional government provides independently. Among these resources and services are financial considerations that defray the costs of officeholding for poorly paid elected officials, and the provision of policy information that shapes the formulation, enactment, and implementation of public policy. This dependency on the part of the government creates vast opportunities for the growth and exercise of interest group power.

Political Parties and Party Competition.   Another important factor in interest group power is the strength of political parties and the nature of party competition.[16] Strong competitive parties provide a countervailing source of power that serves to balance and limit interest group influence. Competition breeds strong party organizations that can provide a source of political support and resources for officeholders independent of interest groups.[17] As we will see in Chapter 7, Texas has historically had a weak party system dominated by a single party, an arrangement that tends not to balance and limit interest group power. Although the party system of Texas has been more competitive during a recent period of transition, this development has not lasted long enough to alter the tradition of interest group power dramatically. The transition may be leading to another era of one-party dominance that, while less complete than the earlier manifestation, will not serve to limit interest group power significantly.

Economic Development.   Finally, states that are or have recently been dominated by a single industry or a small set of industries tend to have strong interest groups.

Dominant industries can convincingly equate their interests with the state generally, giving them a compelling political argument for influence with legislators and other political leaders. Such strong groups help to create and maintain the conditions that protect and promote interest group power, such as a fragmented political structure, unprofessional and weak government institutions, and weak regulations of interest groups and their activities. As we have seen, Texas politics has had a dominant industry for most of its history. Agriculture dominated at the time the Texas Constitution was written, and it was replaced by the oil and gas industry in the twentieth century. In recent years, the Texas economy has dramatically diversified, resulting in the development of many more interest organizations and a reduction in the dominance of any single interest. The tradition of single-industry dominance, however, leaves conditions favorable for the influence of all interest groups in general. For all these reasons, political scientists rank Texas among the states with political systems in which interest groups play a dominant role.

IMPLICATIONS OF INTEREST GROUP POWER

Interest group dominance in politics has important implications for the nature of representation and the vitality of participation in the political system. In Chapter 5, we discussed weak institutions for mobilizing ordinary working Texans, who constitute 80 percent of the families who pay taxes. We suggested that labor unions are rather special kinds of interest groups because of their propensity to organize and mobilize the very people who do not turn out in large numbers in American elections.

In Texas in Context 6.2, we advance this argument with an examination of the interest group dominance scores of the megastates in relation to their labor union membership and voter turnout in an off-year election. A cursory examination of the data suggests that states with strong interest groups seem to have generally lower levels of union membership and lower voter turnout. Subjecting the data to more sophisticated statistical analysis confirms that, indeed, a moderately strong negative relationship between interest group strength and both union strength and voter turnout exists; that is, the stronger the interest groups, the weaker the role of labor unions and the lower the voter turnout in the state. Why are the relationships between interest group strength and both labor union strength and voter turnout so negative?

The first negative relationship exists because of the probusiness and thus antiunion bias of the interest group system. As political scientist Harmon Zeigler has shown, the stronger the interest group system, the stronger the role of business within that system. One of the major political goals of the business community is to weaken labor unions. One of the major features of a business-dominated state political system is a set of laws that make it difficult for workers to organize and thus exercise the right to bargain collectively. The so-called right-to-work laws are only one feature of a set of laws that make it difficult to recruit members and to campaign in collective bargaining elections and that deny protection to individual workers who attempt to promote collective bargaining. According to Zeigler, in states with weak interest group systems, business interest groups constitute 58

TEXAS in Context

6.2 Relationship of Interest Group Strength in the Megastates to Union Membership and Voter Trends

Megastate	Interest Group Score	Union Membership (Millions)	Voter Turnout, 1998 (Percentage)
Michigan	3	20.8	41.3
Ohio	4	17.3	40.8
Massachusetts	3	14.3	37.9
Illinois	4	18.6	37.1
California	4	16.0	33.7
Pennsylvania	3	16.9	32.4
New York	3	25.5	31.8
New Jersey	3	20.8	30.0
Texas	**4**	**5.8**	**24.6**
Florida	5	6.8	10.8

Sources: Clive Thomas and Ronald J. Hrebenar, "Interest Groups in the States," in Virginia Gray and Herbert Jacob, eds., *Politics in the American States: A Comparative Analysis,* 6th ed. (Washington, D.C.: CQ Press, 1996), p. 154; Union Membership 2000: Bureau of Labor Statistics, stats.bls.gov/news.releas/6nion2.t05.htm; Turnout 1998: U.S. Census Bureau, 2000. *Statistical Abstract of the United States: 2000* (Washington, D.C.: U.S. Government Printing Office), p. 292.

percent of the groups in the system. In strong interest group states, business groups constitute 75 percent of the groups in the system. Conversely, the labor union percentage drops from 15 percent in weak systems to 5 percent in strong systems.[18]

The second negative relationship is what one would expect from a set of institutions dominated by the upper class. In strong interest group states, the upper class turns out to vote, but without labor unions and strong parties to mobilize them, the working class does not turn out in large numbers. Thus, the overall turnout rate is low.

WHICH INTEREST GROUPS ARE POWERFUL IN TEXAS POLITICS?

Organization, money, size, and reputation in the political community can contribute to the relative power and influence of individual interest groups.[19] Among these factors, organization and money are especially important because they are instrumental for everything a group does, including maintaining its reputation and making use of its size. A group may be large, for example, but size translates into effective political power only if the membership is coordinated and mobilized. Even a large group cannot clearly and convincingly reward supporters or sanction opponents without an organized membership. Size can sometimes be a liability: the larger the group, the more challenges exist for group leadership to organize and mobilize it effectively.

Even more fundamental is adequate financial resources. Jesse Unruh, a former speaker of the California Assembly, once summarized its importance with the comment, "Money is the mother's milk of politics." This statement is certainly no less true in Texas. Money is instrumental for all other group activities, including organization building. To realize the benefits of size, for example, large groups must have the financial resources to meet the organizational challenges that large size brings. Many interests that have a large potential membership are relatively weak because they lack the resources to mobilize and coordinate the group effectively. Money is also important to creating and maintaining a positive reputation in the political community. As we have seen, grassroots lobbying can be an expensive strategy, but it can greatly improve effectiveness by building general support for a group and its interests or by simply reducing potential resistance. Lobbying effectiveness is also enhanced by the ability to hire professional (and high-priced) lobbyists with well-developed political skills and contacts. Of course, money is more than an instrumental resource in the case of electioneering, where campaign contributions are the most common and effective means of action. As campaigns become more expensive, campaign contributions become more important to politicians. The ability to provide the money that politicians need to get elected gives those groups with great financial resources an increasingly important advantage.[20]

The importance of money goes a long way in explaining the relative dominance of corporate and business interests in Texas politics. These interests can obtain the needed money from their economic activities. They have a natural advantage over other groups because they do not have to depend on membership dues or conduct fundraisers to support their political activity. Their political money comes from the production and sale of the goods and services that constitute their businesses. Using a portion of the company profits to promote and defend political interests is viewed as part of the cost of doing business. It is an investment that can pay great dividends and is thus an effective, and often very profitable, business practice.

Business interests also enjoy other natural advantages. One is that engaging in business fosters and develops the same kind of organizational skills that are useful in interest group politics. Thus, business has a natural pool of organizational expertise and talent to draw on. Management is an important part of the success of any interest group, and management skills are central to the success of business operations. Interest organizations also engage in the marketing of ideas and perceptions. The marketing skills that business marshals for the sale of products and services can be transferred easily to the political arena.

Another natural advantage that business enjoys is general acceptance and legitimacy. Of course, some of this positive reputation is due to the public relations efforts of the businesses themselves and the groups that represent them. But in Texas, it is due mostly to a cultural distrust of government and a trust in private interests. Business interests find it easy to associate themselves with values such as free enterprise, self-reliance, and entrepreneurship, values that are central to the state's culture. As a result, they are more readily accepted than are noneconomic interests, which often call for regulation of various aspects of economic activity.

For all these reasons, business occupies what economist and political scientist Charles Lindblom called a "privileged position" in politics.[21] This observation is also true for national politics, but Texas provides a particularly friendly environment for interest group power and thus for the most numerous and powerful organized interests. Indeed, it has been argued that corporate interests, including oil drillers, bankers, and lawyers, effectively ran the state from the late 1930s to the 1960s.[22] Business and trade groups remain the most powerful interests in Texas today, although they are not as dominant as they once were because of the growth and diversification of the socioeconomic structure of the state. Growth and diversification have divided the economic interests of business and trade groups in more complicated ways than was once true and encouraged the development of a more diverse array of politically active groups. The result is a less united set of business interests in a much more competitive interest group system.

Although business remains powerful and uniquely favored in Texas politics, other organized interests have important resources of their own. If policymakers are faced with a choice between the equally intensely expressed preferences of business and ordinary consumers, they choose the option favored by consumers, despite the advantages enjoyed by business. Consumers represent many more votes than do business leaders. Issues are rarely so clearly drawn, however, and consumers do not usually form a coherent, unified, and organized political force. The power of numbers should not be underestimated, however. It is always politically dangerous to tack opposite the winds of popular opinion, and politicians are reluctant to do so consistently and over a long period of time. Even minimally organized interests with large numbers can be a potent electoral force, providing legions of campaign workers to staff phone banks and walk precincts. When a group has many members who care deeply about their cause and are well organized, they will be both respected and feared by politicians. The success of the NRA and the American Association of Retired People (AARP) has been built more fundamentally on this formula than on money.

Other groups are powerful beyond their numbers or financial resources because of the legitimacy attached by society to their status. Organizations of religious leaders, veterans, mothers (for example, MADD), and the elderly tend to enjoy greater acceptance based on their status in society. General sympathy and respect can help defend the interests of groups that are neither well financed nor well organized. Group leaders understand this fact and trade on it in their political efforts with decisionmakers.

Other groups gain similar legitimacy in the eyes of the public because of their credibility. This credibility may be based on unbiased scholarly expertise or on the perception that the group is altruistic or unselfish in its goals. Think tanks and policy institutes are examples of organizations that rely on a reputation for scholarly accuracy and expertise for their credibility. Their published reports would have little impact on the political process without the credibility that allows them to affect public opinion and the deliberations of decisionmakers. Public interest organizations rely on the perception that they do not expect personal material gain from the policies they advocate. Strategies often involve consciously casting the group's opponents, commonly business interests of various kinds, as illegitimate precisely because they are seeking private gain at public expense. It can be a powerful and compelling argument that allows, in some instances, much weaker and poorly financed organizations to compete successfully with established business interests.

Summary

Interest groups are central players in the policy-making process in Texas. They attempt to shape both the policy agenda and the way decisionmakers perceive the issues on the agenda. These groups try to influence the process in several ways, including lobbying legislators and bureaucratic agencies, influencing the election of officials, pursuing litigation in the courts, and mobilizing public opinion. The relative absence of factors that provide a counterweight to the influence of interest groups, like a consolidated political structure, a professional legislature, strong political parties, and a moralistic cultural environment supportive of political participation, means that interest groups have been an especially powerful influence in Texas politics.

Interest groups that enjoy access to the considerable financial resources required to pursue an effective, multipronged effort to influence political outcomes have been especially powerful in Texas. Business, professional, and trade organizations naturally enjoy these financial advantages. The dominance of the interest group system by business interests means that the extraordinary power of interest groups in Texas has had a generally conservative impact on public policy. Important and basic policy regarding taxation, expenditures, and the distribution of the regulatory benefits and burdens of government reflects the power of the well-organized economic interests.

Although the situation in Texas will not change soon, the future of interest group politics in Texas will certainly be different from what it was in the past. The economy of Texas is on the road to ever greater diversification. As it diversifies, a greater number of economic interests with more diverse political goals will appear. The interest group system will not likely be dominated by one or a few interests again; instead, it will be a more competitive system with far more opportunities for effective representation of less powerful interests.

The party system in Texas is also changing rapidly and is more competitive than it was in the past. If party competition develops and strengthens the party system, parties will play a larger role in the careers of public officials and better serve to balance and channel the influence of interest groups. The course of party development in Texas is still in doubt, and Texas may be headed into another period of one-party dominance. Parties may remain relatively weak counterbalances to the influence of interest groups, although perhaps they will be stronger than they were in the past.

Some trends have led to greater professionalization of the state government, and developments in this direction can be expected to continue. Legislators have provided themselves with more staff support and services, and they have improved their expense allowances, for example. Additional steps to strengthen the independence of legislators, especially in the form of campaign finance regulation, would also help to balance the influence of interest groups. All these changes tend to move Texas away from politics dominated by a few powerful interests, as was true in the past, and toward politics in which interest group activity is merely complementary to the political process, as it is in most other large states.

The key is greater participation and involvement by individual citizens like you. As we have seen, individuals can be important players in politics. They can serve as catalysts for change and help to galvanize opinion on issues. You can affect important political outcomes through involvement in interest group politics. Formation of new groups that represent segments of the population not represented or underrepresented in the interest group system is one important way democracy can be improved in Texas. Lending your active support to a group that helps defend your interests or promotes an issue you care about is also an important way that you can improve Texas politics. Active citizens like you, engaged in politics through a multitude of interest groups, makes the group system work the way it should and provides the policymaking process with a continual input of truly representative information and demands. As a diversified group system develops, decisionmakers are increasingly freed from the dominance of any one or a few interests. As in so many other cases, the quality of our democratic government in Texas is ultimately in your hands, and interest groups provide a useful and established avenue for improving it.

KEY TERMS

Interest group, p. 141
Public policy, p. 141
Free rider, p. 144
Collective benefits, p. 144
Right to work, p. 149

Lobbying, p. 152
Civil disobedience, p. 156
Political action committee (PAC), p. 159
Amicus curiae brief, p. 162

FOR FURTHER READING

Green, George Norris, *The Establishment in Texas Politics: The Primitive Years, 1938–1957* (Westport, Conn.: Greenwood Press, 1979).

Kinch, Sam, Jr., *Too Much Money Is Not Enough: Political Power and Big Money in Texas* (Austin, Tex.: Campaigns for People, 2000).

Mancur, Olson, *The Logic of Collective Action* (Cambridge, Mass.: Harvard University Press, 1971).

Rothenberg, Lawrence S., *Environmental Choices: Policy Responses to Green Demands* (Washington, D.C.: CQ Press, 2002).

Warren, Mark R., *Dry Bones Rattling: Community Building to Revitalize American Democracy* (Princeton, N.J.: Princeton University Press, 2001).

STUDY QUESTIONS

1. Who is Dr. Hector P. Garcia and how has he made a difference in Texas politics?

2. Differentiate how interest groups contribute to and pose a threat to democracy.

3. Identify four features that define interest groups.

4. Identify the major types of interest groups active in Texas politics.

5. Identify three reasons why business interests have a stake in government decisions.

CRITICAL THINKING QUESTIONS

1. Discuss why interest groups are particularly influential in Texas politics and, in light of these reasons, whether you think it a good idea to make the changes necessary to weaken them. Why do you argue as you do?

2. Based on your understanding of the various kinds of groups in Texas politics, discuss which groups you think are more powerful in Texas politics than others, and why.

3. Given the way we have defined interest groups, briefly discuss why some interests are more likely to organize into effective interest groups than are others. Provide some examples to illustrate your points.

4. Discuss the resources that a group would need to be able to use each of the strategies and techniques that interest groups employ to influence public policy.

5. Discuss specific ways that the inequalities in the power of interest groups might be reduced without destroying the positive aspects of interest group activity.

INTERNET RESOURCES

Many websites are available for Texas interest groups. Type the group's name or issue interest into a search engine, along with the word *Texas*, to find them. The following list contains a few common ones to get you started.

www.ccsi.com/~comcause/ The general informational website for Common Cause of Texas, an important public interest organization, includes links to the organization's position papers detailing the causes it regards as "common."

www.politicalindex.com/sect10.htm This general website lists the names of political activist groups on almost any issue. If you have a cause, you will find your organization here.

www.tsra.com/ This website provides information for the state affiliate of the National Rifle Association (NRA), a group for gun enthusiasts. The NRA is the leading opponent of legislative attempts to regulate the manufacture and possession of guns.

www.texascc.org/ The Texas Christian Coalition is a conservative grassroots organization promoting Christian involvement in politics. You can find information about them at this website.

www.tpj.org/ This website provides information about Texans for Public Justice, a nonpartisan, nonprofit policy and research organization that tracks the influence of money in politics.

www.tej.lawandorder.com/ Texans for Equal Justice is an advocacy organization for crime victims that seeks tougher treatment of criminals and greater respect for the rights of victims. This website provides more information about the group and the work that it does.

www.hadenough.net/ This website for the Million Mouse March, an organization for campaign finance reform in Texas, includes events and proposals.

www.aclutx.org/ This website provides information about the American Civil Liberties Union–Texas, an organization that defends the constitutionally guaranteed civil liberties for all citizens, largely through litigation.

Participation, Elections, and Parties

Growing up in Somerset, a small town southwest of San Antonio, Diana Martinez never believed that her future held a role in party politics. Her parents considered themselves Republicans, but politics was not an important topic of family conversation, and she developed no strong partisan identification of any kind. She was interested in being involved in the world around her, however, and that interest led her to activity in student groups in high school and later at the University of Texas. She wanted to make a difference and found working and leading such organizations a satisfying way to accomplish that goal. These experiences brought her into contact with people of differing cultures and beliefs, diversity that she found enlightening, enriching, and invigorating.

She chose to pursue a career in law and attended the University of Texas Law School. In law school, she remained active and found herself developing an interest in issues regarding minorities, women, and the environment. Political activity was an obvious outlet for these concerns, and she realized that she had come to think of herself as a Democrat.

After graduation from law school, she began a law practice in Corpus Christi that brought her into contact with others active in politics, some of whom were officeholders or people seeking office. Her interest in politics, she says, is energized and motivated by her personal friendships. She says that she "first got involved because I wanted to help someone get elected to a judgeship that I knew, cared about, and believed in." These personal connections make politics meaningful for her. Politics, with its shared sense of cause and purpose, is a great way to build and deepen such friendships.

Through her involvement in elections and campaigns, Martinez discovered that many people were detached from the political process. She felt, however, that this detachment reflected a lack of a sense of effectiveness and connectedness rather than cynicism about elections and the political process. It was a problem, though: so many did not vote that the outcome of elections failed to reflect the real interests of the people. The party organization offered a means through which the problem of participation could be addressed, as well as a vehicle to help elect people who would meet her other goals, including environmentally sensitive economic development and the rights of minorities and women. She ran for election as the chair of the Nueces County Democratic party in the hope of uniting the party so that it could be used to stimulate voter turnout and change the direction of government in the region.

She immediately began to attack what she saw as the most fundamental problem: low voter turnout. Her first step was to walk door to door through the precinct neighborhoods where turnout is lowest. A sense of personal connection was key to her involvement in politics, and she felt that such a sense of connectedness would activate others as well. She knows that it is up to the party leadership to make people feel connected to the political process and that meeting them one on one to talk about their concerns is a vital part of accomplishing that goal. She reports that she often hears that party officials have never spoken to the people in the neighborhoods before, but that the people are pleased to meet her and become acquainted. The conversations are not always about public or political matters either but are, she says, surprisingly personal. She hopes that because these citizens are detached and uninvolved rather than alienated and cynical, this personal connection will be rewarded when she, as party leader, asks them to make the effort to vote at election time.

Like young people of generations before her, Martinez has chosen to make a difference concerning the issues she cares about through a party organization. She knows that mobilizing people to elect officials who care about the same issues she does will result in what she believes is a better society. The political party provides Martinez with a vehicle to direct her considerable energy toward shaping a future in tune with her vision.[1]

Parties, Elections, and Democracy

Political party Any group, however loosely organized, seeking to elect government officeholders under a given label.

A **political party** can be defined as "any group, however loosely organized, seeking to elect government officeholders under a given label."[2] Political parties are distinguished from interest groups and other forms of political organization because they offer a slate of candidates competing to win election for public office. Because elections are such a prerequisite of parties and because many elections in

Texas do not officially have party participation, we begin our discussion of participation through parties by examining the nature and variety of elections contested in Texas.

ELECTIONS IN TEXAS

Two of the reasons given for the low voter turnout in Texas are the number of elections and the fact that they are scheduled at different times.[3] Basically six types of elections are held in Texas: general, primary (also referred to as direct primary), runoff, special elections (to fill vacancies), local government (municipal, school district, and special district), and referendums (both binding—recall, bond issue, constitutional amendment, city charter amendment—and nonbonding—a request for policy guidance from voters). Some argue that if elections were scheduled so that more were decided on fewer election days, turnout would be higher. Limiting the number of dates on which elections are held means fewer trips to the polls for people willing to participate once a year or so, but not every three or four months.[4] Two types of elections, primary and general elections, are particularly important for understanding the role of interest groups and political parties in Texas politics. Through these elections, those seeking to wield power in Texas politics by holding office can achieve their goals.

Primary Elections.   As a practical matter, to get elected to government office, one must first get on the general election ballot under the name of a major party. To do so, one must win in the **primary election** of one's party. The use of primaries to nominate candidates (instead of using conventions for those active in the party) was a reform introduced in the early 1900s; it was intended to make the nomination process more democratic and accountable to the people. Although it may have achieved some of its goals, it has also had unintended consequences that are less laudable.

Primary election An election in which voters choose a party's nominees for public office.

One such unintended consequence is that it has dramatically weakened party organization by drastically reducing the ability of leaders in the party to recruit candidates and create a balanced slate of candidates from various support groups of the party. It has also had the effect of giving interest groups another way to influence the political system. From the perspective of those who support strong, cohesive parties offering policies that all the party members will work to enact if party candidates are elected, the direct primary has been a disaster. Actual participation in primaries tends to be dominated by the higher-income members of the party and by people less informed on the issues but strongly influenced by mass media advertising paid for, to a significant extent, by interest groups. As a result, primary participants are typically a decidedly unrepresentative subset of the party.

Primary elections do not work the same way in all states. Two key distinctions involve whether a state's primary is open or closed and whether a state uses a runoff primary. The primary can be thought of as a kind of internal party election in which those who identify with the party can select the candidates they wish to

Closed primary A party nominating election (primary) in which only registered members of the party can participate.

Open primary A party nominating election (primary) in which any qualified voter, regardless of party affiliation, can participate.

Party identification A voter's sense of psychological attachment to a political party.

Runoff primary An election between the top two candidates when no candidate receives a majority in a primary election. A runoff ensures that the eventual nominee will have received a majority vote.

represent the party in the general election. Most states use a **closed primary,** which closely approximates this model of an internal party election. To be effective, a closed primary should be preceded by partisan registration; that is, when registering, the voter declares her- or himself to be a member of one of the parties or chooses to be an independent. Thus, a party's primary is closed to nonparty members.

An **open primary** allows voters, regardless of their partisan affiliation, to participate in selecting the party's candidates. The open primary makes the primary less of an internal party election and reduces the ability of party loyalists to influence the nominating process. People from the other party, independents, and people interested in just one candidate can influence the whole slate of candidates by participating. The more open the primary is, the more the influence of interest groups is likely to be felt.

Technically, Texas has a closed primary system because the two parties' primaries are held in separate places and a voter's card is stamped with the party name at the primary. These characteristics violate a fundamental attribute of open primaries: that the voter's partisan affiliation remains private and is never publicly displayed or made part of the public record. Although Texas's primary system is classified as closed, it functions in practice much like an open primary system. The party-identification stamp is intended primarily to prevent voter fraud, serving only to restrict the voters from voting in more than one party's primary. (Given the low voter turnout in Texas party primaries, it seems unlikely that voters would try to vote in a second one anyway.) Voters are not allowed to vote in more than one party primary in the same election in open systems either, a practice that occurs in the blanket primary used in only a few states.[5] Like an open system, voters in Texas are not asked to register with a **party identification**. Also like an open system, independents can participate in either party's primary. And because voters can choose on Election Day which party primary to vote in without having to change their registration, under the right circumstances, a party primary in Texas can attract a lot of voters who identify with the other party, just like an open system does.

Texas, like most other southern states, also uses a **runoff primary** election when no candidate receives a majority of the vote in the primary. In this system, the two candidates receiving the most votes in the primary face each other in a subsequent runoff election, ensuring that the eventual party nominee for an office will have been nominated by a majority vote of the party. This restriction is a second, and in practical terms more important, reason for stamping the voter's card with a partisan identification the day of the primary. The runoff primary is defended as contributing to the democratic norm of majority rule. Critics of the runoff primary argue that in contemporary politics, it prevents candidates representing ethnic or racial minority groups who might receive a plurality but not a majority from winning nominations. When the Anglo majority vote is split among several candidates and a minority candidate comes in first, that candidate must then run against an Anglo in a two-way race. To no one's surprise, the turnout in a runoff primary is low, the Anglos participate at a higher rate than anyone else participates, and the Anglo candidate often wins.[6]

Primaries and runoffs clearly weaken the ability of party leaders to create a balanced ticket that would appeal to the diverse population of Texas and thus weaken parties as democratic organizations in Texas politics.

General election
Statewide elections held on the first Tuesday after the first Monday of November of even-numbered years. These elections determine who will fill government offices.

General Elections.   **General elections** are statewide elections held on the first Tuesday after the first Monday of November of even-numbered years. These elections determine who will fill county, state, and national government offices. From the candidates nominated in the primaries, the voters of Texas are encouraged by the parties, the media, and various interest groups to make a choice. Turnout is highest in the general election in presidential election years. The general election two years later has a lower turnout and is often referred to as an *off-year election* or a *congressional election.* In Texas, the off-year election is also the gubernatorial election. The governor and several statewide officials are elected in years when voter turnout is not as high as it is in presidential election years. (We wonder what the election results would be if we elected our governors in the same election we choose our president.)

Regardless of how many candidates are contesting a particular office, the winner in the general election is the candidate who receives the most votes. Thus, if more than two candidates participate, the winner needs only a plurality, not a majority, of the votes cast. A runoff is not needed if no candidate receives a majority in the general election.

One of the unnoticed but essential differences between the general election and the primary election is that a politically relevant label does not serve as a cue to the voter in the primary. Nothing tells the voter who the incumbent is, who the most liberal or conservative candidate is, or whether that name you recognize is really the person you think it is. Voters for years nominated Jesse James to be state treasurer in the Democratic primary. And they nominated Warren G. Harding *after* he had died. Voters are often not well informed about less publicized contests farther down the ballot. As a result, they tend to vote with whatever cues are handy on the ballot. In Texas, every candidate voters see on the primary ballot is in the same party, so they have no politically relevant cues to help make a decision in these less publicized contests. Voters are left to rely on nonpolitical cues—for example, position on the ballot, name recognition, or name ethnicity—in making voting decisions in these so-called down-ballot contests. Under such circumstances, voter choices become somewhat arbitrary. Indeed, studies have shown that being listed first on the ballot in such down-ballot contests is worth as much as 7 percent of the vote, even though the order in which candidates are listed on the ballot is simply a matter of chance and has no political meaning.

Those who favor strong parties that have some influence over the selection of their candidates believe that political cues are the best kind. One of the virtues of the general election is that the voter has the important, politically relevant cue of party as a guide. In a primary, whether it is the Democratic or Republican primary, the only cue is the candidate's name. In the general election, the party label is present for every office to serve as a cue. Primaries are, in effect, nonpartisan elections because no party labels guide the voting decision. They are deeply flawed as instruments of democracy because of the absence of politically relevant cues to guide the voter.

Special Elections.

A special election is any election called at a time that does not conform to the regular election calendar. An unexpected vacancy in an elective office is a common reason for a special election. When a vacancy occurs in the state legislature or the Texas congressional delegation, the governor calls a special election to fill the seat. A **special election** is technically nonpartisan, although the parties often endorse and support specific candidates. To win the election and occupy the vacant seat, the candidate must receive a majority of the votes cast. If no one gets a majority, the top two candidates face each other in a runoff election.

A local **bond election,** in which local governments seek permission to borrow money by selling bonds for local projects, may be held concurrent with a city's election of officeholders but is often held at other times as a special election. Referendums and **recall** elections are also normally special elections.

Local Government Elections.

Local elections for city, school district, and special district officials, as well as occasional referendums, add to the list of opportunities for voters to participate. Local governments hold elections for city and school district board positions. State law provides that these elections can be held on one of four election dates: the third Saturday in January or May, the second Saturday in August, or the first Tuesday after the first Monday in November. Many local governments choose to hold their elections in odd-numbered years so that they do not occur amid the statewide primaries and general elections, although some voters find themselves facing local elections, primaries, and general elections in the same year.

Most local contests for public office are nonpartisan elections, which means that only candidates' names, not their party affiliations, appear on the ballot. Nonpartisan elections were introduced in local politics in an effort to avoid the corruption of local party machines that dominated the politics of many big cities in the second half of the nineteenth century and the first part of the twentieth. More recently, nonpartisan elections have been defended as helping to keep local politics local and insulated from state and national partisan controversies.

Removing the partisan guide and motivation may, however, contribute to the extremely low voter turnout that is typical in local elections. Party label is often the most important guide that voters have in making a choice, and those with less means and motivation to access other sources of information will be much less likely to feel compelled to vote. Some argue that this situation particularly discourages lower-income voters, who are likely to depend most heavily on party as a guide in voting. Because they are forbidden from having their labels on the ballot, parties are less likely to spend time motivating voters to participate. Parties are organizations that try to win elections. If they cannot win, they claim, why play?

Interest groups participate in local elections. Their goal is not to take over the government and run it but rather to influence it on a few specific decisions. Thus, in larger cities, candidates sometimes spend a lot of money provided by developers seeking lenient zoning and building regulations, bankers looking for the city's bond-issuing business, or other economic interest groups. One interesting and potentially important way that you can make a difference in the politics of your city might be to investigate the sources of the campaign money given to local candidates. You can determine whether nonpartisan elections come under the influence

---

Special election Any election called at a time that does not conform to the regular election calendar.

Bond election An election for the purpose of obtaining voter approval for a government's incurring debt by selling bonds to private investors.

Recall An electoral procedure for removing an elected official from office before the end of his or her specified term.

of interest groups in your community by looking into the campaign contribution reports of the candidates.

Referendum An election that allows voters to determine a policy issue directly.

Referendums.   A **referendum** is an election in which a decision is referred to the voters. In most referendums, the decision is binding; that is, if the voters approve of the proposition referred to them, then a government must act on it. Among the proposals referred to the voters are borrowing money by issuing bonds, amending a city charter or the state constitution, removing a public official, or approving a local law proposed either by **initiative** (citizen petition) or the local legislature (city council, school board, special district).

Initiative A procedure by which individuals can propose legislation by gathering a specified number of signatures and submitting a petition to a designated agency.

Nonbinding referendums are basically requests from public officials for advice on a matter of public concern. Because they cost money and because public opinion polls are cheaper and less trouble, nonbinding referendums are unusual.

Most referendums take place on one of the regularly scheduled election dates. However, some school districts and special districts attempt to schedule bond referendums at times when the voters opposed to them may not be paying attention. Thus, they schedule special elections in the hope that only their supporters will turn out to pass the bond issue. This tactic is one reason that legislation to eliminate it is introduced in nearly every Texas legislative session.

VOTING: MAKING A DIFFERENCE THROUGH ELECTIONS

To vote, an individual must satisfy four conditions: be eighteen years old, be an American citizen, be a resident of Texas, and be registered. Even those who lose their right to vote because they are convicted of a felony regain eligibility two years after the completion of their sentence. Clearly, these conditions are not difficult to meet, and the vast majority do so. So why do so many of those eligible to vote choose not to?

As we noted in Chapter 5, Texas engages in several electoral practices that tend to discourage voting. Many people are not engaged in the whole political process and don't see voting or any other type of participation as important or worth their while. Some may be disengaged due to cynicism or alienation, others because they calculate the likely impact of a single vote and come to the conclusion that it is unlikely to make a difference.

While it is hard to argue that any individual vote can turn the outcome of an election, it is equally hard to overestimate the importance of holding and exercising the right to vote. If anyone should doubt the importance of this right, they should consider the conscious and concerted efforts that have been made in the past to suppress the vote and disenfranchise some voters. In the months prior to the 2000 election, more than 50,000 black voters were purged from the rolls in Florida.* Like other southern states, Texas once had various obstacles that restricted **suffrage,** that is, the right to vote, for its citizens. In addition to a restrictive voter-registration system that required potential voters to register far in advance of elections and to

Suffrage The right to vote.

*See Chapter 1 in Greg Palast's book, *The Best Democracy Money Can Buy.* You can find more information about his book in the section called For Additional Reading at the end of this chapter.

Property qualification
A requirement that an individual must own property to vote.

White primary A type of nominating election used by the Democratic party in Texas to prohibit African Americans from voting to select the party's candidates for office. The practice was found to be an unconstitutional violation of the Fourteenth Amendment's equal protection clause by the Supreme Court in *Smith v. Allright* in 1944.

Poll tax A voting requirement stipulating the payment of a tax to become eligible to vote. Used as a device to discriminate against minority groups in voting, poll taxes were made unconstitutional by the Twenty-Fourth Amendment to the U.S. Constitution in 1964.

register again each year, devices such as **property qualifications,** residency requirements, a poll tax, and the **white primary** were used to discourage voting. Those that instituted and defended these practices clearly recognized the importance and the power of the vote, and they knew that who voted, in a collective sense, made a profound difference in political and social outcomes.

The Struggle for the Vote. Among the restrictive and discriminatory electoral devices used to limit the rights of some to vote in the South, two were especially important in Texas. The requirement of a payment of a tax to be eligible to vote, a **poll tax,** is worth noting because it symbolizes the class basis of Texas and southern politics. According to V. O. Key, a native Texan and an astute observer of Texas politics, the politics of the South has long been dominated by the planter class (which led poor whites into a devastating civil war to preserve slavery) and their heirs (the merchant bankers, railroad owners, and later the cattle barons and oil billionaires) who constitute the haves in a have and have-not class system.[7] Historian George Norris Green refers to these haves as the establishment.[8] The poll tax is one of several examples of the establishment's efforts to reduce participation by the have-nots and to keep power in the hands of those in the upper-income brackets. When instituted through amendment to the Texas Constitution in 1902, the tax was small by today's standards, ranging from $1.50 to $1.75, depending on the county. For the poor (Anglo, black, and Mexican American) of the era, however, it could easily constitute well over a day's pay. For sharecroppers operating almost without any cash income, it was nearly impossible to pay, which also allowed some land owners to manipulate the vote by paying the tax for their workers, but then directing them how to vote under the threat of job loss.

In addition to making the simple act of voting come at too high a cost for the poor, the burden of having to remember to pay it far in advance of the election constituted another barrier to participation. The poll tax in Texas was payable from October 1 of the preceding year to January 31 of the year in which it applied. This time frame was ideally suited to discourage poorer families from voting because it came during the months when they were concerned with saving and paying for Christmas. Faced with a choice between providing Christmas presents for the family or paying the poll tax for the privilege of voting, it is not hard to imagine which choice most poor families made. After the Twenty-Fourth Amendment ended the poll tax in federal elections in 1964, the practice continued for state and local elections in Texas until the Supreme Court struck it down two years later in *United States v. Texas,* 384 U.S. 155 (1966), as a violation of the equal protection clause of the Fourteenth Amendment.

As a disenfranchisement device, the poll tax discouraged poor whites as well as blacks and Hispanics from voting, but it allowed members of minority groups that paid the tax to vote. If minorities could be barred from participating in the primary elections of the then-dominant Democratic party, however, almost all blacks and Hispanics could be effectively disenfranchised. The disenfranchisement was effective because the dominance of the Democratic party was so complete. Its primary election determined who would ultimately hold office; the general election against token Republican opposition was merely a formality.

After legislation was passed to establish primary elections in Texas in 1903, minorities were discouraged from taking part in the Democratic primary by both informal means and by formal local party rules in many parts of the state. After a decision by the Supreme Court in 1921 (*Newberry v. U.S.*) suggested that the Court would view primaries as private party functions, the Texas legislature passed a law explicitly barring blacks from participation in Democratic primaries in 1923. Several years of legal wrangling ensued, involving the question of the state's role in the Democratic primary.[9] If it did have a role, the Court found that such an exclusion violated the equal protection clause of the U.S. Constitution. In *Grovey v. Townsend*, 295 U.S. 45 (1935) the Court found that the Democratic party was a private organization that could determine membership qualifications and therefore access to the party primary election. The practice was challenged again, however, by the Texas NAACP, and in *Smith v. Allwright*, 321 U.S. 45 (1944) the Supreme Court overturned its earlier decision. The membership of the Court had changed, and this time the Court ruled that various state laws made the primary election an integral part of the general-election process. Therefore, the parties are quasi-public institutions and the party leadership cannot constitutionally prohibit blacks, and by implication other minorities, from voting in the party primary.[10]

Gerrymandering Drawing the boundary lines of electoral districts in a manner that systematically advantages a particular political party, group, or candidate.

Though the legal and constitutional victories that brought an end to the poll tax and the white primary were significant, they did not end all attempts to limit minority participation. The use of other means, ranging from **gerrymandering** to literacy tests, to violence and intimidation, had been common since the end of Reconstruction and continue to be remarkably effective. Various formal and informal practices combined to keep minority registration and voting rates low in states such as Alabama, Louisiana, and Mississippi, and well below white rates in Texas too. Tolerance for the resistance of southern state legislatures to minority voting rights gave way when increasing agitation for such rights was met with overt violence. The murder of voting rights activists in Philadelphia, Mississippi, and the attack by state troopers on peaceful marchers as they crossed the Edmund Pettus Bridge in Selma, Alabama, gained national attention and helped galvanize support for a strong national voting rights law.

Voting Rights Act (VRA) A law passed by Congress in 1965 that made it illegal to interfere with anyone's right to vote. It focused on areas of the country with a history of voting discrimination and has been the principal legal vehicle for protecting and expanding minority voting rights.

The resulting legislation, the **Voting Rights Act (VRA)** of 1965, targeted jurisdictions where the disparity between white and minority registration was great and provided for the suspension of literacy tests and the appointment of federal examiners with the power to register qualified citizens to vote. It also required preclearance for any new voting practices in these jurisdictions from the District Court of the District of Columbia or the U.S. attorney general. The Supreme Court has upheld the constitutionality of the VRA and affirmed a broad range of voting practices for which preclearance was required. Any changes in electoral procedures are examined by the attorney general's office or the federal court before they take place to ensure that they will not adversely affect minority voters. Thus, the extensive protections of the voting rights of minorities currently practiced in election administration are the direct result of the VRA of 1965 and its extension to citizens whose primary language is not English in 1975. The VRA has dramatically reduced the disparity in registration between whites and minority groups, and many view it as the single most effective piece of civil rights legislation passed by Congress. As Box 7.1

BOX 7.1   Redistricting and Voting Rights

Every ten years, after the new census determines the population of each state and therefore the number of representatives to which each is entitled in the U.S. House of Representatives, the state legislature must establish the boundaries of congressional districts. Such a change is one example of an electoral procedure that must be examined by the attorney general's office or a U.S. federal court to ensure that it will not adversely affect minorities before it can go into effect. Indeed, after losing a hard-fought political battle to prevent a congressional redistricting plan favorable to Republicans, Democrats were hoping that the plan would fail the Voting Rights Act test.

The Democrats argue that by giving Republicans a 22–10 or 23–9 majority in the state congressional delegation, the Republican plan disenfranchises minority voters. In the view of Democrats, the plan violates the federal Voting Rights Act (VRA) in at least three ways. First, it makes a previously Hispanic district into a nonminority district by splitting Webb County, in which Laredo is located, and placing tens of thousands of South Texans living in South Texas along the Mexican border into a separate district. Second, the plan destroys the minority district held by Martin Frost in the Dallas area, dividing it five ways. Third, the plan creates an odd shaped district (District 25) that runs from Travis County and includes parts of Austin, all the way to the Mexican border. The Democrats argue that the plan is an example of the classic crack-and-pack gerrymandering strategy, that it cracks minorities in the first two cases and packs them in the third, resulting in a dilution of minority voting power. The plan results in minorities having a majority in one less district—a total of ten rather than eleven argue the Democrats— a clear violation of the VRA. Republicans point to a new Latino district and other minority districts around Houston, and counter that the map actually increases minority representation.

Under Attorney General John Ashcroft, the Justice Department has precleared every redistricting plan presented to it for review under the VRA. As a result, Democrats and associated groups placed most of their hope for overturning the Republican plan in the federal courts. By the time the Justice Department approved the Republican plan as expected, several suits had been filed in federal court in Texas. These cases were consolidated and heard before a special three-judge panel. The lawyers for the state (in favor of the plan) did not base their argument on the contention that the plan did not dilute minority voting strength, but instead that such a result is legal if the purpose of the plan is to produce partisan advantage rather than racial discrimination. The federal judges agreed, clearing the way for the Republican plan to be used in the 2004 elections.

Supporters of the Voting Rights Act fear that, if this decision is allowed to stand, the VRA will lose much of its meaning and take a back seat to the interests of partisan politics. Black and Hispanic voters across the country

(continued)

BOX 7.1   Redistricting and Voting Rights (Cont'd)

could be split among oddly shaped districts and packed into a few minority-dominated ones as long as it serves the interests of the Republican party. The Texas case has been decided in favor of the new map, but cases from other states challenging the legality and constitutionality of partisan gerrymandering are currently pending action by the Supreme Court.

---

suggests, the VRA remains central to political struggles involving issues of partisan advantage and minority representation right up to the present.

Voting: The Continuing Struggle.   Exercising the right to vote is now quite easy for all Texans. All a Texas citizen needs to do is go to the appropriate county office (county tax assessor in some counties, county elections administrator in others) and fill out an application. Applications are also available in other locations, including shopping malls and other public places. As a result of the national motor-voter law, you can also register (in fact, you will be asked) when applying for or renewing your driver's license. In 1991, the Texas Legislature also provided for early voting, which allows you to vote at various sites at your convenience in the weeks prior to Election Day. More and more voters are taking advantage of this opportunity each election.

One might expect, given the relative ease of the process of voting, that a large proportion of those eligible would vote in Texas. Nothing could be further from the truth. The United States has one of the lowest electoral participation rates among the world's industrial democracies, and Texas has one of the lowest participation rates in the United States. Although participation rates for Texas and other southern states are closer to the national average than they were before the elimination of discriminatory electoral practices, Texas continues to rank near the bottom of the fifty states in the proportion of voting-age citizens casting ballots and, with the exception of Florida, at the bottom among the other large states in the Union.

TEXAS ELECTIONS AND YOU

People do not vote in Texas for many reasons. To list them all would be more discouraging than informative. At this point, it seems worth noting a few ways that you can improve the situation. In Chapter 5, we discussed conditions you can influence to increase the participation of others. Keeping those conditions in mind, you might consider engaging in several easy activities: helping people register, helping to get out the vote, providing or organizing transportation to the polls on Election Day, and even helping with election administration. These activities fall under the broader category of electioneering. Registering people to vote is easier than you might think. It is relatively easy to become a deputy voting registrar, but you do not have to be deputized to go door to door with registration forms, wait for them to be filled out, and then deliver them to the appropriate county office. Of course, if you don't want to wait to make sure that they are filled out properly, you can distribute them and hope for the best. You can also help to get out the vote (GOTV). This activity is both easier and more effective than it once was thanks to early voting. With this system, GOTV efforts can be conducted over a period of weeks rather than just on Election Day. You can do it one block or nursing home or homeless shelter at a time, during the early voting period. Along with a pep talk encouraging voting, you either provide transportation or clarify directions on how to get to the polls. In general elections, you would probably volunteer in conjunction with the party of your choice; in other elections, you can work with the volunteers campaigning for a particular candidate.

Election Administration.   The electoral process is regulated by state law, but the actual administration of elections is in the hands of county officials and local party leaders and, of course, you. Plenty of opportunities are available for you to help with election administration because much work must be done in each of the voting precincts. The precinct is the basic electoral unit, and Texas has about 6,600 of these relatively small geographical divisions. Each has a single polling place at which all qualified residents of the precinct (unless they cast early or absentee ballots) will vote. People are needed to work at the polls in each precinct.

In primary elections, the Democratic and Republican county chairs, with the approval of the party executive committees, appoint a presiding judge to run the election in each precinct. They employ several clerks to assist in the primary election. In most cases, a willingness to serve is the only qualification for such positions.

The county government administers the general election more directly. The county commissioners' courts appoint the general election judge to oversee the November election from a list supplied by the county clerk. Partisan considerations also play an important role in the selection of election judges and election clerks for the general election. In addition, parties and candidates can place poll-watchers in whatever precincts they desire.

Helping with election administration by serving as an election clerk or a poll-watcher is vital to ensuring against election fraud. The most common fraud is not the casting of ballots by unqualified voters; it is the denial of the vote to people who are qualified but who will not hold up the line or challenge an authority figure. Out of ignorance, inattention, or laziness, many election clerks and judges fail to use the forms in their packet, called affidavits, that a person can sign if she or he fails to bring a voter card or other form of identification to the polls. If you are at the poll, you can see to it that these forms are used and that the procedure is much more inclusive and democratic. As a poll-watcher, you can make a difference.

Election Campaigns.   Another way that party involvement can lead to broader and more meaningful political participation is through involvement in election campaigns. Of course, parties are active in supporting candidates for statewide and county offices, and they are always seeking volunteers to help their candidates.

What's the worst that can happen? The person who answers hangs up. More often than not, potential voters get information and some become real voters because of your phone call.

Most local elections are nonpartisan, and thus personal candidate organizations seek and organize volunteers for their candidacies. Even partisan elections have become increasingly candidate-centered in recent years. Candidates must create a personal campaign organization to contest the primary election and win the party primary for the office they are seeking. When they win the nomination, they get the help of the party organization in the general election, but they keep their own campaign organization at the center of their campaign. If you are interested in helping a particular candidate and not helping to promote a broader party agenda, plenty of opportunities are available to you.

Campaigns with fewer funds and those for local and regional offices rely on traditional retail, or person-to-person, efforts that in turn rely on volunteers. Even well-financed statewide campaigns need the personal contact that only retail politics can provide. Traditional campaigns are labor-intensive endeavors that can provide a lot of opportunity for hard work, forming strong friendships, and learning about others. Campaign activity may involve preparing mass mailings, staffing phone banks, assembling and distributing signs, and providing transportation on Election Day. Campaigns must also be organized, with someone responsible at the helm to make sure that the information the volunteers gather is used to advantage, bills are paid, and volunteers show up when and where they are needed and that they are fed. Folding literature, stuffing envelopes, licking labels, listening to rude prospective voters on the telephone, and traveling miles putting out yard signs in the rain are all part of the experience. It can be great fun because you can form close and lasting friendships. As you gain experience, you will acquire more responsibility, perhaps making sure that supporters identified by the phone banks are called back on Election Day and that those who were undecided receive one of those carefully stuffed envelopes in the mail.

Contacting potential voters and helping to get out the vote may not seem like important roles, but campaigns do influence votes and affect outcomes, especially in close elections. Campaigns are not designed primarily to change the minds of those who have already decided or have a strong partisan commitment. They are intended to mobilize those who are predisposed to vote for the campaign's candidate and persuade those who are genuinely undecided. Many races are close enough that turnout and undecided voters are crucial and decisive factors in who wins and loses. A candidate must thoughtfully plan campaign strategy, carefully organize to implement the plan, and then work hard throughout the election season to make it pay off.

Different strategies and tactics are appropriate at different levels of election, and the means of campaigning has and will continue to change with advances in technology, but campaigning is certainly a permanent part of our democratic political landscape. Should you find the process exhilarating and rewarding, it can be a significant way to make a difference in politics; with a little training, it can even be the start of a career. Campaigning is professionalizing, especially for state-level campaigns but also at regional and local-level elections. Campaign consultant businesses provide various services, including polling and analysis, media consultation, telephone canvassing, legal advice, and general organizational management. Indeed, a prospective candidate can hire all the expertise needed to launch a complete and thoroughly professional campaign effort. Your training in social science, statistical analysis, law, media, or management could bring you a fulfilling position in a campaign consulting organization. Making a difference can be a full-time occupation if you choose.

Political Parties in Texas

In theory, political parties perform several important functions necessary to the operation of democracy and the expression of the public will through elections. The functions found on the lists of most scholars in this area include recruiting candidates and volunteer activists, organizing campaigns, mobilizing voters, coalition-building, developing a platform of issues on which the candidates run, organizing the government after electoral victory to deliver on the platform, and organizing the loyal opposition after electoral defeat to serve as watchdog on the victors and to offer alternative programs and policies in preparation for the next election.

A party that can perform most of these functions is a strong one. Texas parties traditionally have been weak, and weak parties are one important reason that voter turnout is so low in the state. A brief history of political parties in Texas will provide a context for considering some reforms that might improve the situation.

DEVELOPMENT OF POLITICAL PARTIES IN TEXAS

A prominent characteristic of political parties in the United States is their decentralized structure. Because they are pragmatic organizations, primarily interested in winning elections, and because elections in the United States occur entirely at the state and local levels, the center of party organization has been at the state rather than at the national level. Indeed, the major parties in the United States can be thought of as loose coalitions of state parties. Even the national conventions that meet for a few days every four years to nominate presidential candidates and ratify a national party platform are composed of delegations sent from the largely independent state parties. State parties are not merely branches of a unified national organization; they have a distinct historical development and unique character. Texas parties are no exception.

Texas in the One-Party South.   One important way that party systems have varied from state to state is in the level of interparty competition. If two or more political parties are important for promoting and effecting meaningful democratic choice in elections, the quality of democracy in Texas for much of its history could be called questionable. Texas has traditionally been ranked as one of the states with the least amount of party competition. Although that description is no longer the case today, it is impossible to understand political parties in Texas without examining the state's history of one-party dominance.

During the period of the Republic of Texas, party activity was almost nonexistent. Political competition was largely between those who were for and those who were against Sam Houston. Democrats began to organize seriously in the 1850s. The Democratic party controlled the state through the Civil War, but with Union forces occupying the state during Reconstruction, the Republicans became the dominant party. Republican votes came from newly enfranchised blacks and from the many Anglos (some Republicans and some Unionist Democrats) who had voted against secession in the first place. Republican Edmund Davis, a former Union soldier, was elected governor in 1869.[11]

Facing near-rebellion and continued violence against African Americans by resentful Confederate veterans and Confederate sympathizers, Davis used the militia and an undermanned police force as best he could. Memories of the abuses, real and imagined, suffered under Davis and the Republicans during his one term proved to be fatal to the fortunes of the Republican party. Associated with the freeing of slaves and the Yankee occupation, the Republican party almost disappeared after Davis's defeat in the gubernatorial election of 1873. Except for a serious challenge from the farmers and blue-collar workers of the Populist party in the 1890s, the Democrats maintained one-party dominance in Texas and the rest of the southern states until the 1950s.

One-party dominance had great significance for the nature of Texas politics.

With little competition between two or more parties, party organization tends to put little effort into mobilizing the working class and the have-nots. Without an external threat to the party as an organization, it need not strengthen its organizational structure and services. Indeed, according to V. O. Key, one-party politics really dissolves in significant ways into no-party politics.[12] When all serious candidates share the same party organization, the organization itself becomes politically meaningless.

This situation has two important implications for politics. First, the dominant party becomes merely a shell within which other actors—the interest group system and the Establishment that dominates that system—engage in meaningful political conflict and wield power. As we discussed in Chapter 6, the extraordinary historical power of economic interest groups in Texas is explained in part by the weakness of countervailing political actors such as party organizations. Thus, one-party dominance helps to promote the tradition of influence by the state's establishment.[13]

Second, the weak party organizations that result from one-party dominance also reduce the democratic character of the political process. Without two-party competition, a mechanism does not exist to provide a clear and simple guide to structure the voter's choice. Instead, various political candidates with opposing philosophies and who take opposing views on issues share the same party label, rendering that label meaningless as a guide for voter choice. No mechanism is in place to propose alternative political philosophies or programs of government action and thus differentiate candidates. Nor is there a structure to coordinate the actions of officeholders and provide them with a system of political support. In short, the functions that parties contribute to the democratic process are done less effectively or not at all.

One-party dominance does not imply that political divisions or disagreements did not exist in Texas politics. In the absence of well-defined parties vying for voter support, politics tended to be more fluid and disorderly. New divisions between and associations among voters emerged from election to election, depending on the specific circumstances surrounding the election and the personalities involved. Texas politics was highly fragmented and personalistic, with political contests often driven by support for and opposition to flamboyant personalities, such as James E. "Pa" and Miriam "Ma" Ferguson, and W. Lee "Pappy, Pass the Biscuits" O'Daniel. Despite their folksy labels, these politicians were wealthy members of the upper class. "Pa" Ferguson was a banker and "Pappy" O'Daniel a wealthy flour mill owner.[14]

The Great Depression of the 1930s had a considerable impact on Texas politics and helped move the state toward a two-party system. The economic issues raised by the depression and President Roosevelt's New Deal served as a catalyst for the formation of fairly distinct and stable factions along ideological lines within the Democratic party. Personalities were still important, but now the class dimension became clearer. The conservative establishment hated the idea of Texas workers exercising their right to bargain collectively, were hostile to civil rights, and wanted the tax burdens to remain heavy for the poor and light for the rich. The liberals took the opposite positions. They had to deal with accusations of being un-American and Marxist, however, labels that were taken much more seriously then than they are now.

Alignment along ideological lines had progressed far enough by the late 1940s for V. O. Key to observe that "the terms 'liberal' and 'conservative' have real meaning in the Democratic politics of Texas."[15] These factions, or subgroups within the party, played the role of informal parties to some extent in contesting the Democratic party primary elections for many years after the mid-1930s.

The conservative faction, the establishment, was always the dominant group, finding its identity originally in its dissatisfaction with the liberalism of the national Democratic party's New Deal economic policies and support for an active role for government in promoting civil rights. Conservative Democrats in Texas largely controlled state and local elections from the mid-1930s to the late 1970s, electing nearly all the governors, most of the state's congressional seats, and majorities in both houses of the Texas Legislature during the period. They maintained the state party's independence from the national organization, refusing to support the Democratic party's nominee for president on several occasions.

Several reasons explain the success of the establishment. One is simply that Texas has historically been a socially and economically conservative state, with the lower classes conditioned to defer to the political leadership of their so-called betters. The second reason is that the conservative constituency contains not just the majority of voters—the few regular people who vote—but also the state's economic elite and its considerable power and resources. The conservative faction of the Democratic party, until they became Republicans, was traditionally the home of the state's oil and gas, insurance, banking, ranching and agribusiness, and other corporate interests. The affluent tend to vote in primaries much more often than the general population does, and their financial contributions to these intraparty campaigns also have great impact.

The liberal Democratic faction in the Texas Democratic party is most easily identified as those who have supported the national party presidential ticket and its presidential candidates since the New Deal. Blue-collar workers in and outside unions, the union organizations, African Americans, Mexican Americans, trial lawyers, teachers and other intellectuals, and some small businesspeople and small farmers are the most common representatives of the liberal faction. Liberal Democrats have been successful in elections infrequently and usually for a relatively short period. Notable examples include Ralph Yarborough, who served in the U.S. Senate from 1957 to 1971, and Ann Richards, who was elected governor in 1990 for a single term.

The strength of the liberal faction is increasing within the party, however, and liberals have had more success in capturing party nominations in recent years. This trend is partly due to the growth of the liberal faction but mostly due to the loss of conservative voters and the establishment elite to the Republicans. Indeed, the most recent development in Texas party politics is the rise of the Republican party to challenge the Democratic party in general elections. While liberals have been more successful in winning the nomination of their party, the Democratic party nomination is no longer the sure ticket to election that it once was. Instead, Democrats face a difficult struggle to win office because to do so, they must overcome the conservative establishment and voting bloc, whose considerable resources and votes now go for conservative Republican candidates in the general election, just as they went to conservative Democrats in the past.

The Rise of the Republicans.   The Texas Republican party enjoyed phenomenal electoral success in the 1990s. In 1992, Kay Bailey Hutchison's election to the Senate gave the Republican party control of both the state's Senate seats for the first time since Reconstruction. In 1994, George W. Bush wrested the governor's office from incumbent Democrat Ann Richards. In 1996, Texas was one of the most supportive states in the nation for the Republican presidential nominee, and the party gained a majority of seats in the state Senate. The Republican party was also growing significantly stronger at the grassroots. Republican primaries were held in all 254 Texas counties in 1996, and more voters took part in the Republican primary statewide than in the Democratic primary—both events were historical firsts. In 1998, the party capped its most successful decade of the modern era by winning every statewide election contested. It also reelected a U.S. senator, came within three seats of a majority of the Texas delegation to the U.S. House of Representatives, retained its majority in the Texas Senate, and came within a few seats of a majority in the Texas House.

The roots of this resurgence can be traced back to the 1940s, when the conservative Texas Democratic party and its faithful became increasingly disquieted by the direction of the national party under presidents Roosevelt and Truman.[16] Matters first came to a head in 1948, when President Truman pushed the Democratic party toward a strong civil rights plank in the Democratic national platform. Several state delegations to the Democratic National Convention from the still racially segregated South, including Texas, found the civil rights provisions so objectionable that they walked out of the convention and supported the third-party Dixiecrat candidate, Strom Thurmond of South Carolina.

Four years later, the presidential candidacy of Republican Dwight D. Eisenhower, a highly respected World War II military leader, drew the open support of Texas's Democratic governor, Allan Shivers. Many Texas Democrats followed the governor's lead, voting for the Republican for president and for Democrats in state and local races. Eisenhower carried Texas in 1952 and again in 1956 with the help of these ticket-splitting Democrats, whom political scientists called presidential Republicans. Conservative Democrats became comfortable voting for the more conservative Republican presidential candidates, making Texas a normally Republican state in presidential politics. Presidential Republicans continued to identify with the Democratic party, however, and helped the conservative faction to continue its domination of the Democratic primary elections.

A major milestone in the modern resuscitation of the Republican party came when John Tower, a Republican, was elected to the U.S. Senate in 1961. This early foothold for the Republicans was gained not because of the party's strength at the time but because of the circumstances of the special elections that Texas uses for filling vacant seats. As you recall, these elections are nonpartisan and open to anyone willing to file for election. If no one gets a majority, the top two candidates then face each other to determine who will occupy the office. In the 1961 special election to fill the seat vacated by Lyndon Johnson when he became vice president, seventy-one candidates were on the ballot. The vast majority of these candidates were Democrats, and the divided Democratic vote allowed the Republican Tower to make it into the runoff election against Democrat William Blakley. Blakley was so conservative, however, that most liberal Democrats could not support him and instead helped the Republican win a surprise victory. It was a watershed event, the first statewide office won by a Republican in Texas since Reconstruction. It also marked a significant step in the revival of the Republican party because the Republicans have held the seat ever since.

While they were able to make some modest gains in regional races, electing some members of the U.S. House of Representatives and capturing a few seats in the Texas Legislature, the Republican party had no further statewide success for nearly two decades. In 1978, in what is widely regarded as the party's most significant breakthrough in Texas politics, Republican Bill Clements surprised Democrat John Hill in the race for governor. A representative of the party's liberal faction, Hill had defeated the conservative incumbent Dolph Briscoe in the Democratic primary for the party's gubernatorial nomination. Just as they had done earlier in presidential elections, many conservative Democrats abandoned their party's more liberal nominee for the more conservative Republican candidate, allowing Clements to win by less than 1 percent and become the first Republican elected governor since Reconstruction. Republicans have been competitive in the gubernatorial race ever since, trading victories with the Democrats through the 1980s and winning three times in a row between 1994 and 2002.

By 1980, when John Connally sought the Republican presidential nomination that eventually went to Ronald Reagan, the establishment in Texas was clearly in the process of switching parties. Connally had been a protégé of President Lyndon Baines Johnson and a three-time Democratic governor of Texas. By the 1990s, the process was more or less complete.[17] Wealthy oil producers, cattle barons, corporate executives, and even prominent Baptist preachers who had been Democrats were now proud to call themselves Republicans.

MODERN PARTY COMPETITION IN TEXAS

Texas has become, like most other megastates, a competitive two-party state, with two active parties offering the electorate a choice (see Boxes 7.2 and 7.3). Evidence for competitive two-party politics is clear in election outcomes, participation in primaries, and partisan identification.

Opinion polls indicate that the shift toward two-party politics is not limited to voting behavior but is also reflected in the more fundamental psychological attachment known as party identification. Identification with the Republican party went up from

BOX 7.2 The 2002 Texas Democratic Party Platform Core Beliefs

We believe:

1. In equal opportunity for all Texans to achieve and succeed in their efforts to get a quality education, find a good job, buy a home, provide health care for their families, and exercise their right to vote and participate in our democratic system.

2. In quality public education that puts our tax dollars to work in the classroom to give all Texans the opportunity to reach their potential.

3. In rewarding honest hard work with a livable wage and a tax system that is fair to all taxpayers.

4. In providing economic security for all hardworking Texans through better access to child care, quality health care, affordable insurance, prescription drug coverage, and quality health care for every Texas child.

5. In neighborhoods and homes made safer and more secure through the cooperative efforts of involved citizens and law enforcement officers equipped with the best available technologies to identify and strictly punish dangerous criminals and protect the innocent.

6. In preserving our precious natural resources, clean air and water, and our quality of life.

7. In a strong and secure United States—militarily, morally, economically, and diplomatically.

8. In providing both the basic infrastructure and advanced technology required to support the needs of working families and businesses in an uncertain economy—especially small businesses.

9. In the right of all employees, public and private, to organize, collect dues, designate their income voluntarily to organizations and agencies of their choice, and to negotiate freely with their employers through their elected agents.

10. In freedom from government interference in our private lives and personal decisions and full protection of civil and human rights.

11. In separation of Church and State to preserve the freedom to pursue our beliefs.

12. In the benefits derived from the individual strengths of our diverse population.

Source: Texas Democratic party website at www.txdemocrats.org/.

BOX 7.3   The 2002 Texas Republican Party Platform Core Beliefs

1. We respect and cherish the Declaration of Independence, the Constitution, and our Founders' intent to restrict the power of the federal government over the states and the people. We believe internal self-government is the best government, balanced by limited civil government, which provides for the people those things which cannot be achieved individually.

2. We believe that human life is sacred because each person is created in the image of God, that life begins at the moment of conception and ends at the point of natural death, and that all innocent human life must be protected.

3. We believe that good government is based on the individual and that each person's ability, dignity, freedom, and responsibility must be honored and recognized. We believe that, while equal opportunity is a right and a privilege, equal outcome is not. We insist that no one's rights are negotiable and that individual freedom demands personal responsibility.

4. We believe that government spending is out of control and needs to be reduced. We support fundamental, immediate tax reform that is simple, fair, and fully disclosed.

5. We believe that traditional marriage is a legal and moral commitment between a man and a woman. We recognize that the family is the foundational unit of a healthy society and consists of those related by blood, marriage, or adoption. The family is responsible for its own welfare, education, moral training, conduct, and property.

6. We believe that a well-educated population is fundamental to the continued success of our Republic; and that parents have the right, as well as the duty, to direct their children's education and to have the choice among public, private, and religious schools. Competition improves education, with no child being left behind.

7. We believe that the future of our country depends upon a strong and vibrant private sector unencumbered by excessive government regulation.

8. We believe that a strong America ensures a free America. While we recognize that our nation is a major participant in the global community, we must also vigilantly protect the sovereignty of the United States. Freedom is never free, and we honor all those who have served our nation to protect our liberty.

9. We believe all Americans have the right to be safe in their homes, on their streets, and in their communities. We support enforcement of the laws through the Courts imposing swift and sure justice with stiff penalties, truth in sentencing, and respecting the rights of law-abiding citizens.

BOX 7.3   The 2002 Texas Republican Party Platform Core Beliefs (Cont'd)

10. We believe that personal and public integrity is the cornerstone of a stable and lasting society and it is the key to preserving the freedoms for which our founders pledged their "lives, fortunes, and sacred honor."

Source: Republican party of Texas website at www.texasgop.org/.

---

less than 10 percent in the early 1960s to about 30 percent by the 1990s. During the same period, those who identified with the Democratic party dropped from about 65 percent to around 30 percent. As was true in the nation as a whole, the number of people who did not identify with either party increased significantly during this period, from around 15 percent to about 30 percent of the potential voters. Party identification with the two major parties was at rough parity in the 1990s, so independents have held the balance of power in recent elections. Recent polls suggest that the Republican party is continuing to gain identifiers, however, which bodes well for the competitive position of the party in the coming years.[18] Although the Republicans hold a monopoly on statewide offices in Texas, the Democrats are still quite competitive at the local level, and political scientists continue to rank Texas among the two-party competitive states, along with other large, urbanized, and industrialized states such as California, Florida, New York, Illinois, Ohio, Michigan, and Pennsylvania.[19]

It is also clear, however, that the establishment has rapidly consolidated power in the Republican party and is building it toward dominance. Megastates like California and New York, while considered two-party competitive, are dependably Democratic in voting majorities, and Texas is becoming dependably Republican. Going into the 2004 elections, the Republicans can look back on four consecutive elections in which all statewide Republican candidates have won. After winning control of the Texas Senate in 1996, Republicans have maintained control of that body, building their majority to seven seats (19–12) in 2002, and maintaining that margin in 2004. The 2002 elections also brought the party control of the Texas House of Representatives (88–62) for the first time since Reconstruction. The 2004 state House elections lent some evidence to the Democrats continuing competitiveness as they picked up one seat from the Republicans (the first gain for the party in 32 years) despite the landslide 61-38 margin in the state for President Bush. Republicans set out to do something about that in 2004 (see Box 7.4), and the plan worked, giving their party six additional seats in the Texas congressional delegation, and a 21-11 advantage.

The fact that party competition in Texas is becoming dominated by the Republican Party is indicated not just by the statewide outcome but by the margins of the recent Republican victories. In 2002, despite a lackluster record and mediocre approval ratings, Republican Governor Rick Perry garnered 57.8 percent of the vote, while the Democratic challenger Tony Sanchez mustered just under 40 percent. Republican John Cornyn defeated Democrat Ron Kirk for the U.S. Senate seat vacated by retiring Republican Senator Phil Gramm by 12 percentage points. The Republican candidates won their races for comptroller of public accounts,

BOX 7.4   Redistricting at All Costs

The issue of redistricting, like none other, lays bare base partisan interests. Every ten years, after the new census determines the population of each state and therefore the number of representatives to which each is entitled in the U.S. House of Representatives, the Texas Legislature must establish the boundaries of congressional districts. Always a contentious process in a winner-take-all election system like ours, where even small alterations in the boundaries can make the difference between victory and defeat, redistricting brought new heights of public squabbling between the parties in the wake of the 2000 census in Texas.

The story begins when the Texas Legislature, left with Republicans in control of the Senate and Democrats in control of the House, failed to agree on a new district map for representatives to the U.S. Congress during the 2001 session. As a result, a panel of three federal judges drew a map prior to the 2002 elections. Normally, this solution might have settled the matter until 2010. This map brought more Republicans to Congress from Texas in the 2002 election (fifteen of the thirty-two Texas seats in the U.S. House), and that same election brought a larger majority of Republicans to the state Senate and, for the first time, a substantial majority to the state House of Representatives. In control of both bodies, the Republicans had an historic opportunity to change the balance of party power in the state's congressional delegation, and they were not about to wait until 2010 to exercise it.

Taking the unusual step of mid-decade redistricting (not illegal but by tradition not done for more than 100 years) the Republican-controlled legislature offered a new U.S. Congressional district map in the last weeks of the regular 2003 session. No longer having the votes to defeat the measure, fifty-one House Democrats boycotted a vote on the issue, fleeing to Ardmore, Oklahoma, for several days in May to deny the Texas House the quorum needed to vote. Texans were treated to the spectacle of Speaker Tom Craddick using the Department of Public Safety to try and round up the missing legislators, and Tom DeLay was accused of enlisting the services of the Department of Homeland Security in the search. Despite their efforts, the fifty-one Democrats stayed away until an internal House deadline passed; the issue was killed for the regular session.

Undaunted, Governor Rick Perry then called a thirty-day special session of the Texas Legislature to deal with the issue. One Republican joined eleven Democrats to block the Senate from considering a new map under the rule and tradition that eleven senators can prevent a bill from being debated. Governor Perry then called a second special session, during which Republicans again changed the rules of the game, jettisoning the tradition that allowed the group of senators to block the measure in the first session. This move prompted the eleven Senate Democrats to escape to Albuquerque, New Mexico, to deny the Senate a quorum and block action on the measure.

BOX 7.4   Redistricting at All Costs (Cont'd)

The senators were gone for forty-five days, during which time Governor Perry called yet a third special session. Finally, one of the eleven split with the others and returned, allowing the legislature to vote.

At every pivotal turn, U.S. House Majority Leader Tom DeLay, a Republican from Sugar Land, was in Austin to ensure that state Republican leaders pressed ahead. DeLay's role in the process was unusually overt and heavy-handed, revealing the partisan objectives of the process in several instances. Several less radical redistricting plans considered by the Republicans were rejected when they didn't meet DeLay's apparent objective of removing several specific Democratic representatives—including Austin's Lloyd Doggett, Waco's Chet Edwards, and Dallas's Martin Frost. Indeed, a memo from Jim Ellis, DeLay's lobbyist in Austin for this process, surfaced and caused some embarrassment; it stated that any plan that didn't get those three Democrats out of Congress was not acceptable.[20] The Republican leadership ultimately cooperated in the enterprise, despite this embarrassing revelation about motivation.

The map DeLay insisted upon and ultimately got (see Figure 7.1) reflects many of the more obvious signs of partisan gerrymandering. Many districts are oddly shaped, for example, running from Central Austin to the Rio Grande Valley, or from the Oklahoma state line to south of Fort Worth. It also represents a radical change from previous maps, moving about half of the state's population into a different district to achieve a predicted six- or seven-seat increase in Republican representation. Such a gain, if realized, would have given the GOP nearly 70 percent of the state's congressional seats, far more than their likely share of the popular vote. Even a Republican senator that voted for the final map to help Bush with more Republicans in Congress questioned whether it was "too greedy."[21] Too greedy or not, Mr. DeLay's plan did gain the Republicans six seats in 2004 and ousted one of his Democratic targets—Martin Frost—as well as three other Democratic incumbents.

Both sides sought to legitimize their positions in terms of democratic fairness. Republicans argued that the level of their support in the state was underrepresented in the court-mandated map and that they should have a majority of the state congressional delegation. Democrats argued that the decision had been made and that it was unfair to change the districting map for partisan advantage in response to every shift of power in the state legislature. They felt that the rules had been changed in the middle of the game, both in redistricting and in the state Senate procedures during the consideration of the issue. In many of the so-called democratic districts, voters had elected Democrats to Congress while choosing a Republican governor and lieutenant governor.

Politics is a rough-and-tumble game, and the issue of redistricting brings out the players' baser instincts. Republicans went to extraordinary lengths

(continued)

BOX 7.4   Redistricting at All Costs (Cont'd)

and taxpayer expense to gain a partisan advantage through redistricting that far exceeds their electoral strength, thus weakening their claim of interest in fair representation. Democrats used dramatic and extreme parliamentary devices rather than reason in defending their incumbents and previous political advantage.

No one came out looking good, which raises the obvious question: Isn't there a better way?

The answer is yes. One change, of course, is to have Congress or our state legislature outlaw mid-decade redistricting. Some states already don't allow the practice.

We could also change the way we redistrict. Twelve states have already chosen to assign redistricting to an outside panel rather than to partisan-driven legislative committees.

In Iowa, for example, state law sets the standards for a separate nonpartisan staff to follow in designing district lines for both congressional and state legislative districts. The standards include a ban on the common guides to gerrymandering such as incumbent protection, the addresses of incumbents, the political affiliations of registered voters, or the results of prior elections. Such matters have been central to redistricting in Texas in the past, and to the scandals and shame that have surrounded it.

One Republican state senator, Jeff Wentworth of San Antonio, has introduced legislation several times to create a process more like that in Iowa, without success. One way you might make a difference is to join the effort to help Wentworth succeed the next time.[22]

---

agriculture commissioner, railroad commissioner, commissioner of the General Land Office, and attorney general by more than 10 percentage points. In the first three races, in which the Republicans fielded incumbents, they won by an average margin of more than 20 points. The closest statewide race was for lieutenant governor, and even in that race the Republican David Dewhurst won by almost 6 percent over Democrat John Sharp, a margin that would be considered substantial in a closely competitive state.[23]

Statewide results mask substantial variation, however, in the patterns of party competition in various localities. A high percentage of the state's Republican vote comes from the Dallas–Fort Worth and Houston areas, especially the suburbs.[24] The Republican party is also strong in the Panhandle/High Plains region in the north; the Permian Basin region in the west; the hill country of Central Texas; and the oil-field counties of Gregg, Smith, and Rusk in the east. The Republican party seems to be gaining strength most rapidly in the western region. Populated primarily by conservative farmers and ranchers and people connected with the oil industry, the Panhandle south through the Permian Basin and Davis Mountains to the hill country provides fertile prospects for the Republican Party. Only El Paso

FIGURE 7.1 2003 Congressional Redistricting Map

Source: Texas Legislative Council at http://www.tlc.state.tx.us/research/redist/redist.htm.

remains solidly Democratic in West Texas. Elsewhere, the Republican vote is highest in affluent, largely white suburban neighborhoods like the Highland Park district in Dallas and River Oaks in Houston. The suburbs of San Antonio and Austin also tend to vote Republican.

Democratic voting strength is found in El Paso, South Texas, parts of East Texas, the Golden Triangle area (Beaumont, Port Author, and Orange), and the lower-income areas of the large cities. As this pattern suggests, Democrats have continued to do well with ethnic minorities. Mexican Americans normally vote heavily Democratic, and African American Texans have been most loyal, typically voting 90 percent or more for the Democratic party's candidates. The success of Republican George W. Bush when running for governor of Texas was built substantially on cutting into this Democratic advantage among Mexican American voters. Little

After the Republicans dominating the Redistricting Commission redrew boundaries for House and Senate Districts, Democratic senators and members of the House began to wonder. Sargent © 2004 Austin American-Statesman. *Reprinted with permission of* Universal Press Syndicate. *All rights reserved.*

evidence suggests, however, that Bush's relative popularity with this group of voters has been transferred to the Republican party more generally.

Several reasons explain the development of Republican-dominated two-party competition in Texas. The first is the steady and accelerating shift among conservative middle- and upper-income white Democrats to the Republican party. Having voted Republican in presidential elections but identifying themselves as Democrats for many years, these presidential Republicans (and especially the second generation—the children of the original presidential Republicans) began to think of themselves increasingly as independents or as Republicans. By the time popular Republican president Ronald Reagan arrived on the scene in 1980, the stage was set for these voters to embrace identification with the Republican party more fully. The presidency of Ronald Reagan provided the catalyst for this realignment. The presidency of Texan George W. Bush seems likely to cement it.

In addition to those families and individuals who switched loyalties over the years, broader socioeconomic factors also helped the Republican party become first competitive and then dominant. One such factor was the in-migration from other states that significantly altered the demographic makeup of Texas in the 1970s and 1980s. The newcomers were much more likely to be independents or

Republicans than traditional Texans were, and they significantly altered the pattern of party politics as they made their lives in Texas. They came because of and contributed to more fundamental economic trends that have also brought political opportunity for the Republican party. Texas has become an urban industrialized state with a diverse economy, giving rise to a large, affluent middle class. This fundamental phenomenon has led to the growth of the suburbs in which the Republican party has been able to flourish so well.

A Return to One-Party Dominance? Some would argue that so sweeping has been the growth of Republicanism in Texas and so rapid the decline of Democratic fortunes that Texas soon will become a one-party Republican state. Others attribute the magnitude of recent Republican success to short-term factors such as a uniquely popular Republican governor turned president, the reaction to the 9/11 terrorist attack during his presidency, and the inevitable time lag while the surprised Democrats struggle to catch up organizationally.

Recent polls have suggested that the dramatic shift in party identification toward the Republicans had slowed during the 1990s, and party identification had been stable for some time, with the electorate divided into roughly equal thirds among Democrats, Republicans, and Independents prior to 9/11. After 9/11, however, the Republican advantage in party identification experienced a substantial surge (see Figure 7.2). If this surge proves durable and not dependent on short-term factors associated with events and personalities, it would suggest that the Republican party will continue to dominate Texas politics for the near future.

Will this dominance reach the levels that the Democratic party enjoyed in the past, producing a one-party system that tends to have the same effect on choice and participation as a no-party system? Given the social and economic diversity of the state and the continuing organizational strength of the Democratic party, such a level of one-party dominance seems unlikely. In a winner-take-all electoral system, however, a party locked into what appears to be nearly permanent statewide minority status may find it difficult to maintain organizational strength, partisan loyalty, and member participation. Moderates who might otherwise be Democrats may direct their political activity into the Republican party, making it less cohesive and less conservative, but leaving the Democrats in ever shallower political waters.[25] In such a scenario, might the increasingly isolated Democrats be replaced by a party that is currently a third party in a more competitive party system? Again, this result seems unlikely because the electoral rules are being written by the current major parties and they are in a position to borrow or steal the issues that might popularize a third party. Stranger things have happened, however, and fifty years ago no one could have imagined that the Republican party would be in the position it is today. Box 7.5 describes third parties in Texas. We'll leave to you to choose which third party you think might have the right stuff to be a major competitor in the future.

Many industrial democracies use a system of elections that encourages a multiparty system. By rewarding voters and supporters of parties representing a small

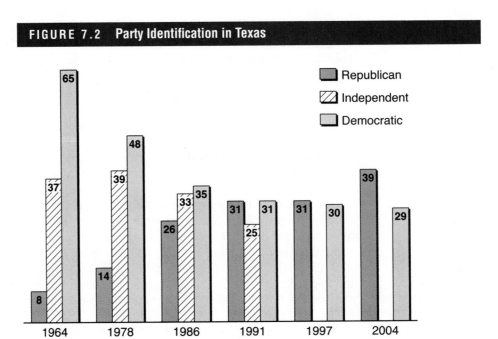

FIGURE 7.2   Party Identification in Texas

The Pew Research Center, http://people-press.org/reports/display.php3?PageID=750 (accessed April 12, 2004).

percentage of the electorate with a similar percentage of seats in the legislature, this electoral system perpetuates third, fourth, and fifth parties. You may also want to consider relative advantages of such an electoral system. Consider the arguments in Join the Debate that follows, and "join the debate!"

The single-member plurality (SMP) system is the most commonly used voting system in the United States, and it is the system by which all national and state government officials are elected in Texas. When Americans think of elections, they commonly think in terms of the SMP system, without giving any thought to its implications or to the possibility that other alternatives may exist. The SMP system uses geographically defined, single-member districts that send one representative to office. Voters cast a ballot for only one candidate for any office, and the candidate receiving the most votes (not necessarily a majority) is elected. (Sound familiar?)

It comes as a surprise to most Americans that very few of the world's major democracies use the SMP system. Most use some form of proportional representation (PR), the major alternative to the SMP system, including those democracies that the United States helped to establish in Europe and Japan in the wake of World War II. Some argue that we should take our own advice and move to a PR system because it will provide more accurate representation and avoid the sort of partisan political manipulation of district boundaries discussed in Box 7.4. Others

BOX 7.5   Do These Third Parties Have a Future in Texas Politics?

Socialist Party of Texas.

The Socialist party of Texas views itself joined in a struggle against the power and greed of giant corporations. Its website states that this power and greed has resulted in "governmental policies more concerned with interest rates than employment rates, stagnating real wages, decaying cores of cities, an intolerable poverty rate, and so on. In short, our problems stem from the control of wealth and government by a select few." This party seeks "no less than a social order where goods will be produced on the basis of human need rather than corporate profit; where cooperation will replace savage competition; and where the fullest potential of every man, woman and child will be allowed to develop."

Constitution Party of Texas.

The orientation of the Constitution party of Texas, a conservative religious organization, is captured in its first platform pronouncement: "We, the members of the Constitution Party, gratefully acknowledge the blessing of the Lord God as Creator, Preserver and Ruler of the Universe and of this Nation. We solemnly declare that the foundation of our political position and moving principle of our political activity is our full submission and unshakable faith in our Savior and Redeemer, our Lord Jesus Christ. We hereby appeal to Him for mercy, aid, comfort, guidance and the protection of His Divine Providence as we work to restore and preserve this Nation as a government of the People, by the People, and for the People."

Green Party of Texas.

The Green party of Texas seeks to build a just and sustainable society through education, direct action, and inclusive electoral politics. Green party members value grassroots democracy, social justice, ecological wisdom, and nonviolence. The Green Party presents itself as "the alternative to the corporately controlled political system that governs and affects all of us."

Libertarian Party of Texas.

The Libertarian party defends the right of individuals to live in whatever manner they choose, as long as they do not forcibly interfere with the same rights of others. Their central argument is that "governments throughout history have regularly operated on the opposite principle, that the State has the right to dispose of the lives of individuals and the fruits of their labor. Even in Texas, all political parties other than our own grant to government the right to regulate the lives of individuals and seize the fruits of their labor

(*continued*)

BOX 7.5   Do These Third Parties Have a Future in Texas Politics? (Cont'd)

without their consent. We, on the contrary, hold that governments must not violate individual rights; we oppose all interference by government in the areas of voluntary and contractual relations among individuals. The resultant economic system, the only one compatible with the protection of individual rights, is the free market."

American Reform Party of Texas.

The American Reform Party declares its mission to be to "stimulate citizen participation in the political process, break the two-party monopoly, and guarantee free elections" and thereby "renew democracy." Key elements of the American Reform party's platform include reducing government spending and size; paying down the national debt; passing a balanced budget amendment; simplifying the tax code with a national sales tax or a graduated flat tax; campaign finance reform to reduce the influence of money and special interests through public funding strategies; ballot access for third-party candidates; term limits for public officeholders; abolition of the Electoral College; elimination of the trade deficit; limits to immigration; and establishment of a universal, single-payer health program.

---

defend the SMP system, reminding us of its virtues of simplicity, stability and constituency representation.

PARTY STRUCTURE AND ORGANIZATION

It's important to note the major components of political parties in Texas and in other states. They all consist of three important components: the party in the electorate, the party in government, and the party organization.[26] The three parts of the party must work together if the party is to perform, at a minimum, the functions of recruitment, mobilization, and delivering on the promises made during the campaign. When the three parts do work together, the party is usually thought of as being cohesive and strong.

When they do not and parties are thus simply labels for a disorganized politics of personalities and factions, then democracy fails to fulfill its promise as a way to bring about effective and responsible government.

According to V. O. Key, "Over the long run the have-nots lose in a disorganized politics. They have no mechanism through which to act and their wishes find expression in fitful rebellions led by transient demagogues who gain their confidence but often have neither the technical competence nor the necessary stable base of political power to effectuate a program."[27]

JOIN the DEBATE

THE ISSUE: We should change from a single-member plurality (SMP) voting system to a proportional (PR) voting system. Are you in favor of single-member plurality (SMP) voting systems or proportional representation (PR) voting systems?

DISAGREE

1. SMP systems are praised for being simple to use and understand. A valid vote requires only one mark beside the name or symbol of one candidate, and the count is easy to administer for electoral officials.

2. SMP provides a clear choice for voters between two main parties. Because minority parties receive no reward in the system, third parties tend to wither away, leaving two clearly distinct parties for voter choice.

3. SMP gives rise to stable, single-party governments. Because the larger party in the system typically receives more representation in the legislature than its proportion of the vote, the system tends to provide a clear (though exaggerated) majority for the winning party. This result produces a strong and stable government, with clear accountability. At the same time, it provides for a clear and coherent opposition, which can present itself as a realistic alternative to the governing party.

4. SMP encourages broad-based political parties. Because a party must seek a plurality to win, it is encouraged to be inclusive. Parties become a vehicle for compromise and cooperation among diverse interests. This advantage is particularly important in societies with many ethnic, racial, regional, or other social divisions. For the same reason, SMP discourages extremist parties representing small ideological minorities. Unless they are geographically concentrated, they are unlikely to win any representation in the winner-take-all SMP system, and thus will be forced to moderate and join with a major party or become politically irrelevant.

5. SMP retains and emphasizes the link between constituents and their representative. Representation is based on defined regions rather than mere party labels. Voters in this geographical region can know who their representative is and keep her or him accountable to the clear regional interests. It allows voters to choose between people rather than just between parties, thus providing a chance for popular independent candidates to be elected. It also allows voters to assess the performance of individual candidates and officeholders rather than having to judge a list of candidates collectively as presented by a party, which can happen under some PR electoral systems.

(continued)

JOIN THE DEBATE

AGREE

1. PR systems are designed to make legislatures reflect more accurately the relative strength of like-minded groupings of voters in the society. For example, PR systems allocate 10 percent of the seats in the legislature to representatives of a party that wins 10 percent of the vote, 35 percent of the seats to a party that wins 35 percent, and 55 percent to a party that wins 55 percent. In an SMP system, the last party would receive 100 percent of the representation, which overrepresents the actual opinion distribution in the electorate.

2. PR systems allow political minorities to have actual representation in the legislature rather than virtual representation. SMP systems assume that the single winner in a district will be able to represent supporters of the losing candidates adequately and accurately. This assumption may have been true when the interests and issues of elections revolved around geographically determined concerns, but it is less so in the modern context, where ideology, ethnicity, and class are key political divisions. Evidence indicates that PR systems produce legislative representation that more accurately mirrors society on all these dimensions and also provides greater representation of women.

3. PR avoids the tendency in SMP systems toward noncompetitive districts and the attendant lower voter turnout. Comfortable majorities for one party or group interest can make elections noncompetitive in an SMP (winner-take-all) system. One consistent winner tends to discourage opposition candidacies and voters, who have no hope of winning representation.

4. Drawing election districts becomes an easy task with PR. It is not necessary to draw artificial districts to ensure that all districts are equal in population. All districts have multiple members, and the number of members assigned to each district depends on its population. Districts can thus be natural areas and communities regardless of population. Gerrymandering is also no longer a problem. Because partisan or racial minorities will win some representation based on their proportion of the vote, regardless of the district they live in, little can be gained by contorting district boundaries. Where a winner takes all, even small adjustments can completely exclude a party or interest. Every vote counts toward electing representation in PR, regardless of where the voter happens to live.

5. PR stimulates parties to conduct active campaigns in all areas of a country or state. This feature contrasts with SMP systems, in which parties tend to concentrate on the relatively few districts that are competitive and tend to neglect districts in which they are either very weak or very strong. This party activity also helps explain the higher turnout in PR systems.

Whether Texas parties move in the direction of organizational strength will depend on whether you participate in one of them and move your party toward cohesion. Two cohesive parties competing for the votes of the majority of the population, who are being mobilized to vote, is certainly one way for the average Texan to make a difference in Texas politics.

The Party in the Electorate.   The party in the electorate is comprised of the citizens who see themselves as members of a party, feel some loyalty to the party, and normally vote for its candidates. One of the most difficult tasks confronting party officials and the people who would like to be candidates for public office in Texas is locating the party in the electorate. Texas does not have party registration, which is significant if, for example, you want to run for county commissioner in your party. To mount your primary election campaign, it would be useful to be able to find volunteers and likely voters in your party. You would discover, however, that the best list of party members available to your campaign is a two-year-old list of those who voted in your party's primary. You have no way of identifying people who did not vote in that primary or people who have recently registered to vote. You would have such a list if we had partisan registration.

Registering to vote as a member of a party may only partially strengthen party identity and increase partisan support, but it certainly makes it much more likely that Texas would have more genuinely closed primaries in which only party members participate. Because it would be easier to reach party members, turnout would more likely increase. As a result, a larger portion of the party membership would elect party candidates.

The Party in Government.   The party in government is comprised of candidates for public office, and both elected and appointed officeholders who share a party label. We devote three chapters (Chapters 8 through 10) to the institutions of government whose members are nominated in party primaries and chosen in the general election. In those chapters, you will learn in more detail the reasons that the party in the majority often has difficulty delivering on its campaign promises, but mostly it's because the parties do not organize the Texas Legislature, unlike the national Congress. They do not make standing committee assignments, the majority party does not choose the chairs of those committees, and thus the parties have little in the way of resources to promote party unity and encourage party members to take the party goals and objectives seriously.

In the U.S. Congress, the best single predictor of how members vote is party membership, which predicts 70 percent of the variance in congressional voting. In some states, party is an even better predictor of a member's vote. According to political scientist Sarah McCalley Morehouse, "Texas is *the only state* where partisanship has absolutely no relationship to support for the governor's program."[28] With no party support for the governor's program, a party cannot deliver on promises made in the gubernatorial campaign. The governor might be able to pull together a coalition of people from both parties;[29] however, the parties are not organizing the legislature to govern. Someone else, or some other actors (the likely candidates being interest groups) perform that function.

The Party Organization.   The party organization is comprised of the activists who work to promote all the party's candidates and issue positions (including those official party officers with titles like state party chair and county committee chair) and party members who are devoted enough to give their time and skills to the party. In a strong party system, the party organization is an important link between the voters and the government. In a weak party system, the party organization consists of people who run the primary as neutral observers and work on the campaign once other actors have decided who the candidates will be. Because parties operate in this fashion in Texas, many of the leaders of the parties are used to the situation and do not want to see it changed. You, of course, can become a party leader, and you can change it.

Texas's two major electoral parties, although different in many ways, are subject to the same set of rules, the Texas Election Code. Each party has both a temporary and a permanent structure. The temporary structure performs important party functions associated with elections in election years, and the permanent structure provides continuity in leadership and organization between elections.

Temporary Organization.   The temporary party organization is the place to begin participating in party activity. The *temporary organization* is basically a series of party conventions that begins at the most basic level of the party, the election precinct, with the precinct convention. Each county is divided into small geographical units called *election precincts,* each having a single polling place, to simplify and localize the election process. The precinct convention is a meeting (or caucus) open to all party supporters in the election precinct who have voted in the party's primary. Texas law currently sets the second Tuesday in March of even-numbered years as the day for party primary elections, and both parties hold precinct conventions in almost every precinct that same day after the polls have closed. To take part, you need only show a voter-registration card stamped to indicate you have voted in the primary, so it is an easy way to begin participating. Also, relatively few people choose to attend, despite the openness of the process, so your presence can immediately be felt and you can easily begin to make a difference.

The precinct caucus provides an opportunity to become involved in party affairs in several ways. You can offer, debate, and vote on resolutions that will be passed on to the county or senatorial district convention. In presidential election years, you would indicate a preference for a presidential candidate; in nonpresidential years, you would indicate support for designations such as a conservative caucus or a progressive caucus, which would be used to evaluate the strength of support for each candidate or caucus. Groups of supporters with the largest numbers may be able to dominate the most significant function of the precinct caucus, selecting delegates to the county or senatorial district conventions.

Factions or candidate supporters who dominate precinct conventions can shape the patterns of factional and candidate support at higher levels in the organization through delegate selection. Thus, precinct conventions are an important battleground for control of the party organization. Because turnout for precinct conventions is usually low, you can often get elected as a delegate to the county convention with the attendance and support of family and some friends. With a little more effort, supporters of a particular issue, ideology, or candidate can bring enough supporters to elect a whole delegation. Activists know how important precinct conventions are and may try to pack precinct conventions around the state with supporters in an effort to control a party.

The next step in the temporary party organization is the county or senatorial district convention held on the second Saturday following the primary and precinct conventions. Counties that are entirely within the boundaries of a single senatorial district hold county conventions. Counties that have more than one state senatorial district, as is the case with large counties like Harris, Bexar, Dallas, and Tarrant, hold conventions in each senatorial district within the county. As in the precinct conventions, these meetings provide an opportunity to offer, debate, and vote on nonbinding resolutions expressing opinion to the state convention and, most important, to help you elect or be elected as a delegate to the state convention.

The state convention is the highest level of temporary party organization. Held in June of even-numbered years, the major parties use these gatherings of thousands of party delegates to certify the official list of the party's nominees chosen in primary elections, adopt a state party platform, elect members of the party's state executive committee, and elect the state party chair and vice chair. In presidential election years, the state convention also elects the state's representatives to the party's national committee, formally selects the state's thirty-four potential presidential electors, and elects some of the state's delegates to the party's national convention (although the vast majority are now selected on the basis of the party's presidential preference primary). Much of this process is routine, but controversy can erupt between factions over the party's platform (the formal statement of the party's position on key issues) and the election of members and officers of the state executive committee. These areas involve the control, direction, and the definition of the party and are often the focus of heated competition that illuminates the divisions within the parties.

Permanent Organization.   In addition to the temporary structures that appear during election years, each of the two major parties in Texas has a permanent organizational structure to keep the party together between elections and plan for future contests. Like the temporary organization, permanent party officials exist at the precinct, county, and state levels.

The basic party official in both the temporary and permanent structures is the **precinct chair,** who serves as party organizer in the precinct. The duties of a precinct chair include keeping in touch with party activists and seeking to find and mobilize potential activists. At election time, the party depends on precinct chairs for locating election judges and poll-watchers, coordinating voter-registration activities, and getting party supporters to the polls. The precinct chair is also responsible for arranging the precinct convention and serves on the county executive committee. Precinct chairs are technically elected by the precinct voters in the party primaries for a term of two years, but in reality, this unpaid position carries little prestige, and these elections are frequently uncontested. Indeed, it is not

Precinct chair The permanent party official at the precinct level.

uncommon for parties to have difficulty finding someone to serve in the position. As the parties become more competitive, however, they make greater efforts to fill out their permanent organizations at the precinct level.[30]

A more active and important position in each party's permanent organization is county chair. As Diana Martinez (whose name you will recognize from the chapter-opening story) knows, this party official is the most important at the local level. Like the precinct chair, the voters in the primary election also choose the county chair for a two-year term. County chair contests are often low-key, lightly contested elections, but occasionally serious factional battles can occur for control of the local party apparatus. The county chair, with the approval of the county commissioners' court, determines where the voting places will be for the party primary and formally appoints primary election judges. The county chair is also responsible for formally accepting candidates for places on the primary ballot, printing ballots or securing voting machines, and (with the county executive committee) certifying the names of official nominees of the party to the secretary of state's office.

The county chair presides over the county executive committee, the second important component of permanent organization at the county level. Composed of all the precinct chairs in the county, the executive committee helps the chair prepare the primary ballot, receive filing petitions and filing fees from primary candidates, and determine the order in which their names will be placed on the ballot. This order can be important in primaries because voters often have such a low level of interest and information that they tend to choose the first name on the ballot. The executive committee also canvasses the returns from the primary for local offices and arranges for county and district conventions.

At the top of the permanent organizational structure of each party is the state executive committee. State law mandates that the state executive committees be composed of one man and one woman from each of the thirty-one senatorial districts and a chair and vice chair. These sixty-four-member committees are selected at each party's state convention. The delegates to the state convention choose the chair and vice chair in an at-large vote for two-year terms. Delegates from each of the thirty-one senatorial districts meet separately to choose two members from their district for subsequent approval by the whole convention.

The state party chairs are the titular heads of their respective parties and serve as media spokespersons. This role is more important for the party chair whose party has not won the governorship because the governor often becomes the informal spokesperson for his or her party. The state chair also provides leadership for the state executive committee, which is responsible for canvassing statewide primary returns and certifying the nomination of party candidates, and for choosing the site of the next state convention. The executive committee seeks to promote party unity and strength, encouraging organizational work in counties and precincts, raising campaign money for party candidates (although most is raised by the candidates themselves), and working with the national party toward common goals. The executive committees of both major parties in Texas have become so busy that they each employ full-time executive directors and staff.

THE FUTURE OF PARTIES IN TEXAS

Although political scientists rank Texas among the states with competitive parties, for reasons we have already discussed, they do not rank Texas as a state with strong, cohesive parties that can recruit candidates and deliver on campaign promises. The establishment-dominated interest group system still plays a major role in Texas politics. Whether Texas parties move in the direction of cohesion and strength will mostly be up to you and future generations. In the following subsections, we present a list of reforms that you may wish to consider if you wish to strengthen the ability of parties to balance the influence of interest groups. When you become active in your party, people already active in that party will welcome your help.

Party Registration.   Party registration strengthens the parties and helps members of the electoral party mobilize registered voters into more active roles. Lists of voters are available, but finding which third of the list identifies with a particular party is a chore. This reform requires the passage of a law that changes the Texas Election Code. Making such a change requires work within the parties explaining and teaching at precinct and county conventions.

Partisan Municipal Elections.   Partisan municipal elections strengthen the parties by linking the party organization to municipal elections. It can create a career ladder from the municipal to the county and state legislative level. It also promotes closer links between county governments, which are elected on a partisan ballot, and municipal governments, which are elected on a nonpartisan ballot. This reform requires changes in the Texas Election Code and grassroots effort from the precinct conventions up through the party levels.

Changed Rules for Organizing the Legislature.   This reform would take the power to make committee assignments from the Speaker of the House and from the lieutenant governor and place it in the hands of party leaders on both sides of each house. The committee assignments would be divided among the parties according to their membership in the whole house, as is the case in the U.S. Congress and many other state legislatures. Party committees would make the assignments for each party. This reform requires changes in the rules of both the House and the Senate, and grassroots efforts would help this process.

Endorsing Conventions.   An endorsing convention takes place before the primaries. Party activists at the convention vote to endorse their choice for the party nomination. After the endorsement decision is made, the other candidates often drop out in the interests of party unity. As a result, precious campaign dollars are saved for the general election. The sixteen states with this procedure use it only for statewide offices at the top of the ticket: the governor or U.S. senator.

As Texas in Context 7.1 indicates, Texas and two other megastates do not use any endorsement mechanisms. You may also note that the states that *do* use them

TEXAS in Context

7.1 Party Strength and Gubernatorial Nominations

Megastate	Party Strength	Endorsing Convention by Law	Endorsement by Party Rule or Practice	No Endorsements
California	Moderate		X	
Florida	Moderate			X
Illinois	Strong		X	
Massachusetts	Moderate/strong		X	
Michigan	Strong		X	
New Jersey	Moderate			X
New York	Moderate	X		
Ohio	Strong		X	
Pennsylvania	Moderate/strong		X	
Texas	Moderate/weak			X

Source: Malcolm E. Jewell and Sarah M. Morehouse, *Political Parties and Elections in American States* (Washington, D.C.: CQ Press, 2001), p. 103.

are those in which parties are stronger than they are in Texas, and voter turnout (as you may have noted in Chapter 5) is also higher. The preprimary endorsing activity has much to recommend it if you want increased voter turnout and mobilization of the working poor and the middle class.

Endorsement procedures accomplish several other goals for the party. First, they increase the likelihood that the party in government will be linked to the party in office. The governor owes his or her election in part to the party endorsement because endorsed candidates tend to win the primaries. Second, they strengthen the party organization and increase participation in it because the endorsing convention clearly plays a meaningful role in the nominating process. Third, they improve the likelihood that candidates for other offices pay attention to and work with the party organization because running for higher office may be part of their plans.[31]

Summary

In this chapter, we have examined elections and political parties, institutions central to the democratic process. The essence of democracy is participation, and voting in elections is our most basic form of participation. Political parties enhance the quality and meaning of participation in various ways. How these basic institutions function in Texas has been the primary focus of this chapter.

Texas has never had a strong record on voting, bringing into question the quality and depth of democracy in the state. Historically, Texas marshaled a wide variety of discriminatory electoral devices to prevent minorities from participating in elections. In addition to restrictive voter-registration practices (symbolized by the poll tax) to limit political participation of ordinary working Texans, the dominant Democratic party employed a white primary to disenfranchise minorities. Because of the efforts of individual Texans and changes in federal rules affecting elections, Texas now has one of the easier methods of registering to vote, and access to the polls is readily available to all. Because of the lack of institutions to mobilize the have-nots and the working class, however, relatively few Texans avail themselves of this right compared to citizens in other industrial democracies and other states.

Political parties are some of the most important institutions for mobilizing the majority of the population in a democracy. In strong-party states, the parties perform several important functions necessary to the operation of democracy and the expression of the public will through elections. These functions include recruiting and nominating candidates, providing structure for voting choice, articulating alternative government programs, and helping to coordinate the actions of officials once in office.

Texas has a long tradition of weak parties. First, we were a one-party state, which in effect is a no-party state. The Republican party has been on the ascendance in Texas for the past four decades and has made rapid gains in the past fifteen years or so. As a result, the state's party system has become more two-party competitive, thus offering alternatives at the polls. Recent elections suggest that the party system may become dominated by a single party once again, this time by the Republicans. It is not yet clear if the Republican dominance in recent elections is due to short-term factors or to fundamental and permanent changes portending a new era of one-party dominance.

What is clear is that the two parties have developed without being able to deliver on campaign promises and without the motivation to become more involved in the recruitment and mobilization processes. A cursory examination of the party platforms indicates that the parties do offer alternatives, but they cannot deliver on the campaign promises they make. With reform, the two parties may be able to make democracy more effective in Texas and counterbalance the influence of the upper-class-dominated interest group system.

We have suggested that all three parts of the party (the party in the electorate, the party organization, and the party in government) must work more cohesively. When they do, voter turnout will increase because parties will have offered meaningful alternatives, mobilized more of the working class to participate, and been able to deliver on the promises made in the campaign after their candidates are elected.

The party organization in Texas is an essential link to this process of delivering on the promise of democracy. Both a temporary and a permanent structure in each party characterize party organization. These structures are open to you and offer the chance to effect change. Throughout this chapter, we have suggested doorways into the system: from campaign volunteer to election worker, to convention delegate. We hope you take advantage of these opportunities and make it possible for parties in Texas to be able to deliver on the promises of democracy through the reforms we have suggested in this chapter or reforms you think of yourself. We also hope that Texans are in for a spirited two-party competition in the immediate future. Although we cannot know the long-term implications of such competition for participation and voter turnout, we can predict that Texas party politics will not be dull.

KEY TERMS

Political party, p. 173
Primary election, p. 174
Closed primary, p. 175

Open primary, p. 175
Party identification, p. 175
Runoff primary, p. 175

FOR FURTHER READING

Jewell, Malcolm E., and Sarah M. Morehouse, *Political Parties and Elections in American States,* 4th ed. (Washington, D.C.: CQ Press, 2001).

Layman, Geoffrey C., *The Great Divide: Religious and Cultural Conflict in American Party Politics* (New York: Columbia University Press, 2001).

Morehouse, Sarah McCalley, *The Governor as Party Leader: Campaigning and Governing* (Ann Arbor: University of Michigan Press, 1998).

Nelson, Albert, *Democrats Under Siege in the Sunbelt Megastates: California, Florida, and Texas* (Westport, Conn.: Praeger, 1996).

Palast, Greg, *The Best Democracy Money Can Buy* (New York: Penguin/Plume, 2003).

Patterson, Thomas E., *The Vanishing Voter: Public Involvement in an Age of Uncertainty* (New York: Alfred A. Knopf, Inc, 2002).

STUDY QUESTIONS

1. List the types of elections used in Texas.

2. Explain the difference between a closed primary and an open primary.

3. Describe how the primary process, including runoff elections, works in Texas.

4. What are the qualifications required to vote in Texas?

5. List all the ways that an individual can participate in Texas elections.

CRITICAL THINKING QUESTIONS

1. Discuss the role and importance of elections for democracy.

2. Discuss the role and importance of parties for democracy.

3. Discuss the implications of Texas's one-party past for the character of contemporary parties in Texas and their role in politics.

4. Speculate on the future of party competition in Texas. Include in your discussion the advantages and disadvantages for each party and the likelihood that the Texas party system will become two-party competitive or slip back into domination by one party.

5. Select one of the reforms discussed in this chapter and explain fully why you would argue that it is the most important for improving Texas politics.

INTERNET RESOURCES

www.texasgop.org/ The website of the Texas Republican party includes information on the party's leadership, membership, latest news, how to get involved, and events, as well as the party's core views and values.

www.txdemocrats.org/ The website of the Texas Democratic party features a guest editorial column, the latest news and upcoming events, the party platform, and a set of media and party links.

www.geocities.com/CapitolHill/Lobby/7013/index.html The central website for the College Democrats of Texas provides resources for Democrats attending colleges throughout the state. Your local campus may have a College Democrats organization, and this website should have a link to it. These organizations provide a way for college-age Democrats to begin to get involved.

www.collegerepublicans.com This website is the Internet home for the Texas Federation of College Republicans, the statewide college auxiliary of the Republican Party of Texas. Your local campus may have a College Republican organization, and this website should have a link to it. These organizations provide a way for college-age Republicans to begin to get involved.

www.cptexas.org/ The website for the Constitution Party of Texas provides information about the party's platform and other related information, a list of party leaders, an events calendar, and information on the next convention.

www.tx.lp.org/ The website for the Libertarian Party of Texas provides the party's platform, an archive of press releases, membership information, officers' names, and links to other related sites.

www.americanreform.org/texas The website for the Reform Party of Texas includes the party's principles, a list of party officers, a calendar of meetings, and a list of related links.

www.txgreens.org The website for the Green Party of Texas includes the party's platform and policy goals, activities, and membership information.

sp-usa.org/lonestar/ The website for the Socialist Party of Texas includes the party's general statement of principles and links to related sites.

www.politicalindex.com/sect9.htm Click on Texas in this comprehensive general political index website for a complete set of links to Texas party organizations.

www.sos.state.tx.us/elections/index.shtml The website for the Texas secretary of state has a wealth of information on Texas voting and elections.

www.austinreview.com/ This website provides insightful coverage of politics, groups, and party activity, with links to Democratic, Republican, and Libertarian party activities and positions.

www.txsdc.tamu.edu A wide variety of online data for Texas and Texas politics is contained on this website for the Texas State Data Center at Texas A&M University College Station.

www.politics1.com/tx.htm The website for the *Directory of Texas State and Congressional Candidates* has links to Texas candidates, elections, political parties, and daily news media.

www.fairvote.org/ The website for the Center for Voting and Democracy has a wealth of information concerning alternative voting systems and their advantages.

CHAPTER 8

The Texas Legislature

Daniel Kulvicki, a freshman at Dickinson High School in northern Galveston County, found a project for his history class that interested not only his teacher but others as well. With all the fuss over the Confederate flag and the tradition of emphasizing the Alamo, why didn't Texans honor an event that is every bit as important to the state and even more long lasting in terms of its historical consequences? That event took place February 19, 1845, when Republic of Texas President Anson Jones officially lowered the Texas flag and raised the twenty-eight-star U.S. flag at the state capitol. Texas, which had been a nearly bankrupt and vulnerable independent country since March 2, 1836, would now be part of a large nation-state that would help Texans defend themselves from the Mexican armies to the south and the Comanches to the west.[1]

Kulvicki suggested State of Texas Anniversary Remembrance Day (STAR Day) as the name for this holiday. His project was to get the Dickinson city council to declare February 19 a city holiday to celebrate the anniversary of Texas joining the Union. The idea was so appealing that the city council passed a STAR Day resolution in October 1995. Mayor John Mitchiner suggested that Kulvicki also go to the Galveston County commissioners court and maybe try the Texas Legislature. The Galveston County commissioners court created STAR Day countywide. Meanwhile, Kulvicki visited with his state representative, Craig Eiland (a Democrat from District 24, Galveston/Harris), who agreed to introduce a STAR Day bill in the Seventy-Fifth Texas Legislature (1997).[2]

The STAR Day proposal died in committee, which is common when bills and resolutions are first introduced in the Texas Legislature. Kulvicki learned from his experience. He realized that getting a bill introduced by a legislator is not enough. He had to help get that bill passed. To raise support for his proposal, he consulted with local political leaders, created a STAR Day committee, wrote letters to county commissioners courts all over the state, and even visited a few of those courts. When he came to lobby the Seventy-Sixth Texas Legislature in 1999, he brought some political ammunition.

Kulvicki had a notebook of resolutions in favor of STAR Day that had been passed by 254 county commissioners courts. As Galveston County Judge Jim Yarbrough observed, "It's tough enough to get all 254 county judges to agree on what day of the week it is." Thus, it was a truly noteworthy accomplishment that Kulvicki got all 254 county commissioners courts to agree that each year, Texas should acknowledge the anniversary of joining the United States. So impressed was the legislature with Kulvicki's accomplishment that the House and Senate unanimously passed Senate Bill 1656, which recognized February 19 as STAR Day. Kulvicki himself was given special recognition for his idea and his hard work. On June 18, 1999, Governor George W. Bush signed the bill into law. Subsequently, the Texas Association of Counties approved a resolution recognizing STAR Day. The day is not a vacation holiday, but the legislation encourages school districts, cities, and counties all over Texas to observe the date.

The story of Daniel Kulvicki demonstrates some noteworthy points about politics and the Texas Legislature. First is that an individual made a difference. This story of one Texan convincing other Texans to celebrate our American heritage complements the story of a Texan helping to amend the U.S. Constitution (recall Gregory Watson's efforts described in Chapter 3). Second, the path of influence may require some effort, and sometimes considerable effort, but that path is available. Dennis Kulvicki and Gregory Watson had to do more than make a few telephone calls. They engaged in intensive letter writing, telephone calling, personal contact, and even traveling some distance to get something done. It paid off for them, and it can for you. Obviously, it will have to be something you believe is important. The point is that you can make a difference if you are willing to try.

Third, members of the Texas Legislature do seek to act as agents for their constituents. Often they cannot do it alone. If State Representative Craig Eiland had been Speaker of the Texas House of Representatives, perhaps one of his constituents would have been more successful the first time the bill was introduced. However, not every one of the 150 members of the Texas House is the presiding officer. Thus, Eiland needed some help. In Chapter 1, we discussed Robert Doerr's conversation with senator Jeff Wentworth. Sometimes the legislator has an agenda that fits your concerns perfectly.

Fourth, if you really want to accomplish something, you sometimes have to let others take credit for it. A detail so minor in the larger picture that we did not mention it in the narrative of the story is the fact that STAR Day was passed by both houses of the Texas Legislature as Senate Bill 1656. Craig Eiland's bill, House Bill 2997, was replaced by the Senate bill authored by state Senator Mike Jackson. What mattered to Eiland and to Kulvicki was STAR Day, not who authored the bill that the governor would eventually sign. Occasionally parking your ego is a good idea in politics, as in life.

Fifth, local legislatures are good places to start—to start learning about getting elected, getting bills passed, how to start building a constituency for a program or idea. Local legislators are also constituents and sometimes fundraisers and advisers to state senators and representatives. U.S. congressmen pay attention when local officeholders speak. Members of the House, in particular, want a warm welcome when they come home to campaign for reelection every two years.

Finally, the Kulvicki story reminds us that local legislatures do many of the same things that the state legislature does. Although this chapter is about the Texas Legislature, it is important to remember that many of the functions performed by the state legislature are also performed by some or many local legislatures: city councils, school boards, and county commissioners courts. The two most important functions that differentiate all legislatures from other types of government agencies are what we call the **parliamentary functions:** taxing and spending.

Parliamentary functions
Taxing and spending.

Parliamentary Functions of Legislatures

It is possible to run a government of a fairly complex political system without a legislature. Modern dictators seldom need them. The emperors of Turkey, China, and India, and the Aztec, Arab, and Songhai emperors, ruled smoothly for long periods of time without popularly elected legislative bodies. An executive branch is essential to run a government; a legislature is important only in a democracy.

The modern legislature evolved from the parliaments that emerged in medieval Europe, at a time when rulers needed more money for defense, to finance public works, and to create the centrally run kingdoms that eventually became nation-states. In most medieval kingdoms, the rulers abolished or weakened parliaments, but the institution survived in England and was later adopted by the American colonies. In other countries, parliaments were revived or created when the age of absolute monarchy ended and the modern era began.[3]

In the British Parliament, representatives of the king discussed issues (that is, parleyed—hence, the term *parliament*) with representatives of the land owners and the common people before levying taxes. Out of these negotiations came demands for expenditures on commodities that the common people wanted, and the power of the purse grew into the power to make new rules for the administration of justice and war and the regulation of the economy.

Parliaments Places where representatives of the people parley (discuss issues) with representatives of the executive branch and decide on taxes and expenditures. All legislatures—state and local—are parliaments because they perform the two parliamentary functions of taxing and spending.

Modern legislatures (national, state, and local) are all **parliaments.** They are places where representatives of the people talk with representatives of the executive branch and decide on taxes and expenditures. Thus, taxing and spending are the parliamentary functions, and they differentiate legislatures from the courts, zoning boards, regulatory commissions, and the rest of the executive branch. City councils, county commissioners courts, and school boards share at least two functions with the Texas Legislature that the governor and the state supreme court do not. Not every legislature performs all the functions that the Texas Legislature does, but all legislatures do perform parliamentary functions.

Legislative Organization

The Texas Legislature has the following major organizational features, and each has important consequences:

- It is functionally bicameral.
- Both houses apply the principles of division of labor and specialization through an extensive committee system.
- One house is small (thirty-one members), and the other is large (150 members).
- It has one biennial regular session.
- Presiding officers make committee assignments.

FUNCTIONALLY BICAMERAL

Bicameral Composed of two houses, as in a legislature.

Article III of the Texas Constitution provides for a structurally and functionally **bicameral** legislature: a legislative body consisting of two chambers, each of which must approve proposed legislation. The bicameral principle found in forty-nine state constitutions (Nebraska is the only state with a unicameral legislative system) was a continuation of the practice in the original thirteen colonies, where one house was elected and the other represented the interests of the crown and colonial aristocracy.[4]

Some countries have two house legislatures in form but not in function. The House of Commons in the United Kingdom, for example, is the only body that has the power to legislate; the House of Lords at best can delay a bill but not keep it from passing. In Texas and forty-eight other states, however, no law can be passed and no money can be spent unless both the state House of Representatives and the Senate pass bills or resolutions in exactly the same language. Not a word, not a comma, not a number can be different.

An important consequence of functional bicameralism is the conference committee. A **conference committee** is appointed for resolving differences on House and Senate versions of a proposed bill. The conference committee, consisting of members from both the House and Senate, is charged with producing a single bill on which both houses will vote.

In some cases, the House or the Senate may pass the version that emerged from the other legislative body without changing it at all, which often happens with bills affecting a small area of the state or bills that are not controversial. On most major pieces of legislation, however, a separate House and Senate bill must go to a conference committee.

Conference committee
A temporary committee formed when the two chambers of the legislature pass separate versions of the same bill. The committee, which consists of members from both the House and Senate, works out a compromise form of the bill.

COMMITTEE SYSTEM

To operate efficiently, the Texas Legislature uses committees to do a great deal of its work. Among the several different kinds of committees are standing committees, select committees, interim committees, joint committees, and (of course) conference committees.

Standing committees are the most important arenas of legislative policymaking. Indeed, the real work of the legislature is accomplished in the standing committee, and many bills die there for lack of action. Hearings, discussions, and efforts by interest groups and governmental agencies to exert political influence take place while the bill is in committee, which helps explain why legislative committees are often called the "little legislatures."

During the 2003 regular session, the Senate had fifteen standing committees and the House had thirty-six (see Table 8.1). Membership in the Senate standing committees ranges from seven to fifteen, and in the House, from five to thirty-two. Most of these committees are substantive; that is, they are responsible for initial consideration of most bills, as well as oversight of the state's administrative agencies. A few committees are procedural, such as the Rules Committee and the Calendars Committee in the House.

Standing committee A permanent committee in the legislature that specializes in a particular policy area, such as agriculture or education.

The various House and Senate standing committees differ significantly in terms of their importance, prestige, and legislative workloads. Some committees play more dominant roles in the lawmaking process than others do, particularly in the House. The House State Affairs, Appropriations, Finance, and Ways and Means committees are powerful and prestigious, and they handle most of the important legislation coming before the legislature. Standing committees may be subdivided into several smaller **subcommittees** to handle specialized subjects. Their number and duration vary with the workload of the individual standing committee.

Subcommittee A division of a larger committee that deals with a particular part of the committee's policy area. Some standing committees in the legislature have several subcommittees.

The standing committees perform the critical functions that make it possible for these large deliberative bodies to function and thus are the core of the legislative process. First, the committee system provides a division of labor in the legislature. With 4,000 to 5,000 or more bills introduced each session, this division of the workload is essential. Second, a committee system—at least in theory—allows

TABLE 8.1   Senate and House Standing Committees: Seventy-Eighth Legislature, 2003

Senate	Number of Members	House	Number of Members
Administration	7	Agriculture	7
Committee of the Whole Senate	31	Appropriations	29
Criminal Justice	7	Border and International Affairs	7
Education	9	Business and Industry	9
Finance	15	Calendars	11
Government Organization	7	Civil Practices	9
Health and Human Services	9	Corrections	7
Infrastructure Development and Security	9	County Affairs	9
Intergovernmental Relations	5	Criminal Jurisprudence	9
International Relations and Trade	7	Defense Affairs and State-Federal Relations	9
Jurisprudence	7	Economic Development	7
Natural Resources	11	Elections	7
Nominations	7	Energy Resources	7
State Affairs	9	Environmental Regulation	7
Veteran Affairs and Military Installations	5	Ethics, Select	7
		Financial Institutions	7
		General Investigating	5
		Government Reform	7
		Higher Education	9
		House Administration	11
		Human Services	9
		Insurance	9
		Judicial Affairs	9
		Juvenile Justice and Family Issues	9
		Land and Resource Management	9
		Law Enforcement	7
		Licensing and Administrative Procedures	9
		Local and Consent Calendars	11
		Local Government Ways and Means	7
		Natural Resources	9
		Pensions and Investments	7

(continued)

Senate	Number of Members	House	Number of Members
		Public Education	9
		Public Health	9
		Public School Finance, Select	32
		Redistricting	15
		Regulated Industries	7
		Rules and Resolutions	11
		State Affairs	9
		State Cultural and Recreational Resources	7
		State Health Care Expenditures, Select	11
		Transportation	9
		Urban Affairs	7
		Ways and Means	9

TABLE 8.1   Senate and House Standing Committees: Seventy-Eighth Legislature, 2003 (Cont'd)

Source: Texas Legislature Online, http://www.capitol.state.tx.us/ (accessed September 10, 2003).

Special or ad hoc committee A temporary committee of the legislature created to conduct studies or investigations.

Interim committee A recess committee created to act as a study or investigatory body between sessions of the legislature.

Joint committee Committee with members from both the House and the Senate.

members to specialize in a certain area of governmental operations. Over time, committee members develop special knowledge about these activities and can provide useful information to their colleagues.

Special or **ad hoc committees** are temporary committees of the legislature created to conduct studies or investigations. They look into temporary problems, such as administrative scandals. Members of these committees are appointed by the respective presiding officers. After the committee makes its report to the chamber, it passes out of existence.

Interim committees are appointed to meet after the regular session. They have been used widely to permit a more detailed study of problems than is possible during the busy day of the regular sessions. Interim committees also allow legislators from all over the state to maintain personal contact by bringing them together periodically in Austin. Although the legislature itself does not meet year-round, several of its standing and interim committees do. Thus, when the legislature convenes, these committees are ready and able to propose some well-researched bills.

Joint committees are legislative committees with members from both the House and the Senate. Some joint committees are appointed for the regular session, and some are created as interim committees. A conference committee is a type of joint committee.

Most of the work of the legislature is done in the committees.

SIZE AND ITS CONSEQUENCES

The House consists of 150 members; the Senate consists of thirty-one members. In theory, all Senators serve four-year terms. As we shall see when we discuss apportionment, the need to redistrict every ten years alters this. Senate elections are staggered so that half of the senators are elected every two years.

Because of its larger size, the Texas House of Representatives needs to regulate the use of its time more carefully than the smaller Senate does. Thus, the House has two committees—the House Rules Committee and the House Calendars Committee—with important roles. As bills are reported out of the standing committees, they are assigned to one of several calendars or schedules for debate by the House Calendars Committee. Each calendar is treated a little differently, but what is important is where on the calendar a bill is located. If a legislator cannot get his or her bill called up before the House from one of the calendars, it dies.

The chair of the Calendars Committee is a powerful and experienced member of the House, and that assignment is as much sought after as is assignment to the Rules Committee, which makes special rules for each bill that will be debated. How long people may speak and what kind of amendments they may offer are all built into the rules for debate on a bill in the House.

Lieutenant governor
The presiding officer and foremost political leader of the Texas Senate. The lieutenant governor is elected statewide for a four-year term in the same general election year in which the governor is chosen.

The Senate, as a smaller body, leaves scheduling decisions to the presiding officer, the **lieutenant governor.** The Senate has a tradition of unlimited debate, which makes it possible for one senator to block a piece of legislation to which he or she is strongly opposed. Another feature of the Senate, the *two-thirds rule,* also gives a small number of senators great influence.

The Senate does not have a Rules Committee or a Calendars Committee. In fact, it does not even use a calendar to schedule debate, although calendars are kept in the Senate to serve as a reference. The Senate's written rules contain the provision that a two-thirds majority is necessary to suspend the rules to bring a bill up for debate. In effect, it means that the bill is brought up out of order from a calendar. The unwritten rules—that is, tradition—require that a senator request permission to move to suspend the rules, and the presiding officer grants this permission only if he or she has been assured that the senator has the necessary votes (twenty-one votes) to pass this motion. Thus, in the Texas Senate, it takes more votes to discuss a bill than it does to pass it. It requires only a simple majority of sixteen votes to pass a bill in the Senate.

As a consequence of the two-thirds tradition (that is, because a relatively small number of senators—eleven—can block a bill), senators trade favors to get a bill debated. Senators who will vote against a particular bill may gain concessions on other legislation by simply voting to allow a bill to be discussed. More important, however, is the fact that this rule makes it easier for someone with a lot of influence to pull together eleven votes to stop legislation. As we will see later in this chapter, the two-thirds rule enhances the influence of the lieutenant governor as the presiding officer of the Senate.

Among the other consequences of the difference in size of the House and the Senate is the fact that senators usually represent much larger and more diverse constituencies than do their counterparts in the House. As a result, senators are somewhat better able than members of the House to represent the interests of groups organized on a regional or statewide basis. On the other hand, the small size and relative homogeneity of their constituencies and the frequency with which they must seek reelection make House members more attuned to the legislative needs of local interest groups.

Because of their larger constituencies, senators are more likely to be prepared to run for statewide office or for U.S. Congress than are members of the House. This feature is one reason that many members of the House attempt to move to the Senate, but few senators ever attempt to move to the House.

ONE BIENNIAL REGULAR SESSION

The Texas Constitution requires that the legislature meet in a regular biennial session, to last no more than 140 calendar days, beginning on the second Tuesday in January in odd-numbered years. The constitution also allows the governor to call additional special sessions as necessary. During a called session, which cannot exceed thirty days, the legislature may consider legislation only on matters specified by the governor. As we shall note later, the ability to craft a special session gives a skillful governor some beneficial bargaining tools. For now, however, we focus on the implications of the 140-day regular session, the only one in the life of a two-year legislature.

First, compressing the work of the legislature into such a short time frame requires centralization of power to get anything done. Thus, the presiding officers of both houses are given great latitude in making decisions. Second, it makes delay an important tactic for any individual or group opposed to change. A bill does not have a second chance in the life of a two-year Texas Legislature, with its one regular session. Third, it almost guarantees that Texas Legislators are part-time, with amateur legislators serving. Until they have been reelected several times, Texas legislators lack experience in the complexities of legislative procedure, the rough-and-tumble of legislative politics, and the demanding knowledge of legislative issues necessary to get work done. The amateurism of junior members serves to strengthen the position of the legislative leadership and of lobbyists, who are often quite knowledgeable about procedure and policy matters.

The merits of annual versus biennial sessions of the state legislature have been debated extensively. Proponents of the current biennial session say that the less the legislature meets, the less time lobbyists and special interests have to congregate in Austin to press for legislation beneficial only to their own narrow interests. Also, it is believed that the more often the legislature meets, the more costly it is to state taxpayers. Annual sessions would require that the House and the Senate keep large year-round staffs on the payroll in Austin rather than scaling back during the long recess, as is now the custom.

Proponents of an annual session, on the other hand, argue that saving a few dollars in legislative costs is a false economy, paid for in tax breaks for business and weak protections for consumers and workers. In the end the penny-wise, pound-foolish approach denies Texans the government they deserve from a megastate. The 140-day session might have been adequate to carry out all necessary business when the constitution was adopted in 1876, they argue, but it seriously compromises the quality of lawmaking and legislative oversight today. Similar restrictions, they point out, were common in many other states 100 years ago, but today forty-three states have annual legislative sessions. See the Join the Debate feature for more arguments for and against the 140-day biennial legislative session in Texas.

Texas, in fact, is the only megastate whose legislature still convenes only biennially.[5] Such restrictions, say proponents of a regular annual legislative session, severely limit not only the legislature's opportunities for deliberation but the effectiveness of its committees. Biennial sessions also limit the ability of less senior members to develop experience and to become acquainted with complex legislative norms. For proponents of a regular annual legislative session, however, the principal reason for having an annual session is to adopt a one-year budget. The two-year budget system is a relic from the nineteenth century, when Texas was a sparsely populated, largely rural state providing relatively few government services. (Legislators themselves recognize the need for an annual session: in a 1991 legislative survey, 68 percent of House members favored an annual session.[6] There is little reason to expect that opinions have changed since then.) Despite compelling arguments, Texas voters rejected an annual session proposal five times between 1949 and 1975.

JOIN THE DEBATE

THE ISSUE: Are you in favor of the 140-day biennial regular legislative session?

AGREE

1. It is less costly for state taxpayers.
2. Meeting less means less time for lobbyists and special interests to congregate and press for legislation beneficial to their interests.
3. It almost guarantees that Texas legislatures are part-time, with amateur legislators serving.
4. It makes delay an effective tactic to anyone opposed to change.
5. It allows legislators to maintain a smaller number of staff on the payroll in Austin.
6. It allows the presiding officers of both houses great latitude in making decisions.

DISAGREE

1. It compromises the quality of lawmaking and legislative oversight.
2. It does not permit legislators to deal with new problems promptly.
3. Representatives in the legislature do not have enough time for discussion, deliberation, negotiation, and bargaining.
4. Committees perform poorly in their consideration of more than 5,000 bills.
5. It results in the frequent use of special sessions to complete the work of the legislature.
6. It allows special interest groups to kill legislation that affects the interest group.

PARTIES DO NOT ORGANIZE THE COMMITTEES OR LEADERSHIP STRUCTURE

Speaker of the House
The presiding officer in the House of Representatives. The Speaker, who is elected at the beginning of the session by fellow representatives, is the most powerful and influential member of the House.

A new legislature is organized every two years. Rules are adopted, leaders are chosen, committee assignments are made, and committee chairs are designated. Political party membership, which is important in the national and most state legislatures, is not a factor in the organization of the Texas Legislature. The **Speaker of the House** is chosen in an open vote, and again party loyalty is not a factor in this process. Once chosen, a Speaker makes committee assignments based on personal loyalty rather than on party loyalty.

The current Speaker of the Texas House is Tom Craddick, a Republican. In the November 2002 election, Texas voters gave Republicans their first majority in the House in 130 years. Republicans picked up sixteen seats for an 88–62 majority. In January 2003, on the opening day of the Texas Legislature, Craddick (from Midland) was elected the first Republican Speaker since Reconstruction. The Speaker makes committee assignments and distributes chair positions to members of both parties on the basis of personal loyalties and his or her perception of who is most qualified to do the job. Under previous rules, one-half of the membership, excluding the chair and vice chair, had been reserved for veteran representatives, who could request a seat based on their years of service in the House. House Speaker Tom Craddick appointed the entire Appropriations Committee under new rules adopted in January 2003. The new rules eliminated seniority assignments to the budget-writing committee. In fact, Craddick broke with tradition, naming two freshmen representatives to the Appropriations Committee over more tenured representatives.

The presiding officer of the Senate is automatically the lieutenant governor, who is referred to as the president of the Senate. In November 2002, voters elected a new lieutenant governor, David Dewhurst, a Republican and former land commissioner. Like Speaker Craddick, he made committee assignments across party lines.

The rules of the House and the Senate provide that in each new legislature, the presiding officer has the authority to choose committee chairs and make most committee assignments. Although some individual committee chairs in both houses are influential by virtue of their reputations for hard work and good judgment, they do not constitute the separate centers of power that committee chairs and committees do in legislatures, where they are chosen by party. Committee chairs are more dependent on the goodwill of the presiding officers for their continuance as leaders of a particular committee. Most committee members are in the same position; the presiding officers decide who continues, and it is in their interest to have some experienced members on each committee from legislature to legislature. In such a system, it becomes difficult for members to develop expertise on the complex subject matter of their respective committees.

One of the consequences of the absence of party in the decisionmaking structure of the Texas Legislature is that no organization seeks to deliver on the promises each party made in the campaign. Legislative leaders may have an agenda, but that agenda is not necessarily the same one chosen by the people who make up the electoral party or by the voters in the party in the electorate. The link between the party in government and the rest of the party in Texas is a matter of personal relationships and loyalties. No process, such as endorsing conventions or assignment of committee chairs and seats to party members, promotes such a link. In fact, Speaker Tom Craddick crossed the aisle to name Representative Sylvester Turner, a Democrat from Houston, as speaker pro tempore.

The last election has brought a major transformation in Texas politics. Now Republicans have a substantial majority in both the Texas House and Senate. However, in the November 2004 election, Democratic challenger Hubert Von unseated incumbent Republican Talmadge Heflin of Houston. At the time of this book's publication, this election was being contested by Heflin. In addition, as illustrated by the recent redistricting and the dramatic walkout by Democrats in the 2003 session, it appears that we can expect a rather sudden shift from an almost nonpartisan atmosphere featuring bipartisan cooperation, to a sharply partisan atmosphere of one-party rule. This shift may make the Texas Legislature even more contentious than the U.S. Congress.

The Legislators

The Texas Legislature, in theory, has become more, not less, democratic in recent years. If by *democracy* we mean rule by the people and political equality, according to an expert on state legislatures, Alan Rosenthal, "then legislatures have been moving in a decidedly democratic direction."[7] State legislatures are stronger and more effective than at any other time in history. These changes did not happen by themselves. Legislators and individuals outside the legislature have worked hard for changes to make the legislature more effective.

CONSTITUTIONAL REQUIREMENTS

The Texas Constitution sets out the formal, or legal, requirements for membership in the House and the Senate. A state senator must be a citizen of the United States, a qualified voter, a resident of the state for five years prior to election, a resident of the district for one year prior to the election, and at least twenty-six years old. The qualifications for House members are the same, except that the state residency requirement is two years prior to the election, and the age requirement is twenty-one years (see Table 8.2).

POLITICAL REQUIREMENTS

The formal requirements are only part of the picture. A successful election campaign also has requirements. Membership in one of the two major political parties is almost essential. So is adequate funding.

The occupational composition of the Texas legislative body is such that those in some occupations have a much better chance of legislative service than others. People in professional and business occupations dominate the legislature in Texas, just as they dominate the interest group system (see Table 8.3).

Some occupations are indispensable for politics; in other words, those engaged in such occupations can take time out from their professional occupational activ-

TABLE 8.2 Constitutional Qualifications for Legislators		
	House of Representatives	**Senate**
Age	21 years	26 years
Citizenship	U.S.	U.S.
State residency	2 years	5 years
District residency	1 year	1 year
Length of term	2 years	4 years

TABLE 8.3	A Portrait of the Seventy-Eighth Texas Legislature, 2003	
Characteristic	House (150 Members)	Senate (31 Members)
Party		
Democratic	62	12
Republican	88	19
Gender		
Male	118	27
Female	32	4
Race		
African American	14	2
Asian American	1	0
Hispanic	30	7
White	105	22
Age		
Under 30	5	0
30–39	18	0
40–49	53	7
50–59	31	19
60–69	35	5
70 and over	8	0
Education*		
University or college degree	120	24
Law degree	46	10
Master's degree	30	7
Doctoral degree	3	1
Some college	20	5
No college	0	0
No response	8	0
Occupation[†]		
Advertising	0	2
Attorney	47	9
Business	41	12
Education	5	2
Farming, ranching	17	2

(continued)

TABLE 8.3 A Portrait of the Seventy-Eighth Texas Legislature, 2003 (Cont'd)		
Characteristic	**House (150 Members)**	**Senate (31 Members)**
Government service	1	0
Insurance	6	1
Real estate	5	2
Other	36	5
No response	0	0

*Some members hold multiple degrees.
†Some members specify more than one occupation.
Source: Texas Legislative Reference Library (Austin: Texas Legislative Reference Library, July 2003).

ity to serve in politics with a minimum of sacrifice. The legal profession, real estate, the insurance industry, farming, and many businesses permit their owners or partners to be away for short periods of time to serve in the state legislature. Some large businesses are happy to release an employee to serve in the legislature because of the customers and tax breaks that may result from their legislative activity. If all business-related occupations—such as insurance and real estate brokers, bank officials, corporate managers, and entrepreneurs—were grouped into a single business category, it would be the most significant bloc in the Texas legislature. No wonder the business lobby (see Chapter 7) does well.

Traditionally, lawyers have constituted the dominant occupational group in the Texas legislature. Today, lawyers hold around 35 percent of the seats. It is widely believed that lawyers bring special skills to politics. The nature of legal training itself may prepare its recipients for legislative roles. Lawyers make no great changes when they move from representing clients in their private practice to representing constituents as legislators. In addition, lawyers often use the legislature as a stepping-stone to higher elected office or judgeships. Some lawyers view legislative service as a means to benefit their private practice.

Other occupational groups, and in particular those in the skilled labor or manual worker categories, are almost unrepresented among Texas legislators. In most cases, employers are not convinced that these employees would be an asset in the legislature and thus do not subsidize their campaigns or give them paid time off to serve. This situation does not mean that some legislators do not attempt to look after the interests of the working poor and blue-collar Texans. It simply means that the salary paid is not enough to enable a working-class Texan to serve as a Texas legislator.

Educationally, socially, and economically, Texas legislators tend to come from the middle and upper classes. Around 93 percent of the legislators have some college education. More than half the members of the Texas legislature have advanced or graduate degrees.

DEMOGRAPHIC CHARACTERISTICS

Women and minorities are no longer absent from the state Senate and House. In fact, women and minority legislators have steadily increased in number since 1975. This growth in their membership has had an impact on the quality of legislation passed, as well as on the behavior of the legislature as a whole.[8]

The application of the Voting Rights Acts in the mid-1970s and the breakup of multimember legislative districts, created by state legislators for states as well as federal seats, into single-member districts have enabled concentrations of minorities to translate their numbers into legislative seats. In 2003, for example, the Texas Legislature included sixteen African Americans, thirty-seven Mexican Americans, and thirty-six women (up from only twenty-two in 1991). Today, nearly 49 percent of the legislature is Hispanic, African American, or female (see Table 8.3). As one might expect, the increased number of women and minority legislators has brought about concomitant growth in the introduction and enactment of gender- and ethnic-related legislation, such as the James Byrd, Jr., hate crimes act.[9] This bill is named after James Byrd, a black man who was chained behind a pickup truck and then dragged to death in Jasper, Texas, in 1998. The bill was signed into law by Governor Perry in May 2001.

PAY AND PERQUISITES

An amendment to the Texas Constitution adopted in 1975 provides annual salaries of $7,200 for both senators and representatives (up from $4,800). Legislators also receive a per-diem allowance to cover room and board expenses when they are in session, just as they do in other states. A constitutional amendment approved in 1991 established the Texas Ethics Commission and allows the commission to propose legislative salary changes to the voters. The work of the commission eliminates the need for the legislature to propose such changes by constitutional amendment. The commission may also set per-diem pay without voter approval at an amount no greater than the daily deduction that the Internal Revenue Service allows legislators living outside Austin to claim as legislative expenses on their federal income tax returns.

As Texas in Context 8.1 indicates, Texas legislators are the most poorly paid among the megastates. In 2003, state legislators in California and New York received annual salaries of $99,000 and $79,500, respectively.[10] As recently as 1989, Texas voters rejected a constitutional amendment to increase legislators' pay from $7,200 to $23,358, which at the time was approximately equal to the fifty-state average.

Are Texas legislators paid enough? The proponents of higher salaries argue that because the salaries of legislators require displacement from jobs that can be hundreds of miles from Austin, legislators often have to be able to afford the diversion of public service. These persons, proponents argue, are likely to be either lawyers, whose business actually benefits from service in the legislature, or persons who are independently well off. Neither category is likely to contain many individuals who relate to the problems of the working poor and the average blue-collar Texan,

TEXAS in Context

8.1 Number of Legislators in Megastates and Their Compensation

State	Number of Senate Members	Number of House Members	Total Members	Annual Salary
California	40	80	120	$99,000
New York	61	150	211	$79,500
Michigan	38	110	148	$77,400
Pennsylvania	50	203	253	$61,889
Illinois	59	118	177	$55,788
Ohio	33	99	132	$51,674
Massachusetts	40	160	200	$50,123
New Jersey	40	80	120	$49,000
Florida	40	120	160	$27,900
Texas	**31**	**150**	**181**	**$ 7,200**

Source: Council of State Governments, *The Book of States, 2003* (Lexington, Ky.: Council of State Governments, 2003), pp. 115, 127–128.

especially when the poor and blue-collar workers tend to be politically apathetic and unorganized. The point is that the financial and time demands of a legislative career, even a short one, constitute a hurdle that only a small and select group of Texans can handle. Turnover in the legislature is about the same as that of the other megastates, and about 90 percent of the legislators who wish to stay usually get reelected. Both facts suggest that the existing circumstances are unlikely to be changed by the current legislators. Why should they open the doors for a new class of people to replace them?[11]

PROFESSIONALISM

Many observers have argued that state legislatures must adapt as the complexity of their work increases and that legislative sessions be longer. All state legislatures have moved in that direction since the early 1970s, but some have made more changes than others have. Texas in Context 8.2 compares the level of professionalization of the Texas Legislature with nine other megastates. This index of professionalization is based on the salary, staff, and time spent in legislative sessions. The number represents the megastate's position relative to all fifty states.

As you can see, nine large states have more professionalized legislatures than does Texas. The Texas Legislature falls somewhere between state legislatures that can be classified as highly professional and those that can be classified as amateur

Texas in Context

8.2 Professionalization of State Legislatures in the Megastates

State	Rank*
New York	1
Michigan	2
California	3
Massachusetts	4
Pennsylvania	5
Ohio	6
Illinois	8
Florida	13
New Jersey	13
Texas	**20**

*The number represents the megastate's position relative to all fifty states.

Source: Peverril Squire, "Legislative Professionalization and Membership Diversity in State Legislatures," *Legislative Studies Quarterly* 17 (February 1992): 72.

or citizen lawmaking bodies. The good news is that the rank of the Texas Legislature has changed over the years: the study that provided the data for Texas in Context 8.2 indicates a rank of 20 for Texas, whereas the original 1971 study comparing state legislatures gave Texas a rank of 38.[12] Clearly, some improvement has occurred. Nevertheless, the Texas Legislature is still a part-time, amateur legislature containing a few experienced and talented public servants.

Legislative Functions

Members of the Texas Legislature have several major responsibilities. Among the most important are apportionment, adjudication, representation, administrative oversight, and (of course) the parliamentary functions performed by all legislatures.

APPORTIONMENT

Apportionment is the process of drawing district boundaries for a legislative body according to agreed-on principles. Several principles have developed over the years to set standards for an ideally apportioned legislative body. The basic principle established by the U.S. Supreme Court is equal representation: one person, one vote. Other principles include the ideas that districts should be compact and contiguous (no separated parts). In some states, the principle of competition has been applied; in other words, districts should not be drawn so that one party can win easily. If districts are not competitive, then safe seats are created to guarantee victory to the dominant party in the general election. They give the voters little choice in influencing the makeup of the legislature.

Every ten years, the U.S. government conducts a census that provides the figures for apportionment that state and local legislatures must use. In the election after the reapportionment (or redistricting) takes place, all seats in the Texas legislature, House and Senate, are up for election according to the new boundaries.

The Texas Legislature is supposed to draw boundaries for seats in four government bodies: the Texas House, the Texas Senate, the U.S. Congress, and the Texas Board of Education. The redrawing is supposed to take place in the year after the census is taken. In 2001, the Texas Legislature failed to complete its task: No redistricting bills were sent to the governor. The governor did not call a special session to redraw the districts; he left the job of drawing new lines to others.

For the seats in the Texas House and Senate, Texas has a procedure in place. The duty falls on the Legislative Redistricting Board, which is composed of the lieutenant governor, the Speaker, the attorney general, the comptroller of public accounts, and the land commissioner. In July 2001, it met to create new districts for the Texas House and Senate. In a split decision, the three republican statewide officeholders voted for a plan that created numerous safe seats and gave the Republicans an opportunity to win an overwhelming majority in both houses. Both members of the board who had legislative experience—the Speaker of the House (a Democrat) and the lieutenant governor (a Republican)—voted against the plan (see Figures 8.1 and 8.2).

Malapportionment exists when the agreed-on principles have not been followed. Usually this condition means that no redistricting has taken place to reflect population changes. Before 1962, many state legislatures were grossly malapportioned; some legislative districts contained many more people than did others. As a result, cities and their minority residents were underrepresented in a legislature that was unfairly dominated by conservative rural and small-town interests.

Following the decision of the U.S. Supreme Court in the famous Tennessee case of *Baker v. Carr* (1962), the membership in the Texas Legislature began to change. In this landmark case, the U.S. Supreme Court suggested that citizens who felt deprived could challenge such redistricting in the federal courts as a violation of the equal protection clause of the U.S. Constitution.[13] Shortly after, in *Reynolds v. Sims* (1964) the Supreme Court ruled, based on the principle of one person, one vote, that congressional as well as state legislative districts must have a substantially equal population.[14] Other principles are that districts be contiguous, that they be compact, and the drawing of districts should avoid splitting communities of interest.

The federal Voting Rights Act prohibits drawing of district lines that would discriminate against racial or language minorities. In 1982, Congress strengthened the Voting Rights Act by outlawing any electoral arrangement that has the effect of

FIGURE 8.1A Texas State House of Representative Districts

FIGURE 8.1B Texas State House of Representative Districts

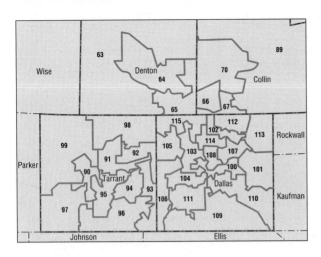

Dallas area inset

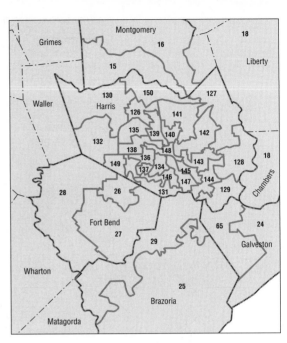

Houston area inset

denying any representation to members of minority groups. In *Thornburg v. Gingles* (1986), the U.S. Supreme Court interpreted the case to require state legislatures to redistrict their states in a way that maximizes minority representation in the U.S. Congress and state legislatures.[15] Since that decision, the U.S. Supreme Court has made several more decisions that have left state legislators somewhat confused about what the Court really wants them to do about representing racial and ethnic communities. The situation is complicated by the fact that in Texas and other states affected by the Voting Rights Act, any voting map—state or local—must be approved by the U.S. Justice Department.

The Voting Rights Act applies to all states and has special provisions (such as approval of district changes by the federal Justice Department) that apply to states like Texas that have traditionally denied blacks the right to vote. In a few cases, the Justice Department has required state legislatures to create districts that the U.S. Supreme Court then found to be unconstitutional.[16]

Many legislators in both parties have adjusted to this predicament by assuming that whatever happens with the districts drawn, a court challenge will ensue. Thus, individual legislators will sometimes ask for votes on amendments to the redistricting bill they have proposed, even when they know they will lose, to establish grounds for suing the state later.[17]

FIGURE 8.2A   Texas State Senate Districts

FIGURE 8.2B   Texas State Senate Districts (continued)

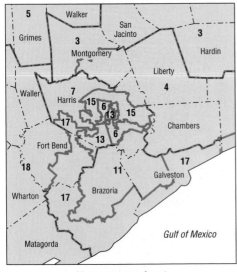

Houston area inset

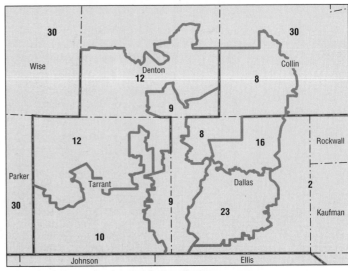

Dallas area inset

Gerrymandering
The practice of drawing legislative district boundaries with the intent of discriminating against a group of people.

Gerrymandering is the drawing of election district lines to gain a partisan advantage. While malapportionment is unconstitutional, gerrymandering is as American as apple pie—unless protected categories of persons are denied representation. When one political party controls both houses of the legislature as well as the governorship, that party is in a position to gerrymander and thus increase its chances of doing well in the next election. The following subsection illustrates a recent case of gerrymandering in Texas.

CONTROVERSIAL APPORTIONMENT IN 2003

Apportionment, or redistricting, is traditionally the most divisive and partisan issue considered by the legislature. It was particularly divisive in the regular session and in the three special sessions of the Texas Legislature in the summer of 2003. Republicans in the Texas legislature were pushed by Tom DeLay, the majority leader of the U.S. Congress, to redraw congressional lines to favor the Republicans, and the Democrats did what they could to prevent it.

Although state legislators are required every ten years to use the new census data to redraw congressional district lines, it did not happen in Texas in 2001. After the regular session of the legislature ended with no redistricting bill, the courts and the Legislative Redistricting Board started the task. Redistricting in sessions after the district maps have been drawn and elections held (in this case, in 2002) is rare without a court order to do so. Redistricting to gerrymander a Republican majority in the Texas delegation to Congress became an unexpected priority in Austin, how-

The process isn't over when the legislature or the Redistricting Commission is finished. Sargent © 2004 Austin American-Statesman. *Reprinted with permission of* Universal Press Syndicate. *All rights reserved.*

ever, after the U.S. House majority leader, Tom DeLay of Sugar Land, began urging the governor and Texas legislative leaders to revisit the matter.

The congressional map in use for the 2002 elections was drawn by a panel of federal judges after the legislature—then split between Republicans and Democrats—failed to draw new congressional lines. The Republican argument for changing the map was that they hold all the state elective offices and a majority in the Legislature, and so they should also have a congressional delegation majority. Democrats held a 17–15 majority in the state's congressional delegation. In several of these districts, the vote for governor was Republican and the vote for Congress was Democratic; in other words, these districts were competitive.

In May 2003, when it was clear there would be no compromise on the congressional redistricting bill, fifty-one Democratic members of the Texas House of Representatives a quorum. They stayed in Ardmore, Oklahoma for four days until a crucial procedural deadline passed. This killed the DeLay designed redistricting bill in the regular session.

However, Governor Rick Perry called lawmakers back to Austin for the first special session in twelve years for the primary purpose of redrawing the congressional boundaries and ending the Democrats' 17–15 majority in the thirty-two-member delegation.

A coalition of senators blocked debate of the bill in the first special session. Although Republicans outnumbered Democrats 19–12 in the Senate, under the chamber's two-thirds tradition, twenty-one members must agree to hear debate on any legislative issue pending on the agenda. This tradition means eleven members can effectively block any legislation.

Lieutenant Governor David Dewhurst announced that he would do away with the two-thirds rule during the second redistricting special session, so only sixteen senators were needed to debate and pass measures. During the second special legislative session, eleven Senate Democrats fled on July 28, 2003, to Albuquerque, New Mexico, and stayed there through the duration of the session. Again, no compromise, no quorum. They crossed the state line so Texas law officers directed by the Senate sergeant-at-arms could not arrest them and force them back to the capital.

At the end of the second special session, state Senator John Whitmire of Houston returned to Texas and said that he would attend a third special session to fight redistricting on the Senate floor. Whitmire's move gave the Senate enough members to achieve a quorum for the third special session, which began on September 15, 2003. After six months, two walkouts, and three special legislative sessions, the Republican majority produced a new congressional redistricting that sent six additional Texas Republicans to Washington on November 2, 2004. Republicans took control of the Texas congressional delegation with the help of a redistricting strategy engineered by House majority leader Tom DeLay. Republicans now hold a 21-11 majority, wiping out Democrats' last toe hold on power in the state.

If voters are to have meaningful choices in legislative elections, our method of redistricting can and should be changed. It is worth considering the solution proposed by state Senator Jeff Wentworth, a Republican from San Antonio. He has offered bills in several sessions that would delegate redistricting to an independent bipartisan citizens' commission, similar to commissions in several other states. His proposed nine-member Texas Congressional Redistricting Commission would be comprised of four Republicans, four Democrats and a nonvoting presiding officer selected by the commission members. Senate Republicans and Senate Democrats would select two commission members each, and House Republicans and House Democrats would do the same. Perhaps redistricting could become an issue that interests you enough to call or write your state legislator about. Then legislators can't claim that constituents haven't expressed an opinion. When legislators behave the way they did in 2003, the state of Texas looks silly, and the public's respect for the political process is likely diminished.

As Kulvicki showed us in the chapter-opening story, influencing the system is hard work, but it can be fun and it can be done. If citizens want to fulfill their responsibilities in a democratic society, they must navigate through a sometimes bewildering maze to understand what government is doing and whether their representatives are fulfilling the promises they made to get into office. Issues such as redistricting affect our ability to influence the process; other issues affect our lives even more directly. Thus, it is important for us to do something about it. Ignoring politics simply ignores an opportunity to take control of our own lives.

ADJUDICATION

The legislature has the authority to judge other officials. They may reprimand or even impeach and try them—that is, adjudicate—judicial and executive officials.

The House of Representatives may impeach (indict) judicial and executive officials. Individuals impeached by the House must be tried by the Senate, with conviction and removal from their department on a two-thirds majority vote. The last time a governor was impeached, his wife was elected twice. After James "Pa" Ferguson was impeached in his second term in 1917, Miriam "Ma" Ferguson was elected governor in 1925 and again in 1933. Her campaign slogan, "Two governors for the price of one," says it all.[18] Adjudication is not a function that the legislature does often or gladly. It is worth noting, however, that the function exists; executive and judicial officials are well aware of it.

REPRESENTATION

Delegate A representative who is expected to mirror the views of those whom he or she represents.

Trustee A representative who acts according to his or her conscience and the broad interest of the entire society.

Legislators are elected to make decisions in the name of their constituents. Political scientists have classified the role of representation in terms of two concepts: delegate and trustee. Some legislators see themselves as **delegates,** instructed to follow their constituency's preferences. Others see themselves as **trustees,** chosen to serve and carry out their own independent judgment, even if that puts them in opposition to a majority of their constituents. Research on individual legislators has shown that some consciously try to achieve one or the other of these two roles, whereas others attempt to move back and forth between the two roles, depending on the policy issue. Some issues may be so salient to the constituency that the legislator must follow the majority preference. Others may provoke so little interest that the legislator feels free to act on his or her independent judgment. You, of course, can make issues salient in your part of Texas and thus influence the role your legislator plays.

In a recent survey, 67 percent of Texas legislators described their role as trustee, 23 percent as delegate, and 10 percent as broker, that is, "to get the most for my constituents.[19] Whether they have developed these perceptions as the product of a philosophy of representative government or as a reflection of the expedient way to stay in office makes little difference. The political reality of making hundreds of policy decisions in a short period of time precludes extensive interaction between constituents and representatives. As a consequence, legislators are forced by circumstances to make decisions on the basis of the facts at hand and an assessment of how the constituents back home want them to vote. Constituency influence is a big factor in decisionmaking. We have heard legislators say, "No one from my district has contacted me on this, therefore they don't care about it."[20]

Casework The practice of individual legislators following up on constituent complaints about their contacts with administrative agencies.

Regardless of their general approach to representation, legislators and their staff pay a great deal of attention to **casework,** that is, personal attention to agency actions that have affected individual constituents. As the details in the laws written by legislators are filled in by the executive branch with rules, regulations, and procedures, the lives of Texans are influenced, and casework results. Members of the legislature and their staff must spend an increasing amount of time helping constituents cut red tape or correct bureaucratic mistakes. A Texas legislator summed it up this way: "One thing I like about politics is the feeling of being useful. I'm fairly religious, and I look upon politics as being a kind of ministry. I am not considered a heavyweight on legislation, but I put a lot of emphasis on . . . constituency casework."[21]

Malcolm Jewell, a political scientist, interviewed many legislators and found that half of their time and that of their staff was devoted to casework.[22] Legislators place great importance on serving their constituents. They believe that their continuation in office depends a great deal on satisfying those who request personal assistance. Thus, do not be shy about contacting your state representative or senator. Most of them believe that casework helps keep them in office.

ADMINISTRATIVE OVERSIGHT

Oversight The effort by the state legislature, through hearings, investigation, and other techniques, to exercise control over the actions of executive agencies.

Sunset review The periodic evaluation of state agencies by the legislature to determine whether they should be reauthorized.

Administrative **oversight** is the legislature's responsibility to make sure the bureaucracy is carrying out the intent of the legislature in administering state programs; thus, it is part of the checks-and-balances principle. Oversight is the process by which the state legislature follows up on the laws it has enacted to ensure that they are being enforced and administered in the way that the state legislature intended. Areas of oversight include committee review of agency action; the legislature's approval of the state budget; approval of executive personnel appointments; and **sunset review,** or the periodic evaluation of state agencies to determine whether they should be reauthorized.

The legislature has the authority to investigate governmental operations through committee hearings and the sunset review. The information gathered may be taken into account in new lawmaking, but sometimes the investigative process itself puts pressure on governmental officials to change their activities, alter the way a law has been interpreted, or simply become more efficient.

Because the legislature controls monetary appropriations, it has the potential to review all agency programs before providing budget items. The Legislative Budget Board, the lawmakers' own budgeting agency, helps the legislature to evaluate all agency appropriations. In particular, new program proposals are closely scrutinized by legislative committees before approval is given. In 1991, the Texas Legislature launched a new budget process based on long-term strategic planning and requiring performance-based budgets measured by specific outcomes. The specific benchmarks that measure spending efficiency may facilitate legislative oversight of state agency spending and permit lawmakers to determine more accurately if the agencies are meeting their performance goals.

Another important instrument of control over state administration is the sunset review. The Sunset Advisory Commission, which was created in 1977, evaluates each state agency and its programs on a rotating basis according to a twelve-year schedule. The commission makes a recommendation about whether the agency should be continued, abolished, or merged with another state agency.

LAWMAKING

Because the Texas Constitution declares that all the legislative power of the state is vested in the legislature, each senator and representative may introduce and help pass legislation designed to promote the general welfare of the state—or at least some special groups within it. Today, the lawmaking function is much more difficult than it was in the past, in part because the legislature must tackle many more problems than it did in the past. The increased demands on the legislature are mostly due to the increased complexity and scope of government. Previously, government touched the life of average citizens on fewer occasions. Today, government profoundly affects the character and quality of every citizen's life. The range of bills considered by the legislature is enormous. The laws that legislators enact create binding new restrictions, new rights, and new programs, and they can repeal or amend existing laws. Many laws also set tax rates and designate the purposes for which public monies are to be expended.

Legislative Process

Chief among the responsibilities of the legislature is its lawmaking function. Proposals for legislation can come from the governor, executive agencies, constituencies, interest groups, or even private individuals, but only members of the House or Senate can formally submit a bill for legislative consideration. As we have already mentioned, the workload of the legislature has increased substantially in the past two decades. In the 140-day regular session of the Seventy-Eighth Legislature, over 5,500 bills were introduced in the House and the Senate; less than 25 percent were enacted into law. In fact, no legislation has a serious chance of success without strong support from the public, the legislative leadership, other legislators, the governor, or important interest groups. The adoption process is much the same in both chambers of the legislature.[23]

The Texas Constitution specifies that a *bill,* that is, a proposed law, be used to introduce a law. In addition to bills, three types of resolutions can be introduced in each house:

- *Joint resolutions* are used to propose amendments to the state constitution and to ratify amendments to the U.S. Constitution.

- *Concurrent resolutions* affect the internal affairs of the legislature, express the opinion of legislators, and require the approval of both the House and the Senate (for example, to set the time of the final adjournment of a session).

- *Simple resolutions* are used in each house and pertain to matters involving that house only (for example, the adoption of rules or the appointment of officers).

A bill must survive five stages before it becomes a law; it may be killed during any of these stages. Thus, it is much easier to defeat a bill than it is to get one passed, which is why your involvement is important. Many bad bills need to be killed, and so many good ones need help. The House and Senate have parallel processes, and often the same bill is introduced in each chamber at the same time. The basic steps in enacting a law are summarized in Figure 8.3.

FIGURE 8.3   How a Bill Becomes a Law

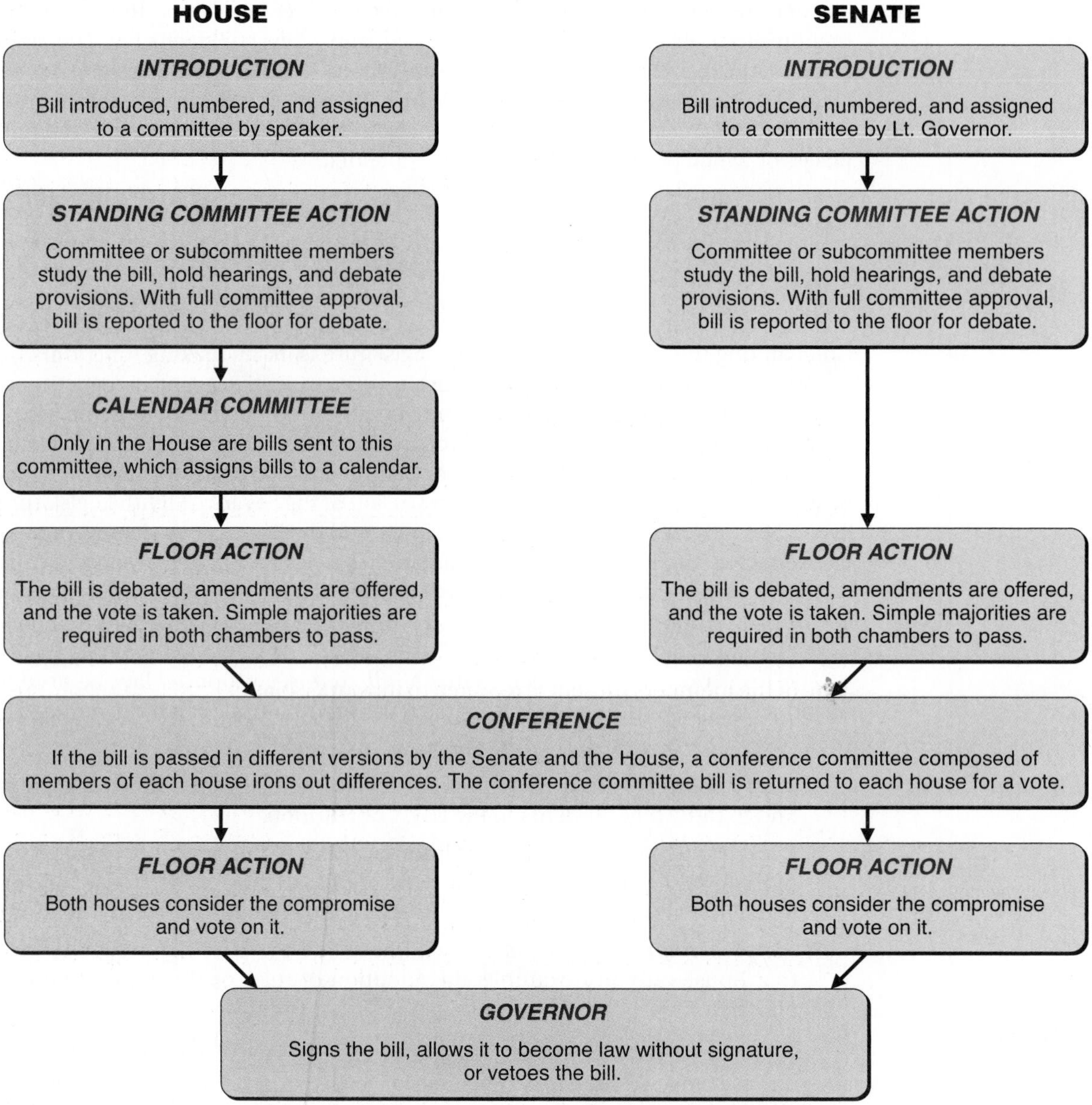

HOUSE

INTRODUCTION
Bill introduced, numbered, and assigned to a committee by speaker.

STANDING COMMITTEE ACTION
Committee or subcommittee members study the bill, hold hearings, and debate provisions. With full committee approval, bill is reported to the floor for debate.

CALENDAR COMMITTEE
Only in the House are bills sent to this committee, which assigns bills to a calendar.

FLOOR ACTION
The bill is debated, amendments are offered, and the vote is taken. Simple majorities are required in both chambers to pass.

SENATE

INTRODUCTION
Bill introduced, numbered, and assigned to a committee by Lt. Governor.

STANDING COMMITTEE ACTION
Committee or subcommittee members study the bill, hold hearings, and debate provisions. With full committee approval, bill is reported to the floor for debate.

FLOOR ACTION
The bill is debated, amendments are offered, and the vote is taken. Simple majorities are required in both chambers to pass.

CONFERENCE
If the bill is passed in different versions by the Senate and the House, a conference committee composed of members of each house irons out differences. The conference committee bill is returned to each house for a vote.

FLOOR ACTION
Both houses consider the compromise and vote on it.

FLOOR ACTION
Both houses consider the compromise and vote on it.

GOVERNOR
Signs the bill, allows it to become law without signature, or vetoes the bill.

INTRODUCTION AND REFERRAL

A bill or a resolution is officially introduced when a representative gives twelve signed copies of it to the chief clerk. A bill may be introduced in either the House or the Senate unless it levies a tax. All tax bills must originate in the House. Once introduced, the bill is given a number (for example, HB 10 or SB 10, indicating, respectively, House or Senate bill number ten for the session).

The Texas Constitution specifies that no bill, except general appropriations bills, may address more than one subject, which must be clearly stated in the caption or title. This regulation is frequently waived, however, which means that the presiding officer may have more than one committee to which he can assign the bill. If it is low on his priority list or he wishes to get the attention of its sponsor, he sends it to a committee that is likely to be unfriendly to the proposed legislation.

Another constitutional provision calls for a regular session to be divided into three specified periods. The first thirty days of the session are reserved for the introduction of bills, resolutions, emergency appropriations, Senate confirmations of recess or interim appointees, appointments made by the governor in the interim, the period between legislative sessions, and emergency matters submitted by the governor.

During the second thirty days, committees must hold hearings to consider pending legislation and emergency matters. During the last sixty days, both houses may act on pending legislation. It has become common practice, however, for the House of Representatives and the Senate to use a constitutional stipulation permitting elimination of this session division by a four-fifths vote at the beginning of a legislative session. In practice, both the House and the Senate permit unlimited introduction of bills during the first sixty days. After the sixtieth day, a four-fifths vote of the members present is required to introduce bills or joint resolutions other than certain emergency matters submitted by the governor, emergency appropriations, or local bills. A local bill affects a single unit of local government (for example, a city, county, or precinct). Following the introduction of a bill, it is assigned a number and gets its first reading. The reading clerk reads aloud the caption, which is a brief summary of the contents, and gives the bill to the speakers. This reading consists of reading only the title of a bill, not the whole bill. Three separate readings on three separate days are required by the Texas Constitution; however, this requirement may be suspended by a four-fifths vote of the house in which the bill is pending. In such cases, the bill is given an immediate third reading following the vote to pass the bill to engrossment or third reading.

COMMITTEE ACTION

After the proposed law is introduced and given its first reading, the Speaker of the House refers the measure to the standing committee with jurisdiction over the subject matter involved in the proposal. In the case of new programs or when bills involve overlapping jurisdiction, the Speaker selects the committee for referral, which leaves the Speaker considerable personal discretion that may be exercised to the advantage of the interests he favors. In the Senate, the lieutenant governor has similar powers. The Senate rules do not define committee jurisdictions.

What happens next is critical to the life or death of a bill. Many bills are pigeonholed, die, and are never reported to the entire House or Senate by the committee. Thus, legislative committees are the place where the bulk of the legislative work is done. Clearly, the size of the legislature, the number of bills it handles, and time constraints preclude much meaningful floor action, especially in the House of Representatives, which is considerably larger than the Senate. Committees make several decisions about proposed legislation. The first is whether to take up the bill at all. Failure to consider a bill usually kills it. The other committee options are to adopt the bill, amend it somewhat, or rewrite it entirely.

In the House, committee chairs may refer legislation to a subcommittee. The subcommittee chair then decides whether the legislation is to be set for a subcommittee hearing. In 1993, several reforms were adopted when Pete Laney was elected Speaker. Included among the reforms were the requirements of advanced public posting of the meetings and opening the meetings to the public and other members. Therefore, hearings are held in open sessions, a change that affords interest groups and citizens a meaningful opportunity to express their opinions. The decisions these committees and subcommittees make affect the lives of millions of Texans. They decide how to raise money and how to spend it, who will pay taxes, and who will receive benefits. With so much at stake, ordinary citizens must make the attempt to testify at these hearings and thus influence legislators' decisions. If you are concerned about a particular issue, you should try to persuade the legislators to take your point of view and mobilize others to do the same.

Mark up Alter the original bill so that it reflects the information the legislature gleaned from the hearing process.

After conducting public hearings, the subcommittee or the full committee meets to **mark up** the bill, that is, draft the bill into the form it wants. Often, each line is amended or rewritten. The full committee receives the marked-up bill from the subcommittee or does the markup itself and then votes on the bill. A majority vote of the committee members is required to approve a motion to report a bill favorably or unfavorably. If a bill is reported favorably out of the committee, it is placed on the calendar of the house from which it originated.

THE CALENDARS SYSTEM

All bills reported favorably from house committees are referred to the Calendars Committee. The Calendars Committee has full authority to make assignments to calendars in whatever order is necessary and desirable. The Speaker, who appoints and controls the Calendar Committee, can have the final word on the matter.

The House of Representatives has six legislative calendars to schedule legislative business:

- *Emergency calendar*—for all bills demanding immediate action, bills submitted as an emergency by the governor, revenue and tax bills, and general appropriations bills.

- *Major state calendar*—for all bills of statewide effect that do not merit emergency designation.
- *Constitutional amendment calendar*—for all proposed amendments to the state constitution or ratification of amendments to the U.S. Constitution.
- *General state and area calendar*—for all bills having less than statewide effect but applying to more than one county.
- *Local calendar*—for all bills that apply to only one county.
- *Consent calendar*—for all bills that are not expected to have opposition.

For bills referred to the Calendars Committee, only those that appear on a daily calendar distributed in advance to House members may be considered on the floor. Once a bill appears on a printed daily calendar, it retains its place in the lineup of bills set for consideration that day and cannot be displaced by any other bill.

The Senate has no Calendars Committee similar to that in the House. Bills and resolutions reported from Senate committees are listed on the daily Senate calendar in the order in which their committee reports are received by the secretary of the Senate. Senate rules require that bills be calendared on a first-come, first-served basis. As a matter of practice, the Senate controls the calendar by lodging a bill at the top of the calendar as a *stopper*. A stopper bill blocks all other bills' access to the floor except by a two-thirds vote to suspend the rules. The stopper bill for the Seventy-Third Legislature, for example, was SB 98 by Haley, a bill that established a county parks compost program.[24] As a result, any bill listed after the first bill reported must be considered out of order and thus requires approval of two-thirds of the members present. As we have seen in the case of the redistricting bill, the lieutenant governor and a few key members can see to it that the first bill on the calendar is the one they want to have discussed. Thus, for that bill, it isn't necessary to vote for treatment out of order.

FLOOR ACTION

Once a bill reaches the floor, it receives its second reading. Reading is again usually by caption only, and the measure is then subject to debate and amendment by the entire House membership. Debate in the House is governed by House rules. Each speaker is limited to ten minutes, except that the representative in charge of the bill is permitted twenty minutes to open and twenty minutes to close debate.

In the Senate, debate is more common, and speaking time has no restrictions. The privilege of unlimited debate can be used to delay legislative action. The **filibuster**—extended debate—is often used to talk a bill to death. In 1977, Senator Bill Meier spoke for forty-three hours against a bill—which nevertheless was passed as soon as he quit the floor. Debate can be limited by simple majority vote, which eliminates the possibility of lengthy filibusters like those that occasionally occur in the U.S. Senate, where a three-fifths vote is required to close off debate. Filibusters in the Texas Senate are most likely to be effective in the closing days of a session, when a delay of a few hours can prevent consideration of important matters.

Filibuster A tactic used by members of the Senate to prevent action on legislation they oppose; it involves continuously holding the floor and speaking until the majority backs down.

When the floor debate is finally concluded, a vote is taken on passage of the measure to engrossment, which requires a simple majority of those voting. The engrossing clerk has the responsibility of typing the bill in the exact form in which it was passed, including all corrections and amendments. A second vote is taken after the third reading. At this stage, the amendments require a two-thirds majority. The third reading consideration of a bill normally occurs the day following second reading consideration. The rules may be suspended to allow second and third readings on the same day.

Once a bill has passed one house, it must be transmitted to the other house for action, and the process begins again. If the bill passes both houses with no changes, it is sent to the governor. In all likelihood, however, the second chamber will have made changes in the bill. The bill is then sent back to the chamber of origin, which may accept the second chamber's amendments or request a conference.

CONFERENCE COMMITTEE

Because most controversial legislation results in conflict between the House and Senate, it is often necessary to call a conference. Conference committees seek to resolve differences between the House and the Senate versions of a bill. They have the power to rewrite legislation.

Either chamber can request a conference, but both chambers must agree to it. The presiding officers appoint members to a joint House-Senate conference committee—five from each house. A conference committee's members are usually drawn from the standing committees that originally handled the bill. The delegation votes as a unit according to how the majority of that delegation feels. A conference committee deals with only a single bill; during a session, there are as many conference committees as there are bills in dispute.

When the conference committee arrives at an agreement, the bill is reported out to both houses for final disposition. The final bill, as reported by the conference committee, may only be approved or rejected; it cannot be amended.

FINAL ACTION

Should a bill survive the process in both houses, it is then enrolled (typed in the exact form in which it was passed), signed by the presiding officer, and sent to the governor. While the legislature is in session, the governor has ten days in which to act and three alternatives for action:

1. Sign the bill, thereby indicating approval. In this case, the bill becomes law ninety days after the end of the session or at another date designated in the bill (for example, at the beginning of the new state fiscal year). If a bill is deemed an emergency matter and passed by four-fifths majorities in both houses, it goes into effect as soon as it is signed by the governor.

Veto The governor's constitutional right to reject a piece of legislation passed by the legislature.

2. **Veto** the bill and return it to the legislature. If the legislature takes no further

Item veto A veto exercised on appropriations bills that gives the governor authority to eliminate unacceptable items while approving the majority of the appropriations.

action, the bill dies. The legislature can override the governor's veto with a two-thirds vote in each house. The governor may also **item veto** separate items in appropriations measures.

3. Do nothing. During the legislative session, and if the governor has not acted after ten days, the bill becomes law without his or her signature. If a bill remains unsigned for twenty days after the legislature adjourns, it becomes law.

Legislative Support System

Now more than ever before, legislators cannot function without help. The range and complexity of the policy issues confronting the legislature have greatly increased in the past 100 years. Lawmakers need clerical assistance and researchers to make sense of and cast votes on the hundreds of complicated measures introduced in every session. Consequently, each legislator is given funds for hiring a personal staff. Although much of a staff's time is devoted to secretarial and clerical work, many legislators have assistants to help them keep track of legislation, research particular problems, and supplement the information provided to them by representatives of interest groups. In addition, legislators can draw on the technical and legal expertise of organizations especially created by the legislature to provide information to its members.

The *Legislative Council,* with fifteen members (five senators and ten representatives), provides a bill-drafting service for individual legislators. It also conducts a short orientation program for new legislators to help inform them on such matters, as does the University of Texas's LBJ School. The ten-member *Legislative Budget Board* (LBB) prepares a detailed operating budget for the state. It is made up of the lieutenant governor (as chair), the Speaker (as vice chair), and four members from each house. The four members from each house are appointed by the respective presiding officers.

The *Sunset Advisory Commission,* established in 1977, assesses the operation of state administrative agencies that are under review for reauthorization or cessation.

The *Legislative Reference Library* provides resource materials for lawmakers, their staff, and the general public. The library houses a large collection of reference works relating to government, economics, politics, and law. It includes 50,000 volumes and 450,000 newspaper clippings dating back to the beginning of the twentieth century.[25]

A key support group in the Texas House of Representatives is the *House Research Organization (HRO).* Originally the House Study group, it is a nonpartisan agency under the direction of a fifteen-member steering committee that is selected independently of the Speaker. This committee provides all members of the legislature with reports on pending legislative issues and bill analyses. During each legislative session, the HRO staff also publishes a daily floor report, which analyzes important bills by providing an objective summary of their contents and arguments for and against each one. The HRO publications are available to all senators and representatives and those who subscribe to those publications.

Summary

Today, legislatures are more representative than they were before. Lawmakers still do not mirror the public they represent, but they come a great deal closer than in the past. Women, African Americans, and Mexican Americans are no longer absent from the Texas House and Senate. As a result of new technologies such as the Internet, e-mail, fax, and cell phones, the legislature has become more accessible and open to ordinary citizens. We now have greater opportunity to influence our representatives' decisions.

Daniel Kulvicki's experience, highlighted in the chapter-opening story, indicates that what sways representatives most is evidence that their constituents care about particular issues. His story also indicates that one convinced legislator is not enough. To get things done, you usually need more ammunition.

The Texas Legislature meets in regular session every other year, in odd calendar years, for 140 days. The governor can call special sessions of the legislature, which may last for a maximum of thirty calendar days. The functions of the legislature include apportionment, adjudication, representation, administrative oversight, lawmaking, and the two parliamentary functions of taxing and spending.

The Speaker of the House, who is elected by a majority vote of its membership, is the chief leader in the House of Representatives; the lieutenant governor is the presiding officer of the Senate. Both the House and the Senate have adopted rules that grant their presiding officers extensive legislative, administrative, and organizational authority.

Most of the actual work of the legislature is handled by committees and subcommittees. The permanent and most powerful committees are called standing committees. Before any bill can be considered by the entire House or Senate, it must be approved by a majority vote in the standing committee to which it was assigned. Some House and Senate committees are also divided into subcommittees.

The Texas Legislature is at the heart of governmental efforts to respond to changing social and economic problems and to do so according to the public will. More than any other branch of government, the legislature is sensitive to popular impulses, preferences, and doubts. Compared to the legislature of a few decades ago, today's legislature is a more diverse body and a serious institution.

Many factors affect how the legislature ultimately decides on legislation. Among the most important influences are constituency preferences. You can write to your legislators by e-mail. We urge you to contact your representatives and inform them of the needs and concerns of your district and community. To learn more about your state legislature, refer to the Internet Resources section at the end of this chapter.

KEY TERMS

Parliamentary functions, p. 216
Parliaments, p. 217
Bicameral, p. 217
Conference committee, p. 218
Standing committee, p. 218

Subcommittee, p. 218
Special or **ad hoc committee,** p. 220
Interim committee, p. 220
Joint committee, p. 220
Lieutenant governor, p. 222

Speaker of the House, p. 224
Gerrymandering, p. 236
Delegate, p. 238
Trustee, p. 238
Casework, p. 239
Oversight, p. 240

Sunset review, p. 240
Mark up, p. 244
Filibuster, p. 245
Veto, p. 246
Item veto, p. 247

FOR FURTHER READING

Calvert, Robert A., and Arnold De Leon, *The History of Texas* (Arlington Heights, Ill.: Harlan Davidson, 1990).

Gray, Virginia, and Russell L. Hanson, *Politics in the American States: A Comparative Analysis,* 8th ed. (Washington, D.C.: CQ Press, 2003).

Jewell, Malcolm E., *Representation in State Legislatures* (Lexington: University of Kentucky Press, 1982).

Norris, George, *The Establishment in Texas Politics: The Primitive Years, 1938–1957* (Norman: University of Oklahoma Press, 1979).

Rosenthal, Alan, *The Decline of Representative Democracy: Process, Participation, and Power in State Legislatures* (Washington, D.C.: CQ Press, 1998).

Volgy, Thomas J., *Politics in the Trenches: Citizens, Politicians, and the Fate of Democracy* (Tucson: University of Arizona Press, 2001).

STUDY QUESTIONS

1. Identify Daniel Kulvicki, STAR Day, and five points about politics that we learn from Kulvicki's story.

2. What are the parliamentary functions of legislatures?

3. Identify the five major organizational features of the Texas Legislature.

4. Name the five different kinds of committees. Which type is the most important?

5. What are the consequences of the two-thirds tradition in the Texas Senate?

CRITICAL THINKING QUESTIONS

1. It is possible to run a government of a fairly complex political system without a legislature. Would Texas be able to operate if it did not have a legislative branch? Why or why not?

2. How can the trading of favors among senators to get bills debated be harmful to legislative effectiveness?

3. Should the Texas salary for both senators and representatives be increased? Why or why not?

4. When representing their constituents, legislators play the role of trustee, delegate, and/or broker. Which role would you like your legislature to play? Why?

5. The Sunset Advisory Commission assesses the operation of state administrative agencies that are under review for reauthorization or cessation. How can the public participate in the sunset review process?

INTERNET RESOURCES

www.capitol.state.tx.us/ Texas Legislature Online provides extensive information on the Texas Legislature.

www.lrl.state.tx.us The Texas Legislative Reference Library home page offers information on bills filed and the Texas document collection, book collection, and legislative council databases.

www.tlc.state.tx.us The Texas Legislative home page offers information on topics relating to state government and the legislative process.

www.ncsl.org/ The National Conference of State Legislatures (NCSL) website provides personalized, comprehensive access to NCSL information and reports for state legislators and legislative staff. It also provides the ability to search more than 500,000 state documents encompassing legislative policy reports, current and past legislation, state statutes, and fifty-state surveys.

CHAPTER 9

The Executive Branch of Texas Government

B ernie Birnbaum's credentials as an individual who made a difference to the insurance industry were already established by October 1998, and they were soon reaffirmed afterward. The insurance industry, which resented Birnbaum's work revealing their redlining practices, went to court to keep him from getting a job. The lawyers for big insurance companies got an injunction to prevent a member of the Texas House of Representatives from hiring Birnbaum. They went to a lot of trouble concerning this opponent.

Redlining is the practice of discriminating against a certain neighborhood. It is like drawing a red line around it and refusing to do business there or to do business at all at the same price as in more upscale neighborhoods. The practice came to public attention in the 1960s when real estate agents and mortgage bankers treated inner-city neighborhoods differently from suburban neighborhoods in terms of who was shown homes where and who obtained mortgages.

Birnbaum, who worked for the Texas Department of Insurance, had noticed the same type of pattern with insurance as early as 1995. Because state law makes auto liability insurance mandatory, everyone has to buy it. However, liability insurance alone is not a moneymaker for insurance companies. They tended to avoid neighborhoods where potential customers were not likely to buy the other insurance features that were profitable to the insurance companies. For those neighborhoods, the companies increased the price of auto liability insurance.

This apparently economic decision had clear consequences for people in lower-income categories who needed transportation to get to work. They found it difficult to find insurance agents who would sell them liability insurance for their automobiles at a fair price. According to *San Antonio Express* columnist Carlos Guerra, "Auto liability insurance—like comprehensive auto, homeowner, renter, health and every other type of insurance—is more expensive for poorer Texans than for those with moderate or high incomes. . . . It's redlining plain and simple and it must be stopped."[1]

The Texas Department of Insurance is an executive agency responsible for preventing discrimination against Texans in the sale of insurance. In 1995, a department investigation recommended that the Nationwide Insurance Company be fined $10 million for illegal discrimination. The fine was never levied because the insurance commissioner who recommended it, Rebecca Lightsey, was replaced when Governor Bush took over from Governor Richards. New rules she had proposed, which would have made it difficult and expensive for insurance companies to engage in redlining, were withdrawn by her replacement, Elton Bomer.[2]

Birnbaum left the Texas Department of Insurance when it became clear that the department under Bomer was not going to be as friendly to consumers as it had been under Lightsey. He began to speak out and use his expertise about the insurance industry to work for ordinary Texans. He wrote many letters and opinion pieces, he testified before legislative committees, and he made a difference. He became so troublesome to the insurance industry that when they learned he was going to get a job and get paid to look into the way they did business—not to mention the way the Texas Department of Insurance under Bomer was letting them get away with it—they went to court to keep Birnbaum from getting a job with State Representative Lon Burnham, a Democrat from Fort Worth. The public reaction to this effort was so strong that the injunction was lifted, and Birnbaum went to work to continue to make a difference on behalf of ordinary Texans.

Birnbaum's story provides us with two useful insights into Texas politics. First, he demonstrates that individuals can both embarrass well-financed interests like the insurance industry and force them to use precious resources, including a bit of their credibility, in doing battle. Public attention causes the powerful to negotiate before there is another public battle. Second, Birnbaum's story points to the good news as well as the bad news about the executive branch in Texas. The bad news is that the executive branch is so much larger than the legislature and has so many points of entry that well-organized interest groups can have a great deal of influence. The good news is that many public servants in the executive branch will listen to reason, will try to do what is right, and sometimes will quit their jobs, as Birnbaum did, before they compromise their principles. In short, you have allies in the many limbs of the executive branch; however, you may have to move a few leaves to find them.

The Executive Branch

The executive branch enforces the laws passed by the legislature. To do so, it often makes rules that spell out general concepts in laws passed by the legislature. Based on its experience with administering laws, the executive branch also influences the making of new laws or the amending of old ones by the legislature.

As we noted in Chapter 2, the Texas Constitution created a divided executive branch and limited the ability of the governor to abuse power. If you don't like the governor, these provisions are great ideas. If you do like the governor, then your view might be that the constitution limits the ability of the governor to use power to serve the people of Texas.

The political system set forth in the Texas Constitution, together with the political culture of Texas, has led to a political system that—when compared to most of the other megastates—appears to have weaker institutions for mobilizing ordinary Texans to participate. It has an executive and a judicial system less well equipped to protect ordinary Texans from those who have economic resources and can convert those resources to political power through the business-dominated interest group system.

STRUCTURE OF THE EXECUTIVE BRANCH

The executive branch of the Texas government contains over 200 agencies, some nearly independent of the chief executive, so we make no claim to providing a comprehensive examination of it in this chapter. Instead, we focus on the three limbs that make up its basic structure (see Figure 9.1):

1. The governorship.
2. The other elected executives and the agencies they run.
3. The agencies without elected officials at the helm, such as the Office of Secretary of State, the Texas National Guard, and other agencies whose executives are either appointed by the governor or by boards, agencies, and commissions created by the Texas Constitution or the Texas Legislature.

Before we examine the limbs of the executive branch, a few observations are necessary about the branch as a whole and the people who work in it.

FIGURE 9.1   Three Limbs of the Executive Branch of the Texas Government

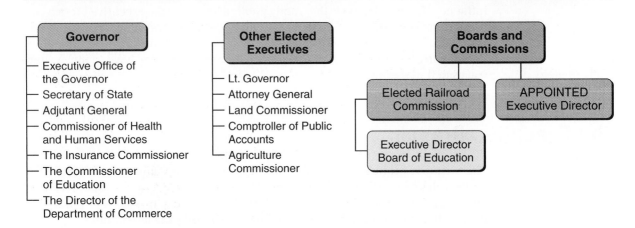

PUBLIC SERVANTS AND THE BUREAUCRACY

Every individual who is employed by the government, from the governor to the person who mows the lawn at the Texas State Capitol, is a public servant. They work for us. They get their jobs in several ways: election, succession, promotion, appointment, nomination, and confirmation. Many tend to refer to employees in the executive branch as bureaucrats. It is worth noting here that any large organization operating on the basic principles of standard procedures, hierarchy, specialization, and merit employment is a **bureaucracy.** The principles of bureaucracy are found in corporations, universities, churches, and other large organizations such as health maintenance organizations (HMOs). Within the legislative branch are bureaucratic structures like the Sunset Commission and the Legislative Budget Board; in the judicial branch, the principle is applied to the people who work for judges.

What differentiates government bureaucrats from corporate bureaucrats is that government bureaucrats are public servants. We emphasize this difference because many people view the word *bureaucrat* as pejorative. It is not. The people who work in many government buildings are public servants. They work in cities of all sizes (even yours) and in large, contemporary buildings, and small quaint ones. In the interests of civility and fairness, we will use the term *public servant* interchangeably with the term *bureaucrat* in this chapter. Now let's briefly examine the key concepts of bureaucracy.

Standardized Procedures.   Standardized procedures refer to the way an agency operates. Many of these procedures are based on the law the agency is carrying out. The public officials elected or appointed to direct the activities of the agency are generally responsible for reading the law and adopting rules and **regulations** that translate the law into the procedures that citizens and other organizations have to

Bureaucracy An organizational system that has a defined hierarchical structure, standardized procedures, and a specialization of duties to carry out public policies.

Standardized procedures The regular procedures an agency uses to carry out state law.

Regulation The use of government authority (and power) to force a course of action.

follow. An example is the procedure you follow to renew your driver's license, or the procedures a corporation must follow to build or significantly remodel an oil refinery.

Merit Principle. Rules and regulations also apply to public servants themselves. Many apply to their hiring and promotion.[3] A requirement usually stipulates that the best-qualified applicant be given the job—something called the merit principle. The **merit principle** is the idea that from a group of applicants, the most qualified one will be chosen on the basis of that person's abilities, skills, and knowledge.

The term *merit* is sometimes oversimplified to mean high test scores. This interpretation can be a problem when someone with experience and other qualifications can do the job, and do it well, but has trouble with tests. This problem is why test scores are not the only criteria for defining merit. If you tend to perform poorly on tests, a good way to get experience in government is through internships in state agencies. Internships can give you experience and allow you to demonstrate the ability to work constructively with other people. Internships are also an ideal way to participate in the day-to-day workings of your government.

Texas has established pay and benefit scales for the various categories of employees, so an office director of one agency makes almost the same as an office director of a different agency. These pay scales and grades are part of the state's budget. In Texas in Context 9.1, you can see how Texas compares to the other megastates on the basis of these government salaries. You can also see the size and cost of the Texas bureaucracy compared to those of the other megastates.

Newly elected officials such as the comptroller or attorney general usually have some changes they want to make. Because of civil service laws, they cannot fire some people in the agencies without good reason. However, executive staff members or policy experts can be let go at any time and for just about any reason. New executives often hire a transition team to oversee the changes at the agency. As the new bosses, they can restructure the agency (to the extent allowed by law) and make sure their supporters (filling **patronage** positions) are in the key positions.[4]

Hierarchy. The principle of **hierarchy** means that jobs are structured in a way that places responsibility and authority for making decisions and giving orders with those at the top of the structure. Any interested party can look at the structure of an agency and determine who in that agency to see about addressing a problem. This structure allows for more opportunities to participate since interested parties can identify the public servants in charge of the various divisions or departments, and who is in charge of those public servants. This can normally be done all the way to the top of an agency—where "the buck stops," so to speak. The structure of an agency may be based on state law or on the rules and regulations that the agency itself has developed. This structure is often a focus in the agency's sunset review when the legislature decides whether some divisions or sections can be cut, or combined, to make them more efficient. Figure 9.2 shows the structure of the Texas Department of Transportation, a typical state agency.

Merit principle The idea that the best-qualified people get jobs and promotions.

Patronage The idea that people are given jobs based on who they know—usually elected officials.

Hierarchy The way a bureaucracy is organized, showing who is in charge of the various departments or divisions.

TEXAS in Context

9.1 The Dynamics of State Employment in the Megastates

State	Employees	Employees per 10,000 Population	Average Salary	Cost of Government
California	476,700	133	$54,597	$26,026,389,900.00
Texas	**345,400**	**156**	**$38,684**	**$13,361,453,600.00**
New York	263,800	137	$50,875	$13,420,825,000.00
Florida	211,600	124	$37,846	$ 8,008,213,600.00
Michigan	171,300	170	$44,942	$ 7,698,564,600.00
Pennsylvania	165,900	134	$43,385	$ 7,197,571,500.00
Ohio	172,600	151	$41,025	$ 7,080,915,000.00
Illinois	161,200	127	$43,001	$ 6,931,671,200.00
New Jersey	149,000	172	$51,451	$ 7,666,199,000.00
Massachusetts	103,300	161	$47,269	$ 4,882,887,700.00

Source: Governing State and Local Sourcebook, 2004, an annual supplement to Governing, The Magazine of States and Localities, pp. 44, 46. Cost of Government column calculated by authors of this textbook.

Specialization of duties
The idea of breaking down the overall work of a bureaucracy into small tasks (duties) and then having those tasks performed by one person as their daily routine at work.

Specialization of Duties.   To be efficient, the overall goal of an agency is analyzed in terms of various tasks or duties. Some of these duties are specified by law— either directly or in the budget. Once the agency has its overall mission, it uses its rules and regulations to assign tasks so that an individual becomes skilled in one or more jobs, a concept called **specialization of duties.** The Department of Public Safety, for example, has employees who are trained to work with the public during the issuing and renewal of driver's licenses, while others receive phone calls, and still others drive the highway patrol cars.

Characteristics of a Democratic Bureaucracy.   One of the characteristics of a democratic bureaucracy is that talented people rise through the ranks by learning more complicated jobs so that eventually they are in charge of offices then possibly divisions and eventually entire agencies. In aristocratic bureaucracies, only the well born or well connected work in the top ranks. In Texas, we have a democratic bureaucracy and a great deal of democracy (some would argue too much democracy with all our elected officials) in determining who is in charge of it. Because of political appointments and recruitment, the Texas bureaucracy is becoming more and more diverse. The person in the executive branch who can encourage both diversity and democracy is the governor, the most visible limb of the executive branch of the government of Texas.

FIGURE 9.2 Texas Department of Transportation Organizational Chart

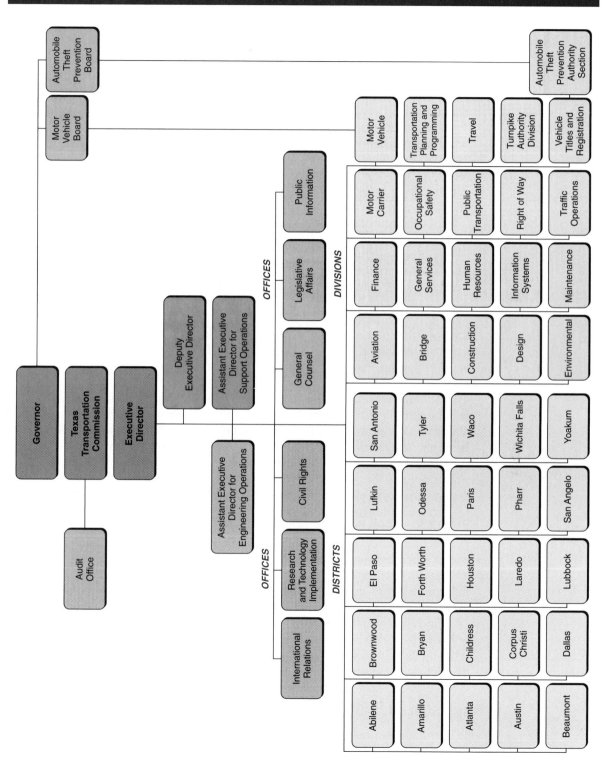

Source: GIF image from the Texas Department of Transportation website at http://www.dot.state.tx.us/.

The Governor

CONSTITUTIONAL AND POLITICAL REQUIREMENTS

The governor of Texas must meet both constitutional and political requirements for election. Over time, the constitutional qualifications have become less detailed through constitutional amendment. For example, the following requirements have been removed: before taking office, the governor must swear that he or she has never fought in a duel, and does not intend to, and that he or she believes in a Supreme Being.[5] Today, the constitutional requirements are that the governor must be at least thirty years old, must have lived in the state for at least five years before election, and must be a citizen of the United States. He or she does not have to be born in Texas.

Political requirements also exist. First is the ability to raise funds for a statewide campaign. The most recent campaign for governor highlighted the need for money. Tony Sanchez used his personal wealth and spent a total of $67 million in a losing effort to Rick Perry, who spent $27 million.[6] The big spenders don't always win; winning a gubernatorial election requires more than money. However, one must have enough money to run a credible campaign to win the primary. Sometimes this requirement involves scaring off the opposition with the size of one's war chest, but just as often it involves a candidate's ability to run a successful campaign and mobilize the constituency to vote. The general election works approximately the same way except that now candidates have a party label and access to the funds and machinery of the electoral party.

In addition to raising money, a candidate must put together a coalition of supporters who can help run a successful campaign. The length of the governor's term allows that coalition to grow or shrink, depending on how the governor uses their position. In Texas politics, personality and personal accomplishment play a large role—perhaps, given the weakness of parties in Texas, a larger role than in other megastates.[7]

A candidate for governor also needs a little luck. Candidate Richards won her first gubernatorial election in 1990 partly because her opponent, Clayton Williams, kept making unfortunate remarks like, "When rape is inevitable, relax and enjoy it," which got into the press and did him a lot of harm. On the other hand, Governor Richards's reelection chances were badly hurt four years later by national events. The Clinton scandals hurt all Democrats up for election in 1994.

Thus, in Texas politics, as in politics everywhere else, a combination of factors influences success in campaigning. In Texas, the major factors are money, the governor's ability to cultivate good relations and thus build his or her campaign coalition, and events on the national level. Once elected, the governor of Texas becomes one of fifty state governors, an influential group of leaders. From governorships, individuals have gone on to the presidency, the cabinet, ambassadorships, and prestigious positions in academia and business.[8]

THE GOVERNOR OF TEXAS IN COMPARATIVE CONTEXT

Many of the features of the governorship of Texas are common to governorships in other states. Most governors, for example, must share executive authority with other elected members of the executive branch. Only the governor of New Jersey is the sole elected executive in the state government. Nevertheless, the Texas governorship displays some significant differences—so significant that during the 2000 campaign for president, political scientists in Texas (including some of the authors of this book) were contacted by the national media to explain why "such a weak governorship would prepare someone to be chief executive of the United States."

For many years, political scientists have compared the formal, or constitutional, powers of the governors of the fifty states.[9] Most of these comparisons examine tenure power, appointment power, budget power, and veto power. We will examine one of the most recent studies available, Thad Beyle's 2002 comparison, which includes a new wrinkle or two—like whether or not the governor enjoys a majority of the same party in the legislature. We examine Beyle's comparisons in Texas in Context 9.2 and in the following subsections.[10]

Tenure Power.   The longer a governor stays in office, the more that person learns about how to be governor, so the ability to remain in office for a long time is an important power. For tenure power, Beyle considered the term of office and the number of terms a governor can serve. A four-year term with no limit on the number of terms a governor can serve gets the highest score. It gives a governor a longer time to be in office and leaves the timing of the decision to leave (that is, not to seek a second, third, or fourth term) up to the governor. Thus, being a lame duck (an official serving his or her last term of office) is a position that governors with unlimited terms can avoid for nearly as long as they choose and can win reelection.

Half of the megastates, including Texas, give their governors four-year terms with no limit on the number of terms, and half limit their governors to two four-year terms. Nevertheless, eight years is a fairly long time to be governor. Some of the other state governors have two-year terms, and some are limited to just one two-year term. In October 2003, the governor of California was recalled by voters—something that is not possible in Texas but otherwise would have an impact on the tenure potential of an elected official that can be recalled.

Appointment Power.   The appointment power category measures the ability of the governor to hire and fire the executives responsible for the major functions in the executive branch. More than fifty of those functions exist in all states. Of the more than twenty ways the corresponding officials may be selected, we look at the five that are relevant to Texas:[11]

- Selected by the governor with no restrictions (needing no one else's approval).
- Nominated by the governor and confirmed or rejected by the Senate.
- Nominated by the governor from a list of names given to him or her, with the Senate confirming or rejecting the nomination.
- Selected by a board or commission.
- Elected by the people.

A governor has the most influence over functions whose executives he can hire and fire without consulting anyone else. The governor of Texas can appoint personal

TEXAS in Context

9.2 Power Rankings for the Megastate Governorships, 2002

Megastate	Tenure	Appointment	Budget	Veto	Party	Average
Pennsylvania	4	4	3	5	2	3.60
Illinois	5	3.5	3	5	4	4.10
Ohio	4	3.5	3	5	4	3.90
California	4	3.5	3	5	4	3.90
New York	5	3.5	4	5	3	4.10
New Jersey	4	3.5	3	5	3	3.90
Michigan	4	3.5	3	5	2	3.90
Massachusetts	4	3.5	3	5	1	3.30
Florida	4	1.5	3	5	4	3.50
Texas	**5**	**1.5**	**2**	**5**	**4**	**3.50**

Source: Data taken from data files on Thad Beyle's website at http://www.unc.edu/~beyle. Accessed August, 2004. Average column calculated by the authors of this textbook. Table does not include Beyle's Separately Elected Officials rankings.

Senatorial courtesy The tradition that senators will vote against a nominee if the senator from the area most affected by the appointment opposes that appointment.

staff. Beyond the members of the personal staff, he or she can only nominate and the Senate then confirms. It takes only one senator to block an appointment. According to **senatorial courtesy,** senators defer to the judgment of a senator whose district would be affected by the nomination or in whose district a nominee resides. Thus, a governor who wishes to fill a position with qualified people needs to have a little staff work done to make sure that senatorial courtesy will not be invoked.

The most important officials whom the governor nominates are probably the secretary of state, who oversees elections, and the adjutant general, who is the head of the Texas National Guard. Also important are the Commissioner of Health and Human Services, the Insurance Commissioner, the Commissioner of Education, and the director of the Department of Commerce. Those six officials are the only major heads of departments whom the governor of Texas appoints. Most of the more than 2,000 other officials the governor appoints are members of boards and commissions.

The secretary of state is the only constitutional office held by an appointed official. The governor nominates the secretary of state, and the Senate confirms the appointment. The secretary holds the office during the term of the governor. The office of the secretary of state has three constitutional divisions: Elections, Statutory Filings, and keeping the Texas State Seal. Governor Perry has increased the responsibility of the office by naming the secretary of state the lead liaison for Texas Border and Mexican Affairs and the state's chief international protocol officer.[12] Of these responsibilities, the Elections Division and Statutory Filing Division command the most attention.

The Elections Division is responsible for implementing the state's election laws. This responsibility includes setting the dates of the elections in Texas and providing assistance and advice to the local officials who conduct the elections. The division provides training for officials and maintains the state's official registered-voter list. It also provides information on upcoming elections to voters. This information includes sample ballots to help the voters make decisions, and information about where to vote.

The Elections Division also provides legal interpretations of the election law. As a college student, it is likely you are living away from home. You may have wondered where you are supposed to register to vote, and where and how you can vote. On January 22, 2004, the secretary of state issued an opinion at the request of Governor Perry regarding students at Prairie View A&M University. The opinion states that a student may elect to establish residency at her or his dorm or apartment and thus be a registered voter in that county for all elections held in that county.[13]

The Statutory Filings Division is the other major part of the office of the secretary of state. This division is basically the filing cabinet of the state. Units within this division include the Administrative Unit, which files all the bills of the Texas Legislature and commissions the executives of Texas. Other units deal with official papers of Texas, notary publics, and several businesses operating in Texas.

The secretary of state publishes the *Texas Register* weekly. It lists all the proposed rules, appointments of the governor, and other official dealings of Texas. This information is made available to the public and is part of the open records of Texas. The *Register* is available on the secretary of state's website at http://www.sos.state.tx.us/texreg/issues.shtml. When you want to find out what an agency is doing, check the *Texas Register*.

Although the secretary of state is a key nomination for a governor to make and is usually confirmed by the Senate with little or no disagreement, the power to nominate people to other positions is sometimes constrained by Texas law or by the Texas Constitution. The governor's nominees must often meet special criteria. A good example is the Board of Vocational Nurse Examiners. According to state law, the board consists of fifteen members appointed by the governor and confirmed by the Senate. The board is made up of the following people: seven licensed vocational nurses who have been practicing nurses for at least five years before their appointment, one registered nurse who is involved in the education of future nurses, one physician who is licensed by the State Board of Medical Examiners and who has been practicing for at least five years before her or his appointment, one hospital administrator who has held that position for at least five years before her or his appointment, and five members of the general public. Neither the doctor nor the administrator can also be a licensed nurse and be on the board.

Most of the members of the boards and commissions in Texas government serve staggered terms. The members of these boards and commissions comprise the majority of the more than 2,000 people nominated by a governor in a four-year term. Thus, halfway through a governor's second term, he or she may have appointed nearly all the members of the boards and commissions. These appointments are also listed in the *Texas Register*. These appointed bodies, not the governor, select the chief executive who then runs the respective agency for which the board is responsible. For example, the Board of Regents appoints the chief executive officer of a university—often called the president of the university. The governor nominates one or two regents per board during his or her term but does not have the authority to hire and fire university presidents. The governor also fills vacancies when judges and many other elected officials fail to serve out their terms of office. In some cases, the governor calls special elections to fill vacant positions. Notices of these special elections are on the secretary of state's website.

In addition to limits on hiring members of the executive branch, the governor needs permission from the Senate to fire one. Furthermore, the governor can dismiss only the people he or she has appointed. These and the other characteristics of the governor's appointive power described here are some of the reasons why Beyle ranks the governor of Texas so low in appointment power.

Budget Power.   The governor of Texas does not have much formal power in creating or adjusting the state budget. The Office of Budget and Planning does help the governor draw up a budget, which is submitted to the legislature at about the time the governor delivers his budget message. However, this budget is not the one that the legislature uses as its first draft. The first draft of the budget is prepared by the Legislative Budget Board (LBB), chaired by the lieutenant governor. The Speaker of the House and chairs of relevant legislative committees appointed by the lieutenant governor and the Speaker serve on that committee. Once again, the governor is ranked low because there are other, more important, players in the budget process.

Veto Power.   The veto power is an important tool for influencing legislation and is thus an important source of political influence in all states, particularly in Texas, where the legislature meets only once every other year for 140 days. Governor Perry set a modern day record of eighty-two vetoes in his first session as governor (during the Seventy-Seventh legislative session in 2001). As a comparison, former Governor Bush vetoed a total of ninety-one bills throughout the six years and three legislative sessions when he was chief executive of Texas. In 2003, Perry vetoed forty-eight more bills. He didn't veto any bills during the three special sessions held in 2003, or the one in 2004.[14]

The governor's regular veto power is not supplemented with the pocket veto that the U.S. president can use. (With the pocket veto, an unsigned bill becomes invalid after a certain period of time because of the president's inaction.) A Texas governor must exercise the veto within twenty days of the end of a legislative session, or a bill becomes law without his or her signature. Thus, the period immediately after the legislature adjourns is a busy one for a governor and his or her staff. Many people have long lists of reasons that certain bills should be vetoed. Remember that every governor needs to veto some bills to look effective. Should you oppose a bill, list your reasons briefly on a single sheet of paper, clearly identify the bill, and submit your letter to the governor's legislative office. You can try e-mail, but hard copy in this case is recommended. For a recent example of an attempt at grassroots lobbying to get support for a veto, see Box 9.1.

Stella Byrd, left, mother of James Byrd, Jr., the East Texas black man who was dragged to his death behind a pickup truck in 1998 by three whites, waits as Governor Rick Perry, center right, signs into law the James Byrd, Jr., Hate Crimes Act at the Texas State Capitol in Austin, Friday, May 11, 2001.

When the legislature is in session, a governor has ten days (excluding Sundays) to veto a bill passed by the legislature. Sometimes the governor will allow a bill that seems rather silly (like the law in the Seventy-Sixth Texas Legislature against insulting Texas vegetables) to become law because he or she does not wish to offend a particular constituency, or because the bill contains something the governor finds useful but not useful enough to sign. HB 752 and SB 1696 each became effective on June 21, 2003, without Governor Perry's signature.[15]

Line-item veto The ability of the governor to strike out and thus cancel parts of appropriations bills with which he or she does not agree.

In addition to the regular veto, the Texas governor can use the **line-item veto.** Most agency budgets consist of dozens, if not hundreds, of separate lines itemizing how the money is to be spent. Some budget items enjoy special protection due to provisions in the constitution or state law, but other items (lines) leave the governor considerable budgetary discretion. Near the end of the session, when the budget is usually finished, no time is available to override a line-item veto—or any other veto, for that matter.[16]

Size of Party Majority. Beyle's comparison of governors includes a measure that is likely to change from election to election: the size of the governor's party majority in the legislature. This characteristic should be particularly noticeable when comparing legislatures before and after the recent redistricting. Beyle's study was

---

BOX 9.1   Grassroots Lobbying for a Veto

After some embarrassing evidence of fiscal mismanagement by the Texas Education Agency had surfaced, the Seventy-Seventh Texas Legislature passed a bill creating some oversight on how the Texas Board of Education invests teacher retirement funds. Some board members were incensed about this move. The following letter, aimed at keeping Governor Rick Perry from signing Senate Bill (S.B.) 512 into law, was circulated by David Bradley, a Republican and the state board of education member from Beaumont.

Dear Fellow Conservative,

   It is understood that a governor's veto is within reach if we will provide Governor Perry with ample evidence of opposition to S.B. 512, legislation which strips more authority from the State Board of Education and, thus, from the voters.

   Now that we have a conservative majority on the board, liberals want to cripple the board and regain control of the school children's $20 billion endowment fund.

   Governor Perry needs to understand that the Republicans on the board are providing the solutions and are not the problem. S.B. 512 penalizes those board members.

   Please handwrite and then fax a letter asking Governor Perry to veto S.B. 512.

   Pick one of the following issues and plug it into the example letter below, or reword your own, as you prefer. . . . [Bradley then lists six issues that present his view of what is wrong with this piece of legislation.]

On June 17, 2001, Governor Perry vetoed S.B. 512. It was one of his record eighty-two vetoes in 2001.

Austin American-Statesman, May 27, 2001; *Austin American-Statesman,* June 18, 2001.

---

conducted in 2002 but this item can be updated at any time because the Texas Legislature has a website. It must be noted that this is the one "institutional power" that is most subject to change over time.

The Megastate Comparison.   As Texas in Context 9.2 indicates, the governorship of Texas is similar to that of the other megastates, but slightly on the lower end of the scale. You should be warned that since political science is a social science, studies such as Beyle's provide useful information only at the present time. As times (and people) change, so will their attitudes toward government and its chief executive. Thus, future studies may show different power rankings, yet the constitutional and statutory powers have not changed. Some still believe that Texas has a weak governor, but there is more to the governorship of Texas than meets the eye. You can

---

JOIN THE DEBATE

THE ISSUE: Does the governor of Texas have enough power?

AGREE

1. The governor appoints large numbers of people to offices.
2. Bills vetoed by the governor stay vetoed.
3. The governor has a large staff to assist with duties.
4. The governor can call a special legislative session and can control its agenda.

DISAGREE

1. The governor can't change the budget alone.
2. The governor has limited authority to remove unwanted appointments.
3. The governor can try to influence only major state agencies.
4. The governor needs significant legislative help to get his or her platform adopted.

---

now Join the Debate about the governor's power to see which side you are on. Next, we look at the various roles the governor plays and then at the governorship as a position for influencing policy and effecting change.

ROLES OF THE GOVERNOR

As part of the checks and balances and the separation of powers of our government, the governor plays several roles in carrying out the duties of the office. Most of these roles are specified in the state's constitution, and some have changed over time. The public has opportunities to participate in the governor's decisions in each of the roles, but you will need to understand the three basic roles of the governor to make your involvement more effective.

Executive. The basic job of the governor is to see that the laws of the state are carried out. The governor is also charged by the Texas Constitution to take care of the business of the state of Texas "in such manner as prescribed by law" (Article IV, Section 10). Because the governor is assigned the role of seeing that the laws of the state are carried out, the governor may sometimes learn of an agency that is not doing its job. As we have seen, the power to fire an agency head is limited for the governor of Texas, but other tools are available.

The behavior of insurance companies in Texas has been an important issue in Texas for some time. It was a major feature of the Perry–Sanchez campaign for governor in 2002. Governor Ann Richards helped to increase gubernatorial influence in this area. She believed that the State Insurance Commission had established regulatory policies that favored the interests of the insurance industry, to the detriment of ordinary Texans. The three members on the commission were appointed for staggered six-year terms. Getting her majority on that commission would take too long, so instead she focused high-visibility attention on the board. She testified at a board hearing, issued press releases, and called for the resignation of commission members. She got one resignation and thus was able to influence the board.

The influence of future governors in this area was strengthened when the legislature responded to her efforts by restructuring the insurance regulation agency. In 1993, it became the Texas Department of Insurance, and the three-member board was abolished. The director of this department is now appointed directly by the governor for a two-year fixed term, subject to Senate confirmation. The governor clearly made a difference in this instance.

Contrary to the belief that the national government is taking power away from the states, the governorship provides an example of a way in which the federal government has augmented the powers of all state governors by making their offices the clearinghouses for all grant-in-aid applications from agencies and local governments in their respective states. Before a grant application from Texas enters the federal system, it must be approved by the governor's Office of Budget and Planning. Because of the clearinghouse role, the governor has some negotiating tools for determining how public policy is administered at the local level and how funds will be spent. At a minimum, a grant application gives the governor's staff opportunities to build goodwill by ensuring that it is handled efficiently. The governor's support for major grant applications is also valued, and this support can increase goodwill for the governor. Some federal grant programs even give the governor discretion to determine how money will be spent. Thus, in addition to the power to say no through the power of the veto, the governor can also say yes through the grant-in-aid process.

The governor also functions as an executive by representing the state of Texas to its own residents, other states, and the wider world. As the leader of a megastate, the governor has the ability to influence corporate decisions about locating plants and congressional decisions about passing legislation.

In the role of chief of state, the governor has impressive symbolic authority to grant recognition to individuals and groups. Using the gubernatorial office to turn media attention on particular issues also brings positive attention to the governor and to Texas. Many gubernatorial proclamations and acts of symbolic recognition, however, do not get much press coverage, although they may be important to those whose issues or activities are being recognized. As an example, on December 4, 2003, Governor Perry issued a proclamation stating that December 7, 2003, would be known as Pearl Harbor Remembrance Day in Texas and urged appropriate recognition of the day.[17]

Legislative.   The ability of a governor to influence legislation beyond the veto is based on the governor's message power, the power to call a special legislative session, the power to determine the agenda of that session, and the ability to give symbolic recognition to legislation by signing it in a well-publicized ceremony—or to allow it to become law quietly without the governor's signature.

Article IV, Section 9 of the Texas Constitution states that the governor must address the legislature at the start of its session and at the end of his or her term of office. The governor may use this time to inform the legislature on the state of the state and may suggest various policies he or she would like the legislature to enact during the session. Most governors use this opportunity to outline their main objectives for the state—bills they would sign into law if given the opportunity and bills they would veto if presented for signature.

In Governor Perry's address to the Texas Legislature on February 11, 2003, one of the items he mentioned as a pressing need for Texas was for institutions of higher learning (colleges) to be able to set their tuition rates. This idea is not new, but colleges and universities could not exceed preset limits—and the tuition rates were the same for every program. HB 3015 was passed by the legislature on June 3, 2003, and was signed by Governor Perry on June 22, 2003. It deregulates tuition so colleges and universities (probably even the one you are paying to attend right now) are free to raise tuition and even to set different tuition rates for different subject matter classes. During the fall 2003 and spring 2004 semesters, several colleges and universities across Texas announced tuition hikes for the fall 2004 semester.

If you didn't think politics mattered to you, we hope that you can now see that it does. Politicians made those tuition decisions claiming no new taxes; instead you, the student, will pay for a greater percentage of your higher education. The governing boards of the state's public colleges and universities are public officials, yet another reason to get involved in politics by going to their meetings or by voting for them.

The tuition example is one of many ways the governor attempts to influence policy. Key legislators are chosen by the governor to introduce legislation, and in some policy areas, nothing is done until the governor's office has drafted the bill to be submitted. The legislature expects the governor to exercise leadership and is sometimes confused and frustrated when a governor does not. A governor's threat to veto a bill often means he or she will never see it because the legislature gives up on it.

The ability to call the legislature into special session is a tool almost unique to Texas. In some cases, a governor calls a special session to help the legislature deal with a problem it has failed to solve during the regular session, such as redistricting in the Seventy-Seventh Legislature. In May 2001, Governor Perry made it clear that he would not force a special session on the legislature if legislative leaders did not think they could draw the districts for Congress and the State Board of Education. Two years later, with a little encouragement from Washington and a Republican majority in both houses, he felt differently. Some special sessions are called in response to court-mandated changes in Texas—educational funding and prison overcrowding are examples from the past decade. In some cases, the threat of a special session can be a bargaining tool, although it has to be used subtly. By mid-April, the weather is getting rather warm in Austin, and the legislators are ready to go home. An additional session in June has little appeal. Thus, if a key piece of a governor's program is bottled up in committee, it may well be jarred loose if the alternative is dealing with it in a special session.

During special sessions, the legislature is allowed to work on only the items the governor assigns them. An astute governor can add an item or two to the charge to the legislature and build his or her coalition with grateful members of the legislature, who might have a bill or two that died during the regular session. These sessions are limited to a maximum length of thirty days, but there is no limit to the number of sessions a governor can call.

Governor Perry made history in 2003 by calling not one but three special sessions. It was the first time in over a decade that a special session had been called. On June 30, 2003, legislators headed back to Austin to consider congressional redistricting.[18] During the special session, Governor Perry added a number of other items to the legislative agenda, but nothing was accomplished because the Democratic senators went to New Mexico and thus denied the Senate a quorum. This tactic effectively shut down one-half of the legislature. Governor Perry then called a second session to start on July 28, and then a third session was called for September 15 because of the Democrats' holdout through the second special session. Finally, on October 13, 2003, Governor Perry signed HB 3 from the third special session into law, ending the string of special sessions.

These special sessions came with a price—about $57,000 per day.[19] During these special sessions, the governor and other elected officials were allowed to collect campaign contributions, an illegal activity during a regular session. Governor Perry was reported to have collected over $400,000, while Lieutenant Governor Dewhurst collected over $1.3 million in just the first special session. These amounts will help fund their future campaigns.

Judicial.   The 2000 presidential campaign revealed the apparent limitations on the governor's power of clemency—the ability to grant mercy after justice has been done. The Board of Pardons and Paroles was created by constitutional amendment after "Pa" Ferguson abused his power of clemency. Now the board reviews sentences of convicted felons and deals with appeals for relief. The Texas Constitution requires that a written recommendation come from the Board of Pardons and Paroles before a governor can grant clemency.

This stipulation appears to be another example of the limits placed on the governor, but one could reasonably argue that it buffers the governor from criticism for not granting clemency and thus saves him or her from having to make a politically damaging decision. Granting clemency could hurt the governor as much in Texas as not granting clemency could. No decision by the governor, no harm to the governor. Thus, the political role of the Board of Pardons and Paroles may be a source of strength for the governor rather than a source of weakness.

The one item the governor may do alone is to grant a stay of execution for up to thirty days. As a matter of note, Governor Perry, on the recommendation of the board, issued a pardon on February 2, 2001, to David Shawn Pope, who was cleared of his crime by DNA testing.[20] This event also prompted Perry to declare Senate Bill 3, making DNA testing available to those convicted of capital crimes, an emergency measure.

POTENTIAL FOR POWER

Because of the potential for influence that a governor may or may not choose to exercise, it does matter who is governor of Texas. Texas governors have (and have not) promoted constitutional change, tax reform, and progressive legislation. The governor is better equipped by the Texas Constitution and by our political system than any other official to influence state policy in Texas, however the governorship is ranked on some national standard.

Salary and Staff.   Unlike the legislators, the governorship is a full-time job. The Texas Constitution originally set the salary for the governor (providing another example of penny pinching and excessive detail in the constitution generally). In 1954, Texas voters amended the constitution to allow the legislature to set the governor's salary, which is currently $115,345; in 1972, another amendment lengthened the governor's term to four years.

Texas in Context 9.3 compares the megastate governors in terms of salary and staff size.[21] Clearly, the governor of Texas has the staff resources to operate independently of the legislature and interest groups for information and research. The official salary may be low, but the governor does have many other resources at his or her disposal.

The Office of the Governor comprises several agencies, the central one being the Administrative Office. Other divisions revolve around functions of the office: Appointments, Criminal Justice, the Legislative Office, and the Budget and Planning Division. In the Budget and Planning Office, for example, the staff advises the governor on grant applications and economic and fiscal issues, prepares the governor's budget, and recommends items in the budget on which he or she might use the veto.[22]

Each governor has the opportunity to reorganize the agencies in the office of governor, and changes occur over time. The Film/Music and Media Office, for example, is a fairly recent addition. For a more complete list, see Box 9.2, or consult the governor's website, which has thousands of pages of information available.

The governor's staff is obviously of great importance to the governor, but the governor's power may be increased in two other ways. The first relies on the cooperation of others, while the second relies on the governor alone.

Streamlining the Executive Branch.   Our chapter-opening story indicated that Governor Richards was able to bring public attention to the redlining problem and institute some changes, but the problem will not be eliminated soon. A governor has the resources to make a difference, one agency at a time. The Texas Constitution is designed for this pace of change. Any reforms have to be introduced slowly. The use of power is difficult because of the checks on its abuse. One way to effect change is to make it possible for a governor to wield more power and then make the judgment about whether the changes were harmful or beneficial in the next election (which is the way democracy works in many other states).

If you want to take this approach, you can work for amendments to the Texas Constitution that would reduce the number of boards and commissions. Some of

Texas in Context

9.3 Megastate Governors: Salary and Staff

Megastate	Salary	Staff
New York	$179,000	180
Michigan	$177,000	56
California	$175,000	86
New Jersey	$157,000	156
Illinois	$150,691	130
Pennsylvania	$144,416	90
Massachusetts	$135,000	70
Ohio	$126,485	60
Florida	$121,171	310
Texas	**$115,345**	**266**

Source: Council of State Governments: *Book of the States, 2004* (Lexington, Ky.: Council of State Governments, 2004), p. 160.

these boards are elected, like the State Board of Education and the Railroad Commission. Others are appointed. Reorganization could place the agencies run by boards or commissions in larger departments, some containing several board- or commission-run agencies. The governor would appoint, with the approval of the Senate, the department executive. Then a governor who wanted to exercise the role of chief executive would not have to attend hearings, issue press releases, and lobby the legislature for reform to get something done. The governor would simply direct the department head to do it.

The interest groups concerned with a particular agency engage in appointmenteering to see to it that appointees make decisions in their interests, whether or not those decisions are in the public interest. Because we cannot hold interest groups accountable, we have to try to hold government accountable—but it is hard to do with so many independently appointed managers to track. The numerous boards and commissions (over 200) present organizational problems simply because of their numbers. A governor or a private citizen must keep track of many organizations. Streamlining the executive branch would be an effective step in strengthening the governor's ability to manage the executive branch and would also enable him or her to serve as the people's representative in running the government. We can hold a governor accountable; interest groups, however, are beyond our reach.

Party Leader.   Political scientists Robert Crew, Lynn Muchmore, and Thad Beyle have surveyed several former governors over the past twenty years and discovered

BOX 9.2   Office of Governor Perry

Appointments. Recommends individuals for the 3,000 appointments to boards, commissions, and advisory committees that a governor makes in a four-year term.

Budgeting, Planning and Policy. Provides fiscal information and analysis related to the state's fiscal policies; works closely with the Legislative Budget Board.

Criminal Justice. Administers and allocates state and federal grants for criminal justice planning.

Governor's Committee for People with Disabilities. Advises the governor about policies and programs subject to the Americans With Disabilities Act. Like many other offices, coordination with others is required because the governor makes appointments to boards and commissions that deal with disabilities and also signs his or her approval for grant programs.

Economic Development and Tourism. Markets Texas to both business looking to relocate or expand, and to individuals looking for a travel destination.

Texas Music Office and Texas Film Commission. Assists the various elements of the entertainment industry in finding Texas locations, talents, and services. Because this activity involves both public relations for the state and economic development, this operation has merited a separate office for several governors.

Texas Military Preparedness Commission. Works with local areas to prevent future base closings and to prepare for the next generation of military in Texas.

Press Office. Responsible for all news media inquiries, news releases and public information, speech writing, correspondence, and the citizens' assistance office.

State Grants. Monitors federal, state, and private funding information resources and alerts state agencies, nonprofit organizations, units of local government, and other entities about funding opportunities.

Texas Workforce Investment Council. Works to promote developing a highly skilled and well educated workforce.

Texas Review and Comment System. Deals with grants and with agencies of the federal government. This department was created in response to the federal requirement that chief executives review and comment on all applications from a state to the federal government.

Governor's Commission for Women. Works to improve the quality of life for Texas women.

www.governor.state.tx.us/divisions (accessed August 10, 2004).

that many of them did not see their role as leader of their state political party to be as important as other duties of the office.[23] Sarah McCalley Morehouse came up with a slightly different result in her classic study, *The Governor as Party Leader*. Party leadership was not important in only half the states she studied. In the 1982 election cycle, she interviewed forty-three prospective gubernatorial candidates in ten states and examined the conditions under which they attempted to build electoral coalitions. After the elections, she followed the ten successful candidates as they attempted to build governing coalitions. One of the states in her study was Texas.[24]

In half of the states studied, the party leaders were unified in fairly strong parties. In comparison to interest groups, they had as much or more influence over the party nomination for governor. Money was not a controlling resource in these contests, whereas it was in states with weak parties.[25]

After the election in strong-party states, the incumbent governors worked closely with the party leadership coalition. Party leadership was important in those states. Candidates for statewide office were more likely to form a combined ticket than they were in weak-party states, where the candidate-centered coalitions tended to run separate campaigns. For voters, electing a single-party team and then holding those elected accountable for running the government is more manageable. Trying to keep track of separate elected officials is analogous to the governor's role of trying to keep track of the executives appointed by 200 or more boards and commissions. We have seen that in Texas, party is less relevant to the conduct of government than are personality and leadership style. To put it another way, the personality and leadership style of not only the governor but of a dozen or more executive officials and elected boards are beyond the average voter's attention span.

In short, parties are not only institutions for mobilizing ordinary Texans to vote; they can also be management teams that can make government more accountable. Morehouse's research indicates that governors capable of building a coalition outside the legislature to win the election are also successful at building a coalition within the legislature to pass their programs. Thus, to strengthen parties in Texas, it makes sense to strengthen the link between governors and their parties. One way to strengthen this link is to allow the parties to hold **endorsing conventions** before the primary (as we discussed in Chapter 5).

At endorsing conventions, the party activists (you could be one of them) vote to endorse their choice for the party nominee for governor. After the endorsement decision is made, the other candidates often drop out in the interests of party unity. Even if they do not, the endorsed candidate usually wins.

This endorsement procedure accomplishes several goals. First, it increases the likelihood that endorsed candidates get the party nomination. Endorsed candidates tend to win the primaries. Second, it strengthens the electoral party and increases party members' participation because the endorsing convention clearly plays a meaningful role in the nominating process. Third, it improves the likelihood that candidates for other offices pay attention to and work with the electoral party because someday they may want to run for higher office.[26]

In Texas today, governors and other statewide officeholders are nominated and elected in elections with relatively low voter turnout. If they were elected in presidential election years, the results might occasionally be different because the parties

Endorsing conventions
Party conventions held before the primary election to have the active party members endorse a candidate they think will be an able representative of the party in the general election. Only the candidates for the one or two top offices are usually subject to this endorsement process.

are more active in presidential election years, and thus they mobilize the have-nots to vote. If Texas parties were stronger, the statewide elections for governor would have more party activity and higher voter turnout.

For most of Texas history, election laws have kept the working poor and minorities from using their numbers to influence the way democracy works in Texas, from the governor's mansion to the county courthouse. Thus, if we simply strengthen the governorship without providing a mechanism for bringing the have-nots into the system that chooses the governor and other public officials, the results will not change much. We will simply have a chief executive in a political system that has a business-dominated interest group system with more influence and victories than it has in most of the other megastates. Stronger parties led by governors who can deliver on their campaign promises might bring more of the have-nots into the political system, to the benefit of average Texans.

Having laid out a grand plan for executive branch reform in Texas, we now examine the other two limbs of the executive branch.

Elected Executives

The second limb of the executive branch consists of elected officials who perform important legislative and executive functions. In their haste to make sure that no other governor abused power, as they believed E. J. Davis had done, the original writers of our current constitution divided executive power among the members of a **plural executive.** Later, the legislature added another elected executive, the agriculture commissioner.

Plural executive The set of several elected state leaders. Each is elected separately by the voters and is accountable only to the voters.

Texas is not alone in its number of elected executives; most states have more than one. In fact, all but three states (Maine, New Hampshire, and New Jersey) have two or more elected executives. Voters in over half of the states choose six or more executives; North Dakota tops the list with eleven.[27]

According to the theory of Jacksonian democracy, electing so many different people to different offices means more opportunities for citizens to get involved in their government. In theory, the candidates need people to work on and to donate to their campaigns, so more people can get involved as candidates and as supporters of other candidates. In practice, however, a long ballot simply turns voters off; it does not mobilize the electorate to engage in multiple decisions. In fact, many Texas voters do not even know what the various offices do. The following sections will introduce you to the offices of the plural executive. Remember that these officials are elected by you state wide for a term of four years.

LIEUTENANT GOVERNOR

The lieutenant governor is the person who becomes governor should the governor leave office. Perry replaced Bush in 2001, when Bush became president of the United States. The governor and the lieutenant governor do not have to be members of the same party. In 1995, the newly elected Republican, George Bush, held the governor's office, while long-time Democrat Bob Bullock held the lieutenant governor's office. Instead of fighting partisan battles, they worked well together during the legislative session.

If the governor leaves the state to attend a meeting or go on vacation, for example, the lieutenant governor takes over and assumes all the responsibilities and duties of the office—and receives the same pay as the governor, not his or her normal legislative salary. Sometimes both the governor and lieutenant governor are out of the state. In that case, the Senate pro tem takes over the office of governor. The members of the legislature select the senator for this office at the start of the legislative session. He or she runs the Senate if the lieutenant governor is absent or is unable to fulfill the duties of the office. Should the governor leave office permanently, the lieutenant governor is promoted, and then the Senate chooses the next lieutenant governor until the next election as they did in 2001.

In the third special session of 2003, David Dewhurst got the Senate to alter its rules in order to get the redistricting bill passed. Instead of the normal two thirds rule, the Senate would require only a majority to bring up a bill for debate. That meant the Democrats could no longer hold up business in the Senate. The power to alter the rules is granted to the lieutenant governor by the Senate when it adopts rules for each session.

ATTORNEY GENERAL

The attorney general (AG) is the state's chief legal representative. Much of the office's work revolves around the first of three constitutional roles: defender of the laws and the Constitution of the State of Texas. The other two roles involve representing the state in litigation and approving public bond issues.

In the first role, the AG offers legal advice to all officials of the state of Texas, but not the private citizens of Texas. The AG fulfills this role by writing opinions, which are interpretations of the law or the constitution. One recent opinion was requested by the district attorney for Leon County. His request revolved around the Leon County Judge who was selling fuel and oil products to the county. The Judge has a substantial interest in the company that was making the sale. The AG ruled that as long as the County Judge filed paperwork stating his interest in the company and abstained from commissioner court deliberations, a conflict of interest did not exist.[28] The AG issued an opinion on January 4, 2004, on the residency requirement of students at Prairie View A&M. This opinion came in response to state Senator Rodney Ellis's request and confirmed the secretary of state's opinion mentioned earlier.[29]

Possibly the most visible set of laws the AG defends are those that deal with child support. The AG's website contains a list of the most wanted child-support evaders in Texas to help generate leads and catch them. Some of the more recent evaders owe over $100,000 in child support.[30]

While the AG does not represent private citizens in legal matters, the AG's office can help private citizens deal with businesses or individuals who may have committed various types of fraud. The AG's office makes announcements when it becomes aware of a new scam or other fraudulent activity in Texas. The AG's office also maintains the open government policies of Texas. These laws allow regular citizens to know what the government officials (both elected and appointed) are doing during their meetings. The AG has even published a booklet dealing with public information. The booklet is available on the AG's website.

Gregg Abbott, the current AG, has been using state tax dollars to help fund the redistricting effort, part of the "representing the state in litigation" responsibility. These lawyers are billing the state at a rate of $300 to $400 an hour to help the legislators draw up districts.[31] Some of these lawyers worked for former AG John Cornyn as state employees. This situation is an example of something called the "revolving door," which will be discussed later in the chapter.

COMPTROLLER OF PUBLIC ACCOUNTS

As the state's chief financial officer, the comptroller is primarily responsible for collecting taxes. Because the office collects the bulk of the state's money, it provides estimates to the legislature of how much money it has to spend. The legislature cannot constitutionally exceed this limit without going to extraordinary measures. Comptroller Strayhorn did not certify the budget passed by the legislature in 2003. On June 19, she stated that the budget was out of balance by some $200 million. Governor Perry then went to work and vetoed a bill and some other items to bring the budget back into balance.[32]

One of the more recent items undertaken by the comptroller has been the review of various agencies that spend the state's money. The state has a separate state auditor, but the comptroller has worked to examine some agencies and even school districts in some detail. The main goal of this review is to see if the state can save money. Governor Perry stated in his State of the State address that the legislature should enact the comptroller's proposals to save the state money.

Current comptroller Carole Keeton Strayhorn has continued the practice started by previous comptroller John Sharp of issuing reports to cut costs. Through various publications like *Texas Innovator* and *Fiscal Notes,* the comptroller points out ways that Texas and other states are saving money. In fact, the office produces over two dozen reports and periodicals devoted to tax and finance issues in Texas—and most are available free from the comptroller's website.

COMMISSIONER OF THE GENERAL LAND OFFICE

This office has been part of Texas since it declared its independence from Mexico. Its original goal was to keep track of the public lands of Texas by recording titles to land and providing maps. Some of the original public lands were sold to pay the revolutionary debt, and other lands were sold or traded to provide various improvements in Texas like railroads and homesteads. The office generates revenue for the Permanent School Fund (PSF) by leasing drilling rights on the 20.3 million acres of public lands. The dividends and interest from the PSF go directly to funding public education.

Like many of the other agencies in Texas, the General Land Office has several divisions. One of these, Archives and Records, serves a historical purpose: it keeps titles of land going back to Spanish holdings. Another division deals with the natural resources of the state; a separate division deals with coastal issues. Texas does not allow private ownership of its beaches, so this office is responsible for the state coastline. The office supports a beach adoption program and an oil-spill prevention and response program. These programs are separate from the duties of the Texas Commission on Environmental Quality.

One of the more notable divisions of the General Land Office is Veterans Programs, created in 1946 by the Texas Legislature. Several programs are available to veterans. One provides loans to help veterans purchase farmland, while others help veterans purchase or remodel homes. All money loaned to veterans is raised from the sale of bonds. This program does not cost Texas taxpayers anything; all the costs are recovered from the veterans who receive the loans.

COMMISSIONER OF AGRICULTURE

This office is the only statewide elective executive office created by the legislature. It was created in 1907, and it has changed and grown over the years like the other agencies. The agency runs several programs—some are service oriented; others are regulation oriented.

The agency is responsible for marketing Texas products and has developed several programs to assist farmers in selling their products. These activities make up the majority of their service programs. They also help farmers diversify their crops to make farms more profitable. These efforts have evolved over time under the leadership of different commissioners. Several publications have been and are produced to help farmers and to educate consumers. Market reports are available free on the website. These reports list the market prices of various agricultural products.

The agency is also responsible for enforcing several state laws aimed at farmers and protecting consumers, and this enforcement comprises its regulatory function. Many of these laws deal with pesticides that farmers can use. Other functions deal with inspecting produce and other products. One area of inspections involves the Weights and Measures Unit. People working for this unit are responsible for checking the accuracy of scales in grocery stores and verifying the amount of gasoline that a pump delivers.

In the spring of 2004, the agency issued new guidelines for school nutrition that will be phased in over a five-year period starting in August 2004. The new rules are aimed at reducing the fat and sugar content in the food distributed to Texas schoolchildren. The new rules also restrict a school district's choice in offering foods that compete with the official guidelines. The Texas Department of Agriculture (TDA) will not allow school districts to be reimbursed if they do not follow the new rules.[33] The fall 2004 school year will start this program by allowing children to eat only school-provided food. This means parents are not allowed to bring a cake to school for their child's birthday, but they can bring a nutritious snack instead. This stipulation is another example of regulation—one you may not have even noticed.

Boards and Commissions

This collection of more than 200 agencies constitutes the third limb of the executive branch. Each agency is led by a group of people—usually a six- to nine-member board or commission. These leaders are like the board of directors of a private corporation. They meet regularly (about every three months) to decide issues affecting the agency and to set its policy. They propose and adopt rules to govern its actions. They choose an executive director who runs the agency on a daily basis. Below the executive director are all the departments and divisions of the agency. Some agencies regulate, some offer services, and some do both. Some regulatory agencies are discussed a little later in this chapter, health and human services agencies are discussed in Chapter 12, and the education agencies are discussed in Chapter 13.

Here we look at two elected boards (the Texas Railroad Commission and the State Board of Education) and two appointed boards (the Texas Department of Transportation and the Texas Commission on Environmental Quality). As you learn about these select agencies, you may think it is difficult to deal with agencies this large, but it isn't, especially in this electronic age. Almost all agencies maintain websites where you can learn about the history of the agency and its leaders, and how to contact the agency. Several agencies have an **ombudsman** to help the average citizen deal with a particular agency. Over 100 agencies have policies for the Compact with Texans to help Texans deal with an agency.

Ombudsman A government official who investigates citizens' complaints against a government agency.

TEXAS RAILROAD COMMISSION

Originally created in 1891 by the Texas Legislature, the Texas Railroad Commission worked to regulate railroad activity in Texas. Its jurisdiction was restricted to the state of Texas; the federal government took care of everything going from one state to another. The agency still does some work with the railroads, but only from a safety standpoint. The main job of the Railroad Commission now is the regulation of various energy industries. It may seem puzzling that a state agency named the Texas Railroad Commission oversees oil, natural gas, and coal mining. In the past, however, many of these commodities were carried on railroads and through pipelines, so the legislature assigned the Railroad Commission the duty of ensuring that these modes of transportation were available to those who needed it, and thus the regulation of these energy industries began.

The Railroad Commission has three members, each elected statewide for overlapping six-year terms of office. The executive director of the commission is hired by and is responsible to the three commissioners. Like the other agencies, the Texas Railroad Commission has several divisions, and most of them have to do with the energy industries.

The Oil and Gas Division is probably what the Railroad Commission is most known for now. This division regulates oil and gas production and distribution. It collects fees from the oil producers that help offset the agency's costs and help clean up abandoned oil wells. Other divisions deal with surface mining and the safety of railroads and pipelines that carry the oil and gas. The agency is expected to develop ways to market propane as an alternative fuel and educate consumers about its use.

The salary for each of the three railroad commissioners is $92,217, the same as the other elected executives. This rather top-heavy payroll has encouraged several people to call for the three commissioners to go the way of the state treasurer, an office that was abolished in 1994. According to journalist Dave McNeely, a long-time observer of events in Austin, the functions of this agency could easily be combined with others. The burden to the taxpayer would be lightened, as would the burden to the voter, who must keep track of these officials to make informed decisions about whether they should be reelected.[34]

STATE BOARD OF EDUCATION

This board and the agency it oversees presents another way—a somewhat intricate way—of organizing government. The commissioner of education, the executive who runs the Texas Education Agency (TEA), is appointed by the governor, not by the board. Although the legislature creates most of education policy, this group of people has the responsibility for interpreting the law and making the policies. Article VII, Section 8 of the Texas Constitution tells the legislature to create such a board but does not specify its size. Currently, the fifteen members of this board are elected from districts drawn by the legislature every ten years. Each board member is elected for four years, and the terms of office are staggered.

Unlike the three railroad commissioners, the more numerous Board of Education members do not receive a salary for their work. As the governing body, the state board meets to perform various activities, including the monumental task of approving the lists of textbooks the state will purchase for use in classrooms; identifying the items to be included in the Texas Essential Knowledge and Skills (TEKS); and granting, revoking, and modifying charters.[35] Texas Essential Knowledge and Skills (TEKS) are the requirements established by the State Board of Education for what a student needs to know to move from one grade to the next. They are established for each course and each grade level, and they generally guide the adoption of textbooks and what a public schoolteacher teaches the students in the classroom.

The Texas Education Agency (TEA) is responsible for public education in Texas. The TEA was responsible for about $15.6 billion of the total spending on education in 2003. While the amount of money is significant, the number of employees is not. Fewer than 850 full-time employees work for the TEA; the state's classroom teachers (about 268,000) are employed by their districts. Chapter 13 contains much more information about how education is handled here in Texas.

DEPARTMENT OF TRANSPORTATION

This agency is generally responsible for the construction and maintenance of the roads we drive on. While many of the roads are city streets (78,648 miles) or county roads (142,477 miles), a considerable number of paved roadways are under the control of the state of Texas—79,513 miles in 2003.[36] The agency came into being in 1917 to get farmers out of the mud and now employs state-of-the-art computers and equipment to plan, build, use, maintain, and manage the state's highways.[37]

Three commissioners constitute the Transportation Commission, the board that oversees the department. They adopt the rules and plans for the agency, and hold meetings every month, unlike some other agencies. They schedule several of their meetings in communities across Texas to make it easier for citizens to talk to the commissioners. One of their more recent meetings was in Tyler in January 2003, a city they had not visited in nearly forty years.[38] While the public is encouraged to attend, any formal presentations to the commission require written arrangements. These arrangements start several months in advance and must go through several steps. The agency points out that the best place to start contacting it is through the district office closest to you—check the phonebook to find out where it is located. See page 257 for the organizational chart of TxDot.

A full discussion of transportation policy is beyond the scope of this chapter, but you do need to be aware that the Texas Department of Transportation (TxDOT) gets money from several sources; the largest is the federal government. Federal tax dollars provide about 51 percent of the $5.2 billion the agency received in FY2003.[39] These tax dollars come from the tax on gasoline and other fuels used by vehicles traveling the state's highways. This tax is a dedicated tax, but not all of the tax money goes toward highways; 25 percent of the state's gasoline taxes are spent on public education. The largest expenditure of funds—about 63 percent in fiscal year (FY) 2002—is for purchasing the rights-of-way and the design, research, and construction of the roads. This process can take anywhere from two to eight years, depending on the size of the project. And the construction phase is about one-fourth of the total project time. The rest of the time is spent studying alternative routes, conducting environmental studies, taking public input (that's you), and purchasing the rights-of-way to the land to build the road on.[40] Most construction projects in cities and counties are paid for with federal, state, and local tax dollars—yet another example of this country's intergovernmental relations.

Finally, with the cooperation of the governor and the legislature, TxDOT is preparing for several new projects. The newest project supported by Governor Perry is called the Trans Texas Corridor. This 4,000-mile project across the state of Texas is aimed at incorporating all modes of transportation: auto, truck and rail. Separate areas are designated for each, and underground space is provided for utilities. The cost for such a project is estimated to be at least $145 billion.[41]

As you well know, transportation affects your daily life. To have input on these or any other projects, you need to get involved. As with all other political endeavors, you have many points of entry: local officials, state representatives, and your local TxDOT office. Interest group leaders know this information, and you should too. Texas in Context 9.4 shows how the spending for transportation and the environment in Texas compares to the spending in other megastates.

Texas in Context

9.4 Comparative Spending on Highways and the Environment*

Megastate	Total Spending	Highway Spending	Highway Percentage	Environment Spending	Environment Percentage
California	$184,928.00	$7,899.00	4.27%	$3,184.00	1.72%
New York	$119,079.00	$3,295.00	2.77%	$ 352.00	0.30%
Texas	**$ 70,426.00**	**$5,219.00**	**7.41%**	**$ 687.00**	**0.98%**
Florida	$ 51,834.00	$4,826.00	9.31%	$1,397.00	2.70%
Pennsylvania	$ 55,166.00	$4,566.00	8.28%	$ 555.00	1.01%
Michigan	$ 49,184.00	$2,717.00	5.52%	$ 508.00	1.03%
Illinois	$ 49,131.00	$3,656.00	7.44%	$ 454.00	0.92%
Ohio	$ 52,594.00	$3,139.00	5.97%	$ 389.00	0.74%
New Jersey	$ 41,988.00	$2,257.00	5.38%	$ 432.00	1.03%
Massachusetts	$ 32,848.00	$2,744.00	9.72%	$ 287.00	0.87%

*All numbers except percentages are in millions of dollars. All numbers are for fiscal year 2002.
Source: Governing: State and Local Sourcebook 2004, pp. 34, 71 and 21. Calculations for Highway Percentage and Environment Percentage are provided by the authors of this textbook.

TEXAS COMMISSION ON ENVIRONMENTAL QUALITY

Few state agencies have gone through as many changes since their creation as has the Texas Commission on Environmental Quality (TCEQ). Because of sunset legislation, the Texas Natural Resources Conservation Commission (TNRCC) was created in 1993 by combining several environmental regulatory agencies, including the Texas Water Pollution Board. In 2002, the name was changed once more to the present one. Now the Texas Commission on Environmental Quality is headed by three gubernatorial appointees and spends some $344 million a year carrying out its duties of protecting air, water, and land from pollution and environmental degredation.[42]

Licensing The most basic form of regulation. A license indicates that a person has met some level of competency.

One of the ways that TCEQ pays for its activities is through **licensing.** A license is the most basic form of regulation. (Your driver's license is one example.) For example, the TCEQ requires a license to design, install, and maintain irrigation systems. To get a license, you must have thirty-two hours of classroom training, pay a $70.00 fee, and score a 70 or more on each section of an exam that covers topics such as hydraulics, backflow prevention, and installation and design.[43]

Like transportation, a full discussion of environmental policy is beyond the scope of this chapter; in fact, it is beyond the scope of this book. The regulatory environment requires that many different fields of expertise work together—chemistry, biochemistry, physics (low-level nuclear radiation is under the jurisdiction of the

TCEQ), as well as agriculture and horticulture. So if you are majoring in one of the natural sciences, you may find employment with the state of Texas in the TCEQ.

As an example of how interwoven the regulatory environment is, both TCEQ and TxDOT report annually to the legislature on the use of scrap tire in Texas. The tires that are taken off your truck or car are no longer thrown into a landfill. Many are shredded and used in playgrounds or as other landscaping. A crumb rubber factory in Baytown can turn your used tires into the roads you drive on.[44] To pay for the transport of used tires to a shredding facility, Texas charges you $2.00 per tire when you put new ones on your vehicle.

Like other agencies, the three TCEQ commissioners hold meetings that are open to the public. Proposed rules are posted in the *Texas Register* and on the agency's website. One example of such rules was required by the legislature in 2001. In December 2002, TCEQ issued a report outlining what is called a Strategically Directed Regulatory Structure. This report outlined a method of providing rewards or incentives to groups to follow the laws, instead of using various methods of punishment to correct bad behavior.[45] The goal, according to some, is to make better use of your tax dollars to protect the environment; to others, such as most environmental interest groups, this method is another example of the government failing to protect you and me by making good corporate citizenship optional—but by golly don't bring birthday cake to your kid's school. That isn't optional.

The Executive Branch and You

In discussing the three limbs of the executive branch, we have noted briefly the ways that you can affect the administration of government and some of the problems that might concern you. Now we will pull them together in one place and introduce a few new ones. We conclude with a list of reforms you may wish to promote should you decide to become more active in Texas politics.

PROBLEMS YOU SHOULD KNOW ABOUT

Iron triangles, agency capture, the revolving door, secrecy, and the abuse of privatization are five problems that could worsen unless more Texans become involved. Fixing some will require legislation, but before such legislation can be passed, more Texans must be made aware of the problems so that political leaders will invest the time in solving them. You can make a difference at this point in the process.

Iron Triangles.   An *iron triangle* is a relationship among an executive agency, an interest group, and a legislative committee. The interest group is concerned about the legislators who serve on certain standing committees and about who leads an executive agency that affects them in some way. This influence on the interest group could involve many possibilities, such as government loans, regulations, or contracts.

From the point of view of businesses, they are simply attempting to protect themselves from unwanted interference. From the point of view of consumers and workers, a little interference is warranted if it protects them from dangerous products, unsafe workplaces, pollution, or contaminated food and water. The political leaders in the legislature and in the executive branch must try to find a workable middle ground. In doing so, they practice the art of politics.

Iron triangles usually tilt the decisionmaking structure in favor of the interest groups that represent business. They make sure that legislators friendly to their concerns are reelected and chosen for committees that affect them and the executive agencies the committees oversee. They use appointmenteering, electioneering, lobbying, and grassroots lobbying to accomplish these goals.

When decisions are made that seem unfair to the public, we depend on the media to let us know about them. But the media cannot be everywhere at once. And as more media corporations merge and buy each other out, news operations are among the first departments to be cut. Thus, your job is to help make the public aware of abuses of power by iron triangles. You can get some help from the media, but once the facts are available, someone needs to increase the size of the issue public and make the issue more salient. In other words, someone needs to explain why the facts are important, as Bernie Birnbaum did in the case of redlining. Someone needs to write to legislators; send letters to the editor; talk about the issue among friends and colleagues; and maybe even join or support an environmental, labor, or good-government group attempting to deal with the problem.

The rules may be about loans to private businesses, individuals, or units of government. They may concern government contracts or eligibility requirements for grants. They may deal with regulating activities that pollute the air, water, land, or food. Clearly, many people do not want any interference as they conduct business, and it is worth a lot of money to them to keep government away, so they join organizations that protect their businesses. These interest groups and political action committees collect money to elect members to the legislature. They give most of their money to the committees that oversee the executive agencies regulating the businesses that contribute to the interest groups.

Agency Capture.   An interest group's influence in an iron triangle can be expanded if it can also directly influence the executive agency itself. This influence can occur using the techniques we mentioned above and in Chapter 5. An agency can be captured if the interest group can get former employees appointed to major decisionmaking positions in it.

An excellent example of agency capture occurred during Governor Bush's administration. According to TxPEER and Molly Ivins and Louis Dubose, Governor Bush asked for resignations of commissioners appointed by previous governors and then made appointments to the three-person Texas Natural Resources and Conservation Commission (now TCEQ), which changed the orientation of the organization to favor polluters. These three appointees have altered several commission policies, including one that took effect ten days after the third commissioner joined the agency. The twenty-three-year-old policy on surprise inspections of suspected polluters was replaced by announced visits—with ten days' notice.[46]

The Revolving Door.   The *revolving door* refers to individuals who leave government service to work for a company where their knowledge and expertise about government regulations and their contacts within government will be useful. The revolving door has been closed for top executives by law.[47] For legislative staff, it remains to be seen whether the present Speaker of the House will continue the policies of former Speaker of the House Pete Laney, who informed staff members that they must wait at least a year after leaving public service before joining a company where their government experience will be put to use. No law prohibits legislators and other elected officials from working for corporations they dealt with as public officials or even becoming lobbyists.

A February 1999 report from Texans for Public Justice, a nonpartisan interest group, identified the top ten former legislators and top ten former agency officials who are now lobbyists. The report also recommends a lifetime ban on elected officials from performing lobbying duties.[48] The group's 2002 update also identified several former legislators now lobbying the legislature, including seven who work for SBC (the parent company of Southwestern Bell).[49] Some sort of ban would help reduce the revolving-door problem, but no agreement exists about how long or what kind of penalties should be imposed on violators.

Secrecy.   The rules for open meetings and open records are under constant threat by interest groups that do not want the public to know about their actions affecting the public. The records on information about insurance company redlining are still not open to the public, although legislative staffs have access to them.

One way to guarantee that the public is represented at hearings, open or closed, is for agencies to have officials called public counsels to represent the interests of the public and to share what they learn with the public. This budget item is easy to cut, however, and it often is.

Be aware of agencies that cite privacy as a reason to close public records. Privacy can be used to close the books on something about which the public has a right to know. As mentioned earlier, the AG has handbooks and other information on open meetings and open records.

Negotiated rulemaking
The procedure whereby a regulatory agency writes proposed rules with the assistance of those who will be affected by the rules.

In 1997, Texas added to state law a new way of making rules, **negotiated rulemaking,** which basically allows those regulated by an agency and members of the agency itself to negotiate what the rules will be. Once a set of rules is worked out and before the public gets involved, the rules are published in the *Texas Register* and public comment is taken.

The whole procedure is subject in theory to most of the open records and meetings laws in Texas. If you are curious about what any of the previous (or other) agency's rules are, you have access to that information. You also have access to comment on the rules themselves. You may find yourself working for a company one day, and part of your job may include negotiating new rules for that company. Political involvement is an ongoing task.

Privatization A government contract with a private company to provide a service to the state.

Abuse of Privatization.   One way to reduce the size of agencies is **privatization.** Public employees are replaced when a public service is offered by a private company. Taxpayer dollars are spent either way, so the question is one of efficiency. The government's employment of public servants is not inherently wrong. For a case study about how this type of abuse occurs, see Dave Mann's article "Getting Rich off CHIP" in the section called For Further Reading at the end of this chapter.

The idea of privatization is that sometimes a business can do the job more cheaply and more efficiently than the government because the business does not have to follow the same rules and regulations that the government does. Texas uses some privatization in its prison system. While the savings may not be as high as in other states, the idea of competition does appeal to some.

Turning public services over to private for-profit companies appeals to legislators who have to balance budgets. Some worry, however, that accountability and responsibility may be compromised. Creating a private monopoly for a service may not be cost-effective in the long run. An effort must be made to promote competition, either with public servants or private companies.

MAKING THE EXECUTIVE BRANCH MORE ACCOUNTABLE

Throughout this chapter, we have mentioned ways for you to influence what goes on in the executive branch. Before summarizing the chapter, we list below some entry points into the political process. You may want to use them to promote better governance and to work for larger-scale reforms.

- *The State of the State Address and the budget message.* Staff and governors are always on the lookout for new ideas and individuals who care enough to get involved. You can write, e-mail, fax, call, or make an appointment to talk to someone personally. You may get your idea on the public agenda.

- *The veto.* The governor needs to hear from you about bills you feel should be stopped.

- *Testimony at public hearings and letters to agencies about proposed rules published in the* Texas Register. Both techniques are effective ways to make your voice heard. It helps if you can persuade a few friends or colleagues to add their voices.

- *Elections.* It matters who serves the public. You can influence election results by appointmenteering or campaigning at election time.

- *Interning.* Today's indispensable volunteer or intern is tomorrow's policy-making employee.

- *Letters to the editor.* Aiming at policies in specific situations is one reason for writing letters to the editor and phoning call-in shows. Another reason is the prevention of threats to open government.

- *Creating or joining an organization that attempts to influence public policy.* This will allow you to focus on a specific policy.
- *Political parties.* Working to strengthen parties and promoting endorsing conventions is a long-term goal well worth engaging in.
- *Working to reduce the number of boards and commissions.* This goal can be accomplished by constitutional amendment and legislative reform.

Summary

The executive branch of Texas government is organized by law and the constitution into three limbs: the governorship, the elected executives, and the boards and commissions that run or appoint executives to run other state agencies. Our examination of the governorship began with comparing the governorship of Texas to that of other states, in particular, the megastates. We then examined the potential for power in the Texas governorship and concluded that several sources of influence make it an important position for Texans. It matters who is governor.

For governors to be more effective chief executives and to make government itself more accountable to the public, we suggested some reforms for which you may wish to work in the years to come. Chief among them are streamlining the executive branch by doing away with the semi-independent boards and commissions and putting the governor directly or indirectly in charge of them. Second, we suggested strengthening the relationship between the governor and the party label he or she competes for in the primary elections.

We examined the limb of the executive branch that consists of the five elected executives and the agencies they run: the lieutenant governor, who runs the Texas Senate; the attorney general, who is the chief legal representative for the state; the comptroller of public accounts, who is the state's chief tax collector and accounting officer; the commissioner of the General Land Office, who oversees the public lands in Texas and programs for Texas veterans; and the commissioner of agriculture, who oversees programs that subsidize some crops and that promote Texas-grown products.

The third limb of the executive branch contains more than 200 state agencies. Among the elected boards and commissions we examined were the Texas Railroad Commission, which oversees much of the oil and gas industry in Texas, and the State Board of Education. The appointed boards and commissions we examined were the Texas Department of Transportation and the Texas Commission on Environmental Quality. The agencies were also examined to see if any of their problem situations can be corrected.

We concluded with an overview of problems that confront all state agencies, regardless of who is in charge of them. We suggested some ways that you can become active in making the executive branch more accountable. One detail to keep in mind about government bureaucracy is that it is open to you. You do not have that kind of access to private bureaucracies.

KEY TERMS

Bureaucracy, p. 254
Standardized procedures, p. 254
Regulation, p. 255
Merit principle, p. 255
Patronage, p. 255
Hierarchy, p. 255

FOR FURTHER READING

Barta, Carolyn, *Bill Clements: Texan to His Toenails* (Austin, Tex.: Eakin Press, 1996).

Beyle, Thad L., and Lynn R. Muchmore, eds., *Being Governor: The View from the Office* (Durham, N.C.: Duke University Press, 1983).

Ivins, Molly, and Louis DuBose, *Shrub: The Short but Happy Political Life of George W. Bush* (New York: Random House, 2000).

Mann, Dave, "Getting Rich off CHIP," *Texas Observer* (September 28, 2003): 4–5.

Morehouse, Sarah McCalley, *The Governor as Party Leader* (Ann Arbor: University of Michigan Press, 2000).

Morris, Celia, *Storming the Statehouse: Running for Governor with Ann Richards and Dianne Feinstein* (New York: McMillan & Co., 1992).

Phares, Ross, *The Governors of Texas* (Gretna, La.: Pelican Publishing Co., 1976).

STUDY QUESTIONS

1. Identify Bernie Birnbaum, define redlining, and identify the agency responsible for protecting Texas consumers on this issue.

2. Identify the three limbs of the executive branch.

3. Identify the basic principles of bureaucracy.

4. Identify the constitutional and political requirements for becoming governor of Texas.

5. Identify the criteria for comparing megastate governors.

CRITICAL THINKING QUESTIONS

1. Texas in Context 9.1 presents information on state government employment. What might explain the differences in average pay between Texas and the other states? Why would Texas have so many employees yet have such a low average salary?

2. Texas in Context 9.2 lists the power ratings of several governors. Using other information in this textbook, explain what factors keep the Texas governor weak in formal powers. List three or four other features of the governorship that might change its power rating.

3. Why does it matter who is governor? Discuss this topic in terms of the traditional analysis of the Texas governorship, the realities of that role, and its formal and informal sources of power. How might the other elected executives use these informal powers?

4. Discuss the ways we might strengthen the role of the governor. What other consequences might this change have?

5. One way to remember who serves on the State Redistricting Board (see Chapter 8) is that it includes the Speaker of the House and, except for the governor, all but two of the constitutionally identified elected executives. Who are they? What two elected executives are not on the State Redistricting Board?

INTERNET RESOURCES

www.oag.state.tx.us   The website for the attorney general's office provides information about victims of crimes and about child support. It also includes information about consumer protection, various legal opinions about Texas government, and publications of the office.

www.cpa.state.tx.us   The website for the comptroller of public accounts provides much of the financial information about the state, including revenues generated from taxes like the sales tax and gasoline tax, and revenue from the many other sources for Texas. It publishes various reports and publications dealing with improving the state of Texas and comparing Texas to the other forty-nine states.

www.glo.state.tx.us   This website for the commissioner of the General Land Office provides information about the public lands of Texas, including coastal cleanup efforts and maps of Texas. The website also includes information about the various veterans' programs administered by the office.

www.agr.state.tx.us   Information by and about agricultural products is the main focus of the website for the commissioner of agriculture. Information about weights and measures and pesticides is provided, as is information for marketing Texas agricultural products. There is a related website at **www.squaremeals.org** for school nutrition information.

www.sos.state.tx.us   Election information is one of the major parts of the website for the secretary of state. You can also find information for businesses and links to the *Texas Register*. Some information on the legislation from the last legislative session is also provided.

www.governor.state.tx.us   This website for the governor's office provides information by and about the governor. Thousands of webpages describe the functions of the office, the press releases and speeches of the governor, and even copies of the vetoes issued by the governor. There is even a section to download applications for appointment to a board or commission.

www.senate.state.tx.us   This webpage for the lieutenant governor's office is really a subsection of the overall Texas Senate website, but information about the office and the text of speeches made by the lieutenant governor are available. You can even find a form to contact the lieutenant governor if you have a question or want to make your opinion known on an issue facing Texas.

www.texasonline.com   This website for the state of Texas links many other Texas websites. A user can also conduct many electronic transactions on this website. It is the place to start when searching for information on the government of Texas.

www.nga.org/   The website for the National Governor's Association provides a wealth of information about state governors and federal issues that affect the states. It also includes information about various state tax and budget policies and other issues facing state governors.

CHAPTER 10

The Texas Court System

Ray Fernandez, a medical doctor, is the Nueces County medical examiner in Corpus Christi, Texas. His grandmother, Maria Rowland Saenz, was the maid to Johnny Jr., an heir of the famous and very wealthy John G. Kenedy family. The Kenedy clan of Kenedy County, Texas, is second only to the Kleberg clan of Kleberg County in landholding, wealth, oil and gas revenues, cattle herds, and political power. Each family at one time basically owned their entire county, including the vaqueros and their families that lived on their ranches, La Parra in Kenedy and King Ranch in Kleberg. The ranches are adjacent to each other along the Gulf Coast in South Texas.

With only months to live, Dr. Fernandez's frail, sickly, and loving grandmother stroked her grandson's face and commented, "You look just like your grandfather, Johnny Kenedy, Jr." Dr. Fernandez was shocked but remained silent. He was puzzled and deeply disturbed by this unsolicited declaration in front of his mother, Ann Matilde Fernandez. For all his life, into adulthood, he thought his grandfather was Disidoro Pena. He dug up his mother's baptismal certificate in Waco, Texas, and it listed Ann Matilde's mother as Maria Rowland, but the space for the father was blank. It did not say Pena.

He dug up his mother's birth certificate, which listed her birth year as 1925, not 1924 as the family had always assumed. Dr. Fernandez and his mother began investigating the life of Maria Rowland Saenz. They found she was raped by Johnny Jr. while she was a maid to the family on the ranch. Once the pregnancy was visible, Maria was shipped by the Kenedys to an unwed mother's home in Waco.

After giving birth to Ann Matilde, she was sent to work at another Kenedy home in Corpus Christi, and the baby girl was placed under the care of a Mexican woman in nearby Kingsville. While in Corpus Christi, Maria became pregnant again by Johnny, Jr., and gave birth to a boy, Raul. Baby Raul and his sister, Ann Matilde, were poisoned in 1931. Raul died but Ann Matilde lived.

In 2001, Dr. Ray Fernandez and his mother, Ann Matilde, and sister, Ester, filed a lawsuit to establish paternity in Austin, in Travis County. Judge Guy Herman heard the evidence on paternity and ordered the body of Johnny Kenedy, Jr., exhumed for DNA testing before the end of February 2004. That decision was appealed and affirmed and is now on appeal to the Texas Supreme Court. If the DNA tests match those of Ann Matilde and her children, Ray and Ester, the court will declare them heirs to the John Kenedy, Jr., estate and possibly the estate of his childless sister, Sarita Kenedy, also. Huge legal battles will likely ensue in probate court over the past disbursements of assets by both estates and the monies owed the newfound heirs, Ray, Ester, and Ann Matilde Fernandez. Together, the trusts and funds from the estates of both Johnny, Jr., and Sarita Kenedy are valued at between $500 million and $1 billion. The lawyers that have represented the estates may face charges in district court of breach of fiduciary duty and negligence in due diligence for not investigating, and perhaps obstructing, the finding of heirs to the millions of dollars they have been handling for large attorney fees for decades.

Ray Fernandez, with his medical know-how of DNA and his keen ear for listening to his old grandmother, found a way to make a difference in the lives of his family, regardless of the final outcome of litigation. He is a Fernandez, maybe a Kenedy. He may be a millionaire or billionaire by winning in court, not the lottery.[1]

Judicial Cases in the News

If you were concerned that a chapter on the judiciary might be a tad dry, we hasten to point out that many interesting cases involve ordinary people, but some involve famous people and well-known companies. Michael Jackson; Martha Stewart; and

Vice President Dick Cheney, former head of Texas oil-drilling company, Halliburton, have all come to the attention of courts somewhere in the world. The following cases, however, all involve Texans.[2]

Millionaire Robert Durst, in a case that involved a record amount of bail, $2 billion, was acquitted of murder in Galveston, Texas, in November 2003. Durst was placed on bail again pending another trial on two charges of bail jumping following indictment in the murder case and bail has been reduced as a result of an appeal. The amount was deemed excessive.[3]

Former Texas attorney general Dan Morales and his lawyer friend Marc Murr were indicted in March 2003 after a four-year investigation into the $17.3 billion settlement by the state with the tobacco industry in 1998. Both men avoided trials by entering into plea bargaining with the prosecutors. In July 2003, Morales pled guilty to mail fraud and filing a false income tax return. He was sentenced to four years in the state penitentiary. Murr pled guilty to mail fraud and received a six-month prison sentence plus a $40,000 fine.[4]

In 1999, forty-six residents of Tulia in West Texas were arrested after an eighteen-month undercover operation involving drug buys conducted by Tom Coleman, an unscrupulous investigator. Thirty-five persons were charged and convicted, and began serving prison sentences. Almost all were African Americans and a couple were Mexican Americans. No drugs or money were ever found in any of these busts. Terry McEachern was the district attorney in charge of prosecution and Coleman's collaborator working on the cases. In August 2003, Governor Rick Perry signed pardons for all thirty-five of the original defendants because Coleman was not a credible witness and because the prosecutor knew this information all along but prosecuted anyway. Both Coleman and McEachern are facing disciplinary and perjury charges for their role in these tragic events.[5]

In Dallas County, a similar situation developed in 2001 after Dallas police officer Mark Delapaz contracted with three nefarious undercover operatives to buy and sell drugs in a sting operation. The targeted population in this case was Mexican immigrants and the operation netted twenty-four arrests, convictions, and sentences; eighty more cases were dismissed.[6]

White-collar criminals have also been busy. Although Chief Executive Officer (CEO) Ken Lay has yet to spend much time in court, some of his associates at Enron Corporation have pled guilty and are starting prison time.[7]

Wal-Mart settled with 450 families hours after the giant retailer lost before the Fifth U.S. Circuit Court of Appeals in its case involving company-owned life insurance. Wal-Mart bought life insurance on the lives of its workers and wrote off the premiums as a business expense. Every four months, its computers would sweep social security numbers in so-called death runs to find out who had died, then file claims for the proceeds. The benefits ranged from $65,000 to $85,000 for hourly wage earners who had died and hundreds of thousands of dollars for deceased management employees. In Texas, a company can benefit from life insurance policies on their workers provided consent is given by the worker or if the company has an insurable interest in the employee, such as a highly paid top executive. Wal-Mart had no such consent or insurable interest.[8]

Local officials (such as the prosecutor in Tulia mentioned earlier) also find themselves on the receiving end of the judicial system for their behavior. District attorney Oliver Kitzman for Waller County does not believe that college students should vote in elections where they reside while attending college at Prairie View A&M University. In the waning days of 2003, Kitzman wrote a letter to the county election administrator advising that these college students were not automatically eligible to vote in county elections. In 1979, in a somewhat related case, the U.S. Supreme Court ruled 5–4 that Prairie View students could vote in county elections. At issue here are not only questions of citizenship, residency, and state police power, but also judicial federalism. Kitzman's actions may involve enough vote dilution to raise issues of protection under the federal Voting Rights Act as applied to Texas since 1975. Now, the Texas secretary of state and attorney general are involved in the fray, as are a state senator and a representative (not to mention the students who are registered to vote).[9]

State representative Jaime Capelo (a Democrat from Corpus Christi) is being investigated by a federal grand jury sitting in Houston for an alleged $100,000 kickback in a civil lawsuit involving an explosion at a CITGO refinery in Corpus Christi. Capelo represented the refinery and another attorney represented the injured police officers on duty when the accident occurred.[10] Representative Capelo lost his re-election bid because copies of the kickback check were used in political advertising by his rivals. Another federal investigation involves state district judge Edward Aparicio presiding in Hidalgo County, Texas (Edinburg). The Federal Bureau of Investigation (FBI) is looking into evidence of bribery, fraud, and racketeering. Judge Aparicio was served a subpoena and boxes of records were removed from his office for evidence.[11]

In a bizarre case out of Texas Tech University in Lubbock, Dr. Thomas Butler was charged with bioterrorism and arrested in early 2003. He had reported the disappearance of thirty vials of bacteria that causes bubonic plague. The professor could not recall whether he lost the vials, threw them away, misplaced them, or had them stolen. The jury acquitted the professor of twenty-two charges, including his false claim of losing the vials and of smuggling, but convicted him of forty-seven other serious misconduct charges, such as exporting plague samples to Tanzania in Africa without authorization. He was sentenced in March 2004 and received a punishment of 330 years in prison and $11 million in fines.[12] He has surrendered his medical license to the Texas State Board of Medical Examiners.

The Judicial Process in Texas

In the chapter-opening story about Dr. Ray Fernandez, the allegations and counter-allegations have not yet resulted in complex and prolonged litigation. Once the official DNA results are made public by the district court, the parties will begin protracted, costly, and extremely complex litigation. The lawyers for the John G. Kenedy, Jr., Charitable Trust and the John G. and Stella Kenedy Memorial Foundation have appealed the trial court ruling exhumation order to the Court of Appeals and most recently to the Texas Supreme Court. They argue that time has run out for the Fernandez's to file lawsuits as heirs, if in fact they are heirs. They argue that Ann Matilde Fernandez knew the story of who her real father was and did nothing. Ray, the lawyers will argue, has no standing to bring this lawsuit so late. If the litigation does move forward, the multiple actions and cross-actions will take years before any closure is possible. Litigation is costly, time-consuming, and personally invasive. Maria Rowland Saenz is dead, Ann Matilde is mentally incompetent, and Ray must carry on the fight alone. Ray and Ester, and their lawyers, individuals making a difference, against many lawyers whose annual income is bolstered by the fees from the estates they administer and that they now want to claim.[13]

THE BEGINNING

Sheriff Highest-ranking law enforcement official in a county, elected by the voters. He or she serves as the custodian of the courthouse.

Common law Laws, principles, and rules of action derived primarily from usage and custom. All the statutory and case law background of England and the American colonies before the American Revolution are considered the common law.

Constable Lowest-ranking law enforcement official in a county, elected by the voters of a given precinct. The person is primarily a process server for the courts; enforces writs; and provides support services to the lower courts as bailiff, security officer, and officer of the court.

Bail An amount sufficient to procure release from confinement. It also serves as insurance of future attendance in court and the intention to remain within the jurisdiction of the court.

A criminal case begins when a person makes an allegation in an original petition or makes an accusation to a local officer capable of arresting someone. Texas Rangers, **sheriffs,** or any officer with prosecutorial power such as a county attorney, district attorney, or attorney general can make an arrest in the case of a violation of the various law codes: penal (crime), family, juvenile, government, business, and municipal (usually traffic and health). Local police officers and even citizens have the power and duty to arrest someone observed committing or about to commit a crime.

In a civil matter, such as a suit to establish paternity, a person simply files an original petition (civil suit) with the county or district clerk alleging a tort, a wrongdoing of the **common law** or the violation of a specific statute. Some examples of wrongdoing are both a violation of the criminal statutes and the common law, such as voting when it involves fraud, corruption, violence, or infringement of civil rights.

A process server, or **constable,** personally serves the accused with official notice of the allegation. In a civil matter, the defendant must respond within a certain number of days to the notice. In a criminal matter, the accused is arrested and jailed.

Once the person has notice and either has posted **bail** or answered the original petition, he or she usually travels to the seat of local government where the principal courthouse is located or the location designated on the notice. Once there, the person enters the courtroom to be physically present, confronts witnesses making the allegations, exercises the right to ask questions, and makes statements or maintains silence while the accusers present their case.

THE TRIAL: SYMBOLISM OF A COURT AND ITS FUNCTIONS

The courtroom is steeped in tradition and symbolism. Every courtroom has a typical layout with a generous use of wood for decoration and finish. The entry doors lead to wood benches, where the public sits to observe the proceedings. Court activity and the records kept of the proceedings are usually open to inspection by the public—with rare exceptions, such as a juvenile matter where privacy is a concern. The prospective jurors summoned for possible service as a jury in a proceeding

Voir dire The preliminary examination undertaken by the attorneys and the judge of persons presented to serve as witnesses or jurors to determine competency, interest, bias, and prejudice. There are two kinds of juries chosen: **petit** and **grand.** A grand jury is comprised of 12 persons and usually hears felony cases although they may also sit for misdemeanor cases. In a criminal case, a grand jury must reach a unanimous verdict. A petit jury is comprised of only 6 persons and they usually sit for lower courts such as municipal, justice of the peace, and county court at law. In Texas a jury trial is a fundamental right but an accused can waive a jury trial and ask for a bench trial meaning trial by the judge.

also sit in this public area initially during jury selection, or **voir dire,** as the legal profession terms the process.

A wooden barrier separates the seating area for the public and the main center, pit, or arena of the courtroom. This physical barrier is the famous lawyer's bar (as in members of the bar) because only licensed lawyers are admitted inside the bar to practice their profession. The accused sit with their legal counsel inside the bar but are not allowed to speak unless spoken to or they are representing themselves.

The other court personnel inside the bar are court reporters, clerks, and the bailiff. Each of these persons has an assigned place to sit or stand at floor level inside the bar and usually in close proximity to the judge. The jury, once selected, sits in a separately enclosed and slightly elevated area with individual chairs for twelve, the maximum number for a jury. The judge also sits in a separately enclosed and highly elevated area above all other persons in the courtroom.

The various elevations and enclosures within the courtroom are used to highlight authority, perspective, and role. The higher the elevation the occupant has within the courtroom, the greater is that person's authority, perspective, and role. The judge is the highest position, commanding the most authority, the highest perspective, and the most important role. The jury is next highest, and all the others are at floor level, with the least authority, limited perspective, and limited role. The judge is the sole interpreter of the law in every case, and the jury is the fact finder. When no jury is requested, the judge assumes both roles: law interpreter and fact finder.

In every trial, the jury or the judge must reach a certain threshold of evidence to make a decision. The lowest level of evidence required in a civil case is referred to as the preponderance of the evidence. The highest level of evidence in a civil case is referred to as clear and convincing. If a mathematical formula were applied to these two thresholds, the former would be more than half on a scale, and the latter would be an overwhelming majority. In a criminal case, the threshold of evidence that must be reached is much higher than in a civil case. The accused must be found guilty beyond a reasonable doubt, which means the doubt that a reasonable person would have in making the most serious of decisions.

The lawyers are the advocates for the state or their clients; all others present inside the bar are support personnel who keep the process functioning in its technical aspects. The public observes the proceedings from outside the bar.

At the conclusion of each case, the accused is found guilty or not guilty in a criminal proceeding, and negligent or not negligent in a civil proceeding. One of the unfortunate features of our legal system is that people are never declared innocent, just not guilty. In juvenile proceedings, the court uses the words *true* or *not true* instead of *guilty, not guilty,* or *negligent.*

Appeals of the outcome by either party involved in a case must allege wrongdoing by the various persons present and involved with the court proceeding. An appeal will not be successful if it simply challenges the outcome; it must raise legal issues. The process continues until resources and appeals are exhausted. Frequently cited grounds for appeal are juror misconduct; attorney misconduct; fundamental error by the judge; perjury by witnesses; conflict of interest; new and relevant evidence not available at the time of trial; and missing, erroneous, or faulty court records.

A case is developing in Bexar County that could hamper future prosecutions of local officials. Justice of the peace Albert McKnight was charged with exposing himself to undercover officers in a local park. His case was heard by Judge Philip Meyer, presiding judge of County Court at Law No. 6, in January 2004 for over four-and-a-half hours of testimony and argument over points of law. The matter of the judge exposing himself is not at the center of the controversy. Instead, the controversy swirls around whether or not a justice of the peace (JP) establishes an attorney-client relationship with the district attorney or the county attorney in carrying out his or her duties.

JPs frequently have prosecutors in their courtrooms. They seek legal advice on matters pending in their courts, they confer with prosecutors on legal points, and the like. State law provides legal representation to any county official or employee named in civil matters by the district attorney's office. Judge Meyer ruled that a conflict of interest exists between Judge McKnight and the district attorney's office. It has been established as an ethical rule that an attorney cannot prosecute someone in a case if he or she has previously represented the person. This legal issue is novel: Is there a conflict of interest based on attorney-client relationship between a county official, a justice of the peace, and the district attorney's office that now seeks to prosecute him on criminal charges?

The matter is now on appeal to the Fourth Court of Appeals. Depending on the decision, the matter could also be appealed to the Texas Supreme Court by the end of 2004. Meanwhile, the state legislature in 2005 may also look at the statutes, both penal and government code, to see if the language can be tightened or revised to permit prosecution of local officials by district and county attorneys. The state bar association may enter the fray on the ethical-rules side to tighten or revise the attorney-client relationship between hired and retained legal-service providers and officials with job descriptions that require provision of legal services without pay. Judge McKnight, the accused, and Judge Meyer, the arbiter, are individuals making a difference.[14]

Contemporary Issues of Tradition and Symbolism

Texas has come a long way from the eras of slavery and Jim Crow. For most of this time, persons of Mexican ancestry and African ancestry were denied their basic civil rights to vote, obtain an education, hold public office, and own property. The legacy of racial exclusion from the political and judicial system continues to this day. The passage of the hate crimes bill in 2001 by the Seventy-Seventh Texas Legislature is a symbolic statement that we are beginning to come to terms with this legacy. The fake drug scandals in Tulia and Dallas in 2003 are reminders that abuse of racial and ethnic minorities by government officials is still a fact of life.

In analyzing the judicial system, this chapter frequently mentions examples of this legacy of exclusion and oppression in the vital areas of judicial selection, court structure, personnel, juries, and several constitutional issues. Not all cases are decided by juries, and much of the work of the courts is conducted before and after a jury is involved. Nevertheless, you are more likely to become a jury member than a judge in the near future, so we begin with jury selection.

"A Jury of One's Peers": Fact or Fiction?

Texas has two types of juries: grand juries and trial juries. The grand jury is both a body of persons and a process. The process is elitist in nature. First, the district judge appoints three to five jury commissioners to prepare a list of eligible jurors, usually fifteen to twenty, from which to pick a twelve-person grand jury. The district judge then chooses twelve jurors from this list. These twelve are the members of the grand jury, which serves a term of three months in most cases. Large counties have more than one grand jury, usually two, sitting at any given time. The members of the grand jury (no fewer than nine) evaluate the evidence presented by the prosecutor to determine if sufficient evidence of a serious crime exists to issue a **true bill** for indicting an individual or to issue no bill. A **no bill** means the grand jury deems the evidence presented insufficient to charge the accused with the crime. The accused, or the person being interrogated by a grand jury and the prosecutor, has no right to an attorney during the proceedings.

True bill An actual bill of indictment by a grand jury indicating that the jury found sufficient evidence and truth to the allegation to bring the accused to trial.

No bill A grand jury does not find sufficient evidence or truth in the allegation to warrant bringing the accused to trial. The opposite of a true bill.

Trial juries consist of six or twelve persons. The smaller number is found in juries hearing cases in the lower courts, such as municipal, justice of the peace, and even county court. District court trials require a jury of twelve members. These trial juries reach decisions on guilt and innocence, truthfulness of witnesses, punishment, and money damages awarded in the civil cases.

SERVICE OR INVOLUNTARY SERVITUDE?

Jury service in Texas is mandatory; refusal to serve is punishable by fine and even confinement in the local jail. The qualifications to serve on a jury are minimal: A juror must be over the age of eighteen, be a resident of the county, be able to read and write, and have no felony conviction or not be under **indictment** for a felony. Certain persons can ask for an exemption from jury service: persons sixty-five years of age and older, full-time students, and persons with children under ten years of age. Judges can also excuse persons from jury service.

Indictment The result of the grand jury process leading to formal charges of wrongdoing against a person. It is also the name of the charging instrument, as in true bill of indictment.

A major problem across the state and nation is absenteeism from jury service. Dallas County, for example, has had an absentee rate of 80 percent in recent years. Young persons, minorities, low-income people, and women with children are seldom found on juries. The faces of jurors seldom mirror the community. Instead, middle-age, white, male, and higher-income persons are overrepresented on juries. At issue is underrepresentation of a distinct group within the community. A jury of one's peers does not mean that each person on trial is entitled to a jury comprised of similar members by gender, race, income, educational attainment, religion, and other characteristics. A jury of one's peers does mean that a jury pool should mirror the population of the community within 5 percentage points and not beyond 10 percentage points. If a variance of more than 10 percentage points is found in a jury pool, some courts have ruled that an impartial jury and a fair trial, as guaranteed by the Texas Constitution and the Sixth Amendment to the U.S. Constitution, are impossible.

A recent study by the *Dallas Morning News* and *Southern Methodist University Law Review* on the jury selection system found several disturbing statistics:

- Hispanics comprised 25 percent of the residents of Dallas County, but only 7 percent appeared in jury pools.
- Young adults between the ages of eighteen and thirty-five years comprised 37 percent of the county's population, but only 8 percent of prospective jurors were in that age group.
- Nearly 40 percent of Dallas County residents had income of less than $35,000 a year, but only 13 percent of jury candidates were in that income bracket.[15]

Jury service is a problem in Texas. The biggest obstacle to jury service is money. The legislature in 1866 set pay for jury service at $2.00 a day. In 1955, the legislature raised the pay to $6.00 a day, and that rate has remained in effect since. At $6.00 a day, the prospective juror is lucky to cover parking expenses. Only Missouri—at $5.00 a day—has a pay rate lower than Texas. Colorado and Connecticut pay $50.00 a day.

Texas law does not require employers to compensate workers while they comply with the jury summons. In El Paso County during 1999, only 22 percent of the people summoned for jury duty showed up. County officials increased juror pay to $40.00 a day, the first Texas county to increase the minimum pay, and thus raised attendance significantly. In the celebrated Harris County probate case involving Anna Nicole Smith and her former husband's estate, jurors were paid for all expenses plus $50.00 a day by the litigating parties; the judge allowed these payments to ensure juror attendance. The case lasted several months during 2000 and 2001.

JURY SELECTION

A jury pool consists of all those persons summoned for service on a given day. All persons who have a driver's license or a department of public safety identification card in a county can be summoned for jury service. The jurors usually gather at a central point to check in and receive instructions and to present their excuses for release from jury duty. Groups of eighteen to forty persons are sent to various courtrooms for the jury selection process of voir dire.

After the bailiff seats the jury panel in the courtroom, the judge administers the oath of service and provides preliminary instructions. The lawyers then begin voir dire, a series of personal questions meant to determine an individual juror's qualifications to serve—for example, an open mind, prejudice, and attitudes toward punishment. If an attorney feels that a prospective juror's answer to a question indicates a preconceived opinion about the defendant's innocence or guilt, the person is challenged **for cause.** The judge determines whether to grant the challenge and excuse the juror for lack of impartiality and fairness. The attorneys and

For cause A challenge for cause to a prospective juror for bias toward, prejudice toward, interest in, or knowledge about the case at hand admitted during voir dire. A successful challenge for cause leads to dismissal from further jury service on that occasion.

Peremptory challenge or **strike** An arbitrary challenge or strike of a prospective juror without need for a reason. Each side is allowed a certain number of strikes, depending on the type of case—usually three per side in smaller misdemeanor cases and six in more serious felony cases.

Hung jury A jury that is unable to agree on a verdict in a case after suitable deliberation. A deadlocked jury.

prosecutors have an unlimited number of challenges for cause. Another type of juror challenge is called **peremptory challenge,** a challenge to a juror without cause. Attorneys refer to these peremptory challenges as **strikes.** Each side in every case has a specified number of strikes, depending on factors such as the nature of the case, the amount in controversy, and the number of parties involved in the litigation. The possibility of attorney bias is inherent in the use of these challenges. Judges monitor attorney challenges to prevent attorneys from striking jurors solely on the basis of race and gender.

Once the jury panel is selected, the members are seated in the jury box and the trial begins. All criminal verdicts in Texas must be by unanimous vote. If only one juror disagrees, the result is a **hung jury,** and the prosecution can retry the case. Unanimity is not required in civil cases. Usually, however, ten of twelve must agree with a verdict in a district case, and five of six must agree on a verdict in the lower courts.

The Texas System of Courts

The Texas Constitution sets out the types of courts in Article V, Section 1 as follows: "The judicial power of this State shall be vested in one Supreme Court, in one Court of Criminal Appeals, in Courts of Appeals, in District Court, in County Courts, in Commissioner's Courts, in courts of Justice of the Peace and in such other courts as may be provided by law." Although the language of this passage sets out seven courts, in reality only six function as courts. The Commissioner's Court is the name given to the legislature of county government in Texas and is not a court that handles cases. Another difficulty with the language of Article V is the designation of a Supreme Court and a Court of Criminal Appeals. In reality, Texas has two supreme courts with different names: the Court of Criminal Appeals is the supreme, or ultimate, court for all criminal matters, and the other supreme court handles all civil matters.

The legislature can and does create additional courts when the need arises. In metropolitan areas with ever-growing populations such as Houston, Dallas, San Antonio, Austin, El Paso, and the Rio Grande Valley, courts must be added regularly to keep up with the volume of cases filed. The first such legislative action to add a court occurred with the county courts. Each of the 254 counties in Texas has a constitutional office of county judge that is filled by election. This public official historically has been the presiding judge at the county level for all misdemeanors and juvenile and probate matters filed with the county clerk of any county. He or she is also the presiding officer of the Commissioner's Court, among other duties. Within a short time after the turn of the twentieth century, many Texas counties had so many case filings that the legislature was compelled to create county courts-at-law. In most large urban centers across the state, numerous statutorily created county courts-at-law and other specialized courts—such as probate courts, domestic relations courts, juvenile courts, criminal district courts, and even auxiliary drug courts—now exist. The legislature has authorized 226 statutory courts in eighty-one counties. As of September 1, 2003, 209 such courts were operating in eighty-one counties, and seventeen statutory probate courts operated in ten counties.[16] Figure 10.1

FIGURE 10.1 Court Structure of Texas

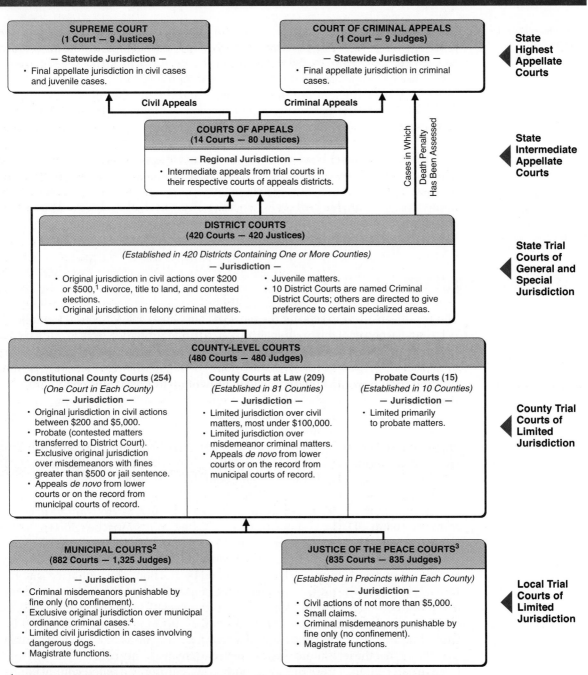

SUPREME COURT
(1 Court — 9 Justices)

— Statewide Jurisdiction —
• Final appellate jurisdiction in civil cases and juvenile cases.

COURT OF CRIMINAL APPEALS
(1 Court — 9 Judges)

— Statewide Jurisdiction —
• Final appellate jurisdiction in criminal cases.

State Highest Appellate Courts

Civil Appeals   Criminal Appeals

COURTS OF APPEALS
(14 Courts — 80 Justices)

— Regional Jurisdiction —
• Intermediate appeals from trial courts in their respective courts of appeals districts.

State Intermediate Appellate Courts

Cases in Which Death Penalty Has Been Assessed

DISTRICT COURTS
(420 Courts — 420 Justices)

(Established in 420 Districts Containing One or More Counties)
— Jurisdiction —

• Original jurisdiction in civil actions over $200 or $500,[1] divorce, title to land, and contested elections.
• Original jurisdiction in felony criminal matters.

• Juvenile matters.
• 10 District Courts are named Criminal District Courts; others are directed to give preference to certain specialized areas.

State Trial Courts of General and Special Jurisdiction

COUNTY-LEVEL COURTS
(480 Courts — 480 Judges)

Constitutional County Courts (254)
(One Court in Each County)
— Jurisdiction —

• Original jurisdiction in civil actions between $200 and $5,000.
• Probate (contested matters transferred to District Court).
• Exclusive original jurisdiction over misdemeanors with fines greater than $500 or jail sentence.
• Appeals *de novo* from lower courts or on the record from municipal courts of record.

County Courts at Law (209)
(Established in 81 Counties)
— Jurisdiction —

• Limited jurisdiction over civil matters, most under $100,000.
• Limited jurisdiction over misdemeanor criminal matters.
• Appeals *de novo* from lower courts or on the record from municipal courts of record.

Probate Courts (15)
(Established in 10 Counties)
— Jurisdiction —

• Limited primarily to probate matters.

County Trial Courts of Limited Jurisdiction

MUNICIPAL COURTS[2]
(882 Courts — 1,325 Judges)

— Jurisdiction —
• Criminal misdemeanors punishable by fine only (no confinement).
• Exclusive original jurisdiction over municipal ordinance criminal cases.[4]
• Limited civil jurisdiction in cases involving dangerous dogs.
• Magistrate functions.

JUSTICE OF THE PEACE COURTS[3]
(835 Courts — 835 Judges)

(Established in Precincts within Each County)
— Jurisdiction —
• Civil actions of not more than $5,000.
• Small claims.
• Criminal misdemeanors punishable by fine only (no confinement).
• Magistrate functions.

Local Trial Courts of Limited Jurisdiction

[1] The dollar amount is currently unclear. See district courts section of Subject Matter Jurisdiction of the Courts.
[2] Some Municipal Courts are courts of record—appeals from those courts are taken on the record to the county-level courts.
[3] All Justice of the Peace Courts and most Municipal Courts are not courts of record. Appeals from these courts are by trial *de novo* in the county-level courts, and in some instances in the district courts.
[4] An offense that arises under a municipal ordinance is punishable by a fine not to exceed: 1) $2000 for ordinances that govern fire safety, zoning, and public health; or, 2) $500 for all others.

Office of Court Administration. September 1, 2003.

shows the court structure in Texas. (Note that redistricting of the justice of the peace courts in Dallas County makes some of the total numbers inconsistent from figure to figure in the 2003 Annual Report of Judicial Council Office of Court Administration.)

MUNICIPAL COURT

De novo A new trial in another court, usually a court of record.

Fines Amounts assessed for specific crimes listed in the Texas Penal Code. Usually a defendant, once found guilty, is assessed fines and court costs, or confinement in jail (or all of these). Probation in lieu of jail sentence also incurs additional costs and conditions imposed by the judge, including restitution to the victim of the crime and community service.

Court costs Assessments made by the court to defray the expenses incurred in the case at hand.

Individuals in Texas have more contact with the municipal court than any other court. In 2003, 8,099,088 cases were filed in these courts. About 1,325 municipal judges sat on the bench of the municipal courts in approximately 883 cities. Larger cities have more than one municipal judge. Municipal judges are appointed for two-year terms by the city council, except in El Paso, which elects their city judges. Only a few municipal courts of record exist, that is, a court in which an official record of the proceeding is taken, usually by a professional court reporter who types a transcript of every word spoken. Any appeal from a municipal court goes to the county-level courts—either the county court or the county court-at-law, both of which are the first level of courts of record. An appeal from a municipal court in which no record was taken is by trial **de novo** in the county-level courts; that is, it is treated as a new case rather than an appeal, but this time with a record of the proceedings.

Cases heard in municipal court do not result in punishment by confinement in jail. These courts have jurisdiction over two types of cases: (1) criminal misdemeanors, usually a traffic offense, with **fines** less than $500 plus **court costs;** and (2) violations of municipal ordinances, usually a fire safety, public health, building code, or zoning infraction, with fines of up to $2,000 plus court costs (see Figure 10.2).

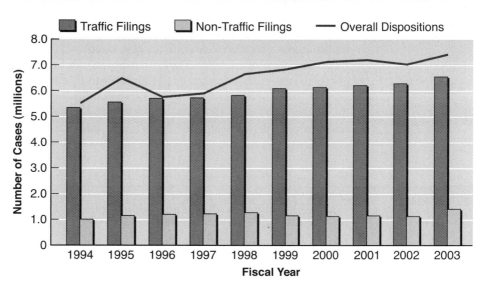

FIGURE 10.2 Docket Composition for the Past Ten Years in the 883 Municipal Courts of Texas

Magistrate A person with limited judicial power who explains to the accused their legal rights and the charges leveled against them; usually a justice of the peace or municipal judge.

Municipal judges may also function as **magistrates.** They can issue arrest and search warrants, set bail, give statutory warnings to the accused, hold examining trials to determine whether enough evidence is available to hold someone for trial, and hold inquests to determine the cause of death. Usually they set bail amounts for those accused of crimes and those seeking liberty from jail confinement.

Cities set the qualifications and salaries of municipal judges in Texas. Most municipal judges do not have to be licensed attorneys. The municipal courts are sources of revenue for the city. For example, in the fiscal year ending August 2003, the city courts in the major cities of the state generated millions of dollars (Houston—$46,255,284; Dallas—$28,503,269; San Antonio—$18,949,026; Austin—$25,061,000; Fort Worth—$19,559,789; El Paso—$22,759,632; Arlington—$11,322,164; and Corpus Christi—$6,129,257).

JUSTICE OF THE PEACE COURTS

People in Texas have their second most frequent court contacts with the justice of the peace courts. Commonly referred to as JP courts (and the judge as a JP), these courts handled 2,957,016 cases in the fiscal year ending August 31, 2003. Unlike the municipal judge, the justice of the peace is elected in a partisan election held every even-numbered year for a term of four years. Like municipal judges, the JP does not have to be a lawyer, but about 5 percent are lawyers.

The Texas Constitution, in Article V, Section 18, requires each county to have at least one and not more than eight JP courts. In 2000, 835 JP courts operated in the state. Each of the 254 commissioners courts set the salary of their JPs, and the salaries vary from county to county. Rural counties have one sitting JP, usually at the courthouse, and the salary is low. Urban counties have up to eight JPs sitting in various locations (called precincts) in the county, and the salaries are much higher than are those for their rural counterparts. Redistricting after 2001 reduced the number of JPs in Dallas County from fourteen to eight, increased the number in Harris County to fifteen, and realigned districts in many counties, such as Bell County.

Forcible entry and detainer Speedy and adequate remedy for obtaining possession of premises by one entitled to actual possession. Usually a matter handled by the justice of the peace courts and involving unpaid rent or lease payment.

JP courts have jurisdiction over criminal misdemeanor cases, usually traffic violations, with fines up to $500. They also handle civil matters, usually small claims involving money damages of $200 up to $5,000, including court costs. The JP courts also hear many other types of cases, such as **forcible entry and detainer** suits, that is, actions to evict someone from a location, usually for nonpayment of rent, and truancy cases (see Figure 10.3). The workload of a justice of the peace varies by precinct and county. The heaviest workload is in the precincts of urban counties. For the fiscal year ending August 2003, Harris County JPs handled 440,826 traffic cases plus others, resulting in revenues of $35.8 million; Dallas County JPs handled 76,903 traffic cases plus others, resulting in revenue of $15.3 million; Tarrant County JPs handled 14,691 traffic cases plus others, resulting in revenue of $3.8 million; and Bexar County JPs handled 45,248 traffic cases plus others, resulting in revenue of $10.6 million. By contrast, rural JPs have small caseloads. For example, Loving County handled thirty-five traffic cases plus others, resulting in revenue of $5,382; and Foard County JPs handled 130 traffic cases plus others, resulting in revenue of $11,581.

FIGURE 10.3 Total Cases Filed Statewide in the 832 Justice of the Peace Courts in Texas

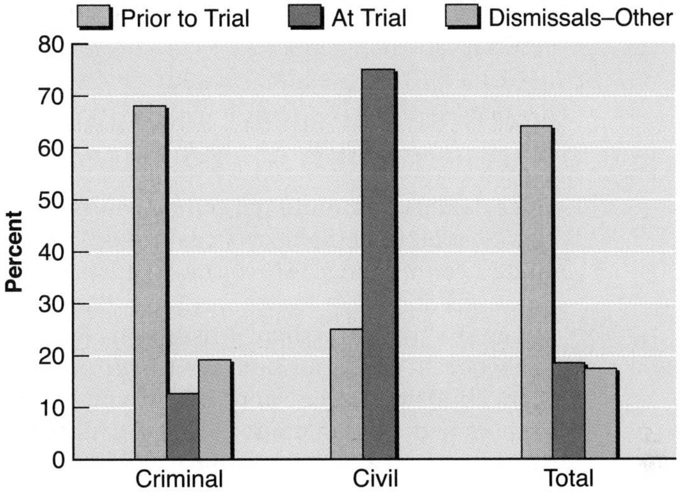

Source: Texas Judicial Council, Office of Court Administration, Annual Report of the Texas Judicial System Fiscal Year 2003.

A person does not risk a jail sentence when appearing before a JP court, only a fine and court costs, unless the matter is for contempt of court. A person can be in contempt of court for failing to appear on a specified court date about which the person had adequate prior knowledge, for acting improperly in the courtroom or before the judge, and for willfully violating a court order about which a person had prior knowledge.

The JP court is not a court of record. No official record of the proceedings is kept by the court; hence, any appeal from this court also must be tried de novo at the next level—county or district. Some persons, certainly lawyers, use the procedural device of appeal to the county courts to prolong, postpone, and delay a final outcome in a case. An appeal from either the municipal or JP court takes time. It is a second chance for a different outcome. The cost of the bond necessary to appeal is minimal, and the evidence, including witnesses, may be lost or may not be as reliable as in the first trial.

In addition to court trials, the JP performs other duties. In many counties, the JP is also the coroner—the person who determines the cause of death in accidents or unattended deaths, as in the case of bodies found. Yet the JP is not a medical expert trained for this task. Even though the law does not require a medical expert, counties sometimes provide their JPs with additional funds to contract for an autopsy by a professional. The JP is also the magistrate for higher-level courts. In this capacity, the JP can set bail, hold inquests, conduct examining trials, and hear administrative law cases such as license suspensions. The most lucrative of the additional duties of a JP is marrying people. Over and above the salary of the justice of the peace set by the Commissioner's Court, a JP can charge a fee for performing a marriage ceremony and keep the fee as separate income. Some JPs perform hundreds of such ceremonies at $100.00 to $150.00 each. Bilingual JPs are especially in great demand.

CONSTITUTIONAL COUNTY COURTS AND STATUTORY COUNTY COURTS-AT-LAW

Texas has 254 constitutional county courts, one per county, as mandated by Article V, Section 15 of the Texas Constitution. The presiding judge of each court is the elected county judge. The term of office is four years, and the Commissioner's Court sets the salary. The county judge does not have to be a lawyer.

The county courts share jurisdiction with the JP courts in civil matters and are the appellate courts for both the municipal and JP courts. The county court also hears criminal misdemeanor cases, particularly driving while intoxicated (DWI) offenses and child-support collection. All county courts are courts of record. A person appearing before a county court or county court-at-law judge may face a jail sentence in addition to a fine and court costs.

At the beginning of this section, we discussed the evolution of county courts-at-law. The jurisdiction of each county court-at-law varies because each was created by separate legislation. The presiding judges of these courts must be lawyers in good standing with the Texas Bar Association. They are elected to four-year terms, and their salaries vary because each Commissioner's Court sets the amount. The county courts-at-law handle probate, juvenile, and domestic relations matters. In 2004, Texas had 209 such statutory county courts, plus the seventeen statutory probate courts. Not all of the county judges for the 254 constitutional county courts have judicial duties; usually only the judges for the rural counties do. Together, these county courts had 798,949 cases pending in the fiscal year ending August 2003, after having disposed of some 698,844 cases during the preceding fiscal year (see Figure 10.4). As the Texas population increases and gets older, the dockets of probate courts and the number of mental health cases will continue to

FIGURE 10.4   Docket Composition in the County-Level Courts of Texas

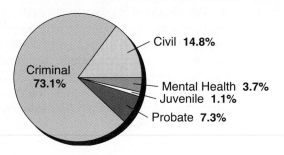

Civil **14.8%**

Criminal **73.1%**

Mental Health **3.7%**
Juvenile **1.1%**

Probate **7.3%**

swell, requiring more courts and more judges. By the end of August 2003, the number of probate cases filed reached 55,716, and the number of mental health cases reached 29,012. Criminal cases still account for the bulk of the caseload in county courts: approximately 70 percent of all cases.

DISTRICT COURTS

In 2004, 420 district courts operated in Texas, many with the same boundaries as other district courts. A district court is created by the legislature for a given geographic area. In rural areas, such a court may cover various counties; urban areas commonly have several district courts in operation.

District judges are elected to four-year terms in partisan elections. They must be lawyers licensed to practice in the state with no less than four years of prior experience as an attorney or judge, and they must be over the age of twenty-five. The base salary of a district judge, at $101,700, is much more than any lower court judge earns, and the salary is supplemented by the county. The supplement plus the regular salary must equal $2,000 less than that received by justices of the court of appeals in which the district court is located. The supplement to the base salary ranges from a high of $23,300 in Harris County to $0.00 in eighteen counties. In Dallas County, it is $9,300; in Travis County, $19,300 to $21,518; in Lubbock County, $10,240; and in Midland County, it is $7,000.

A district judge can hear all criminal misdemeanor and felony cases and all civil cases where the disputed money damages exceed $200. On the criminal side of the docket, most of the offenses involve drugs, burglary, and theft. On the civil side of the docket, over half of the cases are divorces and related family matters. In metropolitan areas, some of the district courts specialize in specific matters such as civil, criminal, family law, or drug cases (see Figure 10.5).

APPELLATE COURTS

Texas has fourteen courts of appeals. Article V, Section 6 of the Texas Constitution authorizes the legislature to divide the state into geographic districts and establish

FIGURE 10.5 Docket Composition in the District Courts of Texas

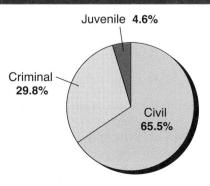

Juvenile **4.6%**

Criminal
29.8%

Civil
65.5%

a court of appeals in each district. Each court of appeals district court can have from three to twelve members—the chief judge and associate justices. The exact number of justices in each appeals court is set by the legislature. Dallas's fifth district has thirteen members and is the largest of all. Houston's first and fourteenth appellate districts have nine justice members each. The thirteenth district in Corpus Christi/Edinburg and the third in Austin each have six members; Waco's tenth, Eastland's eleventh, Tyler's twelfth, Beaumont's ninth, and Texarkana's sixth each have three members. The total number of judges on these appellate courts was eighty in 2004. The term of office for an appeals court justice is six years; therefore, one-third of all justices are up for election in partisan races every two years, in staggered terms, for example, from 2004 to 2006 to 2008.

The salary for an appeals court judge is slightly higher than that of a district court judge. The chief justice earns at least $107,850 per year, and the associate justices earn $107,350 per year, plus any local supplement added by the counties within the district. The supplemental and regular salary must be $1,000 less than that received by a Supreme Court justice and $500 less in the case of the chief justices. Supplements from county funds vary but not as widely as for district judges. In most counties, the supplement is $4,650 for both the chief justice and the justices, except in Amarillo and Tyler, where the supplements are $3,734 and $3,551, respectively, for both positions.

Qualifications to run for a position on this court are higher than for district judge. A candidate for chief justice or associate justice must be a lawyer licensed to practice law in the state and have at least ten years of experience as an attorney or judge, and he or she must be at least thirty-five years of age.

The primary function of the appellate courts is to review the work of the trial courts. A person cannot appeal a case to these courts simply because he or she is dissatisfied with the outcome at the trial court level, as in the case of a municipal or justice of the peace court. A person has to make a case based on error by the trial court that is severe enough to mean justice was not done in that trial or raise a novel legal issue in the case. The appellate court can overturn the prior verdict completely or in part and can dismiss the case or order a new trial. Unlike the lower courts, in which a person can ask for a trial before the court or a jury, the appellate courts rely solely on the record sent from the lower court. No jury is present in an appellate court, and no lawyers are present unless the appellate court grants oral argument on an issue. Attorneys who are skilled and who specialize in procedure and law usually present cases before appellate courts; they are not usually the trial lawyer who litigated in the district court.

Appealing a case to this level is an expensive proposition. The major expenses of an appeal incurred are attorney fees to prepare the appeal; the cost of the official transcript of the entire proceedings at the previous trial; and the cost of a bond and filing fees, if required. In other words, it takes a substantial amount of money to get to the appellate court.

The workload of these appellate courts is growing. The courts of appeal disposed of 12,420 cases in fiscal year 2003, an increase over the 12,399 heard during the same period in 2002. The busiest of all appeals courts are the two in Houston (the first and fourteenth district courts) and the one in Dallas (the fifth district).

Together, they handle about 30 percent of all cases filed for appeal in the state. The workload has not been evenly distributed among the districts across the state; therefore, the state Supreme Court began a docket equalization program to transfer cases in and out and to increase efficiency and workload equity. In 2003, the fifth district in Dallas transferred out 318 cases, the most of all. The eleventh district in Eastland transferred in 206 cases.

The courts of appeal review both civil and criminal matters appealed from trial courts within their district. They have final jurisdiction in some cases, such as divorce, election contests, and slander. All other civil matters reviewed by the court of appeals can be appealed further to the Texas Supreme Court. Only death penalty cases can be appealed directly from the trial court to the other Supreme Court for criminal matters, the Court of Criminal Appeals.

In 2001, clerks assisting the judges in the appellate and supreme court came under scrutiny for accepting signing bonuses with major law firms for positions after their clerkships. Several bills were introduced in the last legislative session to permit this practice provided full disclosure is made. The question remains, however, whether a clerk and judge are impartial to the firm providing the bonus if that firm is a party in a case before the court.

COURT OF CRIMINAL APPEALS

Two courts are positioned at the top of the Texas court structure. The Court of Criminal Appeals, one of the two courts of last resort, was created in 1876. Later in

Texas Court of Criminal Appeals

the nineteenth century, this court's appellate jurisdiction was limited solely to criminal matters, as it remains to this day. Oklahoma is the only other state with two top courts. The Court of Criminal Appeals is comprised of nine justices: a presiding judge and eight associate justices. Like the Court of Appeals, the term of office for these judges is six years. One-third of the judges run statewide in partisan elections every two years. Current terms for Justices Cheryl Johnson, Lawrence E. Meyers, and Mike Keasler are up in 2004. Justices Barbara Parker Hervey and Charles R. Holcomb and the presiding judge, Sharon Keller, are up for election in 2006. The others, Cathy Cochran and Paul Womack, will run in 2008.

Republicans began to win seats on the court in the 1990s and reached total dominance in the 1998 elections. Currently, Republicans hold all the seats on the Court of Criminal Appeals. For the first time in history, the presiding judge will be a woman. No minority judges preside over this court.

The annual salary of the justices of this court is set by the legislature. The salary in 2000 was $115,000 and $113,000 for the presiding judge and judges, respectively. No supplements to the salary are granted for these positions. The qualifications for this position are similar to that of the Court of Appeal justices. A candidate must be at least thirty-five years of age, be licensed to practice law in Texas, and have had at least ten years of cumulative experience as an attorney or judge.

The nine justices can and often do sit in panels of three to handle more cases on appeal. The workload is increasing slightly over time. The Court of Criminal Appeals disposed of 11,257 cases and left pending some 1,830 cases in fiscal year 2003. This supreme court for criminal matters hears all the death penalty cases that are sent directly from the trial court level. They hear cases by petition for discretionary review, which can be filed by any party to the case; cases on their own motion; death penalty cases; and the review of applications for postconviction habeas corpus relief in felony cases without the death penalty. The major sources of cases are the urban counties, which account for 56 percent of all filings. Harris County submitted 513 petitions for review, followed by Dallas County with 313 and Tarrant County with 164.

SUPREME COURT OF TEXAS

The Supreme Court of Texas has statewide final appellate jurisdiction in civil and juvenile cases and original jurisdiction to issue writs. For example, a writ of error is issued to accept a case for review, and a writ of mandamus is issued to order a public official to act in a specific manner. The Supreme Court has general responsibility for the efficient operation of the entire Texas judicial system; is empowered to make and enforce all necessary rules of civil trial practice and procedure, evidence, and appellate procedure; and promulgates rules for the administration of justice in the state. The court has final authority over the involuntary retirement or removal of all judges in the state and the authority to transfer cases between the fourteen courts of appeals.

Qualifications for candidates seeking a position on this court are the same as for the other supreme court for criminal matters and the courts of appeal, as is the salary. This court is also comprised of eight justices and one chief justice. They are elected in partisan, statewide election and run on staggered terms of six years.

Newly appointed Texas Supreme Court Chief Justice Wallace

The Chief Justice of the Supreme Court is Wallace B. Jefferson. He is the first African American to serve in that role. The other six justices are J. Dale Wainwright, whose term expires in 2008; three judges up for re-election in 2004—Steven W. Smith, Harriet O'Neill, and Scott A. Brister. Brister is the only one with an opponent. In the next round of elections in 2006 the terms of Priscilla R. Owen and Nathan L. Hecht expire. The Supreme Court is the only Texas court with two sitting black justices. In filling one of two vacancies pending in late 2004, Governor Perry names his legal counsel, David Medina, 46, and former State District judge to the Texas Supreme Court. Judge Medina was the first Hispanic elected in countywide election from Harris County in 1996 as a Republican.

The Courts and Public Policy

In January 2004, all judges in both of the top statewide courts were Republican and white, except for two African Americans on the Supreme Court. The pendulum of partisan politics has swung completely to the right with a pervasive pro-business philosophy. This court system is the only one in the country, much less the megastates, to decide that worker's compensation is an optional program and that employers are not obliged by law to participate in it. For this reason alone, it makes sense to consider the fact that judges play an important role in making

The Supreme Court of Texas decided that workers did not need to be protected by a state-required worker's compensation plan. We are the only state in which this program is voluntary for employers and not required by state law. Sargent © 2004 Austin American-Statesman. Reprinted with permission of Universal Press Syndicate. All rights reserved.

Compensatory damages
Monetary sum paid to compensate for loss, detriment, or injury to property or person or to a plaintiff's rights under the law from the negligence of another.

Punitive damages
Monetary sum assessed by the jury or court as punishment to the wrong-doer and negligent person for outrageous conduct and to serve as a lesson to others.

Tort reform A political movement whose members oppose large monetary amounts awarded to plaintiffs by juries in negligence cases.

public policy. Judicial elections and judicial selection reform are not abstract issues. They affect the justice that all people receive in Texas.

During the last quarter of the twentieth century, the Texas Supreme Court began to move to the left with a marked proconsumer philosophy. In 1973, for example, the legislature enacted the Deceptive Trade Practices–Consumer Protection Act, which permitted recovery of **compensatory damages** and **punitive damages,** as well as attorney's fees, for aggrieved plaintiffs. The Texas Trial Lawyers Association began to contribute heavily to the campaigns of Supreme Court justices and all other judges. The business community and the Republican party began to attack judges supported by the Trial Lawyers Association as activist judges and demanded **tort reform.** The business community also began to fund the campaigns of Republican candidates who supported their views. In September 2003, a special election was held in the state to determine the status of nearly two dozen proposed amendments to the Texas Constitution, one of which capped noneconomic damages, such as pain and suffering, emotional distress, and mental anguish, for example, at $250,000. It passed. Plaintiffs are in for hard times before juries who now cannot award a sum greater than $250,000 for pain and suffering and punitive damages, for example.

Judicial Selection

Although every district and state judge in Texas is elected in the November general elections, many judges are incumbents in an election because of appointment to a vacancy. It might be advantageous to have all judges appointed, a matter we will examine later.

APPOINTMENTS

Resignations from and appointments to judgeships reveal the musical-chair aspects and politics of the judiciary. For example, Lieutenant Governor Rick Perry served the unexpired remainder of the term of Governor George W. Bush and was elected to a full term in 2002. Governor Perry has made numerous judicial appointments to many courts. Justice Sue Holland resigned from the Court of Criminal Appeals, and Governor Perry filled that vacancy with Cathy Cochran. Governor Perry appointed a successor to the Texas Supreme Court when Justice Greg Abbott resigned on June 6, 2001, to run for and (and subsequently win) the post of Texas attorney general in 2002. For Abbott's seat, Governor Perry appointed a successor, Wallace Jefferson, the first African American chosen for the court. Justice Wallace won election to a full term in 2002. Governor Perry also appointed Xavier Rodriguez, a Latino, to the Texas Supreme Court, but he lost the 2002 election to Steven Smith.

Governor Perry, barely in office six months, appointed one-third of all Texas Supreme Court justices and continues to make appointments during his full term, as required by the Texas Constitution. Justice Craig Enoch, for example, resigned in November 2003 and was replaced by Perry appointee Scott A. Brister, the chief justice of the Fourteenth Court of Appeals in Houston.[18] The Brister resignation from the appellate court also created another appointment for Governor Perry to make. Should he pick a sitting judicial district judge, Governor Perry will get an additional appointment to that position. These three appointments resulted from one Texas Supreme Court resignation.

State law requires judges to retire when they reach seventy-five years of age. Consequently, Justice Sam Bay of the Second Court of Appeals in Fort Worth resigned. Governor Perry appointed Forty-Eighth Judicial District Judge Robert McCoy to the appellate court. McCoy had been appointed district judge by Governor George W. Bush in 1995.[19] Not all judges are required to resign because of age; examples include an appointed associate judge, master judge, and Title IV-D judge. Lawrence Blais, age eighty-three, may be the oldest working judge in the state. He sits as a Title IV-D judge in Tarrant County (Fort Worth).[20]

ELECTIONS AND THE PLACE SYSTEM IN TEXAS

Every judge who is elected in Texas to a court for which there is more than one judge elected runs on the place system. As you may recall from Chapter 4, the place system is used in at-large elections in which more than one office is to be filled. The places create an arrangement in which minorities cannot influence the outcome because a minority runs head-to-head against an Anglo in every electoral place.

Many people erroneously assume that the places are geographic districts. They aren't. Candidates are running at-large in the whole political unit, be it a city, school district, or county. In many urban counties, the county boundaries serve as the boundaries for several separate judicial districts. This setup is nearly the same as the place system. Several judicial districts exist countywide; however, candidates can run for only one district. This system creates a series of district elections in which minority candidates run in one-winner elections against an Anglo candidate and does not allow organized minorities to single shot or to use cumulative elections. Thus, for several countywide judge positions, the state of Texas has created an at-large system that builds in a bias in favor of the Anglo majority and allows that majority to make nearly 100 percent of the decisions.

One solution might be to abandon the place system at all levels and to create large multijudge districts in urban counties. Those districts could either allow cumulative voting or use the generic at-large system, which allows single-shotting (see Chapter 4).

As a participant in the political system in the years to come, you may wish to work for some kind of judicial selection reform. Nonpartisan elections are often touted as a possible reform. If they are instituted with the place system, however, the result will be the same as we have seen in nonpartisan city council elections, where the place system is used.

SINGLE-MEMBER DISTRICT ALTERNATIVE

Single-member districts do not exist for any district judge, court of criminal appeals judge, or supreme court judge. This issue has been raised by minority voters in the recent past. Without single-member districts, ethnic and racial minority candidates find it nearly impossible to win.

The first Mexican American to sit on the Texas Supreme Court was Raul A. Gonzalez. Governor Mark White appointed him to that position in 1984. He won reelection to a full term in 1986 and became the first Mexican American elected statewide in Texas. Today, no Mexican American sits on the Texas Supreme Court. Morris Overstreet became the first and only African American to be elected to the Court of Criminal Appeals in 1990. This underrepresentation is not for lack of qualified African American and Mexican American attorneys who could serve.

In 1988, Mexican American members of the League of United Latin American Citizens (LULAC) filed suit in federal court. *LULAC et al. v. Mattox et al.* challenged the at-large election of district judges in the major counties in the state: Bexar, Dallas, Ector, Harris, Jefferson, Lubbock, Midland, and Tarrant. The plaintiffs alleged that Mexican Americans and African Americans composed 40 percent of the state's population but held only 11 percent of the district judge positions and less than 4 percent of the appellate seats on the various courts of appeal. In 1989, only thirty-five of the 375 district judges across Texas were Mexican American and only seven were African American.

In Harris County (Houston), three Mexican Americans and three African Americans had been elected in 1989 to district judgeships out of fifty-nine district court positions. In Dallas County, one Mexican American held one district judgeship, and African Americans held two of the thirty-six district court benches elected. These two minority groups accounted for 20 and 18 percent of the total population in those counties, respectively.

Various governors had appointed minority judges in both counties when vacancies arose, but they were defeated in the subsequent at-large elections by white voters. LULAC argued in federal court that this polarized voting by whites against minority candidates violated Section 2 of the Voting Rights Act (VRA) of 1965, as amended, by diluting the voting strength of these two minority groups, which are protected classes of voters under the VRA. LULAC prevailed in court, and the judge recommended that single-member districts be drawn by the state legislature. The legislature refused. The case was appealed, and the Fifth Circuit Court of Appeals reversed the federal district court on the grounds that judges were not representatives of the people as were legislators, city council members, school board trustees, community college trustees, and the like.

LULAC appealed that decision to the U.S. Supreme Court, which held that judges are subject to the VRA. Because Texas voters elect their judges, they are indeed representatives of the people. The U.S. Supreme Court remanded the case to the Fifth Circuit for further action. In 1993, the Fifth Circuit upheld the current system of at-large elections, and the following year the U.S. Supreme Court apparently changed its collective mind and rejected the appeal of that decision without comment. Similar lawsuits were filed challenging the at-large place system method of election of the Court of Criminal Appeals and the Thirteenth Court of Appeals (Corpus Christi to Brownsville). All were unsuccessful. In effect, nothing has changed. In the courts of appeals, only twelve Hispanics hold seats out of a total of eighty. No black justices sit on any appellate court at this level. Among the 410 district judges, only eleven are African American and forty-eight are Hispanic. The overwhelming numbers of judges are white males elected by a majority vote in races in which only one candidate can win.

OTHER ALTERNATIVES

In addition to the partisan election system that Texas uses, states select judges in four other ways. Some states use nonpartisan instead of partisan elections; however, partisan and nonpartisan elections can be organized in many ways, as we have seen in Chapter 4. In some states, judges are appointed by the governor or the state legislature. Finally, some states follow a merit plan, sometimes also referred to as the Missouri plan. The megastates are about evenly divided among three of the five methods—partisan election, nonpartisan election, and gubernatorial appointment—as shown in Texas in Context 10.1.

TEXAS in Context

10.1 Judicial Selections in the Megastates

Partisan Election	Nonpartisan Election	Gubernatorial Appointment
Texas	Florida	California
Illinois	Michigan	New Jersey
New York	Ohio	Massachusetts
Pennsylvania		

Source: Council of State Governments, *The Book of the States 2000–2001*, Vol. 33 (Lexington, Ky.: Council of State Governments), pp. 137–139.

THE OTHER SIDE OF THE BIAS ISSUE

Although Texas has not done a good job of creating a judicial system in which ethnic and racial diversity is celebrated, it has done a better job in terms of gender. Women, usually Anglo women, have earned an increasing role in the Texas judicial system.

Women Judges.   The first woman district judge in Texas was Sarah T. Hughes. She was appointed in 1935 by Governor James V. Allred and elected thereafter until 1961, when President John F. Kennedy appointed her to a federal district bench in Texas. By 1989, some fifty-eight women were sitting on district or appellate benches in the state. By 1999, three sat on each of the highest courts in the state, twenty served on courts of appeal, and 276 served on the benches of district and criminal district courts. Carolyn Wright, for example, is the highest-ranking African American woman in Texas; she is justice of the Fifth District Court of Appeals (Dallas). Linda Reyna Yanez is the longest-tenured Chicana in the Thirteenth District Court of Appeals for the Rio Grande Valley.[21] Judge Reyna Yanez sought election to the Texas Supreme Court in 2002. Hundreds of other women judges sit on lower courts across the state, such as county courts-at-law and county judge, probate, justice of the peace, and municipal courts.

According to statistics in the 2003 Profile of Appellate and Trial Judges prepared by the Office of Court Administration, women are making the most dramatic gains in judicial positions. For example, 28 percent of all Texas judges are women (14 percent of all Texas judges are minority; 86 percent are Anglo). From highest percentage to lowest, women comprise 44 percent of judges on the Court of Criminal Appeals, 38 percent of judges on the courts of appeals, 33 percent of all supreme court justices, 29 percent of county court-at-law and probate judges, and 25 percent of all district court judges.[22] Women sit, often in substantial numbers, on

JOIN THE DEBATE

THE ISSUE: Should judges be appointed by the governor from a pool of candidates screened by the state bar or another nonpartisan agency?

AGREE

1. This approach will promote diversity because minorities, even those appointed by governors to fill unexpired terms, are eliminated in the primaries of both parties.

2. In a state where few voters turn out for regular elections, and even fewer turn out for the primaries that nominate the candidates, the selection of judges is in the hands of relatively small ideologically oriented portions of the electorate.

3. The ability to raise political contributions (money) and votes should not be the primary criterion for judicial appointment. The courts should not become the tools of the economic elite.

4. A neutral process, one that is removed from partisan politics, will result in more objective judges.

5. Voters can still vote to keep a judge or vacate that position when renewal of the judge's term comes up.

DISAGREE

1. If the system isn't broken, why fix it?

2. The people should elect those who administer justice in their cases.

3. Judges elected from single-member districts or at-large are more representative of the population they serve.

4. Judicial selection by majority rule of voters is what democracy is all about.

5. Judicial seats ought to remain open to all those qualified for and interested in the position, not just the governor's buddies or campaign contributors.

Recused Removed; a judge with an interest or conflict in a case may be removed (recused) in favor of another, impartial judge. In an election contest case, all judges who sit within the election district being contested must recuse themselves, and a visiting judge must be brought in to hear the case.

every type of court in the state, while minorities (particularly black and brown) do not. And the state of Texas is mostly comprised of browns and blacks, a majority minority population.

Briefly, in 1925, an all-woman supreme court served Texas for one case, *Johnson v. Darr*, which involved a fraternal organization, Woodmen of the World. The all-white, male, elected judges of the supreme court had **recused** themselves due to a conflict of interest in the case: they were members of the Woodmen of the World. Other male attorneys also qualified to be appointed to hear the case recused themselves because they too were members of the Woodmen. Women were not allowed to join the organization, however, so they were the logical appointees.

Governor Pat Neff appointed the women: Hattie Heneberg, Hortense Ward, and Ruth Brazzil. They not only became the first women to sit as members of the Texas Supreme Court, but they also comprised the first all-woman high court in the nation.

The first woman to serve on the supreme court after that time was Ruby Sondock, who was appointed by Governor William Clements in June 1982. She did not seek election when her term ended. Barbara Culver, also appointed by Governor Clements in February 1988 to fill another vacancy, followed her on the court. She was defeated in the general election of 1988. Two women serve on the supreme court in 2004.

Just as important, however, is the pipeline for preparation of future justices and practitioners before the court. Of the eighteen law clerks and briefing attorneys in the supreme court, eleven are (mostly white) female. The Court of Criminal Appeals, with the same pipeline pattern, has nine law clerks and briefing attorneys, eight of which are white females. In the first, second, fourth, and fourteenth courts of appeals, the majority of the law clerks and briefing attorneys are white females. Among the thirty-eight staff attorneys working in the supreme court and Court of Criminal Appeals, twenty-four are females, almost all white.

No women had ever been appointed or elected to the Court of Criminal Appeals until the 1990s. By 1999, three women had been elected to the court in various years: Sharon Keller in 1994, Sue Holland in 1996, and Cheryl Johnson in 1998. In November 2000, Barbara Parker Hervey was elected. Justice Cathy Cochran was appointed to fill the vacancy left by Sue Holland. This court will have four women on the bench, one as presiding judge and the others as justices among the five males.

Women Lawyers.   The number of women attorneys from which candidates for judicial office by election or appointment are selected has more than tripled since 1982. During that year, fewer than 5,000 female attorneys worked in the state. At the beginning of 2004, 24,876 female attorneys were licensed in Texas—approximately 27 percent of the state bar membership. Women are expected to comprise one-third of all lawyers in the state by 2005. Approximately 48 percent of all law students are women in 2004.[23] Women lawyers are also the preferred law clerks, briefing attorneys, and staff attorneys among the fourteen appellate court districts, supreme court, and Court of Criminal Appeals. And women lawyers are taking leadership roles within the profession. For example, Kim J. Askew, with the Dallas law firm of Hughes & Luce, is the chair of the State Bar of Texas; Rhonda Hunter is the ninety-fifth president of the Dallas Bar Association. Both women are also the first African Americans to reach these leadership posts in 2004.[24]

Law clerks at the Supreme Court and other appellate courts have come under scrutiny for accepting signing bonuses with large corporate law firms while they were employed as clerks. Wage disparity is the problem. Clerks earn approximately $37,900 per year for their work, while first-year associates at top law firms typically earn $125,000 per year. Is the practice of paying law clerks a hefty signing bonus to work for top law firms after their clerkship a bribe? Is it a conflict of interest for these clerks to work on cases involving the firms that paid them a signing bonus and will be their future employers? The State Ethics Commission, on August 3,

2001, issued an opinion that found this practice of recruitment did not violate bribery statutes and did not present a conflict of interest.

Tools for Citizen Input

In addition to influencing the composition of the judiciary through participation in elections and serving on a jury, you can influence the degree to which Texas provides all of its citizens with justice in another way: make sure only qualified judges who are behaving correctly serve on the bench.

COMMISSION ON JUDICIAL CONDUCT

Judges—some 3,614 in the state—are subject to compliance with the Texas Code of Judicial Conduct. Complaints against judges are filed with the eleven-member Commission on Judicial Conduct (their toll-free number is 877-228-5750). The commission was created by an amendment to the Texas Constitution in 1965 (Article V, Section 1-a). The eleven-member commission is composed of five judges from each court level appointed by the Supreme Court of Texas, two attorneys appointed by the State Bar of Texas, and four nonlawyer and nonjudge citizens appointed by the governor. The members serve six-year staggered terms. Judges are subject to public censure, reprimand, and judicial oversight; are required to attend additional education; and can be removed from office (see www.scjc.state.tx.us).

During fiscal year 2003, the commission received 1,055 new complaints and had 500 cases pending. During that year, the commission disposed of 1,395 cases. In nineteen cases, the accused judges voluntarily resigned. Several of the 2003 cases are illustrative of the power of person-generated complaints and the power of the commission:

- June 27, 2003—The commission issued a public admonition of municipal judge Alberto Martinez. Judge Martinez, as the complaining witness, issued an arrest warrant and served as magistrate for the defendant in his own case.

- January 17, 2003—The commission issued a public censure of former county court-at-law judge Robert Jenevein for holding a press conference in judicial attire in which he publicly criticized an attorney involved in a high-profile case pending in another court.

- April 10, 2003—The commission issued a public reprimand to justice of the peace Kathryne Gabbert for failing to obtain the required hours of mandatory judicial education for fiscal year 2002.

- June 27, 2003—The commission issued a public warning to appellate judge Paul Womack (Court of Criminal Appeals) for failure to file campaign finance reports for the previous two years, and continuing to refuse to file and pay after he was fined $20,500 by the Texas Ethics Commission (TEC) and efforts to collect were made by the attorney general.[25]

These examples are indicative of the range of coercive police power the commission has over judicial officers. Only the Supreme Court of Texas, however, not the commission, can remove a judge from office after a trial.

PROFESSIONAL POLICE: STATE BAR OF TEXAS

Like most other professionals and law enforcement personnel, attorneys would rather police themselves and not have an agency monitor their behavior. In the case of lawyers, the State Bar of Texas not only examines the qualifications of applicants for the study of law but also the application for a license to practice law. After taking the bar exam and being admitted to practice law, each attorney must also pay membership dues and attend fifteen hours of continuing legal education annually to remain in good standing. Failure to pay and complete the required hours of courses leads to suspension of the license to practice law. Without the bar card, or license, a lawyer should not practice law; to do so would be practicing without a license, a criminal offense.

The Texas Disciplinary Rules of Professional Conduct, adopted January 1, 1990, guide the legal profession. Violation of these rules leads to possible grievances filed against attorneys by clients and other parties. A grievance is filed in writing with the local State Bar Grievance Committee or by a toll-free call to the Chief Disciplinary Counsel's Office at 877-953-5535. A grievance leads to an investigation by the local committee or state bar. After a finding of attorney wrongdoing by an evidentiary panel of specific violations of the disciplinary rules, the lawyer is subject to punishment in the form of monetary sanctions, suspension from the practice of law, public reprimand, and even the loss of the law license (that is, disbarment). *Texas Bar Journal* and other publications, such as the newspaper *Texas Lawyer*, regularly report the results of activity by the various district grievance committees of the state bar and the Texas Supreme Court (see www.statebar.com).

In 1990–1991, a record number of applicants, 300,020, took the Law School Admission Test (LSAT) in the United States. In 2003, a whopping 152,242 persons took the LSAT. The record number of applicants set in the 1990s may fall in the 2000s. In 1980, 530,000 attorneys practiced in the country. One million lawyers practice in the United States today.[26] The number of lawyers in Texas has grown enormously over the years, from 66,000 on January 1, 2000, to a projection of 77,815 in 2005. Not all attorneys licensed to practice law in the state reside in Texas. About 9 percent (approximately 5,700 of the total membership of the state bar) are out-of-state attorneys. The attorney–people ratio in Texas is one for every 330 persons. In Travis County, the ratio is one attorney for every 110 persons. Twice a year, the membership rises when law school graduates take and pass the bar exam.

The overwhelming number of attorneys resides in metropolitan counties, with Harris and Dallas counties having 28 and 21 percent, respectively, of all attorneys. A mere 5 percent of in-state attorneys are located in rural areas. Some rural counties do not have a practicing attorney or one willing to run for the office of county attorney.

JUSTICE OR JUST US?

Lawyers are indispensable to the administration of justice. Minority lawyers are even more indispensable because the criminal and civil justice systems affect overwhelming numbers of minority persons. Currently, 6.4 percent of all Texas lawyers are Latino and 3.8 percent are African American. Minority women are gaining on the minority male lawyers (40 percent to 60 percent, respectively). In the case of African American lawyers in the state, 51 percent are female and 49 percent are male.

Many of the minority lawyers turn to government for employment. In descending order of percentages, 21 percent of all African American lawyers, 18 percent of all Latino lawyers, 12 percent of all Native American lawyers, 12 percent of all Asian–Pacific Islander lawyers, and 10 percent of all white lawyers work for government.[27] One of the favored government programs is legal service to the poor. Most states have federally funded programs through the Legal Services Corporation (LSC), a quasi-governmental agency that provides legal services across the nation to the poor in civil matters, such as divorce proceedings. In the Rio Grande Valley of South Texas and many border counties, the Texas Rural Legal Aid program provides such lawyers. In the Dallas–Fort Worth metro area, the North Texas Legal Services Corporation operates the same type of legal services program (see www.lsnt.org). LSC reconfigured service areas and reduced the number of funded programs from nine to three in Texas as of January 2002.[28]

Summary

The judicial system is important for us to understand because that system is where laws can be declared unconstitutional after they have made it through the legislative process and survived the possibility of a gubernatorial veto. It matters who the judges are; as we have seen, one group of judges on a court makes decisions differently from another group on the same court. We shall soon see if gender makes a difference in the judiciary because women continue to reach positions on the bench and as attorneys.

In this chapter, we have explored the judicial system of Texas by examining the way a judicial case is conducted. We examined the selection of juries and judges and the structure of the court system. Our discussion was presented in the context of making the judicial system even better; several suggestions ranged from making juries more representative to various ways to change the way Texans select judges.

You can also hold judges accountable for their behavior. Like all other parts of the political system, the judicial system should be accountable to the citizens of Texas for administering justice impartially and professionally.

KEY TERMS

Sheriff, p. 292
Common law, p. 292
Constable, p. 292

Bail, p. 292
Voir dire, p. 293
Petit jury, p. 293

FOR FURTHER READING

Fisch, Louise Ann, *All Rise: Reynaldo G. Garza, the First Mexican American Federal Judge* (College Station: Texas A&M University Press, 1996).

Hatley, Allen G., *Texas Constables* (Lubbock: Texas Tech University Press, 1999).

Matera, Dary, *FBI's Ten Most Wanted* (New York: Harper Torch, 2003).

Mauriello, Thomas P., *The Doll House Murders* (New York: PI Press, 2004).

Quezada, J. Gilberto, *Border Boss: Manuel B. Bravo and Zapata County* (College Station: Texas A&M University Press, 1999).

STUDY QUESTIONS

1. Identify the difference between the jurisdiction of a municipal court and that of a district court.

2. List three reasons why persons summoned are reluctant to serve on juries.

3. List three types of courts found in every Texas county.

4. Identify two differences between a petit jury and a grand jury.

5. Indicate the percentage of members of the State Bar of Texas who are (a) women, (b) members of a minority group, and (c) white males.

CRITICAL THINKING QUESTIONS

1. Does Texas have too many courts? If so, what is your solution to this problem?

2. Will the practice of law and the judiciary become a woman's profession?

3. Should the at-large method of the election of judges be replaced with single-member districts, proportional representation, or cumulative voting?

4. Should attorneys and judges be allowed by the State Bar and the Commission on Judicial Conduct to police themselves?

5. What reforms are necessary to guarantee a jury of one's peers in this modern age?

INTERNET RESOURCES

www.courts.state.tx.us   The Texas Supreme Court, all other levels of the state judiciary, plus judicial committees and agencies such as the Office of Court Administration can be reached at this website.

www.info.courts.state.tx.us/juddir.juddir.exe This website lists the courts and judges at the local level. You can also reach them via this website.

www.capitol.state.tx.us/tx-const/tpc.html   You can read the state constitution at this website.

www.capitol.state.tx.us/statutes/statutes.html You can read the state statutes at this website.

www.oag.state.tx.us   The lawyer for the state, that is, the attorney general, can be reached at this website.

www.texasbar.com   The State Bar of Texas, the lawyer's association in the state of Texas, can be reached at this website.

www.abanet.org/publiced   Learn about the national lawyer's association, the American Bar Association, and its public-education programs at this website.

www.txdps.state.tx.us   The state police department, also known as the Department of Public Safety and the Texas Rangers, provides information about its services at this website.

www.fbi.gov   The federal police (the Federal Bureau of Investigation) has its own website.

www.lib.msu.edu/harris23/crimjust/death.htm This website provides information about the issues about and the statistics on the death penalty.

Criminal Justice Policy

In 1983, Richard Ibell's son was murdered, an event that pulled Ibell into a criminal justice system that he had not previously known. He soon discovered it was a system he did not like. From his perspective, it offered too much justice to criminals and too little justice to crime victims. To do something about this imbalance, he joined various victims' rights organizations. While he worked on behalf of victims' rights, he frequently came across organizations known as death penalty resource centers. These centers worked to eliminate the death penalty, a punishment strongly supported by many in the victims' rights movement. Hoping to learn more about death penalty resource centers, Ibell wrote numerous letters and made dozens of phone calls. What he found deeply disturbed him.

Ibell learned that death penalty resource centers owed their existence to a provision in an antidrug law passed by the U.S. Congress in the late 1980s. The law had authorized the federal government to fund nonprofit legal organizations to help convicted murderers with court appeals. It was not this aspect of the centers' work, however, that most upset Ibell. What most upset him was the fact that death penalty resource centers were apparently using public funds to conduct a public relations campaign against the death penalty, a punishment already approved by a majority of Texans. Ibell decided to focus his energy on the death penalty resource centers. Even supporters, however, told him he was tilting at windmills. How could a single individual bring down a politically well-connected, federally funded program with a $20 million annual budget? Richard Ibell didn't believe them.

In 1990, Ibell began a letter and phone campaign that lasted nearly five years. He called and wrote dozens of state and federal legislators to inform them about what he saw as the improper use of public funds by death penalty resource centers. At first, the effort seemed futile, but Ibell persisted, slowly enlisting support from sympathetic congressional representatives like Jack Fields from Texas's eighth congressional district. Still prospects for change were dim. But in 1994, Republicans won the U.S. House of Representatives on a strong anticrime message and suddenly, Ibell's five-year effort paid off. On April 11, 1995, Fields denounced the abuse of public funding by death penalty resource centers on the floor of the U.S. House of Representatives. Later that same year, Congress voted to deny this program any additional funding.

Richard Ibell was not a member of a powerful organized interest group. He was not able to influence criminal justice policy by virtue of large-scale campaign contributions to well-situated congressional representatives. He was an average citizen who was able to right what he perceived to be a significant injustice in the system through years of persistent letter writing and phone calls. He teaches us that even in the complex bureaucratic world of criminal justice, a single committed citizen can make a difference.

The Political Character of Criminal Justice

The goal of the Texas criminal justice system is to provide justice to victims of crime as well as to those accused and convicted of these crimes. Justice is an illusive concept, however; like beauty, it ultimately resides in the eye of the beholder. Because Texans have different and often conflicting views about what constitutes justice, conflict and compromise in Texas politics inevitably shape the meaning and practice of justice in particular situations.

Justice in Texas is shaped by national as well as state politics. Texans are also citizens of the United States. In the earliest years of Texas history, this dual citizenship had little consequence for the practice of justice in the Lone Star State. By the end of the Civil War, however, the consequences of dual citizenship on the practice of Texas justice were impossible to ignore. The Union triumph meant that the justice system in Texas and other states of the Confederacy would no longer support the institution of slavery. In the long run, it also established the broader principle that the practice of justice in any state could not veer too far from the practice of justice in the country as a whole.

Soon after the end of the Civil War, the U.S. Congress formally accepted this principle by adopting the Fourteenth Amendment (1868) to the U.S. Constitution. In part, this amendment reads:

No State shall make or enforce any law which shall abridge the privileges or immunities of citizens of the United States; nor shall any State deprive any person of life, liberty, or property, without due process of law; nor deny to any person within its jurisdiction the equal protection of the laws.

Initially drafted to protect freed slaves in states of the former Confederacy, the Fourteenth Amendment has subsequently been used many times to require states to protect the basic rights and privileges of individuals, both defendants and convicted criminals, brought into the criminal justice system.[1]

In practical terms, the Fourteenth Amendment means that Texans accused, convicted, and sentenced for crimes are often guaranteed important rights as U.S. citizens *even when a majority of Texans believe these rights should be forfeited.* Not surprisingly, imposition of the nation's sense of justice on Texas citizens doesn't sit too well with them. Given the relative power of state and national governments in the American scheme of federalism, however, Texans unhappy with this situation can do as Richard Ibell did and attempt to change what they don't like about the system. Recognizing that the practice of justice in Texas is inevitably a reflection of conflicts and compromises between competing political interests, our task in this chapter is to identify criminal justice issues about which you will have to make decisions in the years to come.

Equal Justice for All?

No single issue of criminal justice has generated greater political conflict in Texas than the issue of equal justice—that is, the expectation that individuals accused of crimes should have the same probability of being judged guilty or not regardless of their race, ethnicity, sex, or economic status. To what extent does criminal justice in Texas compare to this now widely accepted standard?

Adversarial system of justice A system based on the assumption that justice will emerge from conflict between legal adversaries. In criminal cases, the legal adversaries are individuals accused of violating the state's criminal statutes and the state itself.

Criminal cases Cases in which the defendant is accused of violating one or more of the state's criminal statutes.

Like criminal justice systems throughout the United States, the criminal justice system in Texas is an **adversarial system of justice.** It is based on the assumption that justice will emerge from conflict between legal adversaries. In **criminal cases,** the legal adversaries are individuals accused of violating one or more of the state's criminal statutes and the state itself. In these cases, we assume that pitting these adversaries against each other in a court of law will force the defendant's guilt or innocence to emerge.

Such an assumption has always rested on a rather weak reed: a largely unfounded faith that legal adversaries possess roughly equal capabilities. When legal representatives and resources of both antagonists are roughly equal, we have reason to believe that the truth has a good chance of emerging from the legal struggle. On the other hand, when legal representatives and the resources of antagonists are unevenly matched, we have much less reason to believe that truth and justice will emerge from the legal contest.

DOES TEXAS PROVIDE EQUAL JUSTICE FOR THE POOR?

Indigent defendant A defendant who cannot afford to hire a private attorney.

Public defender An attorney employed and paid by the government to represent indigent defendants accused of felonies.

Court-appointed attorney An attorney appointed by the court for indigent defendants.

Because justice is always at risk when two parties of unequal legal representation and resources clash in the legal system, a key test of any state's criminal justice system is the quality of legal representation it provides for **indigent defendants.** How has Texas fared on this key test of its criminal justice system? Judging from recent studies, the answer to this question almost certainly is, "Not well."

In Texas, criminal court judges have been solely responsible for appointing legal counsel for indigent defendants. In some counties, judges have assigned the cases of indigent defendants to a **public defender.** Because only a handful of Texas counties have employed public defenders, however, most Texas judges have relied on **court-appointed attorneys** to represent indigent defendants.[2]

Traditionally, criminal court judges in each Texas county have been free to establish their own system for assigning court-appointed attorneys. Often lawyers who wished to handle cases for indigents simply placed their names on a list maintained by the court. The presiding judge in each case was then free to assign any of these attorneys to any indigent defendant. According to a survey by the State Bar of Texas, a judge's final choice of a court-appointed attorney was typically influenced by a wide range of actors, including court reporters, court clerks, and court coordinators. In some jurisdictions, judges even consulted prosecutors before assigning lawyers to defend indigent defendants.[3]

Has the court-appointed attorney system used so widely in Texas guaranteed poor defendants the same chance of being exonerated as defendants who can afford their own attorneys? A majority of Texas judges and prosecutors claim that the court-appointed attorney system is more than fair to indigent defendants. A recent comprehensive study of indigent defendants in Tarrant County, however, raised serious questions regarding the veracity of this claim. In October 2000, reporters for the *Fort Worth Star-Telegram* revealed the results of a study of over 10,000 felony cases processed in Tarrant County during 1999. Court-appointed attorneys handled roughly half these cases; privately retained attorneys handled the other half. The data published in that analysis is presented here in Table 11.1 and indicates significant differences in the amount of jail or prison time served by defendants who relied on court-appointed legal counsel and defendants who retained their own counsel. This finding was true regardless of the kind of felony or whether or not the defendant had prior offenses. As you can see in Table 11.1, regardless of the crime, defendants with prior offenses who retained their own lawyer were less likely to receive sentences involving jail or prison time than were defendants who used court-appointed attorneys. Defendants accused of sexual abuse of a child, for example, were nearly 40 percent less likely to receive a sentence involving jail or prison if they could afford to retain their own attorneys.

The difference in sentencing outcomes was even greater for defendants with no prior offenses than it was for defendants with a record of prior offenses. Again, as you can see in Table 11.1, defendants accused of sexual abuse of a child were three times less likely to receive jail or prison sentences if they retained their own lawyers. In cases involving property crimes, defendants with retained counsel were four

TABLE 11.1	Percentages of Defendants Receiving Jail or Prison Sentences as a Function of Type of Counsel	
Crime Type	**Appointed Counsel**	**Retained Counsel**
Defendants with prior offenses		
Sexual abuse of a child	96.2%	58.8%
Possession of a controlled substance	90.0	68.0
Property crimes	85.0	74.7
Violent crimes	84.5	68.2
Defendants with no prior offenses		
Sexual abuse of a child	72.6	25.4
Possession of a controlled substance	69.0	22.9
Property crimes	64.7	16.7
Violent crimes	66.3%	25.1%

Source: *"Unequal Justice,"* Fort Worth Star-Telegram, *October 15, 2000.*

times less likely to receive jail or prison sentences than were defendants who relied on court-appointed counsel.

What accounts for these strikingly different sentences for defendants who can afford their own legal counsel and defendants who had to rely on court-appointed attorneys? In part, the answer to this question is found in the manner in which Texas courts traditionally have determined who is entitled to a court-appointed attorney. In most counties, a key test of whether a defendant qualifies for a court-appointed attorney is whether the defendant can afford to post bail for release from jail pending a trial date. Because the court generally has assumed that a defendant who can post bail can also afford to retain an attorney, only a defendant who cannot post bail is typically assigned a court-appointed attorney.

This assumption means that the vast majority of defendants who qualify for court-appointed attorneys remain in jail between the time they are charged with a crime and the time their innocence or guilt is determined in court. A defendant who remains in jail pending trial is at a distinct disadvantage, however, compared to a defendant who posts bail and can return to family and work while awaiting trial. Defendants who return to work and family can continue earning money that can be used in their defense effort. They can also participate actively in their own defense by finding witnesses and collecting evidence. Returning to work and family also provides evidence in subsequent court appearances that defendants are responsible citizens who can be trusted to return to the community.[4]

Perhaps even more important, defendants who return to work and family while awaiting trial are under much less intense pressure to accept an undesirable **plea bargain** from the prosecution. According to reporters from the *Fort Worth Star-*

Plea bargain An agreement that allows a defendant charged with a more serious crime to plead guilty to a less serious crime.

Telegram covering this issue, "Veteran criminal defense lawyers compared what happens to a defendant in jail to water torture. They said the slow drip of time puts 'hydraulic pressure' on the defendants to make and take a deal."[5] Intimidated, physically uncomfortable, away from family, and unable to help support children and spouses, indigent defendants are under heavy pressure to accept a deal offered by the prosecution.

Court-appointed attorneys representing indigents also encourage defendants to plea bargain more readily than do retained attorneys. In part, this tendency is because court-appointed attorneys earn less per hour handling the cases of indigent defendants than they might earn handling cases for defendants who can pay privately for these services. A recent survey by the State Bar of Texas showed that privately retained defense attorneys averaged $136 per hour. Court-appointed attorneys averaged only $40 per hour for this same work. Paid at this lower hourly rate, court-appointed attorneys can maximize their pay by encouraging a plea bargain, even when it is not in the defendant's best interest.[6]

More than simple avarice prompts court-appointed attorneys to push indigent defendants to accept plea bargains prematurely. These attorneys serve at the pleasure of felony court judges who have a vested interest in moving cases through their courts as rapidly as possible. Texas judges are elected officials who must regularly defend their ability to run an efficient court. A judge whose court does not process as many cases as those of his or her colleagues is vulnerable to the charge of sloughing off. The only way for a judge to keep cases moving through court is to encourage court-appointed lawyers to resolve as many cases as possible through plea bargains. Lawyers insufficiently sensitive to the judge's need to maintain an efficient courtroom are unlikely to be court-appointed attorneys for long.

Indigent defendants who have had to rely on court-appointed attorneys faced another disadvantage as well. In each Texas county, felony court judges have traditionally been free to establish their own procedures for assigning court-appointed attorneys to indigent defendants. In some cases, indigent defendants have had to wait several weeks before speaking with their court-appointed attorneys. Yet it is precisely during this critical period immediately following the time one is charged with a crime that a defendant is most in need of an attorney.

During this period, a defendant has the greatest need for legal advice that protects him or her against further self-incrimination. Also, a defendant's recollection about the facts and circumstances surrounding his or her case is most acute at this time. Finally, during this time, an attorney for the defendant has the best chance of successfully completing any investigation needed to support the defendant's case. Eyewitnesses move on, supporting documentation gets lost or thrown out, and physical evidence is destroyed. A defense attorney who cannot collect this exonerating evidence is ill prepared to build the best possible case for his or her client.

EQUAL JUSTICE, INDIGENT DEFENSE, AND THE DEATH PENALTY

Indigent defendants are less likely than their more affluent counterparts to find justice in Texas. Nowhere is this unequal bid for justice more troubling than in cases involving the death penalty. Since the U.S. Supreme Court determined the death penalty to be constitutional in 1976, Texas has led all states in the number of convicted criminals it has put to death. Between 1982 (when the death penalty was reinstated in the Lone Star State) and 2003, the Texas criminal justice system has presided over 321 executions. In 2003 alone, Texas executed twenty-four convicted criminals. The vast majority of those executed were poor, uneducated, and dependent on a court-appointed attorney.[7]

How much did poverty and reliance on court-appointed attorneys influence the death of these indigent defendants? Evidence on this issue is mixed. There is little doubt that a significant number of indigent defendants receiving the death penalty have been represented by less-than-desirable court-appointed attorneys. In May 2000, a comprehensive study by the *Dallas Morning News* of 461 cases of inmates on death row found that nearly one in four condemned inmates has been represented at trial or on appeal by court-appointed attorneys who had been disciplined for misconduct at some point in their careers. Others had been represented by court-provided attorneys who dozed during trials, failed to investigate their case, or provided minimal preparation.[8] Detailed investigations by other national news organizations, including the *New York Times,* the *Chicago Tribune,* and CBS-TV's *60 Minutes,* have also turned up troubling evidence suggesting that indigent defendants were shortchanged during their trials and subsequent appeals. "In one case, a prosecutor acknowledged that a capital murder suspect confessed after relatives were threatened with torture in Mexico."[9]

In another high-profile case, "A disabled oil-field roughneck was unknowingly drugged, denied access to evidence and sentenced to die even though the state's case against him lacked physical evidence, eye witnesses or a motive linking him to the crime."[10] Neither of the two attorneys appointed by the court to represent this defendant, Ernest Willis, had ever defended a death penalty case.[11] They had spent a total of three hours with the defendant before his trial and according to the trial record, they failed to call a single character witness on their client's behalf. When questioned years later, these attorneys were unaware that the prosecutor had given the defendant a psychological examination that could have been used in his defense. They were also unaware that the defendant had been heavily sedated during the trial with antipsychotic drugs that made him appear as though he had no remorse for the crime in question.

Willis spent thirteen years on death row before a large New York law firm volunteered three attorneys to help with his appeal. Drawing on the substantial investigative resources of their firm, these attorneys uncovered enough irregularities in the defendant's initial trial to convince the same district judge who had presided over that trial to set aside the guilty verdict. By the conclusion of the appeal process, the New York law firm that fought for Willis's freedom had invested "thousands and thousands of hours" in the case. According to one of the young lawyers involved, the firm's out-of-pocket expenses totaled "in the low six figures."[12]

The superb legal assistance Willis received in preparing his appeal is the exception rather than the rule for indigent defendants facing death sentences in Texas. The gap between the kind of legal aid offered him and that enjoyed by the average death row defendant in Texas has always been large. Since 1995, however, the Texas Legislature has made some progress in closing this gap. In 1995, for example, the legislature required the state's nine judicial districts for the first time to set minimum standards for attorneys appointed to death penalty cases in their jurisdictions.[13] In 1995, the Texas Legislature also made some key changes in the appeal process designed to provide indigent defendants, especially those facing death sentences, more effective legal defense. Previously, any defendant in a death penalty case who sought a second-level state appeal, known as a **habeas corpus appeal,** had to hire an attorney or hope an attorney would take the case **pro bono.** In 1995, however, the legislature decided to pay court-appointed attorneys handling habeas corpus appeals for indigent defendants.[14]

Although the 1995 reforms were a serious effort to provide indigent defendants more effective legal counsel, by no means do they close the gap between the quality of legal assistance available to indigents facing the death penalty and their more affluent counterparts. Critics point out, for example, that at the same time the state decided to pay for habeas corpus appeals for indigent defendants on death row, it established a cap of only $7,500 that court-appointed attorneys undertaking these appeals could earn.[15] Yet a habeas corpus appeal is an especially difficult and costly process. As experts in the criminal appeals process have pointed out:

> The state habeas process . . . allows defendants to re-examine the entire court record and raise for the first time any issues related to fairness—including the effectiveness of court appointed attorneys. It is a complex area of law, requiring not just a review of the trial record but a search for new evidence.[16]

Because properly conducting a habeas corpus appeal is far more expensive than the state was initially willing to pay, primarily inexperienced attorneys undertook them. Realizing that this system too often left inexperienced attorneys handling life-or-death appeals for indigent defendants, the state increased the cap for habeas corpus appeals to $25,000. Although this figure is clearly an improvement, current state support for habeas corpus appeals still falls far short of the "thousands and thousands of hours" and "six-figure out-of-pocket expenses" that the New York law firm invested in the pro bono appeal it filed on behalf of Ernest Willis.[17]

In 2001, the legislature again attempted to improve the quality of indigent defense in Texas. In that year, the legislature passed the Fair Defense Act, a group of amendments to Texas statutes that further reformed procedures for providing court-appointed defense counsel for indigent defendants. This act set minimum standards for (1) the prompt appointment of defense counsel following arrest, (2) the methods judges use to select counsel for indigents, and (3) fee schedules for attorneys assigned to defend indigents.[18]

TEXAS JUSTICE: A COMPARATIVE PERSPECTIVE

To point out that poor defendants do not enjoy the same opportunity as more affluent defendants in the Texas criminal justice system is in many respects stating the

Habeas corpus appeal An appeal made by a defendant already convicted of a capital crime in state district court. It allows defendants to examine the entire court record to look for procedural or substantive errors.

Pro bono Legal work done on a voluntary basis, with no payment for services rendered.

obvious. Everywhere and always, the poor have had less access to justice than people of means. That this situation should prevail in Texas is not particularly surprising. The more difficult question is, To what extent does Texas, compared to other states, provide justice to its indigent defendants?

To judge from the comments of several nationally known authorities in the area of indigent defense, Texas does less to protect the rights of poor defendants than do most other states. Stephen Bright, director of the Southern Center for Human Rights, recently commented, "What Texas does with its court appointed lawyers is the equivalent of asking chiropractors to do brain surgery."[19] According to Norm Lefstein, Dean of the Indiana University Law School and a nationally known authority on indigent justice, "I think everyone who has looked at indigent defense realizes Texas has farther to go than any other state in the country."[20] Even U.S. Supreme Court Justice Sandra Day O'Connor has recently singled out Texas for the dubious standard its appeal courts have used to determine mental retardation in death sentence cases.[21]

While empirical evidence comparing Texas's record to other states is spotty at best, it does suggest that at least some of this criticism of the indigent defense system in Texas may be unwarranted. As you can see from Texas in Context 11.1, only 12 percent of all death sentences handed down in Texas between 1973 and 2003 have been reversed in state or federal appellate courts. This figure is the lowest percentage of death penalty reversals among any of the megastates. This relatively low reversal rate, of course, may simply be an indication that Texas's appellate courts are unwilling to correct injustices occurring in its trial courts. But it is important to point out that the relatively low reversal rates reflected in the Bureau of Justice data presented in Texas in Context 11.1 are also found in more detailed studies of death penalty reversal rates in federal appellate courts. In a twenty-eight-state study of error and reversal rates in **capital cases** between 1973 and 1995, for example, the study's authors found that 26 percent of Texas capital murder cases appealed to the federal courts were reversed. While that figure seems high, only four of the twenty-eight states in this study had lower reversal rates in federal courts.[22] In short then, available empirical evidence, spotty as it is, suggests that Texas is actually less likely than most other states to sentence a defendant to death when the evidence does not warrant it.

Capital cases Cases in which the defendant is accused of committing a capital crime.

Although these figures do not refute the claim that the system of indigent defense in Texas has serious problems,[23] they strongly suggest that many of these problems plaguing Texas also exist in other states. The authors of the 1999 *Report of the National Symposium on Indigent Defense* concluded:

> Overall . . . indigent defense in the United States today is in a chronic state of crisis. . . . The effects can be severe, including legal representation of such low quality to amount to no representation at all, delays, overturned convictions, and convictions of the innocent.[24]

TEXAS in Context

11.1 Megastate Comparisons of Reversal Rates in Death Penalty Cases, 1973–2002

	Number Sentenced to Death	Percentage Reversed
Texas	**925**	**12**
California	795	15
Pennsylvania	352	25
Illinois	294	33
Ohio	367	37
New York	9	44
Florida	872	46
Massachusetts	4	50
New Jersey	51	51
Michigan*	—	—

* Michigan is not a death penalty state.

Source: "Capital Punishment, 2002," Bureau of Justice Statistics, November 2003, p. 16.

Texas Prisons: "Cruel and Unusual Punishment"?

Cruel and unusual punishment A form of punishment prohibited by the Eighth Amendment to the U.S. Constitution. Exactly what constitutes cruel and unusual punishment ultimately turns on how the Supreme Court interprets this vague concept.

Class action lawsuit A lawsuit in which individuals without adequate personal resources can join together to battle economically more powerful actors in the courts.

A second issue at the core of political struggles over criminal justice policy in Texas is the way that state prisons treat convicted criminals once they are incarcerated. Texans have never been reluctant to send lawbreakers to jail. They have been reluctant, however, to raise taxes to build more jails. By the 1970s, these two proclivities made Texas prisons some of the most crowded and dangerous in the United States. Prison guards in severely understaffed systems allowed the most brutal inmates they could enlist to handle day-to-day disciplinary problems. These building tenders, as they were called, maintained prison discipline largely through a reign of mental and physical violence.[25]

Reacting against these brutal conditions in 1972, David Ruiz, a Texas prison inmate, brought suit against the state for violating his constitutional protection against **cruel and unusual punishment.** Later combined with similar suits brought by other Texas inmates into a **class action lawsuit** filed on behalf of all Texas prison inmates in 1978, the Ruiz case radically changed the face of the state prison system.[26] Most important, it required the state to embark on a massive prison-building campaign that would ultimately cost Texans more than $2 billion over the next twenty years.[27]

Texas Board of Criminal Justice A nine-member board appointed by the governor to oversee the Texas Department of Criminal Justice (TDCJ). Board members are appointed to staggered six-year terms and are responsible for hiring the executive director of the TDCJ.

In spite of the massive prison-building effort undertaken by the state in the late 1980s and early 1990s, Texas prisons were again rapidly approaching their breaking points by 1997. In a meeting of the **Texas Board of Criminal Justice** in November of that year, board chair Allen Polunsky pronounced, "We're projecting we're going to be . . . out of beds sometime in the next sixty days or so." According to Polunsky, the bed shortage resulted from "dropping parole rates during the past three years combined with more parolees being sent back to prison for parole violations." The board's response to this bed shortage was to approve construction of five new prisons capable of housing 990 additional inmates.[28]

Although facilities have improved, operating expenditures and staffing remain dangerously inadequate in most Texas prisons. In 2001, Texas ranked a distant last out of the megastates in prison-operating expenditures, spending only $12,835 a year per inmate. The average per-inmate expenditure for the other nine mega-states in that same year was $29,903, more than twice the amount per inmate spent to operate Texas prisons.[29] With such poorly funded operating budgets, it is no surprise that Texas prison guards are poorly paid, with a starting salary of $18,924 per year.[30] According to the American Correctional Association, this salary puts Texas forty-sixth out of fifty states in terms of prison guard pay.[31] Given the low salary and dangerous nature of the job, turnover is understandably high, which means that a majority of prison guards in Texas are young and inexperienced. At one state prison, more than half the corrections officer staff had less than eighteen months of experience. The low salaries and high turnover rates also make it difficult to keep state prisons fully staffed.[32]

Prior to the Ruiz case, guards relied on co-opted inmate trustees to maintain order in the prisons. Believing this system to be responsible for much of the brutality suffered by inmates, Judge William Wayne Justice, the federal district judge presiding over the Ruiz case, ordered the **Texas Department of Corrections (TDC)** to abandon its use. Specifically, he ordered the TDC to return responsibility for keeping order to prison guards. He also strongly encouraged the TDC to increase the ranks of prison guards sufficiently to compensate for the loss of staff provided by the building tender arrangement.[33]

Texas Department of Corrections Now known as the Texas Department of Criminal Justice, an agency that provides confinement, supervision, rehabilitation, and social reintegration of the state's convicted felons.

The TDC met the first of these requirements without meeting the second, and racial and ethnic gangs emerged to fill this power vacuum. Increasingly, prisoners entering Texas jails have been forced to affiliate with one of these gangs or risk almost daily beatings.[34] The growth of prison gangs combined with an understaffed, young, and inexperienced corps of prison guards have made Texas prisons even more dangerous today than they were a decade ago.

Evidence of the escalating violence in Texas prisons can be seen in Table 11.2. While the number of inmates in Texas prisons tripled between 1988 and 1999, the number of inmate-on-inmate assaults has increased almost tenfold, and inmate-on-staff assaults have gone from only 132 in 1988 to over 1,800 in 1999. These figures indicate that in many Texas prisons, the brutality of the building tender system has been replaced by the brutality of gang warfare.

If justice requires that those convicted of crimes suffer only the punishment imposed on them by society, then Texas prisons are continuing to fall short of that

TABLE 11.2	Criminal Offenses Committed in Texas Prisons, Various Years			
	1988	**1992**	**1996**	**1999**
Inmate-on-inmate assaults	182	366	1,388	1,612
Inmate-on-staff assaults	132	365	918	1,836
Homicides	3	1	5	6

Source: Texas Department of Criminal Justice statistics in John Council, "Prison Bar: An Inside Look at Lawyers Who Handle Big-House Crime," Law News Network, www.lawnewsnet.com/stories/texprchart.html.

goal. As Judge Justice noted at the time of the Ruiz decision, "When the legislature says that you're to be imprisoned, they don't also say that you are to be anally raped or subject to inferior medical care, or have someone assaulting you on a day-to-day basis."[35] By not acting to reduce the level of violence in Texas prisons, state policymakers are, in effect, imposing crueler sentences than society has agreed are fair and appropriate.

We know that Texas prisons are more dangerous today than they were a decade ago, but this finding is true for prisons throughout the United States. Gang violence in particular has become a staple of prison life in all states with large numbers of racial and ethnic minorities in prison.[36] Has gang violence, in combination with poorly paid and inexperienced guards, made Texas prisons more dangerous than others housing comparable inmates? If so, how much more dangerous?

Reliable data on prison violence has always been difficult to obtain. The available evidence suggests that Texas prisons are actually less dangerous than prisons in other comparable states. According to data collected by the Bureau of Justice Statistics, Texas prisons housed 158,008 inmates in 2001,[37] with 673 recorded inmate-on-inmate assaults.[38] In that same year, California prisons held 160,412 inmates[39] but recorded over 4,000 inmate-on-inmate assaults.[40] New York prisons, which held less than 50 percent of the number of inmates in Texas jails in 2001, had 20 percent more inmate-on-inmate assaults than did Texas prisons.[41] Imperfect as these figures are, they strongly suggest that the rising levels of violence seen in Texas prisons are matched in or exceeded by other comparable state prison systems.

How Well Do Incarceration and the Death Penalty Work?

As the costs of large-scale incarceration spiraled ever upward, they precipitated another debate over criminal justice policy in Texas. Has the state's expensive prison-building campaign produced sufficient benefits to compensate for its cost? Opinions

TEXAS in Context

11.2 Percentage of Sentence Served by Violent Offenders Released from Prison in 1997

Megastate	Mean Maximum Sentence, in Months	Percentage of Sentence Served
New York	96	59.6
Florida	84	59.1
Pennsylvania	108	59.0
California	62	58.4
Massachusetts	99	58.4
Texas	**115**	**51.7**
New Jersey	102	45.1
Illinois	106	43.6
Ohio	192	32.6
Michigan	no data	no data
All states	93	52.7

Source: Adapted from D. Wilson and P. Ditton, "Truth in Sentencing in State Prisons," Bureau of Justice Statistics, Washington, D.C., reprinted by the Criminal Justice Policy Council, December 28, 2000.

on this question are mixed. By dramatically increasing prison capacity, state officials ensured that convicted criminals would serve significantly longer portions of their sentences than had previously been the case in the Lone Star State. At one point in the early 1980s, prison space was so limited that even violent offenders were averaging only twenty-one days of jail time for every year of their court-ordered sentence. By 1997, however, the mean time served by violent offenders released from Texas prisons had increased to 51.7 percent of their court-ordered maximum sentences.[42]

Although Texas now requires violent offenders to spend more time in prison than was previously the case, it still ranks slightly below the national average in the percentage of a sentence served by violent offenders. Several states require violent offenders to serve a substantially longer portion of their court-ordered sentences than does Texas. In Vermont, for example, violent offenders on average serve 87.2 percent of their court-imposed maximum sentences. In Texas, the comparable figure is 51.7 percent.[43] Even among the megastates, half require violent offenders to serve a larger portion of their court-imposed maximum sentence than Texas does (see Texas in Context 11.2).

If a goal of the criminal justice system is to ensure that lawbreakers serve sentences imposed on them by society, then building more prisons in Texas has surely

TEXAS in Context

11.3 Incarceration and Violent Crime Rate Changes, 1991–2001

Megastate	Percentage Increase in Incarceration Rate	Percentage Decrease in Violent Crime Rate
Texas	**139**	**31**
Michigan	26	31
Florida	27	33
Massachusetts	70	34
Ohio	23	37
Illinois	44	39
New Jersey	10	39
California	42	43
New York	11	56
Pennsylvania	61	90

Sources: Bureau of Justice Statistics (BJS), "Prisoners in 2001 BJS Bulletin," July 2002, p. 4; BJS data series NPS-1, and BJS FBI Uniform Crime Reports 1991–2001.

contributed to this objective. Whether the state's prison building has contributed to other goals of the criminal justice system is still subject to debate.

Perhaps the most important function of a criminal justice system is to make society safer. Has the state's massive investment in new prison construction and its heavy reliance on the death penalty made Texas a safer place? Those who say yes point to the sharp reduction in crime experienced by Texas during the past decade. As you can see in Texas in Context 11.3, between 1991 and 2001, Texas increased the rate at which it incarcerated its citizens much faster (139 percent) than did any other megastate. Violent crime in Texas did fall significantly during that period, but all of the megastates experienced a significant drop in violent crime during this period. In fact, eight of the ten megastates saw violent crime rates fall even more dramatically than did Texas. New Jersey and New York, for example, both saw more dramatic declines in violent crime, even though these states increased their incarceration rates only 10 percent and 11 percent, respectively. Pennsylvania decreased its violent crime rate three times as fast as Texas did, even though it increased its incarceration rate only half as rapidly as Texas. These figures offer little support for the hypothesis that putting a large number of citizens behind bars is the best way to make Texas a safer state.[44]

Although the link between incarceration and crime reduction remains a subject of intense debate among scholars of criminal justice,[45] the role that the death penalty plays as a deterrent to murder is much clearer. Over the past thirty years, students of criminal justice have conducted numerous studies to determine if

JOIN THE DEBATE

THE ISSUE: Should Texas place a moratorium on death sentences?

AGREE

1. Only God has the right to take human life.

2. The death penalty is just too barbaric for any humane society. The United States is one of only a small handful of advanced societies that continue to permit the execution of criminals.

3. Even if the death penalty itself is appropriate for particularly heinous crimes, the legal justice system in Texas is seriously flawed. The possibility of sending an innocent person to his or her death is simply too great a risk. A growing number of death row inmates have now been cleared of their crimes by post-conviction DNA testing.

DISAGREE

1. The bible itself condones "an eye for an eye" kind of justice.

2. Society has no right to deny family and friends who have been robbed of a loved one the peace of mind that may come from knowing the guilty party has suffered a fate as horrible as the one they inflicted on another.

3. Only a tiny percentage of those sentenced to death have subsequently been proved innocent after their conviction. It is so small that it does not justify withholding the ultimate penalty from the hundreds of individuals who are clearly guilty of committing horrible crimes.

death penalty states have lower homicide rates than non–death penalty states do.[46] They have also investigated whether the increased use of the death penalty within a single state has reduced homicides in that state.[47] The consensus opinion of experts who have looked at this evidence is that the death penalty fails to deter additional homicides. Those who continue to defend the death penalty now typically do so primarily on moral grounds, as our "Join the Debate" for this chapter indicates.

Race, Ethnicity, and Criminal Justice in Texas

We have already noted that indigent defendants face disadvantages in the Texas criminal justice system that are not encountered by more prosperous citizens. Because a disproportionate percentage of racial and ethnic minorities in Texas are

Supporters and opponents of the death penalty demonstrate in Texas.

Racial profiling The practice of factoring race into profiles of suspected criminals that police departments then use to help them determine which citizens should be detained for further questioning or search.

economically disadvantaged, it is not surprising that many minorities believe they are the victims of discrimination in the state's criminal justice system. Most minorities believe this discrimination begins even before they enter the court system with the police practice of **racial profiling.** As a first effort to respond to minority claims of racial profiling, the Texas Legislature in 2001 passed legislation prohibiting this practice and requiring police departments to collect racial data on motorists they stop and search. Early in 2004, researchers analyzing this data concluded that "approximately 3 of every 4 law enforcement agencies reported stopping blacks and Latinos at higher rates than Anglos." These same researchers concluded that blacks and Latinos were also more likely to be searched than Anglos."[48] Researchers from the RAND Corporation were quick to fault the report, however, for its flawed research methodology.[49] Their critique suggests that any claim that Texas peace officers unfairly target minorities must still be regarded primarily as an unproven hypothesis requiring additional research.

While minorities are overrepresented in the ranks of motorists stopped by the state's Department of Public Safety (DPS) and many local police departments in Texas, they are underrepresented on courtroom juries that must judge suspected criminals. Drawing on a survey of 13,612 people summoned to jury duty in Dallas County in March 2000, the *Dallas Morning News* noted that although nearly one in every four Dallas County residents is Hispanic, only one out of every fourteen people reporting for possible jury duty is Hispanic, and although 19 percent of Dallas County's population is African American, only 14 percent of those appearing for jury duty are African American.[50]

There is little disagreement about why minorities are underrepresented on Texas juries. Like all other counties in Texas, Dallas County assembles juries by randomly selecting candidates from lists of registered voters, licensed drivers, and state-issued personal identification cards. Roughly 25 percent of those whose names are picked from these lists never receive their jury summons mainly because they have moved since last registering to vote or getting their license. Because African Americans and Hispanics are disproportionately found in the ranks of lower-income citizens who move more often, they are less likely to receive a jury summons than their white counterparts.[51]

Of those who received their jury summons, nearly 70 percent simply did not show up at court as instructed. Because jurors in Texas are paid only $6.00 per day, low-income workers, particularly those paid on an hourly basis, cannot afford to forgo work to serve on a jury. Because so many of those summoned do not show up, the court cannot enforce the law requiring their attendance. And, because economic hardship and an insufficient command of English are grounds for jury exemptions in Texas, a significant number of Hispanics who show up for jury duty are dismissed. Thus, most juries in Texas courts are underrepresented when it comes to minority citizens. This situation in turn generates the low level of trust that minorities express regarding the jury system in all states, including Texas.[52]

The Changing Landscape of Criminal Justice in Texas

While critics and defenders of the Texas criminal justice system continue to debate its failings, one thing is certain. The impetus for reform generated by the presidential candidacy of George W. Bush in 2000 has largely run its course. In 2001, the legislature passed and Governor Perry signed into law Senate Bill 3, which provides for state-paid, postconviction DNA testing for individuals who can demonstrate that this evidence has the potential to establish their innocence. The legislature also passed and Governor Perry signed into law the Fair Defense Act and the racial profiling legislation described earlier in the chapter.

The 2003 legislative session, on the other hand, produced no major reforms of the Texas criminal justice system. In part this situation can be traced to philosophical conflicts between reform-minded politicians like State Senator Rodney Ellis and hard-line law-and-order advocates like Terry Keel in the House of Representatives. Legislative struggles between these two competing forces accounted for the failure of the Seventy-Eighth Legislature to approve legislation to improve the quality of lawyers appointed to handle death penalty appeals. This legislative conflict also undermined the passage of bills that would have halted executions of seventeen-year-old killers and would have provided for a life sentence without the possibility of parole. Even legislation that would have prohibited death sentences from being imposed on the mentally ill failed to survive the legislative battle between criminal justice reformers and hard-liners, in spite of the fact that just a year earlier the U.S. Supreme Court ruled in *Atkins v. Virginia* that execution of the mentally ill violated a constitutional ban against cruel and unusual punishment.[53]

Summary

We began this chapter by noting that justice is ultimately in the eye of the beholder. Thus, criminal justice policy is largely a reflection of competing beliefs about the fair or right way to treat those accused or convicted of crime. We also noted that justice in Texas is shaped not only by state politics but also by national politics. We then looked more closely at the issue of equal justice for all. We pointed out that traditionally, criminal court judges in Texas have relied on court-appointed attorneys to defend indigent defendants. These attorneys have often been insufficiently trained or experienced to provide their clients with the most competent defense. We also pointed out that court-appointed attorneys have had a strong incentive to encourage their indigent defendants to plea bargain, even when plea bargaining might not be in the best interest of their clients. In general, these factors have meant that indigent defendants do not experience the same measure of justice as more prosperous citizens of the Lone Star State do. This situation has been particularly true in capital murder cases, where the accused faces the death penalty. Many of these injustices continue in spite of legislative efforts in 1995 and again in 2001 to improve the quality of the Texas criminal justice system.

We next looked at the issue of cruel and unusual punishment in Texas prisons. We described the impact that the Ruiz case had on the structure of Texas prisons and analyzed the safety of Texas prisons compared to those in other states. We concluded that although Texas prisons are indeed more dangerous today than they have been previously, they were certainly no more dangerous than prisons in other large and ethnically diverse states.

Finally, we noted that the most obvious factor behind dangerous conditions in Texas prisons is the limited size of prison operating budgets. Limited operating budgets have meant chronic understaffing and reliance on young and inexperienced prison guards.

The last issue we looked at in this chapter was the role of race and ethnicity in the Texas criminal justice system. First, we reviewed the serious underrepresentation of minorities, especially Hispanics, on juries throughout the state. Although this situation is not the result of any conscious effort to exclude minorities from jury duty, we nonetheless underlined the corrosive effect this fact has had on minority trust in the Texas criminal justice system. Second, we looked at the problem of minority profiling. DPS data show that minority drivers are stopped more frequently than are their nonminority counterparts; nonetheless, we concluded that no reliable empirical evidence has yet traced this fact to racial discrimination by state law enforcement officers.

We concluded this chapter by noting that political infighting prevented the Seventy-Eighth Legislature from passing any major reforms in the area of criminal justice. We also noted that this lack of additional reform in the state's criminal justice system was in no small measure due to the fact that Texas was no longer experiencing the intense media scrutiny that accompanied former Governor Bush's run for the presidency in 2000.

In the introduction to this chapter, we saw how a single individual writing to his elected representatives in Congress and the state legislature was able to make policymakers aware of what he saw as abuses in the use of public funds by the death penalty resource centers. Richard Ibell was not the only citizen who was upset about the role of these centers. Individuals in other states were also raising questions about the death penalty resource centers. Without recognizing it at the time, each of these citizen activists was raising the collective awareness of sympathetic lawmakers about this controversial criminal justice program. When shift-ing political fortunes brought these sympathetic policymakers to power, what initially seemed like the futile efforts of individuals like Richard Ibell suddenly altered an important criminal justice policy. His success shows us that a single, persevering individual can make a significant difference in Texas politics.

KEY TERMS

Adversarial system of justice, p. 322
Criminal cases, p. 322
Indigent defendant, p. 323
Public defender, p. 323
Court-appointed attorney, p. 323
Plea bargain, p. 324
Habeas corpus appeal, p. 327

Pro bono, p. 327
Capital cases, p. 328
Cruel and unusual punishment, p. 329
Class action lawsuit, p. 329
Texas Board of Criminal Justice, p. 330
Texas Department of Corrections, p. 330
Racial profiling, p. 335

FOR FURTHER READING

Gainsborough, Jenni, and Marc Mauer, "Diminishing Returns: Crime and Incarceration in the 1990s," in *The Sentencing Project* (Washington, D.C.: The Sentencing Project, September 2000).

Scheck, Barry, *Actual Innocence* (New York: Doubleday, 2000).

Solomon, Amy, et al., *Outside the Walls* (Washington, D.C.: The Urban Institute, 2004).

Texas Defender Service, *A State of Denial: Texas Justice and the Death Penalty* (Austin, Tex.: Texas Defender Service, 2000).

Travis, Jeremy, and Michelle Waul, *Prisoners Once Removed* (Washington, D.C.: The Urban Institute, 2004).

STUDY QUESTIONS

1. Identify three factors that strongly encourage indigent defendants to seek a plea bargain.

2. Name three possible disadvantages faced by indigent defendants when they are assigned a court-appointed attorney.

3. Name two major approaches used in Texas to provide legal counsel to indigent defendants.

4. Name three ways in which economically strapped minorities face a less-than-equal opportunity in the Texas criminal justice system.

5. Name three reforms that policymakers have adopted in the past ten years to provide indigent defendants a more fair trial.

CRITICAL THINKING QUESTIONS

1. Briefly discuss the reasons that criminal justice issues inevitably become political. In addition to those offered in the text, provide at least one concrete example of a criminal justice issue that has become a political controversy, and explain why.

2. Briefly explain why an adequately funded and effective indigent defense program is particularly important in an adversarial system of justice.

3. Briefly discuss the relative advantages and disadvantages of public defender and court-appointed attorney methods of providing legal assistance to the poor.

4. Briefly explain the major flaws in the court-appointed attorney system that Texas has traditionally used to provide legal assistance to indigent defendants.

5. Many familiar with the Texas prison system argue that Judge William Wayne Justice's effort to restructure this system has been a dismal failure. What evidence in this chapter might lead you to support or doubt this claim? Explain your reasoning.

INTERNET RESOURCES

www.ojp.usdoj.gov/bjs/welcome.html The U.S. Department of Justice, Bureau of Justice Statistics, offers online access to a wide range of statistical data on crimes, victims, courts and sentencing, and corrections.

http://www.tdcj.state.tx.us/ The Texas Department of Criminal Justice has primary responsibility for providing public safety in the state of Texas. Its website has a wide range of information on all major state programs in the area of criminal justice.

www.tej.lawandorder.com/index.htm Texans for Equal Justice is a statewide crime victims advocacy group. Its website offers information on stalking, proposed criminal justice reforms, and news about victims' rights.

www.icpst.umich.edu/NACJD The National Archive of Criminal Justice Data acquires, archives, and processes data from a wide range of public and private sources in the field of criminal justice. Many of these data files can be downloaded by researchers for analysis.

www.jrsainfo.org/jjec/index.html The Juvenile Justice Evaluation Center Online provides a categorical listing of juvenile justice programs, summary descriptions, and performance measures used to assess these programs. It also offers a comprehensive list of Internet resources dealing with juvenile justice issues.

bop.library.net/ The Bureau of Prison Library has thousands of books, documents, periodicals, magazines, and newspapers dealing primarily with criminal justice and sociology. The full text or abstracts of many of these publications can be accessed through the library.

www.sentencingproject.org/ The Sentencing Project is an independent source of criminal justice policy analysis, data, and program information for the public and policymakers. The organization is a national leader in promoting alternative sentencing programs.

CHAPTER 12

Texas Health and Human Services

More than 1.23 million Texas children do not have enough to eat. Although several programs in the early 1990s provided emergency food for people in need, none offered a way to help the poor become self-sufficient. To do something about this situation, Kate Fitzgerald founded Sustainable Food Center (SFC) in 1993 in Austin. An employee of the Texas Department of Agriculture, Fitzgerald wanted to help children and their families achieve food security. Today, SFC continues to offer opportunities for Texans to help others and to help themselves through various agricultural and food programs, including the Farmer's Market Network Program, the Happy Kitchen/La Cocina Alegre Cooking and Nutrition School, and the Community and Youth Gardens Program.

The Farmer's Market Network Program brings fresh produce to low-income areas of Austin, thus offering an opportunity for the buying and selling of nutritious farm products. Families may use farmer's market vouchers from the U.S. Department of Agriculture's Women, Infants and Children program to buy food. The Happy Kitchen/ La Cocina Alegre is a bilingual cooking school for low-income people and is held in their own neighborhoods. This program is particularly beneficial for those at risk for diabetes, obesity, and heart disease. After a lesson in healthy food preparation, participants are given a bag of groceries with the ingredients necessary to duplicate the day's recipes at home. The Community and Youth Gardens Program teaches gardening and bee-keeping to at-risk youth and low-income families. Not only do the participants grow food for their own use and for sale, but they also develop marketable skills.

With seven dedicated staff members and twenty-five to thirty volunteers, SFC now serves approximately 8,000 clients in Austin and Central Texas according to Ruth Lauer, the business manager for SFC. Growing up in a family of nine children, Lauer remembers canning beans and visiting farmer's markets. Working with SFC provided the perfect opportunity to join her interests and her affinity for grassroots causes. She had worked as a volunteer for the organization as well as a fundraiser before becoming business manager. Her voice reflects the enthusiasm she feels for the achievements of the staff and volunteers. She believes that the holistic approach of the organization not only fulfills immediate needs but helps the working poor to build skills for the future.[1]

Volunteers for the organization range from youth to college-age individuals, to grandmothers. A University of Texas graduate student, for example, helps SFC improve technology as the organization consolidates with Austin Community Gardens. A university student with a paid internship in public relations designed a public display to take to volunteer fairs and public events and has written press releases and edited the SFC newsletter. Neighborhood grandmothers learn skills from volunteers and serve as liaisons in communities. Almost everyone has a skill that is needed. Organizations such as SFC and individuals like Ruth Lauer and her colleagues demonstrate how individuals can make a difference in the lives of Texans in poverty.

To many people in other parts of the nation, the image of Texans has been formed by the media. Texas has been characterized through movies that portray Texans as gun-toting cowboys and rugged (though feminine) frontier women struggling to master a hostile environment. The glitzy television show *Dallas* in the 1980s introduced another vision of Texas: the world of ruthless millionaires in the upper social strata whose personal lives centered around money interests and sexual escapades. Both of those images fall short of reality. Most Texans today live in urban areas; middle-class and working-class Texans outnumber millionaires, and Texas also has a large number of people living in poverty.

What Is Poverty?

Every year, the U.S. government establishes a guideline that identifies the income threshold below which a person is considered poor. This guideline takes into account family size and the children's ages. In 2004, the threshold for a family of four with children under age eighteen was $18,850 per year; for one person under age sixty-five living alone, the threshold was $9,573 per year.[2] Poverty, in other words, means having insufficient resources to meet the basic needs of shelter, food, clothing, and access to health care. Poverty may mean that children go to bed hungry or sleep in the streets. It may mean that a family cannot pay utility bills. Poverty has consequences that seriously detract from the quality of life and limit opportunities for success.

In essence, poverty is about children. Our political culture makes us less concerned about the poor than people are in the political cultures of most other industrial democracies. We are more disposed to assume that poor adults deserve to be poor because they did not try hard enough. However, many of the people living in poverty in Texas are children. They constitute about 20.5 percent of our entire child population. For that reason alone, we might consider doing something about poverty. (See the Texas poverty website in the Internet Resources section at the end of this chapter.)

The most important reason that people are poor is that they were poor as children. The vast majority of those who have inadequate health care, inadequate diets, and inadequate housing and who are most likely to suffer sexual abuse are poor children. Poor children are more likely to drop out of school and themselves have poor children. Their families are more likely to be crime victims and suffer job losses because of illness, injury, or changes in the economy over which they have no control.

The Texas welfare system, defined in terms of the percentage of the poor reached and the level of support available, places Texas near the bottom among the megastates. Sargent © 2004 Austin American-Statesman. *Reprinted with permission of* Universal Press Syndicate. *All rights reserved.*

There are numerous reasons for being concerned about reducing poverty. Two of the hard-nosed common-sense reasons are economic (wasting the potential talents of poor children is not good resource development) and political (a large class of people for whom the system does not work is a large class of people who could be led into crime or random violence). Both of these reasons are expensive to repair.

How Many People Are Poor in Texas?

The average poverty rate in the United States between 1996 and 1998 was 13.2 percent, compared to 16.1 percent in Texas.[3] By 2001, the national poverty rate had declined to 11.7 percent, but it had increased again to 12.1 percent by 2002. South Texas counties tend to have even higher numbers of poor people; the highest is Starr County, with 49.9 percent of the residents living below the poverty line in 2002.[4] Child poverty throughout the nation is higher than the rate found in the general population. In Texas, 20.5 percent of residents age seventeen and younger are living in poverty. Some areas of the state have exceptionally disturbing numbers of poor children, such as Brownsville, with 45.3 percent, and Laredo, with 38 percent of children living at or below the federal poverty line. Starr County has the highest rate, with 59.5 percent of children classified as poor.

Compared to other states, Texas has a high rate of poverty. It ranks forty-third among the fifty states; that is, only seven states have higher rates of poverty than does Texas.[5] Among the megastates, Texas has the highest rate of poverty. Texas in Context 12.1 shows the average poverty rates in the megastates in 2002.

The Causes of Poverty

Although poverty results from lack of money, money is not the only solution. Hence, the relevance of the self-sufficiency training through the Sustainable Food Center organization described at the beginning of this chapter and the importance of the Valley Interfaith movement mentioned in Chapter 1 are clear. Middle-class people without money are often in a temporary position that they have the skills and contacts to change. Poor people may stay poor for life. Thus, part of the solution to poverty is developing skills and attitudes that make one employable and prepare one to take more control of one's destiny.

In this chapter, we have little to say about programs that help mobilize the poor out of poverty because Texas doesn't have many of them (nor does the rest of the United States, for that matter). Instead, we will examine programs designed to help make it possible for poor children and their families to survive.

About 85 percent of Texans live in cities; most of those people depend on wages earned by working for individuals or large corporations. Throughout the nation, as we changed from a rural, agricultural economy to an urbanized, industrial one,

TEXAS in Context

12.1 Poverty Rates in the Megastates, 2002

Megastate	Poverty Rates
Texas	**15.6%**
New York	14.0%
California	13.1%
Illinois	12.9%
Florida	12.6%
Michigan	11.6%
Massachusetts	10.0%
Ohio	9.8%
Pennsylvania	9.5%
New Jersey	7.9%

Source: U.S. Census Bureau, Current Population Survey. State Poverty Rates and Standard Errors: 3 Year Averages 2000–2003 (Washington, D.C.: U.S. Government Printing Office, 2003).

economic independence diminished. This situation has been especially true in Texas, one of the most urbanized states.

As a largely wage-dependent society, Texas has been affected by trends in the job market. The trend in the past two decades has been an increase in the number of low-paid service-sector jobs, which often do not provide benefits such as health insurance. In more secure areas of employment, there is less and less demand for unskilled workers without a college degree or specialized training. In 2002, 43.2 percent of the poor were employed, while 8.9 percent were unemployed. Another 47.9 percent were not in the labor force (this figure includes children, the retired elderly, the disabled, and other persons unable to work as well as those who are no longer attempting to find work).[6]

Changes in the job market in Texas have produced an increasing separation between those with the highest incomes and those with the lowest incomes. According to the Center on Budget and Policy Priorities, income inequality between the top fifth in income and the bottom fifth grew 43 percent between the late 1970s and the mid-1990s.[7] These data indicate that the average annual income for the poorest one-fifth of Texas families fell by $1,660, while the middle fifth fell by $4,650 during the same period. But the average income of the richest one-fifth increased by $19,120. By 2001, the wealthiest one-fifth of Texans had incomes approximately eleven times larger than that of the poorest one-fifth. Between 1989 and 1999, the average income of the poorest one-fifth increased by $1,590, while that of the richest one-fifth increased by $25,080.

Wages in Texas have historically been lower than in states with strong unions to fight for worker's rights. In the 1960s and 1970s, employers from the strong union states in the North and Midwest were attracted to Texas because of low taxes and weaker unions. During the 1980s and 1990s, many companies, including some in Texas, relocated to areas outside the United States where operational costs were even lower, leaving many people without jobs. Those who lost jobs through company downsizing or relocation often found employment in the service sector at a lower rate of pay. Per-capita income in Texas was $28,860 in 2001 compared to $30,472 nationally. Median household income in Texas also fell below the national average. It is important to note that a person who works full-time at minimum wage and supports a family has an income below poverty.

Another factor affecting wages in Texas has been the increasing number of women in the job market. Women in the United States no longer work only to supplement an adequate family income—in other words, to pay for luxuries. Today, women work for wages to pay for life necessities. Many women are heads of households; they are the sole support of a family. And women from all walks of life make less money than do men, averaging 77 cents for every dollar earned by a male worker.[8] Pay inequities lower the quality of life not just for women but for the men and children who depend on the income earned by women.

Population changes have also played a role in the wages that Texas workers earn. The Hispanic population in the United States, especially in Texas, California, Arizona, New Mexico, and Florida, is rapidly increasing.[9] Hispanics tend to have lower incomes and less education than other groups in the United States. As they become an increasingly larger portion of the workforce in Texas, the average wage tends to decrease and the rate of poverty to increase.

Lack of education is a cause of poverty in our increasingly technology-driven job market. Income tends to increase with education; conversely, lack of education can be a result of poverty. Forty-nine percent of Texans in poverty had less than a high school education in 2001. See Texas in Context 12.2 for the education levels of the adults or heads of families living in low-income households compared to those adults and heads of families not living in low-income households in the megastates (Texas in Context 12.3).[10]

The Consequences of Poverty

Lack of success in education is both a cause and a potential consequence of poverty. Children from poor families (whose wage earners did not do well in school) have less preparation for school than do children from nonpoor families. Even schools in poor districts assume that children come from middle-class families; have been read to frequently; and have adequate toys, coloring books, and story books at home.[11]

Poor people are less likely than middle-class or wealthy people to finish high school. For those who do graduate from high school, attending college is almost

TEXAS in Context

12.2 Education Levels of Heads of Families with Children Living in Low-Income Households (Below 200% of the Poverty Rate) in the Megastates

Megastate	Percentage Less Than High School	Percentage Above High School	Percentage Finishing High School
California	39	28	33
Texas	**36**	**32**	**32**
New York	27	36	38
Illinois	23	39	39
Massachusetts	22	9	38
New Jersey	22	41	38
Florida	20	39	40
Michigan	19	43	38
Ohio	19	43	37
Pennsylvania	19	47	31

Source: National Center for Children in Poverty, Demographics calculated from U.S. Census Current Population Survey, 2001, 2002, and 2003. Available at http://nccp.org/state_detail_demographic_html.

unthinkable. They may need to earn an income to help an extended family, and the cost of tuition and books for college, even in state institutions, may be prohibitive. Because high-paying jobs increasingly demand more education, the inaccessibility of higher education perpetuates poverty.

Poor, uneducated people may not understand the way the educational system works. They may not understand how to apply for financial aid or even know that aid is available. They may not have role models in mothers or fathers, sisters or brothers, who have attended college. They may reason that others without an education have made a successful living. But this reasoning fails to take into account that those people are few in number, and the likelihood of being successful without an education is decreasing rapidly.

On an even grimmer note, there is a greater chance that a poor, uneducated person will end up in prison. That does not mean that the wealthy do not commit crimes or that the poor are more likely to, but as we noted in Chapter 11, a poor person will not be able to marshal the legal defense necessary to be found "not guilty," once accused of a crime.

TEXAS in Context

12.3 Education Levels of Heads of Families with Children Not Living in Low-Income Households in the Megastates

Megastate	Percentage Less Than High School	Percentage Above High School	Percentage Finished High School
California	8	16	76
Texas	**7**	**18**	**75**
Florida	4	19	79
Illinois	4	20	78
Massachusetts	4	17	79
New York	3	24	79
Michigan	2	19	79
New Jersey	2	19	80
Ohio	2	22	76
Pennsylvania	2	26	73

Source: National Center for Children in Poverty, Demographics calculated from U.S. Census Current Population Survey, 2001, 2002, and 2003. Available at http://nccp.org/state_detail_demographic_html.

Poor people tend to have shorter lives and are subject to more health problems than are those with adequate money. The health and development of all people, especially children, is adversely affected by poor nutrition, inadequate or dangerous housing, contaminated water supplies, and inadequate sewage disposal facilities that are often linked with substandard housing. The poor may also have difficulty getting treatment for diseases or obtaining adequate preventive care such as immunizations and checkups.

Texas is a large and diverse state. Health concerns vary across the state and are related to factors such as availability of medical care, economic conditions, racial and ethnic diversity of the area, regional education levels, and variations in lifestyles. The Texas Department of Health Services is particularly concerned with diseases that disproportionately affect some communities or groups in Texas. Recently, the commissioner of health included information about geographic disparities in health on the health department's website. It notes, for example, that people in rural areas may have less access to health care providers than do those in cities. Lack of understanding of health issues (poor health literacy) may cause people to engage in behaviors that are risky, such as tobacco or illicit drug use. Tobacco smoke is the leading cause of preventable death in Texas, with an estimated economic cost of $10 billion in 2003. In that year, 100,000 deaths in Texas were attributed to smoking. Studies show that Texans who have less than a high school education are more likely to smoke than those with a college degree.[12]

Health literacy is related to poor health in other ways. People with a poor understanding of health matters also have reduced ability to read or to communicate in English. The Texas Department of Health Services (TDHS) reports that 42 percent of outpatients did not understand simple instructions regarding taking medicine.

Poverty and lack of access to health care take a heavy toll on the health of Texans. The survival rate (nationwide) of poor victims of cancer is 10 to 15 percent lower than that of others, no doubt because the poor are less likely to receive timely screening and early intervention. Diabetes is the sixth leading cause of death in Texas, where 1.1 million adults were diagnosed with the disease in 2001. Another half million Texans are estimated to have undiagnosed diabetes. Hispanic Texans have the highest rate of death from this disease. Many diseases affect people disproportionately according to race and/or ethnicity. Texans without access to health care often have more severe diseases and have a higher likelihood of dying from disease. For more information about health issues in Texas, visit the Texas Department of Health Services website at http://www.tdh.state.tx.us/.

Lack of access to health care can lower both the quality of life and the length of life. For most Texans, health insurance is provided as a benefit of employment. Thus, an individual who loses his or her job likely loses health insurance benefits as well. In 2001, 57.8 percent of Texans under age sixty-five were insured through a job. The connection of health insurance with employment affects the truly poor and other Americans who are not officially in poverty. Many people work at low-paying jobs that are seasonal or do not provide insurance benefits.[13]

Low-income families are defined as those who live at or below 200 percent of poverty, the minimum level at which resources are sufficient to provide an adequate level of food, clothing, housing, and other necessities—but not costly private health insurance. Among that group in the United States, 56 percent of children live in families in which at least one parent works full-time, while 28 percent have at least one parent who works part-time or full-time, part-year. In Texas, 41 percent of families with children have low incomes. Of those, 63 percent include at least one parent who works full-time, year-round, and 25 percent have at least one parent who works part-time or part-year. Low-income individuals are among those most likely to fall into poverty when the economy falters.[14]

What Government Is Doing About Poverty

As wage dependency increased in the United States, it became obvious that many people could lose their incomes because of periodic fluctuations in the national economy that cause unemployment. The Great Depression, which began in 1929 and lasted through most of the next decade, convinced most U.S. citizens that government programs were needed to protect people from falling into poverty through no fault of their own. As part of President Franklin Roosevelt's New Deal, the national government began several safety-net programs that were intended to provide this economic protection.

The Social Security Act, passed in 1935, established programs to help those who were unable to provide enough money for themselves. Programs such as unemployment compensation and Aid for Dependent Children, later called **Aid to Families with Dependent Children (AFDC),** were begun. In the 1960s, other programs were added, including Medicare, Medicaid, and food stamps.

Aid to Families with Dependent Children (AFDC) A joint federal-state welfare program designed to provide assistance to poor families; it was replaced in 1996 by Temporary Aid for Needy Families. Under AFDC, federal funds were provided to states on the basis of a formula that required the national government to match state monies, with no ceiling on the amount of national contribution.

Entitlement A program that provides benefits to all those who meet the qualifications for the program, with no limit on the number of recipients.

Temporary Aid for Needy Families (TANF) A welfare program whereby federal monies are given to the states in the form of block grants, thus providing a ceiling on the national government's contribution to states. TANF also contains limits on the length of lifetime enrollment and the requirement that recipients actively seek work. TANF replaced AFDC in 1996 when Congress passed the Personal Responsibility and Work Opportunity Reconciliation Act.

In the context of a national budget deficit that was increasing at an alarming rate, many people began to criticize welfare programs in general, focusing primarily on AFDC and Medicaid. Because benefits were intended to support children, the recipients were primarily single parents, and usually mothers. Over time, the programs grew immensely, becoming two of the most costly of all social programs. Because the national government would continue to match the states' contributions regardless of how large the AFDC rolls grew, welfare became an **entitlement**—that is, all those who applied for benefits and met the eligibility criteria would receive assistance. There was no ceiling on the amount that the national government would contribute to the program.

Some critics of AFDC charged that welfare provided a work disincentive because it discouraged recipients from getting jobs. They also believed that welfare encouraged women to have out-of-wedlock babies to increase their AFDC benefits, which were based on the number of children one had. Critics of the program cited cases of fraud and abuse, with ineligible people tapping into the system. Many argued that welfare created a permanent dependency on government assistance that was passed from one generation of welfare recipients to the next.

Defenders of the program argued that benefit levels were so low (approximately $56.00 per month per child in Texas in 1995) that recipient families remained well under the poverty line, and thus the benefits were unlikely to discourage those who could work from doing so. These low benefits, defenders also noted, offered mothers little incentive to have more children for the meager additional sum of money they would receive. Even defenders of AFDC, however, recognized that the link of Medicaid coverage to benefits provided a work disincentive. Mothers of young children might be reluctant to accept a job without health care benefits if doing so meant losing Medicaid benefits. The 1988 Family Support Act required states to continue Medicaid coverage for one year after AFDC benefits were discontinued when the recipient obtained employment. The same act extended coverage to intact families that met eligibility criteria and introduced a mandatory job-training program. In spite of attempts to correct deficiencies in AFDC, criticism of the program continued and resulted in welfare reform. In 1996, the Personal Responsibility and Work Opportunity Reconciliation Act replaced AFDC with **Temporary Aid for Needy Families (TANF).**

| JOIN THE DEBATE |

THE ISSUE: Should welfare benefits stay low to increase incentives to work?

AGREE

1. People who get welfare benefits are poor because they are lazy, don't want to work, and are irresponsible.
2. It is not fair to take money from those who work and pay taxes to support those who won't work.
3. If people can live comfortably on welfare payments, they will choose not to work.
4. People won't appreciate the benefits given to them because they don't work for them.
5. Increasing welfare benefits will just raise taxes on those who are working.
6. Parents who live on welfare benefits are poor role models for their children.

DISAGREE

1. Welfare benefits should be increased to provide a comfortable level of living for recipients because most beneficiaries want to work and will accept a job if they can find one.
2. Welfare benefits are for children, who should not suffer because of a family problem.
3. Welfare benefits are usually spent immediately, pumping money into the economy and thus benefiting all of us.
4. Many welfare recipients are unable to work because of age, disability, or illness. They should be allowed to have a comfortable level of living.
5. Many welfare recipients are mothers of very young children who can't easily work. They should be supported while they take care of their children.

Administration of Social Welfare Programs

Social insurance Social welfare programs that provide benefits to those who have paid into a fund.

Means tested Programs that provide benefits on the basis of demonstrated need.

Some **social insurance** programs are administered by the national government. Recipients of those programs receive benefits whether or not they are poor. Texans receiving benefits from these programs receive the same level of support as recipients in other states do.

Other welfare programs are joint national-state efforts with benefit levels set by the states. These programs are **means tested**; recipients must prove that they are truly poor to be able to receive benefits. Still other programs are supported by state government, local government, and nonprofit agencies.

FEDERAL PROGRAMS

Old Age, Survivors and Disability Insurance (OASDI) A national program funded through lifelong contributions that are deducted from payrolls; commonly referred to as social security.

Social insurance programs sponsored by the national government include **Old Age, Survivors and Disability Insurance (OASDI),** usually referred to as social security, which began in the 1930s; Medicare, which began as part of President Lyndon Johnson's War on Poverty; and Supplemental Security Income (SSI).

Old Age, Survivors and Disability Insurance (OASDI) is funded by payroll taxes paid by employers and employees. The level of benefits received depends on an individual's work history and lifetime earnings. Benefits may also go to survivors of eligible workers and disabled workers or family members of workers. The benefits are not generous, but they have kept many elderly people out of poverty since the program was introduced in the 1930s. Because both rich and poor workers pay into the fund, all receive benefits. Obviously the benefits are more important to poor elderly than to the rich.

Immediately following the 2004 presidential election, George W. Bush identified partial privatization of Social Security as a prime focus of his second term. (Privatization means allowing the money individuals pay into the Social Security fund to be invested in private companies in the hope of gaining higher rates of interest—great if the company stock increases, potentially disastrous if it decreases.) Whether Congress will support the President's proposal in the face of a record national budget deficit is yet to be determined.

Medicare A health insurance program for the elderly funded by payroll contributions. It is not means tested.

Medicare is a federally administered program that was begun in 1965 to provide health insurance to elderly people who have lost their work-related health insurance after retirement. Medicare is a social insurance program that benefits recipients of OASDI. Those who are eligible for OASDI are automatically qualified to receive Medicare Part A benefits free of charge. Medicare Part A pays for care in hospitals, skilled nursing facilities, and hospices. It also covers some home health care. In 2004, recipients paid an annual deductible of $876 and additional copayment requirements for extended stays in hospitals and nursing homes.[15]

Recipients may also expand their coverage by paying a monthly payment of $66.60 (in 2004) for Medicare Part B. This additional insurance helps to pay for doctors, outpatient care, and some other services not covered by Part A, such as physical and occupational therapists and some home health care.

In 1997, a new program was added to Medicare. Medicare Part C, or Medicare + Choice, expands the options open to Medicare beneficiaries, allowing them to choose from several private health plans that may offer greater benefits than are provided by the traditional Medicare plan.[16]

In 2003, Congress passed a bill, the Medicare Modernization Act of 2003, to increase coverage for prescription drugs for Medicare recipients. Some of the bill's provisions will phase in over the next few years. The Medicare Modernization Act of 2003 established the Medicare Prescription Drug Discount Program, which provides poor seniors with a $600 credit for the purchase of drugs in 2004 and an additional $600 in 2005 for Medicare recipients whose incomes are not more than 135 percent of poverty. Insurance companies and pharmaceutical companies will sponsor the discount cards, so the details of coverage may vary. The program requires an initial fee ($30.00 in 2004) and a copayment for purchases. Recipients are not eligible if they receive drug coverage under another plan. The cost to the government of this benefit will exceed what was first predicted, causing controversy within Congress and among many members of the public. Though the program provides needed relief for the excessive costs of drugs, especially for seniors, some analysts fear that the cost to government will jeopardize the Medicare program in the future.[17]

Supplemental Security Income (SSI)
A means-tested program that benefits poor people.

Supplemental Security Income (SSI) is a federally funded and administered means-tested program that was begun in 1972. The benefits, set by the Social Security Administration, are intended to provide a minimum level of income to the aged, blind, and permanently disabled, regardless of work history. To be eligible, one must be at least sixty-five years of age or disabled and have limited assets (income no more than $651 per month for an individual or $950 per month for a couple, with assets of no more than $2,000 for an individual or $3,000 for a couple). The amount of benefit is the difference between 71 percent of the poverty level and the recipient's income, with a maximum of $552 per month (individual) or $829 per month (couple) in 2004. Because benefit levels are extremely low, most states supplement SSI payments from state money, but Texas has not chosen to do so.

JOINT FEDERAL-STATE PROGRAMS

Unemployment compensation
A joint national-state program funded in part by the contributions of employers into a fund.

Unemployment compensation is often called a social insurance program but it is available only to the small percentage who qualify. The Texas Workforce Commission administers the program. Eligibility for unemployment compensation is controlled by the state under guidelines established by the national government. Workers who leave their jobs because they were fired for misconduct or who leave voluntarily are not eligible for benefits, nor are those who have worked fewer than twenty weeks. Only about 25 percent of Texas unemployed workers receive unemployment compensation payments.

Those who are eligible, having lost jobs through company downsizing and cutbacks (in other words, through no fault of their own), must demonstrate that they are searching for work and have not refused suitable work. Even so, benefits are limited, and the duration of coverage is usually twenty-six weeks. Texas's benefits are among the lowest in the nation and are likely to remain so because an increase in benefits would mean an increase in tax on employers.

Lone Star Card
A debit card given to recipients in the Texas food stamp program that can be used to purchase allowable food items.

The food stamp program is funded by the national government through the Department of Agriculture, but the state pays for about half the administrative costs of the program and half the cost of investigations for fraud. In Texas, those who are eligible for food stamps are issued the **Lone Star Card,** which is used as a debit card to purchase food items in grocery stores. Eligibility for the Lone Star Card is keyed to several factors including assets, participation in work programs, and income. To be eligible, a family of three must have a gross monthly income of not more than $1,654.[18] The amount of benefits is calculated by the Department of Agriculture using a formula that includes family income, family size, and the cost of an adequate diet. In Texas, the maximum benefit for a family of three is $371 per month (2003). The program is considered to be successful because it has reduced malnutrition among the poor throughout the nation.[19]

TANF is a means-tested joint federal-state program for the poor who are unable

The Texas Lone Star Card is a symbol of innovation and efficiency in public administration.

to work or find work. Among other features, the program limits lifetime assistance to five years and requires able-bodied adults to work after two years. States may lower the time limits for recipients. Texas in Context 12.4 compares the time limits set by the megastates.

Funding for TANF is provided by the federal government and the states, with the federal share provided through block grants given to the states based on each state's estimated number of eligible poor. Each state sets its own eligibility and benefit levels. Individuals other than pregnant women and adults in drug treatment who have been convicted of felony drug charges may be excluded from benefits. The national government rules deny benefits to illegal immigrants and allow states to deny benefits to legal immigrants under certain conditions. Because the amount of money that the national government contributes to the program is now limited to the amount of the state's block grants, receipt of this assistance is no longer an entitlement. In Texas, benefits are low in comparison to those in other states. Texas has a conservative political culture that does not support generous government programs for the poor. Texas in Context 12.5 compares the amount of TANF benefits among the megastates for a single mother with two children in 2001.[20]

People who are eligible for TANF are automatically eligible for Medicaid (health care benefits). Others who are not eligible for TANF but who have low incomes may also qualify for Medicaid benefits. From 1994 to 1999, Texas had a 53 percent drop in TANF recipients. The trend toward reducing the TANF rolls continued with an additional reduction of 9.3 percent between 2001 and 2002.[21]

While Texas led the nation in the number of children removed from the Medicaid rolls from 1996 to 1999, the Children's Health Insurance Program (CHIP), discussed

TEXAS in Context

12.4 Time Limits for TANF

Megastate	Time Limit
Michigan	No time limit; state funded after 60 months
Illinois	No limit if the recipient has earned income and works at least 20 hours per week; 24 months for a family with no earnings and without a child under age 13
Florida	60 months
New Jersey	60 months
New York	60 months
Pennsylvania	60 months
Ohio	Less than 60 months lifetime
Massachusetts	24 months out of a 60-month period; no lifetime limit
Texas	**12, 24, or 36 months lifetime, depending on employability of the head of household**
California	18–60 months depending on employability, availability of jobs, and recipient's participation in community service work

Source: L. Jerome Gallagher, Megan Gallagher, Keven Perese, Susan Schreiber, and Keith Watson, "One Year After Federal Welfare Reform: A Description of State Temporary Assistance for Needy Families (TANF) Decisions as of October 1997" (Washington, D.C.: Urban Institute, June 1998). Available at newfederalism.urban.org/html/occas6.htm.

Medicaid A means-tested health insurance program for the poor, funded by taxpayers.

below, provided health insurance for many Texas children from 2000 to 2003. The first Republican majority legislature since the end of the Civil War decided to deal with a budget shortfall in 2003 by cutting funding for both Medicaid and CHIP.[22]

Medicaid is a joint national-state program that provides health care to the poor. TANF continues to link eligibility for welfare with eligibility for Medicaid, as did AFDC, and also continues Medicaid benefits for one year to those who leave welfare to go to work. In the late 1980s, federal laws mandated coverage of people ineligible for welfare or SSI, including expanded coverage for the elderly, children, people with disabilities, and pregnant women, adding over 1 million people to the Medicaid rolls between 1990 and 1995. Under the 2004 reorganization, the Texas Health and Human Services Commission administers Medicaid.[23] Welfare reform has tightened the criteria that one must meet to receive Medicaid and has introduced time limits on coverage. In 2003, Texas eliminated Medicaid coverage for adults with mental health problems, leaving almost 200,000 former recipients without access to mental health care. It also discontinued coverage for adult pregnant women who are above 158 percent of the poverty level and discontinued coverage for adults above 17 percent of the poverty level. For adults, eyeglasses, hearing aids, and podiatry and chiropractic services were also eliminated. The Texas Legislature, in 2003, decreased reimbursement rates for physicians, hospi-

TEXAS in Context

12.5	TANF Benefits per Month for a Single Parent with Two Children, 2001
Megastate	TANF Monthly Benefit
Texas	**$201.00**
Florida	$303.00
Ohio	$373.00
Illinois	$377.00
Pennsylvania	$403.00
New Jersey	$424.00
Michigan	$459.00
New York	$577.00
Massachusetts	$626.00
California	$645.00

Source: National Center for Children in Poverty, Columbia University, http://nccp.org/pub_pel04.html (accessed April 4, 2004).

tals, and nursing homes. The latter cut may affect the willingness of health care providers to accept Medicaid patients.[24]

PEOPLE WITHOUT HEALTH INSURANCE IN TEXAS

Although many poor people are helped by Medicaid and many nonpoor have health insurance through their employment, others in Texas have no health insurance coverage at all. Texas residents may lack health insurance because it is not provided by their employment, yet they earn too much money to qualify for Medicaid. Others and their families may lack health insurance because of temporary unemployment or other circumstances. Others may be unable to afford private health insurance. The cost of private insurance increased 13.9 percent between 2002 and 2003, even while coverage was reduced on many plans and copayments were increased. The average cost of private health insurance for a family in Texas was almost $10,000 per year in 2004. In 2002, Texas led the nation in the percentage of uninsured children, with 22.6 percent of residents age seventeen and under without health insurance. Texas in Context 12.6 compares the number of children not covered by any health insurance in the megastates.

To try to alleviate the problem of children without medical coverage, in 1999 the Texas Legislature passed a bill that would provide insurance for about half a million children for as little as a $15.00 enrollment fee and $2.00 per health visit. The program, part of a nationwide state-federal initiative (State Children's Health Insurance Program [SCHIP]) is called CHIP in Texas. The SCHIP program provided 1.8 million low-income children with health benefits between 1999 and 2002, leaving approximately 17.4 million uninsured children nationwide. Even with the in-

TEXAS in Context

12.6   Three-Year Average of Low-Income Uninsured Children in the Megastates, 2000–2002

Megastate	Total Number of Children	Children at or Below 200 Percent of the Poverty Level	Uninsured Children at or Below 200 Percent of the Poverty Level
Massachusetts	1,502,000	458,000	40,000
New Jersey	2,091,000	534,000	277,000
Michigan	2,610,000	840,000	106,000
Ohio	2,923,000	966,000	157,000
Pennsylvania	2,959,000	978,000	162,000
Illinois	3,329,000	1,152,000	228,000
Florida	4,036,000	1,661,000	426,000
New York	4,830,000	1,893,000	277,000
Texas	**6,378,000**	**2,998,000**	**1,013,000**
California	10,096,000	4,226,000	968,000

Source: U.S. Census Bureau, "Low Income Uninsured Children by State: 2000, 2001, and 2002." Available at www.census.gov/html.

creases in coverage, only one in five poor children was insured by 2002. In the 2003 budget crisis, many states reduced funding levels for the program. In Texas, 507,259 children were enrolled in CHIP when funding was reduced in September 2003, resulting in 118,978 low-income children dropped from the rolls. Those not dropped lost dental, vision, hospice, and most mental health services, although Governor Perry restored some mental health benefits in October 2003. Higher co-payments and tighter eligibility requirements are expected to reduce the number of children covered by this program even further and increase the number of Texas children without health insurance.[25]

What do children and adults without health coverage do when illness strikes? The answer is provided by county hospitals and teaching hospitals in Texas. An amendment to the Texas Constitution in 1954 created countywide hospital districts, giving them the responsibility for providing medical and hospital care for the needy inhabitants of the county. The state authorized counties to levy ad valorem property taxes to support these efforts. For counties with an unusually high number of Medicaid and uninsured health care recipients, the state provides disproportionate share hospital funds (DSH) to help offset the high cost of providing care.

Frequently, an individual without health care insurance has no recourse other than to seek medical assistance at a county facility, often going to the trauma center or emergency room. That source of health care tends to be more expensive based on several factors. The cost of an emergency room visit is generally higher than a physician's office visit. In addition, those without access to regular care are more likely to suffer from preventable diseases and may hesitate to seek treatment until an illness is quite advanced. Late diagnosis and treatment increase the financial cost to taxpayers, as well as the costs in terms of human suffering and the possibility of avoidable early death. It also exacerbates the potential of spreading undiagnosed communicable diseases to others. Additional sources of medical assistance and income assistance in Texas are fragmented and perhaps not easily discovered by all who would benefit from them.

STATE PROGRAMS

In 2003, with a budget shortfall threatening, the Texas Legislature passed House Bill 2292 requiring the reorganization of Texas agencies concerned with the delivery of health and human services, thus merging twelve agencies into four new departments under the Texas Health and Human Services Commission (HHSC). By April 2004, the new structure was established, but the details about program delivery responsibilities were still being ironed out. HHSC is charged with centralizing eligibility for programs, establishing the office of inspector general to prevent fraud and waste, and consolidating administrative services.

According to HHSC Executive Commissioner Albert Hawkins, the new organization will save $389 million over the next five years and improve access to services by allowing clients to determine eligibility for multiple programs at one location. He said that, under the old system, the state spent $700 million per year determining eligibility alone, more than is paid out in cash assistance.[26] The savings are expected to occur through both reorganization and privatization of client screening. (For a critique of the theory that privatization always leads to cost savings, see Dave Mann, "Cashing In: Getting Rich off CHIP," which is listed at the end of this chapter in the section called For Further Reading.)

The four new departments are:

1. Department of Family and Protective Services, which includes Child Protective Services, Adult Protective Services, and Child Care Regulatory Services.
2. Department of Assistive and Rehabilitative Services, which includes Rehabilitation Services, Blind and Visually Impaired Services, Deaf and Hard of Hearing Services, and Early Childhood Intervention Services.
3. Department of Aging and Disability Services, which includes Mental Retardation Services, Community Care Services, Nursing Home Services, and Aging Services.
4. Department of State Health Services, which includes Health Services, Mental Health Services, and Alcohol and Drug Abuse Services.

In this reorganization, the longstanding Texas Mental Health/Mental Retardation Agency (MHMR) was split, with responsibilities for mental health and mental retardation going to different agencies, as noted above.[27] In a state which underserves its less fortunate citizens to the extent that Texas does, a lot of work is still being done by many individuals in numerous agencies.

In helping to pay for the needs of children from families both rich and poor, most states are now increasing efforts to improve the collection of child support from spouses who have been delinquent in paying—and thus reduce the amount of support for children that must be paid by taxpayers. In Texas, the agency responsible for this collection is the Child Support Enforcement Division of the Office of the Attorney General. To encourage child-support collections, Texas and many other megastates provide a $50.00-per-month pass-through bonus for TANF-eligible families who receive child-support payments. Texas is serious about child-support payments. The state can withhold income, even Internal Revenue Service (IRS) checks, from a deadbeat parent; it can seize assets from financial institutions; and it can have driver's licenses, professional licenses, and even fishing licenses suspended for failure to pay child support. In the 2002–2003 fiscal year, the Texas attorney general collected a record $1.5 billion in back child support. Over half the money collected was gained through income-withholding orders.[28]

Unlike many other states, Texas does not have a general-assistance program for adults who are not qualified for SSI or any of the other programs already mentioned. Among the megastates, only Texas has no state-supported general-assistance program.[29]

LOCAL PROGRAMS

Many local governments in Texas are responsible for channeling money obtained from federal and state grants to the needy in their communities. Councils of government in some areas coordinate regional meals programs for elderly Texans; cities also may provide senior citizens' centers and summer lunch programs for children.

The Emergency Nutrition and Temporary Emergency Relief Program (ENTERP), partially funded by the state, contracts with local governments to provide services for the poor either directly or on a contract basis, with the contractor paying half the cost of the program. Local utility companies have programs to help the needy with utility bills and other winter needs; they get money for the program through the Oil Overcharge Restitutionary Act, which added oil overcharge funds to ENTERP for this purpose.

OTHER PROGRAMS TO HELP THE POOR

In addition to government-sponsored programs, charitable and nonprofit organizations fill many of the gaps in the assistance provided to poor Texans. Food banks help families who are in immediate need and provide vouchers for other charitable organizations such as churches, which can distribute them to the poor who are seeking assistance. Food banks rely on donations from citizens. Many times, excess produce or food that is good but mislabeled (and therefore not salable) is donated and helps to reduce hunger among the poor. Communities may offer educational programs, such as high school equivalency classes. Literacy Volunteers of America works to assist those whose reading level is too low for the job market.

Countless organizations operate soup kitchens, clothing banks, free clinics, shelters for the homeless, battered women's shelters, and many others. These efforts by individual Texans represent invaluable resources for those who are not eligible for other programs or have needs that are not addressed by government programs.

In spite of the number of programs, many Texans remain poor and in need of assistance. Some are not eligible for the programs that are in place. Others may have incomes that are sharply curtailed because of employer cutbacks, personal tragedies, death, or illness.

Summary

Poverty results at least in part from lack of education and lack of opportunity. It is also a product of changing social and economic conditions. Many people are poor through no fault of their own. Although social programs at national, state, and local levels of government address the problem of poverty, it is unlikely to disappear in the near future.

Those who are concerned about poverty in Texas have several opportunities to improve the condition of those who need assistance. The most obvious course of individual action is volunteerism. Getting involved with a local charity or with a statewide or nationwide group that helps the poor is both personally rewarding and effective in helping those who are less fortunate. Active membership in community-based organizations, such as Communities Organized for Public Service (COPS) in San Antonio, affords citizens the opportunity to affect the lives of the poor. Each of us can use our individual talents to better the condition of others, whether we help Habitat for Humanity build houses, bake cakes for AIDS victims, read to a blind child, or donate excess garden produce to a food bank. The volunteers and staff of Sustainable Food Center illustrate the power of the individual to make a difference and demonstrate the place of innovation in programs to help the needy. Put your ideas to work in your own locality. You may make a tremendous difference in the lives of others.

Perhaps even more effective is getting involved in politics to support programs that will help improve the condition of the poor. Groups have made a difference in the lives of many Texans through political activism. The Mexican American Legal Defense Fund has been successful in gaining benefits for Mexican Americans, including improving access to higher education. Other groups are effective in gaining benefits for the poor. By improving the lives of some Texans, you will improve the quality of life for all.

KEY TERMS

Aid to Families with Dependent Children (AFDC),
p. 349
Entitlement, p. 349
Temporary Aid for Needy Families (TANF),
p. 349
Social insurance, p. 350
Means tested, p. 350

**Old Age, Survivors and Disability Insurance
(OASDI),** p. 351
Medicare, p. 351
Supplemental Security Income (SSI), p. 352
Unemployment compensation, p. 352
Lone Star Card, p. 352
Medicaid, p. 354

FOR FURTHER READING

Folland, Sherman, Allen C. Goodman, and Miron Stano, *The Economics of Health and Health Care*, 4th ed. (New York: Prentice Hall, 2003).

Hancock, LynNell, *Hands to Work: The Stories of Three Families Racing the Welfare Clock* (New York: William Morrow & Co., 2001).

Katz, Michael B., *The Price of Citizenship: Redefining the American Welfare State* (New York: Henry Holt, 2001).

Mann, Dave, "Cashing In: Getting Rich off CHIP," *Texas Observer* (September 26, 2003), www.texasobserver.org.

Sider, Ronald J., *Just Generosity: A New Vision for Overcoming Poverty in America* (Grand Rapids, Mich.: Baker Bytes, 1999).

Weissert, Carol S., *Governing Health: The Politics of Health Policy* (Baltimore, Md.: Johns Hopkins University Press, 2002).

STUDY QUESTIONS

1. Define *poverty* and *low income.*

2. What are Medicare and Medicaid?

3. What is TANF? How is it different, if at all, from AFDC?

4. What criteria must a person meet to qualify for SSI benefits?

5. What is OASDI?

CRITICAL THINKING QUESTIONS

1. Considering all the information you have gathered thus far in this course about the political culture of Texas and the political attitudes of Texans, what changes do you expect to see in the provision of services for the poor in Texas?

2. How can health care for the uninsured in Texas be provided at a lower cost or more effectively?

3. What should be done to reduce poverty in Texas?

4. Do you think the reduction in the TANF rolls is related to the general economy of the state? What would you expect to happen if Texas has a recession and an increase in unemployment generally? What are the other causes of the reduction in the TANF enrollment?

5. What recommendation would you make to increase access to higher education for Texans? How would your recommendations affect the poverty rate in the state?

INTERNET RESOURCES

www.census.gov/   The U.S. Census Bureau website contains statistical and demographic information about residents throughout the United States. The Census Bureau is an authoritative source of information about poverty rates and related data.

www.dhs.state.tx.us/   The Texas Department of Human Services website provides information about state social programs.

www.tdh.state.tx.us/   The Texas Department of Health offers information about state health programs.

www.window.state.tx.us/   The Texas Comptroller of Public Accounts provides various economic facts about Texas.

www.main.org/sfc/   This website for Sustainable Food Center provides information about the organization's programs, mission, and history.

www.cppp.org/products/poverty101.html/   This website provides a succinct profile of low-income residents, their needs, and the state's response.

www.nccp.org/   The National Center for Children in Poverty presents many facts about poverty across the United States and by state.

Education Policy

One June morning in 1990, Bea Salazar walked out to the Dumpster at her apartment complex in Carrollton, Texas, and emptied her trash. She heard a noise down in the Dumpster. When she looked in, she saw a small child scavenging for food. When she asked him why he was there, he told her that there was no food in his apartment. Salazar took the little boy back to her apartment and made him a peanut butter and jelly sandwich. The next day, this boy came back to ask for another sandwich. Soon the boy came to her door accompanied by a few other little boys in her complex. All of them were hungry.

During the school year, these children received a free breakfast and lunch at the local elementary school. But school was closed for the summer, and these children were going hungry. Although disabled and unemployed herself, Salazar began soliciting food donations from local churches and a United Way social service agency in her area. In no time at all, Salazar had collected enough donations to provide free lunches to twelve hungry children in her complex.

When school started in the fall, several of Bea's Kids came to ask her for help with their homework. Gradually, her apartment turned into an after-school study program for children in the complex. Unable to help some of the older children with their more difficult homework, Salazar contacted the principal at a nearby high school, who arranged for honor students to volunteer as tutors for the children. When some of the youngsters became old enough to enter high school, Salazar contacted area colleges for more advanced tutors. Some of Bea's Kids are now college students themselves.

The program Bea Salazar started ten years ago with peanut butter and jelly sandwiches now serves 140 underprivileged children. Relying on an extensive network of volunteers, tutors, and donations, Salazar provides children in her program with an impressive array of educational help and resources: school supplies at the beginning of the year, after-school tutoring, eye exams, new sneakers and underwear, used clothing and toys, and, of course, peanut butter and jelly sandwiches. She has also convinced the apartment complex owners to donate an adjoining empty apartment as a study center, part of which she has turned into a modern computer lab.

Today, area teachers routinely contact her to help with particularly hard-to-reach children. They send these children to Salazar's after-school study program with homework instructions pinned to their shirts. School and area service clubs regularly supply dozens of volunteer tutors and counselors to Bea's Kids. The local school superintendent has even gone so far as to allow school buses to transport Bea's Kids to special school-sponsored functions.[1]

Salazar teaches us an important lesson about making a difference. You do not need to wait for an official go-ahead from the local school board, the Texas Education Agency (TEA), the State Board of Education (SBOE), or even the local parent-teacher association to begin improving the lives and education of children who need help. Once you begin helping children, teachers and school administrators who care about these children will hear about it and will soon contact you to see how they can help.

The Political Character of Education

Education is always and everywhere a political issue. To educate, policymakers must first decide what is important enough and appropriate to teach. Reaching these decisions means that educators invariably must decide to teach some subjects rather than others, some theories rather than others, and some values rather than others. These decisions unavoidably validate and promote the beliefs of some groups and social classes at the expense of others.

Educational policymakers must also decide at what level they will support public education, as well as how to allocate educational resources among various groups, social classes, and geographical regions. These decisions inevitably influence the distribution of future economic and social opportunities. Students educated by competent teachers in good schools go on to prosperous and interesting careers. Students taught by incompetent teachers in poor schools go on to minimum wage, dead-end jobs. Because the economic and psychological stakes are high, political conflict is an inherent part of educational decisionmaking.

Political Issues in Texas Education Policy

Numerous political issues surround educational decisionmaking in Texas. Some issues come and go rather quickly; others are more enduring. Here we examine the most controversial and enduring issues that have plagued educational policymakers in Texas during the past half-century.

WHAT CONSTITUTES EQUAL OPPORTUNITY IN TEXAS PUBLIC SCHOOLS?

The most divisive issue confronting educational policymakers in Texas concerns the extent to which public schools offer equal opportunity to citizens of all races, ethnic groups, and social classes. Soon after the end of the Civil War, Texas instituted a segregated system of public education. During this era, African Americans were prohibited from attending schools with whites and were forced to attend all-black schools and colleges. In 1896, the U.S. Supreme Court legitimized this segregated system of education in the now infamous *separate-but-equal doctrine* issued in **Plessy v. Ferguson.** In this case, the Court held that state laws mandating separate but equal accommodations for blacks and whites in all public facilities, including schools, were constitutional. Constitutionally protected by this doctrine, Texas maintained separate educational facilities for blacks and whites until the 1950s.[2]

In 1954, the U.S. Supreme Court overturned the separate-but-equal doctrine in **Brown v. Board of Education of Topeka, Kansas.** In this landmark case, the Court ruled that separate educational facilities for blacks and whites were inherently unequal.[3] Its segregated system of education now judged to be unconstitutional, Texas was forced to take its first step toward integrated public schools. After years of sometimes ugly resistance to *Brown v. Board of Education,* Texas achieved a legally integrated system of public education by the mid-1960s. Important though it was, the battle for integrated public schools was only the first of several political struggles over equity in Texas public schools.

Even before racially integrated public education became a reality in the Lone Star State, a second controversy over equal educational opportunity was already festering. The root of this conflict was found in the fact that property taxes have always been a major source of funding for public schools in Texas. Because school districts that include valuable commercial and residential property within their boundaries can raise more revenue than those with less valuable properties, property-rich districts can spend more to educate students than their

Plessy v. Ferguson An 1896 Supreme Court case that proclaimed it was constitutional to require blacks and whites to attend separate public schools, as long as these schools were equal. The legal reasoning offered by the Court in this case came to be known as the separate-but-equal doctrine.

Brown v. Board of Education of Topeka, Kansas A 1954 Supreme Court decision that overturned the separate-but-equal doctrine in *Plessy v. Ferguson.* The Court ruled that separate educational facilities for blacks and whites are inherently unequal and therefore unconstitutional.

property-poor counterparts. This situation is true even when property-poor school districts are willing to tax themselves at a higher rate than property-rich districts, and it has made unequal school funding a fact of life in Texas public schools for most of the state's history.[4]

After decades of lobbying the state legislature to implement a fairer system of school funding, property-poor districts took their case to the federal courts in 1971. By 1973, however, the U.S. Supreme Court ruled in ***San Antonio School District v. Rodriguez*** that school finance is a state issue.[5] Rejected by the federal courts, property-poor school districts again returned to the Texas Legislature to lobby for a more equal allocation of school resources. Still unsuccessful, sixty-seven property-poor districts, led by the Edgewood school district of San Antonio, sued the state commissioner of education, William Kirby, in 1984 for a more equitable system of school funding.

In ***Edgewood v. Kirby,*** lawyers for property-poor districts pointed out that property tax bases ranged from $20,000 per student in the poorest district in Texas to $14 million per student in the wealthiest district. This extreme disparity in the property tax base allowed the 100 richest districts in the state to spend an average of $7,233 per student, while the poorest 100 districts were able to spend only $2,978 per student. Because the tax base in the wealthier school districts was so much larger than that in poor districts, the average tax rate in the poorest districts was 50 percent higher than it was in the wealthier districts.[6]

Finding in favor of property-poor school districts in 1987, State District Judge Harley Clark ruled the existing system of public school financing unconstitutional and mandated the legislature to develop a more equitable system to pay for public education. Pressured by the court and delayed by a series of constitutional challenges, the legislature ultimately adopted Senate Bill 7 in 1993.[7] This legislation, still referred to as the **Robin Hood measure** by many Texans, required property-rich districts to transfer a substantial part of their tax revenues to property-poor districts.[8]

The question of exactly how much wealthy school districts should redistribute to poorer school districts continues to be a contentious issue fought anew in every legislative session. Under wealth-equalization rules now in place, some property-rich districts are required to transfer well over half of their property tax revenues to property-poor districts. Never happy with the necessity of transferring a large portion of their property tax revenues to property-poor districts, property-rich districts are now facing another problem: A growing number have now bumped up against the $1.50 per $100 of assessed value cap that the legislature placed on school property taxes.[9] Unable to continue raising tax rates to offset revenue they must redistribute to poorer school district, these property-rich districts are now faced with significant budget cuts. Having failed in their many attempts to get the legislature to revise the Robin Hood measure, four of these property-rich school districts filed a lawsuit against the state in 2001 challenging the constitutionality of this school-funding mechanism.[10] In May 2003, the Texas Supreme Court ruled that the case could be heard in state district court.[11]

San Antonio School District v. Rodriguez A 1973 U.S. Supreme Court decision stating that school finance is a state issue.

Edgewood v. Kirby A 1984 lawsuit by sixty-seven property-poor districts, led by the Edgewood school district of San Antonio, that argued that the state's system of unequal funding of schools violated the Texas Constitution.

Robin Hood measure Legislation passed by the Texas Legislature in 1993 requiring wealthy school districts to transfer part of their property tax revenues to poorer school districts.

A crowded portable classroom at Frey School in Edgewood, Texas.

WHAT CONSTITUTES EQUAL OPPORTUNITY IN TEXAS HIGHER EDUCATION?

While the issue of equal opportunity in Texas public schools has evolved into a struggle over school funding, the most volatile aspect of the equal opportunity debate in higher education concerns college admissions. By 2002, African Americans and Hispanics together made up 46 percent of all high school graduates in Texas.[12] Yet these minorities accounted for only 31 percent of students in state universities.[13] At the state's two flagship universities, the University of Texas (UT) at Austin and A&M College Station, African American and Hispanic students made up only 15 percent and 10 percent, respectively, of the student bodies.[14]

The small number of minority students at prestigious state universities has been an issue for the rapidly growing number of minority legislators in Texas. Prodded by these legislators, college administrators have aggressively recruited minority students in recent years. From the late 1960s until 1996, **affirmative action programs** had been a major part of this effort. The most aggressive of these affirmative action programs gave extra weight to a minority student's college admission application, which allowed more minority students admission to the state's most prestigious universities and professional schools than would otherwise have been the case.

Although affirmative action has been a favorite tool of legislators and other higher education policymakers, it remains extremely controversial. Many Texans see it as providing preferential treatment to minority students. In 1992, Cheryl

Affirmative action programs Programs designed to help minorities by giving extra weight to a minority student's college admission application.

Hopwood **decision** A
1996 decision by the U.S.
Circuit Court of Appeals
for the Fifth District that
declared affirmative action
programs using race as a
criterion of admission
were unconstitutional.
This decision effectively
ended affirmative action
admissions programs in
Texas, Louisiana, and
Mississippi, the three
states within the circuit
court's jurisdiction.

Hopwood and three other white applicants were denied admission to the UT Law
School, so they sued the university, arguing that its affirmative action program
was unconstitutional. In 1994, in what became known as the *Hopwood* **decision,** a
federal district judge ruled in their favor, and in 1996, a three-judge panel of the
federal Fifth Circuit Court of Appeals upheld this decision on appeal.[15]

Faced with a federal circuit court decision prohibiting affirmative action, educational policymakers in Texas looked for an alternate way to increase the number
of minority students at the state's most selective educational institutions. Hoping
to compensate for the generally lower scores earned by minority students on college entry exams such as the SAT, MCAT, and LSAT, policymakers reduced the
weight that these scores would play in the college admissions process. They did so
by requiring college admissions officers to consider intangibles such as any obstacles an applicant might have had to overcome in life, as well as admission test
scores.[16] They also assured any student in the top 10 percent of his or her graduating high school class automatic admission into any state university, regardless of
SAT score.

Grutter v. Bollinger A
2003 U.S. Supreme Court
decision holding that
carefully crafted university
affirmative action programs
are constitutional.

These policies had only a minimum positive effect on student diversity at the
state's two flagship universities.[17] By 2003, however, in the case of *Grutter v.
Bollinger,* the U.S. Supreme Court had ruled that a narrowly crafted affirmative
action program at the University of Michigan Law School was constitutional.[18]
This decision permitted Texas universities the option of once again using affirmative
action as a tool for increasing minority enrollment at selective state universities.
UT Austin has already announced its plans to reestablish an affirmative action
program in 2005. Texas A&M, on the other hand, has decided not to reestablish its
affirmative action plan.[19]

**Permanent University
Fund (PUF)** A fund
established in the Texas
Constitution of 1876 and
paid for by oil-land leases
to provide financial support
for the University of Texas.
Subsequent constitutional
amendments have permit-
ted Texas A&M, as well as
other schools in these two
university systems, to
benefit from the $7.7
billion fund.

Universities as well as school districts struggle over what constitutes an equitable distribution of educational resources. Texas supports thirty-two public
four-year institutions governed by six independent boards. Collectively, these
universities enrolled 455,719 students in 2002. Texas also supports eight public
health–related institutions, which enrolled an additional 13,795 students. Finally,
the state supports fifty-three community colleges, which enrolled an additional
515,771 students.[20] At the beginning of every new legislative session, each of these
institutions of higher education enters into a political struggle for a bigger piece
of the state's higher education fiscal pie.

**Higher Education
Assistance Fund** A fund
established in 1984 by a
constitutional amendment
to provide financial
support for universities
constitutionally excluded
from PUF funds. By 1999,
this fund provided $225
million per year to these
institutions.

State funding for Texas universities comes from student tuition, general state
revenues, and two large public endowments. Historically, the lion's share of these
funds has gone to UT Austin and Texas A&M at College Station. Only these two
flagship universities and some of the smaller schools in these systems are constitutionally entitled to benefit from the $7.7 billion **Permanent University Fund
(PUF)** established in 1876 and paid for by oil-land leases.[21] State universities excluded from PUF money are engaged in a perennial battle for a larger share of
higher education resources. In 1984, these institutions scored a modest victory in
the struggle over state funding when they succeeded in passing a constitutional
amendment establishing the much smaller **Higher Education Assistance Fund**

for schools constitutionally excluded from PUF funds. This fund now provides $225 million per year to these institutions.[22]

While struggles between the state's flagship campuses and its less well-established universities reflect the obvious institutional desire for a bigger piece of the financial pie, they also involve more subtle class and ethnic group struggles. Students attending the state's most prestigious universities are drawn disproportionately from upper-income families. Students attending branch campuses are more likely to be drawn from lower-middle- and working-class families. This situation means that decisions about how to divide the state's higher education budget between its flagship campuses and their smaller counterparts inevitably shape the distribution of educational opportunity among social classes within the state.

Decisions about how to divide the state's higher education dollar between four- and two-year colleges also mask ethnic and racial cleavages. Community colleges are funded by a combination of local property taxes and general state revenue. Together, these funds provide community colleges with less than one-third of the per-pupil resources of the state's four-year colleges.[23] Because working-class and minority students are better represented in community colleges than in universities, choices about how to divide higher education funding between these institutions are also decisions about how to divide higher education dollars between largely working-class minorities and largely middle- and upper-middle-class whites.[24]

In the early 1990s, some of the subtle class and ethnic conflicts that underlie university funding decisions bubbled to the surface when the League of United Latin American Citizens (LULAC) filed suit against education policymakers in Texas. Representing forty communities in South Texas, LULAC argued that the state's decision to concentrate the bulk of its higher education resources in Central and North Texas discriminated against Hispanic communities in the southern part of the state. Ultimately, state policymakers settled this lawsuit by agreeing to undertake the **South Texas Initiative,** which committed the state to invest hundreds of millions of additional higher education dollars in existing and new university campuses in South Texas.[25]

South Texas Initiative
A commitment by the University of Texas to invest millions of additional higher education dollars in existing and new university campuses in South Texas.

Public funding for state universities covers only a portion of the total cost of a university education in Texas. Student tuition and fees cover the remaining cost. Unfortunately for students, in recent years state policymakers have been funding a decreasing portion of the cost of a college education in Texas. In 1980, state general revenue funds constituted 93 percent of all funds appropriated to cover the cost of a college education in Texas. By 2004, state general revenue funds constituted only 72 percent of all funds appropriated to cover the cost of a college education in Texas.[26] The declining state contribution means that students and their families must bear a growing portion of total college costs through increased tuition and fees.[27] This trend will almost certainly accelerate in coming years in part because the legislature granted state universities for the first time in 2003 the right to raise their tuitions without legislative approval.[28] Rising tuition, of course, does not affect all students equally. It is particularly problematic for low-income students and thus inevitably affects equality of educational opportunity in Texas.

HOW DOES THE QUALITY OF EDUCATION IN TEXAS COMPARE TO THAT IN OTHER STATES?

Because conflicts over equal school funding and affirmative action generate so much publicity, they often obscure what many consider an even more fundamental educational issue in Texas. Economists and business leaders are beginning to believe more strongly that states wishing to compete successfully with other states for new and dynamic businesses must be willing to invest in a quality system of public education.[29] How have Texas policymakers responded to this challenge? A cursory look at educational spending suggests that they have not responded well. Texas teachers earn less than teachers in many other states. The average salary earned by public school teachers in all states in 2002–2003 was $45,930. In Texas, the comparable figure was $40,001.[30] Paying teachers less than the national average is a well-established pattern in Texas. Between 1975 and 2000, Texas teachers earned on average 10 percent less than the average salary earned by teachers in all states.[31] Texas also spends less per pupil than many other states to educate its students. The average spending per pupil for public education in all states for 2002–2003 was $7,829. The comparable figure for Texas was only $7,152.32.[32]

Defenders of the state's commitment to public education argue that it is unfair to judge the importance that Texas policymakers place on education by a superficial look at teacher salaries and per-student expenditures. They contend that when one takes into consideration the state's relatively low cost of living, its standing in terms of both teacher salaries and per-pupil expenditures improves considerably. They also note that salary increases for Texas teachers in recent years had brought these salaries, adjusted for state-to-state costs of living, to within 1 percent of the national average by 2001–2002.[33] Finally, defenders of the state's commitment to public education point out that in 2001, the Texas Legislature passed and Governor Perry signed into law a $1.24 billion school employee benefits package, creating the first statewide health insurance program for teachers.[34]

While consideration for the costs of living and providing educational services in Texas brings the Lone Star State close to national averages in both teacher salaries and per-pupil expenditures, it still leaves us in the bottom half of the megastates. As you can see from the data in Texas in Context 13.1, even when cost of living is taken into consideration, Texas still ranks last out of ten megastates in average teacher salaries.

Some defenders of the state's commitment to public education admit that Texas spends less than other states. They argue, however, that lower spending does not necessarily diminish the quality of public education in Texas. In defense of their argument, they point out that researchers have failed to establish any convincing link between educational spending and student achievement. In his summary of research on the relationship between educational spending and student performance, Gary Burtless notes in *Does Money Matter?* that several carefully designed studies have been unable to establish a close correlation between per-student spending and students' in-school performance.[35]

TEXAS in Context

13.1 Teacher Salaries Adjusted for Cost-of-Living Differences in Ten Megastates, 2001–2002

Megastate	Average Teacher Salary Adjusted for Cost of Living, 2001–2002	Average Teacher Salary, 2001–2002
Pennsylvania	$54,960	$50,599
Michigan	$53,822	$52,497
Illinois	$50,436	$49,679
Ohio	$46,953	$44,266
California	$46,043	$54,348
Texas	**$44,110**	**$39,230**
New York	$42,805	$51,020
Massachusetts	$42,051	$48,732
New Jersey	$41,540	$50,115
Florida	$41,401	$39,275

Source: Survey and Analysis of Teacher Salary Trends 2001–2002, American Federation of Teachers, 2003, available online at www.aft.org.

Proponents of the notion that money matters in achieving a quality education question research that denies a link between spending and school performance. They also note that some educational researchers have documented a correlation between per-student spending and out-of-school measures of student perform-ance. They point out, for example, that several studies confirm a significant rela-tionship between per-student spending and the amount of income students earn after they graduate from high school.[36]

Unfortunately, both studies that point to a link between educational spending and those that deny this link have serious methodological limitations. Researchers on both sides of this issue seem willing to concede, however, that if we knew the best places to spend additional money on education and if the money was actually spent where it should be, then additional funding would probably improve stu-dent performance. Until both these conditions are met, however, the fact that Texas spends less on education than many other states does not necessarily mean that the quality of education has suffered accordingly.

A comparison of test scores for Texas students with their counterparts in other states offers some support for this argument, particularly at the elementary school level. Every two years, the U.S. Department of Education conducts the National Assessment of Educational Progress (NAEP) exams to see how well fourth- and eighth-grade students across the country can read, write, and do math. According to the 2003 test results in math for fourth graders, Texas ranked in the top 10 percent of all states in the percentage of Anglo, Hispanic, and black students rated "at or above proficient." While less impressive than the math results, 2003 NAEP reading tests showed Texas ranked in the top third of all states in terms of the percentage of students scoring "at or above proficient."[37] The uniformly positive results one sees in fourth-grade tests of reading and math become more ambiguous when we look at NAEP test results for eighth graders. Texas still ranks among the top states in terms of the percentage of eighth-grade Anglo and black students who score "at or above proficient" in the NAEP reading test. But the state drops to the middle of the pack in terms of the percentage of Hispanic students "at or above proficient." And Texas is below the national average in terms of the percentage of its low-income students who score "at or above proficient." A similar picture of mediocre state performance is revealed by eighth-grade NAEP math scores. According to this data, Texas eighth graders rank no better than the national average, regardless of the racial or ethnic subcategory examined.[38]

Although generally Texas ranks in the top half or better of all states on NAEP reading and math tests, scores within the state vary tremendously by race, ethnicity, and social class. In the 2003 NAEP reading exam, for example, 39 percent of Anglo fourth graders scored at or above "proficient." The comparable figures for Hispanic and black students were 17 percent and 16 percent, respectively. Only 16 percent of Texas fourth graders participating in the Free or Reduced Price Lunch Program scored at or above the "proficient" level, compared to 43 percent of students who didn't participate in this program. As undesirable as these differences are between the performance of Anglo and minority students, Texas has done a better job than most states is narrowing these gaps.[39]

Because NAEP tests have not been given to twelfth graders or the results of these tests have not been sufficiently disaggregated, no reliable comparative assessment of Texas high school students is currently available. Some signs indicate, however, that Texas high schools may not be doing even as well as the state's elementary and middle schools. The state's public high school graduation rate has consistently ranked below the national average. Some studies suggest that as many as 40 percent of students entering the ninth grade in Texas high schools have dropped out by the twelfth grade.[40] Using a more conservative measure of high school dropouts, the Annie E. Casey Foundation estimates that 13 percent of high school–age students in Texas are dropouts. Even according to this measure, however, in 2000 Texas ranked forty-seventh out of fifty states in terms of high school dropouts.[41]

Texas high school students also fare badly compared to their counterparts in other states on standardized college admissions tests like the SAT. As you can see by looking at Texas in Context 13.2, the top 20 percent of college-bound seniors in Texas had SAT I scores that ranked them lower than their counterparts in any of the other megastates. For the latest year these figures were available, Texas's college-bound students ranked forty-seventh out of fifty states on this key indicator of college preparation.[42] Because most highly selective universities weigh these scores heavily in the admission process, Texas high school students are less likely than comparable students elsewhere to gain admission to the nation's best universities.

TEXAS in Context

13.2 Average SAT I Scores for the Top 20 Percent of College-Bound Seniors in Ten Megastates, 1999

Megastate	Average SAT I Score
Illinois	1243
Michigan	1205
Ohio	1171
Massachusetts	1164
New Jersey	1156
New York	1136
Pennsylvania	1127
California	1113
Florida	1107
Texas	**1096**

Source: Scores calculated from 1999 College-Bound Seniors Profile Reports by State, College Entrance Exam Board and Educational Testing Service, 1999, College Board, 2000.

Business and political leaders hoping to attract dynamic new high-tech industries to Texas realize that the state's commitment to higher education is as important as its commitment to good public schools. Dynamic new businesses are attracted to communities that are home to nationally prominent research universities capable of attracting federal research dollars.[43] How have Texas policymakers responded to this challenge? The evidence is mixed. The information in Texas in Context 13.3 shows that the average faculty salary in Texas public universities in 2000 was lower than that in all but one other megastate. In some cases, it was substantially lower. For most of the past quarter-century, Texas has also spent less per student than the national average.[44]

While Texas ranks below the national average in faculty salaries and per-student spending, state policymakers have invested sufficient resources in UT Austin and Texas A&M University at College Station to ensure that these institutions remain in the nation's top tier of research universities.[45] In 1987, Texas was one of the first states to establish large, publicly supported research funds specifically designed to encourage advanced research and technology development at state universities. Until recently, the advanced research and advanced technology programs provided $60 million every two years, primarily to researchers at Texas A&M and UT Austin.[46] By 2003, the legislature had cut back slightly on its commitment to these funds. But at the same time, it had committed $300 million over five years to make UT Dallas one of the nation's premier science and engineering schools.[47]

Although UT Austin and Texas A&M College Station have received sufficient support to rank among the nation's top public universities, most of the state's remaining

Texas in Context

13.3   Average Faculty Salary in Public Universities, 2000

Megastate	Average Faculty Salary
California	$71,208
New Jersey	$69,509
Michigan	$62,794
Pennsylvania	$62,051
Massachusetts*	$61,123
Ohio	$60,408
Illinois	$58,276
New York	$58,216
Texas	**$57,352**
Florida	$56,544

Source: "Average Faculty Salaries (AAUP) Texas and the Ten Most Populous States," Texas Higher Education Coordinating Board (http://www.thecb.state.tx.us); American Association of University Professors, 2001.

*The average salary in Massachusetts was calculated from data published in *Chronicle of Higher Education*, Almanac Edition (September 1, 2000).

Texas Academic Assessment System (TAAS) The educational accountability system used to measure public school performance in Texas until 2002. This system ranks schools according to their dropout rate, their attendance rate, and the percentage of students passing basic skills tests in reading, writing, and math.

Texas Assessment of Knowledge and Skills (TAKS) The Texas educational accountability system. It replaced TAAS in 2002.

universities have struggled to escape second- and third-tier status. Some indication of the gulf between the state's flagship universities and its other less prominent research universities can be seen by comparing UT Austin to the University of Houston. As you can see in Table 13.1, UT Austin, which has fewer than twice as many students as the University of Houston, has more than ten times as many National Merit scholars, awards three times as many doctorates, and receives nearly five times as much federal research money. The gulf between UT Austin and Texas A&M College Station and the other institutions within their respective systems is even greater. The gap between Texas A&M College Station and lesser schools in the A&M system is so great that faculty members on occasion refer to the system as Snow White and the Seven Dwarfs.

DOES THE TEXAS ACADEMIC ASSESSMENT SYSTEM DO MORE HARM THAN GOOD?

As every Texas schoolchild knows, the primary measure of his or her school's performance is the percentage of its students passing a series of standardized tests, the **Texas Assessment of Academic Skills (TAAS),** in reading, writing, and math. The TAAS exams have recently been replaced by the **Texas Assessment of Knowledge and Skills (TAKS).** [48] These standardized exams are at the heart of the educational

TABLE 13.1	A Comparative Look at the University of Texas at Austin and the University of Houston, 2003	
	University of Texas at Austin	University of Houston
Enrollment	50,000	26,024
Average SAT score	1230	1055
Acceptance rate	47 percent	78 percent
Graduation rate (after 6 years)	78 percent	39 percent
Freshman National Merit scholars	259	23
Doctorates awarded	668	202
Federal research grants (1998)	$250 million	$58 million

Source: Offices of Institutional Research at the University of Texas at Austin and the University of Houston.

accountability system in Texas. While simple enough in design, a system of educational accountability using standardized tests as the primary measure of school performance has been controversial since its inception.

Teachers dislike the idea of being assessed on the basis of how well their students perform on a single exam. Pointing out that disproportionate numbers of students in low-income schools fail, they see test results as an indication of the kind of students they teach rather than how well they teach.

Teachers are also unhappy with the drill-and-kill method of instruction that the tests increasingly require of them. Many parents are also unhappy with these tests. Parents of gifted and talented students dislike the fact that their children are bored by spending class time on a minimum-skills test they are able to pass by the eighth grade. Many minority parents are unhappy with a test that their children fail in disproportionate numbers. Is it possible that the test has an economic class bias? Some people think so.[49]

In 1995, the Mexican American Legal Defense and Education Fund (MALDEF), representing both Hispanic and African American students denied high school diplomas because they failed TAAS, challenged the constitutionality of the test in U.S. district court. Pointing to the inordinate numbers of Hispanic and African American students denied high school diplomas because of TAAS, MALDEF argued that the test was unconstitutional because it discriminated against minority students. Late in 1999, the court ruled that Texas was within its constitutional rights to require high school graduates to pass the TAAS.[50]

TAKS and TAAS have supporters as well as critics. Supporters claim that the tests have forced school administrators to put educational performance at the top of their agendas. School administrators now must reward effective teachers and eliminate ineffective ones. Supporters of standardized testing argue that it is directly responsible for the state's strong showing on national standardized tests like the NAEP.

While standardized testing has both harsh critics and strong supporters, it appears to be a permanent fixture of Texas public education. State legislators from both parties, as well as a coalition of powerful business interests, continue to be enthusiastic about a relatively simple and easy-to-understand method of educational accountability. Advocates of the system are now working to expand its scope, hoping soon to be able to use test results not only to identify weak and strong schools but also weak and strong teachers and programs within these schools.[51] One of the state's largest urban school districts is now linking its teacher pay directly to student performance on these tests.[52]

HOW MUCH SCHOOL CHOICE SHOULD WE HAVE IN TEXAS?

Not everyone is happy with the quality of education in Texas public schools. We have already noted the poor performance of minority students on both the state-mandated TAAS/TAKS and the NAEP exams. We have also noted the discontent of parents who have gifted and talented students in the state's public schools. Both groups have pushed hard for greater school choice in Texas, either in the form of a school **voucher program** or a **charter school** program.

A school voucher program provides a publicly funded voucher for use by every school-age child at a school of the parent's choice. Proponents of this system argue that it allows parents greater choice about where to educate their children. They also argue that by allowing parents to choose where to educate their children, public schools as well as private schools are forced to compete with each other for students. This competition, they argue, forces schools to become more efficient.[53]

A second alternative for allowing parents more choice in their child's education is a charter school program. As the name suggests, charter schools are schools chartered by the state to operate under a more relaxed set of regulations than is typically imposed on public schools. Free to teach math, reading, and writing skills however they wish, these schools are required only to meet minimal state curricular requirements and to demonstrate student performance on state-mandated measures of accountability. Proponents believe that by reducing state-imposed educational regulation, these schools will be free to experiment with new and more effective ways to educate children.[54] With few exceptions, groups or individuals outside traditional public school circles operate charter schools.

Popular with some groups, school choice programs are extremely controversial with others. Teachers and public school administrators in particular see school choice as an attack on public schools. Because **school choice programs** allow public education funds to be used by students at private institutions, critics fear these programs will drain much-needed resources from public schools. They also fear that private schools will lure away their strongest students, leaving public schools with a disproportionate number of hard-to-educate students. Finally, opponents of school choice fear that it will undermine the important role that public schools have played in exposing all students to a common set of core political values.[55]

Voucher program A program that provides a voucher valued at a predetermined dollar amount for each school-age child in the state. Parents are then free to use this voucher to pay for all or part of the costs of their child's education at a school of their choice.

Charter school A school chartered by the state to educate Texas school-children. These schools are free to operate with a minimum of state regulation as long as their students can demonstrate competence on state measures of accountability.

School choice programs Programs that allow public school students to attend schools other than their assigned public school.

WHAT CAN AND CANNOT BE TAUGHT IN TEXAS SCHOOLS?

This last political controversy is as old as education itself and as recent as the headlines of yesterday's newspaper. On March 30, 2000, newspapers across the country carried a headline like the following: "Football Prayer Issue Argued Before Supreme Court."[56] Since anyone can remember, prayer had been part of the pregame ceremony at Santa Fe High School near Galveston. But in 1995, two students, one Mormon and one Catholic, filed suit in federal court claiming that pregame school prayer and other religious practices at Santa Fe High were unconstitutional. After five years of appeals, the case was finally argued before the U.S. Supreme Court on March 29, 2000. At issue was whether Santa Fe's policy of student-initiated, student-led prayer at high school football games violated the First Amendment's mandate that "Congress shall make no law respecting an establishment of religion."

Since the 1950s, the U.S. Supreme Court has held that the establishment clause of the First Amendment prohibits efforts by public schools to promote religious instruction or practice.[57] Many religious fundamentalists have characterized the Court's position on this issue as an attempt to keep God out of the schools. In school districts where they compose a substantial portion of students or hold a significant majority of school board seats, fundamentalists have continued to interpret court decisions on religious freedom as narrowly as possible. The question the Supreme Court confronted in the Santa Fe case was whether permitting a student-led prayer over a school-owned public address system violated the wall between church and state established by prior Supreme Court decisions on this issue.[58] On June 19, 2000, the Court ruled by a 6–3 vote that it did.[59]

In Santa Fe, the debate is over school prayer. In other Texas school districts, the debate is about the relative merits of teaching creationism (or as it is sometimes called, creation science) versus the big bang theory and Darwin's theory of evolution. Many Texans believe that God created the universe approximately 6,000 years ago. Relying on a literal interpretation of the Bible, they believe that God created the universe and all its living creatures, including humans, in six twenty-four-hour days. They also believe that modern humans are the same beings God created 6,000 years ago. These views conflict with theories embraced by the vast majority of established scientists about how the universe formed and how humans came to be.

While not denying the possibility that God created the universe, modern astronomers and physicists overwhelmingly accept the view that the universe has existed for much longer than 6,000 years. Using radiometric and other time-measuring techniques, the vast majority of scientists have concluded that the universe is roughly 15 billion years old.[60] These same scientists argue that the universe was created in a single big bang explosion lasting only milliseconds.[61] Finally, these scientists have largely accepted Darwin's updated theory of evolution.[62]

When public school science teachers offer evolution and the big bang theory as explanations for the creation of the universe and modern humans, Texans who subscribe to a literal interpretation of the Bible object vociferously. They argue

---

JOIN THE DEBATE

THE ISSUE: Should creationism be taught alongside the theory of evolution in school science classes?

AGREE

1. The theory of evolution is really just an unproven hypothesis. As such, it should be taught alongside other competing hypotheses such as creationism.

2. Some scholars have pointed out that certain aspects of animal and human development contradict the evolution hypothesis. If certain realities of human or animal development don't fit, then evolution shouldn't be presented as a theory.

3. Like all matters of curriculum, the decision about whether to teach creationism as a science should be left to the local school board.

DISAGREE

1. No theory, including the theory of evolution, explains the real world perfectly. All scientific theories are characterized by certain anomalies.

2. What constitutes an accepted scientific theory is ultimately a consensus decision of the scientific community in a particular field. The same is true for the theory of evolution.

3. Decisions about what should be taught in science classes should be left to experts in this field of study. Among scientists who are experts in this field is an overwhelming consensus that the theory of evolution is the soundest explanation of the origins of the human species.

---

that unproven scientific theories are taught to schoolchildren as accepted facts. At the least, they argue, the biblical view of creation ought to be taught alongside its more scientifically accepted alternative. Science teachers respond to this argument by pointing out that scientists alone have the training to determine which of these competing views of creation is more accurate. They also argue that only explanations of creation embraced by the scientific community should be taught as part of the school's science curriculum.

Like most other decisions about what should be taught in Texas schools, decisions about which view of creation to teach are left largely to local school boards. Some school boards have prohibited the teaching of evolution and the big bang theory altogether. Other school boards have decided that creationism and its more scientifically accepted alternative should be given equal time in public school science classes. Still other school boards have relegated the teaching of creationism to social studies classes.

Much of the conflict over what should be taught in Texas schools appears as a struggle over textbook adoption. Political and social conservatives prefer textbooks that stress the desirability of sexual abstinence before marriage, emphasize traditional family values, and limit the pantheon of national heroes to traditional American icons such as Washington, Jefferson, and Lincoln. Political and social liberals prefer textbooks that include sex education, present homosexuality as an alternate lifestyle, and offer an ethnically and racially diverse pantheon of American heroes. Traditionally, textbook struggles have been fought at the state level in Texas. Members of the State Board of Education (SBOE) decided which textbooks public school students in all public school districts in Texas would use. In 1995, however, state legislators, under the banner of local control, shifted responsibility for textbook decisions to local school boards. This shift to local control did not sit well with conservatives, who were firmly in control of the SBOE by 1995.

A majority of conservative SBOE members believe that in the absence of state-level textbook adoption, Texas school districts are forced to choose among what they see as uniformly liberal textbooks produced primarily for the large California market. California is by far the single largest public textbook market in the country. Textbook publishers necessarily choose and shape textbooks that are likely to sell well there. In 1999, motivated by the desire to bring more traditional textbooks to Texas public schools, SBOE members tried to wrestle control of textbook decisions away from local school boards. Neither the state legislature nor the governor, however, was convinced that the SBOE's concerns were sufficient reason to undermine the principle of local school board autonomy. Without support from these key actors, the SBOE's effort to regain control of textbook selection died a quiet death. Whether made at the state or local level, however, decisions about what constitutes appropriate and important education will continue to be among the most volatile issues in the politics of education.

Key Actors in Educational Politics

Each of the educational conflicts described in this chapter involves various political actors. Some of these actors are formal government decisionmakers. Others are privately organized groups or coalitions that have a vested interest in these issues. Although several different actors play a role in determining educational issues, the particular mix of actors involved depends on the issue at hand. The school-funding issue, for example, involves local school boards, school administrators, TEA administrators, state and federal courts, and the state legislature. Curricular issues like evolution or sex education involve the SBOE, local school boards, and area religious institutions. Struggles over TAAS involve the state legislature, TEA administrators, teacher organizations, and key business leaders in the state. We examine these key actors and seek to explain how they interact with each other to determine the outcomes of political conflicts over educational issues.

THE STATE LEGISLATURE

Who ultimately decides the political conflicts that plague Texas education? First and foremost, state legislators do. The state legislature has consistently funded Texas public schools and universities at levels below the national average. In 1991, it passed legislation requiring implementation of an educational accountability system centered around standardized testing. In 1993, it worked out Senate Bill 7, which spelled out the details of wealth equalization between rich and poor school districts. In 1995, it passed legislation shifting textbook adoption decisions from the SBOE to local school boards. It reformulated admissions standards at state universities in 1997 to compensate for the deleterious consequences of the *Hopwood* decision on minority enrollment. Finally, it was the state legislature in 2003 that decided to deregulate tuition charged by public universities.

Both the state Senate and House have standing committees that specialize in educational issues, and members of these committees necessarily have more influence on education policy than other legislators do. The most influential voices on these committees are the committee chairs. In Texas, however, committee chairs serve at the discretion of the presiding officers in the Senate and House. Thus, the ultimate arbiters of public policy emerging from the state legislature are the lieutenant governor and the Speaker. Education policy is no exception to this general rule. Legislative leaders appoint education committee chairs who promote policies that have at least their tacit approval. The lieutenant governor and Speaker also exercise heavy influence on education policy through their leadership positions on the Legislative Budget Board (LBB), which has broad authority to influence legislative appropriations to education. It also plays a primary role in long-range educational planning.

STATE-LEVEL GOVERNING BOARDS

While the legislature answers broad policy questions about who gets what in Texas education, two state boards, one appointed and the other elected, provide rules and guidelines that direct day-to-day operations of the state's public schools and institutions of higher learning. The SBOE consists of fifteen members elected to four-year terms from single-member districts across the state. It establishes general policies and guidelines for the state's K–12 schools and recommends to the governor possible appointees for the position of commissioner of education.

Whereas the SBOE establishes general policies and guidelines for the state's K–12 schools, the Texas Higher Education Coordinating Board (THECB) establishes statewide policies for institutions of higher education in Texas. THECB is comprised of eighteen members appointed by the governor to six-year terms. As its title suggests, the board attempts to coordinate educational programs offered by the state's two- and four-year undergraduate institutions, as well as its many graduate and professional schools. It has primary responsibility for collecting and analyzing data on Texas universities and providing advice to state legislators contemplating changes in the state's higher education policies. The board approves new degree programs and recently defined forty-two hours of coursework that constitutes a common-core curriculum at all state universities. The board also administers state and federal grant programs for higher education in Texas and more recently has begun serving as an information clearinghouse for college-bound students.

UNIVERSITY BOARDS OF REGENTS

Although THECB coordinates policies for all higher education institutions in the state, each of the seven separate university systems within the state has its own governing board. The governor, with the consent of the Senate, appoints the members of these governing boards to six-year terms. Most of the appointed members of these governing boards are successful business and civic leaders, as well as established professionals who have some political tie to the governor or his or her party. By far, the most prestigious of these governing boards are the UT and A&M boards of regents. These boards have the last word regarding the number of admissions and criteria for admission, the educational priorities within each institution, the faculty who merit promotion and tenure, and, most important, the appointment of administrators who oversee the day-to-day operations of their institutions of higher education.

THE GOVERNOR

As is evident from the large number of gubernatorial appointments that play critical roles in both K–12 and higher education, the governor's influence on Texas education policy is constant, although rarely direct or telling. From time to time, however, Texas governors have played leading roles in shaping education policies. Their greatest influence has come from their ability to raise public awareness of the need for educational reform. In the 1980s, for example, Governor Mark White campaigned hard for increased teacher pay, greater emphasis on teacher competency, and implementation of the infamous no pass–no play policy, which prevented students, including athletes, from participating in after-school activities if they were failing a course. Because of the impact of this rule on the fortunes of high school football teams, it continues to generate controversy. Former Governor Bush championed increased teacher pay, as well as the need for greater school choice.

THE COURTS

Educational issues are inherently divisive. Not wanting to offend an important or vocal constituency, state legislators frequently shy away from making tough educational choices. When state legislators fail to address divisive educational issues seriously, the issues inevitably end up in state or federal courts. A U.S. district court rejected claims by minority groups that forcing students to pass the TAAS was unconstitutional. A U.S. circuit court of appeals finally halted affirmative action admissions in Texas universities. The U.S. Supreme Court ultimately determined whether student-led prayer before Santa Fe High School football games was constitutional. A state district court decision forced the state legislature to equalize school-district wealth in Texas, and another state district court decision forced the University of Texas and Texas A&M to divert millions of dollars to the South Texas Initiative. As these many examples illustrate, federal and state courts are major actors in educational politics.

LOCAL SCHOOL BOARDS

A board of trustees governs each of the 1,054 independent school districts in Texas. The school board, as it is commonly known, is typically composed of five, seven, or nine members elected by popular vote. Historically, voters in the district elected at-large school board members. In smaller, more racially and ethnically homogeneous communities, this system has worked relatively well and continues to this day. In larger, more racially and ethnically heterogeneous communities, the at-large election of school board members has been largely abandoned because it failed to provide adequate representation to ethnic and racial minorities. It was not unusual under the place system of electing school boards to see school districts where Hispanic and African Americans made up 30 to 40 percent of students in a school district without minority representation on the school board.

Because the place system election of school board members discriminated against racial and ethnic minorities, a series of federal court decisions in the 1970s and early 1980s forced Texas school districts with significant minority communities to elect school board members from geographical subunits (districts) within the larger school district. This reform has dramatically transformed the racial and ethnic makeup of school boards in Texas's largest cities. Hispanics and African Americans increasingly dominate school boards in Dallas, Houston, San Antonio, and El Paso, which had been largely dominated by upper-middle-class Anglos.

Regardless of their racial and ethnic makeup, local school boards have enjoyed considerable autonomy in deciding day-to-day policy issues in their schools. They have set personnel policies for school district employees, pay scales for teachers and administrators in the district, and district property tax rates. More recently, they have also provided the last word on textbook selection and curriculum issues. The school board's control over curriculum decisions has made it a major battleground over issues such as evolution and sex education. Last but certainly not least, the school board is responsible for hiring and firing the superintendent, who presides over the day-to-day administration of district policies and personnel.

SCHOOL AND UNIVERSITY ADMINISTRATORS

Working under the nominal direction of state and local governing boards are dozens of educational administrators. The TEA, staffed with over 200 educational administrators, is responsible for carrying out the broad educational directives of the legislature and the SBOE. The staff of the THECB is responsible for carrying out the wishes of the legislature and politically appointed board members. A rapidly growing number of administrators at each state university are charged with following the directives of the politically appointed boards of regents that govern each of these institutions.

As numerous scholars of bureaucracy have taught us, however, public administrators do more than carry out the decisions of their political superiors. Their near-monopoly on information, as well as the lack of educational experience most politically appointed and elected officials bring to office, allows educational administrators to play a central role in shaping state education policy. University presidents, for example, devote considerable time and institutional resources to lobbying legislators and university regents on everything from the need for new campus buildings to the importance of adequate faculty and administrative salaries.

Controlling the flow of information is not the only way educational administrators influence their democratically elected superiors. Typically prohibited from openly engaging in politics, educational administrators are frequently influential behind-the-scenes political actors. It is not uncommon, for example, for a popular principal or school superintendent to orchestrate the electoral defeat of an unsupportive school board member. Nor is it uncommon for educational administrators to make significant financial contributions to political candidates at the state and local levels. Several of the state's wealthiest campaign contributors, for example, are routinely courted by and enjoy special relationships with the University of Texas at Austin and Texas A&M University. Few candidates for statewide office want to risk alienating these power brokers by openly attacking institutions with which they are closely identified.

THE FACULTY

No discussion of education policymakers would be complete without some mention of teacher's organizations at both the public school and college levels. Yet in Texas, one could almost exclude these organizations from such a discussion. Because of state laws prohibiting collective bargaining and an anti-union culture in the state as a whole, faculty organizations have been extremely weak in Texas. Neither the Texas Faculty Association (TFA) nor the Texas Association of College Teachers (TACT), the two principal faculty organizations in Texas, has a membership that approaches even 10 percent of all faculty in the state. The Texas State Teachers Association (TSTA), the principal faculty organization for public school teachers, fares only slightly better than its higher education counterparts.

The organizational weakness of faculty associations in Texas has resulted in faculty salaries that are consistently below the national average. It has also resulted in less faculty involvement in school and university decisionmaking than one finds in many other states. University administrators in Texas rarely even pay lip-service to the concept of shared governance, in which administrators and faculty share decisionmaking authority on the college campus. Public school teachers fare just as poorly as their university counterparts when it comes to shared governance. In spite of educational reform legislation passed in the early 1990s, which required each public school to adopt a form of shared governance known as site-based management, most public school superintendents and principals continue to make key educational decisions unilaterally.

Summary

This chapter began by focusing on major political issues that have continued to define and redefine the nature of education in Texas. We looked first at the issue of equal opportunity in Texas schools and colleges, reviewing the bitter struggle between property-rich and property-poor schools over school finance. We examined the issue of affirmative action and the impact of the *Hopwood* and *Grutter* decisions on admissions programs in Texas universities. Next, we looked at the question of how the quality of education in Texas compares to that in other states. Although Texas falls below the national average in both per-pupil spending and teacher salaries, elementary schoolchildren in Texas have scored above average on national reading and math tests. This better-than-average educational performance falls off significantly, however, as elementary students move on to high school. By the time Texas high school graduates apply to college, they have some of the lowest SAT scores in the nation. Next, we looked at the debate over the issue of school choice and discussed charter schools and school vouchers as possible ways of expanding educational choice in Texas. Although voucher programs offer the greatest degree of school choice, charter schools have attracted much broader political support. Finally, we took up the question of what can and cannot be taught in Texas schools. We looked at the ongoing struggles between religious fundamentalists and their opponents over issues such as school prayer and evolution.

We next focused on the key actors who shape education policy in Texas. The Texas Legislature plays a critical role in deciding how to finance education. State-level governing boards such as the State Board of Education, the university boards of regents, and the Texas Higher Education Coordi-

nating Board play important roles. Popular elections determine membership on the first of these boards, and gubernatorial and legislative appointments determine membership on the latter two boards. In addition, the governor, state and federal courts, and local school boards have educational policy-making roles. The particular mix of actors involved in any educational issue depends on the nature of the issue.

Regardless of the set of actors involved in any single issue, citizens have great opportunities to make a significant impact on education policy in Texas. By design, education policy in Texas is shaped largely in democratic institutions. School boards typically meet several times a year, often once a month, to set policy on a wide range of issues. These meetings are open to the public, and citizens interested in education policy have ample opportunity to express their concerns to board members. Without great expense, a citizen interested in education policy may choose to run for a seat on the school board. School board elections are characterized by voter turnout rates that often fall below 15 percent of the eligible electorate. A candidate who speaks about issues that concern even a relatively small circle of citizens has a reasonable chance of winning a seat on the local school board.

The State Board of Education is also an elected body. Here again, low voter turnout rates for these offices mean that even minimal political activism can have a significant impact on SBOE members. The state legislature, the ultimate arbiter of education policy in Texas, is also a democratically elected body. Most citizens interested in education policy will not have the energy or resources to seek a seat in this institution. Nearly all state legislators, however, establish local committees to advise them on educational issues. Membership on these committees is frequently open to all who ask.

Educational decisions are important because they influence the distribution of economic and social opportunities available to Texas schoolchildren. The institutions making these educational decisions provide numerous avenues of participation to citizens interested in these issues. If Bea Salazar, starting with nothing more than a peanut butter and jelly sandwich, was able to fashion an after-school program that has affected the lives of hundreds of at-risk children in her neighborhood, each of us can make a difference in the quality of Texas education.

KEY TERMS

Plessy v. Ferguson, p. 363
Brown v. Board of Education of Topeka, Kansas, p. 363
San Antonio School District v. Rodriguez, p. 364
Edgewood v. Kirby, p. 364
Robin Hood measure, p. 364
Affirmative action programs, p. 365
Hopwood **decision,** p. 366
Grutter v. Bollinger, p. 366

Permanent University Fund (PUF), p. 366
Higher Education Assistance Fund, p. 366
South Texas Initiative, p. 367
Texas Assessment of Academic Skills (TAAS), p. 372
Texas Assessment of Knowledge and Skills (TAKS), p. 372
Voucher program, p. 374
Charter school, p. 374
School choice programs, p. 374

FOR FURTHER READING

Berliner, David, and Bruce Biddle, *The Manufactured Crisis* (Reading, Mass.: Addison-Wesley Publishing Company, 1995).

Bowen, William, and Derek Bok, *The Shape of the River: Long-Term Consequences of Considering Race in College and University Admissions* (Princeton, N.J.: Princeton University Press, 1998).

Glickman, Carl, ed., *Letters to the Next President: What We Can Do About the Real Crisis in Public Education* (New York: Columbia University Press, 2004).

Ravitch, Diane, *Left Back: A Century of Failed School Reforms* (New York: Simon & Schuster, 2000).

Rochester, J. Martin, *Class Warfare: Besieged Schools, Bewildered Parents, Betrayed Kids, and the Attack on Excellence* (San Francisco, Calif.: Encounter Books, 2002).

STUDY QUESTIONS

1. Name four important court cases that have shaped the history of education policy in Texas during the past century.

2. Identify at least three forms of affirmative action that have been practiced in Texas universities during the past quarter-century.

3. Identify the two principal forms of school choice discussed in Texas education circles.

4. Name at least three different issues that serve as points of conflict for policymakers trying to decide what can and cannot be taught in Texas schools.

5. Identify at least four major actors who play critical roles in shaping education policy in Texas.

CRITICAL THINKING QUESTIONS

1. Briefly discuss the reasons that educational issues often become political controversies. In addition to those offered in this chapter, provide at least one concrete example of an educational issue that has become a political controversy, and explain why.

2. Briefly explain how relying on property taxes to fund public education can lead to inequality in school resources. How has Texas attempted to remedy this problem?

3. Briefly describe the policies that educational decisionmakers have used to increase the number of minorities attending colleges and universities in Texas. What are some of the advantages and disadvantages of these policies?

4. Identify the issues emphasized by critics who charge that policymakers have failed to make quality education a high priority in Texas. What issues do challengers to this claim point to?

5. Identify and briefly discuss the programs that policymakers use to expand school choice for Texas schoolchildren. What are some of the main arguments for and against these programs?

INTERNET RESOURCES

nces.ed.gov/nationsreportcard/site/home.asp
The National Assessment of Educational Progress home page provides a comprehensive and detailed explanation of all aspects of this nationwide testing program.

www-bushschool.tamu.edu/kmeier/teep/   The Texas Educational Excellence Project is a joint program of Texas A&M and the University of Texas, Panamerican. The program is dedicated to original research on the quality and equity of education in Texas.

www.tea.state.tx.us/   The Texas Education Agency home page contains a wealth of basic information on Texas public schools. It offers current press releases, summaries of school law, descriptions of special-education programs in state schools, and information on school finance and grants.

www.thecb.state.tx.us/   The Higher Education Coordinating Board home page offers a wide range of information on Texas colleges and universities, including information about student enrollments, student financial aid, and special-education programs in state universities.

nces.ed.gov/index.html/   The National Center for Educational Statistics is the primary source of statistical information about American education. This home page has links to almost all government agencies collecting statistical information on American schools and universities.

www.NEA.org/   The National Educational Association is the largest teacher organization in the United States. Its home page offers a plethora of information for parents, teachers, and students, including updates on school reforms, new reading and math programs, and bilingual education.

www.tea.state.tx.us/perfreport/aeis/index.html
The Academic Excellence Indicator System is maintained by the Texas Education Agency and provides parents, teachers, and education policymakers with detailed performance data on every school and school district in Texas.

www.edweek.org/   *Education Week* is a popular weekly online publication designed to help raise the level of awareness and understanding among professionals and the public about important issues in American education. It covers local, state, and national news and issues from preschool through the twelfth grade.

The Budget

In late 1998, oil prices were approaching the lowest in decades. For John Bell, this economic reality meant that the wells on his drought-stricken ranch were becoming a liability rather than an asset. The state of Texas charged $4.60 per barrel of oil pumped out of the ground by each well. Because this severance tax was only one of several costs involved in pumping oil (like drilling and exploration costs), it meant that Bell would soon have to consider capping his wells, another expense but one that would stop the losses. Like the wells on many other ranches in West Texas, Bell's were not large producers. In good times, when a barrel brought $40.00, the costs could easily be covered; however, Bell received less than $10.00 a barrel for weeks at a time.[1]

After calling his state legislators and U.S. congressional representatives and sending a note to the Texas Railroad Commission, Bell decided to make the public aware that not all oil-well owners were fabulously wealthy. He called a few friends around Winkler County and beyond and organized a march on Austin. The goal he and the other marchers sought was to build some flexibility in the severance tax. They wanted the tax cut or cancelled if the price of oil dropped below $15.00 a barrel. On January 19, 1999, more than 300 demonstrators marched through downtown Austin to the state capitol to deliver their message.[2]

Someone was listening. A few months later, the state legislature passed a severance tax relief bill by an overwhelming margin, and Governor Bush signed it as soon as it was delivered to his desk. Bell and his marchers had a lot of help: the governor was an oil producer too; so were many legislators; and Exxon-Mobil, Texaco, and others stood to gain some tax relief too. Nevertheless, Bell helped humanize the issue. His demonstration is another example of the fact that individuals can make a difference in Texas politics, and that they usually do not act alone. Their action is essential for the system to continue to be representative of the people. Without Bell's participation, the severance tax reduction effort might have failed in the legislature as a rich man's tax relief bill.

With the price of oil well over $40 dollars a barrel, John Bell's story may seem a little out of date; however, the essentials aren't. One individual made a difference. He also made life better for a lot of wealthy Texans as well as people of modest means who happen to own oil wells. Bell's story illustrates a permanent feature of Texas politics. On many issues, rich and poor Texans are on the same side. The taxes of many wealthy people would go up if we had a fairer tax system. Nevertheless, they support changes to make it fairer. Many people of modest means support tax policies that clearly benefit the well-to-do. They do so not out of self interest but because they uncritically accept the trickle-down view of economics.

Understanding the Budget

Budget A specific itemized monetary plan. It consists of one or more laws that oblige citizens to provide revenue for the government, and oblige government employees to use that revenue in certain ways.

Later in this chapter, in the Join the Debate feature, we will present you with two opposing approaches: percolate up—one that supports the notion that if you give tax breaks to ordinary working folk they will do things that lead to economic expansion; and trickle down—one that promotes the notion that only in the hands of the wealthy do tax breaks lead to economic expansion. The first is associated with a progressive system of taxation, based on the ability to pay. The second requires a regressive system to take tax money from the many to provide a luxurious lifestyle and investment opportunities for the few.

Before we get into that, however, we will present a broader view of how budgets work and some useful terms and concepts for discussing budget and tax policy. A **budget** is a specific itemized monetary plan. It consists of one or more laws that oblige citizens to provide revenue for the government and oblige government employees to use that revenue in certain ways. The budget is produced when legislatures exercise their parliamentary functions of taxing and spending.

It is important to understand that the funds used by government are part of the overall economy. To provide services for the other actors in the economy and to make sure the economy provides a more or less level playing field for businesses small and large, as well as for consumers and employees, government must have the resources to do its job.

It is also important to note that one of the often overlooked facts of life about taxes is that Texans live in a state that puts a minimal burden on its economy, and they live in a country that does the same. On average, Americans are the most lightly taxed people in the industrial world (see Figure 14.1). To say that we are lightly taxed "on average" says little, however, about the burden placed on the ordinary working family. Before we examine that issue, we will discuss the components of a budget and the way it is produced.

Appropriations The portion of the budget that spends money. A single proposed expenditure may be called an appropriation.

The portion of the budget that spends money is usually called **appropriations,** and it consists of one or several appropriations bills. Different agencies of government spend the money and report to the state auditor how they spent it.

State and local governments in Texas have many different sources of revenue. However, a significant portion comes from a system of taxes. The state government determines which taxes local governments can use and how they can use them.

FIGURE 14.1   National, State, and Local Tax Revenue as a Percentage of Gross Domestic Product, Selected Countries

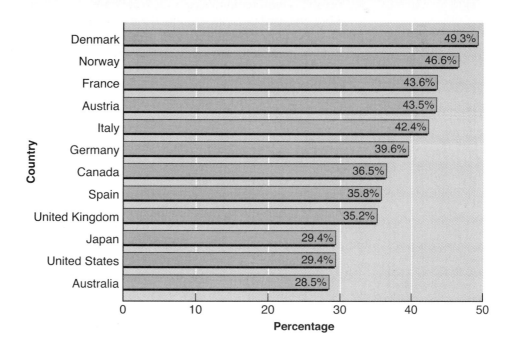

Cities and counties can use the sales tax; school districts cannot. School districts, however, can tax property at a higher rate than other units of government can.

Tax expenditure An analytical tool useful to policymakers and the general public that attempts to put a dollar figure on the tax breaks that special interests have obtained from government or that government has decided are beneficial public policy.

The concept of **tax expenditure** is an analytical tool that is useful to policymakers and the general public.[3] Tax expenditure attempts to put a dollar figure on the tax breaks that special interests have obtained from government or that government has decided are beneficial public policy. It treats money not collected in taxes, and thus money missing from the treasury, as money that has been "spent" by giving the tax breaks. The Texas Legislature now requires the comptroller to prepare an annual report on the value of "each exemption, exclusion, special rate, deduction, and discount available under Texas tax laws."[4] In Chapters 5 and 7, you studied the role of interest groups in seeking laws that grant tax exemptions, so you are well aware of the importance of these gifts from government to special interests.

Note that some of these gifts are the result of the application of common sense. For example, the sales-tax exemption on the purchase of food stamps by the poor is not taxed. This exemption costs the treasury $139 million. This amount pales, however, in comparison to the exemption of food for home consumption, which reduces the treasury by $1.2 billion. The homestead exemption, which means that each homeowner receives a property-tax break, costs the state treasury $1.1 billion. In recent years, the legislature has begun to look carefully at many of these exemptions during each legislative session.[5]

Fiscal note A requirement that each proposed bill containing tax relief, as well as bills proposing expenditures, have a report attached that provides the effective cost to the treasury of Texas.

Incidence Another way of saying impact, it means the effect of a tax on different income categories. We use the concept of tax burden in our text, the comptroller's "incidence" deals with the same idea.

Another change is worth noting. After years of lobbying by organizations such as Common Cause and the Texas Alliance for Human Needs, the Texas House of Representatives has included within its rules a requirement that each proposed bill containing tax relief, as well as bills proposing expenditures, have a report attached that provides the effective cost (how much revenue is lost) to the treasury of Texas. This requirement is called a **fiscal note.**

Although it isn't discussed much in the media, another improvement in the way the budget is treated is that the comptroller now reports the effect of changes on different income categories. You can find this information on the comptroller's website. The comptroller uses the term *incidence*, which means the effect of a tax on income categories.

The Budget-Making Process

When you studied the legislative process in Chapter 8, you covered many of the essential steps in creating a government budget. Both the executive branch and the legislative branch are involved in budget making. One of the facts about taxing and spending that often escapes our attention is that both are laws. Each tax or appropriation exists because a bill was passed by the legislature and either signed by the governor or allowed to become law without his or her signature.

Fiscal year The 365-day period that the state uses to open and close the books on a year's worth of expenditures and revenue collections. It is usually different from the calendar year.

You may recall that the legislature passes a biennial budget. This budget covers two fiscal years. In Texas, the **fiscal year** begins on September 1. A fiscal year is the year the state uses to open and close the books on a year's worth of expenditures and revenue collections. Thus, a fiscal year covers parts of two calendar years.

The 2003–2004 fiscal year started on September 1, 2003, and ended on August 31, 2004. It was the first year of the biennial budget passed by the Seventy-Eighth Texas Legislature in May 2003.

GATHERING INFORMATION

You learned in Chapter 8 that the constitution and laws in Texas do not allow the governor of Texas to control the budget as governors do in many other megastates. Nevertheless, the governor of Texas does have some influence on the budgetary process not only because of the importance of the political and executive roles he or she plays but also because sharing power is still more significant than having none at all. In the budgetary process, the governor and the legislature share power. To some extent, they share it with the comptroller, who must certify that enough revenue will be available to pay for the budget that the legislature proposes.

In March of even-numbered years, the staffs of the Legislative Budget Board (LBB) and the governor's Office of Budget and Planning (OBP) issue guidelines to state agencies calling for their budget submissions. When the numbers from the various agencies are added, they indicate every agency's wish list that will have to be pared down.

During the spring and summer, LBB and OBP staff members hold hearings with individual agencies to discuss the budget requests. In the autumn, the joint appearances end. The LBB and the OBP begin the task of creating the budget that will be presented by its branch of state government. You may not hear much about this process in the news because even-numbered years are election years. However, people who are concerned with how much money the government will tax or spend in the next two years take a great deal of interest in the activities of the LBB and the OBP.

THE GOVERNOR'S BUDGET

The OBP draws up a budget for the governor to present to the legislature. This budget reflects the priorities the governor campaigned on and plans to address early in the legislative session through the budget message. Shortly after the governor's budget speech, a member of the legislature who is friendly to the governor introduces and sponsors the bills that make up the governor's budget. The bill or bills are assigned numbers and sent to the appropriate committees, where hearings are held and the legislative process begins. While some bills in the governor's budget package may set the agenda for legislative hearings, the governor's budget is more often a standard for comparison when it comes time for the governor to respond to the budget bill that emerges from the legislative process.

THE LEGISLATIVE BUDGET

The LBB, led by the lieutenant governor, the Speaker, and the chairs of the relevant committees in each house, prepares the budget that will be the focus of attention in the legislative session. After the hearings and the agency budgets have been submitted, the LBB staff consolidates the submissions into a smaller number of budgets. The LBB leaders discuss their options in terms of areas that need increased spending, recent suggestions for saving money from the comptroller's office, and revenue sources. Then they agree on the budget bill or bills that will be introduced in the legislature.

The legislature's budget is introduced and assigned a number or numbers. The presiding officers of each house send the bill or bills to one or more committees, and the legislative process begins. After months of hearings, meetings, negotiations, and compromises, a single bill or a series of budget bills emerge for the governor's signature. The governor may veto one or more of the bills, veto specific line items, allow the budget to become law without signature, or sign the budget bill or bills into law.

THE ROLE OF THE COMPTROLLER OF PUBLIC ACCOUNTS

Any discussion of the Texas budget-making process would be incomplete without mentioning the comptroller. Like the governor and other major officeholders, the comptroller is elected in the general election in November and is a prominent actor in the Texas political system as well as the budget-making process. Not only is the comptroller in charge of collecting taxes, which provide almost 45 percent of the revenue for the budget, but he or she has also taken on many of the functions of the office of the treasurer, which was abolished by constitutional amendment in 1996. The most significant role of the comptroller in the budgetary process is certification. A budget cannot be submitted to the governor until the comptroller has certified that enough revenue will be available in the budget to cover the proposed expenditures.

Over the years, comptrollers have been able to acquire sufficient funds from the legislature to create a formidable computerized research facility. Starting with Bob Bullock in the 1980s, comptrollers have been able to make the case that "the more staff and equipment you give me, the more taxes I can collect for you to spend." The legislature depends heavily on the comptroller's various reports and studies that indicate the condition of the economy, the effect of expenditures—past and projected, and the effect of changes in the tax system.

In the 2003 legislative session, the independence of the comptroller became such a bother to the governor, the Speaker, and the lieutenant governor that a bill was passed to reduce the responsibilities of the comptroller. That they did not do more is perhaps an indication of their awareness of the fact that the comptroller must certify the budget before the legislature passes it and the governor signs it.[6]

THE JUDICIAL PROCESS

As you learned in Chapter 10, the courts do not intervene in public policy until asked to do so. Thus, the courts become involved in the budget when someone believes strongly that a tax or an appropriation is either in conflict with another law or with the U.S. or the Texas Constitution. This conflict happens often enough for the legislature to be concerned about court cases when they relate to the budget. From time to time, the Texas Courts have declared taxes and expenditures unconstitutional. Recently, a District Court Judge declared the method of financing public schools in Texas to be unconstitutional. This will mean an appeal to the Supreme Court and perhaps several sessions for Texas legislators until the isssue is resolved. If a public official violates the law in the course of levying, collecting, or distributing tax revenue, that official may be sued in court or may be subject to criminal prosecution.

Appropriations

Table 14.1 provides the expenditures for 2003 as reported by the comptroller. The table shows that the cost of running the three branches of government is a

TABLE 14.1 Fiscal Year 2003 Net Expenditures, by Function		
Function	**Amount**	**Percentage**
General government		
Executive departments	$ 1,708,529,827	2.8
Legislative	$ 120,862,790	0.2
Judicial	$ 174,875,112	0.3
Total general government	$ 2,004,267,729	3.3
Education	$20,833,500,871	34.6
Employee benefits	$ 3,149,514,386	5.2
Health and human services	$22,880,243,122	38.0
Public safety and corrections	$ 3,390,806,656	5.6
Transportation	$ 4,933,545,512	8.2
Natural resources		
Recreational services	$ 1,386,770,543	2.3
Regulatory services	$ 241,769,248	0.4
Lottery winnings paid	$ 413,873,103	0.7
Debt service	$ 626,202,105	1.0
Capital outlay	$ 409,954,687	0.7
Total net expenditures	$60,270,447,962	

Source: Texas Comptroller of Public Accounts, "Texas Expenditure History by Function, 1978–2003," Window on State Government, www.window.state.tx.us/taxbud/expend.html (accessed March 7, 2004).

relatively small portion of the budget (3.3 percent). The legislature accounts for a relatively small portion of that amount (0.2 percent of the total budget). Nevertheless, Texans have yet to pay legislators salaries comparable to those paid to legislators in the other megastates. If they were to do so, the dollar amount would still be a minute portion of the state budget.

The top four state government expenditure areas in Texas, as in most other states, are education, health and human services, transportation, and public safety and corrections. Funds for economic development and other activities that promote the economic well-being of the state are found within some of the major spending categories, such as transportation, natural resources, and health and human services. The connection between money spent on education and a well-prepared workforce as an attraction to business is a well-known fact.

EDUCATION

Primary and secondary education receive about three-fifths of the total amount of more than $20 billion, about 34.6 percent of the total budget; the remaining two-fifths (the rest of that percentage) is distributed among the institutions of higher education. The money to be spent by the state in the 2004–2005 period is more than it has ever been.

Nevertheless, this sum represents a smaller percentage of the state budget than the amount spent on education in most previous years; more important, it represents a reduced percentage of the total cost of education. The state of Texas contributes less than 50 percent of the cost when it should contribute, as many observers maintain, about 60 percent of the cost of education. When Governor Perry and the legislative leadership pledged not to increase taxes, they meant state taxes. Local property taxes have increased in many districts to make up for the failure of the state to find tax resources to pay for a growing school population.

HEALTH AND HUMAN SERVICES

Although more attention was given, perhaps, to redistricting in the last regular session of the legislature than to the budget, it did get some coverage. In the view of many observers, that budget was somewhat less than compassionate. Cartoonist Ben Sargent wasn't the only one who believed that the "no new taxes" mantra of the Republican leadership had gone too far. Carole Keeton (Rylander) Strayhorn, a Republican and also the comptroller, agreed:

> In health and human services, like education, Texas is abdicating its responsibilities. And ignoring state challenges is creating local crises. The numbers continue to come in. They are shocking, and they only will get worse if we don't act. At the end of the last regular legislative session, decisions were made that left Texas dead last among states in the percentage of children who have health insurance. And new numbers show that 107,000 children have been dropped from the Children's Health Insurance Program since the beginning of the fiscal year. That's a 21 percent drop in five months.[7]

Sargent © 2004 Austin American-Statesman. Reprinted with permission of Universal Press Syndicated. All Rights Reserved.

While this spending category (health and human services) is the largest, at 38 percent, it is worth noting two characteristics about it. First, about 50 percent of the expenditures in health and human services come from federal matching funds. In other words, of the amount that policymakers in Texas allocate to help each of our less fortunate citizens, only half comes from the state treasury. Should the leadership of Texas choose to allocate more, the federal government would match the figure dollar for dollar.

Second, as Comptroller Strayhorn implies, Texas does not rank high in terms of providing for the less fortunate. Nationally, Texas ranks last in the distribution of food stamps and benefits assistance to needy families.[8]

TRANSPORTATION

Although some of the expenditures for highways come out of the general fund (9 percent of the general budget), most of the money spent on highways comes from a special fund protected by a 1946 amendment to the Texas Constitution. Three-fourths of the money collected from motor fuel taxes goes into this fund, which can be spent only on highways. The interest group that lobbied for the special fund protected by a constitutional amendment, the Good Roads Association, has had a significant impact on transportation policy and budget making. It also is an excellent example of the power of interest groups in Texas.

The legislature and governor are limited in their ability to plan for the transportation needs of the state by the fact that a great deal of the money available must be spent only on highways. Funds for light rail or other solutions to transportation problems confronting the state must come out of the general fund. Because a large amount of money is already dedicated to highways and because so many other needs and programs are underfunded, little enthusiasm can be generated for finding additional transportation funds.

PUBLIC SAFETY AND CORRECTIONS

The largest prison population in the nation is funded by the public safety and corrections portion of the budget (6 percent of the total budget), as are law enforcement and highway safety programs. In this area, as in education, the state contribution is matched by local taxes to pay for sheriff and police departments and the local court systems. Local governments even contribute to the costs of state district courts. The Texas Legislature is not a place where lightening the burdens of local governments is a high priority.

Revenues

As in most other states, revenue comes from sources other than taxes. In Texas, the largest of the big three sources of the state's revenue is the tax system (see Table 14.2). Later in this chapter, we will examine some ways to make that system more fair and more effective.

NONTAX REVENUES

The two major nontax revenues for the states are classified in Table 14.2 as "federal transfers" and "other sources." No single category in "other sources" brings in as much as 10 percent of the state's revenue.

Intergovernmental transfer Funds allocated from one unit of government to another.

Federal Transfers.   Money allocated from one unit of government to another is an **intergovernmental transfer.** The money that a city receives from county government to pay for libraries or fire protection is an intergovernmental transfer. The best-known form of intergovernmental transfer, however, is the grant-in-aid from the federal government. Federal grants-in-aid are distributed to the 80,000 state and local governments and from states to their local governments. As Table 14.2 indicates, the state of Texas received over $20 billion, or about 36 percent of total state revenues, from the federal government in fiscal year 2003. This figure was more than the amount raised in Texas by any single tax source.

TABLE 14.2	Texas Revenues by Source, Fiscal Year 2003	
Revenue Sources	**Amount**	**Percentage**
Total taxes	26,126,675,424	44.81
Federal transfers	20,975,686,726	35.97
Other sources (see details below)	11,207,595,130	19.22
Total revenue	58,309,957,280	100.00
Other sources: details		
Licenses, fees, permits, fines, and penalties	4,785,122,813	8.2
Interest and investment income	1,574,674,327	2.7
Net lottery proceeds	1,405,554,179	2.4

Source: Texas Comptroller of Public Accounts, Texas Revenue History by Source, 1978–2003, www.window.state.tx.us/taxbud/revenue.html (accessed February 27, 2004).

Benefits theory An approach to financing government that assigns the costs of services to those who benefit from them. The problem is in apportioning benefit.

Licenses, Fees, Permits, Fines, and Penalties. Some services are best paid for, at least in part, by those who benefit from them. However, in practice, **benefits theory** is hard to apply with certainty. Families with children are not the only part of society to benefit from education for these children.

Parking fees, the use of overnight facilities in a state park, and tuition at a state university are examples of services that are paid for, in addition to the taxes that are paid, by those who directly benefit from a service or facility. People in various occupations pay a license fee for the privilege of doing business in the state. For many occupations, such as attorneys or certified public accountants, this method is easier than collecting a sales tax on the services they offer, keeping track of it, and then sending it to the state.

The 2003 legislative session found ways besides levying new taxes to balance the budget. Instead, legislators cut services and instituted new fees, such as a $30.00 parking ticket and a fee that single parents must pay to the attorney general before he or she looks for their deadbeat spouses. Some of the new fees, charges, and out-of-pocket expenses for the two-year period include:

- Teachers and school employees: $1.08 billion, including $1,000 less per teacher for insurance premiums.
- Health care: $596 million, including $4.8 million in fees for rural doctors.
- Children: $71.5 million, including $57.9 million in increased costs for CHIP participants.
- Businesses and professionals: $36.4 million, including $3.9 million in new state regulation fees for a wide range of business and industry professionals.[9]

Borrowing.   Many government facilities and some programs are paid for with borrowed money, particularly at the local level, in Texas. In most cases, borrowing means that the unit of government sells bonds to institutions and individuals and promises to pay them back with interest. This interest is then exempt from federal taxation.

Whenever a unit of state or local government borrows money to do something (perhaps build a school) instead of raising taxes or finding some other way to pay for it, U.S. taxpayers help fund it. According to Robert Heilbroner and Peter Bernstein, in their readable book on the federal debt: "Government debt [borrowing by selling bonds] is a net expense for the lower three quarters of [income earners in] the nation and a net benefit for the upper one quarter."[10] Thus, borrowing is usually a subsidy for the wealthy paid for by everyone else. This feature gives additional insight to the refusal of the leadership of Texas to raise state taxes to help local governments pay for new schools, clinics, roads, and hospitals. As a result, local governments must borrow or raise taxes.

Lottery.   Some people see the lottery as a painless way to gain revenue for worthy projects such as education. Others see it as inefficient because the state treasury ends up with barely 35 percent of the money collected. Many feel that it is an extra temptation on the scarce resources of the poor. In 2003, less than 2.5 percent of the state's revenue came from the Texas Lottery.

TAX REVENUES

In 2004, the state of Texas obtained less than half of its revenue from the taxes listed in Table 14.3. Missing from this list is a personal income tax, which is used by forty-three other states. We examine the issues surrounding the personal income tax later in the chapter.

From Table 14.3, you can easily appreciate the heavy dependence of state government on sales taxes. In addition to the $14.6 billion in general sales taxes, the next tax revenue sources include seven taxes that are also sales taxes. The observation that 86.8 percent of the tax revenue for the state is raised by sales taxes is an understatement. Sales taxes (for example, taxes on the sale of mobile homes) constitute many of the taxes that raise $44 million in "other sources" of taxes.

General Sales Tax.   The general sales tax is a tax on items sold by retail establishments. In each legislative session, various interest groups seek exemptions for goods or services they purchase or sell. During the last serious effort to reform the tax system (in 1997), the comptroller reported to the Select Committee on School Finance that more than 34,000 items or organizations were exempt from the general sales tax.[11]

When the sales tax was enacted in 1961, food for home consumption was exempted. This exemption (in addition to exemptions for medicine) somewhat reduces the burden that the sales tax places on the poor and middle class. The next time you visit the supermarket, note how many of the items you purchase that, though necessary, are not food and thus are taxed.

TABLE 14.3	Estimated Texas Tax Collections for 2004, by Major Tax Source	
Tax Sources	**Amount in Thousands of Dollars**	**Percentage of Total**
Sales	14,695,803	56.0
Motor fuel sales	2,886,449	11.0
Motor vehicle sales	2,802,460	10.7
Franchise	1,777,552	6.8
Insurance sales	1,007,093	3.8
Natural gas	923,750	3.5
Tobacco sales	495,894	1.9
Alcoholic beverage sales	574,527	2.2
Oil production	358,911	1.4
Inheritance	112,480	0.4
Utility sales	337,274	1.3
Hotel occupancy	236,333	0.9
Other sources	44,657	0.2
Total	26,253,183	

Source: Texas Comptroller of Public Accounts, 2004–2005 Certification Revenue Estimate, window.state.tx.us.80/taxbud/cre0405/tablea16.html (accessed February 26, 2004).

Property Tax. The property tax is a tax on items owned. The state government does not use this tax but local governments do. This tax focuses on land and improvements on the land rather than on household furnishings or personal items. Some jurisdictions annually tax motor vehicles. The property tax collected by the several thousand school districts, municipalities, counties, and special districts in Texas produces about 40 percent of the tax revenue collected by state and local government.[12]

Excise Taxes. Excise taxes are also known as selective sales taxes, and some—but not all—are referred to as sin taxes. They are sales taxes on specific items such as tobacco products and alcoholic beverages (the so-called sin taxes), jewelry, motor vehicles and fuels, and motel and hotel room rentals. They constitute nearly one-third of the state's tax revenue. While general sales taxes can be levied by local governments in addition to the 6.25 percent that the state levies, they have not been given permission by the Texas Legislature to use excise taxes.

Franchise Tax. The franchise tax is paid by corporations that do business in Texas, whether their home base is here in Texas or not. The tax is based on the higher of two amounts: 4.5 percent of profits (*or* income) or 0.25 percent of net worth (buildings, refineries, electric generators, manufacturing plants, etc.). The fact that corporations pay a tax on profits and other businesses do not is one of several reasons that the Texas tax system is considered by many observers (liberal and conservative, Democrat and Republican) to be unfair.[13]

Severance Taxes.   The severance tax is levied on the removal of natural resources from the earth (so-named because people are breaking the connection between the earth and the natural resources found on or within it). Oil production, gas, coal, and stone quarries are the resources that yield most of this revenue. The severance tax used to be a major source of revenue for the state. In 1981, when oil prices were higher, these taxes provided 28 percent of the state's tax revenues.

Evaluating Taxes and Tax Systems

Tax system A mix of taxes used to raise revenue for a unit of government or a system of governments.

Some state constitutions allow state and local governments to use a wide variety of taxes; others do not. Few governments of any size can depend on one tax. The problems that arise in some parts of Texas because school districts (no matter how large) can use only one tax (the property tax) provides some evidence for the problems that can arise from this dependence. Thus, in discussing state and local taxes, we need to address the concept of a tax system.

A **tax system** is a mix of taxes used to raise revenue for one or more governments. The notion of a system of taxes is important because raising one tax in the system can make it possible to lower others. A change in economic conditions that radically reduces revenue from one tax may require that other taxes be raised so that the amount in the budget can remain the same or simply keep up with population growth.

Economists and political scientists working with the National Conference of State Legislatures (NCSL) have conducted numerous studies of state tax systems and arrived at a set of ten principles of a "high-quality state revenue system."[14] Discussing all ten is beyond the scope of this book, so we will address the most important one: equity, or fairness.

ADAM SMITH AND TAX EQUITY

While there are many ways of deciding what is fair, there is a definition of tax equity that has been around at least since 1776. In that year, Adam Smith (1723–1790), the first philosopher of capitalism, published *The Wealth of Nations*. In that well-known work, Smith sets forth the principles of tax equity:

> The subjects of every state ought to contribute towards the support of the government, as nearly as possible, in proportion to their respective abilities; that is in proportion to the revenue which they respectively enjoy under the protection of the state.[15]

Subsistence The income necessary to live at the level of bare existence: meager food, clothing, shelter; a minimal standard of living.

Surplus The income beyond subsistence. From surplus, one can buy higher quality subsistence items, enjoy luxuries, and have money left over for saving, speculation, and investment.

Smith thus advocated a tax system based on the ability to pay. Two important concepts are associated with his definition. The first is **subsistence.** If one's income allows one to live only at a modest level, to subsist, then one should not have to pay much, if anything, in taxes. Smith stated that subsistence—food, shelter, clothing, and the tools of craftsmen—should not be taxed.

The second concept is **surplus.** Those with income in excess of subsistence have surplus. Somebody has to pay for government, and those with surplus should pay for it, according to Smith. The more surplus one has, the more one should contribute to the cost of government.

It is important to understand that it was the first philosopher of capitalism who suggested a tax system in which the rich pay at a higher rate than the poor do. Although you may recognize this principle from Luke 21 in the New Testament, the idea of taxes based on the ability to pay is one to which some wealthy individuals and organizations claiming to represent tax fairness are violently opposed. They label those who support that idea as socialists or Marxists.

While it is true that Marx agrees with Luke 21 and with Adam Smith on tax fairness, he didn't invent the notion. The first English-speaking person to put in writing "the ability to pay" as a definition of fairness was Smith, not Marx. Smith was dead for over a quarter of a century before Karl Marx was born. As a future leader in Texas, you may have to point out this fact to a few people. In other words, Marx was a Smithist, not the other way around.

THE TEXAS TAX SYSTEM

We can now examine the Texas tax system, beginning with Smith's definition of an equitable tax system: one that shields subsistence income from taxation. To do so, we need to understand a few more terms. To round out your knowledge, refer to Box 14.1. The first term in the box is *tax bill*—an amount of money. The second term is *tax burden*—the percentage of income used to pay your tax bill. If you know your tax bill (sales tax bill, property tax bill, the bill you pay to operate your vehicle), divide it by your income to find out your tax burden on that tax. Adam Smith is concerned with the tax burden, not the tax bill. If you tax a poor person at 10 percent and a millionaire at 1 percent, clearly the millionaire will have a bigger tax bill but a much lighter burden.

Three terms that build on the notion of tax burden are *proportionate*, *progressive*, and *regressive*. These terms can be used to examine tax systems or particular taxes. They help us see past the sticker shock of the tax bill that a millionaire would face if he or she bore the same tax burden as the poor person taxed at 10 percent. *Proportionate* means that everyone bears the same burden. Again, the tax bills may not be the same, but the burdens will be. *Progressive* means that the tax burden grows lighter as income decreases, heavier as income increases. *Regressive* means the reverse. The poor pay more. A regressive tax is one that results in a lighter burden for the wealthy and a heavier burden for the poor. With these conceptual tools in place, let's look at the Texas tax system.

BOX 14.1   Conceptual Tools for Discussing Taxes

Tax Bill. The amount of money a unit of government collects to pay for services and facilities.

Tax Burden. The portion of one's income used to pay one's tax bill. The bigger the percentage, the heavier the burden. To determine your tax burden for a particular tax (for example, the property tax), divide your tax bill by your annual income. You can also add all your tax bills and divide them by your income to arrive at your annual tax burden.

Proportionate. A tax or tax system in which the tax burden is the same for everyone regardless of their income. Achievement of this goal is nearly impossible in the real world. Tax systems usually miss on one side or the other; that is, they are either regressive or progressive.

Regressive. A tax or tax system in which one's tax burden increases as one's income decreases. Some taxes are clearly regressive. Sales taxes are regressive because the proportion of household income spent on taxable consumption is typically higher for low-income than it is for high-income households. Say that you chew one pack of gum a day, for which you pay a sales tax; if your income doubles, you are unlikely to double your gum consumption and thus pay twice as much in sales tax on that item.

The Declining Propensity to Consume. The concept based on the notion that consumption of taxable items does not increase at the same rate that incomes increases.

Progressive. A tax system in which one's tax burden decreases as one's income decreases (or increases as one's income increases). In a progressive system, tax burdens and incomes increase or decline together. In short, someone with no income pays no taxes in that system. A progressive tax or tax system is based on the ability to pay.

Tax System Equity. The ultimate effect of a mix of regressive and progressive taxes. If no progressive taxes are in place to balance the effect of sales taxes and other regressive taxes, then the system as a whole will be regressive, and the poor will pay more.

Subsistence. The basic necessities of life (enough food to nourish us, clothing, tools for our occupation, and so on). According to the NCSL and to Adam Smith, the items of subsistence should not be taxed.

Surplus. Income beyond subsistence. It makes possible a better lifestyle, as well as saving, speculation, and investment.

Dependence on a Regressive Tax. Texas depends on sales taxes (general and selective) for nearly 90 percent of its tax revenue. Unfortunately for the poor, sales taxes are regressive. Why? Because the wealthy do not spend most of their income on items that are taxed, the poor do. The wealthy buy more and better items, but they spend a relatively smaller proportion of their income to do it, and they have money left over for speculation and investment. Some items they do spend money on (that the poor probably don't) aren't taxed—services by orthodontists, landscape architects, travel planners, financial planners, tax consultants, and attorneys; *The Wall Street Journal*; and country club memberships—to list a few.[16]

The belief that the sales tax is fair because everyone pays it is contradicted by the patterns of spending for rich and poor families. A recent analysis of these patterns in each of the fifty states by the Institute on Taxation and Economic Policy shows that in Texas, a family with an income in the lowest 20 percent bears a sales tax burden of 8.5 percent, while a family with an income in the top 1 percent bears a sales tax burden of 1.2 percent. Thus, the burden for the poor family is almost eight times as heavy as the burden for the wealthy family.[17]

Texas in Context 14.1 puts the regressive nature of the Texas tax system in comparative perspective: Texas has the second most regressive tax system among the megastates. Our measure of regression is the ratio between the tax burden on the poorest 20 percent of families in Texas to the tax burden on the families in the top 1 percent. For Texas, this ratio is 11.4 divided by 3.5, which tells us that the bottom 20 percent bear a burden that is 326% heavier than that borne by the top 1 percent. (In the previous edition of this book, the ratio was 3.14.)

Robin Hood and Property Taxes. Until now, we've been dealing with vertical equity, that is, fairness of the tax system among families with different incomes. However, Adam Smith didn't have to deal with horizontal equity in the 1770s: the fact that a single large political unit (for example, Texas) may have many small political units with different tax rates (for example, Edgewood School District and Alamo Heights School District).

Thus, two families with the same income living in houses valued exactly the same may pay different property-tax bills and thus bear unequal tax burdens. The National Conference of State Legislatures (NCSL) defines vertical equity the same way Adam Smith does, but the NCSL also defines horizontal equity as a system in which all households with the same income bear the same burden.

To provide horizontal equity, Texas requires 118 school districts to share resources with 916 districts—the Robin Hood plan. The use of that name—Robin Hood—for the Property Tax Equalization Act is fairly obvious. It implies, however, that robbery is taking place. That implication is not the only misunderstanding about the Property Tax Equalization Act. Contrary to the many myths about it, the transfers of funds provide only about 4 percent of the money used to fund public education in Texas. Another myth is that abolishing the Property Tax Equalization Act will mean that everyone's property taxes would go down, but taxes would go down only in the 118 districts that send property tax money to other districts. The large tax base of these districts is used to educate only 10 percent of the state's

TEXAS in Context

14.1　The Heavier Tax Burden of the Working Poor in Texas*

Megastate	Bottom 20 Percent	Top 1 Percent	Bottom to Top Ratio
Florida	14.4	3.0	4.80
Texas	**11.4**	**3.5**	**3.26**
Pennsylvania	11.4	4.8	2.38
Illinois	13.1	5.8	2.26
Michigan	13.3	6.7	1.99
New Jersey	12.5	8.4	1.49
New York	12.7	10.6	1.20
Massachusetts	9.3	8.2	1.13
Ohio	11.0	9.7	1.13
California	11.3	10.6	1.07

*In Florida, for example, the working poor bear a tax burden that is 4.8 times as heavy as the tax burden on the top 1 percent.

Source: Institute on Taxation and Economic Policy, *Who Pays? A Distributional Analysis of the Tax Systems in All 50 States*, 2d ed. (Washington, D.C.: Institute on Taxation and Economic Policy, 2003.).

population. In light of these facts, one might reasonably ask, Why should a small portion of the state's students benefit just because their homes are in the same districts as shopping malls, business centers, and industrial plants?

The real problem of funding education in Texas is that the state provides only 40 percent of the resources; school districts have to come up with the other 60 percent. Those currently in office seem bent on making sure that this split stays in place. As we noted earlier, in the $2.7 billion in new nontax revenue that the 2003 state legislature "found" in the 2003–2004 budget are cuts in retirement benefits for teachers and cuts in the school textbook budget. As a college student, you are doubtless paying the increase in tuition that resulted in the reduced state support for higher education. If the state doesn't find new revenue, the situation is likely to get worse.[18]

Looking to the Future: A Personal Income Tax?

Because the political system in Texas is bound to change, the issue for the next generation of leaders is whether the situation will get better or worse for middle-class families and the working poor. The only progressive tax available is a personal

JOIN THE DEBATE

THE ISSUE: Do you favor the idea of trickle-down economics?

AGREE

1. Millionaires should not be punished for their economic success by paying taxes at a higher rate than the poor pay.

2. A regressive tax system means more money for millionaires to invest in businesses, which produces jobs for everyone else.

3. Millionaires will use the money resulting from their light tax load wisely and will not spend it on a luxurious lifestyle.

4. Even if the rich do spend their money on a luxurious lifestyle, they will provide jobs for waiters, dog walkers, pool cleaners, and people in various service and construction businesses.

5. If the poor are allowed to keep more of their money, they will squander it on fattening food, drugs, gambling, and alcohol.

DISAGREE

1. Taxation isn't punishment; it is paying for something—government—that we all need, rich and poor alike. If punishment is involved, is it right to punish the poor for their lack of economic success? Not everyone can be born to wealthy or even middle-class parents who help prepare one for economic success.

2. A tax system that protects the incomes of the working poor will result in spending on homes, furniture, and appliances. This spending will create demand, which in turn will provide profits for businesses and encourage them to invest and provide more jobs for the working poor and the middle class.

3. Millionaires will still be better off than the working poor in a progressive tax system.

4. Millionaires and their children are better prepared to use the resources that a stable political system provides and thus should pay for it at a higher rate than the working poor. The wealthy have more property and possessions for the police and fire departments to protect, and they use the courts and the legal system to enforce their contracts and business agreements.

5. The lifestyle of millionaires clearly indicates that they enjoy a luxurious lifestyle and have surplus money to support politicians who do what they want.

income tax. All of the megastates except Florida and Texas use the personal income tax as part of their tax systems. During the past few legislative sessions, many observers have noted that a personal income tax seems the most logical solution to the unfairness of the tax system for both families and the business community. We examine three of the many arguments that have been put forth in favor of adding a personal income tax to the mix of taxes.

A LEVEL PLAYING FIELD FOR THE BUSINESS COMMUNITY

The most important reason given for the personal income tax is that it is the only way to tax businesses that are not corporations. Corporations pay a corporate income tax; it is built into the corporate franchise tax and has been declared a corporate income tax by the U.S. Supreme Court. Because the owners of businesses that are not corporations do not pay a business profit tax, the only way to get their business to contribute to the cost of government is to tax the personal income of those business owners. According to *The Austin Business Journal* about 4,000 corporations in Texas have restructured themselves as partnerships to avoid the franchise tax. San Antonio Based SBC may have saved as much as $50 million a year by restructuring.[19]

The economy of Texas includes thousands of businesses organized as sole proprietorships and partnerships that generate large profits for their owners. These businesses pay no profits tax, whereas corporations do. It is no wonder that many corporations are reorganizing to become partnerships. If we wait until only a few corporations remain, it could be too late.

ABILITY TO PAY

Adam Smith believed that government should be paid for by those who can afford to do so. If a progressive tax is added to the mix of taxes used in Texas, other taxes that tend to hit working people and the middle class could be lowered. Remember, we have a tax system, not just one or two taxes. In other words, the sales tax could be lowered (or even eliminated), and the regressive nature of the Texas tax system would be significantly reduced.

No one seriously proposes a state personal income tax that would apply to the first $150,000 of income for small businesses because the first $150,000 of gross receipts is exempt.[20] Other exemptions for small corporations would have to be made available to individuals and small business owners. Thus, a state personal income tax would be more of a millionaire's tax than a tax on ordinary Texans.

Also, it is highly unlikely that a state income tax would be applied to any income less than $100,000. Even with that exemption, the resulting tax package would include significant reductions in property and sales taxes. As it stands now, according to the Advisory Commission on Intergovernmental Relations, if Texas were to levy a personal income tax at the average state rate, it would raise more than $5 billion a year. That money could be used to reduce the heavy sales tax burden that families in the bottom 20 percent of income earners bear now.

AN END TO SUBSIDIZING OTHER STATES

Taxpayers in the forty-three states where the personal income tax is used can deduct part of their state tax from their federal taxable income. Because Texas does not have a state income tax, it is subsidizing the states that do. A taxpayer who deducts payment of state income tax from his or her federal income tax is, in effect, paying about two-thirds of their state income tax bill, not the whole amount. This effect is referred to by tax experts as the **federal deduction offset**.

Federal deduction offset
A way of looking at a state tax that can be deducted from the federal income tax. For sales taxes there is no deduction, although there are bills in congress to change that.

For state property taxes and for state income taxes there is a reduction in one's income tax bill. Thus, money paid to the state is offset (counterbalanced, made up for) by a corresponding reduction in one's federal tax bill. Naturally, this only affects people who use the long 1040 form to compute their federal income taxes.

THE BOTTOM LINE

The best kept secret about fixing our regressive tax system is that lawmakers do not have to increase the burden for the top 1 percent of income-earning families all that much to lower the burden for the lowest 20 percent of income-earning families from 11.4 percent to 3.5 percent. We certainly would not have to place an 11.4 percent burden on the top 20 percent because so much money is available at the top income levels.

The Institute on Tax Policy has estimated that the top tax burden in Texas would be about 7 percent if the tax system were to add a progressive income tax. The beauty of this change for the well-to-do is that they can pass about 2 percent on to the federal government because state income taxes are deductible from the federal income tax. Thus, a 7 percent income tax in Texas would effectively cost a wealthy person only 5 percent.[21]

By applying Adam Smith's principle of taxation, which is based on the ability to pay, a personal income tax in Texas would have the following impact on individuals in the various income categories:

1. It would require the wealthy to pay additional taxes from their surplus, that is, the money left over after they have paid for food, shelter, and clothing. Thus, their tax bills would go from 4 percent of their income to about 6 percent of their income (keep in mind that state personal income taxes are deductible from one's federal income tax bill—the federal deduction offset).
2. It would not make much difference to the middle class. Few members of the middle class, in any given year, would have income beyond $100,000, and that income would be surplus, not subsistence. By adding a personal income tax to the mix, the sales taxes and property taxes paid by the middle class would be lowered somewhat. Thus, the overall effect would probably be a slight drop in their tax bills.
3. A personal income tax would have no direct effect on the poor because they would not have to pay it. It would have a dramatic indirect effect, however, on their overall tax burden. By lowering sales taxes, the state would no longer tax their subsistence as heavily. A state personal income tax could reduce their overall burden from 11.4 percent to about 3.9 percent.

Why a State Personal Income Tax Would Be Hard to Enact

A reform that appears to be so beneficial to the poor, so harmless to the middle class, and so minimally inconvenient for the wealthy is nevertheless difficult to enact into law. To understand why it would be difficult, we must—in part—review some of the material we have discussed in earlier chapters.

1. Political socialization in and the political culture of Texas have created a belief system about a personal income tax that associates it with punishing the successful and with introducing Marxism into Texas politics. You have only to write a letter to the editor of your local paper about why we ought to have a state personal income tax to see what we mean. The letters responding to it will contain one or the other of the above objections. Those responses don't mean that you shouldn't write those letters. It takes time to walk people through the concepts we have covered in this chapter. The task of explaining these concepts could be one of your jobs as a future leader. Explaining the vocabulary of tax equity takes time. So does reminding people that in 1776, Adam Smith, the first philosopher of capitalism, advocated a tax system based on the ability to pay, long before Karl Marx (1818–1883) was born.

2. Our discussion of the interest group system in Texas indicates that it is biased in favor of the business community. The majority of businesses in Texas are not corporations. Most corporate leaders would have to pay the personal income tax, as would the leaders of the major business interest groups. It was easier to institute a corporate income tax than a personal income tax fifteen years ago because the tax did not come out of the pockets of any wealthy individuals. Thus, until a significant portion of the population gets involved in favor of a personal income tax to counterbalance the weight of the interest group system, it is unlikely to happen. Even common-sense solutions to problems are not enacted into law unless someone acts. Want an example? Compare smoking regulations in the United States and Europe. Why are they so tough in the United States? Ordinary people got involved.

3. An argument against a personal income tax that we have heard former governor George Bush offer is that it is "an engine of government growth." He's right. Any new source of revenue is a potential "engine of government growth." The government of Texas certainly grew after we instituted the sales tax; however, so did the population and the economy. We are, after all, a megastate. And because we are a growing megastate, government in Texas will have to grow, which is why many lobbyists and political leaders in Texas readily admit that the personal income tax seems inevitable. They just don't see how the inevitable will occur. In this chapter, we have not advocated government growth. We have discussed taxes in terms of keeping the budget the same size while making the tax system a fair one. However, if you recall from Chapters 11, 12, and 13 some of the problems that need solutions, then you may want to have some parts of government grow.

TABLE 14.4 Texas State Taxes Repealed or Abolished Since 1972	
Tax	**Year Repealed**
Express Company Tax	1976
State Ad Valorem Tax [Property Tax]	1982
Occupation tax on Pistol Dealers	1983
Occupation tax on Billiard Table Owners or Operators	1983
Occupation tax on Quotation Services	1983
Occupation tax on Ship Brokers	1983
Car Company Tax	1985
Telegraph Tax	1985
Telephone Company Tax	1988
Bingo Tax—State	1993
Interstate Motor Carrier Sales and Use Tax	1997

Source: Carole Keeton (Rylander) Strayhorn. Sources of Revenue Growth: A History of State Taxes and Fees in Texas 1972-2001. *May 2002 Austin: Texas Comptroller of Public Accounts. p.6.*

4. A final point about the difficulties facing your efforts to reform the tax system of Texas is that when people begin talking about taxes, they throw in a lot of other myths and facts into the debate that are beside the point. For example, they start talking about their mistrust of government and they often become rather angry. You have to remain calm in these situations and guide people back to the point.

When discussing mistrust of government, one point often made is that no legislature ever lowers a tax once it has been instituted. That charge is patently false, as Table 14.4 indicates. Furthermore, a cursory examination of the tax chapter in *The Book of the States,* which is published every two years by the National Council of State Governments, will show that more than one state lowers as well as raises taxes. As Table 14.4 shows, the reason we do not have a state property tax today in Texas is that the legislature proposed—and voters ratified—an amendment abolishing it in 1982

Summary

In this chapter, we have explored the components of government budgets and how the budget is related to the economy. We have examined the process of budget making and learned about various ways governments acquire money and how they use most of it. We have also examined one of several ways to evaluate a tax system.

By focusing on fairness, we raise several questions about the current tax system of Texas and how to change it. Naturally, if you like it the way it is, then you must simply defend the status quo and continue to pay more or less than your fair share. If you want to effect change in the direction of equity, then you must put to work some of your new knowledge about participating in the political system of Texas.

As we have suggested throughout this book, you can make a difference on many issues. Why not start this week? Other Texans have. You can make the system work even better than it already does.

KEY TERMS

Budget, p. 386
Appropriations, p. 387
Tax expenditure, p. 388
Fiscal note, p. 388
Incidence, p. 388
Fiscal year, p. 388

Intergovernmental transfer, p. 394
Benefits theory, p. 395
Tax system, p. 398
Subsistence, p. 399
Surplus, p. 399
Federal deduction offset, p. 405

FOR FURTHER READING

Beamer, Glenn, *Creative Politics: Taxes and Public Goods in a Federal System* (Ann Arbor: University of Michigan Press, 1999).

Brunori, David, *State Tax Policy: A Political Perspective* (Washington, D.C.: Urban Institute Press, 2001).

Heilbroner, Robert L., *The Essential Adam Smith* (New York: W. W. Norton & Co., 1986).

Heilbroner, Robert L., and Peter Berstein, *The Debt and the Deficit* (New York: Norton, 1989).

Michael P. Ettlinger, John F. O'Hare, Robert S. McIntyre, Julie King, Elizabeth A. Fray, and Neil Miransky, *Who Pays? A Distributional Analysis of the Tax Systems in All 50 States,* 2d ed. (Washington, D.C.: Institute on Taxation and Economic Policy, 2003).

Tokin, Albert, ed., *Internet Taxation* (New York: Novinka Books, 2003).

STUDY QUESTIONS

1. Define the following terms: budget, appropriations, tax expenditure, and fiscal note.

2. In terms of tax revenue as a percentage of gross domestic product (GDP), how many countries in Figure 14.1 place a heavier burden on the economy than the United States does?

3. What are LBB and OBP? The budget drawn up by which organization is taken most seriously by the Texas Legislature?

4. Approximately what percentage of the state budget comes from the federal government? What percentage comes from the lottery?

5. Define the terms presented in Box 14.1.

CRITICAL THINKING QUESTIONS

1. Discuss the roles of the different actors who influence the budget of Texas.

2. Why is the sales tax regressive?

3. How do taxes in Texas repel or attract businesses?

4. How does the Texas tax system compare to that of the other megastates?

5. Who was Adam Smith, and how would he evaluate the tax system of Texas?

INTERNET RESOURCES

www.ufenet.org/ United for a Fair Economy. This site deals with issues affecting working class families. To Fox News it would be a socialist site. To the New York Times, it would be a liberal site.

www.inequality.org/ This website serves as a network of journalists, writers, and researchers concerned with economic policy as it affects ordinary working families.

www.ctj.org/ Citizens for Tax Justice is a nonpartisan, nonprofit research and advocacy organization dedicated to fair taxation at the federal, state, and local levels. The website contains data and tables.

www.cppp.org/ The Center for Public Policy Priorities, located in Austin, Texas, conducts advocacy research dealing with children and the working poor.

www.window.state.tx.us This website for the Texas Comptroller of Public Accounts provides a comprehensive overview of the Texas budget, expenditures, and taxes. The comptroller's office is the major data source on Texas government.

Chapter 1

1. Klein, Genevieve. "Other Universities Speak Out on Name Change." *The University Star*. February 27, 2002.
2. Green, Erin. "ASG Passes Bill Regarding Name Change." *The University Star*. Feb 11, 2003.
3. Green, Erin. "Alumni Protest Name Change." *The University Star*. March 5, 2003.
4. Interview David Doerr, Editor, *University Star*. January 14, 2003. (No Relation to Robert Doerr).
5. Jeremy Schwartz, "Texas State University Signed into Being." *Austin American Statesman*. June 20, 2003.
6. *University Star*, Summer Issue 2003.
7. Robert Doerr, Telephone interview, February 22, 2004.
8. George W. Bush, "Inaugural Address," *New York Times*, January 21, 2001, pp. 12–13.
9. U.S. Census Bureau, *Statistical Abstract of the United States, 2000* (Washington, D.C.: U.S. Government Printing Office, 2000), p. 159.
10. John Naisbitt, *Megatrends* (New York: Warner Books, 1982), p. 97.
11. U.S. Census Bureau, *Statistical Abstract of the United States, 2000* (Washington, D.C.: U.S. Government Printing Office, 2000), p. 32
12. Jim Suydam. 2002 "Teacher Shortage Worsening in Texas." *Austin American Statesman*. May 28, 2002.
13. A. Ray Stephens and William M. Holmes, *Historical Atlas of Texas* (Norman: University of Oklahoma Press, 1989), p. 28.
14. Ibid., p. 30.
15. Robert A. Calvert and Arnoldo De Leon, *The History of Texas* (Arlington Heights, Ill.: Harlan Davidson, 1990), p. 91.
16. John Sharp, *Bordering the Future: Challenge and Opportunity in the Texas Border Region* (Austin: Texas Comptroller of Public Accounts, 1998), p. 5.
17. *World Almanac and Book of Facts 2000* (Mahwah, N.J.: Primedia, 2000), p. 566, and U.S. Census Bureau, *Statistical Abstract of the United States: 1999* (Washington, D.C.: U.S. Government Printing Office, 1999), p. 12.
18. Steve H. Murdock, Md. Nazrui Hoque, and Beverly A. Pecotte, "Texas Population Growth Leads Nation," in *Texas Almanac: 1998–1999* (Dallas: Dallas Morning News, 1997), pp. 293–295.
19. Texas Comptroller of Public Accounts, "Direct Returns," in *Fiscal Notes* (Austin: Texas Comptroller of Public Accounts, 1999), pp. 1–4.
20. *Texas Almanac: 1998–1999*, p. 61.
21. Ibid., p. 576.
22. Dave McNeely, "Ric Williamson Might Be Roads' Best Guardian," *Austin American Statesman*, March 22, 2001, p. B-1.
23. *Texas Almanac: 1998–1999*, p. 444.
24. Councils of Governments (Austin: Texas Association of Regional Councils, 2000), p. 3.
25. *Texas Almanac: 1998–1999*, p. 591
26. http://www.txpeer.org/toxictour/pilgrim.html. accessed Februrary 10, 2004. Also of interest is a May 2000 Consumers Union report on "Animal Factories: Pollution and Health Threats to Rural Texas." http://www.consumersunion.org/other/animal/pilgrims.htm, Nancy Flores. 2002. "Chicken Plant's Water Plan Lays an Egg with Neighbors. *Austin American-Statesman*. November 19, 2002. See also, Robert Bryce, "Not Plucking Around," *Texas Observer*, December 8, 2000, pp. 8–13.
27. Calvert and De Leon, *History of Texas*, pp. 216–217.
28. Texas Public Employees for Environmental Responsibility, "PANTEX: Pollution in the Panhandle," www.txpeer.org/toxictour/, March 22, 2001. See also James Kimberly, "Pollution from Pantex Causes Panhandle Fears," *Houston Chronicle*, May 21, 2000.
29. *Texas Almanac: 1998–1999*, p. 242.
30. Lawrence Goodwyn, *The Populist Movement: A Short History of Agrarian Revolt in America* (New York: Oxford University Press, 1978), p. 47.
31. Melissa Millecam and Mark B. Taylor, "Lucius D. Bunton III: A Giant of a Texan," *Austin American-Statesman*, January 21, 2001, p. 21.
32. *Texas Almanac: 1998–1999*, p. 5.
33. Calvert and De Leon, *History of Texas*, pp. 5–7.
34. Ibid., p. 18.

35. *Texas Almanac: 1998–1999*, p. 484.

36. Ken Herman. 2003. "House Gets Picky with Gambling Measures. *Austin American-Statesman* May 28, 2003.

37. Had we used the term *Native American*, we would have been including 721 Eskimos and 807 Aleuts, for a total of 65,877 Native Americans. Texas Data Center, Texas A&M University, "1990 Census Lookup (1.4a)," http://txsdc.tamu.edu/txprof.html.

38. Associated Press. "Demographic Trends Paint Dismal Picture for Texas," *Austin American-Statesmen,* July 29, 1996, pp. BI/BS.

39. Calvert and De Leon, *History of Texas,* p. 175.

40. Steve H. Murdock, "Texas Challenged: Implications of Population Change for Public Service. Demand in Texas. A Report Prepared for the Texas Legislative Council." January 2001, p. 62.

41. Ibid., p. 87.

42. Stephens and Holmes, *Historical Atlas of Texas*, p. 8.

43. Calvert and De Leon, *History of Texas*, p. 100.

44. Molefi K. Asante and Mark T. Mattson, *Historical and Cultural Atlas of African Americans* (New York: Macmillan, 1992), p. 100.

45. Ibid., p. 148; Calvert and De Leon, *History of Texas,* p. 235.

46. Bob Barton, "Smitty's Clout Carried the Day," *Free Press,* February 15, 2001, p. 1.

47. Maurey Maverick, Jr., "The Mayor of La Villita," *Texas Observer*, November 20, 1998, p. 30.

48. Daniel Elazar, *American Federalism: A View from the States*, 3rd ed. (New York: Harper & Row, 1984), pp. 114–122.

49. Calvert and De Leon, *History of Texas*, p. 74

50. See Daniel J. Elazar, *The American Mosaic: The Impact of Space, Time, and Culture on American Politics* (Boulder, Colo.: Westview Press, 1994), pp. 229–255, for Elazar's most recent explication of his influential analysis

51. Goodwyn, *The Populist Movement*, p. 206.

52. Robert A. Caro, *The Years of Lyndon Johnson: Means of Ascent* (New York: Knopf, 1990), p. 389.

53. Ibid., p. 189.

54. Elazar, *American Federalism*, pp. 115–116.

55. For a start at the rugged individualism literature, consult T. R. Fehrenbach, *Lone Star: History of Texas and Texans* (New York: Macmillan, 1968) and almost any edition of *The American Spectator* For the populist and cooperative literature, see Lawrence Goodwyn, *Democratic Promise: The Populist Moment in America* (New York: Oxford University Press, 1976), and Chandler Davidson, *Race and Class in Texas Politics* (Princeton, N.J.: Princeton University Press, 1990), Chap. 2.

56. Davidson, *Race and Class in Texas Politics*, pp. 34–35.

57. Mody C. Boatright, "The Myth of Frontier Individualism," *Southwestern Social Science Quarterly* 22 (1941): 14–32.

58. Calvert and De Leon, *History of Texas*, p. 216

59. John Kincaid, ed., *Political Culture, Public Policy and the American States* (Philadelphia: Institute for the Study of Human Issues, 1982), p. 21.

60. Ibid., pp. 28–35.

61. Calvert and De Leon, *History of Texas*, p. 396.

62. Jake Bernstein and Dave Mann, "Sharpstown II ?" *Texas Observer*. February 27, 2004. 4–7. On the web, Mike Haley. "*The Sharpstown Standard: A Yardstick for Scandal.*" *Capitol Inside site*, http://www.capitolinside.com/ accessed 2/28/04.

63. Robert Putnam, *Making Democracy Work* (Princeton, N.J.: Princeton University Press, 1993).

64. Tom W. Rice and Alexander F. Sumberg, "Civic Culture and Government Performance in the American States," *Publius* (Winter 1997): 100–101.

65. Ibid., p. 109.

Chapter 2

1. Frank M. Stewart and Joseph L. Clark, *The Constitution and Government of Texas* (Boston: D. C. Heath, 1949), p. 4.

2. Fred Gantt, Jr., *Governing Texas: Documents and Reading* (New York: Crowell, 1966), p. 35.

3. Robert A. Calvert and Arnoldo De Leon, *The History of Texas* (Arlington, Ill.: Harlan Davidson, 1990), p. 36.

4. Ibid., p. 75.

5. Ibid., p. 92.

6. For a better understanding of the 1845 Constitution, see Annie Middleton, "Donelson's Mission to Texas in Behalf of Annexation," *Southwestern Historical Quarterly* 24: 247–291.

7. George D. Braden, *Citizens' Guide to the Texas Constitution* (Austin: Texas Advisory Commission on Intergovernmental Relations, 1972), p. 11.

8. T. R. Fehrenbach, *Lone Star: A History of Texas and Texans* (New York: Macmillan, 1968), pp. 398–399.

9. Calvert and De Leon, *The History of Texas*, p. 135.

10. Fred Gantt, Jr., Irving O. Dawson, and Luther G. Hagard, Jr., eds., *Governing Texas: Documents and Readings* (New York: Crowell, 1966), p. 39.

11. Ibid.

12. George E. Shelley, "The Semicolon Court of Texas," *Southwestern Historical Quarterly* 48 (April 1945): 449–468.

13. John Walker Mauer, "State Constitution in a Time of Crisis: The Case of the Texas Constitution of 1876," *Texas Law Review* 68 (1990): 1627.

14. Rupert Norval Richardson, Ernest Wallace, and Adrian N. Anderson, *Texas: The Lone Star State* (Englewood Cliffs, N.J.: Prentice Hall, 1981), p. 269.

15. Mauer, "State Constitution in a Time of Crisis," p. 1641.

16. Richardson, Wallace, and Anderson, *Texas*, p. 274.

17. Ibid., p. 271.

18. A. J. Thomas, Jr., and Ann Van Wynen Thomas, "The Texas Constitution of 1876," *Texas Law Review* 35 (1957): 917.

19. *Texas Constitution*, Art. 1, sec. 12, 29.

20. *The Book of the States, 2003*, vol. 35 (Lexington, Ky.: Council of State Governments, 2003), p. 3.

21. John J. Harrigan, *Politics and Policy in States and Communities, 6th ed.* (New York: Longman, 1998), pp. 240–241.

22. Thomas R. Dye, *Politics in State and Communities* (Englewood Cliffs, N.J.: Prentice Hall, 1981), p. 26.

23. Janice C. May, *The Texas Constitutional Revision Experience in the 70s* (Sterling Swift Publishing Co., 1975), p. 25.

24. *Statistical Abstract of United States, 1986* (Washington, D.C.: Government Printing Office, December 1985), p. 440.

25. Ibid., p. 10.

26. G. Stanford, "Constitutional Revision in Texas: A New Chapter," *Public Affairs Comment* 2 (February 1974): 1–6.

27. See May, *The Texas Constitutional Revision Experience.*

28. John E. Bebout, "The Meaning of the Vote on the Proposed Texas Constitution," *Public Affairs Comment* 14 (February 1978): 1–4.

29. See Nelson Wolff, *Challenge of Change* (San Antonio: Naylor Co., 1975), pp. 45–46.

Chapter 3

1. Stephen F. Frantzich, *Citizen Democracy: Political Activism in a Cynical Age* (Boulder, Colo.: Rowman & Littlefield, 1999), p. 12.

2. Ibid., p. 17.

3. U.S. Census Bureau, *Statistical Abstract of the United States, 2000* (Washington, D.C.: U.S. Government Printing Office, 2000), p. 299.

4. Willard B. Stouffer, Cynthia Opheim, and Susan B. Day, *State and Local Politics: The Individual and the Intergovernments*, 2nd ed. (New York: HarperCollins, 1996), p. 55.

5. Roy B. Flemming, Canadian studies expert, personal communication, April 6, 2001.

6. *Texas v. White*, 74 U.S. 700 (1868).

7. Daniel J. Elazar, *American Federalism: A View from the States*, 3rd ed. (New York: Harper & Row, 1984).

8. David C. Nice and Patricia Fredericksen, *Federalism: The Politics of Intergovernmental Relations* (New York: St. Martin's Press, 1987), pp. 101–102.

9. *Roe v. Wade*, 410 U.S. 113 (1973).

10. Catherine Drinker Bowen, *Miracle at Philadelphia* (Boston: Little, Brown, 1986), pp. 255–256.

11. *Garcia v. San Antonio Metropolitan Transit Authority*, 469 U.S. 528 (1985).

12. *U.S. v. Lopez*, 115 S. Ct. 1624 (1995).

13. Council of State Governments, "Supreme Court Confirms the Role of States in U.S. Federal System," *Issue Alerts*, July 25, 1997.

14. *City of Boerne, Texas v. Flores*, 117 S. Ct. 2157 (1997).

15. Russell I. Hanson, "Intergovernmental Relations," in Virginia Gray and Herbert Jacob, *Politics in the American States* (Washington, D.C.: Congressional Quarterly Press, 1996), p. 57.

16. *New York Times*, May 21, 1990, p. A11.

17. Michael C. Tolley and Bruce A. Wallin, "Coercive Federalism and Search for Constitutional Limits," *Publius: The Journal of Federalism* 25 (1995): 79.

18. Hanson, p. 58.

19. Ellen Perlman, "The Gorilla That Swallowed State Laws," *Governing* (August 1994): 46–48.

20. Robert A. Calvert and Arnoldo De Leon, *The History of Texas* (Arlington Heights, Ill.: Harlan Davidson, 1990), pp. 371–372.

21. John F. Dillon, *Commentary on the Law of Municipal Corporations* (Boston: Little, Brown, 1911), vol. 1, sec. 237.

22. Jerry Thompson, *Work in Progress: Texas: A History of Six Countries* (New York: Longmans).

23. SB 1857 76(R) (www.senate.tx.gov) passed by 76th Legislature in 1999.

24. Calvert and De Leon, *History of Texas*, pp. 114–115.

25. David Saffell and Harry Basehart, *State and Local Government: Politics and Public Policies*, 7th ed. (New York: McGraw-Hill, 2001), pp. 310–311

26. Texas Association of Regional Councils, *Councils of Governments* (January 2000), pp. 6–7. State of Texas Publication, Austin, Texas.

27. Barrales, Ruben . "Federalism in the Bush Administration" in *Spectrum: The Journal of State Government.* Summer, 2001, 5–6.

28. Plotz, David. 2003. "The New, New, New Federalism" http://slate.msn.com/toolbar.aspx?action= print&id=110785

29. Symposium Series Number 2, *The Role of "Home" in Homeland Security, The Federalism Challenge* March 24, 2003. Albany, New York: The Rockefeller Institute of Government.

Chapter 4

1. Information about Blue Sky gathered from telephone interviews and written correspondence with Nita Van Cleave and from media accounts: Michael Beachum, *Louisville Leader,* September 11, 1999; Thomas Korosec, "Burnt Offering: When Dallas' Major League Soccer Team Wanted to Come to Hickory Creek, the Folks There Just Weren't Buying," *Dallas Observer,* August 26–September 1, 1999; Kevin Lahner, "Citizens Protest Soccer Complex," *Denton Record-Chronicle,* August 8, 1999; Jason Roberts, "HC Council Delays Talk on Blue Sky," *Lake Cities Sun,* July 14, 1999; Josh Renn, "Westlake to Host Blue Sky," *Lake Cities Sun,* July 21, 1999; Annette Reynolds, "Soccer Fans Enthusiastic about Proposed Complex But Some in Hickory Creek Fear Traffic," *Dallas Morning News,* July 15, 1999, Lake Cities Sun, July 28, 1999, paid advertisement; and Annette Reynolds, "Developer Revises Soccer Complex Goal" *Dallas Morning News,* September 2, 1999.
2. W. B. Stouffer, Cynthia Opheim, and Susan Bland Day, *State and Local Politics: The Individual and the Governments,* 2nd ed. (New York: HarperCollins, 1996). Counties are called boroughs in Alaska and parishes in Louisiana. Ibid.
3. *Avery v. Midland County,* U.S.S.C. 474,482 (1968).
4. H.B. 2009, amending sec. 86.0021, Local Government Code.
5. Texas Local Government Code, sec. 85.006.
6. Texas Department of Housing and Community Affairs and Texas Association of Counties, *Guide to Texas Laws for County Officials* (Austin: State of Texas, 1997–1998).
7. John F. Dillon, *Commentaries on the Law of Municipal Corporations* (Boston: Little, Brown, 1911).
8. Texas Local Government Code, Chap. 9, sec. 9.002(a).
9. Bernard H. Ross, Myron A. Levine, and Murray S. Stedman, U*rban Politics: Power in Metropolitan America,* 4th ed. (Itasca, Ill.: F. E. Peacock Publishers, 1991).
10. Ibid.
11. TASB online: www.tasb.org
12. *Harris County Water Control and Improvement District No. 110 v. Texas Water Rights Commission,* 593 S.W. 2d 852 (Tex.Civ. APP. —Austin 1980)
13. Analysis of Proposed Amendment, SJR No. 30, Author: Jon Lindsay; Sponsor: William Callegari. "Allowing municipal utility districts to develop parks and recreational facilities. http://www.tlc.state.tx.us/research/analyses072403/amd4.htm
14. Lani Guinier, *The Tyranny of the Majority: Fundamental Fairness in Representative Democracy* (New York: Free Press, 1995), pp. 75, 239, n. 11.
15. Croteau, Roger. "Some Vote 3 Times, Legally" 04/12/2002. San Antonio Express-News. http://news.mysanantonio.com/global-includes/printStory.cfm?xla='saen'&xlb=0&xlc=66 11/29/2003.
16. Texas Local Government Code, Chap. 42, sec. 42.001.
17. Texas Local Government Code, Chapter 43.028.
18. Kirk, Bryan. "Court takes issue with NB annexation" *The Seguin Gazette.* September 21, 2003. http://www.seguingazette.com/print.lasso?wcd=5028. 11/16/2003
19. Perryman Group, April 2003. http://www.perrymangroup.com
20. Baugh, Josh. "Hickory Creek rejects zoning change" *DentonRC.com* Wednesday, September 17, 2003. http://www.dontonrc.com/cgi-bin/bi/gold_print.cgi Accessed 9/22/03.
21. Bishop, Bill. "Senate Tax Swap May Come to Pass" Sunday, May 25, 2003. *Austin American-Statesman.* http://statesman.printthis.colckability.com/pt/cpt?action=cpt&expire=&urlID=6404649&f... 11/29/2003.
22. Center for Public Policy Priorities. 11/9/2003. http://www.cppp.org/products/reports/ttexecsum.html
23. Strayhorn, Carole Keeton. "Homestead Tax Deferral Changes" October, 2003. Window on State Government. http://www.window.state.tx.us/taxinfo/proptax/stmt/stmt0310/stme0310_3.html
24. "School Finance System Ruled Unconstitutional," http://www.cnn.com/2004/law/09/16/school.finance.tnal.ap. Accessed 9/16/04.
25. Meyers, Robert and Christina Prkic. 2002. Dade County Commission on Ethics and Trust.
26. Katherine Barrett and Richard Greene, "The Government Performance Project, Grading the Cities: A Management Card" (February 2000), in Governing, an online publication of Congressional Quarterly, Inc.
27. Roger L. Kemp, "Cities in the Twenty-First Century: The Forces of Change," *Texas Town and City* 87 (October 2000): 18–25.
28. www.ci.arlington.tx.us/carf/actionrequest/
29. Strayhorn Report. November 12, 2003. www.window.state.tx.us/news/31112tamiu.html

Chapter 5

1. Laura Washington. "The Online Pension Activist," *Money* (April 2000): 142–143.
2. Andrew Clark, "CALPERS Back IBM Workers in Pension Dispute," Austin American Statesman, March 27, 2000.
3. Brian Tumulty. "Pension Decisions Boost Case for New Regulations." Gannett News Service. June 8, 2003.
4. Washington, "The Online Pension Activist," p. 143.

5. Thomas E. Patterson. 2002. *The Vanishing Voter: Public Involvement in an Age of Uncertainty*. New York: Random House. 130–131.
6. Patterson. 133.
7. Patterson. 138.
8. Patterson. 137.
9. Hedrick Smith, "The Unelected—The Media and Interest Groups," PBS-TV, 1995. The People and the Power Game. Vol. 2
10. Anthony J. Nownes and Patricia Freeman, "Interest Group Activity in the States," *Journal of Politics* 60 (February 1998): 92.
11. José Angel Gutierrez, *The Making of a Chicano Militant: Lessons from Cristal* (Madison: University of Wisconsin Press, 1998). 59.
12. Gutierrez. 47.
13. Bingham Powell, "American Voter Turnout in Comparative Perspective," *American Political Science Review 80* (1986): 184.
14. Powell. 185.
15. U.S. Department of Commerce, *Statistical Abstract of the United States* 2000 (Washington, D.C.: U.S. Government Printing Office, 2000), p. 292.
16. Glenn Mitchell II and Christopher Wlezien, "The Impact of Legal Constraints on Voter Registration, Turnout, and the Composition of the American Electorate," *Political Behavior* (June 1995): 179–202.
17. Adam Clymer, "Class Warfare? The Rich Win by Default," *New York Times*, August 11, 1996. See also Reinhard Bendix and Seymour Martin Lipset, eds., *Class, Status, and Power: A Reader in Social Stratification* (New York, Free Press, 1966) and Lipset, Seymour Martin Lipset, and Stein Rokkan, eds., *Party Systems and Voter Alignments: Cross-National Perspectives* (New York, Free Press, 1967).
18. See for example Table 5.1 on.
19. According to *Business Week* the ratio is now 531 times what the typical hourly worker takes home. *Business Week*, "Spreading the Yankee Way of Pay," April 16, 2001.
20. Center for Responsive Politics, cited in *Congressional Quarterly: Guide to Current American Government*, Spring 1998 (Washington D.C.: Congressional Quarterly Press, 1998), p. 32.
21. U.S. Census Bureau. "Income Inequality (Middle Class)—Narrative," December 13, 2000. See also www.censusgov/hhes/income/midclass/midclsan.html/and Nancey Green Leigh, *Stemming the Middle Class Decline* (New Brunswick, NJ.: Center for Urban Policy Research Press, 1994).
22. Jo-Ann Mort, ed., *Not Your Father's Union Movement: Inside the AFL-CIO* (New York: Verso, 1998), p. 35.
23. Steven Greenhouse, "AMA Delegates Vote to Unionize," *The New York Times*, June 24, 1999.
24. Sarah McCally Morehouse, *The Governor as Party leader: Campaigning and Governing* (Ann Arbor: University of Michigan Press, 1998), p. 236. See also Robert Harmel and Keith E. Hamm, "Development of a Party Role in a No-Party Legislature," *Western Political Quarterly 39 (1986):* 79–92.
25. Mark R. Warren, "Creating a Multi-Racial Democratic Community: A Case Study of the Texas Industrial Areas Foundation" (paper presented at the Conference on Social Networks and Urban Poverty, Russell Sage Foundation, New York, March 1–2, 1996), p. 2.
26. Ibid., p. 6.

Chapter 6

1. "Dr. Hector P. Garcia: A Remembrance," *Corpus Christ Caller Times*, August 11, 1996.
2. See, for example, Robert Dahl, *Democracy and Its Critics* (New Haven, Conn.: Yale University Press, 1989).
3. David B. Truman, *The Governmental Process* (New York: Knopf, 1951), traces this group theory of politics to Arthur F. Bentley's *The Process of Government* (Chicago: University of Chicago Press, 1908).
4. Berry, Jeffrey M. *The Interest Group Society*, 3rd Ed. (New York: Longman, 1997), pp.1–2.
5. Mancur Olsen, *The Logic of Collective Action* (Cambridge, Mass.: Harvard University Press), p. 64.
6. E. E. Schattschneider, T*he Semisovereign People: A Realist's View of Democracy in America* (New York: Holt, Rinehart & Winston, 1960), p. 35.
7. For some interesting insights on business in the interest system in Texas, see Keith E. Hamm and Charles W. Wiggins, "Texas: The Transformation from Personal to Informational Lobbying," in Ronald J. Hrebenar and Clive S. Thomas, eds., *Interest Group Politics in the Southern States* (Tuscaloosa: University of Alabama Press, 1992).
8. L. Harmon Zeigler, "Interest Groups in the States," in Virginia Gray, Herbert Jacob, and Kenneth N. Vines, eds., *Politics in the American States: A Comparative Analysis*, 4th ed. (Boston: Little, Brown, 1983), pp. 97–131.
9. For an interesting discussion of some of the special problems in interest organization in agriculture, see Allan J. Cigler, "From Protest Group to Interest Group: The Making of the American Agriculture Movement, Inc.," in Allan J. Cigler and Burdett A. Loomis, eds., *Interest Group Politics,* 2nd ed. (Washington, D.C.: Congressional Quarterly, 1986), pp. 46–69.
10. For a thorough history and discussion of LULAC, see Benjamin Marquez, *LULAC: The Evolution of a Mexi-*

can American Political Organization (Austin: University of Texas Press, 1993).

11. Allen D. Hertzke, "The Role of Churches in Political Mobilization," in Allan J. Cigler and Burdett A. Loomis, eds., *Interest Group Politics,* 3rd ed. (Washington, D.C.: Congressional Quarterly, 1991), pp. 177–198.

12. For a good summary of the goals of the Christian Coalition in Texas, see Chuck Lindell, "Pulpit to Polls Movement Gathers Steam," *Austin American-Statesman,* March 6, 1994, p. A1; and James Lamare, Jerry L. Polinard, and Robert D. Wrinkle, "Texas: Religion and Politics in God's Country," in *The Christian Right in American politics: Marching Toward the Millenium,* edited by John C. Green, Mark j. Rozell, and Clyde Wilcox (Washington, D.C.: Georgetown University Press, 2003), pp. 59–78.

13. Keith E. ham and Charles W. Wiggins, "Texas: The Transformation from personal to Informational Lobbying," in *Interest Group Politic in the Southern States,* edited by Ronald J. Hrebenar and Olive S. Thomas (Tuscaloosa: University of Alabama Press, 1992).

14. "Money in Politics: A Guide to Money in the 2002 Texas Elections," (Texans for Public Justice, 2003), www.tpj.org.

15. Clive S. Thomas and Ronald J. Hrebenar, "Interest Groups in the States," in Virginia Gray and Herbert Jacob, eds., *Politics in the American States: A Comparative Analysis,* 6th ed. (Washington, D.C.: CQ Press, 1996), p. 147.

16. Ronald J. Hrebenar and Ruth K. Scott, *Interest Group Politics in America* (Englewood Cliffs, N.J.: Prentice Hall, 1982), p. 197.

17. Majorie R. Hershey and Paul A.Beck, *Party Politics in America,* 10th Ed., (New York, NY: Addison-Wesley, 2003), p. 66.

18. Zeigler, "Interest Groups in the States," p. 103. p16.

19. Hrebenar and Scott, "Interest Group Politics in America," p. 197.

20. Jeffrey M. Berry, *The Interest Group Society,* 3rd ed. (New York: Longman, 1997), pp. 218–240.

21. Charles Lindblom, *Politics and Markets* (New York: Basic Books, 1977), p. 175.

22. For a discussion of political influence in Texas during the middle of the twentieth century, see George Norris Green, *The Establishment in Texas Politics: The Primitive Years, 1938–1957,* (Westport, Conn.: Greenwood Press, 1979).

Chapter 7

1. Diana Martinez, in an interview with the author, August 15, 2000.

2. Leon Epstein, *Political Parties in Western Democracies* (New York: Praeger, 1967), p. 9.

3. For a discussion of the impact of election frequency and timing, see Richard W. Boyd, "Election Calendars and Voter Turnout," *American Politics Quarterly* 14 (January–April 1986): 89–104.

4. In fact, the Texas Legislature did address this matter in 2001, nearly passing a bill that would have limited to four the number of dates on which elections could be held.

5. The blanket primary takes the concept of openness a step further in California, Washington, and Alaska. In this form, all voters receive the same ballot with the names of all the candidates and their respective parties. The voter can choose to vote in one party's primary for governor, for example, and another party's primary for senator. For each office, the top vote getters in each party go on to face each other in the general election. The future of the blanket primary is in great doubt due to the U.S. Supreme Court's decision in *California Democratic Party v. Jones* (2000), which found the arrangement a violation of political parties' right to assemble that is protected by the First Amendment.

6. For an extensive discussion of the nature and impact of runoff elections, see Charles S. Bullock and Loch K. Johnson, *Runoff Elections in the United States* (Chapel Hill: University of North Carolina Press, 1992).

7. Chandler Davidson, *Race and Class in Texas Politics* (Princeton, N.J.: Princeton University Press, 1990), pp. 5–6.

8. George Norris Green, *The Establishment: The Primitive Years, 1938–1957* (Norman: Oklahoma University Press, 1979).

9. Texas's white primary law was declared unconstitutional in *Nixon v. Herndon,* 273 U.S. 536 (1927) as an obvious violation of the equal protection clause of the Fourteenth Amendment. When the Texas Legislature then tried to protect the practice by providing statutory protection for the parties to "prescribe qualifications of its own members," the U.S. Supreme Court again struck down the Texas statute in *Nixon v. Condon,* 286 U.S. 73 (1932). The legislature then repealed all laws dealing with primaries, leaving the Democratic party to declare itself a private organization whose membership was restricted to whites. This passed the Supreme Court's Fourteenth Amendment test in *Grovey v. Townsend,* 295 U.S. 45 (1935), but the white primary was finally dealt a death blow in *Smith v. Allwright,* 321 U.S. 45 (1944), in which the Texas

practice was found unconstitutional as a violation of the Fifteenth Amendment's grant voting rights.

10. For a good thorough discussion of the history of the White Primary in Texas see: Darlene Clark Hine, *Black Victory: The Rise and Fall of the White Primary in Texas* (Millwood, New York: KTO Press, 1979).

11. Robert A. Calvert and Arnoldo De Leon, *The History of Texas,* 2nd ed. (Wheeling, Ill.: Harlen Davidson, 1996), pp. 139–141.

12. V. O. Key, *Southern Politics* (New York: Knopf, 1949), pp. 298–311. Davidson, *Race and Class in Texas Politics,* p. 7.

13. Green, *The Establishment,* p. 3.

14. Calvert and De Leon, *History of Texas,* p. 270; Green, *The Establishment,* pp. 23, 42–44.

15. Key, *Southern Politics,* p. 255.

16. For a more thorough discussion of the rise of the Republican party in Texas, see Roger M. Olien, *From Token to Triumph: The Texas Republicans Since 1920* (Dallas: SMU Press, 1982).

17. John R. Petrocik, "Realignment: New Party Coalitions and the Nationalization of the South," *Journal of Politics* 49 (May 1987): 347–375.

18. The Pew Research Center data indicates that Republicans may have about a 10 percent advantage in identification in Texas in 2004 (39%–29%) http://people-press.org/reports/display.php3?PageID=750 accessed April 12, 2004.

19. John F. Bibby and Thomas M. Holbrook, "Parties and Elections," in Virginia Gray and Herbert Jacob (eds.), *Politics in the American States,* 6th ed. (Washington, D.C.: CQ Press, 1996), p. 105.

20. "DeLay's involvement in Texas redistricting: pure partisan politics," *Austin-American Statesman,* December 12, 2003. at http://www.fairvote.org/redistricting/reports/remanual/frames.htm Accessed April 7, 2004.

21. Laylan Copelin, "Final map passes; legal battles on the way Senate's approval sends controversial redistricting issue toward review by Justice Department, court challenges," *Austin-American Statesman,* October 10, 2003 at http://www.fairvote.org/redistricting/reports/remanual/frames.htm Accessed April 7, 2004.

22. "Change Needed in the Way Texas Redraws Districts," *Austin-American Statesman,* January 7, 2004 at http://www.fairvote.org/redistricting/reports/remanual/frames.htm Accessed April 7, 2004.

23. Office of the Secretary of State http://204.65.104.19/elchist.exe Accessed April 12, 2004.

24. For a discussion of the development of two-party competition focusing on Houston, see Richard Murray and Kent L. Tedin, "The Emergence of Two-Party Competition in the Sunbelt: The Case of Houston," in William Crotty, ed., *Political Parties in Local Areas*

(Knoxville: University of Tennessee Press, 1987), pp. 39–62.

25. For a good general discussion of the development of two-party politics in Texas and other sunbelt megastates, see Albert Nelson, *Democrats Under Siege in the Sunbelt Megastates: California, Florida, and Texas* (Westport, Conn.: Praeger, 1996).

26. V.O. Key, *Politics, Parties, and Pressure Groups* (New York: Cromwell, 1958.) Key used this "tripartite" conception of parties to organize his classic text on parties and it has had great influence on the scholarship of parties since.

27. Cited in Davidson, *Race and Class in Texas Politics,* p. 7.

28. Sarah McCalley Morehouse, *The Governor as Party Leader: Campaigning and Governing* (Ann Arbor: University of Michigan Press, 1998), p. 236.

29. Indeed, it is just this skill, uniquely important and possible for a Texas governor, that George W. Bush promised to bring to Washington during his campaign for president. His promise to be a "uniter, not a divider" will prove harder to keep in Washington, however, where parties are strong in the Congress and partisanship is a powerful predictor of support for the president's program.

30. For more information on the current state of party organization in Texas and other megastates, see John F. Bibby, "State Party Organizations: Coping and Adapting to Candidate-Centered Politics and Nationalization," in L. Sandy Maisel, ed., *The Parties Respond: Changes in American Parties and Campaigns,* 3rd ed. (Boulder, Colo.: Westview Press, 1998), pp. 23–49.

31. For an extended discussion of endorsing conventions see Morehouse, *The Governor as Party Leader,* pp. 23–35, 197–198.

Chapter 8

1. Robert A. Calvert and Arnoldo De Leon, *The History of Texas* (Arlington Heights, Ill.: Harlan Davidson, 1990), p. 79.

2. Daniel B. Kulvicki, "The State of Texas Anniversary Remembrance Day Story," STAR DAY Museum and Park exhibit, 2000. See www.StarDay.org.

3. George H. Sabine, *A History of Political Theory,* 3rd ed. (New York: Holt, Rinehart, and Winston, 1961), p. 325.

4. Belle Zeller, ed., *American State Legislatures* (New York: 1954), chap. 4.

5. Council of State Governments, *The Book of the States: 2003* (Lexington, Ky.: Council of State Governments, 2003), p. 128.

6. Gregory S. Thielemann, Texas Legislative Survey, University of Texas at Dallas, April 1, 1991), p. 2.

7. Alan Rosenthal, *The Decline of Representative Democracy: Process, Participation, and Power in State Legislatures* (Washington, D.C.: CQ Press, 1998), p. 6.

8. Arturo Vega, "Gender and Ethnicity Effects on the Legislative Behavior and Substantive Representation of the Texas Legislature," *Texas Journal of Political Studies* 19 (1997): 7.

9. "Hate Crimes Bill Sent to Governor," *Austin American Statesman*, May 10, 2001.

10. Council of State Governments, *Book of the States: 2003*, p. 84.

11. Kendra Hovey and Harold Hovey, *Congressional Quarterly's State Fact Finder 1999: Rankings Across America* (Washington, D.C.: Congressional Quarterly Press, 1999)

12. Citizens Conference on State Legislatures, *The Sometimes Governments: A Critical Study of the Fifty American Legislatures* (New York: Bantam Books, 1971), pp. 52–53.

13. *Baker v. Carr*, 369 U.S. 186 (1962).

14. *Reynolds v. Sims*, 377 U.S. S33 (1964).

15. *Thornburg v. Gingles*, 478 U.S. 30 (1986).

16. *Shaw v. Reno*, 509 U.S. 630 (1993); *Miller v. Johnson*, 515 U.S. 900 (1995). See, for example, David T. Canon, *Race, Redistricting, and Representation: The Unintended Consequences of Black Majority Districts* (Chicago: University of Chicago Press, 2000), Chap. 2.

17. Dave McNeely. "Craddick Hopes to End Dems' Reign as Speaker," *Austin American Statesman*, May 10, 2001, p. B1.

18. George Norris Green, *The Establishment in Texas Politics: The Primitive Years, 1938–1957* (Norman: University of Oklahoma Press, 1979), p. 13.

19. Thielemann, Texas Legislative Survey, p. 1.

20. Texas Senate Archives, "Select Committee on Public Education Hearings," March 14–17, 1999.

21. Quoted in Malcolm E. Jewell, "Legislative Casework in Serving the Constituents, One at a Time," *State Legislature* (November 1979): 16.

22. Malcolm E. Jewell, *Representation in State Legislatures* (Lexington, Ky.: University of Kentucky Press, 1982), p. 141.

23. "Legislative Wrapup," *Austin American Statesman*, June 1, 2001, p. A1.

24. House Research Organization, "How a Bill Becomes Law: Rules for the 73rd Legislature," Special Legislative Report No. 180 (Austin: House Research Organization, February 1993), p. 26.

25. *Texas Legislative Manual* (Austin: Texas State Directory, 1993), p. 58.

Chapter 9

1. *Austin American-Statesman*, April 22, 1995, p. A10

2. Ibid., May 13, 1995, p. A11.

3. American Political Science Dictionary, 10th Edition, by Jack Plano and Milton Greenberg. Harcourt Brace Publishers, Ft. Worth, TX, 1997, page 230

4. "On Your Mark, Get Ready, Reorganize" Texas Government Newsletter, November 23, 1998, page 2.

5. *The Texas Almanac: 1998–1999* (Dallas: Dallas Morning News, 1997), p. 371.

6. Houston Chronicle, Jan 16, 2003 (Electronic database)

7. Sarah McCalley Morehouse, *The Governor as Party Leader* (Ann Arbor: University of Michigan Press, 2000), p. 23.

8. Thad Beyle, "Governors: The Middlemen and Women in Our Political System," in Virginia Gray and Herbert Jacob, eds., *Politics in the American States*, 6th ed. (Washington, D.C.: CQ Press, 1996), p. 250

9. One of the first was Joseph A. Schlesinger, "The Politics of the Executive," in Herbert Jacob and Kenneth N. Vines, eds., *Politics in the American States* (Boston: Little, Brown, 1965).

10. Thad Beyle, "The Governors: Chapter 6" in Virginia Gray, Russell Hanson, and Herbert Jacob. *Politics in the American States,* 7th edition (Washington, D.C., CQ Press, 1999), pages 210, 211.

11. Council of State Governments, *The Book of the States: 2000–2001* (Lexington, Ky.: Council of State Governments, 2000).

12. SOS web page: http://www.sos.state.tx.us/about/duties.shtml

13. Election Law Opinion GSC-1, dated 1-22-04.

14. Texas Legislative Website, Legislative Statistics at: http://www.capitol.state.tx.us/cgi-bin/db2www/tlo/billhist/statistics.d2w/report

15. Signature Message of Governor Rick Perry on HB 752, dated 6-21-03, from http://www.governor.state.tx.us/divisions/press/bills2003/bills/message.2003-hb-752

16. Glenn Abney and Thomas P. Lauth, "Research Notes: The Item Veto and Fiscal Responsibility," *The Journal of Politics*, 59:3 (1997): 889–890.

17. Governor's website: http://www.governor.state.tx.us/divisions/press/proclamations/proclamation.2003-12-04

18. Source- Governor's Proclamation of June 21, 2003

19. Ft. Worth Star-Telegram, 9-21-03 (Electronic database)

20. *Austin American-Statesman,* February 22, 2001, p. B1.

21. Kendra Hovey and Harold Hovey, *State Fact Finder 1999,* CQ Press Washington D.C. page 101 and Council of State Governments, *The Book of States: 2000–2001* (Lexington, Ky: Council of State Governments, 2000), page 18.

22. "Key Duties of the Office of Budget and Planning," http://www.governor.state.tx.us/Budget/budget/keyduties.html [Accessed 6-6-2000].

23. Thad L. Beyle and Lynn R. Muchmore, eds., *Being Governor: The View from the Office* (Durham, N.C.: Duke University Press, 1983), p. 48.

24. Morehouse, *The Governor as Party Leader.* The weak party states were California, Kansas, Oregon, Tennessee, and Texas; the strong party states were Colorado, Connecticut, Minnesota, Illinois, and New York.

25. Ibid., p. 197.

26. For an extended discussion of endorsing conventions, see Ibid., pp. 23–35, 197–198.

27. Council of State Governments, *Book of the States,* p. 24.

28. Opinion number GA-0136 dated Jan 15, 2004.

29. AG opinion GA-0141 dated Feb 4, 2004.

30. AG's website at: http://www.oag.state.tx.us/evaders/evader_all_arrested.php

31. Ft. Worth Star-Telegram, 9-21-03 (Electronic database)

32. Governor's press releases 6-9-03 & 6-20-03

33. *Houston Chronicle* "State orders schools to serve less junk food" by Polly Ross Hughes. Also, Texas Department of Agriculture Press Release, March 3, 2004.

34. Dave McNeely, "Texas Can Do Without Railroad Commission," *Austin American Statesman,* December 13, 1994, p. A11.

35. Mary Ramos, ed., *Texas Almanac, 2000–2001* (Dallas: *Dallas Morning News,* 2000), pp. 533–534.

36. TxDOT 2002 Annual Summary, page 15

37. TxDOT 2002 Annual Summary, page 3

38. *Tyler Morning Telegraph*, Jan 25, 2003. (Electronic database)

39. TxDOT website graphic

40. TxDOT website

41. TxDOT 2002 Annual report, pages 6,7.

42. TCEQ website history page, and HB1 (2003)

43. TCEQ website

44. "Progress Report on Using Scrap Tires and Crumb Rubber in Highway Construction Projects," TCEQ report, January 2003

45. Strategically Directed Regulatory Structure, December 2002

46. www.txpeer.org/Bush/Quiet_Little_War.html; Molly Ivins and Louis DuBose, *Shrub: The Short But Happy Political Life of George W. Bush* (New York: Random House, 2000).

47. Texas Government Code, chap. 572.054–.056, effective 2001.

48. "Texas Revolvers: Public Officials Recast as Hired Guns," Texans for Public Justice, February 1999, page 6.

49. "Austin's Oldest Profession: Texas' Top Lobby Clients and Those Who Serve Them", TPJ 2002, page 5.

Chapter 10

1. John MacCormick, "South Texan rattles skeletons in a famous closet," *San Antonio Express-News,* February 8, 2004, p. 1A, 12A.

2. *Houston Chronicle,* January 23, 204, p.21A.

3. *Fort Worth Star-Telegram,* December 19, 2003, p. 5B.

4. *The Dallas Morning News,* December 20, 2003, p. 6A.

5. *The Dallas Morning News,* November 22, 2003, p.4A and December 19, 2003, p.10A and *Fort Worth Star-Telegram,* September 27, 2003, p. 5B. Coleman was interviewed on *60 Minutes* September 28, 2003.on this scandal.

6. Enron's former Chief Financial Officer Andrew Fastow, and his wife, Lea, entered guilty pleas and have been sentenced in Houston, Texas; Richard Causey, former chief accounting officer was charged with five counts of securities fraud and one count of conspiracy and has pled not guilty as of this writing. See *San Antonio Express-News,* January 23, 2004, p.1D.

7. *Houston Chronicle,* January 9, 2004, p. 1C.

8. *The Dallas Morning News,* December 31, 2003, p. 6A. See also *Houston Chronicle,* January 23, 2004, p. 25A, 34A for statistical information on number of students claiming to live on campus but list out of county mailing addresses; more than 2,700 student voters list Prairie Viwe's University Village campus housing as their residence but the facility only has capacity for 1,836; and, the same three postal box addresses have been used by 220 students. The U.S. Department of Justice, civil rights division, has launched an investigation as well.

9. *San Antonio Express-News,* January 12, 2004, p.7B.

10. *San Antonio Express-News,* January 24, 2004, p. 5B.

11. *The Dallas Morning News,* December 14, 2003, p. 35A. See also *San Antonio Express-News,* January 8, 2004, p. 9B.

12. Ihosvani Rodirguez, "DA's office barred from JP McKnight case," *San Antonio Express-News,* January 23, 2004, p.1B, 8B.

13. Gary Cartwright, "Sarita's Secret," *Texas Monthly,* September 2004, pp. 130–133, 239–245.

14. Mark Curriden and Allen Pusey, "A Poor Reflection," *Dallas Morning News,* October 22, 2000, p. A1.

15. Texas Judicial Council, "Court Structure of Texas Descriptive Outline September 1, 2003" in *Annual Report of the Texas Judicial System, Fiscal Year 2003* (Austin: Texas Judicial Council, 2003)).

16. *The Dallas Morning News,* November 22, 2003, p. 3A.

17. John Moritz, "Historic Appointment," Ft. Worth Star-Telegram, September 15, 2004, p. 5B.

18. *Fort Worth Star-Telegram*, November 22, 2003, p.2B.

19. *Fort Worth Star-Telegram*, October 25, 2003, p. 12B.

20. *Chicana*, for females, and *Chicano*, for male, are terms in vogue during the Chicano Movement of the 1960s, 70s and 80s. Most dictionaries define the terms as a U.S. citizen of Mexican ancestry and many older elected officials and influentials still use the self-descriptor, as does Justice Reyna Yanez.

21. Statistical Profile of Texas Judges (2002–2003) State Bar of Texas, October 2003.

22. Lisa Kalakanis, "Statistical Profile of the State Bar of Texas Membership (2002–2003), State Bar of Texas, May 2003.

23. The Dallas Morning News, December 21, 2003, p.2E and Dallas Bar Association HEADNOTES, January 1, 2004, p. 1.

24. "2003 Annual Report," State Commission on Judicial Conduct, Austin, Texas., pps. 23–28.

25. Del Jones, "Lawyers, wannabes on the rise," *USA Today*, December 26, 2003, p.5B.

26. Lisa Kalakanis, "Annual Report on the Status of Racial/Ethnic Minorities in the State Bar of Texas (2002–2003). State Bar of Texas, May 2003, pps. 1–4.

27. *Lawstreet Journal,* newsletter of Legal Services of North Texas, 3 (Spring 2001):8.

Chapter 11

1. Sheldon Goldman, *Constitutional Law and Supreme Court Decision-Making: Cases and Essays* (New York: Harper and Row, 1982), pp. 319–320, 484–496.

2. "Unequal Justice," *Fort Worth Star-Telegram,* October 15, 2000.

3. Ibid.

4. Ibid.

5. Ibid.

6. Ibid.

7. "Death Row Information ," Texas Department of Criminal Justice, 2004

8. "Defense Called Lacking for Death Row Indigents," *Dallas Morning News,* September 10, 2000.

9. "State's Death Penalty Procedures 'Grossly Flawed,' Report Says," *Fort Worth Star-Telegram,* September 21, 2000.

10. "Judge Says Inmate Wrongly Convicted," *Dallas Morning News,* September 10, 2000.

11. For a detailed look at the case of Ernest Willis, see Ibid.

12. Ibid.

13. "Texas Death Penalty Practices: Quality Regional Standards and County Plans Governing Indigent Defense in Capital Cases," The Equal Justice Center and Texas Defender Service, Austin, November 2003, p.1.

14. "Judge says inmate wrongly convicted," Op.cit.

15. Ibid.

16. Ibid.

17. Ibid.

18. "The Texas Fair Defense Act's Answers to frequently Asked Questions," Equal Justice Center and Texas Appleseed, Austin, 2003, p.2.

19. "Little justice for those living under the death penalty," San Antonio Express/News, December 8, 2002.

20. "Unequal Justice—Part III: Poor More Vulnerable to Death Penalty, Critics Say," *Fort Worth Star-Telegram,* October 17, 2000.

21. "Texas death sentences scrutinized," Dallas Morning News, March 23, 2004.

22. James Liebman, Jeffery Fagan, and Valerie West, "A Broken System: Error Rates in Capital Cases, 1973–1995," Appendix A-10, The Justice Project, Justice. policy.net/jpreport/index.html.

23. For a detailed description of the continuing problems in indigent defense in Texas see "A State of Denial:Texas Justice and the Death Penalty," Texas Defender Service, October, 2000.

24. *Improving Criminal Justice Systems Through Expanded Strategies and Innovative Collaborations: Report of the National Symposium on Indigent Defense* (Washington, D.C.: U.S. Department of Justice, February 25–26, 1999), p. ix.

25. "Inside America's Toughest Prison," *Newsweek,* October 6, 1986, pp. 46–61.

26. Ibid.

27. "State Board Approves Two New Maximum-Security Prisons," *Abilene Reporter-News,* November 22, 1997.

28. Ibid.

29. Corrections Yearbook 2002, Criminal Justice Institute, Middleton, Conn p.94; Bureau of Justice Statistics BJS)Bulletin, p.4.

30. "Guards Complain of Work's Challenges as Prison Officials Lobby for Better Pay," *Dallas Morning News,* January 22, 2001.

31. Ibid.

32. Ibid.

33. "Inside America's Toughest Prison," p. 48.

34. Michael Berryhill, "Prisoner's Dilemma," *New Republic,* December 27, 1999, pp. 18–23.

35. "Inside America's Toughest Prison," p. 51.

36. See, for example, Joel Samaha, *Criminal Justice* 2nd ed. (St. Paul, Minn.: West Publishing Company, 1991), p. 478, or Jay Albanese, *Criminal Justice* (Boston: Allyn and Bacon, 1999), p. 395.

37. U.S. Department of Justice, Bureau of Justice Statistics, *Census of State and Federal Adult Correctional Facilities, 1995* (Washington, D.C.: Government Printing Office, 1995).

38 Corrections Yearbook 2002. Criminal Justice Institute, Middleton, Conn., p.6.
39. Bureau of Justice Statistics, "Prisoners in 2001," p.4.
40. Corrections Yearbook 2002. p.6.
41. Ibid.
42. D. Wilson and P. Ditton, *Truth in Sentencing in State Prisons* (Washington, D.C.: Bureau of Justice Statistics, January 1999).
43. Ibid.
44. Jenni Gainsborough and Marc Mauer, "Diminishing Returns: Crime and Incarceration in the 1990s," in *The Sentencing Project* (Washington, D.C.: The Sentencing Project, September 2000), p. 4.
45. For competing explanations of the role of incarceration on crime reduction, see George Kelling, *Fixing Broken Windows: Restoring Order and Reducing Crime in Our Communities* (New York: Simon & Schuster, 1996); Andrew Karmen, *New York Murder Mystery: The True Story Behind the Crime Crash of the 1990s* (New York: New York University Press, 2001).
46. B. E. Forst, "The Deterrent Effect of Capital Punishment: A Cross State Analysis of the 1960's," *Minnesota Law Review* 61 (1977): 743–767.
47. Scott Decker and Carol Kohfeld, "Capital Punishment and Executions in the Lone Star State: A Deterrence Study," *Criminal Justice Research Bulletin* (Criminal Justice Center, Sam Houston State University) (1988).
48. "Racial Profiling: Texas Traffic Stops and Searches," The Steward Research Group, The Texas Criminal Justice Reform Coalition, February 2004, p.4.
49. "Police search statistics don't lie, but statisticians can," Dallas Morning News, February 2004.
50. "A Poor Reflection—Number of Minority, Low-Income Jurors Doesn't Mirror County Population," *Dallas Morning News*, October 22, 2000.
51. Ibid.
52. Ibid.
53. "Turning a blind eye to justice reform," Austin American-Statesman, July 6, 2003.

Chapter 12

1. Sustainable Food Center, *www.main.org/sfc/*; telephone interview by Carol Waters with Ruth Lauer, March 12, 2001.
2. U.S. Census Bureau. 2003 Poverty Threshold. www.census.gov.
3. U.S. Census Bureau, *Current Population Survey: Poverty* 1999 (Washington, D.C.: U.S. Government Printing Office, 2000). Available at www.census.gov/hhes/poverty/povanim/pvmaptxt.html
4. Anne Erickson *Legal Services Journal*. October, 2003 "New Census Data Shows Increase in Poverty Children, Minorities, Married Couples Hit Hard."
5. U.S. Census Bureau Historical Poverty Rates 1980 to 2002. www.census.gov.hhes/poverty/histpov/hstpvo21.html.
6. National Center for Children in Poverty. Demographics calculated from the US. Census Current Population Survey, 2001, 2002, and 2003. http://nccp.org/state.detail.demographic.html.
7. "Pulling Apart: A State by State Analysis of Income Trends," December 6, 1997. Center on Budget and Policy Priorities. Available at http://www.cbpp.org/pa-tx.htm.
8. LIFT Economic Conditions Cross-state. *www.nccp.org*. Accessed 4/7/04.
9. U.S. Census Bureau. "Texas Quick Facts, 2001." http://quickfacts.census.gov/qfd/states/06000.html.
10. National Center for Children in Poverty. Demographics calculated from the US. Census Current Population Survey, 2001, 2002, and 2003. http://nccp.org/state.detail.demographic.html.
11. Ruby K. Payne, *Poverty: A Framework for Understanding and Working with Students and Adults from Poverty* (Baytown, Tx., RFT Publishing, 1995, pp. 2–3, 8–10.
12. Texas Department of Health "National Public Health Week-Geographic Disparities" April 2, 2004. www.tdh.state.tx.us/ophp/pubs/phw.Factsheets.pdf.
13. The Henry Kaiser Family Foundation. "State Health Facts Online" www.statehealthfacts.kff.org/
14. National Center for Children in Poverty. "Parental Employment in Low-Income Families. http://nccp.org/pup-pel04.html.
15. U.S. Department of Health and Human Services. "Medicare" www.hhs.gov/
16. Terry Savage "Introduction to Medicare, part C," *Chicago Sun Times*, August 30, 1998.
17. Center for Medicare and Medicaid Services. "Medicare Prescription Drug Discount Card and Transitional Assistance Programs" March 26, 2004. *www.cms.hhs.gov/media/press/release.asp?Counter=990*.
18. Food Research and Action Center. Jan. 2004. "A Guide to the Supplemental Security Income/Food Stamp Program Combined Application Projects."
19. State of Texas. "The Food Stamp Program." *www.dhs.state.tx.us/programs/Texas Works.Foodstamp*.html.
20. State of Texas. "The Food Stamp Program." *www.dhs.state.tx.us/programs/Texas Works .Foodstamp.html*
21. Center for Law and Social Policy. "State TANF Caseload Data, Annual Change, Sept 2001-Sept 2002. www.clasp.org.
22. Texas Health and Human Services Agency. *www.hhsc.state.tx.us/*. "Medicaid History," Thursday, March 25, 1999.

23. Texas Health and Human Services Agency, "Medicaid Policy Changes, 78th Legislature, Regular Session, 2003. www.hhsc.state.tx.us/April 2, 2004.

24. Campaign to Restore Chips. "What cuts were made to CHIPS as a result of the 78th Texas Legislature? May, 2004.

25. Guerra, Carlos. San Antonio Express News. "If Texas new uninsured numbers seem high, stick around." 10/05/03. http://news.mysanantonio.com.

26. Texas HHSC. "HHS Transformation FAQ" 4/04/04.www.hhsc.state.tx.us/consolidation/cons/_FAQ.html

27. *San Antonio Business Journal*. October 24, 2003. sanantonio.buzjournals.com/sanantonio/stories/2003.

28. L. Jerome Gallagher. "A Shrinking Portion of the Safety Net: General Assistance from 1989 to 1998" in New Federalism Issues and Options for the States (Washington, D.C.: Urban Institute: September, 1999). Available at newfederalism.urban.org/pdf/anf_a36pdf.

Chapter 13

1. The information on Bea Salazar's program was gathered in a personal interview by Barry Price conducted in April 2000.

2. Sheldon Goldman, *Constitutional Law and Supreme Court Decision-Making: Cases and Essays* (New York: Harpers & Row, 1982), pp. 205–207.

3. Ibid., pp. 498–500.

4. "The Educational Gap," *Dallas Morning News,* June 5, 1988. "$5 Billion Divides Richest, Poorest School Districts," *Fort Worth Star-Telegram,* February 15, 1987.

5. Goldman, *Constitutional Law,* pp. 702–706.

6. "Texas' Poor Schools—Not Just on the Border," in Texas Comptroller of Public Accounts, *Fiscal Notes* (March 1988).

7. For a detailed chronology of judicial and legislative decisions leading up to Senate Bill 7, see "School Finance Rulings," *Dallas Morning News,* January 31, 1992.

8. The Texas Supreme Court ruled the original "Robin Hood" legislation unconstitutional in January 1992. Senate Bill 7 was a subsequent effort by the state legislature to develop a constitutionally permissible plan to transfer property tax wealth from rich to poor school districts.

9. "Fed up with school funding, Austin joins suit," Dallas Morning News, October 26, 2003

10. West Orange-Cove Consolidated ISD., et. al. v. Alanis. No.02-0427.

11. "Dallas to join wealthy school districts' lawsuit", Fort Worth Star-Telegram, September 26, 2003.

12. "Graduate Reports 2001–2002", Public Education Information Management System.Texas Educational Agency.

13 Texas Higher Education Coordinating Board, *Statistical Report,* FY 2003-.

14. Ibid.

15. David Savage, "Court Lets Stand Ruling Against Race Preference," *Los Angeles Times,* July 2, 1996.

16. "Colleges Weigh Diversity Options," *Fort Worth Star-Telegram,* January 24, 1999.

17. "Study: Top students not hurt by admissions law" Dallas Morning News, January 20, 2004.

18. GRUTTER v. BOLLINGER (02-241) 288 F.3d 732, affirmed.

19. "Texas Returns to Affirmative Action", CROSSTALK, Winter 2004.

20. Statistical Report, FY 2003", Texas Higher Education Coordinating Board 2003. 21. "2003 Annual Report," University of Texas Investment Management Company, Online at www.utimco.org

22. "Higher Education Assistance Fund Allocation Model, 1998," Texas Higher Education Coordinating Board, October 1998.

23. National Center for Educational Statistics, *State Comparisons of Educational Statistics* (Washington, D.C.: National Center for Educational Statistics, 1998).

24. "Statistical Report, FY 2003," Texas Higher Education Coordinating Board, February 2000.

25. "Bordering the Future," in Texas Comptroller of Public Accounts, *Fiscal Notes* (July 1998).

26. Statistical Reports: 1980, 2004.Texas Higher Education Coordinating Board.

27. Losing Ground: The Texas State Budget for 2004–2005. Center for Public Policy Priorities, January 2004, p.5.

28. Ibid.

29. "Public Universities Get Money to Attract High-Tech Industry," *Chronicle of Higher Education,* February 25, 2000.

30. Rankings and Estimates: Report of School Statistics. National Education Association, Fall 2003, p.3.

31. "Estimates of School Statistics," and unpublished data, National Education Association, Washington, D.C., 2000.

32. Rankings and Estimates: Report of School Statistics. National Education Association, Fall 2003, p.5.

33. F. Howard Nelson, Rachael Drown. Survey and Analysis of Teacher Salary Trends 2002, American Federation of Teacher, 2003, p.13. www.aft.org.

34. "Legislators Reach Deal to Fund Health Insurance for Teachers," *Dallas Morning News,* June 25, 2001.

35. Gary Burtless, ed., *Does Money Matter?* (Washington, D.C.: Brookings Institute, 1996), pp. 4–12.

36. Ibid., pp. 12–16.

37. National Assessment of Educational Progress: 4th grade Math and Reading Results 2003, National Center for Educational Statistics.

38. National Assessment of Educational Progress: 8th grade Math and Reading Results 2003, National Center for Educational Statistics.

39. National Assessment of Educational Progress: 4th grade Math and Reading Results 2003, National Center for Educational Statistics.

40. "The State of School Dropouts in Texas Public High Schools," Roy Johnson, Intercultural Development Research Associates Newsletter, October 1998.

41. Kids Count 2003 Data Book Online. Annie E. Casey Foundation available online at aecf.org/kidscount/databook.

42. College Board, 2000. See Table 13.2.

43. "How Many Research Universities Does a State Need?" Chronicle of Higher Education, February 11, 2000.

44. National Center for Educational Statistics, State Comparisons of Educational Statistics (Washington, D.C.: National Center for Educational Statistics, 1998).

45. Chronicle of Higher Education, Almanac Issue, August 27, 1999.

46. Texas Higher Education Coordinating Board, "Advanced Research Program, Advanced Technology Program Fiscal Year 1998 Progress Report" (Austin: Texas Higher Education Coordinating Board, November 1998).

47. Texas Budget Highlights Fiscal 2004–05, House Research Organization, Texas House of Representatives, November 17, 2003, pp 20–23.

48. For a detailed explanation of the Texas accountability system, see Texas Education Agency, 2000 Accountability Manual (Austin: Texas Education Agency, 2000). Also see "Schools in Dark on Rating System".

49. For a thorough discussion of the deleterious consequences of TAAS testing, see Linda McNeil and Angela Valenzuela, The Harmful Impact of the TAAS System of Testing in Texas; Beneath the Accountability Rhetoric (Cambridge, Mass.: The Civil Rights Project, Harvard University, January 2000).

50. "Judge Errs Upholding Texas TAAS High School Exit Test," press release, Mexican American Legal Defense and Education Fund, San Antonio, January 7, 2000.

51. "The Public School Fix, Dallas Morning News, March 14th, 2004.

52. "Moses raises stakes for teachers," Dallas Morning News, December 17, 2003.

53. For a good overview of arguments for and against school vouchers see John Witte.The Market Approach to Education, Princeton University Press, 2000.

54. "Charters Challenge Traditional Notions of 'School,'" Fort Worth Star-Telegram, September 7, 1998.

55. For a summary of arguments questioning the promise of charter schools, see Richard Rothstein, "Charter Conundrum," American Prospect (July–August 1998): 46–60.

56. "Football Prayer Issue Argued Before Supreme Court," Fort Worth Star-Telegram, March 30, 2000.

57. This case history is briefly summarized in Doe v. Santa Fe Independent School District, 168 F.3d 806 (5th Circuit, 1999).

58. "Marian's Prayer", Fort Worth Star-Telegram, April 2, 2000.

59. Santa Fe Independent School District v. DOE, Supreme Court of the United States, June 19, 2000.

60. John Gribban, The Birth of Time: How Astronomers Measured the Age of the Universe (New Haven: Yale University Press, 1999).

61. Alan Guth, The Inflationary Universe: The Quest for a New Theory of Cosmic Origins (Reading, Mass.: Perseus Books, 1997).

62. Steve Jones, Darwin's Ghost: The Origin of the Species Updated (New York: Random House, 1999).

Chapter 14

1. Bruce Hight, "Texas Oil Producers Caught in Bind," Austin American Statesman, February 1, 1999, p. A1.

2. Monahans News, January 21, 1999, p. 1.

3. Richard D. Pomp, "State Tax Expenditure Budgets—and Beyond," in Steven D. Gold, ed., The Unfinished Agenda for State Tax Reform (Washington, D.C.: National Conference of State Legislatures, 1988), pp. 65–83.

4. "Message from the Comptroller," January 29, 2003. Letter of Transmittal in Preface to: Tax Exemptions and Tax Incidence: A Report to the Governor and the 78th Texas Legislature (Austin: Texas Comptroller of Public Accounts, 2003).

5. The Texas Comptroller of Public Accounts. Tax Exemptions and Tax Incidence.: A Report to the 78th Texas Legislature. Austin: 2003. pp 4 and 39.

6. Dave McNeely, "Strayhorn's Always Full of Surprises." Austin American Statesman. August7, 2003.]

7. Carole Keeton Rylander. "Texas Can be Leaner without being Meaner." Opinion Editorial. March 11, 2004. www.window.state.tx.us/oped/040311hhs.html

8. Texas Comptroller of Public Accounts. "Texans to Pay $2.7 Billion More Under New State Laws ." Window on State Government. www.window.state.tx.us/news/30827fees.html. Accessed 3/15/04.

9. Center for Public Policy Priorities, 'Texas Poverty Fact Sheet,' June 28, 2001, www.cppp/products/fastfacts/poverty.html.

10. Robert Heilbroner and Peter Berstein, *The Debt and the Deficit* (New York: Norton, 1989), p. 26.

11. John Sharp, Comptroller of Public Accounts, *Sales Tax Exemptions* (Austin: Office of the Comptroller, 1997), 1:18.

12. George R. Zodrow, *State Sales and Income Taxes: An Economic Analysis* (College Station: Texas A&M Press, 1999), p. 105.

13. Ibid., p. 104.

14. Gold, *Unfinished Agenda,* pp. 47–57.

15. Adam Smith, 1776. *Wealth of Nations*, Book V, Part IV, Chapter 2. Quoted in Robert L. Heilbroner, *The Essential Adam Smith* (New York: W. W. Norton & Co., 1986), p. 313.

16. For 2004, according to the The Comptrollers Exemption and Incidence Report newspaper exemptions from the sales tax will cost the state $20.6 million, another exemption for newspaper inserts is another $27 million. p. 5

17. Institute on Taxation and Economic Policy. 2003. Who Pays? A Distributional Analysis of the Tax Systems in All 50 States. 2nd Edition. Washington, D.C. p.102.

18. "Finding 'Robin Hood' in School Finance Forest. Austin American Statesman. February 16, 2003.

19. Michael P. Ettlinger, John F. O'Hare, Robert S. McIntyre, Julie King, Elizabeth A. Fray, and Neil Miransky, *Who Pays? A Distributional Analysis of the Tax Systems in All Fifty States* (Washington, D.C.: Citizens for Tax Justice and institute on Taxation and Economic Policy, 1996). Appendix 3.

CREDITS

Chapter 1
p. 18: Photo © Ariel Skelley/Corbis

Chapter 2
p. 35: Photo © Bob Daemmrich Photography, Inc.

Chapter 3
p. 55: Cartoon, *Sargent* © 2004 *Austin American-Statesman*. Reprinted with permission of *Universal Press Syndicate*. All Rights Reserved.
p. 60: Photo © Bob Daemmrich Photography, Inc.
p. 73: From *Federalism: The Politics of Intergovernmental Relations*, by David Nice. Copyright © David C. Nice. Reprinted with permission of Palgrave.

Chapter 4
p. 107: Photo © Bob Daemmrich Photography, Inc.

Chapter 5
p. 123: Photo © Bob Daemmrich Photography, Inc.
p. 125: Photo, Jim Watkins/*Lubbock Avalanche-Journal*/AP-Wide World Photos
p. 127: Photo by Brian K. Diggs © *Austin American-Statesman*. Photo courtesy of C.O.P.S. (Communities Organized for Public Service)—Metro Alliance, San Antonio, Texas.

Chapter 6
p. 153: Photo © Bob Daemmrich/The Image Works
p. 157: Photo © Bob Daemmrich Photography, Inc.
p. 159: Photo © Bob Daemmrich/The Image Works
p. 160: Cartoon, *Sargent* © 2004 *Austin American-Statesman*. Reprinted with permission of *Universal Press Syndicate*. All Rights Reserved.

Chapter 7
p. 184: Photo © Bob Daemmrich/The Image Works
p. 198: Cartoon, *Sargent* © 2004 *Austin American-Statesman*. Reprinted with permission of *Universal Press Syndicate*. All Rights Reserved.

p. 210: Table, "Party Strength and Gubernatorial Nominations," from Malcolm E. Jewell and Sarah M. Morehouse, *Political Parties and Elections in American States,* © 2001, CQ Press, pg. 103.

Chapter 8
p. 221: Photo, Robert White/Texas Senate Media Services
p. 239: Cartoon, *Sargent* © 2004 *Austin American-Statesman*. Reprinted with permission of *Universal Press Syndicate*. All Rights Reserved.

Chapter 9
p. 263: Photo, Deborah Cannon/AP-Wide World Photos

Chapter 10
p. 305: Photo © Bob Daemmrich/The Image Works
p. 307: Photo © Bob Daemmrich Photography, Inc.
p. 308: Cartoon, *Sargent* © 2004 *Austin American-Statesman*. Reprinted with permission of *Universal Press Syndicate*. All Rights Reserved.

Chapter 11
p. 335: Photo, Brett Coomer/AP-Wide World Photos

Chapter 12
p. 342: Cartoon, *Sargent* © 2004 *Austin American-Statesman*. Reprinted with permission of *Universal Press Syndicate*. All Rights Reserved.
p. 353: Photo © Bob Daemmrich Photography, Inc.

Chapter 13
p. 365: Photo © Bob Daemmrich Photography, Inc.

Chapter 14
p. 393: Cartoon, *Sargent* © 2004 *Austin American-Statesman*. Reprinted with permission of *Universal Press Syndicate*. All Rights Reserved.

Ad valorem taxes   Taxes levied on real property, that is, land and buildings, based on the assessed value of the property.

Adversarial system of justice   A system based on the assumption that justice will emerge from conflict between legal adversaries. In criminal cases, the legal adversaries are individuals accused of violating the state's criminal statutes and the state itself.

Affirmative action programs   Programs designed to help minorities by giving extra weight to a minority student's college admission application.

Aid to Families with Dependent Children (AFDC)   A joint federal-state welfare program designed to provide assistance to poor families; it was replaced in 1996 by Temporary Aid for Needy Families. Under AFDC, federal funds were provided to states on the basis of a formula that required the national government to match state monies, with no ceiling on the amount of national contribution.

Amicus curiae brief   A legal brief filed by an individual or group that has an interest in a court case but is not a party to that case in an effort to influence its outcome.

Annexation   The practice of a city extending its borders to include areas that were formerly not within the city limits.

Appointmenteering   An attempt to influence appointments to public office.

Appropriations   The portion of the budget that spends money. A single proposed expenditure may be called an appropriation.

Astroturf lobbying   The use of various techniques by public relations firms to simulate lobbying by individuals. It is regarded as artificial grassroots lobbying.

At-large election   One in which the entire political unit—for example, a city—votes for a candidate for office. The winner thus represents all citizens in the political unit.

Bail   An amount sufficient to procure release from confinement. It also serves as insurance of future attendance in court and the intention to remain within the jurisdiction of the court.

Benefits theory   An approach to financing government that assigns the costs of services to those who benefit from them. The problem is in apportioning benefit.

Bicameral   Composed of two houses, as in a legislature.

Bill of rights   Amendments to the constitution that define basic liberties such as freedom of religion, speech, and the press, and offer protections against arbitrary searches by the police and being held without legal representation.

Bond election   An election for the purpose of obtaining voter approval for a government's incurring debt by selling bonds to private investors.

Brown v. Board of Education of Topeka, Kansas   A 1954 Supreme Court decision that overturned the separate-but-equal doctrine in Plessy v. Ferguson. The Court ruled that separate educational facilities for blacks and whites are inherently unequal and therefore unconstitutional.

Budget   A specific itemized monetary plan. It consists of one or more laws that oblige citizens to provide revenue for the government, and oblige government employees to use that revenue in certain ways.

Bureaucracy   An organizational system that has a defined hierarchical structure, standardized procedures, and a specialization of duties to carry out public policies.

By-district election   One in which the political unit is divided into parts or districts. A candidate for office is selected by the citizens of each district and thus represents only that part of the political unit.

Capital cases   Cases in which the defendant is accused of committing a capital crime.

Casework   The practice of individual legislators following up on constituent complaints about their contacts with administrative agencies.

Charter school   A school chartered by the state to educate Texas schoolchildren. These schools are free to operate with a minimum of state regulation as long as their students can demonstrate competence on state measures of accountability.

Checks and balances   A major principle of the U.S. government system whereby each branch of the government exercises a check on the actions of the other branches.

Civic culture   A culture that demonstrates four characteristics:
1. civic engagement;
2. political equality;
3. solidarity, trust, and tolerance
4. social structures of cooperation.

   Political units with a civic culture are most likely to have democratic political systems and effective, responsive governments.

Civic Culture Index score   A number that Rice and Sumberg compute by using data on the four elements of civic culture. Without accurate polling data, they use somewhat crude but sometimes interesting and creative measures, such as the percentage of schoolteachers who are men; the percentage of state legislators who are women; how well a state cares for the poor, especially children; the fairness of its tax system; and the existence of consumer-protection laws.

Civil disobedience   The intentional, public, nonviolent violation of a law to protest the unjustness of the law or a public policy related to or represented by the law.

Class action lawsuit   A lawsuit in which individuals without adequate personal resources can join together to battle economically more powerful actors in the courts.

Closed primary   A party nominating election (primary) in which only registered members of the party can participate.

Collective bargaining   The right of workers, after winning a majority in an organizing election, to bargain with management on working conditions such as safety, wages, and benefits.

Collective benefits   Benefits we enjoy whether we helped obtain them or not.

Colonias   Residential developments found in South Texas, particularly along the Texas-Mexico border, that are lacking in acceptable water and sewer services and contain substandard structures.

Common law   Laws, principles, and rules of action derived primarily from usage and custom. All the statutory and case law background of England and the American colonies before the American Revolution are considered the common law.

Compensatory damages   Monetary sum paid to compensate for loss, detriment, or injury to property or person or to a plaintiff's rights under the law from the negligence of another.

Confederacy   A league of independent states in which the central government has only limited powers over the states.

Conference committee   A temporary committee formed when the two chambers of the legislature pass separate versions of the same bill. The committee, which consists of members from both the House and Senate, works out a compromise form of the bill.

Constable   Lowest-ranking law enforcement official in a county, elected by the voters of a given precinct. The person is primarily a process server for the courts; enforces writs; and provides support services to the lower courts as bailiff, security officer, and officer of the court.

Constitution   A basic law that sets forth the institutional structure of

government and the tasks these government institutions perform.

Cooperative federalism   A system of government in which powers and policy assignments are shared between states and the federal government.

Councils of government (COGs) Voluntary associations of local governments formed under state law to deal with the problems and planning needs that cross the boundaries of individual governments or that require regional attention.

Court costs   Assessments made by the court to defray the expenses incurred in the case at hand.

Court-appointed attorney   An attorney appointed by the court for indigent defendants.

Criminal cases   Cases in which the defendant is accused of violating one or more of the state's criminal statutes.

Cruel and unusual punishment A form of punishment prohibited by the Eighth Amendment to the U.S. Constitution. Exactly what constitutes cruel and unusual punishment ultimately turns on how the Supreme Court interprets this vague concept.

Cumulative   To increase by adding on instead of increasing by substituting new activities for old ones.

De novo   A new trial in another court, usually a court of record.

Delegate   A representative who is expected to mirror the views of those whom he or she represents.

Demonstrating   Group attempts to bring public attention to an issue and make public officials aware of the intensity of group feelings.

Dual federalism   A system of government in which states and the national government remain supreme within their own sphere.

Edgewood v. Kirby A 1984 lawsuit by sixty-seven property-poor districts, led by the Edgewood school district of San Antonio, that argued that the state's system of unequal funding of schools violated the Texas Constitution.

Electioneering A wide range of activities involved in getting someone elected to public office.

Endorsing conventions Party conventions held before the primary election to have the active party members endorse a candidate they think will be an able representative of the party in the general election. Only the candidates for the one or two top offices are usually subject to this endorsement process.

Entitlement A program that provides benefits to all those who meet the qualifications for the program, with no limit on the number of recipients.

Extraterritorial jurisdiction (ETJ) The geographical area outside the boundaries of a city over which the city has some control and some responsibility.

Federal deduction offset A way of looking at a state tax that can be deducted from the federal income tax. For sales taxes there is no deduction, although there are bills in congress to change that.

For state property taxes and for state income taxes there is a reduction in one's income tax bill. Thus, money paid to the state is offset (counterbalanced, made up for) by a corresponding reduction in one's federal tax bill. Naturally, this only affects people who use the long 1040 form to compute their federal income taxes.

Federalism The philosophy that describes the governmental system in which power is divided between a central government and regional governments.

Filibuster A tactic used by members of the Senate to prevent action on legislation they oppose; it involves continuously holding the floor and speaking until the majority backs down.

Fines Amounts assessed for specific crimes listed in the Texas Penal Code. Usually a defendant, once found guilty, is assessed fines and court costs, or confinement in jail (or all of these). Probation in lieu of jail sentence also incurs additional costs and conditions imposed by the judge, including restitution to the victim of the crime and community service.

Fiscal note A requirement that each proposed bill containing tax relief, as well as bills proposing expenditures, have a report attached that provides the effective cost to the treasury of Texas.

Fiscal year The 365-day period that the state uses to open and close the books on a year's worth of expenditures and revenue collections. It is usually different from the calendar year.

For cause A challenge for cause to a prospective juror for bias toward, prejudice toward, interest in, or knowledge about the case at hand admitted during voir dire. A successful challenge for cause leads to dismissal from further jury service on that occasion.

Forcible entry and detainer Speedy and adequate remedy for obtaining possession of premises by one entitled to actual possession. Usually a matter handled by the justice of the peace courts and involving unpaid rent or lease payment.

Free rider Someone who enjoys collective benefits without making a contribution to obtaining or defending them.

General election Statewide elections held on the first Tuesday after the first Monday of November of even-numbered years. These elections determine who will fill government offices.

General law charter A city charter that establishes the legal status of smaller cities, setting down the type of government the city has and establishing the powers of the city.

General-purpose governments Governments that provide various services and perform various functions. The most common general-purpose local governments are counties and cities.

Gentrification A term used to describe the renovation of an older area of a city to make it attractive to middle-class people.

Gerrymandering Drawing the boundary lines of electoral districts in a manner that systematically advantages a particular political party, group, or candidate.

The Grange An organization of farmers. The Texas Grange was organized in 1873.

Grassroots lobbying Attempting to influence others to contact a public official personally.

Gross state product The gross market value of the goods and services produced and delivered in a state.

Grutter v. Bollinger A 2003 U.S. Supreme Court decision holding that carefully crafted university affirmative action programs are constitutional.

Habeas corpus appeal An appeal made by a defendant already convicted of a capital crime in state district court. It allows defendants to examine the entire court record to look for procedural or substantive errors.

Hierarchical Arranged in order of increase or decrease according to a characteristic. Political participation can be arranged in a hierarchy according to increasing opportunity costs and decreasing percentages of the population involved.

Hierarchy   The way a bureaucracy is organized, showing who is in charge of the various departments or divisions.

Higher Education Assistance Fund   A fund established in 1984 by a constitutional amendment to provide financial support for universities constitutionally excluded from PUF funds. By 1999, this fund provided $225 million per year to these institutions.

Home rule charter   A city charter that may be adopted by larger cities. It allows the city greater self-governing power.

Hopwood **decision**   A 1996 decision by the U.S. Circuit Court of Appeals for the Fifth District that declared affirmative action programs using race as a criterion of admission were unconstitutional. This decision effectively ended affirmative action admissions programs in Texas, Louisiana, and Mississippi, the three states within the circuit court's jurisdiction.

Hung jury   A jury that is unable to agree on a verdict in a case after suitable deliberation. A deadlocked jury.

Incidence   Another way of saying impact, it means the effect of a tax on different income categories. We use the concept of tax burden in our text, the comptroller's "incidence" deals with the same idea.

Indictment   The result of the grand jury process leading to formal charges of wrongdoing against a person. It is also the name of the charging instrument, as in true bill of indictment.

Indigent defendant   A defendant who cannot afford to hire a private attorney.

Initiative   The power of citizens to draft a proposal through a process of collecting signatures on a petition favoring the proposal. It is a way in which citizens can write or change law themselves.

Interest group   A formal organization through which individuals seek to promote or defend a shared interest by influencing public policy.

Intergovernmental relations   A term that describes the working relationships of governments in modern American federalism as they interact with each other at all levels.

Intergovernmental transfer   Funds allocated from one unit of government to another.

Interim committee   A recess committee created to act as a study or investigatory body between sessions of the legislature.

Item veto   A veto exercised on appropriations bills that gives the governor authority to eliminate unacceptable items while approving the majority of the appropriations.

Joint committee   Committee with members from both the House and the Senate.

Layer cake   A phrase that is used to describe federalism in which the top layer is the national government and the bottom layer is comprised of all the state governments. This picture of federalism indicates a formal, legal separation of the activities of the national government and the state governments.

Licensing   The most basic form of regulation. A license indicates

that a person has met some level of competency.

Lieutenant governor   The presiding officer and foremost political leader of the Texas Senate. The lieutenant governor is elected statewide for a four-year term in the same general election year in which the governor is chosen.

Limited government   A government with limited authority. Usually the bill of rights and other provisions throughout the constitution place limits on governmental authority and power.

Line-item veto   The ability of the governor to strike out and thus cancel parts of appropriations bills with which he or she does not agree.

Litigating   Using the legal system to influence public policy.

Litmus test of American federalism   Does the Constitution protect the states by giving them a role in amending it?

Lobbying   Any attempt to influence public policy decisions through direct contact with decisionmakers.

Lobbying   Personally contacting a public official to influence a decision.

Lone Star Card   A debit card given to recipients in the Texas food stamp program that can be used to purchase allowable food items.

Magistrate   A person with limited judicial power who explains to the accused their legal rights and the charges leveled against them; usually a justice of the peace or municipal judge.

Marble cake   A phrase used to describe the relationships among governments in which national, state, and local government activities are swirled together with no clear lines of separation. This picture of federalism incorporates the idea of all governmental levels sharing in making and carrying out decisions.

Mark up   Alter the original bill so that it reflects the information the legislature gleaned from the hearing process.

Means tested   Programs that provide benefits on the basis of demonstrated need.

Medicaid   A means-tested health insurance program for the poor, funded by taxpayers.

Medicare   A health insurance program for the elderly funded by payroll contributions. It is not means tested.

Megastate   States that have large, highly urbanized populations and a large gross state product, which indicates a complex economy.

Merit principle   The idea that the best-qualified people get jobs and promotions.

Municipal corporation   Another name for an incorporated city.

Negotiated rulemaking   The procedure whereby a regulatory agency writes proposed rules with the assistance of those who will be affected by the rules.

No bill   A grand jury does not find sufficient evidence or truth in the allegation to warrant bringing the accused to trial. The opposite of a true bill.

Nonpartisan elections   Elections in which the candidates are not identified by a political party label. This type of election is the most common city election.

Old Age, Survivors and Disability Insurance (OASDI)   A national program funded through lifelong contributions that are deducted from payrolls; commonly referred to as social security.

Ombudsman   A government official who investigates citizens'
complaints against a government agency.

Open primary   A party nominating election (primary) in which any qualified voter, regardless of party affiliation, can participate.

Oversight   The effort by the state legislature, through hearings, investigation, and other techniques, to exercise control over the actions of executive agencies.

Parliamentary functions   Taxing and spending.

Parliaments   Places where representatives of the people parley (discuss issues) with representatives of the executive branch and decide on taxes and expenditures. All legislatures—state and local—are parliaments because they perform the two parliamentary functions of taxing and spending.

Party identification   A voter's sense of psychological attachment to a political party.

Patronage   The idea that people are given jobs based on who they know—usually elected officials.

Peremptory challenge or strike   An arbitrary challenge or strike of a prospective juror without need for a reason. Each side is allowed a certain number of strikes, depending on the type of case—usually three per side in smaller misdemeanor cases and six in more serious felony cases.

Permanent University Fund (PUF)   A fund established in the Texas Constitution of 1876 and paid for by oil-land leases to provide financial support for the University of Texas. Subsequent constitutional amendments have permitted Texas A&M, as well as other schools in these two university systems, to benefit from the $7.7 billion fund.

Plea bargain   An agreement that allows a defendant charged with a
more serious crime to plead guilty to a less serious crime.

Plessy v. Ferguson   An 1896 Supreme Court case that proclaimed it was constitutional to require blacks and whites to attend separate public schools, as long as these schools were equal. The legal reasoning offered by the Court in this case came to be known as the separate-but-equal doctrine.

Plural executive   The set of several elected state leaders. Each is elected separately by the voters and is accountable only to the voters.

Political action committee (PAC)   An organization created by an interest group, corporation, labor union, or other organization to raise money for the purpose of spending on and contributing to political campaigns.

Political culture   A pattern of attitudes toward and beliefs about politics, participation in politics, and the purpose of government.

Political participation   Any activity that seeks to influence public decisions.

Political party   Any group, however loosely organized, seeking to elect government officeholders under a given label.

Political socialization   The process of learning about politics as we learn our language and culture.

Poll tax   A voting requirement stipulating the payment of a tax to become eligible to vote. Used as a device to discriminate against minority groups in voting, poll taxes were made unconstitutional by the Twenty-Fourth Amendment to the U.S. Constitution in 1964.

Popular sovereignty   A political concept in which the voters in a political system are the ultimate and supreme source of all authority.

Powell's paradox Despite the fact that they are more predisposed to participate and that they participate in some activities more than people in other countries do, Americans vote at a lower rate than do citizens in other industrial democracies.

Precinct chair The permanent party official at the precinct level.

Primary election An election in which voters choose a party's nominees for public office.

Privatization A government contract with a private company to provide a service to the state.

Pro bono Legal work done on a voluntary basis, with no payment for services rendered.

Property qualification A requirement that an individual must own property to vote.

Public defender An attorney employed and paid by the government to represent indigent defendants accused of felonies.

Public hearing A meeting at which decisionmakers listen to the public to gather information.

Public policy Decisions that determine what government does or does not do.

Punitive damages Monetary sum assessed by the jury or court as punishment to the wrongdoer and negligent person for outrageous conduct and to serve as a lesson to others.

Racial profiling The practice of factoring race into profiles of suspected criminals that police departments then use to help them determine which citizens should be detained for further questioning or search.

Recall An electoral procedure for removing an elected official from office before the end of his or her specified term.

Recused Removed; a judge with an interest or conflict in a case may be removed (recused) in favor of another, impartial judge. In an election contest case, all judges who sit within the election district being contested must recuse themselves, and a visiting judge must be brought in to hear the case.

Referendum An election that allows voters to determine a policy issue directly.

Regulation The use of government authority (and power) to force a course of action.

Retail politics Personal contact with citizens by telephone or door-to-door canvassing to mobilize them to vote or participate in some other way.

Right to work The legal prohibition of collective bargaining agreements that contain any provisions for compulsory union membership.

Robin Hood measure Legislation passed by the Texas Legislature in 1993 requiring wealthy school districts to transfer part of their property tax revenues to poorer school districts.

Runoff primary An election between the top two candidates when no candidate receives a majority in a primary election. A runoff ensures that the eventual nominee will have received a majority vote.

Salience The condition of being strikingly conspicuous; prominent.

San Antonio School District v. Rodriguez A 1973 U.S. Supreme Court decision stating that school finance is a state issue.

School choice programs Programs that allow public school students to attend schools other than their assigned public school..

Senatorial courtesy The tradition that senators will vote against a

nominee if the senator from the area most affected by the appointment opposes that appointment.

Separation of powers The principle of dividing governmental power among the executive, legislative, and judicial branches.

Sheriff Highest-ranking law enforcement official in a county, elected by the voters. He or she serves as the custodian of the courthouse.

Social insurance Social welfare programs that provide benefits to those who have paid into a fund.

Socioeconomic status (SES) The rank one has in a hierarchy that is determined by occupational prestige, income, education, and wealth.

South Texas Initiative A commitment by the University of Texas to invest millions of additional higher education dollars in existing and new university campuses in South Texas.

Speaker of the House The presiding officer in the House of Representatives. The Speaker, who is elected at the beginning of the session by fellow representatives, is the most powerful and influential member of the House.

Special election Any election called at a time that does not conform to the regular election calendar.

Special or **ad hoc committee** A temporary committee of the legislature created to conduct studies or investigations.

Special-purpose governments Governments that provide only one or just a few related services.

Specialization of duties The idea of breaking down the overall work of a bureaucracy into small tasks (duties) and then having those tasks performed by one person as their daily routine at work.

Spillover effects Unintended effects of the policies or practices of a government that may produce negative or positive consequences on those outside the policy area.

Standardized procedures The regular procedures an agency uses to carry out state law.

Standing committee A permanent committee in the legislature that specializes in a particular policy area, such as agriculture or education.

Statutory law Statutory law is created by the legislature rather than established in the state constitution.

Subcommittee A division of a larger committee that deals with a particular part of the committee's policy area. Some standing committees in the legislature have several subcommittees.

Subsistence The income necessary to live at the level of bare existence: meager food, clothing, shelter; a minimal standard of living.

Suburb A residential community that has grown up outside the city limits of a larger city and may exist as one of many contiguous suburbs.

Suffrage The right to vote.

Sunset review The periodic evaluation of state agencies by the legislature to determine whether they should be reauthorized.

Supplemental Security Income (SSI) A means-tested program that benefits poor people.

Surplus The income beyond subsistence. From surplus, one can buy higher quality subsistence items, enjoy luxuries, and have money left over for saving, speculation, and investment.

Tax expenditure An analytical tool useful to policymakers and the general public that attempts to put a dollar figure on the tax breaks that special interests have obtained from government or that government has decided are beneficial public policy.

Tax system A mix of taxes used to raise revenue for a unit of government or a system of governments.

Temporary Aid for Needy Families (TANF) A welfare program whereby federal monies are given to the states in the form of block grants, thus providing a ceiling on the national government's contribution to states. TANF also contains limits on the length of lifetime enrollment and the requirement that recipients actively seek work. TANF replaced AFDC in 1996 when Congress passed the Personal Responsibility and Work Opportunity Reconciliation Act.

Texas Academic Assessment System (TAAS) The educational accountability system used to measure public school performance in Texas until 2002. This system ranks schools according to their dropout rate, their attendance rate, and the percentage of students passing basic skills tests in reading, writing, and math.

Texas Assessment of Knowledge and Skills (TAKS) The Texas educational accountability system. It replaced TAAS in 2002.

Texas Board of Criminal Justice A nine-member board appointed by the governor to oversee the Texas Department of Criminal Justice (TDCJ). Board members are appointed to staggered six-year terms and are responsible for hiring the executive director of the TDCJ.

Texas Department of Corrections Now known as the Texas Department of Criminal Justice, an agency that provides confinement, supervision, rehabilitation, and social reintegration of the state's convicted felons.

Tort reform A political movement whose members oppose large monetary amounts awarded to plaintiffs by juries in negligence cases.

True bill An actual bill of indictment by a grand jury indicating that the jury found sufficient evidence and truth to the allegation to bring the accused to trial.

Trustee A representative who acts according to his or her conscience and the broad interest of the entire society.

Unemployment compensation A joint national-state program funded in part by the contributions of employers into a fund.

Unitary system A system of government in which all powers reside in the central government.

Veto The governor's constitutional right to reject a piece of legislation passed by the legislature.

Voir dire The preliminary examination undertaken by the attorneys and the judge of persons presented to serve as witnesses or jurors to determine competency, interest, bias, and prejudice. There are two kinds of juries chosen: **petit** and **grand**. A grand jury is comprised of 12 persons and usually hears felony cases although they may also sit for misdemeanor cases. In a criminal case, a grand jury must reach a unanimous verdict. A petit jury is comprised of only 6 persons and they usually sit for lower courts such as municipal, justice of the peace, and county court at law. In Texas a jury trial is a fundamental right but an accused can waive a jury trial and ask for a bench trial meaning trial by the judge.

Voting Rights Act (VRA)   A law passed by Congress in 1965 that made it illegal to interfere with anyone's right to vote. It focused on areas of the country with a history of voting discrimination and has been the principal legal vehicle for protecting and expanding minority voting rights.

Voucher program   A program that provides a voucher valued at a predetermined dollar amount for each school-age child in the state. Parents are then free to use this voucher to pay for all or part of the costs of their child's education at a school of their choice.

White primary   A type of nominating election used by the Democratic party in Texas to prohibit African Americans from voting to select the party's candidates for office. The practice was found to be an unconstitutional violation of the Fourteenth Amendment's equal protection clause by the Supreme Court in *Smith v. Allright* in 1944.

Wholesale politics   The use of the mass media to reach voters.

Zoning laws   The control of land use and development in a particular area.